Microeconomics
Second Edition

Microeconomics

Second Edition

B. Curtis Eaton

Simon Fraser University

Diane F. Eaton

W. H. Freeman and Company
New York

Library of Congress Cataloging-in-Publication Data

Eaton, Buford Curtis, 1943–
    Microeconomics / B. Curtis Eaton, Diane F. Eaton. —2nd ed.
      p.   cm.
    Includes index.
    ISBN 0-7167-2082-5:   — ISBN 0-7167-2168-6 (pbk.):
    1. Microeconomics. I. Eaton, Diane F. II. Title.
 HB172.E23 1991
 338.5 — dc20   90-39335
                                                  CIP

Printed in the United States of America

1 2 3 4 5 6 7 8 9 0 RRD 9 9 8 7 6 5 4 3 2 1

To Brett and Sarah

CONTENTS

PREFACE

To the Student

Why do you sometimes find two or three gas stations at the same intersection? Why does the value of a new car plummet the instant you drive it off the lot? Why do we have bosses? Why do people have to spend so much time searching for an apartment in rent-controlled areas? Why do amusement parks often charge a whopping admission price to the park and almost nothing for the rides? Why does McDonald's break down the job of making hamburgers into so many little tasks and hire different workers to do each one? Why does IBM produce a whole spectrum of products? Why are some markets — such as the market for local telephone services — monopolized, and others — such as the markets for haircuts or carpet shampooing — highly competitive? What is the best way to alleviate the annoying traffic congestion that plagues so many North American cities?

As you work your way through this book, you'll discover the answers to these and many other questions. But microeconomics is not just a listing of specific economic questions and their answers. Rather, it is a systematic way to set out and solve virtually any question that you might encounter in everyday economic life. Our primary goal in writing this book is to help you

learn how to formulate intriguing economic questions and then start finding the answers.

In Chapter 1, we explain the working methodology of the microeconomic theorist — not by talking about it, but by showing you how to create and explore a specific economic model. This "hands on" approach is used throughout the book and is reinforced by many in-chapter problems and end-of-chapter exercises aimed at engaging you in active, participatory reading. (We provide answers to the in-chapter problems at the end of the book.) Our philosophy is that the only way to learn microeconomics is to do it — every step of the way.

Doing economics well means understanding economic analysis thoroughly. We present all the standard topics of microeconomic analysis in a series of carefully sequenced steps. The narrative style of presentation means that each topic flows naturally from what came before it and leads smoothly into what follows. By working actively through the text and the accompanying problems, you will come away with a solid understanding of the major topics of microeconomics.

Of course, microeconomics is a field that is still changing — and that is its real challenge. We provide you with an overview of current research in representative areas, including the theory of the firm, the theory of oligopoly and market structure, the economics of information, and the address (or characteristics) approach to product differentiation. In exploring these topics, you will be able to reach the frontiers of microeconomic research — and to see just how much exciting work in microeconomics remains to be done.

To the Instructor

This book is intended for use in undergraduate courses in intermediate microeconomics. We do not use calculus in the text itself, where we rely on carefully explained graphic techniques. However, we do provide complete calculus footnotes.

The approximately 180 in-chapter problems, all of which are answered at the back of the book, are reinforced and extended by a similar number of end-of-chapter exercises. Especially difficult exercises are marked with an asterisk. You will find answers to all the end-of-chapter exercises in the *Instructor's Resource Book*. The *Instructor's Resource Book* also contains a series of easy-to-administer classroom experiments that illustrate the power of economic analysis and transparency masters for all graphs in the text. A *Test Bank* of multiple-choice questions is available on computer disk for the IBM PC and compatibles and in booklet form.

In the accompanying study guide, *Problem Solving in Microeconomics*, Second Edition, Nancy Gallini of the University of Toronto has done a superb job of providing supplementary material that will help the student to develop a thorough understanding of microeconomics. Each chapter contains a chapter summary, case studies, a list of key words, multiple-choice questions, and true-false questions. In addition, the study guide offers a wide range of useful and fascinating real-world problems designed to teach students how to think as economists do.

How to Use This Book

We have designed this book so that a number of differentiated courses can be taught from it. Note that chapters and sections of chapters that are marked with an asterisk in the table of contents and the text can be skipped with no loss of continuity. Note, too, that the order in which this material can be assigned is often quite flexible. For example, Chapter 6 (Choice Making Under Imperfect Information) can fit neatly just after Chapter 10 (The Theory of Perfect Competition), since it deals with both competitive insurance markets and Akerlof's lemons model. Alternatively, it can be used at the very end of the course, as an introduction to a set of issues that will be covered in detail in more advanced courses. To cite one further example, Sections 8.5, 10.8, and 11.10 make up a comparative institutional package that can be taught conveniently at any point after Chapter 11.

Chapters 1 through 5 and Chapters 8 through 11 form the core of a standard one-semester course. A number of differentiated courses that build on this core are described below.

- *Nonspecialized:*
  Suggested chapter assignments: 1–5, 8–11, 14–15
  Optional chapter assignments: 12, 16

- *Comparative institutional analysis, or property rights:*
  Suggested chapter assignments: 1–5, 7–11 (highlight Sections 2.3, 5.6, 8.5, 10.8, 11.8, 11.10)
  Optional chapter assignments: 6, 13

- *Labor economics:*
  Suggested chapter assignments: 1–5, 7–11, 14 (highlight Section 5.5)
  Optional chapter assignment: 16

- *Consumer theory:*
  Suggested chapter assignments: 1–5, 6–11, 16 (highlight Sections 3.3, 3.4, 4.10, 5.2)

On the Second Edition

Broadly speaking, the organization and content of the first edition are unchanged in the second edition. However, specific material in many chapters has been substantially reorganized, and all but four chapters have been completely rewritten. All these revisions are aimed at making the book more user-friendly for students. In addition, a number of other changes have been made in the interests of liveliness, clarity, and accessibility:

- The graphs have all been streamlined and relabeled.

- The mathematical notation has been thoroughly overhauled and simplified.

- The end-of-chapter exercises have been completely revised, and many new exercises that reinforce basic concepts have been added.

- New and up-to-date examples have been added throughout.

- Economic concepts that students typically find abstract or difficult are presented in terms of specific illustrations that are concrete and easy to understand.

- All of the general equilibrium material has been pulled together in one chapter.

Acknowledgments

We would like to thank our colleagues Judy Alexander, Larry Boland, Jack Knetsch, and Denton Marks for their many valuable comments and suggestions. Our thanks, too, to Kevin Wainwright for his assistance in developing the problems and exercises, and to George D. Brower for reworking the multiple-choice test questions. Finally, we'd like to acknowledge all the people at W. H. Freeman who have contributed so much of their time, talent, and energy to the making of the second edition, especially Gary Carlson, Cynthia Farden, Susan Landry, and Diana Siemens.

Reviewers

We would like to acknowledge all the useful suggestions and generous encouragement from our reviewers for both the first and second editions. Reviewers for the first edition include

George Borjas, University of California, Santa Barbara
Oscar T. Brookins, Northeastern University
Norman Clifford, University of Kansas
William T. Dickens, University of California, Berkeley
Joseph C. Gallo, University of Cincinnati
Charles Geiss, University of Missouri
Edward Greenberg, Washington University
Richard Hofler, University of Tennessee
Joseph Hughes, Rutgers University
Michael Jones, Yale University
Edward C. Kienzle, Boston College
Anthony Y. C. Koo, Michigan State University
Martin McGuire, University of Maryland
Paul L. Menchik, Michigan State University
Paul Glen Munyon, Grinnell College
Jack Ochs, University of Pittsburgh
William B. O'Neil, Colby College

Paul Roman, St. Louis University
William Schaffer, Georgia Institute of Technology
John Schroeter, Iowa State University
Alan Slivinski, University of Western Ontario
Paul M. Sommers, Middlebury College

Reviewers Thomas Barthold (Dartmouth), Edward Greenberg (Washington University), and Michael Morgan (College of Charleston), whose detailed and thoughtful comments at various stages were invaluable, deserve special recognition.

Reviewers for the second edition include

Arlo Biere, Kansas State University
George D. Brower, Allegheny College
Mukesh Eswaren, University of British Columbia
Larry Herman, Kenyon College
Anthony Y. C. Koo, Michigan State University
James P. Lesage, University of Toledo
Lynne Pepall, Tufts University
Malcolm Rutherford, University of Victoria
Nicolas Schmitt, Simon Fraser University
Alan Slivinski, University of Western Ontario
Roger Ware, University of Toronto
Douglas S. West, University of Alberta

We would especially like to thank Robert A. Becker (Indiana University), whose thoughtful comments were so useful in shaping this edition.

Microeconomics

Second Edition

P A R T

I

An Introduction to Microeconomics

In Chapters 1 and 2, we'll trace out the working methodology of the microeconomic theorist, define the terms *economy* and *economics*, review some of the key tools from principles of economics, and outline the remainder of the book.

The purpose of economic modeling or theorizing is to explain everyday economic activity. In Chapter 1, we'll show how the economic theorist creates and evaluates the relatively simple (and therefore necessarily abstract) models used to interpret economic affairs by building a particular model from the ground up. Then we'll use that model to explore the differences between positive and normative economics, to consider Pareto optimality and cost-benefit analysis, and to look at ways of evaluating economic models.

In Chapter 2, we'll see what an economy is and does, and we'll pay special attention to the role played by economic institutions. We'll then outline the sequence of topics to be covered in the remainder of the book and provide a quick review of demand and supply analysis.

1

DOING MICROECONOMICS: A WORKING METHODOLOGY

Economic textbooks often begin by asking "What is economics?" Thorough definitions of economics and microeconomics await us in Chapter 2. In this chapter, we'll simply invoke economist Jacob Viner's tongue-in-cheek but sensible reply to that standard question: "Economics is what economists do." In fact, encouraging you to learn economics by doing is our central aim. As you work through this book, you not only will become acquainted with important concepts forming the core of the microeconomist's knowledge but also will be practicing microeconomics by doing it.[1]

The real economic environment poses so many complex questions that we cannot expect to find ready-made answers to them all. The only way to do microeconomics successfully is to find a method for setting out and then solving microeconomic problems. Throughout the book, you are encouraged to learn how to set up intriguing questions and to use economic tools of analysis to discover their answers. As social scientist Kenneth Boulding once remarked, a really well educated person is one who, when seeking answers, picks up a pencil and begins working toward a solution.

Once you have taken pencil in hand, however, you need a systematic method for proceeding from question to solution. Microeconomic theorizing provides just such a systematic framework within which economic behavior can be understood.

1.1 The Methodology of Economic Theory

Because microeconomic theory addresses ordinary economic reality, a working methodology begins with questions about what goes on in the world at large. Here are a few of the many questions you will encounter in this book: Why do major retailers stock so many models of portable radios, ranging from pocket-sized Walkmans to awesome "boom boxes"? Why do airline companies

---

[1] See Boland (1987) for an accessible discussion of modern views on methodology.

charge different fares for the same flight? What are the economic effects of access to university racquetball courts on a first come, first served basis? Why are some businesses owner-managed, others partnerships, and yet others publicly held corporations? Why are some athletes offered multimillion-dollar contracts?

We begin the process of economic theorizing by selecting an intriguing, often casual observation from our own real experiences — for instance, that the audio retailer Bay-Bloor Radio has in stock about 24 different portable radios. If we then ask *why* Bay-Bloor Radio stocks so many models of portable radios, we are inevitably dealing with theory, not with fact. Even the most superficial reply to our question is a tentative theory, although not necessarily a carefully formulated, accurate, or even conscious one. Suppose we reply, "Not everybody wants the same kind of radio, so it pays the retailer to carry a selection of models." If we look closely, we'll discover that this reply is not plain fact but a tentative theory based on a series of implicit assumptions from which we've derived a conclusion or prediction. We have implicitly made the following assumptions:

- Human beings have diverse preferences.

- Portable radios are significantly different.

- Sellers of sound equipment are motivated by profit.

From implicit assumptions such as these we've made a very loose deduction: the retailer will offer a wide range of models because by doing so it can sell more radios and thereby make more profit. Our deduction is also a prediction about what we would discover if we attempted to verify our casual observation by systematically observing the behavior of many audio retailers. That is, we've made the loose prediction that audio retailers in general will offer a number of different models for sale. But is this hunch or tentative theory sound?

The basic method of thinking through an economic theory or model is by using deductive reasoning, in which conclusions are drawn from carefully chosen and clearly defined assumptions. First, we explicitly select and state the assumptions that we think are relevant. Then we draw deductions from those assumptions. The deductions we draw, like deductions in geometry, must satisfy the rules of logic by following from the assumptions. These deductions are also the predictions of our model; they are the statements about what we would actually expect to find in the world. We can test their accuracy by conducting rigorous empirical investigations that will tend either to support or to refute them.

1.2 Choosing the Assumptions of a Model

Now let's begin to construct an economic theory by considering some other intriguing questions based on casual observation. Why do two, three, or even four gas stations sometimes locate at the same intersection? Why do large grocery stores seem so similar in the range and quality of goods they offer us? Why do supposedly different brands of premium beer or tennis rackets or economics textbooks seem almost indistinguishable?

These were the sorts of questions that Harold Hotelling attempted to answer in a now classic paper, "Stability in Competition" (1929). Just as we began with a casual observation about the range of models offered by an audio retailer, so Hotelling began with the observation that firms tend to cluster together in their locations or in the range or quality of their goods. Gas stations "cluster" at certain intersections, or premium beer makers "cluster" along certain characteristics of the beer they produce. In short, Hotelling began with the casual observation that firms seem to produce minimally differentiated products — products that are only slightly different from one another.

Our challenge, then, is to create a model or theory that helps us to understand the phenomenon of clustering, or **minimum differentiation.** Be aware, though, that any particular model is not the final or "right" one in any absolute sense. Your role, therefore, is to think through this model actively rather than to accept it passively.

Reducing an Economic Problem to Its Simplest Form

Because the multitude of economic "facts" relevant to any economic question is overwhelming, we need to reduce the question to manageable proportions; that is, we need to choose a few simple assumptions that seem to approximate the fundamental elements of the complex reality we are attempting to understand. Although you may object that the process of abstraction is "unrealistic," you probably would agree that many abstractions in noneconomic contexts are practical and even necessary. City road maps are one example. Although real cities look nothing like maps of cities, city maps are useful precisely because they ignore such superfluous information as the color of the second house from the corner on Main and First Streets. Maps give us only what we need to know to get from one point to another. Similarly, economic models abstract what we hope is the relevant information from a welter of economic details.

Let's begin this process of abstraction by thinking about the different ways in which products can cluster, or be minimally differentiated, and then selecting the simplest or most manageable kind of product

differentiation. Firms can cluster in *geographic space* by locating their stores together, or they can cluster in *characteristics space* by producing products that have similar mixes of characteristics. Gas stations located at the same intersection are clustered in geographic space. Different brands of tennis rackets that are similar in weight, balance, size, and strength are clustered in characteristics space. Because choosing a location in geographic space is easier to understand than choosing a point, or location, in characteristics space, let's ask where in a particular geographic market firms will choose to establish their businesses.

Having chosen to focus on clustering in a geographic space, we naturally arrive at the following questions: How many firms are there? What are the potential geographic locations of their stores? With what kinds of firms are we concerned? What goods do they sell, and at what prices? What are the firms' costs? What characterizes the customers who buy the firms' goods? What motivates these buyers and sellers?

Our next step is to reduce the vast number of firms and of goods that they sell to the most rudimentary case possible: What is the smallest number of firms with which we can deal? Because we are building a theory to understand minimum differentiation, we need at least two competing firms — a duopoly. We can also reduce the vast array of products these two firms might sell to identical goods. We'll assume that both firms offer exactly the same good, which we'll call groceries, for sale. Because prices, even for the same good, can vary widely from firm to firm and from time to time, we'll also assume that no price competition exists between the two firms and that both sell groceries at the same *fixed* price, denoted by P. We'll assume, too, that the cost to firms of each unit of groceries, denoted by C, is exactly the same for both firms, and that the price P is greater than the cost C. We can combine these restrictions in our first assumption.

ASSUMPTION 1

There are two firms selling an identical good, groceries, at a fixed price P per unit. The firm's cost of groceries is C per unit, and P is greater than C $(P > C)$.

PROBLEM 1.1

How much profit does a firm earn on each unit sold? Alternatively, what is the firm's profit per unit sold?

Where firms choose to locate obviously has a great deal to do with where their potential customers live. Our model, therefore, must include a geographic space that locates potential buyers in a particular pattern. Reducing the actual geographic space to manageable proportions is part of producing an economic model. Let's imagine that all the consumers live along one long street called Main Street. We can then graphically represent the geographic space that consumers inhabit by a straight line that, for simplicity, is 1 mile long. This brings us to the second simplifying abstraction in our theory.

ASSUMPTION 2

The geographic space is a street, Main Street, that is 1 mile long.

In Figure 1.1, we've represented Main Street by a line segment extending from 0 to 1. We can then think of numbers between 0 and 1 as addresses on Main Street — $\frac{1}{2}$, for example, is the address at the midpoint or middle of Main Street.

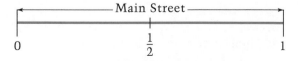

FIGURE 1.1   Main Street.

The geographic space is a line 1 mile long, Main Street.

Now, what assumptions should we make about the number and distribution of these buyers? We know, of course, that population density differs from place to place and even from block to block. For instance, a thousand people may be living in a high-rise development on one block but only a hundred people may be living in large, single-family houses on the next block. Nevertheless, to assume that the customers are spaced evenly, or uniformly, along Main Street is a useful simplification. Imagine, then, that a specific number of customers, N, are uniformly distributed along Main Street.

ASSUMPTION 3

There are N customers uniformly distributed along Main Street.

PROBLEM 1.2

Suppose that N is equal to 128. How many customers live between addresses $\frac{1}{2}$ and $\frac{3}{4}$? Between addresses $\frac{1}{4}$ and 1? Between addresses 0 and $\frac{1}{8}$?

Although in reality customers buy groceries at different times and places and in different amounts, we can simplify this analysis by making a fourth assumption: each customer buys one unit of groceries at the fixed price P from one of the two firms described in assumption 2.

ASSUMPTION 4

In each period, each customer buys one unit of groceries at the fixed price P.

We'll also assume that getting to the store and back is expensive for the customer and that the farther it is to the store, the more expensive it is to make the trip back and forth.

ASSUMPTION 5

Travel to either store is costly for the customer, and the customer's cost of travel increases with the distance traveled.

The Role of Self-Interested Behavior

Finally, we need to identify the basis on which firms and customers make their respective decisions. What motivates a firm in choosing its location, and customers in choosing the store they patronize? The economist's answer to any such question concerning motivation is self-interest. Our final assumption is that consumers and firms alike choose what seems best for themselves.

ASSUMPTION 6

All economic agents, both firms and their customers, are motivated by self-interest.

The precise meaning of the term *self-interest* varies from model to model. In this model, it is in the firms' self-interest to make the largest possible profit, and it is in the customers' self-interest to minimize their travel costs. The assumption of self-interested behavior is universal in economics. Indeed, as we'll see in the next section, self-interest is the driving force of economic analysis.

1.3 Positive Economics

Now that our assumptions are in place, what predictions can we derive from them? How will our two grocery stores pursue their own self-interest? We can safely assume that each would like to generate as much profit as possible. Notice that location is the only variable under their control because our other assumptions have equalized prices, products offered, and other relevant variables. According to assumption 6, our two grocery stores—let's call them All-Valu and Bestway—will attempt to maximize their profits through the *locations of their stores.*

Let's concentrate on All-Valu's choice of location. Notice that All-Valu's profit in any period is just profit per unit times number of units sold in the period; that is,

All-Valu's profit
$$= \text{(profit per unit)(units sold)}$$

As you already know, profit per unit is just $P - C$ since All-Valu pays C for a unit of groceries and sells it for P. Because each customer buys exactly one unit, the number of units sold is equal to the number of customers whom the store attracts; therefore,

All-Valu's profit
$$= (P - C) \text{ (number of All-Valu's customers)}$$

To discover the number of customers who choose to shop at All-Valu, we need to look at the locations of the two stores. In Figure 1.2, the line from address 0 on the left to address 1 on the right represents Main Street. We'll refer to addresses 0 and 1 as the **market boundaries** of Main Street. Let's arbitrarily locate Bestway at point b, somewhere to the right of the halfway point on Main Street $(b > \frac{1}{2})$. Now let's arbitrarily locate All-Valu's store at point a, somewhere to the left of Bestway's store $(a < b)$. Given the locations represented in Figure 1.2, how many customers will shop at All-Valu?

To answer this question, we need to derive a prediction about how individual customers will choose the stores where they shop. According to assumption 6, the grocery shoppers—like the grocery stores—are motivated by their own self-interest. Because the stores' prices are identical and because travel to the store is costly, self-interest will lead customers to buy their gro-

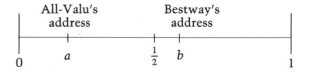

FIGURE 1.2 Firms' locations.

All-Valu's location or address is a, and Bestway's address is b.

ceries at the nearer store. We can now state the first prediction of our model:

PREDICTION 1

Customers will patronize the nearer store.

Knowing that customers will choose the closer store, we can calculate the number of shoppers who will patronize All-Valu. Let's begin by identifying the address of the customer who is indifferent between the two stores. Notice that in Figure 1.3, the address $(a + b)/2$ is *midway* between points a and b, or equidistant from All-Valu and Bestway. The customer at address $(a + b)/2$ is therefore **indifferent** between shopping at All-Valu or at Bestway. However, customers to the left of this point prefer All-Valu because it is closer. Customers to the right of this point prefer Bestway for the same reason. We'll call the address $(a + b)/2$ the **point of market segmentation** since it divides the total market into All-Valu's and Bestway's market segments. All-Valu's market segment extends from 0 to $(a + b)/2$, and Bestway's market segment extends from $(a + b)/2$ to 1. Because the N customers are uniformly distributed from 0 to 1, the number of All-Valu's customers is equal to the length of its market segment, $(a + b)/2$, multiplied by the total number of customers in the market, N; that is,

number of All-Valu's customers

$$= N\left(\frac{a + b}{2}\right)$$

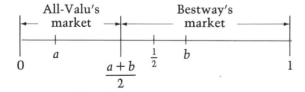

FIGURE 1.3 Firms' markets.

Shoppers patronize the nearest firm. Since the point $(a + b)/2$ is equidistant from a and b, All-Valu's market extends from 0 to $(a + b)/2$, and Bestway's market extends from $(a + b)/2$ to 1.

Combining this expression with the previous one for All-Valu's profit, we have

All-Valu's profit

$$= (P - C)\left[N\left(\frac{a + b}{2}\right)\right] \quad \text{when } a < b$$

PROBLEM 1.3

Suppose that N is 128, b is $\frac{3}{4}$, and $P - C$ is 1. When a is 0, what is the point of market segmentation? How many customers shop at All-Valu? What is All-Valu's profit? When a is $\frac{1}{4}$? When a is $\frac{1}{2}$? Does the number of All-Valu's customers increase or decrease as a increases?

Given that the only decision All-Valu can make that affects its profit is where to locate, which value of a maximizes All-Valu's profit? As you saw in Problem 1.3, as a increases, the point of market segmentation, $(a + b)/2$, moves to the right and All-Valu's market segment increases. Because All-Valu's profit is *directly* proportional to its market segment, its profit increases as a increases. Thus, our model predicts that when $a < b$, All-Valu will locate as close to b as possible; that is, a will be just less than b.[2] Of course, All-Valu is also free to locate anywhere *to the right* of Bestway; that is, to choose $a > b$. If it does so, All-Valu's profit is expressed by

All-Valu's profit

$$= (P - C) N\left[1 - \left(\frac{a + b}{2}\right)\right] \text{when } a > b$$

PROBLEM 1.4

Draw a diagram similar to Figure 1.3 in which $a > b$. First, find the point of market segmentation, and show that the length of All-Valu's mar-

---

[2] In this exercise, All-Valu is choosing its location a to maximize its profit. The partial derivative of this profit function with respect to a is $[(P - C)N]/2$, which is positive. All-Valu's profit is thus an increasing function of a. All-Valu will therefore locate as near to b as possible.

ket segment is $[1 - (a + b)/2]$. **Now derive the expression for All-Valu's profit. Finally, suppose again that N is 128, b is $\frac{3}{4}$, and $P - C$ is 1, and find the point of market segmentation, the number of All-Valu's customers, and All-Valu's profit when a is 1. When a is $\frac{7}{8}$.**

When All-Valu locates to the right of Bestway $(a > b)$, it is clear that as it relocates farther and farther to the right, it loses customers to Bestway, and its profit drops. Thus, when $a > b$, All-Valu's profit is largest when a is just to the right of b.

In Figure 1.4, we've used the two algebraic expressions for All-Valu's profit to graph its profit as a varies from 0 to 1. Possible locations for All-Valu along Main Street are on the horizontal axis, and its profit is on the vertical axis. So that you can verify the details, in drawing this figure we've sup-

posed that N, b, and $P - C$ are the values specified in Problems 1.3 and 1.4. We've also assumed that when a is equal to b, the stores split the market evenly. From Figure 1.4, we see that—because we have assumed that b exceeds $\frac{1}{2}$—All-Valu will locate just to the left of Bestway. However, if b is less than $\frac{1}{2}$, All-Valu will instead decide to locate just to the right of b. The general inference that we have drawn is that All-Valu will locate adjacent to its competitor on one side or the other. Whether it chooses to be on the right or on the left will depend on whether b is smaller or larger than $\frac{1}{2}$. It will choose whichever side gives it the larger segment of the market. Of course, Bestway will choose its location in exactly the same way. As a result, we have

PREDICTION 2

When a store is relocating, it will always choose to establish itself adjacent to its competitor on the side farther from a market boundary (points 0 and 1).

Prediction 2 begins to make sense of our earlier observations about how gas stations tend to cluster at the same intersection.

Finding the Equilibrium of Locations

From prediction 2, we can deduce the equilibrium of locations in our model. By **equilibrium,** we mean a location for All-Valu and one for Bestway such that neither store can increase its profit by changing its own location. (We'll have more to say about notions of equilibrium in Chapter 2.) We can find the equilibrium by discovering what would happen if both stores were to locate to one side of the midpoint $(\frac{1}{2})$ of Main Street.

In Figure 1.5, Bestway is initially located at b_1. Because it is closer than its competitor to the midpoint and therefore commands the larger share of the market, it will stay put. However, because All-Valu is ini-

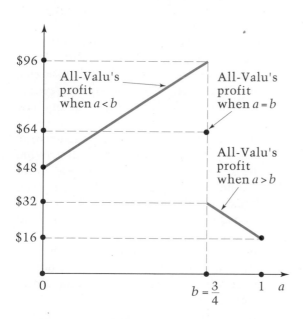

FIGURE 1.4 Profit as a function of location.

The green line gives All-Valu's profit for all addresses a from 0 to 1, given that Bestway is located at $\frac{3}{4}$. When $a < \frac{3}{4}$, All-Valu's profit increases as a increases. When $a > \frac{3}{4}$, All-Valu's profit decreases as a increases. Because All-Valu's profit is largest when a is just less than $\frac{3}{4}$, it will locate there.

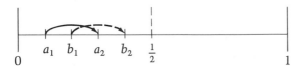

FIGURE 1.5   The equilibrium of locations.

The firms are initially located at a_1 and b_1. All-Valu relocates at a_2, inducing Bestway to relocate at b_2. This process of relocation by leapfrogging stops only when the firms are both located at the midpoint of the market; that is, $a = b = \frac{1}{2}$ is the equilibrium pair of locations.

tially located at a_1, it will "leapfrog" its competitor and relocate adjacent to its competitor on the side closer to the midpoint at a_2. As a result of All-Valu's move, Bestway's share of the market will drop. It will then leapfrog All-Valu to recapture its market advantage.

This process will continue until both grocery stores are finally *located together at the center of Main Street.* Of course, this leapfrogging is not something we would actually expect to see, but rather something these two firms would play out in their minds before choosing their equilibrium locations at the center of the market. (In Exercise 4 at the end of the chapter, you can explore how a store might think through the leapfrogging game before it chooses its location.)

PREDICTION 3

Both stores will locate together at the center of the market.

In the following problem, you can show that the locations just predicted actually represent an equilibrium.

PROBLEM 1.5

If both grocery stores are located at address $\frac{1}{2}$, can either store increase its profit by choosing some other location? Assume that N is 128, b is $\frac{1}{2}$, and $P - C$ is 1, and then construct a graph like Figure 1.4. Notice that because All-Valu's profit is largest when a is $\frac{1}{2}$, it will stay put. Will Bestway also stay put?

Although prediction 3 is limited to how two stores will locate in geographic space, economists such as Hotelling and Boulding believe that the prediction about clustering at a central position can be generalized to a significant range of other economic and even noneconomic problems. For instance, Kenneth Boulding (1966) has listed observations that illustrate what he calls the **principle of minimum differentiation:**

> It explains why all the dime stores are usually clustered together, often next door to each other; why certain towns attract large numbers of firms of one kind; why an industry; such as the garment industry, will concentrate in one quarter of a city. It is a principle which can be carried over into other "differences" than spatial differences. The general rule for any new manufacturer coming into an industry is: "Make your product as like the existing products as you can without destroying the differences." It explains why all automobiles are so much alike. . . . It even explains why Methodists, Baptists, and even Quakers are so much alike, and tend to get even more alike, for if one church is to attract the adherents of another, it must become more like the other but not so much alike that no one can tell the difference. (p. 601)

Our locational model is just one among many economic models. Its abstractions are tailored to the problem of minimum differentiation that it addresses. Its purpose is to explore the forces that generate minimum differentiation or, more generally, to *ex-*

plain minimum differentiation. In this sense, economic models are like maps—*constructed for particular purposes.* Think of the differences between city street maps, underground utility maps, road maps, atlases, topographical maps, weather maps, celestial navigation maps, and electrical circuit maps. Economic models vary just as maps do, depending on what kinds of questions they are designed to answer.

Self-Interest: The Engine of Economic Analysis

Despite their individual variations, all economic models are based on the assumption that economic agents pursue their own self-interest—a psychological assumption that lies at the very heart of our model. The model's first prediction—that customers will shop at the nearer grocery store—arose from the self-interested behavior of consumers trying to save themselves the additional expense of traveling to the more distant store. Similarly, the second and third predictions—that one store will locate next to its competitor on the side associated with the larger market segment and that both stores will ultimately locate side by side in the center of the market—arose from the self-interested behavior of firms attempting to maximize their private gain. At the core of any economic model is the assumption that economic agents pursue their own self-interest; that is, positive economic analysis is driven by self-interested behavior. Indeed, this approach is so pervasive that economics can be described accurately as the study of the implications of the assumption of self-interested behavior.

1.4 The Evaluation of Models

Our location model illustrates the central function of microeconomic theory: to provide models that allow us to understand and interpret economic behavior in the real world. But how do we decide whether a particular economic model is a useful one? Although evaluating economic models is still a matter of debate among economists, we can distinguish "good" models from less useful ones by isolating three characteristics: simplicity, fruitfulness, and robustness.

Simplicity

We have seen that, in some sense, our location model is a simple one. Yet that reduction to stark simplicity is the source of its power. It has cut away a great deal of messy detail and left us with a key insight: firms tend to cluster at the center of their markets. This seemingly simple insight is extraordinarily powerful. It reveals why some firms—whether gas stations, grocery stores, car dealerships, or movie theaters—choose to cluster together at certain geographical locations.

Fruitfulness

Simpler models are also preferred to more complex ones because they are potentially more generalizable, or fruitful. They can be applied to a wider range of economic events.[3] In explaining clustering, our model not only tells us something about why firms tend to locate together, but also helps to explain why competitors also tend to imitate one another in the qualities or the range of goods they offer and in other essential ways

---

[3] Hotelling's original location model stimulated a good deal of subsequent research. These are but a few of many papers inspired by Hotelling's model: Lerner and Singer (1937); Smithies (1941); Eaton and Lipsey (1975); and d'Aspremont, Gabsewicz, and Thisse (1979).

as well. Our location model thus generalizes from the clustering of locations in geographic space to the clustering of products in other domains. Many economic activities that display a tendency toward clustering or mutual imitation can be accounted for by the basic model, although we may need to reinterpret one or more of the model's assumptions.

To explore the potential fruitfulness of our model, we can reinterpret it in another context: the morning scheduling decisions made by competing airlines on the route from, say, Chicago to Atlanta. Let's assume that most people prefer to arrive within an hour of 8 A.M., a time neither too early for most travelers to arrive nor too late to leave them a good part of the day to spend in Atlanta. The assumption is, then, that most morning passengers prefer to fly in the early morning but will accept arrival times before or after their most preferred time.

If one airline picks 8 o'clock as its arrival time, when will its rival schedule its morning arrival? As we discovered in the leapfrogging exercise, the competitive strategy is to get between one's rival and the mass of customers by locating just next to the rival on the side with the larger market segment. If more customers prefer to arrive after rather than before 8 o'clock, we can predict that the rival airline will schedule an arrival just slightly after 8 o'clock. Notice that we have implicitly modified the assumption about distance: we have substituted *time* — the stretch of time within which morning arrivals are acceptable to air travelers — for *distance.* (How have we also implicitly redefined our assumption about what constitutes the self-interest of airline passengers?)

By scheduling a flight that arrives just after 8 A.M., the rival airline picks up all the midmorning traffic — passengers who have no later choice — yet it does not forfeit customers who prefer times closer to 8 A.M. We

then predict that the two rivals will locate at the center of the market for morning air travel.

We can test the prediction in a rough way by looking at how airlines actually schedule flights. For example, one day at Atlanta's Hartsfield Airport, 45 commercial flights were scheduled to land between 8 A.M. and 8:10 A.M.

From the airline example, we can see that a fruitful model can provide an agenda for further research. Reasoning by analogy, we extended a spatial model to a temporal one while preserving its essential features. Again reasoning by analogy, we can apply our locational model to noneconomic phenomena. Political scientists have used the spatial model to analyze political platforms in a two-party system. Political parties — like rival firms — tend to choose politically central positions. In our location model, the two competing stores located together in the middle of their market. By analogy, we can predict that both parties in a two-party system will establish themselves side by side at politically centrist positions. According to the principle of minimum differentiation, although one party will be politically more to the "left" and one more to the "right," both will shun extremist positions.[4] A fruitful theory, then, is one that generalizes, inviting extensions by means of analogy.

Robustness

When applying an existing model in a new context, however, we must rework the assumptions of the original model scrupulously. (How must we reinterpret each of

---

[4] The most ambitious application of this type of model to politics is Downs (1957), a readable and enlightening book.

the assumptions in our location model to achieve logically consistent predictions about the similarities between the Republican and Democratic parties?) The ability of a given theory to account for a variety of economic phenomena depends on the model's robustness, how well its predictive value stands up to changes in the initial assumptions.

To test our model for robustness, let's make a change in one of its assumptions. Does changing the assumption radically alter our model's predictions? If it does, we can be confident that the assumption is critical to our result. By questioning and reinterpreting the original assumptions of a theory, we can very often gain new insights or arrive at more accurate formulations of the problem. For example, what happens to the equilibrium of our location model if we change the geographical assumption? Suppose that the population of N individuals is not uniformly distributed on a *linear street* beginning at 0 and ending at 1. Instead, suppose that the population is uniformly distributed on a one-unit-long *circular road* stretching around the perimeter of a volcanic island.

PROBLEM 1.6

Draw a circle and locate the two grocery stores at any two points on it. How do the two stores divide the market? Now shift one of the stores to any other location and see what happens to the pattern of customer patronage. Do they divide the market differently? Show that any pair of locations is an equilibrium in this model. What does your result suggest about the driving force behind minimum differentiation?

As you found in Problem 1.6, the principle of minimum differentiation does not arise in a circular market. The division of customer patronage does not change when the locations of the two stores are changed. For our location model's predictions to hold, we need *market boundaries* — a be-

ginning and an end to the market for customers. In the circular case, the market is *unbounded*; that is, there are no points at which the geographical market begins and ends. The assumption of boundaries is therefore critical, and the theory is not robust when this assumption is altered.

By contrast, if we substitute *variable density* for uniform density, this alteration does not substantially affect the predictions of the model.

PROBLEM 1.7

Replace the uniform density of population on Main Street with the *variable density* illustrated in Figure 1.6. Location along Main Street is measured along the horizontal axis. Population density is measured along the vertical axis. Therefore, the height of the density curve gives the density of population at any location on Main Street. The area under the curve between two points is the number of customers living between those points. For example, the green area under the density curve from addresses 0 through $\frac{1}{4}$ in Figure 1.6 represents the population living between 0 and $\frac{1}{4}$. Similarly, the area under the curve from $\frac{1}{4}$ to 1 represents the population to the right of address $\frac{1}{4}$. What will be the equilibrium of locations given this variable-density function?

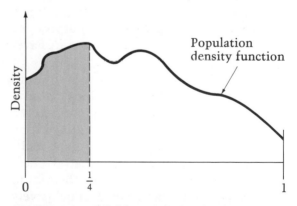

FIGURE 1.6   Variable population density.

The height of the density function reflects the population density. The population between any two points is therefore the area below the density function (and above the horizontal axis) between the two points. For example, the green area is the population between 0 and $\frac{1}{4}$.

As you just discovered, the most interesting prediction of our location model — minimum differentiation — is robust with respect to changes in the density of consumers. The uniform-density assumption is not crucial to minimum differentiation. By playing with the assumptions of a model, we discover its strengths and weaknesses, the situations in which it is potentially applicable and those in which it is not.

Testing Economic Models

We know that the goal of constructing economic theories is to get accurate predictions about the real world. If economic theory is to be useful, it must yield predictions that can be tested. When such theories are empirically tested, a number of special constraints must be added. Because a theory can be empirically tested only against a specific set of data, the theory must be respecified to accommodate the data. In fact, some economists reserve the term *theory* for the general statement containing the assumptions and deductions and use the term *model* for a specific instance of the theory that they constructed to test it against a particular set of data. (Notice that this process of creating a specific version of a theory for purposes of empirical testing once again provides avenues for fruitful research.)

A particular economic model is evaluated by confronting its predictions with evidence from the real world. How accurately a model forecasts economic events, therefore, is a measure of its value. Yet significant difficulties attend such empirical testing.[5] Economic theories — like scientific theories in general — cannot be proved conclusively true. One problem is that most economic tests are not conducted in the laboratory. As a result, one or more variables that were assumed to have been held constant may not have been and, therefore, may influence the results. Nevertheless, one of the exciting developments in economics in recent years is the emergence of experimental or laboratory economics as a means of testing basic economic models. We will look at some of this laboratory evidence in later chapters. A related problem is that because most economic data occur in a natural, not an experimental, setting, economists cannot repeat historic economic events in order to produce new evidence to retest the predictions. **Econometrics** is a specialized field of economics that attempts to overcome these empirical difficulties.

1.5 Normative Economics

In our location model, we have been trying to understand the real-world phenomenon of minimum differentiation. This is the domain of **positive economics.** We can also ask if we *like what we see.* In terms of our model, this means asking whether we find minimum differentiation desirable. This is the domain of **normative economics.** Although economists sometimes find it difficult to separate normative economics from positive economics — and indeed debate whether the distinction can accurately be made — we can arrive at generally acceptable working definitions of the two concepts.

Positive Versus Normative Economics

Positive economics tells us what is or has been and attempts to predict on that basis what will be. It involves questions about the *facts* of economic activity; therefore, "positive" answers to microeconomic questions

[5] For a discussion of the methodological issues raised by testing, see Friedman (1953), Samuelson (1963), and Boland (1979).

are always supported or refuted by reference to facts: What happens to the price of butter when the price of margarine falls? What happens to the stock of rental housing when rent controls are imposed? Do we, in fact, observe minimum differentiation? The supporting evidence for answers to such positive questions is produced by conducting scrupulous observations of the facts of the real world, however difficult those facts might be to collect and interpret. Building models to explain real phenomena, as we have done in creating this particular location model, is positive analysis.

By contrast, normative questions involve *value judgments* and cannot be answered by reference to objective facts alone. Answers also depend on our commitment to *values* that are essentially outside the scope of positive economics. Should we have a system of free public education? Should we guarantee a minimum income to all our citizens? Should we require businesses to hire specific percentages of certain minority groups? These normative questions are answered by citing ethical statements of value, such as "All people are created equal." They are based on ethical judgments we as members of society make about what is good or evil, right or wrong, desirable or undesirable.

Normative Questions in the Location Model

We have seen how our location model can be used to illustrate positive analysis. Now we'll see how normative analysis works with the model. Issues of social welfare — of what contributes to and detracts from the common good — are clearly normative. How do economists evaluate different social states to determine whether, from a societal perspective, one state is better, or more desirable, than another? And what value judgments do such comparisons (at least implicitly) invoke?

Let's return to our location model to explore these questions by asking if minimum differentiation is socially desirable. Rather than provide a general definition of **social state,** we'll use the model to illustrate what it means. (The term will be defined in Chapter 2.) In our model, any pair of locations defines a social state because the pair determines what transport cost each customer must pay and what profit each grocery store owner will realize. In short, any locational configuration determines the well-being of all individual economic agents, shoppers and store owners alike.

Two social states are illustrated in Figure 1.7. State 1 in Figure 1.7a is the equilibrium of locations from our location model. The point of market segmentation is at $\frac{1}{2}$.

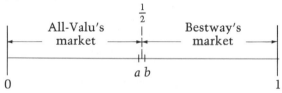

(a) State 1

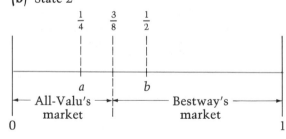

(b) State 2

FIGURE 1.7 Comparing social states.

In state 1, both firms are located at $\frac{1}{2}$. In state 2, Bestway is located at $\frac{1}{2}$ and All-Valu at $\frac{1}{4}$. Shoppers in interval $(0, \frac{3}{8})$ prefer state 2 because they are closer to their preferred store. Shoppers in interval $(\frac{3}{8}, 1)$ are indifferent between states 1 and 2. All-Valu prefers state 1 because its profit is larger in state 1, whereas Bestway prefers state 2 because its profit is larger in state 2.

The customers from addresses 0 through $\frac{1}{2}$ shop at All-Valu, and the customers from addresses $\frac{1}{2}$ to 1 shop at Bestway. State 2 in Figure 1.7*b* is a locational configuration in which All-Valu is located at address $\frac{1}{4}$ and Bestway is at address $\frac{1}{2}$. The point of market segmentation is at $\frac{3}{8}$. The customers from addresses 0 to $\frac{3}{8}$ shop at All-Valu, and customers from $\frac{3}{8}$ to 1 shop at Bestway.

The Primacy of the Individual

What information would we want to have to compare — or *rank* — the *desirability* of these two social states? To economists, the answer is clear. The only relevant information is data about the well-being of the individual members of the society. You can see what the underlying value judgment is in this choice of data: what counts is the welfare of individuals.

In Chapter 3, we will define individual welfare more precisely. Here, we'll use our location model to illustrate its meaning. Who are the individuals whose well-being is at stake? They are the owners of the two grocery stores and the grocery shoppers. (For simplicity, we'll assume that each grocery store is owned by a single individual.) What affects the fortunes of these two groups of individuals? An owner is better or worse off, respectively, as the store's profit is larger or smaller. A customer — who always buys one unit of groceries from the nearer store at the fixed price P — fares better or worse as the distance to the nearer store is smaller or larger.

Let's consider what happens to individual welfare in a move from state 1 to state 2 in Figure 1.7. We can organize the relevant information about individual welfare by assigning each person to one of three possible groups. Group I (indifferent) is composed of owners and shoppers who are equally well off in either state 1 or state 2. All of Bestway's customers in state 2 — those located between $\frac{3}{8}$ and 1 — fall into this group because in both states they travel the same distance to buy groceries. Group W (winner) is made up of all those who do better in state 2. All of All-Valu's customers in state 2 — those between addresses 0 and $\frac{3}{8}$ — are in this category because they travel a shorter distance than in state 1. In addition, the owner of Bestway is a winner because the store's profit increases by $\$[N(P - C)]/8$. Group L (loser) is composed of those individuals whose welfare is adversely affected by a move to state 2. The obvious (and only) loser is the owner of All-Valu, because that store's profit drops by $\$[N(P - C)]/8$. In effect, in the move from state 1 to state 2, this amount of profit has been taken away from All-Valu's owner and handed over to Bestway's owner. (You should verify these changes in the firms' profits.)

The Pareto Criterion

How can we use this individual welfare data to determine — from the perspective of the entire society — which of the two states is better, or "preferred"? One pervasive and almost universally accepted criterion used by economists to rank social states is the **Pareto criterion.** Vilfredo Pareto, a turn-of-the-century Italian economist, argued that one social state is better than another if everyone is as well off and if at least one person is better off in the first state than in the second. Although the Pareto criterion is a value judgment, it is not hard to accept. Moreover, it plays such a central role in economic analysis that we will be invoking it at many points throughout the book. Let's define the Pareto criterion in terms of two arbitrary social states, state I and state J.

D E F I N I T I O N: Pareto Criterion

In comparing any two social states, say I and J, we will say that state I is *Pareto-preferred* to state J if no one is worse off and if at least one person is better off in state I than in state J. If state I is Pareto-preferred to state J, we say that a move from state J to state I is *Pareto-improving*.

Returning to our location model, we see first that the Pareto criterion does not rank the two social states described in Figure 1.7. Even though there are many winners in a move from state 1 to state 2 (Bestway's owner and the grocery shoppers from addresses 0 to $\frac{3}{8}$), there is also a loser (All-Valu's owner). To rank social states, the Pareto criterion requires not only that at least one person gains by the move but also that no one loses out. Because All-Valu's owner is made worse off by the move, we cannot conclude that state 2 is Pareto-preferred to state 1, or vice versa. This does not mean that the two states are therefore equivalent. It means only that the Pareto criterion is silent about their relative social desirability.

Notice that the Pareto criterion will rank state 2 as Pareto-preferred to state 1 under one condition: if the move to state 2 is combined with a transfer of $\$[N(P - C)]/8$ from Bestway's owner to All-Valu's owner. Because All-Valu's owner is exactly compensated for the loss of profit incurred in the move from state 1 to state 2 by receiving the money transfer, and because the welfare of Bestway's owner is now precisely the same in either state, our model has no losers. It has only winners (all of the customers from 0 to $\frac{3}{8}$) and those whose welfare remains the same (both store owners and the customers from $\frac{3}{8}$ to 1). If we call this state-2-with-transfer "state 2T," we can say that state 2T is *Pareto-preferred* to state 1, or that a move from state 1 to state 2T is *Pareto-improving*.

PROBLEM 1.8

What does the Pareto criterion tell us about the relative desirability of states 2 and 2T?

Another important economic concept used repeatedly throughout this book — **Pareto optimality** — follows directly from the Pareto criterion.

DEFINITION: Pareto-Optimal

We call a social state Pareto-optimal if no other social state is Pareto-preferred to it.

Pareto optimality plays so important a role in economics that it is synonymous with economic efficiency. Accordingly, we will use the terms **Pareto-optimal, Pareto-efficient,** and **efficient** interchangeably.

Although the concept of Pareto optimality, or efficiency, is a central idea in economics, it does not identify the best possible social state; it only rules out certain states as being inefficient. To see why Pareto optimality does not answer all the tough questions in economics, consider the following problem.

PROBLEM 1.9

Two gluttons must split a pecan pie. A social state in this context is simply a particular division of the pie: X% to one glutton and $(100 - X)$% to the other. What values of X are Pareto-optimal, or efficient?

Economic policymakers are invariably confronted with making choices between social states: they must either choose the status quo or implement a new policy. Yet few, if any, policies are free of adverse consequences for at least some individuals. In a choice between two states, whenever we find that some people prefer the first state and that others prefer the second, the Pareto criterion tells us only that neither state is Pareto-preferred to the other. You can see that this information is not manifestly useful to policymakers who must recommend for or against a particular policy. Guided solely by the Pareto criterion, they might always opt for the status quo, evaluating the best policy as no policy change.

Cost-Benefit Analysis

Do we have any alternative criterion to Pareto's? A deceptively simple but less widely accepted criterion that some economists use to compare social states is cost-benefit analysis. The **cost-benefit criterion** is particularly attractive to policymakers because it will rank social states where the Pareto criterion will not.

To see how cost-benefit analysis is done, let's consider a move from any social state to any other; say, from state I to state J. In calculating the social benefits from such a move, we first identify the winners, those whose fortunes improve as a result of the move, and then place a dollar value on each winner's private benefit. (One way to compute the dollar value is to determine by what amount we would have to increase the winner's income in state I to make him or her indifferent between the two states.) Finally, we add up all the measures of private benefit to arrive at the *gross social benefit.*

In calculating the social costs of the move from state I to state J, we identify the losers, those whose fortunes are adversely affected, and place a dollar value on the private cost to each of them. (How would you determine each loser's private cost?) We then add all the measures of individual cost to arrive at the *gross social cost.*

If we then subtract the gross social cost from the gross social benefit, we have the *net social benefit.* We can use net social benefit to define the cost-benefit criterion.

DEFINITION: Cost-Benefit Criterion

In the move from social state I to social state J, if net social benefit is positive then the cost-benefit criterion ranks state J as preferred to state I. On the other hand, if net social benefit is negative then the cost-benefit criterion ranks state I as preferred to state J.

In our location model, we can calculate customers' costs and benefits by comparing transportation costs for each customer in the two social states, and we can calculate store owners' costs and benefits by comparing the profits for each in the two states. As you will see in the following problem, the cost-benefit criterion speaks where the Pareto criterion is silent.

PROBLEM 1.10

Using the cost-benefit criterion, compare states 1 and 2; states 1 and 2T; and states 2 and 2T.

As you now know, the cost-benefit criterion ranks state 2 as more desirable than state 1; state 2T as more desirable than state 1; and states 2 and 2T as equally desirable. By contrast, the Pareto criterion ranks only state 2T relative to state 1.

The cost-benefit criterion is clearly more powerful because it provides more answers than does the Pareto criterion. Why? Because the cost-benefit criterion is blind to the distribution of costs and benefits over individuals, whereas the Pareto criterion is not. Which individuals enjoy greater benefits or incur greater costs is not at issue. What matters is that the *net social benefit is positive.* In moving from state 1 to state 2T, both criteria rank state 2T as more desirable because there are no losers. By contrast, in a move from state 1 to state 2, the Pareto criterion refuses to rank the two states because the welfare of All-Valu's owner is adversely affected. Yet the cost-benefit criterion does rank state 2 as better than state 1 because the cost borne by All-Valu's owner — the only loser in the move from state 1 to state 2 — is *exactly offset* by the gain to Bestway's owner and because all of the customers from addresses 0 to $\frac{3}{8}$ *gain* by the move to state 2.

A strong — and to many economists, strongly objectionable — assumption of cost-benefit analysis is that "a dollar is a dollar." In cost-benefit calculations, a dollar of cost to one person can always be offset by a dollar of benefit to any other person. This assumption, like the Pareto criterion, is clearly a value judgment. Many economists refuse to endorse it and consequently decline to use the cost-benefit criterion. We will use the Pareto criterion at many points throughout the book. We will also use cost-benefit analysis, but less often — and always with the understanding that it carries the troublesome "a dollar is a dollar" assumption.

Both the Pareto and the cost-benefit normative criteria tell us that state 1 — the equilibrium of our location model — is less socially desirable than state 2T. Using the cost-benefit criterion, we can go one step further and identify the single best configuration of locations in the model. The aggregate profit of the two stores is independent of their locations because aggregate profit is $N(P - C)$, regardless of where they locate. Therefore, the best configuration is the one that *minimizes travel costs.* If we suppose that the relationship between distance traveled and costs incurred is proportional to distance and is the same for all customers, then the configuration of store locations that minimizes transport cost — illustrated in Figure 1.8 — is one in which one store is located at address $\frac{1}{4}$ and the other store at address $\frac{3}{4}$. Consequently, the social state illustrated in Figure 1.8 is *cost-benefit optimal.* In this configuration, no customer is

farther than $\frac{1}{4}$ mile from the nearer store. By comparison, in the equilibrium of our location model, half the population (the customers located between 0 and $\frac{1}{4}$ and between $\frac{3}{4}$ and 1) must travel more than $\frac{1}{4}$ mile.

Summary

The principal objective of this chapter has been to set out the working methodology of the microeconomic theorist. Because microeconomic theory attempts to explain economic reality, what often sparks the theorist's interest is an intriguing observation from ordinary life coupled with the question why: Why are premium beers or national politicians so much alike, for example?

The theorist then builds a model (or theory) to explain the phenomenon. This model building is the process of judiciously selecting a set of assumptions that capture the essential features of that economic reality and of logically deriving conclusions, or predictions, from those assumptions. The force that drives this deductive process is invariably the self-interest of the individual economic agents. In fact, the systematic application of this method of analysis distinguishes economics from other social sciences.

The usefulness of economic theories can be evaluated. Three widely accepted standards for judging economic models are simplicity, fruitfulness, and robustness. Other things being equal, a simpler model is preferred to a more complex one because it is easier to comprehend. A model is fruitful if it explains a wide range of economic phenomena. A model is robust if its major predictions do not vary as the assumptions are changed.

The real test of any model is its ability to explain and predict economic reality. Testing therefore confronts the predictions

FIGURE 1.8   Cost-benefit optimal locations.

Because the aggregate profit of All-Valu and Bestway is independent of their locations, the cost-benefit optimal locations minimize shoppers' travel costs. The pair of locations that minimizes aggregate travel costs is $\frac{1}{4}$ and $\frac{3}{4}$.

of a model with the facts of economic life. Econometrics is a field of economics devoted to empirically testing economic models. Experimental, or laboratory, economics has recently begun to contribute to empirical testing of models as well.

In doing microeconomic theory, it is important to distinguish between positive economic analysis (supported or refuted by objective fact) and normative economic analysis (supported or refuted by reference to ethical judgments outside the scope of economics per se). Building models to explain real events is an exercise in positive economics. Evaluating, or ranking, different social states is a normative exercise.

Economists almost universally accept the value judgment that the only data necessary to evaluate the relative desirability of different social states are data about the welfare of individuals. Economists also typically accept the Pareto criterion for ranking social states: one state — say, state I — is Pareto-preferred to another state — say, state J — if no one is worse off and at least one person is better off in state I than in state J. The Pareto criterion is used to define Pareto optimality, a concept so fundamental to economics that it is synonymous with economic efficiency. A social state is Pareto-optimal, or efficient, if no other state is Pareto-preferred to it.

Unfortunately, the Pareto criterion is not often helpful in choosing between social states. For this reason, policy economists are often willing to make value judgments stronger than, but not as widely acceptable as, the judgments supporting the Pareto criterion. One such value judgment is that in evaluating a move from one social state to another, a dollar of private benefit (or private cost) should be counted as a dollar of social benefit (or social cost), regardless of who gains (or loses). This value judgment gives rise to the cost-benefit criterion for comparing social states, a criterion that will

rank social states where the Pareto criterion will not.

Exercises

1   "In economics any equilibrium is always optimal; in fact, the terms equilibrium and optimum are synonymous." Discuss.

2   Suppose that in our location model there are three firms on Main Street. Show that an equilibrium of locations does not exist.

3   In our location model, show that any pair of locations is Pareto-optimal. To do so, consider any pair of locations for the two firms, and then show that any change in the location of one firm, or of both firms, makes someone worse off. What pairs of locations are Pareto-optimal in the circular version of the location model described in Problem 1.6?

4   In finding the equilibrium of Hotelling's duopoly model, we assumed that the two grocers could change their locations at no cost. Consider the opposite extreme: assume that once they have chosen a location, the grocers cannot relocate their stores. Let All-Valu choose its location first and assume that it understands that once its location is chosen, Bestway will choose the location that maximizes its own profit. Which locations will the firms choose?

*5   When we analyzed the circular model with a *uniform* customer density, we discovered that any pair of locations was an equilibrium. Let's consider what happens in the circular model with a *variable* density. Think of locations on the circle in terms of times on a clock face, and suppose that the variable density is greatest at 12 o'clock, smallest at 6 o'clock, and symmetric about 12 o'clock. Density at 9 o'clock is then equal to density at 3 o'clock, which is less than density at 12 o'clock and more than density at 6 o'clock. What is the equilibrium of locations in this model?

---

* Throughout this book, the more difficult problems are marked by an asterisk.

References

Boland, L. (1979), "A Critique of Friedman's Critics," *Journal of Economic Literature*, 17:503–522.

Boland, L. (1987), "Methodology," in *The New Palgrave*, vol. 3, J. Eatwell, M. Milgate, and P. Newman (eds.), London: Macmillan, 455–488.

Boulding, K. (1966), *Economic Analysis*, New York: Harper & Row.

d'Aspremont, C., J. Gabsewicz, and J. Thisse (1979), "On Hotelling's 'Stability in Competition,'" *Econometrica*, 47:1145–1150.

Downs, A. (1957), "An Economic Theory of Political Action in a Democracy," *Journal of Political Economy*, 65:135–150.

Eaton, B. C., and R. G. Lipsey (1975), "The Principle of Minimum Differentiation Reconsid-

ered: Some New Developments in the Theory of Spatial Competition," *Review of Economic Studies*, 42:27–49.

Friedman, M. (1953), "The Methodology of Positive Economics," *Essays in Positive Economics*, Chicago: University of Chicago.

Hotelling, H. (1929), "Stability in Competition," *The Economic Journal*, 39:41–57.

Lerner, A., and H. Singer (1937), "Some Notes on Duopoly and Spatial Competition," *Journal of Political Economy*, 45:145–186.

Samuelson, P. A. (1963), "Discussion of Problems of Methodology," *American Economic Review*, 53:231–236.

Smithies, A. (1941), "Optimum Location in Spatial Competition," *Journal of Political Economy*, 49:423–439.

2

THE ECONOMY AND ECONOMICS

In Chapter 1, you plunged into doing microeconomic theory. In this chapter, we'll systematically explore the meaning of terms such as *economy*, *economics*, and *microeconomics*. We'll ask: What is an economy? How does microeconomics differ from macroeconomics? What is economic policy? What role do property rights and other institutions play in coordinating economic activity? Precisely what do we mean by the term *equilibrium*? Along the way, we'll develop another simple, but powerful, model to illustrate answers to some of these questions, and we'll introduce two extremely important tools: comparative institutional analysis and comparative statics analysis. Finally, we'll trace out the path followed in the remainder of the book and do a quick review of the tools of supply and demand.

2.1 Economics Informally Defined

The purpose of economic activity is to transform resources into goods and services. Goods and services — or **goods,** for short — are what individuals value: artichokes, T-shirts, haircuts, 18 holes of golf, and so on. **Resources** are what are used to

produce such goods. Land in the Salinas Valley of California, for instance, is a resource because it can be used to produce artichokes (or cotton or a shopping mall or recreational facility). Your time is another resource because it can be used in growing artichokes (or manufacturing cotton fiber or building a shopping center or playing golf). With these concepts, we have an informal but useful definition:

Economics is the study of the allocation of scarce resources to the production of alternative goods.

Two words in this definition deserve special attention: *scarce* and *alternative.* It is almost impossible to think of a resource that is not scarce. Rainwater in January on the Olympic Peninsula in Washington State is perhaps one of the few examples of a resource effectively in unlimited supply. From an economist's perspective, how to share out the Olympic Peninsula's January rainwater is a not an interesting question because no tough allocative decisions must be made: there is more than enough water to go around.

Because resources are normally in limited supply, understanding how they are allocated to alternative uses is a fundamental economic question. It is difficult to imagine a resource with only one possible use. Think of the many ways water and oil are used in different production processes. Because resources almost invariably can be used in any number of productive processes, understanding how they are allocated to alternative ends becomes a difficult economic problem. Indeed, our dominant concern throughout this book is to discover the principles that direct resources to alternative uses in a **market economy,** an economy in which the dominant mode of economic activity is voluntary exchange.

2.2 Describing an Economy

Our informal definition of economics is useful but limited. To develop a deeper understanding of what economics is all about, we first need to know just what an economy is. We can describe any economy by breaking it down into four basic building blocks: a *resource endowment*, a *technology*, *preferences* of individuals, and *institutions.*

As you read about these building blocks for the first time, think in terms of an economy with a short time horizon of one or two periods. You may then want to reread the material, putting it into a richer intertemporal frame of reference. In doing so, you will need to recognize that goods, resources, and technologies must be described in terms of time: "artichokes today" and "artichokes tomorrow" are different goods; an hour of your time today and an hour of it tomorrow are different resources.

A Resource Endowment

A **resource endowment** consists of all the resources available to an economy. We could describe it by listing the quantities of all available resources: for example, X thousand acres of land in the Salinas Valley, Y cubic yards of coal in the Appalachian Mountains, Z hours of your time.

A Technology

An economy's **technology** specifies how resources can be used to produce goods. Figuratively speaking, it is the economy's cookbook. Suppose that we were thinking about producing 1000 tons of artichokes. The economy's technology would tell us all the different combinations of resources that could do the job: all the land-intensive techniques, all the labor-intensive techniques, all the hydroponic techniques, and so on. Our technological cookbook differs from an ordinary cookbook in that it provides not just one but a potentially large number of resource combinations that will all achieve a given result.

Production Possibilities Set

Taken together, the first two building blocks—a resource endowment and a technology—describe the economy's productive potential, or its **production possibilities set.** The production possibilities set is composed of all combinations of goods that the economy could produce with its resource endowment, given its technology. Figuratively speaking, if the economy's technology is its cookbook, then the production possibilities set is its menu.

To illustrate the production possibilities set, we'll focus on a very simple model in which there are just two periods—this year and next year—and two goods—fish consumed this year and fish consumed next year. The economy's resource endowment consists of 180 fish. We'll imagine that these fish are stored in fish pens, just as Maine lobstermen store their lobster catch in lobster pens. These fish can be consumed this year or they can be released into a river. If they are released, they will reproduce and their numbers will increase. For convenience, let's suppose that for every fish released this year, $\frac{5}{3}$ fish will be available for consumption next year. The technology of this fish economy is then described by the following statements:

One fish taken this year produces one fish for consumption this year.

One fish released this year produces $\frac{5}{3}$ fish for consumption next year.

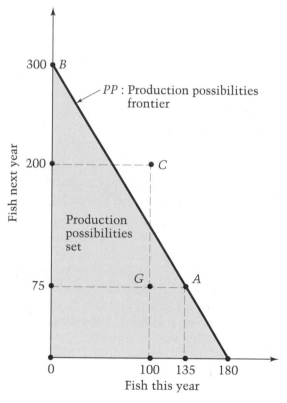

FIGURE 2.1   The production possibilities set.

The green area on and below the production possibilities frontier is the production possibilities set. Any combination of fish this year and fish next year in the green area can be produced. For example, (135, 75) at point A and (100, 75) at point G are combinations that can be produced, but (100, 200) at point C, above the production possibilities set, is a combination that cannot be produced.

Figure 2.1 illustrates our fish economy's production possibilities set. The quantity of fish consumed this year is measured on the horizontal axis, and the quantity of fish consumed next year is measured on the vertical axis. The green area represents the economy's production possibilities set. Any combination of this year's and next year's fish that lies on the line labeled PP or below and to the left of it can be produced in this economy. On the other hand, any combination of fish above and to the right of PP cannot be produced. For instance, the economy can produce 135 fish this year and 75 next year at point A in Figure 2.1, or it can produce 0 fish this year and 300 next year at point B. But it cannot produce 100 fish this year and 200 next year at point C. The upper boundary of the production possibilities set, labeled PP in Figure 2.1, is of special interest. It is called the **production possibilities frontier.**

PROBLEM 2.1

First, indicate which of the following combinations are in the production possibilities set for our fish economy and which are on the production possibilities frontier: 90 fish this year and 150 next year; 150 fish this year and 60 next year; 60 fish this year and 190 next year. Then find an algebraic expression for the production possibilities frontier.

Economic States

The production possibilities set, derived from the economy's resource endowment and its technology, describes the choices open to the economy as a whole. However, economics is concerned with more than an economy's aggregate production figures. To describe what we called in Chapter 1 a social state, or economic state, we also need to know how the aggregate output of goods is distributed among the individual members of the society. Thus, a **social state** is a specific allocation of goods to individuals. A description of a particular social state is simply a list of the individual members of a society and the quantities of each good allocated to each person.

Let's use our fish economy model as an illustration. Let's limit our attention to the case in which there are just two people in the economy — say, Ted and Amy. Now, if we pick a particular point from the production possibilities set in Figure 2.1 — say, point A, where 135 fish are consumed this year and 75 next year — we can illustrate an *array of possible social states.* The dimensions of the box in Figure 2.2 correspond to the combination of goods produced in our two-good economy. Its horizontal sides are 135 (fish) long, and its vertical sides are 75 (fish) long. The lower left-hand corner of the box is labeled 0_T because it is the origin for the allocation of goods to Ted. Relative to this origin, Ted's allocation is plotted in the standard way. A move to the right in the box corresponds to an increase in Ted's fish con-

sumption this year, and a move upward in the box corresponds to an increase in his fish consumption next year. The upper right-hand corner of the box, labeled 0_A, is the origin for Amy's allocation of goods. Relative to this origin, Amy's allocation is plotted in a slightly unorthodox way. A move to the left in the box corresponds to an increase in Amy's fish consumption this year, and a move downward corresponds to an increase in her fish consumption next year.

Any point in this box represents a social state: an allocation of goods to Ted and Amy that completely uses up the available goods. In the social state at point S, for instance, Ted consumes 100 fish this year and 25 next year, and Amy consumes 35 fish this year and 50 next year.

PROBLEM 2.2

What social state does point 0_A in Figure 2.2 represent? What social state does point B represent?

Each point in the production possibilities set gives rise to an array of social states analogous to those presented in Figure 2.2. The whole collection of such diagrams — one for every point in the production possibilities set — represents all possible social states in our simple two-person, two-good economy.

In Chapter 1, we discussed the differences between *normative* and *positive* economics. Here it's useful to highlight these different orientations relative to social states. Positive economics seeks to determine the social state an economy will actually attain. Normative economics compares social states to determine which state is "better" from a social welfare perspective. Before we can say more about these issues and about the interesting interplay between them, we need to introduce the third and fourth building blocks of an economy: preferences and institutions.

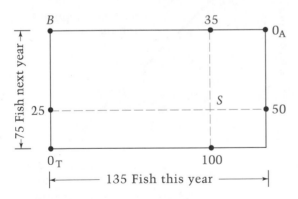

FIGURE 2.2   An array of social states.

Points in the box are allocations of the 135 fish this year and 75 fish next year. Ted's allocation is plotted relative to 0_T, and Amy's allocation is plotted relative to 0_A. At point S, Ted's allocation is (100, 25) and Amy's is (35, 50). In this two-person economy, an allocation is also a social state.

Preferences of Individuals

As you'll soon see, individuals' preferences about the goods and services they are allocated form the keystone of the economist's description of an economy. We'll consider preferences very carefully in Chapter 3. In the meantime, a quick preview, combined with some simple illustrations drawn from our fishing model, will do. In principle, to describe any person's preferences we would construct a **preference ordering**—a list of bundles of goods and services in which bundles are ranked in terms of relative desirability. Bundles appearing higher on an individual's list are preferred by that person to bundles lower on the list. For example, if Ted prefers the bundle containing 50 fish this year and 30 next year to the bundle containing 40 fish this year and 35 next year, then the first bundle of goods would appear above the second bundle in Ted's preference ordering.

To keep our fish economy as simple as possible, we'll assume that both Ted's and Amy's preferences are such that they always prefer the bundle with the larger total number of fish. In other words, given a choice between any two bundles, they will always choose the bundle containing more fish.

PROBLEM 2.3

Indicate how Amy would rank the following bundles: 10 fish this year and 140 next year; 160 fish this year and 0 next year; 78 fish this year and 78 next year; 90 fish this year and 70 next year.

Preferences are the keystone of the economist's edifice for two reasons. First, preferences are critical in *positive* economic analysis because they tell us how individuals will act. At the highest level of abstraction, the assumption of self-interested behavior means that each person will undertake actions that allow him or her to obtain the most preferred bundle attainable in his or her preference ordering. Second, prefer-

ences are central to *normative* economics because they give meaning to the expressions "worse off" and "better off." As we saw in Chapter 1, the only data economists use to evaluate social states are data about the well-being of individual people in each state. A person is better off (or worse off) in one state than in another state if the allocation of goods in one state is higher (or lower) in his or her preference ordering than is the allocation in the other state.

The simplifying assumption about preferences in our fish economy allows us to describe the essential features of social states in that economy more simply than in Figure 2.2. Because Ted and Amy care only about the *total number of fish each is personally allocated*, we can illustrate the resulting social states in Figure 2.3, where the total number of fish allocated to Ted is mea-

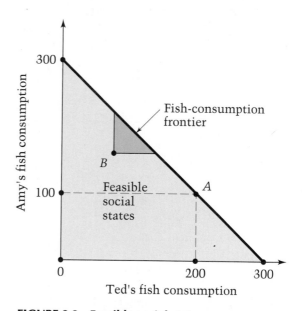

FIGURE 2.3   Feasible social states.

The light green area represents all the feasible social states in this economy. Social states on the fish-consumption frontier are Pareto-optimal, whereas social states below it are not. The dark green area represents the social states that are Pareto-preferred to *B*.

sured on the horizontal axis and the total number allocated to Amy is measured on the vertical axis. Since the economy's resource endowment is 180 fish and since one fish released in the water this year produces $\frac{5}{3}$ fish next year, the total number of fish to be allocated to the two individuals cannot exceed 300 (180 multiplied by $\frac{5}{3}$). The feasible social states in this fish economy therefore lie in the green area on or below the line labeled fish-consumption frontier in Figure 2.3:

Ted's fish consumption
+ Amy's fish consumption = 300

Notice first that any social state on the fish-consumption frontier is Pareto-optimal. For example, suppose that the economy is initially at point A on the fish-consumption frontier, where Ted has 200 fish and Amy has 100 fish. If we wanted to make Ted better off, we would have to give him more fish. Because the economy is already on the fish-consumption frontier, however, we would have to take those fish away from Amy — thereby making her worse off. In other words, once the economy is on the fish-consumption frontier, it is impossible to make one person better off without making the other worse off. Therefore, we know that point A — and indeed any point on the fish-consumption frontier — is Pareto-optimal.

On the other hand, as you'll discover in the following problem, any point below the fish-consumption frontier is not Pareto-optimal.

PROBLEM 2.4

Suppose that Ted and Amy are at point B in Figure 2.3. Identify the points that are Pareto-preferred to point B.

From this problem, we see that according to the Pareto criterion, the economy should be on the fish-consumption frontier. If the economy is initially below the frontier — say, at point B in Figure 2.3 — any point in the dark green area is Pareto-preferred to B. The Pareto criterion therefore ranks any such point higher than B. By contrast, if the economy is initially on the fish-consumption frontier, then the initial allocation is Pareto-optimal. In other words, no other feasible allocations are Pareto-preferred to the initial allocation. Now you can perhaps begin to see why the terms *Pareto-optimal* and *efficient* have come to mean the same thing in economics.

Institutions

Notice that all three of the building blocks we have so far considered — an economy's resource endowment, its technology, and individuals' preferences — are not easily changed over short periods of time. Indeed, in most economic theory, these building blocks are assumed to be unchangeable. They are treated as the primal constituents with which any economy has to work.[1]

By contrast, **institutions** — the fourth building block — are subject to change. They can be and are altered in significant ways from time to time. Let's briefly consider a few such institutions. The United States and Canada recently entered a free-trade agreement that calls for the elimination of tariffs on goods traded between the two countries. In Montreal in 1987, the nations of the world negotiated a new treaty designed to control the production of chlorofluorocarbons (CFCs) to protect the earth's ozone shield, and just 2 years later in Helsinki, they negotiated much tougher standards. The city of Los Angeles is now

---

[1] In an intertemporal framework, technology changes from period to period. Furthermore, it is possible to promote technological change by appropriate policy measures. Nuclear power is just one example of a policy-promoted technology.

considering major institutional changes to alleviate its air pollution problems, including the elimination of free parking and a ban by 2009 on cars fueled by petroleum products. (How will the elimination of free parking help to improve air quality in Los Angeles?) As part of the effort to control acid rain, the United States is considering the creation of a market for emission rights, an institutional innovation that would allocate such emission rights to the polluters who face the highest costs of reducing emissions. (As we'll see in Chapter 17, this is a sensible way to achieve a given reduction in emissions at minimum social cost.) In essence, any change in economic policy means the substitution of one institution (or set of institutions) for another. In this sense, the study of economic policy is equivalent to the study of institutions. Because institutions are changeable, they play an especially interesting role in economics.

What is that role? If we think of economic activity as a game in which the objective of each player is to reach the highest possible level in his or her own preference ordering, then economic institutions are the rules by which the game in that particular economy must be played. In terms of our two-person fish economy, this means that each person (constrained and directed by an as-yet-unspecified set of institutions) strives to maximize the total number of fish he or she consumes. In terms of the real economy, for instance, it means that automobile firms strive to maximize their profit. In the recent past, that pursuit of profit led them to use the relatively inexpensive refrigerant freon-12 — one of the more virulent CFCs — in air conditioners for cars. It now seems likely that laws (one form of institution) will be revised to discourage the use of this ozone-destroying substance. Indeed, as of 1993 it will be against the law in Vermont to sell new cars that use CFCs in their air conditioners.

In short, institutions modulate and direct economic activity. Indeed, institutions determine which of the infinitely many possible economic states will be achieved. Indirectly, then, a choice of economic institutions is also a choice of the state an economy will actually attain.

Such institutions may be formally codified in law or privately created. For example, property law formally specifies how ownership of property may and may not be acquired and transferred. It therefore directs and constrains economic activity. Other significant legal institutions that modulate economic behavior include tax laws, antitrust laws, labor laws, minimum-wage laws, and rent-control laws.

PROBLEM 2.5
Governments often require retailers to collect from their customers a 10-cent deposit on pop bottles taken from the store. What is the purpose of this institution, and how does it work?

Less conspicuous but also important are the private, often informal institutions that govern everyday transactions in an economy. For example, private rental deposit schemes of various kinds are very much like the public institution you considered in Problem 2.5. If you want to rent certain kinds of merchandise such as furniture, VCRs, ski equipment, ice skates, or power tools, you will probably be asked to leave a hefty deposit to guarantee the return of the good. If you've rented an off-campus apartment, you've probably been asked to pay a damage deposit — a similar institution. And if you ever pass through the Phoenix airport, you will be able to rent a baggage cart by depositing four quarters in a coin box, which then releases your cart from a special lock. The clever twist is that you can get one quarter refunded if you replace your cart in the machine, where it is once again locked up. (What is the special function of the quarter-refund-for-cart-return institution?)

These informal institutions, like formal ones, are aimed at controlling and directing private economic behavior.

As we saw earlier in this chapter, positive economics is concerned with the social state that an economy actually attains. Traditionally, economists express this concern in terms of three fundamental questions: What goods will be produced? (What point in the production possibilities set will the economy achieve?) How will those goods be produced? (Which of the many possible production techniques will actually be used to produce the goods?) For whom will these goods be produced? (What social state will the economy attain?)

2.3 Comparative Institutional Analysis

One particularly interesting type of question in positive economics concerns the relationship between an economy's institutions and the state the economy actually attains. Given a set of institutions and the hypothesis of self-interested behavior, if we are clever enough we ought to be able to predict what social state actually will be attained. And if we can perform this sort of analysis for one set of institutions, we can do it for another. This means that we can then compare social states attained under alternative institutional arrangements. This is the method of **comparative institutional analysis,** which is the very essence of much of modern economics.

Comparative institutional analysis is in the domain of positive economics, since it attempts to predict which social states will actually follow from different institutional arrangements. It is also the most important economic technique used in policy-making, which involves the often subtle interplay between positive and normative economics. In such policy-making, normative consider-

ations dictate what are and are not desirable social states, and comparative institutional analysis reveals what are and are not sensible ways of trying to attain a particular desirable social state. To put the point about policy-making differently, formulating social and economic goals is clearly in the realm of normative economics. Deciding how to implement those goals and, indeed, discovering whether those goals can actually be implemented are comparative institutional problems and therefore in the realm of positive economics.

We can return to our fish economy model to illustrate both comparative institutional analysis itself and the interplay between positive and normative economics involved in a policy choice concerning a set of institutions. We will begin by specifying the property institution that prevails in the first year of our fish economy. Then we will compare the outcomes that result under two different property institutions in the second year. Let's begin by assuming that *private-property rights* prevail in the first year, perhaps because Ted and Amy own the fish pens in which the 180 fish are stored. In fact, let's assume that each privately owns half of the resource endowment of 180 fish, or 90 fish. In the first year, Ted and Amy must then individually decide how many of their 90 fish to eat and how many to release into the river—knowing, of course, that each fish released will produce $\frac{5}{3}$ fish next year.

Now let's describe two different property institutions that will prevail in the second year. Under one institution—which we'll call a **common-property institution**—Ted and Amy will each harvest half of all the fish in the river in the second year. Under the alternative institution—which we'll call a **private-property institution**—Ted and Amy will each harvest in the second year only those fish that are available as a result of the fish each personally released in the first year.

PROBLEM 2.6

Suppose that Ted releases 30 fish in the first year and that Amy releases 60 fish. Under the common-property institution, how many fish will each harvest the second year, and how many fish in total will each consume? Under the private-property institution, how many fish will each harvest the second year, and how many fish in total will each consume?

A Common-Property Institution

Given the common-property institution, what will self-interest lead Ted and Amy to do? Let's begin with Ted's decision. For every fish he releases in the first year, $\frac{5}{3}$ additional fish will be available next year. However, under the common-property institution, he will personally harvest only half of those additional fish; that is, releasing a fish this year means that Ted will harvest an additional $\frac{5}{6}$ of a fish to eat next year. But it also means that he has one less fish to eat this year. Thus, Ted's total fish consumption is smaller by $\frac{1}{6}$ $(1 - \frac{5}{6})$ if he does decide to release the fish in the first year. Putting it another way, Ted's fish consumption is larger by $\frac{1}{6}$ if he harvests the fish in the first year instead of releasing it. Because we have assumed that Ted's preferences are such that he wants to maximize his total fish consumption, under the common-property institution, Ted's self-interest will lead him to harvest rather than to release a fish in the first year.

Because one fish is just like another in this economy, we can predict that Ted will harvest rather than release all his fish in the first year. Similarly, we can predict that Amy will also harvest all her fish in the first year. Therefore, the total fish consumption under the common-property institution will be 90 fish apiece.

The social state in which each person consumes 90 fish *lies below the fish-consumption frontier* in Figure 2.3 and is there-fore *not Pareto-optimal.* In particular, Ted and Amy could have eaten a total of 150 fish $(90 \times \frac{5}{3})$ apiece if both had released all their fish in the first year — and both clearly would have been better off. Yet under the common-property institution, the pursuit of self-interest does not lead to this Pareto-preferred outcome.

A Private-Property Institution

Now let's see what self-interest will lead Ted and Amy to do when we substitute the private-property for the common-property institution. If Ted releases rather than harvests a fish this year, he will harvest $\frac{5}{3}$ additional fish next year — and his total fish consumption will be larger by $\frac{2}{3}$ $(\frac{5}{3} - 1)$. Once again, because one fish is just like another in this economy, we can predict that under the private-property institution, Ted will release all his fish in the first year and harvest 150 fish the second year. Amy will likewise release her 90 fish the first year and harvest 150 fish the second year. This allocation of 150 fish apiece *is on the fish-consumption frontier* and is therefore *Pareto-optimal.* We see, then, that by producing an outcome that is Pareto-optimal, or efficient, the private-property institution succeeds where the common-property institution fails.

PROBLEM 2.7

Suppose that one fish released in the first year produces not just $\frac{5}{3}$ but three fish in the second year. Show that under the common-property institution, self-interest now leads Ted and Amy to release all their fish. Still supposing that one fish released in the first year produces three fish in the second year, find the equilibrium under the common-property institution when the economy is composed of four people rather than two people. To do so, assume that in the four-person economy, each person harvests $\frac{1}{4}$ of the total fish available the second year.

Simple as this model is, the insight it offers is apparently difficult to learn. It may be useful here to reinterpret the insight. Notice first that this model is really concerned with *investment decisions.* Not harvesting one fish this year means that an additional $\frac{2}{3}$ of a fish will be available next year; therefore, the activity of releasing a fish is, in essence, an investment activity. Because individuals are concerned only with the total number of fish they eat, the socially desirable outcome is for everyone concerned to release, or "invest," all their fish in the first year. Under the common-property institution, however, they choose not to invest their fish because they cannot personally capture all of the returns to their investment decisions for themselves. By contrast, under the private-property institution, they do invest their fish because they are able to personally capture all of these returns. The point is this: if we want to induce self-interested individuals to make socially desirable investment decisions, we must design institutions that recognize the self-serving nature of individual decisions and attempt to direct individuals' private pursuit of self-interest toward socially desirable goals.[2]

It would be a serious mistake, however, to assume that individuals should be allowed to pursue their own self-interest without restraint. It does not take much exposure to the air-pollution problems of almost any large city in North America to see that the unfettered pursuit of self-interest does not produce socially desirable results. Sensibly designed institutions do not simply allow individuals to pursue their private objectives free of restraints of any kind. Instead, they acknowledge the power of self-interest as a motivator of economic behavior and then seek to harness and direct private self-interest toward socially useful ends.

Like our location model in Chapter 1, our fish economy model in this chapter is also a fruitful model because it can be interpreted in a number of ways. For example, we might have substituted corn for fish. The choice in this case would then be to decide how much to eat in the initial period and how much to plant. We chose to use fish as our example because so many very real common-property problems crop up in a number of fisheries throughout the world. Indeed, some formerly productive fisheries, such as the California sardine fishery that so fascinated John Steinbeck, have been completely destroyed by overfishing. Today the cod fishery off the Grand Banks of Newfoundland—for 400 years one of the world's most productive fishing grounds—is plagued by a common-property problem. Many countries exploit this fishery, including Canada, the United States, France, Norway, Spain, and Portugal. Because the property rights over the fish are imperfect, the fishery is being seriously overfished. As a result, the fish stock has become seriously depleted. For example, one Portuguese cod-fisherman who had fished on the Grand Banks since he was 16 years old recently lamented that he was forced to give up his life's work at the age of 52 because he was, in his own words, "a victim of the decreasing cod stocks." In contrast to our simple fish model, this real-world common-property problem is not easily solved. As a former prime minister of Canada put it, "The problem with fish is that they swim around." Consequently, devising enforceable private-property rights is very difficult to do.

[2] See Alchian (1987) and Coase (1960) for a general discussion of the role of property rights in economics, and Cheung (1987) for a discussion of the problems associated with common property.

2.4 The Market Economy

For our purposes, the set of institutions characterizing a free-enterprise, or pure-market, economy is the baseline model of the economy. These are the institutions of private property. They create and enforce property rights and promote unrestricted voluntary exchange as the primary mode of economic interaction. In this baseline model, then, the only role government plays is to enact and enforce the requisite laws.

We'll consider a great many alternative institutions at intervals throughout the book. These will include taxes and subsidies of various kinds, such as income taxes, welfare payments, and minimum-wage regulations; a number of restrictions on property rights, such as rent-control legislation; a diversity of common-property institutions, such as unrestricted access to racquetball courts; and a variety of institutional forms for the firm, including the partnership and the owner-managed firm.

In most cases, however, we will analyze an alternative institution in a context in which all others are free-enterprise institutions. Questions about alternative institutions will therefore take the following form: Relative to the pure-market economy, what are the implications of minimum-wage legislation?

The market economy thus serves as the benchmark in all the comparative institutional exercises in this book. By using comparative institutional exercises, economists can answer many real economic questions. If a social goal is to alleviate poverty among the working poor, for example, comparative analysis allows us to say that in a market economy, minimum-wage legislation tends to create unemployment and is therefore a less effective remedy for poverty than is an income-transfer program.

Why do we choose a pure-market economy as our baseline case when it is plainly not the observed economic reality? First, it is perhaps the simplest economy in which interesting economic problems arise. It therefore provides a clear context in which to stage and examine a variety of problems. Second, a good share of economic activity in countries such as Australia, Canada, Great Britain, and the United States is coordinated through markets. Understanding a pure-market economy is therefore necessary in interpreting the economic activity we see around us. Third, private enterprise institutions, as we've already seen, sometimes produce a Pareto-optimal social state. From a normative perspective, then, market institutions give us a meaningful yardstick for making comparisons.

The Circular Flow of Economic Activity

A useful way to conceptualize a market economy is the circular-flow diagram in Figure 2.4. In this scheme, two sets of economic actors play the crucial roles: individuals and firms. From an economist's perspective, each individual to the left in Figure 2.4 can be described by his or her preferences and by the resources each owns. In a pure-market economy, all resources, including resources nominally owned by firms, are ultimately owned by individuals because individual people own the firms. Each firm to the right in Figure 2.4 can be described by its technology (the terms on which it can transform resources into goods) and its organizational structure (the set of internal institutions used to organize the firm).

These individuals and firms interact in two sets of markets: resource markets and goods markets. In the resource markets at the bottom of the figure, individuals are the suppliers of labor and other resources; firms

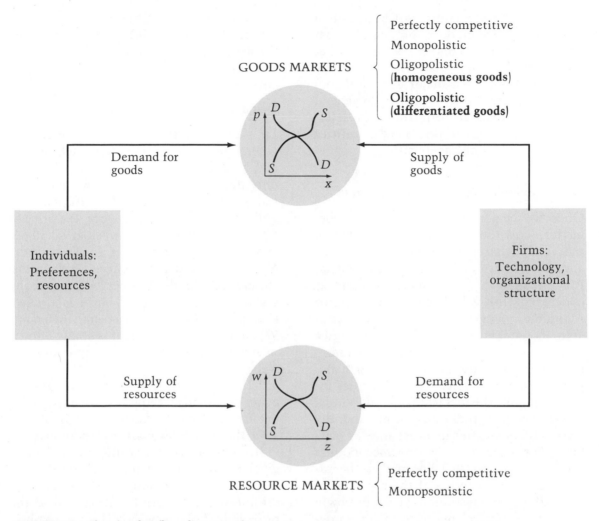

FIGURE 2.4   The circular-flow diagram of an economy.

Individuals, whom we describe by their preferences and the resources they own, supply resources to firms and demand goods from firms. Firms, which we describe by their technology and their organizational structure, demand resources from individuals and supply goods to them. Firms and individuals interact in resource markets and in goods markets, in both of which prices and quantities are determined.

are the demanders. In the goods markets at the top of the figure, firms are the suppliers of goods and services; individuals are the demanders. In equilibrium, there is a price and a quantity in every resource market and in every goods market.

Partial Equilibrium and General Equilibrium Analysis

We can analyze that equilibrium in two ways. When we undertake **partial equilibrium analysis**, we determine what the equilibrium price and quantity will be in a small number of these markets, holding all other prices constant. This market-by-market partial equilibrium analysis is extremely useful and will be a major analytical tool throughout the book. When we do **general equilibrium analysis,** our aim is to determine the entire set of prices and quantities in all markets simultaneously.

Microeconomics Versus Macroeconomics

Once we begin to analyze economic behavior, how do we distinguish between the issues that occupy macroeconomists and those that concern microeconomists? **Macroeconomics,** as its name suggests, is concerned with economics-in-the-large, or economic aggregates. Macroeconomic variables include the national product, the price level, the unemployment rate, consumption, and investment. On the other hand, **microeconomics** focuses on economics-in-the-small, or the decisions of individual consumers and individual firms and the prices and quantities in a vast array of markets. For example, the macroeconomist thinks in terms of the labor market; the microeconomist, in terms of the markets for baseball players, systems analysts, or newly graduated electrical engineers. The macroeconomist works on monetary policy and other broad policies that influence the price level or the rate of unemployment; the microeconomist, on rent-control or minimum-wage policies, which affect the price, quantity, and allocation of rental housing or the level of unemployment among teenagers.

2.5 A Review of Supply and Demand

By reviewing how the forces of supply and demand determine price and quantity in a single market, we can reinforce your understanding of an important piece of microeco-

nomics, clarify the difference between partial and general equilibrium analysis, and illustrate another useful tool — comparative statics analysis.

Demand

Let's consider the market for avocados, where individual demanders such as you and I have no real control over price. The only decision we make is how many avocados to buy at a given price p. At present, I will buy 10 avocados per week at a price of $0.10 per avocado, 2 per week at $0.50 per avocado, and none at all at $1 per avocado. My individual demand curve for avocados simply specifies the number I will buy at any given price. This demand curve is a reflection of my own self-interested behavior. When the price of avocados is $0.50, I find it in my self-interest to buy 2 avocados per week.

If we add up the demand curves for every person in an economy, we have a **market demand curve,** labeled DD in Figure 2.5a. It tells us how many avocados all individual demanders are willing to buy at any given price in any given week. For example, if the price of avocados is $0.36, then 2.6 million avocados will be demanded. If the price is higher — say, $0.60 — then only 1 million will be demanded. Demand curves are ordinarily thought to be *downward-sloping:* the higher the price, the smaller the quantity demanded.

Supply

Individual suppliers of avocados, like individual demanders, exercise no appreciable control over price. The only decision each supplier makes is how many avocados to produce at a given price. An individual firm's supply curve simply indicates the number of avocados that it will put on the market at any given price. Just as an individual's demand curve reflects that individual's

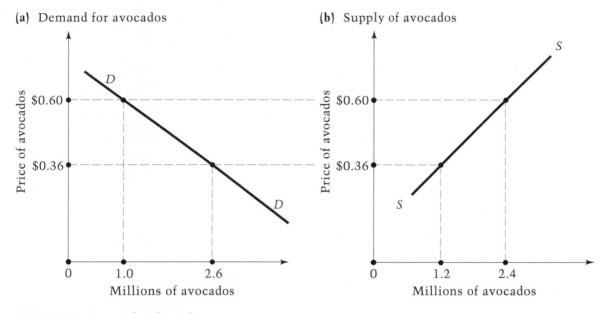

(a) Demand for avocados

(b) Supply of avocados

FIGURE 2.5   Demand and supply.

The demand curve *DD* tells us the quantity of avocados that will be demanded at any price, and the supply curve *SS* tells us the quantity that will be supplied at any price. If price is $0.36, for instance, 2.6 million avocados will be demanded and 1.2 million will be supplied. If price is $0.60, 1 million will be demanded and 2.4 million will be supplied.

self-interested behavior, so, too, a firm's supply curve reflects that firm's self-interested, profit-maximizing behavior.

If we add up the supply curves for all firms, we have a **market supply curve,** labeled *SS* in Figure 2.5*b*. It tells us how many avocados all suppliers will produce at any given price. If the price per avocado is $0.60, then 2.4 million avocados will be supplied. If the price is lower—say, $0.36—then only 1.2 million will be supplied. Supply curves are usually thought to be *upward-sloping:* the higher the price, the larger the quantity supplied.

Equilibrium Price and Quantity

By combining the demand and supply sides of the avocado market into a single diagram in Figure 2.6, we can identify the **equilibrium price and quantity**—p^e (equal to

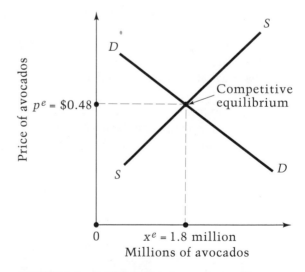

FIGURE 2.6   Equilibrium price and quantity.

A market is in equilibrium when quantity demanded is equal to quantity supplied. The equilibrium price is $p^e = \$0.48$ because 1.8 million avocados are demanded and supplied at that price. At higher prices, there is excess supply; at lower prices, there is excess demand.

$0.48) and x^e (equal to 1.8 million). At prices higher than the equilibrium price, we find excess supply: not all the avocados supplied can be sold. As a result, price will tend to drop toward the equilibrium price p^e. At prices lower than the equilibrium price, we find excess demand: more avocados will be demanded than are available. As a result, price will tend to rise toward p^e.

In the demand-supply model, price serves to coordinate economic decisions. As we have seen, suppliers and demanders base their supply and demand decisions on price. If their decisions are not mutually consistent — that is, if there is either excess demand or excess supply — a pressure will arise that pushes price either up or down. Only at the equilibrium price are the decisions of suppliers and demanders mutually consistent, and therefore only at this price is there no pressure for price to change.

In this brief sketch of the theory of price and quantity in a single competitive market, we have implicitly assumed that all other relevant prices are held constant. Because the price of avocados is only one of the many determinants of the demand for and supply of avocados, this analysis is called partial equilibrium analysis.

Factors other than a good's own price, however, play important parts in determining the demand for any good. For example, because many people who buy avocados like to serve them stuffed with shrimp, the price of shrimp — a **complement** to avocados — is an important determinant of the demand for avocados. Furthermore, because many people ordinarily choose between avocados and artichokes as appetizers, the price of artichokes — a **substitute** for avocados — is also an important determinant of the demand for avocados. In drawing the demand curve in Figure 2.5, we not only implicitly held the prices of all complements and substitutes constant, but in principle held all other prices in the entire economy constant.

2.6 Comparative Statics Analysis

If the price of a complement such as shrimp increases, we would expect the demand curve in Figure 2.6 to shift downward and to the left, as shown in Figure 2.7, since for any given price of avocados, the package "shrimp-stuffed avocados" is now more expensive. If the price of shrimp rises from $5 to $10 per pound, for example, then the demand curve for avocados in Figure 2.7 shifts from DD to $D'D'$, and the equilibrium shifts from E to E'. As a result, both equilibrium price and equilibrium quantity fall. Equilibrium price drops from $0.48 to $0.36, and equilibrium quantity drops from 1.8 million to 1.2 million.

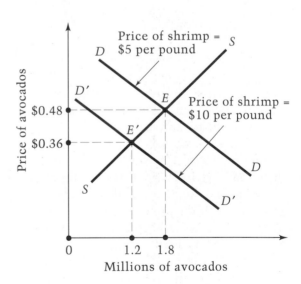

FIGURE 2.7 Comparative statics analysis.

Initially, when the price of shrimp is $5 per pound, the equilibrium price of avocados is $0.48 and the equilibrium quantity is 1.8 million. When the price of shrimp increases to $10 per pound, the avocado demand curve shifts to the left from DD to $D'D'$ because avocados and shrimp are complements. As a result, the equilibrium price of avocados falls to $0.36, and the equilibrium quantity falls to 1.2 million.

Similarly, if the price of a substitute such as artichokes increases, we would expect the demand curve for avocados to shift upward and to the right because for any given price of avocados, artichokes are now relatively more expensive.

PROBLEM 2.8

What happens to the equilibrium price and quantity of any good as the price of a substitute increases?

In constructing the supply curve for avocados, we have taken into account only one of many determinants of supply. In particular, we ignored the prices of all the resources used to produce avocados, even though these have an important bearing on supply. For example, if the price of fertilizer or of farm labor goes up, we would anticipate an upward and leftward shift in the supply curve for avocados.

PROBLEM 2.9

How would such a resource-price increase affect equilibrium price and quantity in the avocado market?

These demand-supply exercises are examples of partial equilibrium analysis because we have restricted our attention to determining a limited set of prices and quantities, holding all others constant. By constrast, general equilibrium analysis involves the simultaneous determination of all prices and quantities.

The exercises surrounding Figure 2.7 and in Problems 2.8 and 2.9 are examples of **comparative statics analysis.** In these exercises, we examined the response of variables determined in the theory — the equilibrium price and quantity of avocados — to a change in a variable that the theory does not determine — the price of shrimp, artichokes, or fertilizer.

In this model, as in any model, certain variables are determined within the model and others are not. This seemingly simple distinction is an important one. Within the context of a particular model, the variables that are determined by the model are called **endogenous,** and the variables that are determined outside the model are called **exogenous.** In the model of demand and supply of avocados, the price and quantity of avocados are endogenous variables, and the prices of shrimp, artichokes, and fertilizer are exogenous variables. In our location model of Chapter 1, the locations of firms and the shopping decisions of consumers are endogenous, whereas the price of the good and the distribution of consumers, among other things, are exogenous.

In a comparative statics exercise, we examine the response of variables that are endogenous in a particular model to a change in a variable that is exogenous to that model. You may have noticed that we've used this important tool repeatedly. In answering Problem 2.7, for example, you saw how the equilibrium of our fish model responds to changes in two exogenous variables: the fertility of released fish and the number of individuals in the economy. In Problem 1.7, you saw how the equilibrium of our location model changed when we substituted a variable customer density for a uniform customer density.

The distinction between endogenous and exogenous variables in a model and the tool that the distinction gives rise to — comparative statics analysis — are fundamental in economics and indeed in any science. To reinforce your own understanding of the distinction, take 5 or 10 minutes to think through the following problem.

PROBLEM 2.10

Return to the fish model and make a complete list of the variables that are exogenous and of the variables that are endogenous.

2.7 Equilibrium

We've now looked at three different models: our location model, our fish model, and the demand-supply model of a competitive market. In each model, we've identified an equilibrium and considered a number of comparative statics exercises. From this sampling, you can begin to see just how dominant equilibrium analysis is in economics. Before proceeding, it will be useful to discuss just what *equilibrium* means.

Note first that the term *equilibrium* has nothing to do with the variables that are *exogenous* in a particular model. Rather it concerns the variables that are determined within the model — that is, the model's *endogenous* variables. In both our location model and the fish model, all of the endogenous variables are determined directly by the decisions of individual agents, and in the equilibrium of those models, no agent can improve its position by changing its own decision. In the equilibrium of the fish model under a common-property institution, for example, both individuals chose to harvest all their fish in the first year because neither could increase the total number of fish he or she consumed by releasing fish. Again, in the equilibrium of our location model, both grocery stores located side by side in the center of the market because neither store could earn a larger profit by changing its location.

In models such as these, where all of the endogenous variables are directly determined by the decisions of individual agents, the meaning of the term *equilibrium* follows immediately from the hypothesis of self-interested behavior. The model is in equilibrium when no individual agent can improve its position by changing its decision or decisions. This concept of equilibrium is called *Nash equilibrium*, after the American game theorist John Nash.

DEFINITION: Nash Equilibrium

If all the endogenous variables in a model are directly chosen by individual agents, the model is in equilibrium when no agent can improve its position by changing its decision (or decisions).

The demand-supply model of a competitive market is somewhat different because price — a crucial endogenous variable — is not directly determined by any individual agent in the model. Economists often say, somewhat loosely, that price is determined by "market forces." But market forces represent nothing other than the collection of all the decisions made by the relevant agents. In a competetive model, then, price is determined by the collective decisions of all agents. In equilibrium, price — the collectively determined endogenous variable — is such that aggregate quantity supplied is equal to aggregate quantity demanded. But this definition of equilibrium is superficial. If we dig deeper, we see that quantities demanded and supplied are directly determined by individual agents — that is, by the demanders and suppliers whose individual demand and supply curves we aggregated to form the market demand and supply curves. In equilibrium, these individual agents cannot make themselves better off by changing their decisions. Firms, for example, cannot earn a larger profit by choosing to supply some other quantity.

DEFINITION: Competitive Equilibrium

In competitive models, where prices are determined by market forces, the model is in equilibrium when prices are such that no agent can improve its position by changing its decision (or decisions).

2.8 The Plan of the Book

Figure 2.4 provides a handy reference point for previewing the rest of the book. In Part Two, Individual Choice, we'll concentrate on the individuals on the left side of our circular-flow diagram. In Chapter 3, we'll set out the standard economic theory of individual preferences. In Chapter 4, we'll add to this theory of preferences the assumption that individuals maximize their utility. We can then analyze the equilibrium of the individual household. In the process, we'll derive demand curves for goods and supply curves for resources, thereby providing the demand side of the markets for goods at the top and the supply side of the markets for resources at the bottom of Figure 2.4.

In Chapter 5, we'll use the tools created in earlier chapters to explore a range of institutional questions drawn from everyday life. In Chapter 6, we'll extend the theory of preferences to include economic decisions that have "risky" outcomes. We'll then use this theory to explain some otherwise puzzling real-life phenomena.

In Part Three, The Firm, we'll turn our attention to the firms on the right in Figure 2.4. In Chapter 7, we'll try to understand why firms exist and why they take the particular organizational forms they do. In Chapters 8 and 9, we'll introduce the idea of a production function and then use it to derive a number of cost relationships for a firm in the short run and the long run.

In Part Four, Goods Markets, we'll discuss the forces that determine both the prices of the goods available in the goods markets at the top of Figure 2.4 and the quantities in which they are produced. In Chapter 10, we'll look at perfectly competitive markets; in Chapter 11, at monopolistic markets; in Chapter 12, at an undifferentiated oligopoly, a market in which a small number of firms sell an identical good; and in Chapter 13, at a differentiated oligopoly, a market in which a small number of firms sell differentiated goods.

In Part Five, Resource Markets and General Equilibrium, we'll turn at last to the resource markets at the bottom of Figure 2.4. Chapter 14 takes up both perfectly competitive and monopsonistic resource markets. Chapter 15 draws together many of the concepts in the preceding chapters to build a model of general equilibrium, equilibrium in all markets at once.

In Chapter 16, we'll concentrate on the distribution of income and examine the conflict between economic efficiency and equity in the distribution of income. Finally, in Chapter 17, we'll explore externalities and, more briefly, public goods.

Summary

The purpose of an economy is to use resources to produce goods. Economics is the study of the process whereby scarce resources are allocated to the production of alternative goods. To say more, we need a more precise description of an economy. Any economy can be described by breaking it down into four building blocks: a resource endowment, a technology, the preferences of individuals, and institutions.

A resource endowment and a technology jointly determine the production possibilities set: the set of all combinations of goods that an economy could produce. If we imagine all the possible ways to distribute all possible combinations of goods to individual members of a society, we then have the set of possible social states. Ultimately, the social state that a given economy attains is the subject matter of economics.

The preferences of individuals play two key roles in economic theory. First, preferences are critical building blocks in positive economic analysis, since the economist's theory of behavior is that each individual will pick the path of action that appears to make him or her as well off as possible. Second, in normative economics, preferences give meaning to the expressions "better than" and "worse than" in characterizing the well-being of individual members of society.

Three of an economy's building blocks —the resource endowment, the technology, and individual preferences—are assumed to be fixed in most analyses. Only the fourth building block—institutions—is changeable, which makes institutions particularly interesting. Indeed, the most interesting exercises in economics are comparative institutional exercises: What happens when we substitute one institution for another? To answer such questions consistently, however, we need a point of comparison: a baseline set of institutions. In this book, the baseline model is the set of institutions defining a pure-market, or free-enterprise, economy.

Economic problems can be approached by using partial equilibrium analysis, in which a limited set of prices and quantities is determined and all others held constant, or by using general equilibrium analysis, in which all prices and quantities are determined simultaneously. Partial equilibrium analysis is the primary tool used in this book, and supply and demand analysis is an important illustration of it.

Exercises

1 Consider the following supply and demand functions:

$$x_D = 20 - p \quad \text{(demand)}$$
$$x_S = p - 6 \quad \text{(supply)}$$

where x_D and x_S are quantity demanded and supplied, respectively, and p is price.
a Find the competitive equilibrium price and quantity.
b Now suppose that consumers' incomes increase, shifting the demand curve up and to the right as follows:

$$x_D = 28 - p \quad \text{(demand)}$$

Find the new equilibrium price and quantity. Illustrate both equilibria on a carefully constructed diagram.

2 One of the social problems associated with the use of illegal drugs is street crime. Drug addicts sometimes become muggers and thieves as they seek to raise money to support their addiction. If the police manage to restrict the supply of illegal drugs, what will be the effect on the price of illegal drugs? On the level of street crime?

3 Until very recently, the money prices of most consumer goods in the Soviet economy were fixed, and goods were allocated to consumers on a first come, first served basis. If money prices are not allowed to perform the role of allocating consumer goods to consumers, on what basis will such goods be allocated?

4 Suppose that the U.S. government convinced Japanese automakers to voluntarily restrict the number of Japanese cars they sold in the U.S. market. What effect would these voluntary export restraints have on the price of Japanese cars in the United States? On the price and quantity of American cars sold in the United States?

5 Explain the following statement. Even though the costs of collection are as large as the revenue collected, parking meters should be retained because of the allocative function they perform.

6 The disposal of household refuse is now a major problem all across the United States. In most cities, refuse disposal is provided by the city free of charge. (The cost of disposal is financed by tax revenue in these cities.) In contrast, some cities use a refuse disposal fee, charging the household, let's say, $2 per bag of trash. Under which system will the quantity of trash hauled to the official trash dump be larger? Under which system will the quantity of trash illegally dumped by the roadside be larger?

7 By volume, paper is the single largest source of household refuse in the United States, accounting for 40% of the total volume of trash by some estimates. Newspapers alone account for 15% of the total volume.
a For purposes of argument, suppose that the total cost of disposal is $\frac{1}{10}$ of a cent per

page of newspaper. What would be the effect of a law requiring newspapers to pay a refuse disposal tax equal to $\frac{1}{10}$ of a cent per page printed on the price and quantity of newspapers? On the size of newspapers? On the format of newspapers? On the size of magazines? On the demand for radio and television ads?

b More generally, what would be the effects of such a disposal tax levied on the sale of all paper products?

c What sorts of institutions would encourage recycling of paper?

References

Alchian, A. (1987), "Property Rights," in *The New Palgrave*, vol. 3, J. Eatwell, M. Milgate, and P. Newman (eds.), London: Macmillan, pp. 1031–1034.

Cheung, S. N. S. (1987), "Common Property Rights," in *The New Palgrave*, vol. 1, J. Eatwell, M. Milgate, and P. Newman (eds.), London: Macmillan, pp. 504–505.

Coase, R. H. (1960), "The Problem of Social Cost," *Journal of Law and Economics*, **3**:1–44.

Individual Choice

In Part Two, we will turn to our circular-flow diagram (Figure 2.4, p. 33) to see how consumers decide which goods to buy in the goods market (top of diagram) and which labor services and other personal resources to sell in the resource markets (bottom of diagram).

In Chapter 3, we will set out the most widely accepted, but not the only possible, theory of self-interest. This theory allows us to use a *utility function* to analyze individual decision-making behavior.

In Chapter 4, we will see how a consumer allocates a limited income across consumption goods to maximize his or her own utility. The solution to this problem is a set of demand functions specifying how much of each good a consumer buys, given the consumer's income and any set of prices for consumption goods.

In Chapter 5, we will apply the techniques of Chapter 4 to a grab bag of situational problems. For example, we'll ask, Why is the allocation of court time at the University of Colorado Recreation Center wasteful, and how could it be improved? Our intention is to let you see just how fruitful the theory of choice actually is.

Because the theory of self-interest developed in Chapter 3 does not apply to situations that are "risky," we will extend the theory in Chapter 6 to include risk. This *theory of expected utility* will allow us to explain decision making in several specific situations. For example, we'll ask, Why does the market price of a new car drop by $1500 or more the minute it is driven off the car lot?

3

A THEORY OF SELF-INTEREST: SELF-INTEREST, PREFERENCES, AND UTILITY FUNCTIONS

Key elements in both positive and normative economics, we argued in Chapters 1 and 2, are the closely related concepts of preferences and self-interest. Precisely what do we mean by self-interest? Any answer to this question is of course a theory, and in this chapter we'll set out the most widely accepted, but not the only possible, theory of self-interest.

We'll begin by considering three assumptions about individual preferences that establish a clear meaning for the concept of **self-interest**: they imply that individuals can always make choices and that the choices they make are consistent. To complete the theory, we'll make two additional assumptions that allow us to represent an individual's preferences by a *utility function*, which is defined fully in Section 3.4. Finally, we'll add two assumptions that are not necessary to the theory but are very convenient because they allow us to define and explore the *marginal rate of substitution*, a

concept we'll use in Chapter 4 to analyze individual choice making.

3.1 The Psychological Assumption of Self-Interest

Chapters 1 and 2 emphasized the central role that two different kinds of assumptions play in economic theorizing. When we talked about individuals as being motivated from within by self-interest, we were dealing with a psychological assumption. All the other assumptions we made were technical. They concerned the external environment—the physical and institutional framework within which economic behavior takes place. Our technical assumptions will vary from one economic theory (or model) to another, depending on the type of problem we choose to investigate. The psychological assumption of self-interested behavior, however, appears in some form in every economic model. Self-interest is assumed to be the propelling force behind all economic behavior.

Yet, such unobservable entities as human motives pose special problems because they are difficult to measure. If we use self-reports to test assumptions about economic motives — for example, by asking individuals why they behave the way they do — the evidence we get is entirely subjective. Indeed, we may wonder if human beings are actually motivated by "self-interest"—and if so, what we mean by the concept. Is our concept a self-evident truth about human conduct? Is it merely a useful abstraction? Is it perhaps a typical behavior pattern under capitalism? Or is it something else? Economists continue to disagree about what stance to take vis-á-vis self-interested behavior. We do not want to enter into the debate here, but we do need to know what self-interest means in the context of a specific theory.

You may already be familiar with a standard operational definition of self-interest: many economic questions are posed as problems of maximizing something, subject to some constraint. In the context of consumer theory, the individual consumer's problem is to choose the quantities of various goods that maximize his or her utility, subject to a budget constraint. Almost invariably, introductory economics courses treat the utility function in this problem as a given. Yet how did this utility function come into being? To discover what we mean by the **utility** that a utility function represents, we will build one from the ground up. We'll see how to derive a utility function from more primitive, or basic, ideas about individual *preferences.*

To analyze consumer choice, we need to create a theory (or model) that captures the essential elements of individual decision making. How do individual people decide how to allocate their leisure time to alterna-

tive activities and their income to alternative consumption goods, for example?

Such judgments are obviously based on preferences: I prefer car rides to bus rides, watching television to playing squash, butter to margarine, and giving money to charities over contributing to political organizations. Notice that *self-interest* is not synonymous with *selfish.* Charitable actions of all kinds are consistent with self-interested behavior.

The mathematical tool we use to represent these preferences is a utility function. Thus, the assumptions of consumer-preference theory will necessarily be assumptions about individual preferences coupled with assumptions that allow us to represent these preferences by a utility function.

The theory we'll develop is just that — one of many possible theories.[1] In fact, we will modify this theory in Chapter 6 when we explore decision making when outcomes are risky rather than certain. As we develop this theory, you will also discover that even though a utility function is very useful because it gives us a compact and convenient way to write down preferences, it is also arbitrary in the sense that we can identify any number of different utility functions that all convey the same information about preferences. As we proceed, you will find that the basic stuff of consumer theory is not utility, but individual preferences.

3.2 Individual Preferences

All theories of self-interest in economics are predicated on the simple notion that individuals have preferences: they know what

---

[1] Students interested in a mathematical treatment of this theory should consult Arrow (1959) or Chapter 3 of Debreu (1959). The basic elements of the theory are attributable to Slutsky (1915) and to Hicks and Allen (1934).

they like. Simple as this idea is, its systematic use is what differentiates economics from other social sciences.

Preferences as Primitives

In modern treatments of self-interest, economists take statements of preferences as primitives; that is, statements such as "Mary prefers soft rock to heavy metal" are taken as *meaningful* or as requiring no explanation. The question "Why does Mary prefer soft rock to heavy metal"— interesting as it may be — is not treated in ordinary economic science.

Human likes and dislikes cover a vast range of preferences. We express preferences over ways to spend our leisure time (skiing, jogging, watching television, eating out); possible occupations (carpentry, dentistry, accounting); social relations (living in the hometown among old friends or traveling around the country meeting new people); various forms of charitable behavior (donating money to a food bank or driving a car for a "meals on wheels" program); and different climates or weather conditions.

In this chapter, for simplicity, we'll limit our attention to preferences over consumption goods (over goods and services such as pizzas, T-shirts, VCRs, haircuts, TV shows, and public transportation). As you'll see, however, the theory of preferences can be easily extended to encompass any number of possibilities other than consumer goods and services. Again for simplicity, we'll concentrate on the case in which there are just two goods. At the end of the chapter, we'll indicate what is involved in extending the theory to the case in which there are any number of goods.

Consumption Bundles

Let's begin by considering consumer preferences over all imaginable consumption bundles composed of just two goods. We'll use the terms good 1 and good 2 to represent the goods themselves. For example, good 1 might be T-shirts and good 2 might be haircuts. We'll use the symbols x_1 and x_2 to denote corresponding quantities, or amounts of good 1 and good 2. Thus x_1 is the quantity of good 1, and x_2 is the quantity of good 2. For example, $x_1 = 2$ means two T-shirts and $x_2 = 5$ means five haircuts.

A **consumption bundle** is simply an *ordered pair* of specified amounts of the two goods. We'll denote a consumption bundle symbolically in two different ways: by (x_1, x_2) to indicate that the bundle is composed of specified amounts of the two goods, or by B, simply because this notation is more compact. The word *ordered* in this description of a consumption bundle is important. For example, if good 1 is T-shirts and good 2 is haircuts, the ordered pair (10, 6) means that this bundle is composed of 10 T-shirts ($x_1 = 10$) and 6 haircuts ($x_2 = 6$). It does not mean 10 haircuts and 6 T-shirts.

Because negative quantities have no natural meaning in the context of consumption bundles — the "consumption of -5 T-shirts" is meaningless — the set of conceivable consumption bundles is the set of all ordered pairs $B = (x_1, x_2)$ in which the amounts of both goods are either positive or equal to zero, $x_1 \geq 0$ and $x_2 \geq 0$. For example, the bundle composed of 7 T-shirts and 5 haircuts (7, 5) is a conceivable consumption bundle, as are bundles composed of no T-shirts and 15 haircuts (0, 15) and no T-shirts and no haircuts (0, 0). But neither a bundle composed of -5 T-shirts and 3 haircuts $(-5, 3)$ nor one composed of -8 T-shirts and -1 haircuts $(-8, -1)$ is a conceivable consumption bundle. The set of conceivable consumption bundles is simply the set of all bundles that imaginably could be consumed.

Implicit in our choosing one consumption bundle over another is our ability to express preferences, to say either "I like this bundle better than that one" or "I like both equally well." In principle, at least, we can make use of any person's ability to make these preference statements to construct that individual's **preference ordering** — a ranking from top to bottom, from most preferred to least preferred of all conceivable consumption bundles.

More precisely, we want to find a set of assumptions about individual preferences that will allow us to construct such an ordering. Why? Because we cannot analyze an individual's consumption choices unless we know what his or her preferences look like. Also, we want to construct a function — a utility function — that will mirror that individual's preference ordering. Again, why? Because we can then use powerful graphic techniques to analyze any individual's consumption decisions.

3.3 Constructing a Complete Preference Ordering

Let's start with the problem of constructing a complete preference ordering. First, we need some notation to represent two primitive statements of preference. The two statements are (1) the individual prefers one consumption bundle to another, and (2) the individual is indifferent between two consumption bundles:

D E F I N I T I O N: Preference

Given two consumption bundles, B_1 and B_2, the statement

$$B_1 \; P \; B_2$$

means that the individual prefers consumption bundle B_1 to consumption bundle B_2.

Of course, the symbol **P** is just shorthand for "is preferred to." Notice that we will be using the notation B_1 and B_2 to denote particular consumption bundles. For example,

B_1 might denote the bundle (10, 5) and B_2 the bundle (5, 7). To indicate that (10, 5) is preferred to (5, 7), we could write $B_1 \; P \; B_2$ or equivalently, (10, 5) **P** (5, 7).

The notion of preference is intuitive. If we suppose that individuals act on their own self-interest in making decisions, then we can infer that given a choice between B_1 and B_2, the individual will actually choose B_1 whenever $B_1 \; P \; B_2$.

D E F I N I T I O N: Indifference

Given two consumption bundles, B_1 and B_2, the statement

$$B_1 \; I \; B_2$$

means that the individual is indifferent between the two bundles B_1 and B_2.

Again, the symbol **I** is shorthand for "indifferent." The statement $B_1 \; I \; B_2$ is also intuitive. If this statement is true, then the individual likes both bundles equally well.

Notice that we can use these notions to compare consumption bundles and that by making a series of such comparisons, we may be able to construct a preference ordering. Let's consider a particular person — say, Eleanor — who has made a series of preference statements about bundles composed of specific amounts of good 1 — say, hours of watching TV — and of good 2 — say, hours of aerobic exercise. She has made the following preference statements: (14, 10) **P** (14, 9); (14, 9) **I** (9, 14); and (9, 14) **P** (8, 20). Can we rank, or *order*, Eleanor's preferences over these four consumption bundles? The obvious candidate for such an ordering is

- First: (14, 10)
- Second: (14, 9), (9, 14)
- Third: (8, 20)

But we cannot be sure — given only the preference statements Eleanor has made —

that $(14, 10)$ **P** $(8, 20)$, $(14, 10)$ **P** $(9, 14)$, or $(14, 9)$ **P** $(8, 20)$. To be sure that these statements are correct, we need to know that Eleanor's preferences are in some sense *consistent*.

We lack not only assurance that Eleanor's preferences are consistent but also information that will allow us to construct or even to think about a complete ordering of her preferences over the infinite number of conceivable consumption bundles composed of TV viewing and aerobic exercise. We clearly need some assumptions about preferences—a theory of preferences—if we are to infer that such a complete ordering of Eleanor's preferences can be constructed.

Completeness

The first assumption is that an individual's preferences are *complete*; that is, that an individual can compare any pair of consumption bundles.

ASSUMPTION: Completeness
Given any two consumption bundles, B_1 and B_2, one of the following statements is true:

$$B_1 \text{ P } B_2 \qquad B_2 \text{ P } B_1 \qquad B_1 \text{ I } B_2$$

The *completeness assumption* says that for any two consumption bundles, an individual can say that he or she prefers the first to the second, prefers the second to the first, or is indifferent between them.

This is a *strong* assumption because it implies that any individual has complete knowledge. It seems necessary that an individual must have at least some experience of the goods included in the consumption bundle. A person who has never eaten fresh lichee nuts cannot be expected to satisfy this assumption if lichee nuts are one of the goods included in the consumption bundles. Thus, the assumption rules out some interesting economic issues concerning how individuals explore their own preferences.

Our theory cannot address these issues; we would need to build a different theory—one that does not assume complete knowledge—to address them.

Two-Term Consistency

Common sense suggests that the three statements in our first assumption must be mutually exclusive; that is, for any two consumption bundles, only one of the three statements is true. If Eleanor tells us that $(9, 14)$ **P** $(8, 20)$, then she cannot consistently tell us that $(8, 20)$ **P** $(9, 14)$ or that $(9, 14)$ **I** $(8, 20)$. The assumption that only one of the statements in our first assumption is true is therefore called the assumption of two-term consistency.

ASSUMPTION: Two-Term Consistency
Given any two consumption bundles B_1 and B_2, only one of the following statements is true:

$$B_1 \text{ P } B_2 \qquad B_2 \text{ P } B_1 \qquad B_1 \text{ I } B_2$$

To see why this assumption is necessary, let's suppose it did not hold. Suppose Eleanor tells us that $(9, 14)$ **P** $(8, 20)$ and that $(8, 20)$ **P** $(9, 14)$. Eleanor's first statement leads us to place $(9, 14)$ above $(8, 20)$ in her preference ordering, but her second statement leads us to place $(8, 20)$ above $(9, 14)$. In this case, we are forced to conclude that Eleanor has no preference ordering—and therefore no well-defined self-interest. To be sure that we can construct a preference ordering, we need to assume two-term consistency.

Three-Term Consistency, or Transitivity

To guarantee a *complete* preference ordering, we need one further assumption: the three-term-consistency, or transitivity, assumption. Notice that this assumption has four parts.

ASSUMPTION: Transitivity

Given any three consumption bundles, B_1, B_2, and B_3:

1 If B_1 P B_2 and B_2 P B_3, then B_1 P B_3.

2 If B_1 P B_2 and B_2 I B_3, then B_1 P B_3.

3 If B_1 I B_2 and B_2 P B_3, then B_1 P B_3.

4 If B_1 I B_2 and B_2 I B_3, then B_1 I B_3.

To see why the transitivity assumption is necessary, let's suppose Eleanor says that (14, 10) **P** (14, 9), that (14, 9) **P** (8, 20), and —contrary to part **1** of our transitivity assumption—that (8, 20) **P** (14, 10). Eleanor's first statement leads us to place (14, 10) above (14, 9) in her preference ordering, and her second statement leads us to place (14, 9) above (8, 20). Therefore (14, 10) must precede (8, 20) in the ordering. Yet her third statement, on the contrary, leads us to place (8, 20) above (14, 10). Once again, Eleanor has no well-defined preference ordering because the three preference statements violate transitivity.

PROBLEM 3.1

Does the following set of four preference statements violate the transitivity assumption? (10, 19) P (14, 21); (14, 21) P (15, 8); (15, 8) P (0, 0); (15, 8) I (11, 17)

Four-Term Consistency

Although assumptions of two-term and three-term consistency are needed to construct a preference ordering, a four-term-consistency assumption is not necessary because it is implied by the three-term-consistency assumption. In Problem 3.2, you can show that three-term consistency implies four-term consistency.

PROBLEM 3.2

Eight statements are needed to describe four-term consistency. This is one statement:

If B_1 P B_2, B_2 P B_3, and B_3 P B_4, then B_1 P B_4.

Show that this statement is true if the transitivity assumption is satisfied. Seven other statements are also needed to describe four-term consistency. What are they?

Existence of a Complete Preference Ordering

Just as we can use three-term consistency to show four-term consistency, we can use four-term consistency to derive five-term consistency, and then use five-term consistency to derive six-term consistency, and so on, as we derive an endless chain of consistency results. In combination with the two-term-consistency assumption, this chain of consistency results means that an individual is incapable of making any inconsistent set of preference statements.

Now we have reached our first goal: these three assumptions imply that the notion of self-interest is a precise, well-defined concept. As we just saw, the first assumption guarantees that an individual can always make preference statements, and the second and third assumptions guarantee that he or she is incapable of making inconsistent preference statements. Thus, an individual can consistently rank any set of consumption bundles. In other words:

Taken together, these three assumptions imply the existence of a complete preference ordering.

3.4 Constructing a Utility Function

Now that a complete preference ordering is in place, we want to construct a mathematical representation of that ordering. This preference function—or utility function, as it is commonly called—will assign a number to each consumption bundle. These numbers will reflect an individual's ordering of the consumption bundles from top to bottom, from most preferred to least preferred.

Indifference Curves

Let's begin by defining an indifference curve. Looking back at the ordering that we tried to construct for Eleanor, we realize that, by definition, the bundles among which she is *indifferent* will occupy the *same position in her preference ordering.* The complete list of bundles that occupy the same position in a preference ordering is called an **indifference curve**.

DEFINITION: Indifference Curve

Pick any bundle B. The associated indifference curve is the set of all consumption bundles that are indifferent to B.

Thus, any two consumption bundles on the same indifference curve — say, B_1 and B_2 — must satisfy the indifference statement $B_1 \mathbf{I} B_2$. A representative indifference curve, I, is presented in Figure 3.1. Because I is an indifference curve, by definition any two bundles on it — say, $(10, 5)$ and $(4, 12)$ — satisfy the indifference statement $(10, 5) \mathbf{I} (4, 12)$. Notice, too, that this indifference curve can be identified by bundle $(10, 5)$ because the consumption bundle $(10, 5)$ is on it. It could just as easily be identified by bundle $(4, 12)$ because this consumption bundle is also on the indifference curve I.

Indeed any consumption bundle on a given indifference curve can be used to identify that indifference curve. Accordingly, in Figure 3.1 we have given the indifference curve the label $J(10, 5)$ because the consumption bundle $(10, 5)$ lies on it. However, the label $J(4, 12)$ — which we have also attached to that indifference curve — will do just as well because the consumption bundle $(4, 12)$ also lies on that indifference curve. Because we will be using this method of labeling indifference curves at a number of key points, be sure that you understand it.

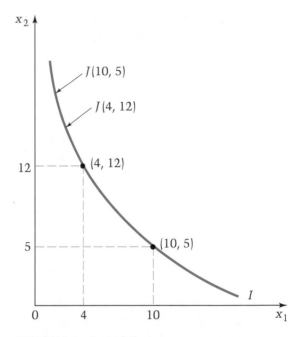

FIGURE 3.1 An indifference curve.

Line I is an indifference curve because the individual is indifferent between any two consumption bundles on it. For example, $(10, 5) \mathbf{I}$ $(4, 12)$. The labels $J(10, 5)$ and $J(4, 12)$ are equally appropriate because bundles $(10, 5)$ and $(4, 12)$ are both on the indifference curve.

The Continuity of the Indifference Curve

At this point, we cannot say anything about the *shape* of indifference curves. In fact, in constructing Figure 3.1, we have tacitly assumed that each point — or consumption bundle — is on what can be called a nontrivial indifference curve. In other words, we have treated consumption bundles as if there were other bundles that an individual finds equally acceptable. Is it conceivable that there are consumption bundles for which an individual finds no acceptable substitutes?

PROBLEM 3.3

Clem is a single-minded person who is obsessed with good 1.

1 Given any two bundles with unequal quantities of good 1, Clem prefers the bundle with the larger quantity of good 1.

2 Given any two bundles with equal quantities of good 1, Clem prefers the bundle with the larger quantity of good 2.

Consider bundle (2, 3), and show that there is no other bundle B for which Clem will state B I (2, 3). Now, consider an arbitrary consumption bundle and show that it, too, is a single-point indifference curve.

As you know, Clem's "indifference curves" are simply points; that is, the indifference curve defined by some arbitrary consumption bundle B is composed of only one point — namely, B itself. As you'll see, no utility function exists that represents these single-point preferences, even though such preferences are not ruled out by our three assumptions. Because we want to represent preference orderings by utility functions, we clearly need an additional assumption: the continuity assumption.

ASSUMPTION: Continuity of Preferences

Through any consumption bundle in which the quantity of at least one good is positive, there is a continuous indifference curve.

To see what the continuity assumption means in graphic terms, place your pencil on some consumption bundle in Figure 3.1. The continuity assumption means that you can draw the indifference curve through that bundle without lifting your pencil from the paper — that is, the indifference curve is continuous.

Nonsatiation

One further assumption is useful, but not necessary, in constructing a utility function: the assumption that more is better, which we'll call the *nonsatiation assumption*. If I am not satiated, I would rather have two glasses of Perrier and two Ritz crackers than one Perrier and one cracker. And I would rather have two Perriers and two crackers than two Perriers and only one cracker.

ASSUMPTION: Nonsatiation

Given two consumption bundles, B_1 and B_2, if B_1 contains more of one good than does B_2 and if B_1 does not contain less of the other good, then B_1 is preferred to B_2.

To check your understanding of the nonsatiation assumption, try the following problem.

PROBLEM 3.4

Indicate which of the following preference statements violate the nonsatiation assumption: (12, 35) P (10, 30); (17, 98) P (17, 97); (10, 9) P (10, 10); (42, 67) P (42, 60); (6, 9) P (7, 8); (99, 43) P (101, 45).

The Slope of the Indifference Curve

As you can see from Figure 3.2, the nonsatiation assumption implies that the slope of

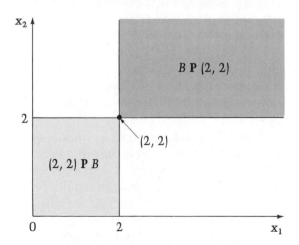

FIGURE 3.2 Implications of nonsatiation.

Nonsatiation implies that any bundle in the dark green area is preferred to bundle (2, 2) and that bundle (2, 2) is preferred to any bundle in the light green area. Accordingly, the indifference curve through (2, 2) cannot pass through either the dark green or the light green area, and its slope is therefore negative.

any indifference curve is *negative*. For any bundle *B* in the dark green area of Figure 3.2, the nonsatiation assumption implies that *B* **P** (2, 2), because the bundles in that area contain *at least* 2 units of both goods and *more than* 2 units of at least one good. Similarly, for any bundle *B* in the light green area, the nonsatiation assumption implies that (2, 2) **P** *B*, because those bundles contain *less* of at least one good and *no more* of the other good than consumption bundle (2, 2). Now, try to draw an indifference curve through *B*. Because it cannot enter the dark green (more preferred) area or the light green (less preferred) area, the curve must slope downward and to the right. In other words, it must have a negative slope.

The nonsatiation assumption implies that indifference curves have a negative slope.

The Indifference Map

One additional observation is important. Because the preference ordering is a complete ordering, we know that there is an indifference curve through every bundle. The (x_1, x_2) plane, or quarter plane, is filled with indifference curves such as the ones illustrated in Figure 3.3.

Because of the nonsatiation assumption, bundles with more of both goods are preferred to those with less. As a result, we know that bundles on indifference curves farther from the origin are preferred to bundles on curves closer to the origin. For example, as we move upward and to the right in Figure 3.3 from indifference curve $J(2, 2)$ to $J(3, 3)$ to $J(4, 4)$ to $J(5, 5)$, we encounter indifference curves containing more-preferred consumption bundles. Any bundle on $J(3, 3)$, for example, is preferred to any bundle on $J(2, 2)$. Notice, too, that the indifference curves in Figure 3.3 do not cross or even touch each other. Because this is an

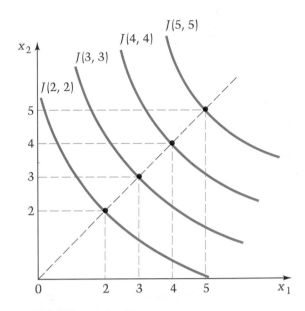

FIGURE 3.3   An indifference map.

The space of consumption bundles is filled with indifference curves, four of which are illustrated. Any bundle on $J(5, 5)$ is preferred to any bundle on $J(4, 4)$, any bundle on $J(4, 4)$ is preferred to any bundle on $J(3, 3)$, and any bundle on $J(3, 3)$ is preferred to any bundle on $J(2, 2)$.

important property of indifference maps, pay close attention to the following problem.

PROBLEM 3.5

Show that the two consistency assumptions imply that indifference curves cannot intersect. Hint: Assume that they do intersect and then show that the intersection violates the transitivity assumption.

As you will soon see, these five assumptions allow us to represent an individual's preferences by a utility function.

Utility Function Defined

The term *utility function* may be a bit intimidating, but the basic concept is simple. A **utility function** assigns a number—which we call a *utility number*—to every consumption bundle in a person's preference ordering. The utility function must assign utility numbers in accordance with two rules. First, if an individual prefers one bundle to another, the utility function must assign a larger number to the preferred bundle. Second, if an individual is indifferent between two bundles, the utility function must assign the same number to both bundles. Since a utility function assigns numbers to consumption bundles, we'll denote such a function by $U(x_1, x_2)$ or, more compactly, by $U(B)$.

D E F I N I T I O N: Utility Function

A function, $U(x_1, x_2)$, or $U(B)$, is a utility function if it assigns a utility number to all consumption bundles and if it satisfies the following conditions:

Condition 1: If $B_1 \, P \, B_2$, then $U(B_1) > U(B_2)$.

Condition 2: If $B_1 \, I \, B_2$, then $U(B_1) = U(B_2)$.

To see just what utility functions and utility numbers are and do, let's return to Amy's preferences in the fish model of Chapter 2. Recall that Amy consumed bundles containing what we will now think of as good 1 — "fish this year" — and good 2 — "fish next year." Recall, too, that when one consumption bundle contained a larger total number of fish than another bundle, Amy preferred the consumption bundle containing the larger total number of fish. (So did Ted, but that is of no concern to us at this point.) For example, given a choice between (80, 34) and (37, 80), Amy preferred (37, 80) to (80, 34). When two consumption bundles contained the same total number of fish, Amy was indifferent between the two bundles. For example, Amy was indifferent between (30, 20) and (25, 25). Letting x_1 and x_2 denote quantities of fish this year and fish next year, we can capture Amy's preferences by the following function:

$$U(x_1, x_2) = x_1 + x_2$$

Does this function meet the definition of a utility function? It does assign a number to all consumption bundles containing fish this year and fish next year. To see that it satisfies condition 1, consider two bundles with different quantities of total fish — say, bundles (10, 45) and (15, 20). The first bundle is preferred to the second because it contains 55 fish and the second contains only 35. According to condition 1, it should therefore be assigned a higher utility number. This function does meet that condition because it assigns the larger utility number, 55 (10 + 45), to the first bundle and the smaller utility number, 35 (15 + 20), to the second bundle. Now to see that it satisfies condition 2, notice that bundles with the same total number of fish are assigned the same utility number. For example, the two bundles (10 + 45) and (20 + 35) are both assigned the utility number 55.

Utility Numbers

Now let's establish a rule for assigning utility numbers to consumption bundles that will allow us, in principle at least, to construct a utility function for any set of individual preferences that satisfy the five assumptions we've made. Notice that now we are not dealing with specific preferences such as the preferences from our fish model, but rather with any preferences that satisfy the five assumptions made in this chapter. Therefore, our objective is not to find a particular utility function — such as the utility function $U(x_1, x_2) = x_1 + x_2$ — but to show that some utility function exists for any preferences that satisfy these five assumptions.

In Figure 3.4, we have constructed a ray through the origin (the line $x_2 = x_1/2$), which we will be using in setting out our rule for assigning utility numbers. What is the rule for assigning utility numbers? For any bundle on the ray, first identify the as-

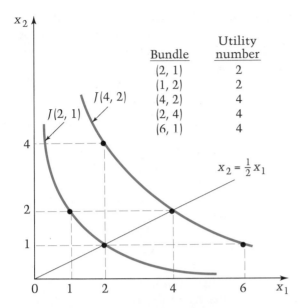

Bundle	Utility number
(2, 1)	2
(1, 2)	2
(4, 2)	4
(2, 4)	4
(6, 1)	4

FIGURE 3.4   Constructing a utility function.

To construct a utility function, for every bundle on the ray $x_2 = x_1/2$, identify the associated indifference curve, and assign the quantity of good 1 in the bundle as a utility number to all bundles on the indifference curve. This rule assigns utility number 2 to all bundles on $J(2, 1)$ and utility number 4 to all bundles on $J(4, 2)$.

sociated indifference curve. For example, if the bundle is (2, 1), identify the continuous indifference curve that passes through (2, 1) and label it $J(2, 1)$. Next, note the quantity of good 1 in the original bundle on the ray, and use this quantity as the utility number for every bundle on the indifference curve. For example, if the bundle is (2, 1), assign the number 2 as the utility number for every bundle on $J(2, 1)$. From Figure 3.4, you can see that both the consumption bundles (2, 1) and (1, 2) are assigned the utility number 2. Now let us consider a different indifference curve — say, $J(4, 2)$. This rule assigns the utility number 4 to every bundle on $J(4, 2)$. For example, consumption bundles (2, 4), (4, 2), and (6, 1) are all assigned the utility number 4. As you will see, if you follow this rule for every bundle on the ray, you will have a utility function.

DEFINITION: Rule for Assigning Utility Numbers

For every bundle on the ray $x_2 = x_1/2$, first identify $J(x_1, x_2)$, and then assign the number x_1 to all bundles on $J(x_1, x_2)$.

Since other rules will do the job, this particular rule is not fundamental to the theory of utility functions; it simply allows us to assign utility numbers to consumption bundles in a manner consistent with the definition of a utility function.

Does this rule meet the definition of a utility function? We know that it meets condition 2. Because indifference curves are negatively sloped and because the ray is positively sloped, any indifference curve will intersect the ray once and only once. Thus, this rule does assign the same utility number to all bundles on the same indifference curve — just as condition 2 demands.

But do these utility numbers meet condition 1 by preserving the preference ordering from lowest to highest? In other words, does the rule assign a higher number to a more preferred bundle and a lower number to a less preferred bundle? To find out, let's consider two bundles on the ray in Figure 3.4 — say, bundles (2, 1) and (4, 2). The nonsatiation assumption implies that (4, 2) **P** (2, 1) because (4, 2) contains more of both goods. Furthermore, the consistency assumptions imply that any bundle on $J(4, 2)$ is preferred to any bundle on $J(2, 1)$. Thus, the consumption bundle (6, 1) is preferred to (2, 1) and to (1, 2), for example, because it is on $J(4, 2)$ and the other bundles are on $J(2, 1)$. This rule assigns the utility number 4 to bundles on $J(4, 2)$ and the utility number 2 to bundles on $J(2, 1)$. Because 4 exceeds 2, it does satisfy condition 1 of the definition of a utility function: a larger utility number is assigned to the bundles on the preferred indifference curve.

More generally, given any two indifference curves, the nonsatiation assumption implies that the preferred bundles are on the indifference curve that is farther from the origin. Because this rule assigns a larger utility number to bundles on the indifference curve farther from the origin, it satisfies condition 1.

Finally, we need to check that the rule assigns a utility number to all bundles. To see that it does, let's consider some consumption bundle in Figure 3.5 that is *not* on the ray $x_2 = x_1/2$, bundle $(4, 5)$ for instance. The continuity assumption implies that there is a continuous indifference curve, labeled $J(4, 5)$, that passes through this bundle. Furthermore, the indifference curve $J(4, 5)$ must intersect the ray $x_2 = x_1/2$ because it is negatively sloped and the ray is positively sloped. Because $J(4, 5)$ intersects the ray at $(6, 3)$ in Figure 3.5, the rule assigns utility number 6 to consumption bundle

$(4, 5)$. In other words, our rule for assigning utility numbers does in fact assign a number to every consumption bundle. We have now reached our second goal:[2]

If preferences satisfy our five assumptions, there is a utility function that represents those preferences.

We can also begin to see why we need the continuity assumption. Suppose that we tried to use this rule to construct a utility function to represent Clem's single-minded preferences from Problem 3.3. Recall that, for Clem, each consumption bundle is a one-point indifference curve. Yet our rule assigns utility numbers only to consumption bundles on indifference curves that *intersect* the ray $x_2 = x_1/2$. In Clem's case, our rule therefore uses up all the positive real numbers in assigning utility numbers to bundles on the ray $x_2 = x_1/2$; that is, the rule does not assign utility numbers to any bundles that are not on the ray. Of course, we might try using negative numbers as utility numbers, but there just are not enough negative numbers to go around. We adopted the continuity assumption because it rules out these awkward preferences, and making this assumption — or one very close to it — is essential if we are to represent preferences by utility functions.

We have used these five assumptions to show that there is a utility function that represents an individual's preference ordering. But this discovery tells us only that such a function exists. In Problem 3.6, you will be asked to identify a utility function that actually represents the preference ordering specified in the problem.

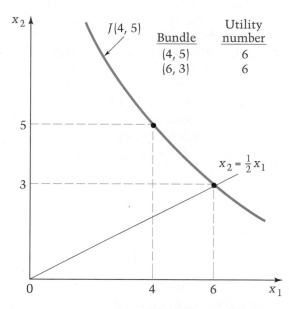

FIGURE 3.5 A utility number for each bundle?
To see that the rule assigns a utility number to each bundle, pick any bundle not on the ray $x_2 = x_1/2$ — say, bundle $(4, 5)$ — and identify the associated indifference curve, $J(4, 5)$. Since $J(4, 5)$ is downward sloping, it intersects the ray at bundle $(6, 3)$. The rule therefore assigns utility number 6 to bundle $(4, 5)$.

---

[2] Notice also that we have shown that there is a *continuous* utility function that represents any preference ordering that satisfies our five assumptions.

PROBLEM 3.6

Suppose that for any positive value of c, all bundles on $x_1 x_2 = c$ satisfy the indifference statement. For example, $x_1 x_2 = 1$ is an indifference curve. Furthermore, any bundle on an indifference curve $x_1 x_2 = c_1$ is preferred to any bundle on $x_1 x_2 = c_2$ if $c_1 > c_2$. For example, any bundle on $x_1 x_2 = 6$ is preferred to any bundle on $x_1 x_2 = 3$. Using our rule for assigning utility numbers, construct a utility function that represents these preferences.

Now we have achieved our initial two goals. Our first three assumptions guarantee that the concept of the individual's self-interest is well defined. That is, these assumptions assure us that a complete preference ordering does exist. Our fourth and fifth assumptions guarantee that the preference ordering can be represented by a utility function. Next, we want to argue that, given preferences satisfying these assumptions, any number of utility functions can be constructed that represent these preferences.

PROBLEM 3.7

Consider the following rules for constructing functions. For any consumption bundle B on the ray $x_2 = x_1/2$, identify the associated indifference curve, $J(B)$. Then assign to each point on $J(B)$ the number

1 $10x_1$

2 $x_1^{1/2}$

3 $(x_1 - 5)^2$

4 x_2

Show that the functions defined by rules 1, 2, and 4 are utility functions and that the function defined by rule 3 is not a utility function.

From Problem 3.7, you know that many functions will represent a preference ordering. This is an important point because it helps us to see what utility numbers do and do not mean. For example, consider a utility

function $U(x_1, x_2)$ and two consumption bundles, $(17, 9)$ and $(15, 10)$. Suppose that $(17, 9)$ is preferred to $(15, 10)$. Because $(17, 9)$ P $(15, 10)$, we know that the utility number $U(17, 9)$ exceeds the utility number $U(15, 10)$. Keep in mind that $U(17, 9)$ and $U(15, 10)$ are just the utility numbers that emerge when the utility function is evaluated first at $(17, 9)$ and then at $(15, 10)$. Now let's form a new function by multiplying the utility number associated with any bundle by some constant c. The new function, $V(x_1, x_2)$, is simply

$$V(x_1, x_2) = cU(x_1, x_2)$$

Is $V(x_1, x_2)$ also a utility function? It is if it always assigns a larger utility number to the preferred bundle. In particular, does $V(17, 9)$ exceed $V(15, 10)$? Or, equivalently, does $cU(17, 9)$ exceed $cU(15, 10)$? If c is positive, it does. Therefore, when c is positive, $V(x_1, x_2)$ is also a utility function. The point is this: if we have one utility function, we can generate others that represent the same preference ordering by multiplying the original utility function by a positive constant. This is not the only way to construct a new utility function. For example, squaring utility numbers instead of multiplying them by a constant would generate yet another utility function.[3]

---

[3] In general, we can form a new function $V(x_1, x_2)$ from $U(x_1, x_2)$ by feeding utility numbers into another function, which we'll call f. Symbolically, the new function is

$$V(x_1, x_2) = f[U(x_1, x_2)]$$

If f has the property that the larger the number you feed into it, the larger the number that comes out, then $V(x)$ is also a utility function. (Any function f that has this property is said to be a *monotonically increasing* function.) Suppose that f is monotonically increasing. Then (1) when $U(B_1) > U(B_2)$, $V(B_1) > V(B_2)$, and (2) when $U(B_1) = U(B_2)$, $V(B_1) = V(B_2)$. In other words, the functions $V(x_1, x_2)$ and $U(x_1, x_2)$ represent the same preference ordering. Thus, given a utility function, we can create others by operating on it with any monotonically increasing function.

The Meaning of Utility Numbers

These observations should make it clear that the particular numbers any utility function assigns to consumption bundles are arbitrary except for their order. The utility number assigned by one utility function to a given indifference curve will ordinarily be different from the utility number assigned by another utility function.

Utility numbers are therefore ordinal, not cardinal. They reveal only the *relative ordering* of consumption bundles (first, second, or third) and nothing about the "distance" between bundles in terms of desirability (twice as desirable or one-third as desirable). Utility numbers do not depend on any physical or psychological measure, as was once proposed by Jeremy Bentham and other utilitarian theorists; these numbers cannot be interpreted as measures of "happiness" or "satisfaction." As we have seen throughout, the notion of preference — not happiness — is the primitive, or irreducible, concept at the heart of our analysis. In comparing two bundles, we find that utility numbers tell us one of three things: the first bundle is preferred to the second, the second bundle is preferred to the first, or the individual is indifferent between the two bundles — and *nothing more.*

Furthermore, we cannot use utility numbers to make comparisons among individuals. Given the way in which we have constructed the utility function, any utility number — 3, for example — is intelligible only within the context of a single individual's preference ordering and a particular representation of that ordering.

3.5 Trade-offs and the Marginal Rate of Substitution

In the rest of this chapter, we'll provide the final touches as we introduce some new concepts and add two more useful and simplifying assumptions to the theory. These last two assumptions are often used in economic theory, but they are not essential, and in subsequent chapters we will consider a number of interesting illustrations in which they do not hold.

Basic to the theory of consumer choice in Chapter 4 is the rate at which an individual is willing to *trade off one good for another:* the rate at which the quantity of one good must be increased as the quantity of another is decreased in order to keep an individual on the same indifference curve. Our purpose in this section is to develop a measure of the willingness of an individual to substitute one good for another: **the marginal rate of substitution (MRS).**

Let's pick a consumption bundle on indifference curve I in Figure 3.6 — say, the bundle at point A. Now suppose that we decrease the amount of good 1 in this bundle by Δx_1. What increase in the amount of good 2 will offset this decrease in good 1 — that is, will keep this individual on indifference curve I? From Figure 3.6, we see that the answer is Δx_2. We can call the ratio $\Delta x_2 / \Delta x_1$ the *nonmarginal rate of substitution* since it is a measure of the rate at which good 2 must be substituted for good 1 to keep this individual on I. Notice that the nonmarginal rate of substitution is simply the slope of the dashed line segment BA multiplied by -1. (We must multiply by -1 because the slope of the dashed line is negative and $\Delta x_2 / \Delta x_1$ is positive.)

To find MRS, just imagine what happens to the nonmarginal rate of substitution as Δx_1 gets smaller and smaller. As Δx_1 gets smaller, the consumption bundle B moves along the indifference curve I toward bundle A, and the dashed line BA approaches the line labeled TT tangent to indifference curve I at bundle A. Therefore as Δx_1 approaches zero, the nonmarginal rate of substitution approaches the slope of TT multiplied by -1. The slope of TT multiplied by

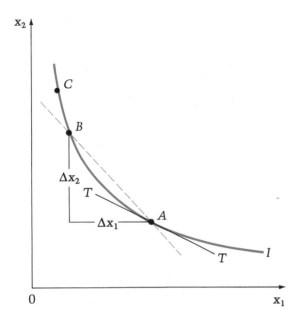

FIGURE 3.6   The marginal rate of substitution.
Beginning at bundle A, if we reduce the quantity of good 1 by Δx_1, we must increase the quantity of good 2 by Δx_2 to get back to the indifference curve. The rate of substitution of good 2 for good 1 is therefore $\Delta x_2 / \Delta x_1$, or -1 times the slope of the dashed line from bundle A to bundle B. To find MRS, let Δx_1 approach zero. As it does, the rate of substitution approaches -1 times the slope of the tangent line TT, which is MRS at bundle A.

-1 is the marginal rate of substitution of good 2 for good 1 at bundle A; that is, the rate at which good 2 must increase as good 1 decreases (by an infinitesimal amount) to keep the individual on the same indifference curve.

D E F I N I T I O N: Marginal Rate of Substitution
The marginal rate of substitution of good 2 for good 1 at any point (x_1, x_2), denoted by $MRS(x_1, x_2)$, is the slope of the indifference curve at point (x_1, x_2), multiplied by -1.

Notice that if we had picked some point on the indifference curve in Figure 3.6 other than point A, we would have derived a dif-

ferent value for $MRS(x_1, x_2)$ because the slope of this indifference curve varies from point to point. For instance, because its slope is steeper at point C than at point A, we know that MRS is larger at point C than at point A. This means that $MRS(x_1, x_2)$ ordinarily takes on different values at different bundles along an indifference curve, or that MRS is a *function*, and not simply a number.[4]

In the following problem, you can explore the interesting case in which MRS is the same at all bundles. Be sure to pay particular attention to the unusual shape of the indifference curves.

---

[4] We can use the implicit function theorem to express MRS in terms of the partial derivatives of $U(\cdot)$. An indifference curve can be written as

$$u' = U(x_1, x_2)$$

where u' is fixed and x_1 and x_2 are free to vary. Since the indifference curve defines x_2 as an implicit function of x_1, we can use the implicit function theorem to express this indifference curve as

$$x_2 = g(x_1)$$

MRS is, of course, just $-g'(x_1)$, where $g'(x_1)$ is the derivative of $g(x_1)$. Combining these equations, we have the following identity

$$u' = U[x_1, g(x_1)]$$

Differentiating the identity with respect to x_1 gives us

$$U_1[x_1, g(x_1)] + g'(x_1)U_2[x_1, g(x_1)] = 0$$

where $U_1(\cdot)$ and $U_2(\cdot)$ denote the partial derivatives of $U(\cdot)$ with respect to x_1 and x_2. (The partial derivative $U_i(\cdot)$ is sometimes called the marginal utility of good i.). Rearranging this equation, we get

$$-g'(x_1) = \frac{U_1(x_1, x_2)}{U_2(x_1, x_2)}$$

But the left side of this equation is just MRS; hence

$$MRS(x_1, x_2) = \frac{U_1(x_1, x_2)}{U_2(x_1, x_2)}$$

Thus, for example, for the utility function $U(x_1, x_2) = x_1 x_2$, $MRS(x_1, x_2) = x_2 / x_1$.

PROBLEM 3.8

First, consider Amy's utility function from our fish model, $U(x_1, x_2) = x_1 + x_2$. Draw the following indifference curve, and then find its MRS.

$$2 = x_1 + x_2$$

Now consider another utility function for which MRS is just a number:

$$U(x_1, x_2) = 9x_1 + 3x_2$$

Draw an indifference curve for this utility function, and find its MRS.

Kinked Indifference Curves

Even though MRS is a very useful concept, it is not always well defined. Figure 3.7 represents a case in which an indifference curve has a *kink* at point K. At any point to the right or to the left of the kink, it is possible to construct a unique line tangent to the indifference curve; consequently, MRS is well defined for any such point. Through point K, however, any number of straight lines can be constructed — such as the two dashed

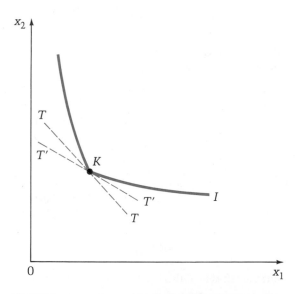

FIGURE 3.7   MRS and kinked indifference curves.
The indifference curve I has a kink at bundle K. Any line through K that is steeper than $T'T'$ and flatter than TT does not intersect I. Hence, there is no tangent line to the indifference curve at bundle K, and MRS is not defined.

lines labeled TT and $T'T'$ in Figure 3.7 — that do not intersect the indifference curve. This means that the MRS at point K cannot be defined. In the following problem, you can consider another case in which MRS is not everywhere well defined.

PROBLEM 3.9

Suppose the utility function is $U(x_1, x_2) = \min (2x_1, x_2)$, where *min* means "the minimum of." For example, if x_1 is 4 and x_2 is 2, then $U(x_1, x_2)$ is 2, since "the minimum of 8 (2×4) and 2" is 2. Draw the following indifference curve: $2 = \min(2x_1, x_2)$. To get started, notice that bundle $(1, 2)$ is on this indifference curve and that the indifference curve has a right-angled kink at bundle $(1, 2)$. What is MRS to the right of the kink? Above the kink? At the kink itself?

If indifference curves are *smooth* — that is, if they have no kinks — then MRS is well defined. Because it is so convenient to use MRS in analyzing consumer choice, we will often make the assumption that indifference curves are smooth:

ASSUMPTION: Smooth Indifference Curves
Indifference curves are smooth.

From time to time, however, we will instead use kinked indifference curves, such as the one you just constructed.[5]

Convexity of Indifference Curves

Finally, we want to introduce an assumption regarding the shape of indifference curves. This assumption will eliminate indifference curves such as those in Figures

---

[5] Mathematically, smoothness of indifference curves is related to differentiability of the utility function. From footnote 4, we know that $MRS(x_1, x_2) = U_1(x_1, x_2)/U_2(x_1, x_2)$. If these partial derivatives are continuous functions, then so is their ratio, $MRS(x_1, x_2)$; hence, if $U(x_1, x_1)$ is differentiable and if its partial derivatives are continuous, then its indifference curves are smooth.

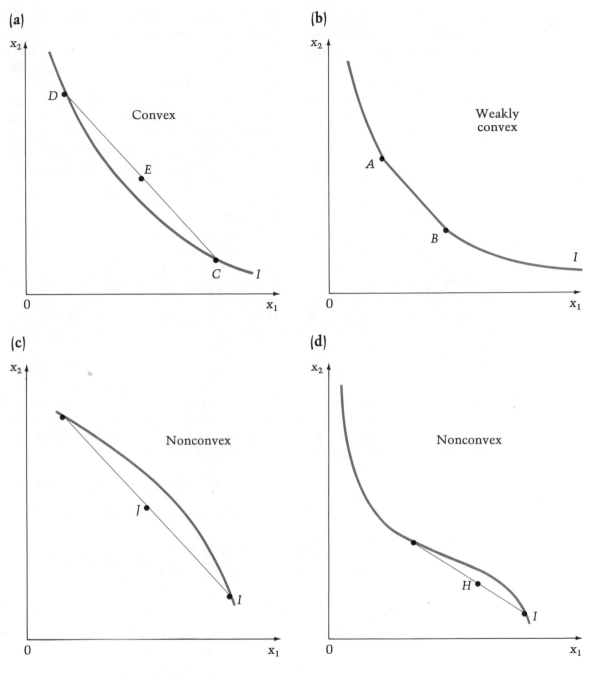

FIGURE 3.8 Convexity of indifference curves.

The indifference curve in (a) is convex, the indifference curves in (c) and (d) are nonconvex, and the indifference curve in (b) is weakly convex.

3.8*b*, 3.8*c*, and 3.8*d* and leave us with only **convex indifference curves,** such as the one in Figure 3.8*a*.

To see what this assumption entails, consider Figure 3.8*a* for a moment. Let's choose two bundles on indifference curve

I—say, bundles C and D—and then construct the line segment connecting these two bundles. Notice that with the exception of the original bundles C and D, any bundle on this line segment lies above the indifference curve. By nonsatiation, we know that any bundle on the line segment is preferred to bundle C and to bundle D—and indeed to any other bundle on indifference curve I. For example, bundle E at the midpoint of the line segment is preferred to any bundle on indifference curve I. Notice, too, that this property—that any bundle in the interior of a line segment connecting two bundles on indifference curve I is preferred to any bundle on that indifference curve—holds regardless of which two bundles on indifference curve I are chosen. This is what we mean by saying that indifference curve I is convex.[6]

We have a simpler criterion to show that an indifference curve is *nonconvex*. Simply identify one pair of bundles on the indifference curve and one bundle on the line segment connecting those two bundles that is less preferred than a bundle on the indifference curve. For example, because any bundle on the indifference curve in Figure 3.8c is preferred to bundle J, we know that this indifference curve is nonconvex. Similarly, because any bundle on the indifference curve in Figure 3.8d is preferred to

bundle H, we also know that this indifference curve is nonconvex.

The indifference curve in Figure 3.8b is slightly more complex. Because this indifference curve has a linear segment—segment AB—it fails to satisfy the convexity criterion. Yet it also fails to satisfy the nonconvexity criterion. To see why it fails to satisfy either criterion, suppose we begin by picking bundles A and B at the ends of the linear segment of the indifference curve. Because the line segment connecting these two bundles is then *coincident* with segment AB of the indifference curve, we know that bundles on this line segment are neither more preferred nor less preferred than the bundles on the indifference curve. Because neither the criterion for convexity nor the criterion for nonconvexity is satisfied, this indifference curve is said to be *weakly convex to the origin*.

The standard assumption is that indifference curves are like the one in Figure 3.8a. Generally, we will be making this assumption, but occasionally we will use weakly convex indifference curves like the one in Figure 3.8b.

ASSUMPTION: Convexity of Indifference Curves

Indifference curves are convex.

PROBLEM 3.10

Construct the following indifference curves and indicate whether they are convex, weakly convex, or nonconvex.

$$2 = x_1 + x_2$$
$$1 = x_1 x_2$$
$$1 = (x_1)^2 + (x_2)^2$$

Because MRS for smooth indifference curves is well defined, we can express the convexity assumption for such curves in this way: in any move from left to right along the indifference curve, MRS diminishes. In other words, *for smooth indiffer-*

---

[6] Convexity of an indifference curve can be defined in more mathematical terms. Pick any two bundles on the same indifference curve, say B' and B''. Form a new bundle B''' as follows:

$$B''' = tB' + (1-t)B''$$

where t is any number larger than 0 and less than 1. The bundle B''' is said to be a convex combination of B' and B''. Suppose, for example, that $B' = (2, 4)$, $B'' = (4, 0)$, and $t = \frac{1}{2}$; then the convex combination B''' is $(3, 2)$. If for all B' and B'' on the indifference curve and for all permissible values of t the convex combination B''' is preferred to the original bundles B' and B'', the indifference curve is convex.

ence curves, convexity and diminishing marginal rate of substitution are equivalent concepts.

What is the justification for the convexity assumption? First, like the smoothness assumption, the convexity assumption is convenient because it allows us to set aside tedious problems that would otherwise arise. Second, as you will see in Chapter 4, the nonconvex portions of indifference curves are in a sense irrelevant to choice making because no utility-maximizing individual would ever choose to buy a consumption bundle on a nonconvex portion. Because nonconvex segments are irrelevant, we can safely assume them away. (You will have the opportunity to explore this justification in Exercise 22 at the end of Chapter 4.) Finally, in many cases the assumption seems plausible. Suppose that x_1 is quantity of shelter and x_2 is quantity of food. It seems likely that the more shelter a particular person has relative to the amount of food, the less willing he or she will be to give up food for even more shelter. In other words, the larger x_1/x_2 is, the flatter the indifference curve will be, but this is nothing other than a diminishing MRS.

---

*3.6 Many Goods

Since most real consumption bundles contain a large number of goods, what could we possibly learn about real consumption choices by reducing them to this simple two-good case? As it turns out, we can learn a great deal. In Chapter 4, we will see that a vast number of real consumer decisions can be legitimately reduced to the two-good case. Yet this answer raises another, closely related question: Reduced from what? In this last section of the chapter, we will briefly indicate how the theory can be extended to the case in which there are an arbitrary number of goods — the *n*-good case.

In this *n*-good case, a consumption bundle is an ordered list of quantities of *n* goods, written as $(x_1, x_2, \ldots, x_n)$. Here, x_1 is the quantity of good 1, x_2 is the quantity of good 2, and x_n is the quantity of good *n*. A conceivable consumption bundle is just a bundle in which there are no negative quantities. To see how the core theory extends to this *n*-good case, let's consider two questions: What assumptions guarantee that the notion of self-interest is well defined? What additional assumptions guarantee that preferences can be represented by a utility function?

The first question is easily answered. The three assumptions that guarantee a complete preference ordering in the two-good case do the same job in the *n*-good case. If an individual can compare any pair of bundles, and if those comparisons exhibit two- and three-term consistency, then that individual's preference ordering is complete; that is, the existence of many goods creates no new wrinkles in this part of the theory.

As in the two-good case, a continuity assumption is required if a preference ordering is to be represented by a utility function. In this case, however, the assumption is more technical and therefore harder to understand. Nevertheless, it serves the same purpose. Given any consumption bundle — say, bundle *B* — we can define the set of bundles that are either preferred to *B* or indifferent to it. This set is called the **no-worse-than set** because the bundles in it are no worse than *B*. Similarly, we can define the **no-better-than set,** which contains all the bundles to which *B* is preferred or to which *B* is indifferent. The continuity assumption in the *n*-good case is that the no-worse-than and the no-better-than sets are closed sets — that is, sets that contain their boundaries.

As in the two-good case, it is convenient to make the assumption of nonsatiation. If bundle B_1 contains more of at least one good than bundle B_2, and if it contains no less of any good, then B_1 is preferred to B_2.

If these five assumptions are satisfied, then a preference ordering can be represented by a utility function, which we can write as $U(x_1, x_2, \ldots , x_n)$. The core of the theory of self-interest in the n-good case is therefore essentially the same as in the two-good case. The only new feature is the more technical continuity assumption.

Finally, we should briefly indicate how the concept of MRS is defined in the n-good case and what the smoothness and convexity assumptions mean in this case. Suppose that from the list of n goods, we pick two goods — say, good i and good j — and then hold constant, or fix, all other quantities in the utility function. For example, we might fix all these quantities at zero or fix some at zero and others at one or, indeed, at any values. What matters is that all quantities other than x_i and x_j are fixed. As a result, we have a function with just the two variables x_i and x_j — that is, a utility function very much like those we explored earlier in this chapter. The only difference is that this utility function with just two variables has been created from a utility function with n variables by fixing the values of all but two of the n variables. Like the two-variable utility functions explored earlier, the indifference curves associated with this utility function also can be plotted in a two-dimensional diagram with x_i on one axis and x_j on the other. We can then use this type of diagram to define MRS(x_i, x_j) and to understand the smoothness and convexity assumptions.

In this type of diagram, the absolute value of the slope of an indifference curve at some point is the MRS of good j for good i at that point. The smoothness assumption means that these indifference curves are smooth, and the convexity assumption means that they are convex. In essence, nothing more is needed to extend the theory of self-interest to the n-good case.

The following problem will reinforce your understanding of a very simple utility function in the three-good case — a utility function in which marginal rates of substitution are constant.

PROBLEM 3.11

The following function is Brett's utility function for good 1, \$100 bills; good 2, \$20 bills; and good 3, \$10 bills. (It may also express your preference ordering over these goods.)

$$U(x_1, x_2, x_3) = 100x_1 + 20x_2 + 10x_3$$

Fix x_1 at 10, and plot an indifference curve of the resulting function with x_2 on the horizontal axis and x_3 on the vertical axis. What is MRS of good 3 for good 2? Now fix x_2 at 10, and plot an indifference curve with x_1 on the horizontal axis and x_3 on the vertical axis. What is MRS of good 3 for good 1?

Summary

The hypothesis that self-interest motivates individual choice is the psychological assumption that underlies consumer-preference theory. We defined self-interest in consumption by developing a theory built on three assumptions: (1) individuals can compare any two consumption bundles (completeness); (2) their preferences are consistent over any pair of consumption bundles (two-term consistency); and (3) their preferences are transitive (three-term consistency). These assumptions imply the existence of a complete preference ordering, or complete listing of consumption bundles from most preferred to least preferred.

This preference ordering can be represented by a utility function by adding two more assumptions. The first assumption (continuity of preferences) is essential; the second (nonsatiation) is useful. We then showed how to construct a utility function that faithfully represents an individual's preference ordering when these five assumptions hold.

The proposition that preferences that satisfy these assumptions can be captured by a utility function is important in choice theory because it justifies the standard analysis of consumer choice—the topic of the next chapter. As we discovered, utility functions are arbitrary, in the sense that if we can construct one utility function to represent some preference ordering, we can construct any number of utility functions to represent that preference ordering.

Finally, we introduced some additional concepts and two additional assumptions useful in analyzing individual choice making in Chapter 4. The marginal rate of substitution of good 2 for good 1 is the rate at which the consumption of good 2 must be increased as the consumption of good 1 is decreased in order to keep an individual on the same indifference curve. At any point, MRS is equal to the absolute value of the slope of the indifference curve through that point. To ensure that MRS is always well defined, we assumed that indifference curves are smooth. Finally, we assumed that indifference curves are convex.

Although this theory is widely used in economics, it is only one theory of self-interest. Others are clearly possible and necessary for the exploration of some important issues; for example, the completeness assumption rules out the possibility that individuals are ignorant about their own preferences. Thus, this theory cannot address any issues concerning, for example, how students might determine what their preferences actually are by sampling different courses in the first week of the term.

By developing this consumer-preference theory in some detail, we have seen both its limitations and its possible modifications and extensions. As we noted in Chapter 1, knowing a theory's limitations helps us to isolate its range of application. Furthermore, in the absence of some set of assumptions—and therefore of some set of limitations—the concept of self-interest is meaningless.

Exercises

1 Could the following two equations represent two different indifference curves for the same individual?

$$x_1 + x_2 = 100$$

$$x_1 x_2 = 100$$

2 Given a choice between two bundles containing good 1 and good 2, Dizzy says that (1) he prefers the bundle with the larger quantity of good 1 and (2) if the quantity of good 1 is the same in the two bundles, he is indifferent between them.
 a Draw one of Dizzy's indifference curves.
 b Construct three utility functions that represent Dizzy's preferences.
 c Can you find two goods such that your preferences are like Dizzy's?

3 Construct a representative indifference curve for each of the following situations. In so doing, you are creating a theory of preferences for each situation. A good theory is one that you can defend.
 a The two goods are $5 bills and $20 bills. (What is the marginal rate of substitution of $20 bills for $5 bills?)
 b The two goods are right shoes and left shoes, and the consumer has two feet; the consumer has only one foot.
 c The two goods are money and cocaine, and the more cocaine the individual consumes, the more money he or she is willing to give up to get even more cocaine.
 d The two goods are money and lobster tails, and eating more than a certain number of lobster tails makes the consumer sick. (Assuming that the consumer can dispose of unwanted lobster tails at no cost, how do the indifference curves change?)
 e The two goods are Coke and Pepsi, and the consumer perceives no difference between the two soft drinks.
 f The two goods are effort and income, and the individual doesn't enjoy working.

4 Consider the following utility functions:

$$(1)\ U(x_1, x_2) = x_1 x_2$$

$$(2)\ U(x_1, x_2) = 10 x_1 x_2$$

$$(3)\ U(x_1, x_2) = (x_1 x_2)^2$$

a Construct an indifference curve for each of these functions. For equation 1, use utility number 20; for equation 2, use utility number 200; for equation 3, use utility number 400.

b Do these utility functions represent different preference orderings?

5 Althea's preferences are captured in the following utility function:

$$U(x_1, x_2) = \min(2x_1, 7x_2)$$

a Draw an indifference curve for Althea.

b Which of the assumptions in Chapter 3 do not apply to Althea?

c Does more of good 1 always make Althea better off?

6 Consider the following utility function:

$$U(x_1, x_2) = x_2 + x_1^{1/2}$$

a Carefully draw the indifference curves associated with utility numbers 64, 49, and 36. For all three indifference curves, find the quantity of x_2 when x_1 is 0, 1, 4, 9, 16, 25, and 36.

b How does MRS change as you move from one indifference curve to another along the *vertical line* $x_1 = 4$? Or $x_1 = 16$? Or any vertical line?

7 Suppose that someone's preferences satisfy all the assumptions made in this chapter. Suppose, too, that for any value of x_1, MRS is the same regardless of the value of x_2. Draw two indifference curves. Do the indifference curves you constructed in Exercise 6 meet these conditions?

8 Jack's preferences over goods 1 and 2 can be described as follows: bundle (x_1', x_2') is preferred to bundle (x_1'', x_2'') if the maximum of x_1' and x_2' is larger than the maximum of x_1'' and x_2''; if the maximums are equal, he is indifferent between the bundles.

a Show that Jack is indifferent between (10, 8) and (2, 10). Draw the entire indifference curve through these two bundles.

b Find a utility function to represent these preferences.

c Which of the assumptions in Chapter 3 do not apply to Jack's preferences?

9 Jo says that (1) she has convex indifference curves for bundles that contain more than three units of good 1; (2) she prefers any bundle with more than three units of good 1 to any bundle with three or less units of good 1; and (3) for bundles with three or less units of good 1, the function $U(x_1, x_2) = x_1$ represents her preferences. Illustrate Jo's indifference map.

References

Arrow, K. J. (1959), "Rational Choice Functions and Orderings," *Economica*, 26:121–127.

Debreu, G. (1959), *Theory of the Value*, New York: Wiley.

Hicks, J. R., and R. G. D. Allen (1934), "A Reconsideration of the Theory of Value," *Economica*, 1:52–75, 196–219.

Slutsky, E. (1915), "Sulla teoria del bilancio del consumatore," *Giornale degli Economisti e Rivista di Statistica*, 51:1–26. English translation: "On the Theory of the Budget of the Consumer," in *Readings in Price Theory*, G. J. Stigler and K. E. Boulding (eds.), Homewood, Ill: Richard D. Irwin, pp. 27–56.

4

GETTING AND SPENDING: THE PROBLEM OF ECONOMIC CHOICE

During the nineteenth century, the English poet William Wordsworth lamented his countrymen's overriding concern with "getting and spending." However lamentable such getting and spending may still appear today, economic choice making threads its way through our ordinary lives. Some choices are minor: Should I spend the evening watching television? Should I buy a new pair of running shoes? Some are more significant: Should I spend the next 8 years of my life studying to be a physician? As we'll see in this chapter, all economic decisions, large or small, have certain elementary but important factors in common. In this chapter, we'll analyze consumer choice-making behavior by formulating the individual's constrained-choice problem; finding its solution, a system of demand functions; exploring the restrictions on these demand functions; and then developing a set of graphic tools to analyze a range of such choice problems.

4.1 Economic Choices

In the theory of choice, the word *constrained* is critical: constraints are basic to all economic choices. These include limits on income, time, and human resources. Moreover, when we make choices about getting and spending our limited resources, we have only imperfect information to guide us.

Choice and Scarcity: Getting and Forgoing

Implicit in the word *choice*, then, is the notion that we must make economic choices among competing alternatives. *Income* is one limitation. If I choose to buy a pair of running shoes, I have implicitly decided to give up other consumption possibilities — maybe a tennis racket or dinner at a favorite Italian restaurant. I can't afford all three because my income — my command over goods — won't stretch that far.

Time is another constraint. By deciding to spend the evening watching television, I am giving up other activities that compete for my time — say, studying economics or reading a murder mystery. Indeed, the most fundamental economic problem we all face is what to do with the one life span we have. By deciding to become a physician, I give up the chance to become a carpenter, a writer, an accountant, or a restauranteur.

Our endowment of *human resources* also limits our choices. For example, someone who tips the scales at 95 pounds can't choose to become a heavyweight boxer. We can augment the human resources we do have — for example, by choosing further schooling — but we make this choice at the cost of other opportunities such as getting work experience or traveling.

Because our endowments of income, time, and human resources necessarily restrict the possibilities open to us, we must make choices. We are therefore unavoidably engaged in getting and spending: getting skills, getting income, spending income, and spending time.

Imperfect Information and Intertemporality

To make these kinds of choices, we should know just what our alternatives are. Yet we usually have to make such choices without having the relevant information at hand. In other words, most choice problems are choice problems under *imperfect information*. Usually, we don't know the complete list of alternatives available to us — for example, all the movies that are currently showing or all the jobs that are now open. Nor do we have complete information on the prices of these alternatives.

Even more conspicuously, we cannot be perfectly informed about future alternatives and their prices. For example, the jobs of bank teller, secretary, and automobile assembly line worker, as we know them today, will almost certainly not exist in 20 years.

However, we can't know precisely how and when these occupations will change. Similarly, determining the wage that a computer scientist will command 10 or even 5 years from now is problematical. Yet this information, or "guesstimates" about it, is essential to those who are now choosing careers as computer scientists (or bank tellers or secretaries). Such choices are inherently *intertemporal* (we spend time today to acquire skills that we hope to market in the future), and we make them using imperfect information (we can't know the future). In fact, all economic decisions are intertemporal. By spending income today, I am giving up the chance to spend it later. By acquiring the skills of a computer scientist today, I am passing up the opportunity to study electrical engineering and therefore the chance to be an engineer in the future.

These simple observations illustrate what a complex affair economic choice making is. In a sense, making a choice today affects all the economic choices we must make in a lifetime — and we make each choice in an environment about which we have imperfect information. To understand those choices, we once again need to simplify the bewildering complexity of individual choice problems, in much the same way that we simplified the complexity inherent in the firm's choice of location in Chapter 1.

4.2 The Static Choice Problem

In this chapter, we'll examine a relatively simple choice problem: an individual consumer's choice of a consumption bundle in some period (this week, for instance) when the consumer knows his or her budget and the prices of all goods. Unlike the real problems consumers actually face, this choice problem is *atemporal* rather than intertemporal and involves *perfect information* rather than imperfect information. Thus, we're supposing that this person has already decided to devote a particular sum of money to the consumption of two goods in a given period; that is, he or she has somehow resolved the potentially complex interactions between today's consumption decisions and tomorrow's. We are therefore abstracting from the intertemporal aspect of individual choice. In addition, when we suppose that this person knows all relevant prices, we are abstracting from the economic problem of how individuals generate such information. We'll introduce intertemporal decision making and imperfect information into our model in subsequent chapters, but in this chapter we'll be operating in a static environment with perfect information.

With a few exceptions that will be quite obvious, we'll also assume that this person's preferences satisfy the seven assumptions of Chapter 3. Recall that these seven assumptions imply that individuals can always rank consumption bundles and that their rankings are consistent; they allow us to represent preferences by utility functions; they let us use the marginal rate of substitution (MRS).

Finally, we need to highlight one last, apparently quite restrictive, assumption. Until the last section of the chapter, we'll confine our attention to the case in which there are just *two goods*. In that final section, you'll see why the two-good case is not as restrictive as it appears to be at first.

Attainable Consumption Bundles

We'll begin this examination by identifying the consumer's **attainable consumption bundles** — that is, the bundles that our consumer can actually afford to buy. We distinguish between attainable consumption bundles and conceivable ones by noting that we can all imagine owning a Ferrari or buying a ride on a Russian space shuttle for $12 million, but — John Denver excepted — few of us can actually afford to do so. Our choices are circumscribed by our budgets and by the prices of the goods we want to buy. An attainable consumption bundle, then, is one that doesn't break the budget.

Some notation will allow us to define attainable bundles more precisely. As in Chapter 3, we will call the two goods good 1 and good 2, and we will denote their respective prices as p_1 and p_2. In addition, we will denote the consumer's budget or income by M. The total cost of bundle (x_1, x_2) is just the sum of prices multiplied by quantities, $p_1x_1 + p_2x_2$, and attainable bundles are just bundles whose total cost does not exceed M. Thus, **any consumption bundles that satisfies the following inequality is attainable:**

$$p_1x_1 + p_2x_2 \le M$$

This inequality is referred to as the **budget constraint.** In case it is unfamiliar, the symbol $\le$ means "less than or equal to."

In Figure 4.1, the set of attainable bundles is indicated by the green area. The attainable bundles on the line

$$p_1x_1 + p_2x_2 = M$$

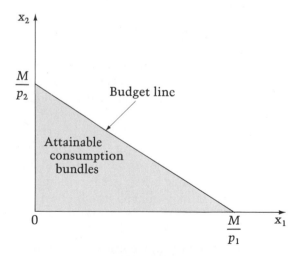

FIGURE 4.1 Attainable consumption bundles.
Any bundle in the green area on or below the budget line is an attainable bundle because the money required to buy it is no larger than the budget M. Any bundle above and to the right of the budget line is unattainable.

use up all of the individual's budget, whereas attainable bundles below the line do not. The line itself is commonly referred to as the **budget line**. Because it is an important one, give the following problem careful attention.

PROBLEM 4.1

Why does the budget line intersect the x_1 axis at M/p_1 and the x_2 axis at M/p_2? What is the slope of the budget line? On the budget line, how many units of good 2 must the consumer give up to get an additional unit of good 1? What happens to the budget line as p_1 approaches zero? What happens as p_2 approaches zero?

For many purposes, it is useful to think of the prices of goods in terms of real alternatives or opportunities forgone, rather than in monetary terms. In Problem 4.1, you discovered that on the budget line, the individual must give up p_1/p_2 units of good 2 to get an additional unit of good 1. Thus, the real cost of good 1 — or the **opportunity cost** of good 1 — is p_1/p_2 units of good 2. Conversely, the opportunity cost of good 2 is p_2/p_1 units of good 1.

Stating the Choice Problem

Consumer theory is built on the assumption that individual consumers make the most of their opportunities in light of their preferences. Because higher indifference curves contain bundles that are preferred to those contained by lower indifference curves, an individual consumer's problem is to find the highest indifference curve permitted by the budget constraint — that is, the highest attainable indifference curve. However, given the assumptions about individual preferences from Chapter 3, we know that preferences can be represented by a utility function, which we'll write as $U(x_1, x_2)$. This allows us to reformulate the consumer's problem. Rather than seeing this individual as trying to find the highest attainable indif-

ference curve, we can think of him or her as maximizing utility, given the budget constraint.

More precisely, we can think of the consumer as choosing the quantities of the two goods that maximize utility, subject to the budget constraint. We'll call the consumption bundle that the consumer chooses the **utility-maximizing bundle**, denoted by (x_1^*, x_2^*).

We can infer one important characteristic of the utility-maximizing consumption bundle: it must lie on the budget line. Why? Consider, for example, bundle A in Figure 4.2, which lies inside the budget line. This cannot be the utility-maximizing bundle (x_1^*, x_2^*) because the nonsatiation assumption implies that any bundle on segment CD of the budget line — every one of which contains more of both goods — is preferred to the bundle at A. Therefore, the assumption implies that a consumer will always pick a consumption bundle on the budget

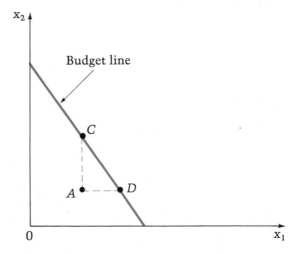

FIGURE 4.2 Nonsatiation and the utility-maximizing consumption bundle.

Nonsatiation implies that the utility-maximizing consumption bundle will be on the budget line. For example, bundle A could not be the utility-maximizing bundle because any bundle on segment CD of the budget line is preferred to it.

line. In other words, he or she will spend the whole budget on consumption.

Using this result, we can write the consumer's problem as follows:

maximize $U(x_1, x_2)$ by choice of x_1 and x_2

subject to the constraint $p_1x_1 + p_2x_2 = M$

This expression is really just a compact way of writing out the consumer's choice problem. It tells what the consumer's objective is — maximizing utility. It tells what the consumer is choosing — a consumption bundle. And it tells what constraint the consumer faces — the budget line.

4.3 Demand Functions: The Solution to the Choice Problem

Just what does the solution to a consumer's choice problem look like? It is very much like the solution to that recurring problem, What should I wear today? In New York, for example, late fall weather is notoriously unpredictable. One day may be warm and sunny, the next cold and dry, the next very rainy, and the next snowy. Before choosing clothing to venture out, the sensible New Yorker looks out the window to see what the weather is like.

We could describe the solution to the New Yorker's choice problem by a series of rules of thumb. If it's warm and sunny, wear a light windbreaker. If it's raining, wear rain gear. If it's cold and dry, wear a down jacket. This example recalls a distinction made in Chapter 2: the items that we choose are always **endogenous variables** because we do the selecting, but the items we actually select are determined by **exogenous variables** over which we have no control. That is, according to the New Yorker's rules for choosing what to wear, the endogenous variable (clothing) is a function of the exogenous variable (the weather).

The solution to the consumer choice problem in this chapter has the same form because here, too, the endogenous variables are determined by the exogenous variables. Of course, in the consumer's utility-maximizing problem, the endogenous variables are the quantities of the two goods to be chosen: x_1 and x_2. The exogenous variables are the two prices p_1 and p_2 and the budget M. These are the givens, the constraints within which an individual consumer must operate. In the solution to this choice problem, then, the utility-maximizing values of x_1 and x_2 are determined by p_1, p_2, and M.

Before taking up this general choice problem, it may be helpful to actually solve a specific choice problem — that is, to find (x_1^*, x_2^*) for a specific utility function. We'll use the following utility function, which captures Amy's preferences from our fish model of Chapter 2:

$$U(x_1, x_2) = x_1 + x_2$$

Notice that even though the indifference curves associated with Amy's utility function are only weakly convex to the origin and therefore fail to satisfy all the assumptions made in Chapter 3, Amy's choice problem nevertheless provides an instructive illustration.

The two goods are perfect substitutes because an additional unit of either good is equally attractive. In effect, Amy sees no real difference between the two goods. Therefore, she maximizes her utility by spending her whole budget on the cheaper good; that is,

$$x_1^* = \frac{M}{p_1} \quad \text{and} \quad x_2^* = 0 \quad \text{if } p_1 < p_2$$

$$x_1^* = 0 \quad \text{and} \quad x_2^* = \frac{M}{p_2} \quad \text{If } p_1 > p_2$$

If the prices are identical, *any* bundle on the budget line is utility-maximizing since the budget line is then coincident with an indifference curve.

Notice how similar the solution of this problem is to the solution to the New Yorker's what-to-wear problem. Both solutions have the same essential form: the variables that are to be chosen (the endogenous variables) are determined by the variables that are given (the exogenous variables). If it's raining, wear rain gear (and leave the down parka in the closet). If $p_1 < p_2$, spend M/p_1 on good 1 and nothing on good 2.

In fact, the solution to any consumer choice problem has this form. Hence, we'll write the solution to the general two-good choice problem in the following symbolic way:

$$x_1^* = D_1(p_1, p_2, M)$$
$$x_2^* = D_2(p_1, p_2, M)$$

The functions D_1 and D_2 are **demand functions**.[1] The first of them says that the utility-maximizing quantity of good 1 (denoted by x_1^*) is some function D_1 of the exogenous variables p_1, p_2, and M. This equation is simply a symbolic way of saying that the choice of x_1^* is determined by (or depends on) the prices of all items in the consumption bundle and the budget to be devoted to the whole bundle. (Notice that we actually found the demand functions associated with Amy's utility function $U(x_1, x_2) = x_1 + x_2$.)

A single demand function, then, describes the functional relationship between the quantity of a good demanded and all the factors that influence demand: the price of that good, the prices of other goods, and the size of the individual consumer's budget. A system of demand functions, D_1 and D_2, tells us how much of both goods will be chosen, given the exogenous variables. In the following problem, you are asked to solve another relatively simple utility-maximization problem, thereby generating the demand functions for another specific utility function.

PROBLEM 4.2

Consider the following utility function:

$$U(x_1, x_2) = \min(x_1, x_2)$$

The budget constraint is, of course, $p_1x_1 + p_2x_2 = M$. Show that the demand functions are

$$x_1^* = \frac{M}{p_1 + p_2}$$
$$x_2^* = \frac{M}{p_1 + p_2}$$

Hint: First draw an indifference curve and observe that it is not smooth. It has a right-angled kink where it intersects the line $x_2 = x_1$. Then show that the utility-maximizing bundle lies on the line $x_2 = x_1$. Finally, use this information in combination with the budget line to derive the demand functions.

[1] One method for solving the consumer's choice problem when the utility function is differentiable is the method of Lagrange multipliers, developed in most basic calculus texts. The mechanics of the method are simple. First, combine the utility function and the budget line by introducing a Lagrange multiplier λ to form what is called the Lagrangian function, as follows:

$$L(x_1, x_2, \lambda) = U(x_1, x_2) - \lambda(M - p_1x_1 - p_2x_2)$$

Now, differentiate with respect to x_1, x_2, and λ and set these derivatives equal to zero to obtain

$$U_1(x_1^*, x_2^*) - \lambda^*p_1 = 0$$
$$U_2(x_1^*, x_2^*) - \lambda^*p_2 = 0$$
$$M - p_1x_1^* - p_2x_2^* = 0$$

(The symbol U_i denotes the partial derivative of U with respect to x_i.) We then have a system of three simultaneous equations in three unknown endogenous variables, x_1^*, x_2^*, and λ^*. Solving for these unknown endogenous variables in terms of the three exogenous variables, p_1, p_2, and M, yields two demand functions and a function that determines a value for λ^*. For example, if

$$U(x_1, x_2) = x_1x_2$$

then

$$x_1^* = \frac{M}{2p_1}$$
$$x_2^* = \frac{M}{2p_2}$$
$$\lambda^* = \frac{M}{2p_1p_2}$$

4.4 Two General Properties of Demand Functions

It is clear that the precise form of an individual consumer's demand functions will be determined by his or her preferences. For example, regardless of the values of the exogenous variables in the utility-maximizing problem, a nonsmoker won't buy cigarettes and a nondrinker won't buy alcohol. Yet we can easily derive two general propositions about the properties of demand functions.

Homogeneity of Degree Zero

One important property of demand functions—homogeneity of degree zero—is easy to establish. Suppose that all the exogenous variables in a demand function change proportionately. For instance, suppose that both prices and the budget increase by a factor of 2. How will the individual consumer respond to this change in the exogenous variables? How will his or her consumption decisions change? Let's consider the two budget lines

$$p_1 x_1 + p_2 x_2 = M$$

$$2p_1 x_1 + 2p_2 x_2 = 2M$$

Of course, we can derive the second budget line from the first by multiplying the first by 2, or the first from the second by dividing the second by 2. But this means that these two budget lines are, in fact, identical. (You may want to choose specific values for the exogenous variables and actually plot these two budget lines.)

Because the budget lines are identical, so, too, are the solutions to the utility-maximizing problems. We know, then, that the individual's consumption decisions *will not change* in response to a proportional increase in all prices and income. We can write down this result more precisely:

Select arbitrary values for the exogenous variables p_1, p_2, and M, and then multiply these values by some positive constant $a > 0$ to determine a new set of values ap_1, ap_2, and aM. The quantities demanded of both goods at these two sets of prices and incomes are identical; that is,

$$D_1(p_1, p_2, M) = D_1(ap_1, ap_2, aM)$$
$$D_2(p_1, p_2, M) = D_2(ap_1, ap_2, aM)$$

This property of demand functions simply means that if prices and income all change by the same factor of proportionality, the consumer's choices are unchanged. To borrow terminology from mathematics, we have learned that demand functions are **homogeneous of degree zero** in prices and income. The importance of this simple result is that it tells us the types of functions that could and could not be demand functions. For example, the demand function derived in the previous problem,

$$x_1^* = \frac{M}{p_1 + p_2}$$

is homogeneous of degree zero in the variables p_1, p_2, and M since

$$\frac{M}{p_1 + p_2} = \frac{aM}{ap_1 + ap_2}$$

PROBLEM 4.3

Which of the following could not be demand functions? In other words, which of these functions is not homogeneous of degree zero in p_1, p_2, and M?

1 $x_1^* = \dfrac{M}{p_1}$

2 $x_1^* = \dfrac{Mp_2}{p_1}$

3 $x_1^* = \dfrac{M}{(p_1 p_2)^{1/2}}$

4 $x_1^* = 1 + p_2 - 5p_1 + \dfrac{M}{20}$

Engel's Aggregation Law

The observation that individual consumers will use up their budgets allows us to derive another important restriction. In this case, the restriction applies not to demand functions individually but to the entire system of demand functions. We know that the utility-maximizing bundle is on the budget line, or that

$$p_1 x_1^* + p_2 x_2^* = M$$

Rewriting this expression gives us the following proposition:

A system of demand functions must satisfy the property that the sum of prices multiplied by quantities demanded equals income:

$$p_1 D_1(p_1, p_2, M) + p_2 D_2(p_1, p_2, M) = M$$

This proposition, known as **Engel's aggregation law**, is just a formal way of saying that people spend what they spend. Like homogeneity of degree zero, it imposes a strong restriction on acceptable systems of demand functions. To see the sorts of demand systems that Engel's aggregation law does and does not permit, consider the following problem.

PROBLEM 4.4

Which of the following cannot be systems of demand functions? That is, which of these systems do not satisfy Engel's aggregation law? For each system of equations, simply ask: Does $p_1 x_1^* + p_2 x_2^*$ equal M?

1   $x_1^* = \dfrac{M}{3p_1}, \; x_2^* = \dfrac{2M}{3p_2}$

2   $x_1^* = \dfrac{M}{5p_1}, \; x_2^* = \dfrac{3M}{4p_2}$

3   $x_1^* = \dfrac{M}{2} + p_2 - p_1, \; x_2^* = \dfrac{M}{2} + p_1 - p_2$

These two restrictions—homogeneity of degree zero and Engel's aggregation—are

quite useful to economists who use data to estimate demand functions.

4.5 Graphic Analysis of Utility Maximization

Neither of the two utility-maximizing problems we've solved so far satisfies all seven of the assumptions that we laid out in Chapter 2. The indifference curves associated with Amy's utility function are not convex to the origin, and the indifference curves in Problem 4.2 are not smooth. In this section, we will use powerful graphic techniques to describe, or characterize, the solution to the utility-maximizing problem when all seven assumptions do hold.

We'll distinguish two types of solution to the problem—interior and corner solutions—and two kinds of goods—essential and inessential goods. An **interior solution** to the utility-maximizing problem is one in which the quantities of both goods are positive. A **corner solution** is one in which the quantity of one good is positive and the quantity of the other good is zero. An **essential good** is one that is indispensable, such as water or air. Regardless of how high the price of an essential good may be, the consumer will still decide to buy some of it. In contrast, an **inessential good** is one like a joy ride in a Russian space shuttle or cut flowers on the kitchen table. If the price of an inessential good is high enough, the consumer will decide not to buy any of it.

Interior Solutions

As you already know, the nonsatiation assumption implies that the solution to the utility-maximizing problem will lie on the budget line. This is one of the two statements that describe, or characterize, an interior solution:

$$p_1 x_1^* + p_2 x_2^* = M$$

For example, the utility-maximizing bundle in Figure 4.3 lies on the budget line at point A.

The second statement tells us just which bundle on the budget line maximizes utility. Notice that at the utility-maximizing bundle in Figure 4.3, the indifference curve I_2 is *tangent* to the budget line. As long as indifference curves are smooth and the solution is an interior rather than a corner solution, this tangency result always holds: an indifference curve is tangent to the budget line at the utility-maximizing bundle. Why? The indifference curve through any bundle on the budget line will (1) intersect the budget line from above, (2) intersect it from below, or (3) be tangent to it. The first case is shown at point D in Figure 4.3. Because bundles along the budget line to the right of D (and to the left of F) are preferred to it, D cannot be the utility-maximizing

bundle. The second case is shown at point F in Figure 4.3. Because bundles along the budget line to the left of F (and to the right of D) are preferred to it, F cannot be the utility-maximizing bundle. This means that the third case, where the indifference curve is tangent to the budget line at point A, must be the utility-maximizing bundle.

This tangency result is the second statement that characterizes an interior solution. As you learned in Problem 4.1, the slope of the budget line is -1 multiplied by p_1/p_2, and as we learned in Chapter 3, the slope of an indifference curve at any point (x_1, x_2) is $MRS(x_1, x_2)$ multiplied by -1. Because the budget line and the indifference curve are tangent at point A, their slopes must be identical at this point. In other words,

$$MRS(x_1^*, x_2^*) = \frac{p_1}{p_2}$$

This is the second statement that characterizes an interior solution.[2]

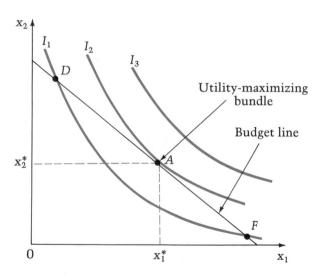

FIGURE 4.3 The utility-maximizing consumption bundle.

The utility-maximizing consumption bundle (x_1^*, x_2^*) at point A is the point on the budget line where an indifference curve is tangent to the budget line. That is, at the utility-maximizing bundle, the budget line and the indifference curve have the same slope.

---

[2] Let's derive this characterization of the utility-maximizing solution by using the method of Lagrange multipliers introduced in footnote 1. The Lagrangian function is

$$L(x_1, x_2, \lambda) = U(x_1, x_2) - \lambda(M - p_1x_1 - p_2x_2)$$

Differentiating with respect to x_1, x_2, and λ and setting the results equal to zero, we obtain

$$U_1(x_1^*, x_2^*) - \lambda^*p_1 = 0$$
$$U_2(x_1^*, x_2^*) - \lambda^*p_2 = 0$$
$$M - p_1x_1^* - p_2x_2^* = 0$$

The last condition is familiar — the utility-maximizing bundle is on the budget line. It is the first half of our characterization of an interior solution. Eliminating λ^* by combining the first two conditions, we get

$$\frac{p_1}{p_2} = \frac{U_1(x_1^*, x_2^*)}{U_2(x_1^*, x_2^*)}$$

But, as we saw in footnote 4 in Chapter 3, the right side of this expression is just $MRS(x_1^*, x_2^*)$. Hence, we have

$$\frac{p_1}{p_2} = MRS(x_1^*, x_2^*)$$

which is the second half of our characterization of an interior solution.

But what does this tangency condition really mean? Suppose that the consumer is thinking about choosing some bundle on the budget line where MRS is less than p_1/p_2 — say, at point F in Figure 4.3. As we argued in Chapter 3, MRS is the rate at which good 2 must be substituted for good 1 to keep the consumer on indifference curve I_1. On the other hand, p_1/p_2 is the rate at which the consumer *can* substitute good 2 for good 1. At point F, MRS is less than p_1/p_2 and the consumer will be better off as he or she substitutes good 2 for good 1. Accordingly, the consumer will move to the left from F along the budget line, substituting good 2 for good 1. A corresponding argument tells us that if the consumer is at some point on the budget line where MRS exceeds p_1/p_2, he or she will move to the right along the budget line, substituting good 1 for good 2.

We can summarize these results in the following equations:

When indifference curves are smooth, an interior solution is characterized by two conditions:

$$p_1 x_1^* + p_2 x_2^* = M$$

and

$$\text{MRS}(x_1^*, x_2^*) = \frac{p_1}{p_2}$$

We can summarize these two conditions equally well in plain English:

When indifference curves are smooth and when the quantities demanded of both goods are positive, the utility-maximizing bundle is on the budget line at the point where the budget line is tangent to an indifference curve.

Corner Solutions

The characterization just discussed presumes that the consumer decides to buy some of both goods. It is called an interior solution because graphically it always lies somewhere in the space between the two axes. But this characterization does not apply if the consumer decides not to buy even the smallest amount of a particular good. This case is sometimes called a corner solution, because graphically it lies not in the interior between the two axes but at a corner where the budget line intersects one of the two axes.

In fact, deciding not to buy a particular good is not an isolated or perverse choice. Imagine taking a walk through several large stores that offer various kinds of merchandise — hardware, groceries, clothing, electronic equipment, books, records, cosmetics — and tabulating the number of goods you will never buy, out of all the items for sale. Chances are that your list will be extraordinarily long. Of the vast array of goods available in developed economies, most of us choose not to buy many — perhaps most — of them. In this section, we'll explore choice problems in which such corner solutions are possible.

With two goods, two kinds of corner solutions are possible. We'll focus on the case in which the consumer decides not to buy any of good 1 and instead to spend the entire budget on good 2. In this corner solution, the utility-maximizing bundle is at point $(x_1 = 0, x_2 = M/p_2)$ — the point at which the budget line intersects the x_2 axis. You can explore in Problem 4.6 the other sort of corner solution in which the consumer spends the entire budget on good 1.

What types of indifference curves give rise to corner solutions, and what types do not? If indifference curves do not intersect the x_2 axis, then we will never see a corner solution. In other words, no matter how expensive good 1 becomes, the consumer will persist in buying a positive quantity of it. This case is illustrated in Figure 4.4. Even when the price is relatively high, as in Figure 4.4b — the steep slope of the budget line is a

(a)

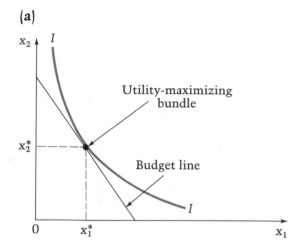

(b)

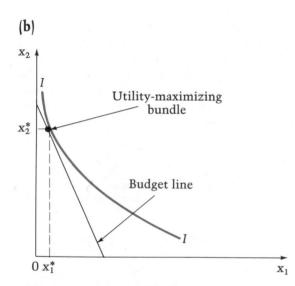

FIGURE 4.4   Essential goods.

If indifference curves do not intersect the x_2 axis, then x_1^* is always positive, and good 1 is therefore an essential good. In both (a), where p_1 is moderate, and (b), where p_1 is high, x_1^* is positive.

then a corner solution is possible. This case is illustrated in Figure 4.5. When the price of good 1 is moderate, as in Figure 4.5a, the consumer will decide to buy some of both goods. As you now know, the utility-maximizing bundle is on the budget line at the point where the budget line is tangent to an indifference curve.

However, when good 1 becomes relatively expensive—once again, the steep budget line in Figure 4.5b indicates a relatively high price—the consumer decides not to buy any of good 1. That is, this con-

(a)

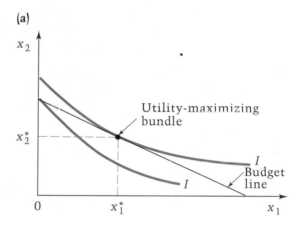

(b)

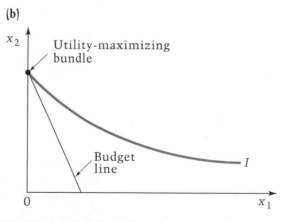

FIGURE 4.5   Inessential goods.

If indifference curves intersect the x_2 axis, then there is always a p_1 large enough that $x_1^* = 0$, and good 1 is therefore an inessential good. In (b), for example, p_1 is so large that $x_1^* = 0$. In (a), p_1 is low enough that x_1^* is positive.

telltale sign that good 1 is expensive relative to good 2—the consumer still buys some of good 1. By definition, then, it must be an essential good.

On the other hand, if the indifference curves do intersect the x_2 axis and if they are not vertical where that intersection occurs, sumer's utility-maximizing solution is this: $x_1^* = 0$ and $x_2^* = M/p_2$. The consumer in this circumstance, perhaps deciding that "Good 1 is too rich for my blood," chooses to spend the whole budget on good 2. As we noted, graphically the solution is at the corner where the indifference curve intersects the x_2 axis, indicating the consumer's decision to forego good 1 completely in favor of good 2. In the case illustrated in Figure 4.5, good 1 is an inessential good. If its price is too high, the consumer decides not to buy any.

PROBLEM 4.5

Suppose that indifference curves intersect the x_2 axis and that they are vertical at the point of intersection. Is good 1 essential or inessential?

When good 1 is an inessential good, what determines whether the result is an interior or a corner solution? The determining factor is the relationship between the opportunity cost of good 1, p_1/p_2, and MRS at the point where the budget line intersects the x_2 axis. If $MRS(x_1, x_2)$ at the point $x_1 = 0$ and $x_2 = M/p_2$ is greater than p_1/p_2, as in Figure 4.5a, the result is an interior solution. If it is less than p_1/p_2, as in Figure 4.5b, the result is a corner solution.

Notice that in Figure 4.5, we have been assuming not only that good 1 is inessential but also that good 2 is essential, since the indifference curves in Figure 4.5 do not intersect the x_1 axis. We therefore have found a characterization for the case in which good 2 is essential and good 1 is inessential.

If good 2 is an essential good and good 1 an inessential good, then the solution to the consumer's utility-maximizing problem is characterized in the following way:

1 If $MRS(x_1, x_2)$ at the point $x_1 = 0$ and $x_2 = M/p_2$ is greater than p_1/p_2, the result is an interior solution:

$$p_1 x_1^* + p_2 x_2^* = M$$

and

$$MRS(x_1^*, x_2^*) = \frac{p_1}{p_2}$$

2 If $MRS(x_1, x_2)$ at the point $x_1 = 0$ and $x_2 = M/p_2$ is less than p_1/p_2, the result is a corner solution:[3]

$$x_1^* = 0 \text{ and } x_2^* = \frac{M}{p_2}$$

In the following problem, you can look at the case in which the other type of corner solution is possible.

PROBLEM 4.6

Suppose that indifference curves intersect the x_1 axis but not the x_2 axis and that the slope of any indifference curve at the point of intersection is strictly negative. Show that good 2 is inessential and good 1 is essential, and describe the conditions that characterize the solution to the utility-maximizing problem.

---

[3] We can use calculus techniques to see when we have a corner solution. We know from footnote 4 in Chapter 3 that

$$MRS(x_1, x_2) = \frac{U_1(x_1, x_2)}{U_2(x_1, x_2)}$$

Hence, we have a corner solution if

$$\frac{U_1(0, M/p_2)}{U_2(0, M/p_2)} < \frac{p_1}{p_2}$$

For example, suppose that $U(x_1, x_2) = x_2 + x_1 x_2$. Then

$$\frac{U_1(0, M/p_2)}{U_2(0, M/p_2)} = \frac{M}{p_2}$$

Hence

$$x_1^* = 0 \text{ and } x_2^* = M/p_2 \qquad \text{if } M < p_1$$

As you may want to verify,

$$x_1^* = \frac{(M - p_1)}{2p_1}$$

and

$$x_2^* = \frac{(M + p_1)}{2p_2} \qquad \text{if } M \geq p_1$$

4.6 Comparative Statics Analysis of Demand

When we differentiated between essential and inessential goods, we were creating a classification — or *taxonomy* — based on the kind of consumption response a consumer makes to a change in the price of a good. The response in the case of an inessential good is to give it up if the price goes too high; in the case of an essential good, to continue to buy some amount regardless of price. If consumer demand theory is to be useful, it must provide a framework for asking and answering questions like these about how a consumer responds to such changes: How does an increase in a consumer's income affect his or her consumption decisions? How does an increase in the price level affect consumption decisions? What happens if the price of one good goes up and all other prices remain the same? Will consumer demand for that good necessarily decline? Will demand for all other goods necessarily increase?

We can generate a great number of such questions. However, to find the answers, we first need to reduce them to three fundamental questions:

1 How will a consumer's demand for some good — say, good 1 — change in response to an increase (or decrease) in income?

2 How will a consumer's demand for good 1 change in response to an increase (or decrease) in the price of that good?

3 How will a consumer's demand for good 1 change in response to an increase (or decrease) in the price of some other good?

Notice that all three questions are about a consumer's response to a change in the value of an exogenous variable in a demand function. By altering the values of exogenous variables, we can compare solutions to the utility-maximization problem before and after the change. As we saw in Chapter 2, this procedure, *comparative statics analysis*, is termed static because it is concerned with stationary equilibrium points rather than with the dynamic adjustments between these points. It is termed comparative because it allows us to compare consumer choices in different circumstances.[4]

PROBLEM 4.7

Consider the following demand function — one that you first encountered in Problem 4.2: $x_1^* = M/(p_1 + p_2)$. Suppose that initially $M = \$120$, $p_1 = \$1$, and $p_2 = \$1$. How does x_1^* respond to a $1 increase in p_1? To a $1 increase in p_2? To a $2 increase in M?

Because in Problem 4.7 you had in hand a specific demand function — one derived from a specific utility function — you were able to provide *precise* answers to the comparative statics questions posed in the problem. For example, given p_1 and p_2 equal to $1, you discovered that whenever M increases by $2, consumption of good 1 increases by one unit. In the following sections, we'll be concerned with more general questions, which presume only that a consumer maximizes his or her utility. As a result, we will look not for precise answers to comparative statics questions, but instead for qualitative answers — indicating the direction but not the magnitude of the demand response. For instance, we will ask: Does utility maximization imply that a consumer will buy less of a particular good when its price rises?

---

[4] These qualitative comparative statics questions are simply questions about the signs of partial derivatives of demand functions. For example, is the partial derivative of the demand function for good 1 with respect to M always positive?

4.7 Consumption Response to a Change in Income

We'll begin by asking, What will happen to the demand for good 1 as income M changes? More precisely we'll ask, If the prices of both goods are held constant and if income rises, is the change in the quantity demanded, x_1^*, positive, negative, or zero? In other words, will a consumer buy more, less, or just the same amount of a good when prices remain the same and his or her income goes up?

Normal Goods and Inferior Goods

The answer depends on just what that good is. Casual observation suggests that as consumers become wealthier, they buy less of some goods and more of others. For example, many students eat lots of relatively inexpensive pasta for dinner before they graduate, but switch to relatively more expensive meat once they leave school and find well-paid, full-time employment. This observation provides us with a taxonomy: a good is a **normal good** if consumption of the good *increases* as income increases. It is an **inferior good** if consumption *decreases* as income increases.

In Figure 4.6a, good 1 is a normal good. We've constructed three budget lines corresponding to income levels $100, $150, and $200. Notice that the budget lines have the same slope (and are therefore parallel) since prices are held constant. Only income changes. Notice, too, that as this consumer's income increases from $100 to $150 to $200, his or her consumption of good 1 increases from 6 to 9 to 12. We know, then, that for this consumer, good 1 is a normal good. The line labeled *IC* in Figure 4.6a, which passes through the utility-maximizing bundles that are generated as this consumer's income increases (holding prices constant), is called an **income-consumption**

(a) A normal good

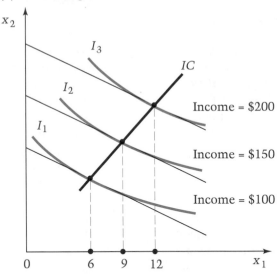

(b) An inferior good

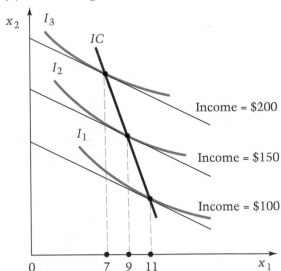

FIGURE 4.6 Normal and inferior goods.

In (a), as income increases, so does quantity demanded of good 1; good 1 is therefore a normal good. The income consumption path *IC* is positively sloped for a normal good. In (b), as income increases, quantity demanded of good 1 decreases; good 1 is therefore an inferior good. *IC* is negatively sloped for an inferior good.

path. In Figure 4.6*a*, its slope is positive because both good 1 and good 2 are normal goods. (Do you see why good 2 is also a normal good?)

In Figure 4.6*b*, good 1 is an inferior good. As this consumer's income increases from $100 to $150 to $200, his or her consumption of good 1 decreases from 11 to 9 to 7. Notice that the slope of the income-consumption path *IC* is negative in this case. (Is good 2 a normal or inferior good in Figure 4.6*b*?)

PROBLEM 4.8

Are the following statements true or false?

1 When *IC* is negatively sloped, good 1 is invariably inferior.

2 When *IC* is negatively sloped, one good is inferior and the other is normal.

3 Both goods cannot be inferior.

4 Both goods cannot be normal.

Engel Curves

In Figure 4.7, we have used the information from each of the cases in Figure 4.6 to construct a relationship between income and the utility-maximizing quantity of good 1. This relationship is called an **Engel curve**, after the nineteenth-century Prussian statistician Ernst Engel. In effect, we have plotted the demand function for good 1 when income is allowed to vary and prices are held constant. For a normal good, the Engel curve is positively sloped because, by definition, x_1^* increases as M increases. For an inferior good, the Engel curve is negatively sloped because, again by definition, x_1^* decreases as M increases.

PROBLEM 4.9

Suppose that MRS depends only on x_1. Then MRS is identical at all points on any vertical line in (x_1, x_2) space. (Recall that you considered this case in Exercises 6 and 7 at the end of Chapter 3.) Show that good 1 is neither inferior nor normal

(a)

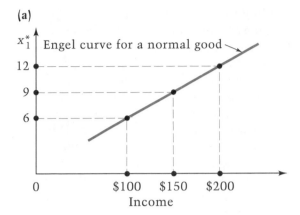

(b)

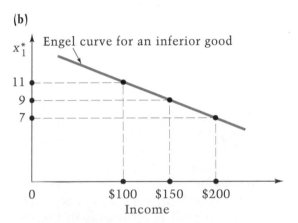

FIGURE 4.7 Engel curves.

An Engel curve is a graph of a demand function, holding all prices constant and allowing income to vary. Income is plotted on the horizontal axis and quantity demanded on the vertical axis. The Engel curve for a normal good, illustrated in (a), is positively sloped. The Engel curve for an inferior good, illustrated in (b), is negatively sloped.

—that is, show that the utility-maximizing quantity of good 1 is independent of income. Illustrate the Engel curve for such a good.

4.8 Consumption Response to a Change in Price

Now let's take up the second question: What will happen to the demand for a good —say, good 1—as its own price changes, holding the price of the other good p_2 and income M constant? What happens to a particular consumer's demand for Darjeeling tea, for instance, as its price rises or falls?

In Figure 4.8a, we've drawn three budget lines and marked the three resulting utility-maximizing bundles at points E, F, and G. For clarity, we have not included the indifference curves, which are tangent to the three budget lines at these points. In constructing this figure, we have held p_2 constant at $2 and M constant at $60. And we have used three different values for p_1: p_1 is $4 on the lowest budget line, $3 on the intermediate budget line, and $2 on the highest budget line.

The Price-Consumption Path

The line labeled PC is called a **price-consumption path**. It connects the utility-maximizing bundles that arise as p_1 is successively decreased from $4 to $3 to $2 in Figure 4.8a (holding the other exogenous variables, p_2 and M, constant). The price-consumption path is analogous to the income-consumption path, with this difference: in the income-consumption path, only income varied; here, only the price of good 1 varies.

The Demand Curve

We can use the price-consumption path to construct a relationship between the price of good 1 and the quantity demanded in much the same way that we used the income-consumption path to construct an Engel curve. This relationship — which we will call the consumer's **ordinary demand curve** for good 1 — is presented in Figure 4.8b. The three points E', F', and G' on the demand curve correspond to the utility-maximizing points E, F, and G in Figure 4.8a. The demand curve is a graph of the demand function when p_1 is varied and p_2

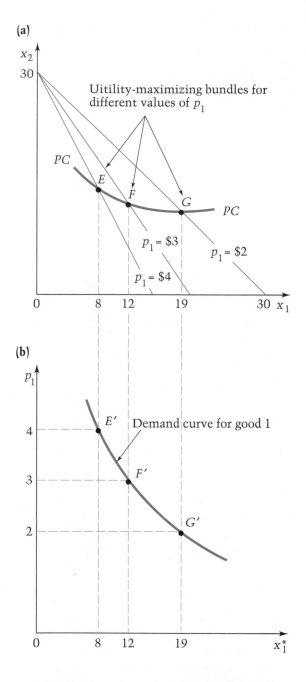

FIGURE 4.8 The price-consumption path and the demand function.

The price-consumption path PC in (a) passes through the utility-maximizing consumption bundles that are generated as the price of good 1 changes, holding income and all other prices constant. The demand curve in (b) is the graph of the demand for good 1 as its price changes.

and M are held constant. Just as common sense suggests, price and quantity demanded are negatively related in this case. As price increases from $2 to $3 to $4, the quantity demanded decreases from 19 to 12 to 8.[5]

Intuition strongly suggests that the quantity demanded of any good is *negatively* related to that good's price. In other words, it seems reasonable to suppose that as the price of a good continues to drop, the consumer decides to buy more and more of it. For example, most of us would expect that as compact discs become less expensive, people who own compact disc players will buy more discs. Graphically, the consumer's demand curve would then be downward sloping, as it is in Figure 4.8*b*. As Figure 4.9 reveals, however, it is at least theoretically possible for the quantity demanded to be *positively* related to price. In other words, as the price of some good rises, the consumer decides to buy more of it. As p_1 increases from $2 to $3 in Figure 4.9, the quantity demanded of good 1 increases from 12 to 14. When price and quantity demanded of a good are positively related, the good is called a **Giffen good**.

To develop some understanding of this surprising theoretical possibility, we'll decompose the quantity response to a change in price into (1) a pure price or **substitution effect** and (2) an **income effect**. We'll see that — just as our intuition suggests — the substitution effect is negatively related to the price change. Yet we'll also discover that the income effect may be either negatively

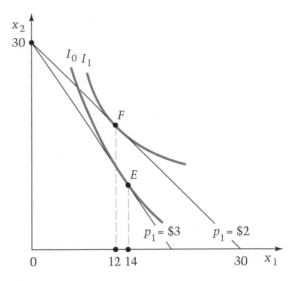

FIGURE 4.9 A Giffen good.

As p_1 increases from $2 to $3, quantity demanded of good 1 increases from 12 to 14. Because quantity demanded increases as price increases, good 1 is a Giffen good.

or positively related to the change in price. For normal goods, the income effect is negatively related to the price change. But for inferior goods, it is positively related to the price change. As a result, the demand curve for a normal good is always downward sloping, but the demand curve for an inferior good may be either downward or upward sloping.

4.9   Income and Substitution Effects

A change in p_1 (holding p_2 constant) alters the relative price, or opportunity cost, of good 1 in terms of good 2. If p_1 increases, good 1 is relatively more expensive, and if it decreases, good 1 is relatively less expensive. The substitution effect is associated with this *change in the opportunity cost* of good 1.

In addition, a change in p_1 (holding p_2 and M constant) affects the consumer's purchasing power, or real income. If p_1 goes up,

---

[5] It is customary in plotting this sort of relationship to put the exogenous variable on the horizontal axis and the endogenous variable on the vertical axis. Although we followed this custom when we plotted the Engel curve, tradition dictates that we violate it when we plot the demand curve. The demand curve has quantity demanded (the endogenous variable) on the horizontal axis and price (the exogenous variable) on the vertical axis.

real income goes down, and if p_1 goes down, real income goes up. The income effect is associated with this *change in real income.*

Imagine, for example, the reaction of a student sitting at a bar with $10 in her pocket to a drop in the price of beer from $2 a bottle to $1. Beer is suddenly a better buy because its price relative to wine has decreased. In addition, she also feels richer because she can now buy more beer and wine if she wants to. The substitution effect is associated with the change in the price of beer relative to wine, and the income effect is associated with the fact that the student now feels richer.

Two Effects Associated with a Price Increase

Let's look at the income and substitution effects graphically. In Figure 4.10, M is held constant at $60, and p_2 is held constant at $1. When the price of good 1 is $1, this particular consumer decides to buy the utility-maximizing bundle containing 30 units of good 1 at point A on the indifference curve labeled I_2. When the price of good 1 rises to $3, however, this consumer now switches to the bundle containing 12 units of good 1 at point C on the indifference curve labeled I_1. For the individual preferences illustrated in Figure 4.10, then, the quantity demanded is negatively related to price. In other words, this consumer's response to an increase in the price of good 1 is to buy less of it.

Now let's break this quantity response — the drop from 30 to 12 units of good 1 — into a substitution effect and an income effect. To isolate the substitution effect, we'll eliminate the income effect by giving the consumer just enough additional income to allow him or her to get back to the original indifference curve, I_2. We will call the resulting budget line the **compensated budget line**. The compensated budget line is the dashed line in Figure 4.10. (It is parallel to the budget line through C because in both instances p_1 is $3.) Given the compensated

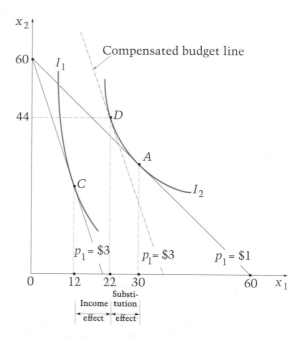

FIGURE 4.10   Income and substitution effects for a price increase.

As the price of good 1 increases from $1 to $3, quantity demanded decreases from 30 to 12. To isolate the substitution and income effects, increase income by just enough that the original indifference curve I_2 is attainable at price $p_1 = $3 — the resulting budget line is the compensated budget line. The substitution effect is the reduction in consumption from 30 to 22, and the income effect is the reduction in consumption from 22 to 12.

budget line, this consumer switches to the utility-maximizing bundle containing 22 units of good 1 at D. The substitution effect associated with the price increase in this case is a drop in consumption of good 1 from 30 to 22; hence, the substitution effect is negatively related to the price change.

To isolate the income effect, we'll hold p_1 constant at $3 and take back the added income. As a result, the budget line shifts downward from the dashed budget line through D to the solid budget line through C. Once the consumer's added income is removed, he or she switches to the bundle containing 12 units of good 1 at C, and consumption of good 1 drops from 22 to 12. Notice that the income effect in this case is also negatively related to the price change. This negative relationship reflects the fact that good 1 is a normal good in Figure 4.10. (When income decreases, the consumer buys less of it.)

PROBLEM 4.10

In Figure 4.10, income M is \$60 and p_2 is \$1. D contains 22 units of good 1 and 44 units of good 2. What, then, is the compensated budget line? What is the *added income* associated with the compensated budget line?

Two Effects Associated with a Price Decrease

Now let's perform the same sort of decomposition for a price decline instead of a price hike. In Figure 4.11, when p_1 is \$2, the consumer picks the utility-maximizing bundle containing 3 units of good 1 at A on indifference I_1. When p_1 then drops from \$2 to \$1, the consumer switches to the bundle containing 9 units of good 1 at C on indifference curve I_2. Once again price and quantity demanded are negatively related. How can we decompose this increase in consumption into a substitution effect and an income effect?

To isolate the substitution effect, we'll alter the consumer's income just enough so that he or she can attain the initial indifference curve, I_1. Because the price of good 1 has dropped, this time we have to take income away from the consumer. The dashed line in Figure 4.11 is the compensated budget line, and the consumer picks the utility-maximizing bundle containing 14 units of good 1 at D, increasing consumption of good 1 from 3 to 14 units. Thus, the substitution effect is again negatively related to the price change.

Now, to isolate the income effect, we'll keep p_1 at \$1 and restore the income that we have just taken away. The solid line through

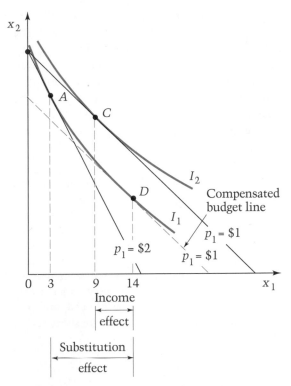

FIGURE 4.11 Income and substitution effects for a price decrease.

As the price of good 1 decreases from \$2 to \$1, quantity demanded increases from 3 to 9. To isolate the substitution and income effects, decrease income by just enough that the original indifference curve I_1 is attainable at price $p_1 = \$1$. The substitution effect is the increase in consumption from 3 to 14, and the income effect is the reduction in consumption from 14 to 9.

C is the resulting budget line, and the consumer chooses the bundle containing 9 units of good 1 at C. Since this income effect — a decrease in consumption of good 1 from 14 units to 9 — is associated with a price decrease — p_1 decreased from \$2 to \$1 — the income effect is *positively* related to the price change. This positive relationship reflects the fact that good 1 is an inferior good in Figure 4.11.

Notice that in Figure 4.11, the income and substitution effects work in opposite directions. Because the substitution effect is larger than the income effect, however, the *total* effect is negatively related to the price change. In the following problem, you will see that when good 1 is an inferior good, the income effect may — in theory at least — be larger than the substitution effect. When it is, the good is a Giffen good.

PROBLEM 4.11

Consider again Figure 4.9, in which the price and quantity demanded of good 1 are positively related. Suppose that initially the price is $3 and that it subsequently drops to $2. First, decompose the change in quantity of good 1 demanded into income and substitution effects. Then notice that the substitution effect is negatively related to the price change, that the income effect is positively related, that good 1 is an inferior good, and that the income effect is larger than the substitution effect.

The Negative Substitution Effect

In all of these decompositions, the substitution effect is negatively related to the price change. In the first exercise, when the price climbed, the substitution effect generated a decline in the consumption of good 1. In the second exercise, when the price dropped, the substitution effect generated an increase in consumption. The negative relationship between the substitution effect and the price change is always true when indifference curves are convex and smooth and when the consumer buys a positive amount of both goods.

To see why this result is a general one, let's isolate the substitution effect by imagining two points of tangency between two budget lines that reflect different prices of good 1 and one indifference curve. One budget line is the consumer's real budget line in the initial situation; the other is the compensated budget line. If the indifference curve is convex and smooth, its point of tangency with the budget line that re-

flects the lower price of good 1 will be to the right of the other point of tangency. The result is a negative relationship between the change in price and the change in quantity of good 1.

If indifference curves are smooth and convex and if the consumer buys a positive quantity of both goods, then the substitution effect is negatively related to the price change.

The Ambiguous Income Effect

Unlike the substitution effect, however, the income effect of a price change may be either negatively or positively related to the price change. If the good is normal, the relationship is negative.

For a normal good, the income effect is negatively related to the price change.

If, as in Figure 4.11, the good is inferior, however, the relationship is positive.

For an inferior good, the income effect is positively related to the price change.

The Slope of the Demand Curve

We can now fit these various pieces together to develop a deeper understanding of the slope of the demand curve, or the qualitative relationship between the price and the quantity demanded of a good. If the good is normal, the substitution and income effects of a price change are both negatively related to the price change and are therefore complementary.

If a good is normal, then its demand curve is downward sloping: price and quantity demanded are negatively related.

If the good is inferior, the income effect of a price change is positively related and the substitution effect is negatively related to the price change; the slope of the demand curve then depends on the relative strengths of the two effects.

If a good is inferior and if the substitution effect is larger than the income effect, then its demand curve is downward sloping: price and quantity demanded are negatively related.

If a good is inferior and if the income effect is larger than the substitution effect, then its demand curve is upward sloping: price and quantity demanded are positively related.

The last statement clearly describes the Giffen good case. Although Giffen goods are theoretically possible, there is no systematic empirical evidence to indicate that they actually exist. So, we'll set Giffen goods aside in the rest of this book and simply assume that demand curves are downward sloping.

---

*4.10 The Compensated Demand Curve

We used the assumptions that indifference curves are smooth and convex — in conjunction with the other assumptions from Chapter 3 — to derive the result that the substitution effect is negatively related to the price change. In this section, we'll drop the assumptions of smoothness and convexity and instead use only minimal assumptions from Chapter 3 to show that the substitution effect is never positively related to the price change. We'll do so by introducing the *compensated demand curve*, which reflects only the substitution effect, and then showing that — unlike the ordinary demand curve — it cannot be upward sloping.

The Substitution Effect Revisited

To show that the substitution effect cannot be positively related to the price change, we need only four of the assumptions from

Chapter 3 — completeness, two-term consistency, three-term consistency, and nonsatiation. As you saw, the first three assumptions guarantee that individuals do make consistent choices. The fourth assumption — nonsatiation — will also be satisfied in any interesting choice situation. Because we're now using only minimal assumptions, we are essentially discovering an implication — in fact, a very important one — of the assumption that individuals are motivated by self-interest.

Recall that when we identified the substitution effect, we identified the minimum income that allowed the consumer to attain the original indifference curve. Let's call this minimum income the **compensatory income.** The associated budget line is, of course, the compensated budget line. The dashed budget lines in Figures 4.10 and 4.11 are compensated budget lines.

In Figure 4.12, the indifference curves have been omitted because their shapes now play no role in the analysis. In the initial situation, given the lower value of p_1 — reflected by the flatter budget line LAF — this consumer chose the utility-maximizing bundle at A. Now suppose that p_1 goes up. If this consumer's income goes up to M_1, the resulting budget line will now be JAE, and he or she will still be able buy the original bundle at A. We know, then, that the compensatory income — because it is the income that just allows the consumer to attain the original indifference curve — can be no greater than M_1.

Suppose for the moment that the compensatory income is M_1. (It's unlikely to be this large, but as you'll see in Problem 4.12, it can be.) The compensated budget line is then JAE in Figure 4.12. Notice that on segment AFE of the compensated budget line, only bundle A can be on the original indifference curve. Why? If another bundle on AFE were on the original indifference curve — say, the bundle at F — then, by nonsatiation, any bundle on segment CD of the origi-

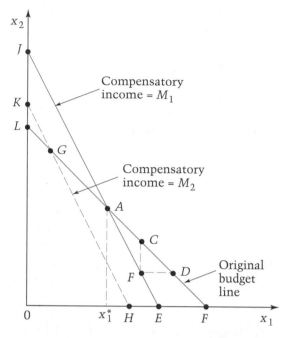

FIGURE 4.12   The nonpositive substitution effect.
The initial utility-maximizing bundle is at point A on the original budget line. Given the price increase (reflected in the slope of the two compensated budget lines), the compensatory income is no greater than M_1. If the compensatory income is in fact M_1, then the utility-maximizing bundle is on segment JA of the compensated budget line JAE, and the quantity of good 1 in the utility-maximizing bundle does not exceed x_1^*. If the compensatory income is less than M_1—say, M_2—then the utility-maximizing bundle is on segment KG of the compensated budget line KGH, and the quantity of good 1 in the bundle is less than x_1^*. In either case, the substitution effect is nonpositively related to the price change.

the substitution effect in this instance is *nonpositively related* to the price change. In other words, given the compensated budget line, the quantity demanded of good 1 will not increase. Instead, it will either remain the same or decrease.

Now let's suppose that the compensatory income is something less than M_1—say, M_2—in Figure 4.12. This lower compensatory income gives rise to the lower compensated budget line KGH. By simply revising the argument above, we can establish that, given the higher price of good 1 and compensatory income M_2, the consumer will now pick a bundle on segment KG of the compensated budget line. Because the quantity of good 1 in all these bundles is *strictly less than* x_1^*, we know that the substitution effect in this instance is *negatively* related to the price change.

In sum, we now know that the substitution effect cannot be positively related to the price change.

If the completeness, two- and three-term consistency, and nonsatiation assumptions are satisfied, then the substitution effect is nonpositively related to the price change.

The Compensated Demand Function

In the preceding analysis, we have held p_2 constant while allowing p_1 to vary. We have also adjusted the consumer's income up or down so that he or she remains on the same indifference curve. And for each value of p_1, we have identified the quantity of good 1 in the consumer's utility-maximizing bundle. If we now plot these price-quantity pairs, we'll have what is called a **compensated demand curve**. The adjective *compensated* indicates that the consumer has been given the compensatory income needed to keep him or her on the original indifference curve.

In Figure 4.13a, we have held p_2 constant at $2 and considered three different

nal budget line would be preferred to bundle A. But this is impossible because bundle A is the original utility-maximizing bundle. Thus, we know that given the higher price of good 1 and the compensatory income M_1, this consumer will choose a bundle on segment JA of the compensated budget line. Because the quantity of good 1 in these bundles *does not exceed* x_1^*, we also know that

values of p_1—$1, $2, and $4. This has allowed us to identify the corresponding points of tangency between the three compensated budget lines and the indifference

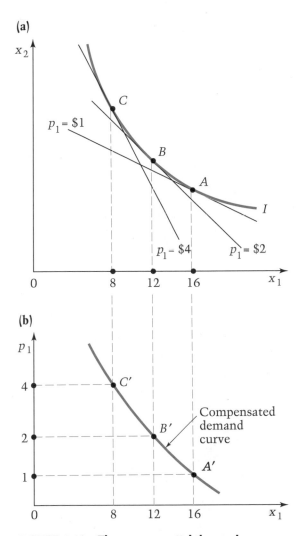

(a)

(b)

FIGURE 4.13   The compensated demand curve.
In (a), three compensated budget lines, associated with three prices for good 1, are tangent to indifference curve I at points A, B, and C. These points of tangency are used to construct the compensated demand curve in (b). For example, when p_1 is $4, the compensated budget line is tangent at bundle C, which contains 8 units of good 1; therefore, one point on the compensated demand curve is point C', where 8 units are demanded at price $p_1 = $4.

curve I. We have labeled these points A, B, and C in Figure 4.13a, and we have plotted the corresponding points A', B', and C' on the compensated demand curve in Figure 4.13b. For instance, when p_1 is $1 in Figure 4.13a, the compensated budget line is tangent to the indifference curve I at the bundle containing 16 units of good 1 at A. Therefore, point A' in Figure 4.13b is one point on the compensated demand curve. Similarly, when p_1 is $2 (or $4), the compensated budget line is tangent to I at bundle B (or bundle C), which gives rise to point B' (or C') on the compensated demand curve.

Since the compensated demand curve reflects only the substitution effect, it cannot be upward sloping. That is, when p_1 increases, quantity demanded on the compensated demand curve will ordinarily decrease, and it cannot increase. Thus, our intuition that demand functions are downward sloping is correct for compensated demand functions.[6]

In the following problem, you'll see that the substitution effect is not always

[6] Notice that to find the compensated demand functions, in essence, we solved a cost-minimization problem by minimizing the cost of attaining a specified indifference curve; that is, we implicitly solved

$$\text{minimize } (p_1x_1 + p_2x_2) \text{ by choice of } x_1 \text{ and } x_2$$

$$\text{subject to the constraint } U(x_1, x_2) = u$$

where u is a fixed utility number. (The Lagrange multiplier method can be used to solve this problem.) The solution gives us x_1 and x_2 as functions of p_1, p_2, and u. Symbolically,

$$x_1 = H_1(p_1, p_2, u)$$
$$x_2 = H_2(p_1, p_2, u)$$

The functions H_1 and H_2 are the compensated demand functions. We have shown that the partial derivative of $H_i(p_1, p_2, u)$ with respect to p_i is nonpositive. In other words, as the price of a good increases, the quantity of that good in the bundle that minimizes the cost of getting to a designated indifference curve does not increase.

negative — that it can be zero — and you'll get a chance to construct a compensated demand curve.

PROBLEM 4.12

Suppose we have the following utility function: $U(x_1, x_2) = \min(x_1, x_2)$. Initially both prices are $1, and income is $30. Find the utility-maximizing bundle. Now let p_1 increase to $2. What is the compensatory income? Show that the substitution effect is zero. Construct the compensated demand curve for good 1. Now use your answer to Problem 4.2 to find the ordinary demand curve for good 1, given $p_2 = \$1$ and $M = \$30$, and plot both demand curves on the same diagram.

We now have two demand curves: the ordinary demand curve, which arises from the consumer's real choice problem, and the compensated demand curve, which arises from the fictional choice problem in which the consumer is given a different income — the compensatory income — every time the good's price changes. In the remainder of the book, when we use the term *demand curve*, we'll mean the ordinary demand curve. When we talk about the *compensated demand curve*, we'll always add the adjective *compensated* to distinguish it from the ordinary demand curve.

4.11 Complements and Substitutes

Now let's turn to the last comparative statics question: how will consumer demand for a good change in response to a change in the price of some other good? For example, how does a consumer's demand for Pepsi (or a ski bus ticket) change when the price of Coke (or a ski pass) changes? More generally, how does x_1^* respond to a change in p_2, holding p_1 and M constant?

Two possibilities are illustrated in Figure 4.14. When p_2 is $1, the consumer chooses the bundle containing 6 units of good 1 at point A in both Figures 4.14*a* and

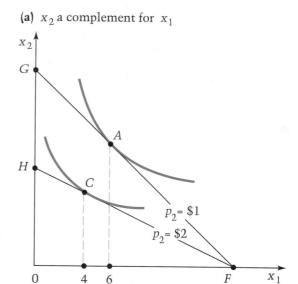

(a) x_2 a complement for x_1

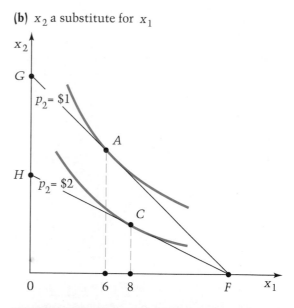

(b) x_2 a substitute for x_1

FIGURE 4.14 The consumption response to a change in the price of another good.

In (a), the quantity demanded of good 1 decreases from 6 to 4 as the price of good 2 increases from $1 to $2, and good 2 is said to be a complement for good 1. In (b), the quantity demanded of good 1 increases from 6 to 8 as the price of good 2 increases from $1 to $2, and good 2 is said to be a substitute for good 1.

4.14b. Now what happens when p_2 rises to $2? The higher price for good 2 causes the budget line to pivot around point *F*, shifting it from *GAF* to *HCF*. Because of the increase in p_2, the quantity demanded of good 1 *decreases* to 4 in Figure 4.14a, but it *increases* to 8 in Figure 4.14b. In other words, the consumer's response depends on the consumer's preferences. When p_2 increases, the consumer may decide to buy either more or less of good 1. Both possibilities are consistent with utility-maximizing behavior.

What have we learned? Although our theory gives us no qualitative result, it does provide us with a useful taxonomy. If x_1^* decreases in response to an increase in p_2 as in Figure 4.14a, we say that good 2 is a **complement** for good 1. Ski bus tickets and lift tickets, movies and popcorn, computers and software, and tennis balls and tennis rackets are all examples of complements. When the price of a movie goes up (or down), a consumer might decide to go to fewer (or more) movies *and* buy less (or more) popcorn. The utility function $U(x_1, x_2) = \min(x_1, x_2)$ — one you already explored in Problems 4.2 and 4.12 — is the case of *perfect complementarity*. Right skis and left skis, for instance, are perfect complements since you do not decide to buy one ski without buying the other.

On the other hand, if x_1^* increases in response to an increase in p_2 as Figure 4.14b, we say that good 2 is a **substitute** for good 1. Coke and Pepsi, coffee and tea, or Mercedes and BMWs might be thought of as substitutes. The utility function $U(x_1, x_2) = x_1 + x_2$ — the one we used to capture Amy's preferences in our fish model — is the case of *perfect substitutibility*. As you know, when p_1 is equal to p_2, these preferences imply that any bundle on the budget line is a utility-maximizing bundle. However, if p_2 decreases ever so slightly, the consumption of good 1 goes to zero. For example, if the price of one brand of soft drink rises by just a bit, a consumer will switch to a substitute brand

—if they are perfect substitutes and if the consumer is initially indifferent between them.

4.12 Measuring Comparative Statics Responses

In the preceding section, we looked for *qualitative* comparative statics results. For example, we asked if our theory of preferences inevitably implies an inverse relationship between the price and the quantity demanded of any good. The only qualitative result we discovered was that the substitution effect is nonpositively related to the price change, or that the compensated demand curve cannot be upward sloping. In this section, we'll be measuring and comparing *quantitative* comparative statics responses. To do so, however, we need a *units-free* measure that is not based on a particular yardstick such as pounds or kilowatt-hours.

Why must the measure be units-free? To find out, let's look at two demand curves in Figure 4.15. One demand curve is for oranges and the other for electricity. In Figure 4.15a, the price per pound of oranges is on the vertical axis and pounds of oranges demanded on the horizontal axis. In Figure 4.15b, the price per kilowatt-hour of electricity is on the vertical axis and kilowatt-hours of electricity demanded on the horizontal axis.

In which of these two cases is the response of quantity demanded to a $1 change in its own price larger? A glance at the two figures suggests that the appropriate answer is oranges because the demand curve for oranges is less steeply pitched than is the demand curve for electricity. But if we take the 5-pound bag to be the unit in which we measure oranges, we get the much steeper, dashed demand curve *D'D'* in Figure 4.15a, and the appropriate answer then seems to be electricity.

(a)

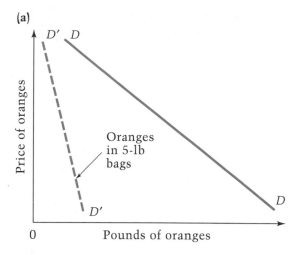

(b)

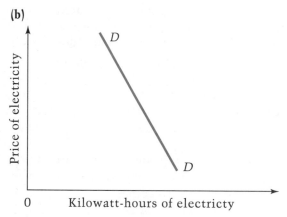

FIGURE 4.15   The need for a units-free measure of responsiveness.

Although the demand *DD* for oranges in (a) appears to be more responsive to changes in price than the demand *DD* for electricity in (b), the appearance is deceiving. For example, when we measure oranges in 5-pound bags instead of pounds, the demand for oranges appears to be less responsive. Meaningful comparisons require a units-free measure of responsiveness.

    The point is that in Figure 4.15, we can't compare demand responsiveness by comparing slopes of demand curves because the units of measurement are not the same. Furthermore, we can't make the comparison meaningful by choosing the same unit of measurement for each, because oranges

can't be measured in kilowatt-hours (or kilowatt-years or kilowatt-minutes) or electricity in pounds (or ounces or tons). What we need is a *units-free measure of responsiveness.*

Elasticity

A general units-free measure of responsiveness that is used for many different purposes is called **elasticity**. To illustrate the concept, suppose that we have some arbitrary demand curve

$$x_1 = D(p_1)$$

Now let's evaluate this function at two points: $x_1' = D(p_1')$ and $x_1'' = D(p_1'')$. We want a units-free measure of the change in x_1, $x_1' - x_2''$, induced by the change in p_1, $p_1' - p_1''$. If we expresses each of these changes as a proportionate change, $\Delta x_1/x_1'$ and $\Delta p_1/p_1'$ (where $\Delta x_1 = x_1' - x_1''$ and $\Delta p_1 = p_1' - p_1''$), then the units cancel and what remain are pure numbers. We can now form the ratio of the proportionate change in x_1 to the proportionate change in p_1.

DEFINITION

$$E = \frac{(\Delta x_1/x_1')}{(\Delta p_1/p_1')}$$

This ratio is called the **arc price elasticity of demand**.

PROBLEM 4.13

Suppose we have the following demand function: $x_1 = 10 - p_1$. Compute the elasticity of this demand function as price decreases from 9 to 8 and again as price decreases from 3 to 2. Notice that because the changes in prices are positive—but the changes in quantities are negative—the elasticity is a negative number.

The Point Price Elasticity of Demand

Beginning with the expression for the arc price elasticity of demand, we'll derive the more useful *point price elasticity of demand.* By rearranging the arc elasticity expression above, we get

$$\left(\frac{\Delta x_1}{\Delta p_1}\right)\left(\frac{p_1'}{x_1'}\right) = \left(\frac{1}{\Delta p_1/\Delta x_1}\right)\left(\frac{p_1'}{x_1'}\right)$$

Because the demand curve has a negative slope, this formula gives us a negative value for price elasticity. To get a positive value, it is traditional to use the *absolute value* of $\Delta p_1/\Delta x_1$, denoted by $|\Delta p_1/\Delta x_1|$, when computing arc price elasticity.

To identify the point elasticity of demand, we'll begin with the arc elasticity between points B and F on the demand curve in Figure 4.16 and ask: What happens as Δx_1 and Δp_1 get small? Notice first that

$$\left|\frac{\Delta p_1}{\Delta x_1}\right| = |\text{slope of line } BF|$$

As Δx_1 and Δp_1 get smaller and smaller, the slope of the line BF approaches the slope of the dashed line HBG, which is tangent to the demand function at point B. But

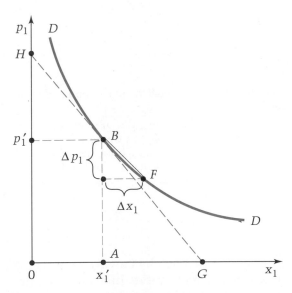

FIGURE 4.16   Computing the price elasticity of demand.

The point price elasticity of demand at point B is equal to $AG/0A$.

$$|\text{slope of } HBG| = \frac{AB}{AG}$$

where the distances AB and AG are defined in Figure 4.16. We can therefore write the **point elasticity of demand** at point B, denoted by η, as

$$\eta = \left(\frac{1}{(AB/AG)}\right)\left(\frac{p_1'}{x_1'}\right)$$

Notice that because p_1' is equal to distance AB and x_1' is equal to distance $0A$, the expression above can be rewritten as

$$\eta = \left(\frac{1}{(AB/AG)}\right)\left(\frac{AB}{0A}\right)$$

or, by rearranging and canceling terms,

$$\eta = \frac{AG}{0A}$$

Notice what a simple graphic trick we've found for computing the elasticity of demand at any point on any demand function. First, construct the line — analogous to HBG in Figure 4.16 — that is tangent to the demand function at the desired point. Then, to identify point A, drop a vertical line from the desired point down to the quantity axis. To identify point G, extend the tangent line until it intersects the quantity axis. In the following problem, you can try your own hand at this graphic trick.

PROBLEM 4.14

Construct a linear demand function and identify its midpoint—the point halfway along the demand function between the price axis and the quantity axis. Show that η is greater than 1 to the left of the midpoint and that it is less than 1 to the right of the midpoint. What is η at the midpoint? At the point where the demand function intersects the price axis? At the point where it intersects the quantity axis?

Price-Elastic and Price-Inelastic Demand

We can use the value of elasticity of demand to create another taxonomic distinction.

When η exceeds 1, we say that demand is elastic with respect to price, or **price elastic**. The adjective *elastic* is used because η greater than 1 means that the proportionate increase in quantity demanded is greater than the proportionate price decrease that induced it. If price drops by, say, 10%, then quantity demanded rises by more than 10% if demand is elastic with respect to price.

This suggests a relationship between price elasticity of demand and a consumer's total expenditure on the good — or price multiplied by the quantity demanded. Since a consumer's expenditure is inevitably some firm's revenue, we can substitute for the term total expenditure the more familiar term **total revenue**. When demand is price elastic, a decrease in price results in an increase in total revenue. Conversely, an increase in price results in a decrease in total revenue.

On the other hand, when η is less than 1, we say that demand is inelastic with respect to price: it is **price inelastic**. The adjective *inelastic* is used here because the proportionate increase in quantity demanded is less than the proportionate decrease in price that induced it. If price drops by, say, 10%, then quantity demanded rises by less than 10% if demand is inelastic with respect to price. Furthermore, when demand is price inelastic, total revenue decreases as price decreases. Conversely, total revenue increases as price increases.

To help you understand the relationship between price elasticity of demand and total revenue, we've plotted a linear demand curve in Figure 4.17a, and we've constructed the associated total revenue curve in Figure 4.17b. Because in Figure 4.17a the quantity demanded at point B on the demand curve is zero, in Figure 4.17b the total revenue is also zero. The total revenue curve in Figure 4.17b therefore passes through the origin. Now begin at point B in Figure 4.17a and imagine continually decreasing the

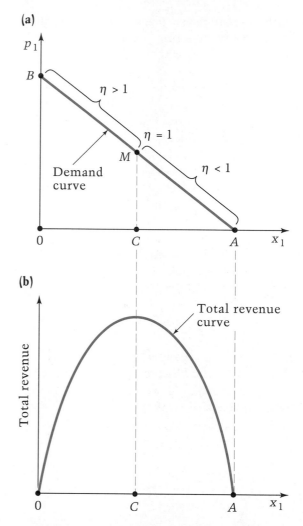

FIGURE 4.17   Price elasticity of demand and total revenue.

The linear demand curve in (a) generates the total revenue curve in (b). As we move down the demand curve, total revenue increases when $\eta > 1$, and it decreases when $\eta < 1$. Total revenue is a maximum when $\eta = 1$.

price of good 1, thereby moving to the right down this demand curve. In the elastic portion of the curve, from points B to M, total revenue increases as the price drops. But in the inelastic portion of the curve, from points M to A, the total revenue decreases as the price drops. At point M, η is 1, and total revenue attains its maximum value. Because at point M price elasticity is 1, M is sometimes called the *point of unitary price elasticity*.

Other Elasticity Measures

The general notion of elasticity can be used to measure the responsiveness of quantity demanded to other exogenous variables in the demand function. Here we'll look at two *arc elasticity* concepts: the **income elasticity of demand** and the **cross-price elasticity of demand**. (However, we will not derive the corresponding point elasticity concepts.) If we choose two points on the Engel curve for good 1 (M', x_1') and (M'', x_1''), the income elasticity of demand for the change in income from M' to M'' is

$$\left(\frac{(x_1' - x_1'')/x_1'}{(M' - M'')/M'} \right)$$

For a normal good, income elasticity of demand is positive because the Engel curve for a normal good is upward sloping. On the other hand, the income elasticity for an inferior good is negative.

To measure the consumption response of good 1 to a change in the price of good 2, we can construct the cross-price elasticity of demand. Given p_2', suppose that the consumer buys x_1' of good 1. Now change p_2 to p_2'' and suppose that the consumer now buys x_1''. Then the cross-price elasticity of demand for good 1 with respect to p_2 is

$$\left(\frac{(x_1' - x_1')/x_1'}{(p_2' - p_2'')/p_2'} \right)$$

Good 2 is a substitute for good 1 if the cross-price elasticity is positive. It is a complement for good 1 if the cross-price elasticity is negative.

4.13 The Composite Commodity Theorem

Throughout this chapter, we've focused on consumer choice problems in which there are just two goods. In this last section, we'll briefly discuss the **composite commodity theorem**, independently discovered by Hicks (1939) and by Leontief (1936). The theorem is useful because it allows us to reduce complicated choice problems that involve many endogenous variables to much simpler problems that involve just two endogenous variables. As we have seen throughout this chapter, these simpler problems can be analyzed graphically.

Let's first write down a complex choice problem, and then see how the theorem can be used to simplify it. When there are n goods, instead of just two, the utility-maximizing problem is

maximize $U(x_1, x_2, \ldots, x_n)$
    by choice of $x_1, x_2, \ldots, x_n$

subject to the constraint
    $p_1 x_1 + p_2 x_2 + \cdots + p_n x_n = M$

Now suppose that we are interested, *not* in all goods in this problem, but in just one or two goods. For example, suppose we want to know how the quantity demanded of good 1 changes in response to a change in p_1. That is, suppose we wanted to explore the demand curve for good 1. If we could write down a utility function and a budget constraint with just two goods — x_1 and quantity of some "composite good" representing all other goods — we could use familiar graphic techniques to analyze this choice problem. To preview another example, we'll see in Chapter 5 that labor-supply decisions can be usefully regarded as simple choices between income and leisure, with income representing a composite of all consumption goods — that is, all goods other than leisure. The composite-commodity theorem provides a theoretical justification for the use of these sorts of composites of consumption goods.

Let's consider the first illustration. How could we reduce the complex utility-maximization problem with n goods to a manageable problem with only two goods — x_1 (quantity of good 1) and y (expenditure on all other goods)? To write down the simplified utility-maximization problem, we need both a pseudobudget constraint and a pseudoutility function in which the variables x_1 and y appear. The pseudobudget constraint is straightforward:

$$p_1 x_1 + y = M$$

That is, expenditure on good 1 plus expenditure on all other goods is equal to income.

To make sense, the pseudoutility function must tell us, for any bundle (x_1, y), the *maximum utility* the individual could attain by allocating the expenditure y to all other goods: good 2 through good n. That is, this pseudoutility function arises from the solution to a utility-maximizing problem:

maximize $U(x_1, x_2, \ldots, x_n)$
  by choice of $x_2, \ldots, x_n$

subject to the constraint
  $p_2 x_2 + \cdots + p_n x_n = y$

In this problem, the exogenous variables are $p_2, \ldots, p_n$; x_1; and y; and the endogenous variables are x_2 through x_n. In particular, note that x_1 and y are exogenous variables in this problem. As in the other utility-maximizing problems we've considered, in the solution to this problem the endogenous variables can be expressed as functions of the exogenous variables. Let's call these functions *pseudodemand functions*. Imagine, then, that we have these pseudodemand functions that give us the utility-maximizing values for x_2 through x_n, given the exogenous variables $p_2, \ldots, p_n$, x_1, and y.

Here's the crucial step: to find the pseudoutility function, we would substitute these pseudodemand functions for x_2

through x_n in the ordinary utility function, $U(x_1, \ldots, x_n)$. The arguments of the pseudoutility function would then be $p_2, \ldots, p_n, x_1$, and y. Notice that the prices of good 2 through good n appear in the pseudoutility function. If we write this utility function as $U'(x_1, y, p_1, p_2, \ldots, p_n)$, the form of the simplified utility-maximization problem is

maximize $U'(x_1, y, p_1, p_2, \ldots, p_n)$
  by choice of x_1 and y

subject to the constraint
  $p_1 x_1 + y = M$

The composite commodity theorem guarantees that the demand for good 1 can be analyzed with this simplified problem. That is, it assures us that there is a pseudoutility function that accurately represents the individual's preferences. Furthermore, given the preference assumptions of Chapter 3, the theorem guarantees that the pseudoutility function will have indifference curves that are smooth and convex to the origin. The demand curve arising from this simplified problem is therefore the individual's demand curve for good 1.

The theorem allows us to simplify complex choice problems by writing a pseudoutility function with x_1 and y (expenditure on all other commodities) as its arguments. Remember though that this utility function also includes the prices of all goods in the composite commodity. Thus, whenever we use a composite commodity, we are implicitly assuming that the prices of all goods included in the composite are held constant.

We'll use this theorem extensively in the following chapter, and indeed you can use it right now to reinterpret what you've learned in this chapter. In particular, all the material in Sections 4.8 through 4.10 can be reinterpreted by regarding good 2 not as some other good but as a composite of all goods other than good 1. If good 2 is expenditure on all other goods, its price is just $1.

As you reinterpret this material, you must therefore set p_2 equal to $1.

Summary

We began this chapter by considering the constraints—wealth, time, and human resources—on individual decision making and by noting how complex rational decision making can be, because the individual's economic decisions are inherently intertemporal and because they necessarily involve imperfect information. To analyze decision making in this complex world, we created an ideal case; we defined a choice problem involving just one period, perfect information, and two goods.

We then characterized and solved the individual's constrained-choice problem in this static framework. Given the prices of consumption goods and the consumer's income, the solution—a system of demand functions—yields the utility-maximizing quantities of those goods.

In investigating the implications of the theory of consumer choice for these demand functions, we discovered two important general properties that act as restrictions on demand functions. First, each demand function is homogeneous of degree zero in prices and income. For instance, if all prices and income double, the consumer's real situation is unaltered. Consequently, his or her utility-maximizing choices do not change. Second, the entire system of demand functions must satisfy Engel's aggregation law. This law is simply a reflection of the truism "We spend what we spend." These restrictions are of significant practical use to economists who use data to estimate demand functions.

We then graphically analyzed a range of choice problems, beginning with the demand for essential and inessential goods. A consumer will always buy some amount of an essential good, regardless of how high its price is. By contrast, a consumer will not necessarily buy a positive amount of an inessential good; if the price is high enough, he or she will choose not to buy any. This distinction helps us to understand why most individuals choose not to buy many—perhaps most—of the goods available in advanced economies.

Next, we characterized normal and inferior goods in terms of the consumer's demand response to a change in income. As income goes up, the consumption of a normal good also increases, but the consumption of an inferior good declines.

We then explored the relationship between a good's own price and the quantity demanded of that good, which we called the demand curve. Surprisingly, the demand curve can be upward sloping (in the theoretically possible case of Giffen goods) or downward sloping (in the standard case for all other goods). The fact that we lack a label for the standard case, in which the consumption of a good goes down when its price goes up, reflects how pervasive this case seems to be. In fact, the Giffen good—the case in which consumption increases as price increases—has never been convincingly identified and remains a theoretical curiosity.

To understand why the Giffen good is theoretically possible, we decomposed the quantity response to a price change into income and substitution effects. We found—just as intuition suggests—that the substitution effect for all goods and the income effect for normal goods are negatively related to the price change. However, the income effect for inferior goods is positively related to the price change. Giffen goods are therefore inferior goods for which a positive income effect dominates a negative substitution effect. We then introduced a new demand curve, the compensated demand curve, which—because it incorporates only the substitution effect—can never be upward sloping.

98 — Individual Choice

Next we looked at how demand for one good changes in response to a change in the price of some other good. We called goods complements when consumption moves up or down in tandem (right shoes and left shoes) and substitutes when an increase in consumption of one good is paired with a decline in consumption of another (chocolate mousse and lemon meringue pie). More precisely, good 2 is a complement (or a substitute) for good 1 if quantity demanded of good 1 decreases (or increases) as the price of good 2 increases.

We then introduced the concept of elasticity—a units-free measure of responsiveness—and saw how to use it to measure and compare quantitative comparative statics responses. We used this concept to define the price elasticity of demand, the income elasticity of demand, and the cross-price elasticity of demand.

Finally, we discussed the composite commodity theorem, which allows us to reduce complex choice problems with many endogenous variables to relatively simple problems that can be solved graphically.

A major thrust of this chapter has been to create a set of useful analytical tools for exploring consumer choice problems. In the next chapter, we'll put these newly developed tools to work as we analyze a number of varied and interesting problems.

Exercises

1 A normal good at one level of income need not be a normal good for all levels of income. To see why not, draw an Engel curve that initially rises and subsequently falls as income increases. Then construct an indifference map that would generate the Engel curve you drew. Begin by constructing the income-consumption path corresponding to this Engel curve.

2 Consumption bundles (10, 20) and (15, 40) are both on the income-consumption path. What, if anything, can you say about the

MRS at these two bundles? Illustrate your answer.

3 Rita's indifference curves are smooth and convex. Given prices $p_1 = \$2$ and $p_2 = \$4$, Rita bought consumption bundle (100, 50).
   a If p_1 increases to $3 and Rita's income increases by $100, can you tell if she will be better off or worse off?
   b If p_1 increases to $3 and Rita's income increases by $97, can you tell whether she will be better off or worse off?

4 Good 1 is not a Giffen good, and bundles (10, 23) and (15, 40) are both on the price-consumption path that is generated by changing p_1. What, if anything, can you say about the MRS at these two bundles? Illustrate your answer with a carefully drawn graph.

5 Nancy spends all her income on good 1 and good 2, and her income-consumption path is downward sloping. Is it possible that both goods are normal? That both are inferior? That good 1 is normal? That good 1 is inferior? That one of these goods is inferior and the other normal?

6 Smiling Jack's utility function is

$$U(x_1, x_2) = x_2(1 + x_1)$$

   a Carefully plot the indifference curve that passes through the bundle (2, 1).
   b Is good 1 essential or inessential? What about good 2?

7 The revenue that wheat farmers as a group receive for their crop tends to be larger when there is a poor harvest than when there is a bumper crop. What does this observation suggest about the price elasticity of demand for wheat?

8 Ted lives in a two-good world. He always spends 40% of his income on good 1 and 60% on good 2.
   a What are his demand functions?
   b Suppose that both prices are $1, and construct Ted's income-consumption path and the Engel curves for both goods.

9 Suppose that MRS of good 2 for good 1 depends only on the quantity of good 1. What is the relationship between quantity demanded of good 1 and income? What is the

income elasticity of demand for good 1? (You may want to review your answers to Exercises 6 and 7 at the end of Chapter 3.)

10 Consider any two linear demand functions that intersect the quantity axis at the same point and that have different slopes. Show that when quantities demanded are equal, so are the elasticities of demand and that when prices are equal, the elasticity of the lower demand function is larger.

11 Nancy spends all her income on good 1 and good 2. As p_1 increases while p_2 remains fixed, Nancy's price-consumption path is horizontal.
a How does Nancy's expenditure on good 1 respond to changes in p_1?
b Show that Nancy's demand for good 1 is proportional to $1/p_1$.
c Is good 1 a complement or a substitute for good 2?
d What is Nancy's price elasticity of demand for good 1?

12 It is sometimes argued that demand for medical services is perfectly inelastic with respect to the price of medical services. By considering the limitations imposed by a finite income, show that no demand curve can be perfectly inelastic for all prices.

13 Ronald spends all his income on good 1 and good 2, and good 1 is *not* a Giffen good. As p_1 increases while p_2 remains fixed, Ronald's price-consumption path is downward sloping.
a What can you say about the price elasticity of demand for good 1?
b Is good 1 a complement or a substitute for good 2?

14 Brett's MRS is given by the following function:

$$MRS = \frac{x_2}{x_1}$$

What are Brett's demand functions? Is either good inferior? Is either good a Giffen good? Is either good inessential?

15 Norma spends all her income on good 1 and good 2, and her income-consumption path is upward sloping.
a What if anything can you say about the demand response for good 1 and good 2 to an increase in income?

b Is it possible that good 1 is a Giffen good?

16 Consider the following price schedule for electricity. The price of each unit of electricity up to 10 units is $1. The price for each unit in excess of 10 is $1.50. Construct the implied budget line for electricity and a composite commodity (expenditure on all other goods). Assuming that both electricity and the composite are essential goods, illustrate three sorts of utility-maximizing solutions.

17 Mr. Lucky intends to spend a recent inheritance of $1000 over the next two periods. He has no other source of income. Let x_1 and x_2 be two composite commodities: expenditure on consumption in this period and in the next period. Suppose that the rate of interest that Mr. Lucky can get on his savings is 25%; that is, for every $1 invested in this period, he will have $1.25 in the next period. What is Mr. Lucky's budget line? That is, what combinations of x_1 and x_2 does his inheritance allow him to have? What is the opportunity cost of consumption in the first (second) period in terms of foregone consumption in the second (first) period?

18 Mr. Lucky's cousin Not-So is broke, but his grandmother has left him in trust an inheritance of $1250. Let x_1 and x_2 be two composite commodities, expenditure on consumption in this period and in the next period. The terms of the trust specify that he can't have the money until the next period, but his banker will lend him money at a 25% interest rate (thereby frustrating his grandmother's intentions). For every $1 borrowed today, Not-So must pay back $1.25 tomorrow. What is Not-So's budget line? How does it compare with Mr. Lucky's?

*19 "The demand for any good tends to be more elastic with respect to price in the long run than in the short run." Explain why this statement might be true, and name some goods to which you think the statement applies.

*20 Consider the following scheme devised by the parent of an overweight child to reduce the child's consumption of candy bars. The parent offers to sell candy bars to the child at their market price of $1 plus a parental tax of $0.50 per candy bar. To induce the child to cooperate, the parent offers to increase the child's allowance by A dollars. If the child accepts the deal, he or she agrees not to buy candy from anyone else. Draw a diagram in which you identify the minimum value of A that will induce the child to cooperate. Assuming that the parent does increase the child's allowance by that amount and that the child accepts the offer, will the child's consumption of candy bars decrease? Will the amount of tax the parent collects from the child be as large as the increase in the child's allowance?

*21 Suppose that the indifference curves between x_1 and x_2 are concave (as opposed to convex) to the origin. Show that the point on the budget line where $MRS(x_1, x_2)$ is equal to p_1/p_2 is not a solution to the utility-maximizing problem. What points on the budget line are preferred to this point? Show that utility maximization implies that the consumer will spend all of his or her income on good 1 or good 2.

*22 Show that a utility-maximizing consumer will never choose a consumption bundle (in which both quantities are positive) on a nonconvex portion of an indifference curve.

References

Hicks, J. R. (1939), *Value and Capital*, London: The Clarendon Press.

Hicks, J. R., and R. G. D. Allen (1934), "A Reconsideration of the Theory of Value: Parts I and II," *Economica*, 1:52–75, 196–219.

Leonteif, W. W. (1936), "Composite Commodities and the Problem of Index Numbers," *Econometrica*, 4:39–59.

Slutsky, E. (1915), "Sulla teoria del bilancio del consumatore," *Giornale degli Economisti e Rivista di Statistica*, 51:1–26. English translation: "On the Theory of the Budget of the Consumer," in *Readings in Price Theory*, G. J. Stigler and K. E. Boulding (eds.), Homewood, Ill.: Richard D. Irwin, pp. 27–56.

5

VICARIOUS PROBLEM SOLVING: APPLICATIONS OF THE THEORY OF CHOICE

In Chapter 4, we first defined the choice-making problem from the consumer's perspective and then tried to anticipate how each consumer would solve that problem. The analysis created in Chapter 4 is thus meant to do what Thomas Schelling calls *vicarious problem solving:*

> If we know what problem a person is trying to solve, and if we think he can actually solve it, and if we can solve it too, we can anticipate what our subject will do by putting ourself in his place and solving his problem as we think he sees it. This is the method of "vicarious problem solving" that underlies most of microeconomics. (1978, p. 18.)

As we try our hand at vicarious problem solving in this chapter, the central question is just how much territory we can cover — that is, how wide-ranging or fruitful our theory of consumer choice will prove to be. The time has come, as the Walrus said, to talk of many things. Not of shoes and ships and sealing wax, perhaps, but of Polaroid cameras and private clubs, ski holiday packages, racquetball court assignments, and more.

5.1 Taxation: Lump-Sum Versus Excise Taxes

One issue that is bound to induce heated discussion anywhere is the question of taxation. Can our analytical tools help us to shed some light on this highly charged subject? The basic issue — given that governments are going to dip their hands into private pockets to pay for public services — is what sort of taxation scheme would the taxpayer prefer? In other words, given that someone must pay a particular sum of money to the government, what sort of tax institution would leave him or her better off?

Excise Tax Versus Lump-Sum Tax

We'll compare two taxes: an **excise tax** and a **lump-sum tax.** An excise tax is one in which a given tax surcharge is added to the price of each unit of a particular good. Excise taxes on gasoline, liquor, and perfume are common examples. By contrast, a lump-sum tax is a fixed tax liability. Under this scheme, a government simply demands that an individual remit a certain sum. Britain recently introduced a quite controversial tax that has many of the features of a lump-sum tax—the Community Service Tax.

Imagine, then, that a government wants to raise a specified sum of money by imposing either a lump-sum tax or an excise tax on some commodity—gasoline, for example. From the taxpayer's point of view, which is preferable? The first thing to notice is that an excise tax increases the *opportunity cost* to the consumer of the taxed commodity. By contrast, a lump-sum tax *alters the budget* available to the individual.

Let's suppose that good 1 is gasoline and that an excise tax on gasoline has been imposed. Because we'll be using the composite commodity theorem to simplify the problem, good 2 will be a *composite commodity* (expenditure on all other goods). Since good 2 is expenditure, it's measured in dollars (or pounds or yen) and its price is therefore $1.

Let's begin by considering some consumer—say, Ms. C—before any tax is imposed. Her pretax budget line is the dashed line ACG $(p_1x_1 + x_2 = M)$ in Figure 5.1, where x_1 is quantity of gasoline, and x_2 is quantity of the composite commodity.

Now let's impose an excise tax t per unit of gasoline. Ms. C's budget line is now the solid line ADH $[(p_1 + t)x_1 + x_2 = M]$. We know from Chapter 4 that the new budget line is represented graphically by a line rotated downward from the point at which the pretax budget line intersects the x_2 axis. In other words, the same budget is still available (indicated by the intersection of both budget lines at the same point on the x_2 axis), but the cost to the consumer of gasoline is higher once an excise tax is in effect (indicated by the steeper pitch of the new budget line).

Once the excise tax is in place, Ms. C chooses the consumption bundle at point D on indifference curve I in Figure 5.1. The tax take, or the amount of tax the government

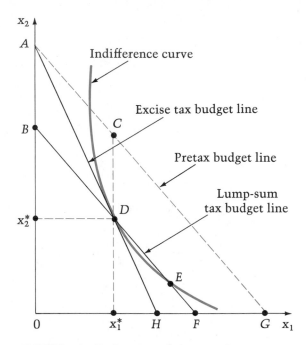

FIGURE 5.1   Excise versus lump-sum taxes.

Given the excise tax budget line ADH, the utility-maximizing bundle is point D, and the tax revenue is equal to distance DC. A lump-sum tax that yields the same tax revenue gives rise to the flatter lump-sum tax budget line $BDEF$. Given this budget line, the individual will choose some point on segment DE on a higher indifference curve. The lump-sum tax is therefore preferred to the excise tax even though both taxes yield the same tax revenue.

collects, is just tx_1^* because x_1^* is the amount of gasoline Ms. C buys and t is the tax per unit of gasoline. Let's identify the tax take graphically. In the absence of the excise tax, Ms. C could have bought the bundle at point C on the pretax budget constraint. The tax take is therefore equal to the distance DC in Figure 5.1.

Now, what about the alternative scheme, in which a lump-sum tax yields the same revenue—that is, one in which tx_1^* is equal to distance DC? Once the lump-sum tax is imposed, Ms. C's budget constraint is the solid line $BDEF$ in Figure 5.1. The new budget line is below, but parallel to, the pretax budget line since Ms. C's income — but not the prices she pays — has changed. Notice that the lump-sum tax budget line passes through point D. Why? In the absence of any tax, the bundle at point C is attainable and, since the lump-sum tax is equal to distance DC, the bundle at D is attainable after the lump-sum tax has been deducted from her income.

Although Ms. C could buy the bundle at D, she will choose instead some bundle on segment DE of the lump-sum budget line because this segment lies above and to the right of the indifference curve in Figure 5.1. By nonsatiation, any point on segment DE is preferred to the bundle (x_1^*, x_2^*) at D. Of course, this means that Ms. C. is better off with the lump-sum tax than she is with the excise tax.

In other words, a lump-sum tax is the preferable form of taxation:

Given a choice between a lump-sum tax and an excise tax that raise the same revenue, the consumer will choose the lump-sum tax.

In this analysis, we've implicitly assumed that Ms. C's indifference curves were convex and smooth and that she buys a positive amount of gasoline. For her, the substitution effect is therefore nonzero. Yet in Section 4.6, we saw that when indifference curves are kinked, the substitution effect may be zero. Is the lump-sum tax still preferred when the substitution effect is zero? To find out, try the following problem.

PROBLEM 5.1

Suppose that Kinky's preferences can be represented by the following utility function: $U(x_1, x_2) = \min(x_1, x_2)$. As you discovered in Problem 4.12, the substitution effect is zero for this utility function. Show that Kinky will be indifferent between an excise tax and a lump-sum tax that raise equal revenue.

Government Subsidies

Governments not only take money out of people's pockets but also, in some cases, put money back through a variety of subsidy schemes. In Canada, for instance, parents are given monthly family allowance checks, whose size depends on the number of children in the family. In the United States, many schoolchildren receive lunches subsidized by the government. So, too, in the United States, the tax deductibility of mortgage interest payments is a significant subsidy to home buyers. Welfare payments, public-housing projects, and many other programs are examples of government subsidies. Any such subsidy is, in effect, just a tax whose value is *negative*. As you'll see in Exercise 2 at the end of this chapter, the sort of analysis we've just done for taxes also applies to subsidies — and the outcome is similar. Given a choice between a lump-sum subsidy and a per-unit subsidy on some good, which cost the government the same amount, the consumer will prefer the lump-sum subsidy.

At the outset of this section, we were careful to discuss the question of the preferred form of taxation in the context of a single person, Ms. C. To extend the result directly to a larger group of taxpayers in a municipality, province, state, or nation, we'd have to assume that the group is composed of taxpayers whose individual preferences and income are all identical. Yet taxpayers in any particular jurisdiction are probably not so much alike. We therefore must be cautious in applying these principles of taxation to real situations.

An Application to the Theory of Clubs

Nevertheless, we can identify certain groups in which the assumption of a **representative consumer** — the assumption that the preferences and income of an individual randomly selected from the group will be characteristic of each person in that group — is likely to be more nearly true. Private clubs, for example, cater primarily to people who seek the same amenities and can all afford the membership fee. Because club members can, in a rough way, be viewed as self-selecting according to certain preferences and income levels, any individual club member we select is likely to be representative of the whole membership.

Let's broaden the meaning of *taxation* to apply to any circumstances in which sums are taken out of someone's pocket and used to fund some project of a group to which that person belongs. If the project is a private club, then, what is the preferred way for such a club to assess its membership fees? Of course, this is a comparative institutional question about the taxing arrangements that are preferable from the perspective of the club members. In Problem 5.2, you can adapt what you've learned about the relative desirability of excise and lump-sum taxes to discover what that preferred arrangement will be.

PROBLEM 5.2

Suppose that a private dining club, composed of 100 members with identical preferences, incurs an overhead cost of $100,000 each year and that the cost of each meal is $50. (If the club sells one meal in a year, for example, its total costs are $100,050; if it sells five meals, its total costs are $100,250.) The club is considering two possible fee structures designed to generate just enough revenue to cover its costs. Its first option is to charge members a fixed price p_1 per meal. Let x_1^* denote the number of meals per year that each member buys at price p_1. If the club is to cover costs, it must choose p_1 so that $100x_1^*(p_1 - 50) =$ $100,000 or so that $x_1^*(p_1 - 50) = 1000. The club's second option is to charge each person a membership fee equal to $1000 and then to sell meals at a price of $50 per meal. Show that from the point of view of the club members, the second option is preferred to the first if indifference curves are smooth and convex. Hint: $p_1 - 50 is

analogous to an excise tax on club meals, and the $1000 membership fee is analogous to a lump-sum tax.

Many private clubs actually use fee structures like the one chosen by the hypothetical club in Problem 5.2 by selling a membership fee that just covers their overhead and then selling their services at marginal cost. That membership fee is analogous to the lump-sum tax we examined previously.

5.2 Measuring Benefits and Costs

As we indicated in Section 1.5, cost-benefit analysis is a very important tool in any economic policymaker's toolkit. But how can we measure the benefits and costs to individuals arising from a particular policy or institution? We'll begin by asking a specific question: What value does Mr. Polo, a potential member of an exclusive dining club, place on the right to be a member of the club? More precisely, what is the value to him of the right to buy meals in the club at some specified price p_1?

If we can devise adequate benefit measures for this specific problem, we can then adapt those measures to a range of similar benefit questions. In the context of a proposed rural electrification project, for instance, we could measure the value a farmer places on the right to buy electricity at some specified price. And we can adapt these measures to gauge costs as well as benefits. For example, we could measure the cost to an individual smoker of the now very large excise tax on cigarettes.

We'll make the realistic assumption that "meals at the club" is an inessential good and begin the analysis by identifying Mr. Polo's equilibrium in two circumstances. In the first situation, he is not a member and therefore does not buy meals at the club. In the second situation, he is a club member and can now buy meals at price p_1. In Figure 5.2, x_1 is the number of meals he eats at the club, and x_2 is his expenditure on all other goods. Because in the first situation Mr. Polo is not a member, he spends his entire income $\$M$ on the composite commodity. The initial equilibrium is therefore M units up the vertical axis at E_0 on indifference curve I_0. In the second situation, however, he can buy club meals at price p_1, and his budget line is now the solid line E_0E_1 in Figure 5.2. The subsequent equilibrium is therefore at E_1 on indifference curve I_1. In essence, our problem is to measure the value that Mr. Polo places on the move from indifference curve I_0 to indifference curve I_1. Furthermore, we want to measure this value in dollars or, equivalently, in units of the composite commodity.

Equivalent Variation for a New Good

By taking the subsequent indifference curve I_1 as our point of reference, we get a measure called the **equivalent variation** and labeled EV in Figure 5.2. This measure answers the following question: What is the *variation* in income that is *equivalent* to the right to buy club meals at price p_1? The answer is distance EV in Figure 5.2. Why? Because if Mr. Polo had $\$EV$ of additional income instead of a club membership, he would still be on indifference curve I_1. In other words, that additional income is *equivalent* to the right to buy club meals.

Compensating Variation for a New Good

On the other hand, by taking the initial indifference curve I_0 as our point of reference, we get a measure called the **compensating variation**, labeled CV Figure 5.2. This measure answers the following question: What *variation* in income *compensates* for the right to buy club meals at price p_1? The answer is CV. Why? Because if Mr. Polo had a club membership but his income had been reduced by $\$CV$, he would still be on indifference I_0 at point E_3. In other words, the reduction in income exactly *compensates* for the right to buy club meals.

Another interpretation of CV is useful. Since $\$CV$ exactly compensates for the right to buy meals in the club, it is the *maximum price* that Mr. Polo will pay for meal privileges. Therefore, if he is offered meal privileges for any price less than $\$CV$, he will buy it—and end up on an indifference curve higher than I_0. We'll use this interpretation in Section 5.3 where we consider the demand for consumer capital.

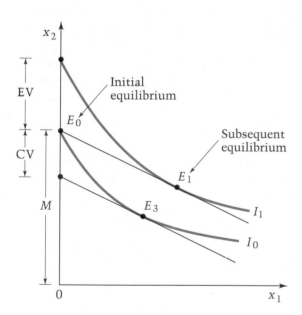

FIGURE 5.2   Measuring economic benefits 1.

Mr. Polo's initial equilibrium, when he is not a club member, is at E_0 on indifference curve I_0. His subsequent equilibrium, when he is a member, is at E_1 on the higher indifference curve I_1. What is the value of club membership to Mr. Polo? The *variation* in income that is *equivalent* to club membership is distance EV since, given that he is not a member, this additional income would put him on indifference curve I_1. The *variation* in income that *compensates* for club membership is distance CV since, given that he is a member, if his income were reduced by CV he would be on indifference curve I_0.

PROBLEM 5.3

Show that as p_1 increases, CV decreases. In other words, show that the larger is p_1, the smaller is the maximum amount a consumer will pay for the right to buy good 1 at price p_1.

So far, we've been focusing on measures of the benefit associated with the introduction of a specific *new good* — access to meals at a private club. These measures are

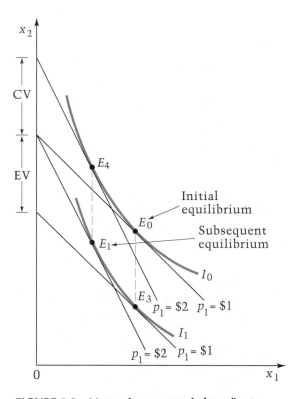

FIGURE 5.3   Measuring economic benefits 2.

The initial equilibrium, associated with the lower price of good 1, is at E_0 on indifference curve I_0. The subsequent equilibrium, associated with the higher price of good 1, is at E_1 on the lower indifference curve I_1. The *variation* in income that is *equivalent* to the price increase is distance EV since, given the lower price, this reduction in income would put the individual on indifference curve I_1. The *variation* in income that *compensates* for the price increase is distance CV since, given the higher price, if income were increased by CV the individual would be on indifference curve I_0.

obviously applicable to other new goods. For example, what value would someone in Flagstaff, Arizona, place on the privilege of being able to listen to a symphony orchestra to be based in Flagstaff? These measures are also applicable to the costs associated with the *disappearance* of goods. For example, what value would a New Yorker place on the loss of the New York Yankees to Dallas, Texas? We could easily adapt these concepts to measure the resulting costs borne by a New York resident as well as the benefits enjoyed by a Dallas resident.

Many interesting policies and institutions, however, involve not the introduction of a new good, but a change in the price of some existing good. For example, every time the government raises the excise tax on cigarettes, a smoker faces a higher price for smoking. Every time your university increases tuition fees, you face a higher price for your education. Let's adapt the equivalent and compensating variations to measure the costs and benefits of such price changes.

Let's begin with a price increase, and again suppose that good 2 is a composite commodity. In Figure 5.3, p_1 is initially \$1 and the initial equilibrium is at E_0 on indifference curve I_0. The price of good 1 then rises to \$2, and the subsequent equilibrium is at E_1 on indifference curve I_1.

Equivalent Variation for a Price Change

To identify the equivalent variation of this price change, we'll use the subsequent indifference curve I_1 as a point of reference and ask: What variation in income is equivalent to the price increases? The answer is distance EV in Figure 5.3. If this consumer has to give up \$EV of income but can still buy good 1 at the initial price of \$1, he or she will remain on indifference curve I_1. In other words, a \$EV decrease in income is equivalent to a price increase from \$1 to \$2.

Compensating Variation for a Price Change

To identify the compensating variation of this price change, we'll use the initial indifference curve I_0 as a point of reference and ask: What variation in income compensates for the price increase? The answer is distance CV in Figure 5.3. Even though the price of good 1 has increased from $1 to $2, if this consumer's income is increased by $CV, he or she will remain on indifference curve I_0 at E_4. In other words, a $CV increase in income compensates for the price increase.

In Problem 5.4, you can find the equivalent and compensating variations for a price decrease. But do keep two things in mind:

1 The indifference curve attained in the subsequent situation is the point of reference for the equivalent variation.

2 The indifference curve attained in the initial situation is the point of reference for the compensating variation.

PROBLEM 5.4

In Figure 5.3, suppose that the initial price is $2 and the subsequent price is $1. The initial equilibrium is therefore at E_1 and the subsequent equilibrium at E_0. What is the equivalent variation of this price reduction? What is the compensating variation?

Comparing Equivalent Variation and Compensating Variation

Are these two measures ever the same? They are the same when the good in question is neither normal nor inferior and the quantity demanded is therefore *independent of income.* (You considered this case in Problem 4.9.) To see why, notice that in Figure 5.3 (but not in Figure 5.2) the vertical distance between the two indifference curves is constant. For example, $E_3 E_0$ is equal to $E_1 E_4$. This reflects the property that MRS depends only on x_1 for the preferences pictured in Figure 5.3. In other words, along any verti-

cal line in this figure, MRS is constant. We therefore know that the quantity demanded of good 1 is independent of income. When quantity demanded of good 1 is independent of income, we say that there are *no income effects.*

Since there are no income effects in Figure 5.3, CV measures the distance between the two indifference curves along one vertical line (through E_1 and E_4), and EV measures the distance between the two indifference curves along another vertical line (through E_3 and E_0). Of course, these distances are identical:

In the no-income-effects case, EV is identical to CV.

Consumer's Surplus[1]

The CV and EV benefit measures share one major drawback: to use either of them, we must know what a consumer's preferences look like. A more practical measure of benefit, known as **consumer's surplus** (CS), can be calculated simply by observing what consumers actually buy and then estimating their demand functions from their consumption behavior.

How can we use CS to measure the value to Mr. Polo of the privilege of buying meals at price p_1 at his private club? Mr. Polo's demand curve for club meals is illustrated in Figure 5.4. At price p_1, the price at which meals are actually sold in the club, Mr. Polo buys six meals per period. Now suppose that we interpret the prices along this demand curve as the value Mr. Polo places on successive meals. He values the first meal at $300, the second at $280, and so on. Notice that even though Mr. Polo values the first meal at $300, he pays only p_1

---

[1] Hicks (1943) provides a thorough graphic analysis of consumer's surplus.

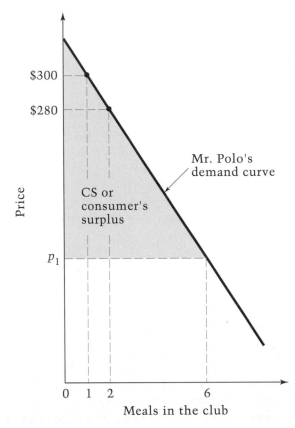

FIGURE 5.4   Consumer's surplus 1.

The consumer's surplus (CS) measure of the benefit of the right to buy good 1 at price p_1, instead of being unable to buy it at any price, is the light green area.

Because the only information needed to calculate CS is an individual's demand curve for the good in question, CS is more practical as a benefit measure. But is it a good measure compared with CV and EV, which have more solid theoretical foundations? Surprisingly:

In the no-income-effects case where the vertical distance between indifference curves is constant,[2]

$$EV = CV = CS$$

When we use the consumer's surplus measure at various points in the following chapters, we'll assume that we are in the no-income-effects case.

PROBLEM 5.5

Suppose that for Ms. J the demand for good 1 is independent of income and is given by the following demand curve:

$$p_1 = 100 - 2x_1$$

What is the benefit to her of a decrease in the price of good 1 from $60 to $40? If good 1 is initially unavailable, what is the benefit to Ms. J if it is subsequently available at

$$p_1 = \$50$$

*5.3   The Demand for Consumer Capital

Let's now turn our attention to the vast array of decisions that people make about buying what is called **consumer capital**: the very significant class of goods valued for the services they yield. We buy beds, chairs, and television sets for what they allow us to do: sit, sleep, and watch TV. We buy refrigerators to get refrigeration, telephones to get

for it. He therefore receives a surplus of ($300 − p_1) on that first meal. His surplus on the second meal is ($280 − p_1), and so on. Mr. Polo's total surplus on the six meals that he actually buys at p_1 — his CS — is therefore the entire light green area in Figure 5.4.

We can also use CS to measure the benefit of a price reduction or the cost of a price increase. In Figure 5.5, for example, the light green area can be interpreted either as the benefit to the consumer of a price reduction from $15 to $10 or as the cost borne by the consumer of a price increase from $10 to $15.

---

[2] Although indifference curves do not always display this very convenient property, Willig (1976) provides a convincing argument that even when they do not, CS remains a useful measure of individual benefit.

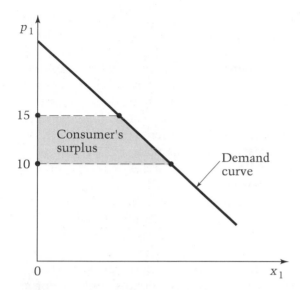

FIGURE 5.5   Consumer's surplus 2.

The consumer's surplus (CS) measure of the benefit of the right to buy good 1 at price $p_1 = \$10$, instead of price $p_1 = \$15$, is the light green area.

telephone service, and personal computers to do word processing and play video games.

Notice that the items themselves have only indirect value. Few of us find a refrigerator intrinsically appealing; we simply use it to keep our meat and milk cold. Some of us are nearly phobic about flying; nevertheless, we still buy plane tickets as a means to an end — say, a holiday in Puerta Vallarta. Consumer capital, then, is valued only indirectly, as a necessary means of producing a valued service or good. Notice, too, that producing a desired service from consumer capital often means buying *complementary*, or interdependent, goods. We buy both cars and gasoline to get transportation; both televisions and electricity to get TV programming; both a printer and computer paper to get computer printouts; and both skis and lift tickets to go skiing.

As economists, our problem is to determine the conditions under which a consumer will decide to buy a particular item of consumer capital. In other words, we want

to analyze the demand for consumer capital.

Imagine being a theorist who is trying to derive the demand for cameras. You begin by noticing two things. First, cameras are items of consumer capital because the buyer values not cameras but photographs. Second, producing photographs involves an interdependency because the photographer must buy both a camera and some film.

Because our potential purchaser, whom we'll call Buff, directly values photographs, but not film or cameras, we'll need to write her utility function as $U(x_1, x_2)$, where x_1 is the quantity of photographs and x_2 is a composite commodity. We'll assume for convenience that one unit of film will produce one photograph. Therefore, the number of photos produced will be equal to the quantity of film, and we can then interpret x_1 as the number of photos *or* the amount of film.

Buff's budget constraint in this consumer-capital framework is novel. It is

$$p_1 x_1 + x_2 = M - n p_c$$

where p_1 is the price of film, x_1 the quantity of film (or photographs), n the number of cameras bought, and p_c the price of a camera. The constraint simply says that expenditure on film and the composite commodity $(p_1 x_1 + x_2)$ is equal to Buff's total income less the expenditure on cameras $(M - n p_c)$.

To further simplify things, let's assume that Buff can produce all the photographs she wants with just one camera and that she can't rent a camera. Then, it's clear that she will buy one camera, or none — that is, n^* will be 0 or 1. Furthermore, if she doesn't buy a camera, she can't produce any photos. Our problem, then, is to figure out when she will buy a camera and how the price of the camera, p_c, and the price of film, p_1, affect her decision making.

In Figure 5.6, we can easily deduce that if Buff doesn't buy a camera, she will end up at point G, with no photos and M units of the composite commodity, since if she has no camera, she won't buy any film. On the

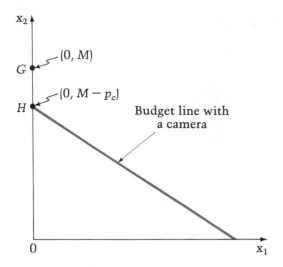

FIGURE 5.6 Consumer capital and the budget line.

If she has no camera, Buff will choose point G. If she has a camera, she will choose a point on the green budget line.

ure 5.7—then the relevant budget constraint $p_1 x_1 + x_2 = M - p_c''$ lies everywhere below the green indifference curve and the consumer decides against buying a camera: that is, $n^* = 0$. But if the price of a camera is not too high—p_c' in Figure 5.7—then the budget constraint $p_1 x_1 + x_2 = M - p_c'$ intersects the green indifference curve and Buff decides to buy a camera. That is, $n^* = 1$. Why? Because Buff prefers any bundle on segment DE to point G.

Let's be more precise about the relationship between the price of and the demand for a camera. Draw a budget line in Figure 5.7 parallel to the existing budget lines and just tangent to the green indifference curve. Use p_c^r to denote the price of a camera defined by this budget line. Of course, p_c^r is equal to the distance from the point at which the budget line you drew intersects the x_2 axis to point G. We know that $n^* = 0$ if the price of a camera is greater than

other hand, if she does buy a camera, she'll choose the bundle on the green budget line that maximizes her utility. These observations reveal the general principle that determines whether she'll buy a camera or not. If Buff's utility at point G is larger than her utility from the utility-maximizing bundle on the green budget line, she will not buy a camera. If it's smaller, she will. Supposing, quite reasonably, that photos are inessential, we can restate this principle:

If the indifference curve through point G lies above the green budget line, she will not buy a camera, but if it intersects the budget line, she will buy one.

Now let's use Figure 5.7 to discover how the camera's price influences Buff's decision. The green indifference curve is pivotal because it passes through point G. If the price of the camera is too high—p_c'' in Fig-

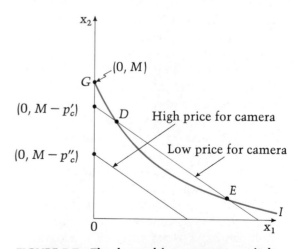

FIGURE 5.7 The demand for consumer capital.

If the price of a camera is low enough, p_c' in the figure, Buff will buy one and end up somewhere on segment DE of the "low price for camera" budget line. If the price of the camera is high enough, p_c'' in the figure, she will buy no camera and will end up at point G on indifference curve I.

p_c^r and that $n^* = 1$ if the camera's price is less than or equal to p_c^r. (We have arbitrarily assumed that when $p_c = p_c^r$, Buff will buy a camera, even though she is actually indifferent between buying or not buying it.) The price p_c^r—clearly the critical one—is termed a **reservation price**. If the price of a camera exceeds Buff's reservation price, she will not buy it. If it is less than or equal to her reservation price, she will buy it.

Because owning a camera effectively confers the privilege of buying photographs at price p_1, p_c^r is the maximum price that Buff is willing to pay for the right to buy photographs at price p_1. In this context, you can then see that the reservation price is just our old friend CV, the compensating variation. That is, p_c^r is the reduction in income that exactly compensates for the privilege of buying photographs at price p_1.

Since p_c^r is simply the consumer's CV, we know from Problem 5.3 that it is inversely related to p_1. In Figure 5.8, the black line RR', which gives the reservation price for the camera associated with any price of film, is therefore downward sloping. If the market prices for film and camera are in the dark green area above this downward-sloping line, Buff will not buy a camera. If prices are below the line in the light green area, she will buy the indirectly valued camera so that she can get the directly valued photographs.

A great many consumer decisions conform to the structure of our camera and photographs problem. Most decisions about consumer durables—items such as VCRs, personal computers, electric crepe makers, water beds, or backpacks—can be interpreted in this framework. Other less obvious consumer choice decisions can also be understood in this way. For example, suppose you're considering a ski holiday in Aspen, Colorado. You can interpret p_c as the cost of airfare to Aspen, p_1 as the price per day of accommodation and lift tickets, and x_1 as the number of days on the mountain.

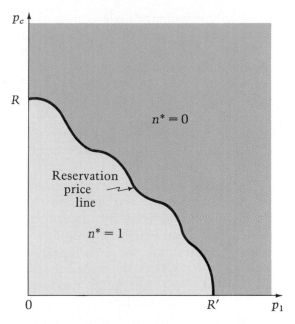

FIGURE 5.8   Reservation prices.

The line RR' gives Buff's reservation price for the camera, given any price p_1 for film. Therefore, for combinations of the price of film p_1 and the price of a camera p_c in the light green area, Buff will buy a camera $(n^* = 1)$; otherwise, she will buy none $(n^* = 0)$.

5.4   Two-Part Tariffs: The Polaroid Corporation's Price Dilemma

Knowing something about the demand for consumer capital should tell us something about the other side of the coin: the pricing policy of firms. In particular, if a firm could exploit the interdependent demand between the complementary items needed to produce a directly valued good, what pricing strategy would it follow? Walter Oi, a pioneer in the study of what are usually called **two-part tariff** questions, was curious about this pricing problem. Specifically, Oi (1971) asked how executives of Disneyland would exploit their monopoly power in setting the price of admission to the park and the prices of each of the amusements inside the gates: "If you were the owner of Disneyland, should you charge high lump-sum admission fees and give the rides away, or should you let people into the amusement park for nothing and stick them with high monopolistic prices for the rides?" (p. 77). Insofar as the Disneyland executives want to extract the largest possible profit in choosing the two sets of tariffs, or prices, involved, they face a fairly tricky pricing problem.

The Polaroid Land Corporation faced a similar pricing dilemma in the 1950s. The introduction of the Polaroid camera gave birth to a new commodity, the "instant photograph." At that time, the corporation had a monopoly on both the camera and the film it used. Because the demand for its camera and its film were so clearly interdependent, the Polaroid Corporation's pricing predicament was closely analogous to the pricing dilemma faced by the owners of Disneyland. Should the corporation attach a high price tag to the camera and essentially give the film away, or should it sell the camera cheaply and charge a high price for the film? Here, the Disneyland entry fee is analogous to the price of the Polaroid camera. We can think of the price of the camera as an entry fee into the world of instant photographs and the price per exposure as analogous to the price per amusement ride.

We can learn a great deal about this pricing problem by adopting three assumptions. The first assumption is quite realistic: instant photographs are inessential. And so is the second: all the photographs desired can be taken with one camera. The third is a *representative-consumer* assumption: Polaroid's potential customers all have preferences and income identical to Buff's in the preceding section. This last assumption allows us to focus on Polaroid's profit from just one consumer, Buff.

Now, what combination of the price of the camera, p_c, and the price of film, p_1, will maximize the profit Polaroid Corporation

can exact from Buff? Specifically, let's suppose that Polaroid's cost of producing a camera is $5 and its cost of producing a unit of film is $1. Polaroid's profit from Buff can then be written in the following way:

$$\text{profit} = x_1^*(p_1 - 1) + n^*(p_c - 5)$$

Here, n^* is Buff's demand for cameras (0 or 1), and x_1^* is her demand for film, given the two prices p_1 and p_c. Because the firm will choose p_1 and p_c so that n^* is 1, we can rewrite the profit function as

$$\text{profit} = x_1^*(p_1 - 1) + (p_c - 5)$$

If we assume for simplicity that Buff's demand for instant photos is independent of her income, we can then solve this profit-maximization problem easily. Buff's demand curve for instant photos is presented in Figure 5.9. Let's start by supposing that Polaroid charges $3 for its film. Given this price, if Buff had a camera, she'd buy 5 units of film. Polaroid's profit on the film would be $10 = 5($3 − $1), or the light green area in Figure 5.9. Given $p_1 = \$3$, Polaroid will clearly decide to price its camera at Buff's reservation price. Yet, from Section 5.2, we know that because Buff's demand for instant photos is independent of her income, her reservation price for the camera is simply the consumer surplus associated with $p_1 = \$3$. If Polaroid decides to sell its film at $3, it will then sell its camera at price p_c^r, represented by the dark green area in Figure 5.9. Its profit will then be equal to the sum of the two shaded areas in Figure 5.9, minus the cost of producing the camera, $5.

But Polaroid can do better than that. As you can easily verify, as long as the price of film exceeds $1 — the cost of producing a unit of film — Polaroid can increase its profit by decreasing the price of its film and correspondingly increasing the price of its camera to reflect Buff's increasing reservation price. When p_1 is equal to $1, Polaroid's profit from its film is zero [15($1 − $1)], but

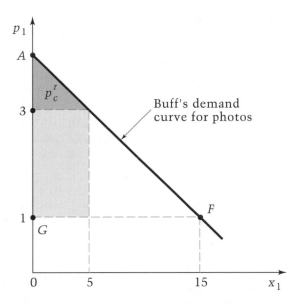

FIGURE 5.9   The Polaroid pricing problem.

If Polaroid sells its film at price $p_1 = \$3$, it will sell its camera at price p_c^r, equal to the dark green area, because Buff's reservation price is identical to her consumer surplus. Polaroid's total profit in this case is the dark green area, plus the light green area, which represents its profit on the sale of film, less $5, the cost of producing the camera. As long as p_1 exceeds $1 (the cost of producing a unit of film), its profit increases as p_1 decreases. To maximize profit, Polaroid should therefore sell film at cost ($p_1 = \$1$) and the camera at a price equal to the triangular area *GAF*.

the profit from its camera is the area of the triangle *GAF* minus $5, the cost of producing the camera. In Problem 5.6, you can show that Polaroid's profit decreases as it lowers the price of film below $1.

The profit-maximizing strategy is therefore to sell film at cost and to charge the corresponding reservation price for the camera.[3]

---

[3] See Schmalensee (1982) for a more complete analysis of this type of pricing problem.

PROBLEM 5.6

Consider any p_1 less than $1, and the associated reservation price for the camera. Show that profit is smaller than it is when Polaroid sells its film at $1 and its camera at area *GAF*.

We now have a positive prediction about Polaroid's profit-maximizing strategy: it will sell its film at cost and will charge the corresponding reservation price for the camera. What was the Polaroid Corporation's actual pricing policy? A Polaroid camera in 1955 cost approximately $1100 in 1990 U.S. dollars — surely an order of magnitude greater than the cost of producing the camera. Because it had a monopoly in selling instant cameras and instant film, Polaroid could exploit the obvious interdependence in the demand for cameras and film. Its dual monopoly position permitted it to extract aggregate profits in excess of the aggregate profits that independent monopolists in film and (separately) in cameras could have managed.

We cannot examine here the robustness of this pricing model with respect to the obviously restrictive assumption that consumers are identical. However, the model does seem to generate some insight into Polaroid's actual pricing behavior. By analogy, we can generalize from the model to illuminate any pricing strategy that conforms to the two-part-tariff pricing structure. For example, using the two-part-tariff model, we can analyze the pricing strategies chosen by the owners of Disneyland; by computer companies selling hardware and software; and by copy-machine companies selling machines and all the fluid, paper, and other paraphernalia that go with them. The telephone company, the cable TV company, and the utilities company all use similar pricing structures: a hook-up fee and a separate fee based on use. (If you've rented an off-campus apartment, you've probably encountered this sort of strategy.) Unlike Polaroid, these firms are regulated and their ability to extract profit is therefore constrained. Nevertheless, they do choose to use two-part tariffs.

Our model may also help to shed light on other pricing phenomena. For example, as we noted in the preceding section, the demand for ski holidays at Aspen and air transport to Colorado are interrelated in precisely the same way as the demand for Polaroid cameras and film. Of course, neither ski resorts nor airlines can independently exploit this interrelationship in demand. Enter travel agencies that sell package deals: their role in economic life seems to be to exploit the profit potential arising from this demand interdependence. You can probably think of other firms that aim at exploiting such demand interdependency.

5.5 Getting and Spending Revisited: The Demand for Leisure and the Supply of Labor

Although we remarked at the outset of Chapter 4 that choosing how to distribute our time among all the available alternatives is a fundamental decision, so far we have omitted time from our formulation of the consumer-choice problem. Let's remedy that oversight by reformulating the choice problem to include the element of time.

Work, Leisure, and Income

One useful way of conceptualizing the problem is to imagine that we choose to divide our time between work and leisure. In a rough way, then, we divide our time between activities that do and don't bring in money. Let T be time available in some period, h be hours of work, and x_1 be hours of leisure. Because the hours of work and at leisure must add up to total time, the **time constraint** (analogous to the budget constraint) is

$$h + x_1 = T$$

How we choose to divide our time between work and leisure obviously determines our work-generated income; that is, the time at work multiplied by the wage rate determines earned income. Here we are assuming (somewhat unrealistically) that an individual — let's call the worker Jan — can choose her hours of work. Letting w be the wage rate at which Jan can sell her labor and assuming that she has A dollars of income from other sources, we can write Jan's income as $A + wh$. We'll assume that Jan spends her income on a composite commodity, x_2. Her choice problem can then be written in the following way:

maximize $U(x_1, x_2)$
  by choice of x_1, x_2, and h

subject to the time constraint
  $h + x_1 = T$

subject to the budget constraint
  $x_2 = A + wh$

Here we are using the composite-commodity theorem to write Jan's preferences over two goods: hours of leisure x_1 and expenditure on all goods x_2.

Notice that there are two constraints in this choice problem — a time constraint and a budget constraint — and three endogenous variables — hours of leisure, expenditure on the composite commodity, and hours of work. To simplify the problem, we can eliminate hours of work h by combining the two constraints. Notice that the first constraint can be rewritten as $h = T - x_1$. Combining this equation with the budget constraint yields $x_2 = A + w(T - x_1)$. In other words, Jan's expenditure on the composite commodity is simply her nonwork income plus her wage rate w multiplied by her hours of work, $T - x_1$. Rearranging this combined constraint, we can rewrite Jan's problem as

maximize $U(x_1, x_2)$
  by choice of x_1 and x_2

subject to the combined constraint
  $wx_1 + x_2 = A + wT$

Now we can interpret w as the price of leisure and $A + wT$ as potential or **full income.** We can think of Jan, then, as spending her full income $(A + wT)$ on leisure and consumption. Notice what we've achieved by combining these constraints: we've turned an apparently complex problem, with three endogenous variables and two constraints, into a relatively simple and familiar form. The solution to this choice problem is illustrated in Figure 5.10. Jan demands x_1^* hours of leisure and spends x_2^* on consumption goods.

Labor Supply

Notice that we have also derived Jan's supply of labor. Because the time she devotes to work and leisure is equal to total time available $(h + x_1 = T)$, her supply of labor is $h^* = T - x_1^*$. This particular view of labor supply will play a central role in analyzing labor markets in Chapter 14.

PROBLEM 5.7

Historically, as wages rates have increased in Western societies, the work week has declined. A hundred years ago in the United States, for instance, the average work week was more than 70 hours. Today it is less than 40. Using the framework just developed, diagram the case in which the quantity of labor supplied decreases as the wage rate increases. In this case, is leisure a normal or an inferior good? This case is sometimes called the *backward-bending supply curve of labor.*

Consumption and the Opportunity Cost of Time

Usually, consumption and leisure are interrelated activities. Leisure activities, for example, often require the expenditure of in-

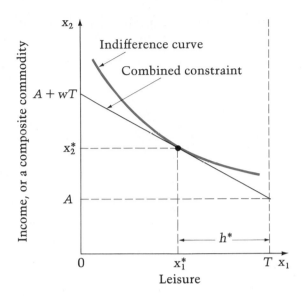

FIGURE 5.10   The demand for leisure and the supply of labor.

Given the combined constraint, which reflects her nonlabor income A and her wage rate w, Jan chooses to work h^* hours. Her income is therefore $A + wh^*$ (or x_2^*) and she enjoys $T - h^*$ (or x_1^*) hours of leisure.

come: green fees for golfing, the cost of specialized equipment for backpacking, or the price of a ticket for a concert. Conversely, consumption requires the expenditure of time: to shop for clothes, see a movie, or buy and use a personal computer. This observation led Gary Becker (1965) to formulate the consumer choice problem in an enlightening way by including in the full price of a good both a time price and a money price.

Time and Money Prices

Let's explore Becker's formulation by briefly considering the case in which consumption requires both time and money. Let p_1 and p_2 be money prices and z_1 and z_2 be time prices for goods 1 and 2. Consuming one unit of good 1, for example, requires p_1 units of money and z_1 units of time. The consumer's choice problem again involves two constraints: the budget constraint,

$$p_1 x_1 + p_2 x_2 = A + wh$$

and the time constraint,

$$z_1 x_1 + z_2 x_2 + h = T$$

Because the consumer's nonwork income is once again A — and total income therefore $A + wh$ — the first constraint is simply the standard budget constraint. Notice, however, that money prices may be zero. Meditating or sleeping may be valued activities, for example, but they cost nothing. The second constraint is the time constraint. Notice that even though money prices may be zero, virtually all time prices are positive because consumption invariably requires some expense of time. Meditating or sleeping do take time. Once again, let's combine the two constraints. From the time constraint, we have

$$h = T - z_1 x_1 - z_2 x_2$$

The time devoted to work is simply the total time available T minus the time devoted to consumption. When we combine this with the budget constraint, we have

$$p_1 x_1 + p_2 x_2 = A + wT - wz_1 x_1 - wz_2 x_2$$

We can rearrange the equation as

$$(p_1 + wz_1)x_1 + (p_2 + wz_2)x_2 = A + wT$$

Again, we can interpret $A + wT$ as potential or full income, and — this is the crucial point — we can interpret $p_1 + wz_1$ as the **full price** of good 1 and $p_2 + wz_1$ as the full price of good 2.

What have we learned? Because consumption takes time, the opportunity cost of that time must be included in the full price of any good. In this model, the opportunity cost of time is the amount required to consume a unit of a good multiplied by the value of time, the wage rate w. We have discovered a simple but very important principle: consumption costs time as well as money. If we are to fully understand consumption decisions, we must take into account the opportunity cost of that time. In the next section, we'll see just how significant a role this insight can play.

---

*5.6 Limited Resources and the "Tragedy of the Commons"

Many interesting economic problems involve the use (and potential overuse) of a limited resource by those who have access to that resource. A limited resource is one that can accommodate only a certain level of use before its utility or value is effectively extinguished. Only so many swimmers can comfortably swim laps in a pool and only so many sun lovers can happily sunbathe on a beach before overcrowding takes all the fun out of these activities. And only so many drivers can converge on Manhattan before gridlock sets in.

Common-Property Problems

Economists often speak of such problems collectively under the label **common-property problems.** They sometimes call the overexploitation of a common-property resource "the tragedy of the commons," after an article of the same name by biologist Garrett Hardin (1968). In this article, Hardin compares the problem of uncontrolled population growth to the historical problem of the overgrazing of the pastures held in common by villagers in colonial New England and in England. Hardin predicted that just as individual farmers continued to add one cow and then another to the commons until the pastureland was devastated by overgrazing, human beings, too, might well produce one child and then another until the resources of the world were completely overtaxed by a population too large to be sustained by the earth's limited capacity.

Hardin mentions several other activities that could result in the tragedy of the commons: the cattle owner's overgrazing on U.S. national forestry lands; the insistence of maritime nations on upholding the freedom of the seas; a New England city council's decision to provide free downtown parking during the Christmas-shopping rush; and the "fouling of our own nest [because we are putting] sewage, or chemical, radioactive, and heat wastes into water: noxious and dangerous fumes into the air: and distracting and unpleasant advertising signs into the line of sight" (p. 1245).

Racquetball and the Tragedy of the Commons

Let's look at a familiar common-property problem. At community centers, private clubs, and universities around the world, racquetball court time is often allocated on a first come, first served basis. Sometimes the scheme works well. At Yale University a few years ago, for example, courts were usually available at any time of the day: court time was not a scarce good.

A problem arises, however, in places where there are lots of ardent racquetball players and limited court space. When we last visited the University of Colorado, for example, we were told to sign up in person sometime after 7 A.M. on Wednesday to reserve a court for Thursday. "Tragically," we actually had to show up considerably before 7 A.M. because a lineup began to form about 6 A.M. At the Jewish Community Center in Vancouver, British Columbia, allocation of court time was a slightly more civilized affair. We could book a court on Thursday by phoning the center after 9 A.M. on Wednesday. Still, to guarantee ourselves a court, we had to start dialing at 9 A.M. in the expectation of getting through by 9:30 A.M. The first come, first served allocation mechanism—whatever form it might take—makes signing up for court time a common-property problem.

First Come, First Served Allocation

What can we learn about the implications of this allocation mechanism by applying the tools we've developed? Let's imagine a situation in which 200 avid players have common access to a racquetball court facility, perhaps because they are students in a particular university. We'll use a representative-player assumption to simplify the analysis—that is, we'll suppose that these players have identical preferences and that they value their time at $10 per hour. To make the problem quite specific, we'll assume that the racquetball facility has the capacity to accept 3000 bookings a month and that the duration of a booking is one hour. The facility can therefore accommodate up to 15 bookings per player per month ($15 \times 200 = 3000$). The value of the time spent playing racquetball by one player is then $10 per booking. Suppose, too, that the players have free access to the courts, in the sense that they need not pay a fee for booking court time.

We'll adapt the approach developed in the preceding section by letting x_1 be the number of bookings the player makes per month and x_2 be the now-familiar composite commodity, and by supposing that nonwork income is zero. If access to the courts really is free, we can write the player's choice problem as

maximize $U(x_1, x_2)$
    by choice of x_1 and x_2

subject to the constraint
    $10x_1 + x_2 = 10T$

Although access may be free, we must account for the value of time spent on the court. Thus, the implicit price of each booking is the value of an hour of time, $10. The constraint then says that the value of the time spent on the court each period, $10x_1$, added to the value of the composite commodity, x_2, must add up to full income, $10T$.

In the solution to this problem, if each player demands a relatively small number of bookings, say 10, then the total number of bookings demanded each month, $2000 = 10 \times 200$, will be less than the facility's capacity, 3000, and everyone can be accommodated without difficulty. But what happens when the demand for court time is greater than the facility's capacity? What happens, for example, when each player demands 20 bookings per month, so that total demand, $4000 = 20 \times 200$, exceeds capacity, 3000?

Excess Demand and Lineups

Just what occurs in this circumstance will be determined by the booking scheme used by our imaginary university. If players must show up in person to book, excess demand implies that lineups will form before the appointed hour. If players must phone for a booking, excess demand implies that they will be forced to spend time on the telephone trying to get through. In this case, the amount of time actually spent on the phone will be random: some will be lucky and get through on the first try; others will be unlucky and spend a significant amount of time dialing.

Under either booking procedure, however, access to bookings is not really free even though the university doesn't charge for the use of its courts. The time required to make a booking—which we can regard as the time price of making a booking—will increase until the excess demand is eliminated; that is, until the total number of bookings demanded is just 3000 or until each player demands exactly 15 bookings per month (since $15 \times 200 = 3000$).

How do we confirm that an equilibrium will be reached when the time price is just large enough that demand for bookings is equal to the fixed supply? We need to look at the individual player's choice problem once the implicit price per booking includes both

the time required to make a booking and the time actually spent on the court. Let q represent the time necessary to make a booking. Then the total time spent per booking is $(1 + q)$, since the game itself takes an hour to play and since it takes q hours to make a booking. The total time price per booking is then $\$10(1 + q)$, and the revised constraint for the player's choice problem is then

$$10(1 + q)x_1 + x_2 = 10T$$

In Figure 5.11, we have illustrated the solution to the player's choice problem when q is large enough that each player demands 15 bookings. The total number of bookings demanded is therefore 3000, and the excess demand has been eliminated. The player's equilibrium is at point A on the in-

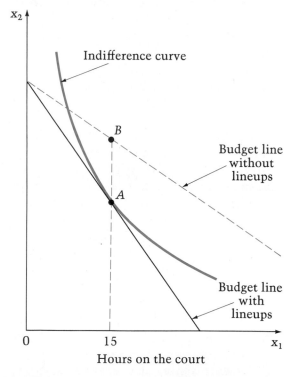

FIGURE 5.11   Racquetball and the tragedy of the commons.

The individual chooses to spend 15 hours on the court and $15q$ hours waiting in line to book courts. The value of time spent in line is distance AB.

difference curve. To identify graphically the value to the individual player of the time spent acquiring a booking, we've also included the constraint that would arise if q were equal to zero—the dashed line in Figure 5.11. The value of the time spent in the lineup each month is then the distance AB.

Institutional Mechanisms for Allocation

Notice that when there is excess demand, it is time in the lineup that discourages players from attempting to use the facility so frequently and thereby establishes an equilibrium between demand and supply. Yet, as we know from the foregoing section, time is a valuable resource. The "tragedy" of spending time in the lineup needlessly uses up this valuable resource. That is, spending time to acquire bookings is avoidable. It is the consequence of using a first come, first served institution for allocating bookings.

Can we think of other institutional arrangements that are clearly superior? Yes. Imagine substituting a money price for the time price. Specifically, suppose that the university charged a dollar price equal to $10q$ for each booking. Then the player's constraint would still be $10(1 + q)x_1 + x_2 = 10T$—since we've just substituted for a time price an equivalent money price—and the player's equilibrium would still be at point A in Figure 5.11. Note that there would then be no excess demand for bookings since each player again demands 15 per month. Thus, this price institution produces an equilibrium in which the player is just as well off, and it completely avoids the waste of time that occurs with the first-come, first served institution.

With this price institution, the time resources that would have been spent in lineups have instead been spent working, and the income generated by this work has been transferred to the university as court fees. Under one institutional arrangement,

the university could earmark those revenues for acquiring more recreational facilities. Even if the university chose to put the revenues into its general fund, resources would not be needlessly used up in lineup time.

Alternatively, let's imagine that the racquetball players at this university are a cooperative and resourceful group. They could collectively design a system that would allow each of them to attain the more desirable point B in Figure 5.11. For instance, one very simple mechanism would be to issue individual players the right of access to 15 bookings. Each player gets the same number of bookings as under a first come, first served arrangement and avoids the time price involved in the queuing system.

The point of this exercise is to show that free access is not really free when we consider the time price of access. Relative to a price mechanism, a first come, first served institution substitutes time prices for money prices. The "tragedy" is that the time price is a real resource cost: the lineup time of individuals is needlessly wasted.

Although lineups may not be a significant problem in your own life, in countries such as the Soviet Union, where the price mechanism is not used to allocate consumer goods, they are a pervasive feature of economic life. Historically, the excess demand for consumer goods at state-administered prices has resulted in a colossal amount of time spent lining up to buy scarce products. In fact, in many Soviet families, the full-time "job" of the retired members is to stand in lines to buy household goods.

*5.7 Index Numbers

We are continually bombarded by index numbers. We may be told, for example, that in the third quarter of some year, real disposable income grew at x% per year or that the consumer price index has increased at $y\%$ per year. The first statement is about a **quantity index**—an indicator of the amount of real disposable income available to consumers. Ordinarily, an increase in real disposable income is interpreted as an increase in the average consumer's economic welfare, since he or she can buy more. The second statement is about a **price index**—an indicator of the price level that consumers face in the marketplace. If a consumer's income is unchanged, then an increase in the consumer price index is ordinarily interpreted as a decline in the average consumer's economic welfare, since he or she can buy less with the same income.

In this section, we'll see precisely what quantity and price indexes are, and we'll learn two important things about them. First, given the same data, two different quantity (or price) indexes can send different qualitative messages—for example, that disposable income (or the price level) is both increasing and decreasing. Second, when two different indexes do send different messages, it may be impossible to determine which message is correct. The setting we'll use to develop an understanding of index numbers is deceptively simple, but the understanding itself is profound.

Let's begin by imagining that we can observe the consumption decisions of an individual, Norm, in two different periods. Let's also assume that Norm's preferences are identical in both periods.[4] A natural

question then presents itself: In which period was Norm better off? If we can answer this question, a second question then arises: By how much was he better off?

Quantity Indexes

There can be no direct answer to the second question. Even if we knew Norm's utility function, we couldn't say how much better off he was in one period than another, because a direct answer requires cardinal information. As we indicated in Chapter 3, a utility function contains only ordinal information. Nevertheless, we may be able to use the information at hand to construct an indirect answer: a *quantity index* that will give us some indication of how the aggregate quantity of the goods Norm consumed has changed from period to period.

Analogous questions arise at the macroeconomic level. Were U.S. citizens better off in 1990 than in 1989? If so, by how much was the average person better off? If we again adopt the assumption of a representative consumer, we can reinterpret this microeconomic exercise—which focuses on one person, Norm—in a macroeconomic context. If we assume that the economy is composed of individuals with preferences identical to Norm's, we can then interpret the indexes discussed below as indexes of real national income per capita.

We can see the sorts of problems that arise with any index number by using the two-good case. The notation is necessarily a little clumsy: subscripts denote goods, and superscripts denote time periods. Thus, in period 0, Norm buys the bundle $B^0 = (x_1^0, x_2^0)$ at prices (p_1^0, p_2^0). From these quantities and prices, we can compute his income in period 0: $M^0 = p_1^0 x_1^0 + p_2^0 x_2^0$. In period 1, he buys the bundle $B^1 = (x_1^1, x_2^1)$ at prices (p_1^1, p_2^1), and his income is $M^1 = p_1^1 x_1^1 + p_2^1 x_2^1$.

If this information on prices and quantities is available, it obviously reveals something about Norm's preferences and there-

---

[4] We can be more precise about the assumption that Norm's preferences are identical in the two periods. His utility function has four arguments—$x_1^0, x_2^0, x_1^1, x_2^1$—because a good today and the same good tomorrow must be regarded as different goods. We are assuming, then, that Norm's utility function can be written in the following way:

$$U(x_1^0, x_2^0, x_1^1, x_2^1) = U'(x_1^0, x_2^0) + U'(x_1^1, x_2^1)$$

The function $U'(x_1, x_2)$ is then Norm's utility function in each period.

fore something about his well-being. But exactly what does it tell us? The first step is to answer the following question: In what circumstances can we infer that either B^0 is preferred to B^1 or that B^1 is preferred to B^0? If we can infer that one or the other of these statements is true, we can develop a quantity index indicating the extent to which aggregate quantity consumed in one period exceeds aggregate quantity consumed in the other.

Let's begin by looking at the case in which Norm is definitely better off in period 1. Suppose that B^0 is inside Norm's period-1 budget constraint, as in Figure 5.12. That is, suppose that

$$p_1^1 x_1^0 + p_2^1 x_2^0 < p_1^1 x_1^1 + p_2^1 x_2^1 \qquad (= M^1)$$

The left-hand side of this inequality is the expenditure required to buy B^0 at period-1 prices, and the right-hand side is Norm's ac-

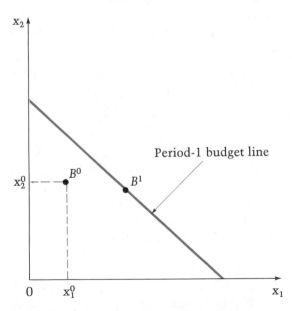

x_2

x_2^0 — — B^0 B^1

Period-1 budget line

0   x_1^0 x_1

FIGURE 5.12   The Paasche quantity index.

Norm bought bundle B^0 in period 0 and B^1 in period 1. He could have bought bundle B^0 in period 1 since it lies below the period-1 budget line. Therefore, B^1 is preferred to B^0. In other words, if the Paasche quantity index P exceeds 1, then B^1 is preferred to B^0.

tual expenditure in period 1. Because bundle B^1 is revealed by Norm's choice to be the utility-maximizing bundle in period 1 and because bundle B^0 is attainable in period 1, we infer that B^1 is preferred to B^0:

If $p_1^1 x_1^0 + p_2^1 x_2^0 < p_1^1 x_1^1 + p_2^1 x_2^1 \ (= M^1)$, then B^1 is preferred to B^0.

The inequality that allows us to make this inference suggests a quantity index known as a **Paasche quantity index.** If we divide Norm's actual expenditure in period 1 by the expenditure required to buy B^0 in period 1, we have an index of the extent to which Norm's aggregate consumption in period 1 exceeds his aggregate consumption in period 0:

DEFINITION

$$P = \frac{p_1^1 x_1^1 + p_2^1 x_2^1}{p_1^1 x_1^0 + p_2^1 x_2^0}$$

We can then restate the proposition above:

If the Paasche quantity index exceeds 1, then B^1 is preferred to B^0.

As we'll see, if this index is less than 1, we can't be sure that Norm is worse off in period 1. As a result, this quantity index is not always an accurate indicator of Norm's well-being.

Notice that the Paasche quantity index uses period-1 prices for aggregating quantities in both periods. By substituting period-0 prices for aggregating quantities in both periods, we have another quantity index, known as the **Laspeyres quantity index:**

DEFINITION

$$L = \frac{p_1^0 x_1^1 + p_2^0 x_2^1}{p_1^0 x_1^0 + p_2^0 x_2^0}$$

By simply reversing the argument of the previous paragraph, we can restate the proposition:

If the Laspeyres quantity index is less than 1, then B^0 is preferred to B^1.

In other words, if L is less than 1, Norm was better off in period 0 because he could have bought B^1 in period 0 but chose instead to buy B^0.

As you'll discover in the following problem, P can be less than 1 and L greater than 1 at the same time. In this case, which is illustrated in Figure 5.13, the two indexes send conflicting messages. P indicates that Norm's consumption has fallen and L that it has risen. Furthermore, neither of these two propositions is applicable, and without more information on Norm's preferences, we can't know in which period Norm was better off.

PROBLEM 5.8

Given the information in Figure 5.13, show that P is less than 1 and that L is greater than 1. In addition, draw one indifference map in Figure 5.13 such that B^1 is preferred to B^0 and another such B^0 is preferred to B^1.

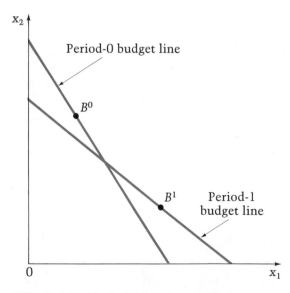

FIGURE 5.13 An index-number puzzle.

For the case illustrated, P is less than 1 and L is greater than 1, and it is impossible to tell in which period Norm was better off.

Price Indexes

In the preceding section, we used fixed sets of prices (period-0 prices or period-1 prices) to define two quantity indexes. In this section, we'll reverse the procedure and use fixed sets of quantities to define *price indexes*. Price indexes are supposed to measure the extent to which the *price level* — as opposed to the prices of individual goods — changes from one period to another. We'll discover that the commonly used price indexes, like the commonly used quantity indexes, are not entirely satisfactory.

The Paasche price index, denoted by P', uses period-1 quantities:

DEFINITION

$$P' = \frac{p_1^1 x_1^1 + p_2^1 x_2^1}{p_1^0 x_1^1 + p_2^0 x_2^1}$$

If P' is 2, for example, it takes twice as many dollars to buy B^1 at period-1 prices than at period-0 prices.

The Laspeyres price index, denoted by L', uses period-0 quantities:

DEFINITION

$$L' = \frac{p_1^1 x_1^0 + p_2^1 x_2^0}{p_1^0 x_1^0 + p_2^0 x_2^0}$$

If L' is 2, for instance, it would cost twice as much to buy B^0 at period-1 prices than at period-0 prices.

We can use these price indices in combination with information about Norm's relative money income in the two periods to restate the conditions under which we know for certain that Norm is better off in one period than in the other. The case in which Norm has the same income in both periods is an interesting point of reference: when L' is less than 1, then P' is also less than 1, and Norm is better off in period 1; when P' is greater than 1, then L' is also greater than 1, and Norm is better off in period 0. The difficulty is that the situation is not always so clear-cut. It's entirely possible that L' is greater than 1 and, at the same time, that P' is less than 1. When this happens, the two indices convey different messages. L' indicates that the price level has risen and P' that it has fallen. Which message is correct? There is no way of knowing, given only the information we have. Price indexes, like quantity indexes, are not always what they appear to be.

PROBLEM 5.9

In period 0, $p_1 = \$4$ and $p_2 = \$3$, and Norm bought the bundle (15, 20). In period 1, $p_1 = \$5$ and $p_2 = \$2$, and Norm bought the bundle (10, 35). Compute the two quantity indexes and the two price indexes. In which period was Norm better off?

5.8 Intertemporal Choice and Present Value

In answering the questions about Mr. Lucky and his cousin at the end of Chapter 4, you discovered that interest rates play a fundamental role in intertemporal choice problems. In this section, we'll generalize some of your results and introduce some other choice problems. We'll adopt two simplifying assumptions: that individuals can both borrow and invest at a single, or common, interest rate i, and that this interest rate does not change from period to period. An interest rate of 10% is written as $i = .1$, an interest rate of 50% as $i = .5$, and so on. For instance, think of i as the rate at which you can borrow money from your bank and the rate you'll receive on money deposited in your savings account.

Suppose that you deposit $1 in your savings account. At the end of one period, your balance will be the original dollar plus interest i on that dollar, or $1 + i$. At the end of two periods, it will be

$$(1 + i)^2 = (1 + i) + i(1 + i)$$

The first expression on the right, $(1 + i)$, is the balance at the end of the first period, and the second expression, $i(1 + i)$, is the interest earned in the second period. As you can easily verify, at the end of t periods, the balance will be $(1 + i)^t$. Similarly, if you borrow $1 today, promising to repay the original dollar plus interest in t periods, you'll have to repay $(1 + i)^t$ dollars.

In other words, $1 today is equivalent to $(1 + i)^t$ dollars in t periods. Or, to put it the other way around, the value today of $1 payable in t periods—called the **present value** of $1 received t periods in the future—is $1/(1 + i)^t$. Why? If you deposited this amount today, you would have a $1 balance in t periods. Alternatively, if you borrowed this amount today, you would have to repay $1 in t periods.

Mortgages

Let's consider the present value of D dollars in each of t periods: D dollars at the end of period 1, period 2, period 3, and so on. The present value of this stream of dollars, PV, is

DEFINITION

$$\mathbf{PV} = \frac{D}{1+i} + \frac{D}{(1+i)^2} + \cdots + \frac{D}{(1+i)^t}$$

This present-value expression, which should be familiar to any home buyer unlucky enough to have taken out a mortgage, gives the present value in today's dollars of D dollars payable at the end of each of the next t periods. If PV is the amount the homeowner borrows and if t is the term of the mortgage, then D is the amount that the buyer must pay the mortgage company in each period. For example, using the present-value formula to calculate the yearly payment on a 3-year mortgage of $1000, we find that if $i = .05$, then the yearly payment will be $367.21; if $i = .10$, it will be $402.11; and if $i = .30$, it will be $550.63.

Bonds

The present-value expression also plays an important role in the bond market. To borrow money from the public, firms sell **bonds.** These are just pieces of paper that promise to pay the bondholder a fixed sum of money in each of a fixed number of periods. If the promise is to pay D at the end of each period for t periods, then

$$PV = \frac{D}{1+i} + \frac{D}{(1+i)^2} + \cdots + \frac{D}{(1+i)^t}$$

will be the price of a bond (assuming, of course, that the firm's promise to pay is believed with certainty). To understand this result, suppose first that the price was higher than PV. In this case, everyone prefers to deposit money in a savings account at interest rate i to buying the bond, because the same stream of payments (D at the end of each of t periods) can be generated by investing the smaller sum PV. In other words, $D/(1+i)$ deposited for one period will generate D dollars at the end of period 1, $D/(1+i)^2$ deposited for two periods will generate D dollars at the end of period 2, . . . , and $D/(1+i)^t$ deposited for t periods will generate D dollars at the end of period t. On the other hand, if the price of a bond is lower than PV, everyone now prefers buying the bond to depositing money at interest rate i. The price of a bond is therefore the *present value of the stream of payments.*

PROBLEM 5.10

Use the present-value expression to calculate the price of a bond that pays $100 at the end of years 1, 2, and 3: when $i = .05$; when $i = .1$; when $i = .3$.

Present Value with an Infinite Horizon

Because one special case of the present-value formula is simple, it deserves particular attention: the present value of D dollars in every future period. In this case,

$$PV = \frac{D}{1+i} + \frac{D}{(1+i)^2} + \frac{D}{(1+i)^3} + \cdots$$

Factoring out $1/(1+i)$, we have

$$PV = \frac{1}{1+i}\left[D + \frac{D}{1+i} + \frac{D}{(1+i)^2} + \frac{D}{(1+i)^3} + \cdots\right]$$

Combining these two expressions, we have

$$PV = \frac{1}{1+i}\left(D + PV\right)$$

Finally, we can solve for PV to get

$$PV = \frac{D}{i}$$

A bond that pays a fixed sum in every future period is called a *consol.* From the last expression above, we can see that the price of a consol is simply the fixed payment per period divided by the interest rate, or D/i. The higher the interest rate, the lower the price of such a consol.

Intertemporal Choice

Present values play a central role in intertemporal choice making. To see just what that role is, let's consider a relatively simple choice problem. Sarah is given the choice between two inheritance bundles. The first bundle offers her a combination of I_1 now and J_1 at the end of period 1 (or the beginning of period 2), and the second bundle offers a combination of I_2 now and J_2 at the end of period 1. She has no other income and she wants to spend all her money in these two periods. Which inheritance bundle should she choose? The key to the answer lies in the budget lines associated with the two inheritance bundles. Let x_1 and x_2 be two composite commodities: expenditure on consumption this period and expenditure on consumption next period. These budget lines satisfy the following equation:

present value of expenditures
  = present value of inheritance bundle

If Sarah chooses the first inheritance bundle, her budget line will be

$$x_1 + \frac{x_2}{1+i} = I_1 + \frac{J_1}{1+i}$$

Similarly, if she chooses the second inheritance bundle, her budget line will be

$$x_1 + \frac{x_2}{1+i} = I_2 + \frac{J_2}{1+i}$$

In (x_1, x_2) space, the two budget lines are parallel, and the right side of each budget line is the present value of the inheritance bundle. Sarah will therefore choose the inheritance bundle that offers the larger present value.

Notice that because Sarah can borrow and invest at a common rate of interest, we can determine which inheritance bundle she will choose without reference to her utility function $U(x_1, x_2)$. She simply picks the inheritance bundle associated with the larger present value.

Unless she can borrow and lend at a common rate of interest, however, we cannot determine which inheritance bundle she will choose without reference to her utility function. To see why, let's suppose that the interest rate at which she can borrow, i', is greater than the interest rate she earns on her savings, i''. The budget constraint implied by the first inheritance bundle—I_1 now and J_1 at the end of period 1—is described by the solid line in Figure 5.14. Notice that it is composed of two segments. If $x_1 < I_1$, her budget constraint can be written as

$$x_1 + \frac{x_2}{1+i''} = I_1 + \frac{J_1}{1+i''}$$

because in this case she is earning interest at rate i'' on $I_1 - x_1$: the portion of I_1 that she does not spend in the first period. On the

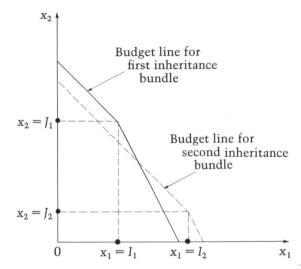

FIGURE 5.14 Choosing an inheritance bundle.
Sarah must choose between two inheritance bundles. In one inheritance bundle, she gets I_1 now and J_1 at the end of one period; in the other bundle, she gets I_2 now and J_2 at the end of one period. Because the rate of interest at which she can borrow, i', exceeds the rate she earns on her savings, i''', the budget lines are kinked. Consequently, we need her utility function to determine which inheritance bundle she will choose.

other hand, if $x_1 > I_1$, her budget constraint can be written as

$$x_1 + \frac{x_2}{1+i'} = I_1 + \frac{J_1}{1+i'}$$

because in this case she is borrowing $x_1 - I_1$ at interest rate i'.

Now, suppose that $I_1 < I_2$ and $J_1 > J_2$, so that she has a nontrivial choice problem. The implied budget line associated with the second inheritance bundle—I_2 now and J_2 at the end of period 1—is then the dashed line in Figure 5.14. You can see from Figure 5.14 that to determine which inheritance bundle Sarah will choose, we need to know her utility function. Roughly speaking, if she has a strong preference for consumption today relative to consumption tomorrow, she'll pick the second inheritance bundle; if she has a strong preference for consumption tomorrow relative to consumption today, she'll pick the first.

As this exercise reveals, the analysis of intertemporal choice problems is enormously simplified by assuming that the two rates of interest are identical. We'll be using the assumption of an identical, or a common, interest rate — sometimes called the *perfect capital markets assumption* — at various points in the book.

tive consumer. We simplified the real diversity of individual tastes and incomes to those of a representative individual and then analyzed only this person's choice problem. This abstraction is an extremely useful one, as long as we recognize the need to reintroduce diversity when confronting real situations. The most general conclusion we can draw is that these tools can yield insights into a wide range of economic problems from everyday experience: they help us to do vicarious problem solving.

Summary

In this chapter, we wanted to see just how widely applicable the tools of Chapter 4 would prove to be. We also extended the theory of self-interest to include time prices as well as money prices. And we looked at how to construct index numbers and at intertemporal choice and present value. We can draw two important general lessons from the wide-ranging economic problems explored in this chapter.

First, the presence of a nonzero substitution effect is the crucial factor in a broad range of interesting theoretical problems in economics. For instance, in the absence of a substitution effect, we saw that taxpayers would be indifferent between a lump-sum tax and an excise tax that produced the same tax revenue. Similarly, it is easy to show that in the absence of a substitution effect, private club members would not care which of two arrangements they used to cover their overhead costs. As you'll discover in Exercise 13, it is also true that the economic puzzles associated with constructing index numbers are generated by a nonzero substitution effect. The presence of a nonzero substitution effect, then, influences in a crucial way the results in these applications.

Second, we were able to reduce very complex problems to manageable ones by employing the useful fiction of a representa-

Exercises

1 The government wants to raise $50 a month from Joe Blow. A $1 sales tax per package of cigarettes will raise the required revenue, as will a lump-sum tax of $50 per month. Which tax would Joe prefer? Will he smoke more cigarettes under the sales tax or the lump-sum tax?

2 Suppose that the government has decided to transfer income to some individual. Draw a graph analogous to Figure 5.1 and compare the implications of a program that subsidizes the consumption of some good — food or shelter, for example — with the implications of a lump-sum transfer of cash.
   a Show that if the two programs involve an equal expenditure of public revenues, the recipient will never prefer the first scheme.
   b Supposing that the two programs involve an equal expenditure of public revenues, illustrate the case in which the individual would be indifferent between them.

3 The 50 students in Dunnell's Boardinghouse have formed a club to buy a coffee vending machine that costs $500. They currently pay $0.75 per cup at the café next door, and figure that coffee from the machine will cost them just $0.25 per cup. The problem is that no one except Jane has $10 to pay his or her share of the $500. Jane has agreed to either (1) lend each of the other students $10, in which case they can get coffee at $0.25 per cup immediately, or (2) buy the machine herself and charge $0.75 per cup until she

recovers the $490. Only then will the price drop to $0.25 per cup. Which option would you recommend to these students?

4 Buff recently bought a camera that produces instant photographs. The film costs $2 per exposure. A new camera model on the market is identical to Buff's camera in every way but one: the film for the new model costs only $1 per exposure. Let p'_c denote the price of the new model and p''_c the price at which Buff could sell her camera.
   a Use a graphic argument based on indifference curves to determine the price differential $p'_c - p''_c$ at which Buff will be indifferent between keeping the camera and selling it so that she can buy the new model.
   b Now suppose that her demand for instant photographs is independent of her income, and use a graphic argument based on her demand curve to determine the same price differential.

5 Jay's income elasticity of demand for garlic is zero, and his demand curve for garlic is

$$p = 150 - 2x_1$$

   a What is the maximum sum that Jay will pay in order to have 50 units of garlic rather than none?
   b If he currently can't buy garlic at any price, what is the maximum amount that he will pay for the opportunity to buy it at a price of $30 per unit?
   c What is the maximum amount that he is willing to pay for the opportunity to buy garlic at a price of $10 rather than $30 per unit?

6 Each of the 100 kids in Ess Cee has the following demand for rides on Walt's Magic Merry-Go-Round:

$$p = 10 - x$$

where x is the number of rides per week and p is the price per ride. Demand is independent of income. What is magical about Walt's Merry-Go-Round is that it costs nothing to run and has unlimited capacity. What two-part tariff maximizes Walt's profit? How much profit does Walt earn? How many rides does each kid take in a week?

7 Unions commonly bargain for a basic wage rate w and an overtime rate. Assume that the overtime rate is $1.5w$ and that it is paid for hours worked in excess of 40 per week.
   a Construct the relevant budget line between leisure and a composite commodity.
   b Assuming that the union member would choose to work 40 hours per week at wage rate w, will he or she want to work overtime?
   c Assuming that members are contractually obligated to work at least 40 hours per week, illustrate the conditions under which the union member would prefer no overtime work?

8 Ralph currently has two jobs. His primary job pays well, $20 per hour, but he can work only 40 hours per week at it. His secondary job pays only $15 per hour, but he can work as few or as many hours as he wants. For Ralph, leisure is a normal good. If the wage rate for his primary job increases to $22 per hour, will Ralph increase or decrease the number of hours he works in the secondary job?

9 Helga currently gets a $1000 weekly investment income, and she works 10 hours each week at $50 an hour, thereby earning an additional $500. Leisure is neither an inferior nor a normal good for Helga. If offered the choice between a 10% increase in her investment income and a 20% increase in her hourly wage rate, which would Helga choose? Assume that she is free to choose her hours of work.

10 At many universities, students are admitted free to football and basketball games. Because seating is on a first come, first served basis—and because the number of good seats is usually limited—the good seats are often taken 1 to 2 hours before game time. What would happen if more good seats were made available to students? If the average quality of the seats in the student section were improved? Can you devise a better institution for allocating seats to students?

11 Buford buys consumption bundle (4, 8) when the prices of good 1 and good 2 are both $1 and buys bundle (8, 2) when the

price of good 1 is $1 and the price of good 2 is $2. Is it possible to infer from this information which of the two bundles Buford prefers?

12 Howard's income was $10,500 in both periods 0 and 1. For which of the following three cases was Howard better off in period 1? For which was he worse off in period 1? For which cases are you uncertain? (1) Both P' and L' exceed 1. (2) Both P' and L' are less than 1. (3) L' exceeds 1 and P' is less than 1. Construct a diagram consistent with case (1) in which you indicate Howard's budget line and consumption bundle for both periods. Do the same for case (3).

13 When we used Norm's consumption decisions to develop quantity indexes for him, we supposed that we knew nothing about his preferences. Suppose now that his preferences in both periods are captured by the following perfect-complements utility function:

$$U(x_1, x_2) = \min(x_1, x_2)$$

Supposing that Norm always chooses the utility-maximizing bundle, show that (1) if one quantity index is less than 1, then so is the other; (2) if one quantity index is greater than 1, then so is the other; and (3) if one quantity index is equal to 1, then so is the other. Explain these curious results. Hint: Ask yourself why the situation pictured in Figure 5.13 cannot arise with this utility function.

14 Howard can borrow against future income at a 10% rate of interest and he can earn 10% on his savings. His rich uncle has given him the choice between $50,000 now or $72,000 in 4 years. If he put it all in his savings account, how much would the original $50,000 be worth in four years? What is the present value of the $70,000? Which option should Howard choose?

15 A certain plot of agricultural land is scheduled to be developed into a shopping mall in 3 years. The developer who now owns the land is no farmer; however, she knows that if the land is farmed, it will generate $100,000 in revenue per year and that any farmer's costs are only $75,000 per year. She has

therefore decided to sell the right to farm the land for the next 3 years.
a If the interest rate is 10%, what price should she ask? If it's 20%?
b Suppose that the interest rate that farmers can earn on their savings is less than the rate they must pay to borrow money. Show that the opportunity to farm this land is more valuable to a farmer with lots of money in the bank than to one with very little.

*16 Let's generalize the basic insight regarding lump-sum versus excise taxes. Suppose that Laura's indifference curves are smooth and convex and that both good 1 and good 2 are essential. Consider her choice between (1) a system of excise taxes, composed of separate excise taxes t_1 and t_2 on goods 1 and 2, or (2) a lump-sum tax, and suppose that both raise equal tax revenue.
a Show that she is never better off with the system of excise taxes.
b When will she be indifferent to the two tax regimes?
c How would your answer to part b change if her indifference curves were not smooth?
d How would your answer to part b change if good 1 were inessential?

*17 I buy gasoline only when my tank is virtually empty, and I always fill it up because it takes 10 minutes of my valuable time to buy 5 gallons, 10 gallons, or the full 20 gallons. Show that my behavior is utility-maximizing. Hint: Using Becker's full-income apparatus, consider my budget lines between gasoline and a composite commodity when I buy 5 gallons at a time, 10 gallons at a time, 20 gallons at a time.

*18 An economist decided to take the train rather than an airplane from California to a convention in Colorado. Even though the train fare was about half the airfare, most other travelers chose to fly. What factors bear on their choice of transportation? Suppose that travelers place no value on the experience of traveling by rail or by air. Develop a model that determines which passengers go by train and which by plane.

*19 The recently abandoned 55-mph speed limit in the United States was imposed to reduce the nation's fuel consumption. Because most automobiles get better gas mileage at 55 mph than at higher speeds, the idea behind the legislation was that the lower speed limit would reduce gas consumption even if drivers didn't reduce the number of miles they drove. Yet the lower speed limit actually tends to reduce the number of miles driven as well. Explain why. Is this a sensible way to reduce fuel consumption? Hint: Suppose first that all consumers have identical preferences, identical nonwage incomes, and identical wage rates, and find a better institution for achieving a specified reduction in fuel consumption. What considerations arise when you drop the representative-consumer assumption?

References

Becker, G. (1965), "A Theory of the Allocation of Time," *The Economic Journal,* **75**:493–517.

Hardin, G. (1968), "The Tragedy of the Commons," *Science* (Dec):1243–1248.

Hicks, J. R. (1943), "The Four Consumer's Surpluses," *Review of Economic Studies,*" **11**:31–41.

Oi, W. (1971), "A Disneyland Dilemma: Two-Part Tariffs for a Mickey Mouse Monopoly," *Quarterly Journal of Economics* **85**:77–96.

Schelling, T. (1978), *Micromotives and Macrobehavior,* New York: W. W. Norton.

Schmalensee, R. (1982), "Monopolistic Two-Part Pricing Arrangements," *Bell Journal of Economics,* **85**:77–76.

Willig, R. (1976), "Consumer's Surplus Without Apology," *American Economic Review,* **66**:589–97.

*6

Choice Making Under Imperfect Information

So far, we have assumed that individual economic actors are *perfectly informed:* that is, that they know the outcome of any economic decision they make. Yet, for most of us, the outcomes of everyday decision making are risky, or *probabilistic,* rather than riskless or certain. Every time I drop two quarters into a vending machine to buy some gum, for example, there is at least some probability that I'll walk away empty-handed and 50 cents poorer; some other probability that I'll get both the gum and my 50 cents back; and some third, larger, probability that I'll get the gum but not the 50 cents. Indeed, a whole class of economic choice questions — including problems in gambling, insurance, occupational choice, speculation, and the internal organization of firms — cannot be treated in our initial theory of consumer choice making.

In this chapter, we'll relax the assumption of perfect information and extend our theory to include risky decisions. We'll reconstruct the theory so that all possible risky choices can be compared with one another and with all possible riskless choices. How can we begin? Using the methodology set out in Chapter 1, we'll select a familiar situation with a risky outcome — a TV game show. We'll look for an initial hypothesis that explains our observations, then restructure the hypothesis into a rigorous model, and finally apply the model to a range of risky situations to see how useful and widely applicable it actually is.

6.1 The Expected-Utility Hypothesis

Imagine a TV game show in which a certain player — say, Chauncey — is given the choice between walking away with a fixed sum of money A or staking it on a game, Risk. If Chauncey decides to play Risk, the game show host will toss a coin. If a head appears, Chauncey wins $2; if a tail appears, he wins nothing. What principles govern Chauncey's choice in this situation? If we can answer this question, we'll have learned something about the principles governing human behavior in general under risky circumstances.

We have purposely focused on the apparently trivial case of a simple game of chance because we all understand precisely what is going on in games such as these. Once we analyze choice making in this elementary environment, we can consider applications of the theory in the more complicated environment of the real world.

Whether Chauncey chooses to take *A* or to play Risk clearly depends on just how large *A* is. We can think of *A* as the *opportunity cost* of playing Risk. Our problem, then, is to derive Chauncey's demand function for Risk. We can describe this demand function completely by a *reservation price R:* if *A* is less than or equal to *R* (if the opportunity cost of Risk is not too high), Chauncey will play; if *A* exceeds *R* (if the opportunity cost of Risk is too high), he'll take *A*.

Clearly, Chauncey's reservation price *R* will satisfy $0 < R < 2$. If *A* exceeds $2, he'll take *A*, because the best possible outcome if he plays is that he'll win $2, and the probability is 1/2 that he'll win nothing. On the other hand, if *A* is zero—and if Chauncey has no scruples about gambling—he'll play because he loses nothing by playing, and the probability is 1/2 that he'll win $2.

Calculating Expected (Monetary) Value

Chauncey's reservation price thus satisfies $0 < R < 2$. How can we pin down that reservation price? We might calculate for Chauncey the expected (monetary) value of the payoffs to Risk. An **expected (monetary) value** is simply a weighted average of the payoffs to the possible outcomes, where the weights are the probabilities of occurrence assigned to each of those possible payoffs. Because in Risk the probability of winning $2 is 1/2 and the probability of winning nothing is 1/2, the expected (monetary) value of the payoff to Risk is $1:

$$1 = (1/2)2 + (1/2)0$$

On any single play of this game, Chauncey would win either $2 or nothing. However, if he played the game repeatedly—say, *n* times—he could be expected to win approximately *n* dollars, winning $2 half the time and $0 half the time.

Having done this expected-value calculation, we are tempted to guess that Chauncey's reservation price is $1. Does $R = 1$? More generally, do reservation prices reflect expected monetary values? To find out, try the following problem.

PROBLEM 6.1

You now have a chance to play Risk—but the stakes are better: you can walk away with *A* dollars, or you can gamble on the outcome of a coin toss. If a head appears, you get $2 million, but if a tail appears, you get nothing. Calculate the expected (monetary) value of the game. Is this value your reservation price? What value of *A* would make you indifferent between taking *A* or playing this version of Risk?

If past experience is any guide, the number you wrote down as a reservation price in Problem 6.1 is certainly less than $1 million—the expected (monetary) value of Risk in this problem—and is probably less than $100,000. The empirical reality you have just discovered is that the reservation price associated with a risky game may be very small, relative to the game's expected payoff.

Calculating expected (monetary) value, then, does not seem to account for our behavior. It seems that risk itself somehow plays a role in shaping our behavior. What is that role? Daniel Bernoulli, a contemporary of Adam Smith's, proposed the **expected-utility hypothesis** to resolve the paradox that reservation prices are not necessarily equal to expected payoffs.[1] Because it plays a dominant role in modern theories of choice in risky situations, we'll carefully construct a modern version of Bernoulli's expected-utility hypothesis and provide a set of assump-

---

[1] Bernoulli's version of this paradox, known as the Saint Petersburg paradox, is treated in Exercise 4 at the end of this chapter. Bernoulli's original work has been recently reprinted. See Bernoulli (1954, pp. 23–36).

tions under which the hypothesis is a theorem.

Before you consider the theory of expected utility, however, try the following problem to reinforce your understanding of expected (monetary) values.

PROBLEM 6.2

Imagine that your rich uncle offers you the chance to toss a die. He promises to pay you $1800 if you toss a 1 or a 3 and $3000 if you toss a 2. On the other hand, if you toss a 4, 5, or 6, you must pay him $300. What is the expected (monetary) value of your winnings from this die-tossing game.

Calculating Expected Utility

Before getting down to the essence of the theory, let's look at the mechanics of it. Bernoulli argued that in evaluating risky prospects, individuals compare not the expected (monetary) values of payoffs but the **expected utilities** of payoffs. An expected utility is calculated in the same way as an expected (monetary) value, except that the utility associated with a payoff is substituted for its monetary value. To calculate an expected utility, then, you simply compute a weighted average of the utilities associated with the payoffs, using the appropriate probabilities as weights.

What is Chauncey's expected utility for Risk? If we think of wealth (command over goods) as a composite commodity, we can write utility as a function of wealth:

$$u = U(w)$$

where u is Chauncey's utility, w is his wealth, and U is the utility function. For example, let's suppose that Chauncey's wealth before he makes his choice about playing Risk is $0. In other words, he is flat broke. If he decides to play, one of two possible outcomes will occur: (1) he'll win $2 with probability 1/2, his wealth will then be $2 = $2 + $0, and his utility will be $U(2)$; or (2) he'll win $0, again with probability 1/2,

his wealth will then be just $0, and his utility will be $U(0)$. Taking the *probability-weighted average* of these utilities gives us Chauncey's *expected utility* of playing Risk: it is just $(1/2)U(2) + (1/2)U(0)$. Of course, his other option is to walk away with A. If he chooses to take A rather than play Risk, his wealth will be A with probability 1. The expected utility associated with this outcome is just $U(A)$.

According to the expected-utility hypothesis, Chauncey will choose to play Risk in preference to taking A if the expected utility of playing Risk is greater than the expected utility of taking A, or if

$$(1/2)U(2) + (1/2)U(0) > U(A)$$

Of course, he'll take A if the inequality is reversed.

Furthermore, his reservation price R satisfies

$$U(R) = (1/2)U(2) + (1/2)U(0)$$

In this case, the two expected utilities are equal; therefore, Chauncey will be indifferent between playing Risk and taking R. The following problem will help you understand the mechanics of the expected-utility theory.

PROBLEM 6.3

Suppose that Chauncey's utility function is

$$U(w) = 12 - \frac{12}{1 + w}$$

and that his initial wealth is zero. What is Chauncey's expected utility of playing Risk? What is his reservation price R? If A is $0.75, will he play Risk or take A? Finally, suppose that his initial wealth is $1. Now what is the expected utility of Risk?

6.2 The Expected-Utility Theorem

To make this expected-utility hypothesis really usable, we need to create a rigorous theoretical model. Interestingly, even though the hypothesis is over 200 years old, its solid theoretical grounding dates from the 1920s and 1930s, and its widespread application in economics to the 1960s and 1970s.[2]

Our purpose here is much the same as it was in Chapter 3. We are attempting to give precise meaning to the notion of self-interest in risky choice situations, so that you'll understand exactly what lies behind any application of expected-utility theory. As in Chapter 3, we'll look very closely at the assumptions used to justify the expected-utility theorem because this procedure will reveal precisely what maximizing expected utility means and will allow you to pinpoint potential weaknesses in the theory.

To keep the discussion relatively simple, we'll see how the hypothesis is justified in an environment in which any risky situation has at most three possible outcomes. That is, we'll be talking about lotteries, or what we'll call **prospects**, which offer at most three different prizes, or *outcomes* — say, $10,000 with probability 1/2, $6,000 with probability 1/4, and $1000 with probability 1/4. First we'll set out the notation used in the three-outcome case, then we'll consider the assumptions necessary to prove the expected-utility theorem, and finally we'll see how to construct the implied utility function.

The Three-Outcome Case

The assumptions of the expected-utility theorem are about the way that individuals make choices in risky situations. As we've said, to make the problem manageable, we'll consider only risky prospects that have three possible outcomes. For the moment, these outcomes can be interpreted simply as

dollar magnitudes. Specifically, let's suppose that the three money prizes, or outcomes, are $10,000, $6000, and $1000. Once we've laid out the expected-utility theorem for this case, we'll be able to generalize it to *any number of outcomes* — and also to outcomes *other than dollar magnitudes.*

Prospects

First, we need notation to represent risky prospects. Suppose, then, that some game offers $10,000 with probability p_1, $6000 with probability p_2, and $1000 with probability p_3. From our understanding of probability, we know that p_1, p_2, and p_3 are numbers greater than or equal to 0 and less than or equal to 1:

$$0 \leq p_1 \leq 1 \qquad 0 \leq p_2 \leq 1 \qquad 0 \leq p_3 \leq 1$$

In addition, since these are the only possible outcomes, these three probabilities must sum to one:

$$p_1 + p_2 + p_3 = 1$$

We'll use the term *prospect* to refer to any set of three probabilities — p_1, p_2, and p_3 — assigned to their respective outcomes — $10,000, $6000, and $1000 — and we'll denote a prospect by

$$(p_1, p_2, p_3: 10000, 6000, 1000)$$

or, more simply, by

$$(p_1, p_2, p_3)$$

with the understanding that the first probability (p_1) pertains to the first prize ($10,000), the second probability (p_2) to the second prize ($6000), and the third probability (p_3) to the third prize ($1000). For example, if a game offered $10,000 with probability 1/4, $6000 with probability 1/2, and $1000 with probability 1/4, we'd write (1/4, 1/2, 1/4: 10000, 6000, 1000) or, equivalently, (1/4, 1/2, 1/4). The notation can also

[2] See von Neumann and Morgenstern (1944). For a more accessible treatment, see Luce and Raiffa (1957).

represent riskless, or *assured*, outcomes: outcomes that occur with probability 1. For example, either (1, 0, 0: 10000, 6000, 1000) or (1, 0, 0) denotes the assured outcome, $10,000.

To be certain you understand this notation, try the following problem.

PROBLEM 6.4

Describe in words exactly what each of the following objects is, and calculate its expected (monetary) value. (.25, .25, .50), (.2, .5, .3), (.5, .4, .1), (0, 1, 0).

The Challenge

Now, we know that the objects in Problem 6.4 are prospects (or lotteries) that offer the three outcomes (or prizes) of $10,000, $6000, and $1000, and that these prospects can be represented by (p_1, p_2, p_3), where p_1 is the probability of winning $10,000, p_2 is the probability of winning $6000, and p_3 is the probability of winning $1000. Our task is to find a set of assumptions about preferences over these objects and a utility function such that whenever one prospect is *preferred to* another, the expected utility of the preferred prospect is *larger than* the expected utility of the other prospect.

The utility function $U(w)$ will assign utility numbers to each of the three outcomes — $10,000, $6000, and $1000. The utility numbers themselves can be written as $U(10,000)$, $U(6000)$, and $U(1000)$. To see where we're headed, let's look at two specific prospects, (.2, .5, .3) and (.3, .3, .4), and suppose that the person whose preferences we are considering prefers the first prospect to the second one. Using our notation for "preferred to" from Chapter 3, we have

$$(.2, .5, .3) \ \mathbf{P} \ (.3, .3, .4)$$

We want to find a utility function — the three numbers $U(10,000)$, $U(6000)$, and

$U(1000)$ — such that the expected utility of the first prospect is greater than the expected utility of the second prospect:

$$.2U(10,000) + .5U(6000) + .3U(1000)$$

$$> .3U(10,000) + .3U(6000) + .4U(1000)$$

To find such a function, we'll need to adapt four familiar assumptions from Chapter 3 and add three new ones.

The Expected-Utility Assumptions

First, we'll reinterpret the familiar assumptions. To guarantee a complete preference ordering over these prospects, we simply have to substitute *prospect* for *consumption bundle* in the completeness assumption, the two-term-consistency assumption, and the three-term-consistency assumption from Chapter 3. We will also use a version of the nonsatiation assumption. Specifically, we'll assume that $10,000 is preferred to $6000, which is preferred to $1000. Or, using our prospect notation,

$$(1, 0, 0) \ \mathbf{P} \ (0, 1, 0) \ \mathbf{P} \ (0, 0, 1)$$

In the following three sections, we'll look at the *three new assumptions* concerned explicitly with risk.

The Continuity Assumption

The first assumption concerning risky prospects is called the **continuity assumption**. (Note that this assumption is different from the assumption of the same name in Chapter 3.) To see what our new continuity assumption means, let's consider another simple game. Suppose that Chauncey is given a choice between the following two prospects:

$$(0, 1, 0) \quad \text{and} \quad (e, 0, 1 - e)$$

On the right, e and $1 - e$ are probabilities of the $10,000 and $1000 prizes. If e is

1/4, for example, Chauncey faces a choice between the assured prospect $6000 and the risky prospect that offers either $10,000 with probability 1/4 or $1000 with probability 3/4.

If $e = 0$ and therefore $1 - e = 1$, then both prospects are riskless, or assured. The first prospect offers $6000 with probability 1, and the second prospect offers $1000 with probability 1. Hence, when $e = 0$, the first prospect is preferred to the second. Notice that as e increases, the risky prospect becomes increasingly more attractive. When $e = 1$, both prospects are again assured, but now the second is preferred to the first.

It seems plausible to assume, then, that there is some value of e — let's call it e^* — greater than zero but less than 1, such that Chauncey would be indifferent between the certain and the risky prospect. This is our first assumption:

A S S U M P T I O N: Continuity

There is a unique number e^*, $0 < e^* < 1$, such that

$$(0, 1, 0) \, I \, (e^*, 0, 1 - e^*)$$

Since e^* must be greater than 0 and less than 1, this assumption guarantees that individuals are willing to make trade-offs between risky and assured prospects: they are willing to bear some risk. As you'll see, the probability e^* plays a very significant role in our theory, so you should be certain that you understand the continuity assumption. In particular, notice that for any individual, e^* is a number and that this number will vary from individual to individual. What is e^* for you?

P R O B L E M 6.5

Jack says that he is indifferent between $6000 and a lottery that pays $10,000 with probability .75 and $1000 with probability .25. His sister Jane says that she prefers $6000 to this lottery. What can you say about the number e^* for Jack? For Jane?

The Substitution Assumption

The substitution assumption concerns the ability of individuals to evaluate compound prospects. A **compound prospect** is one that has as one of its outcomes (or prizes) *another risky prospect* (or lottery). The wheels of fortune on the streets of Paris that offer as prizes lottery tickets in the French National Lottery are one example of a compound prospect. The accumulator bet in horse racing is another example. When the bettor places a "double," it means that the payout for winning one race is to be used as a stake for betting on the next race.

Now let's create a compound prospect and see how to represent it in our notation. We'll call (.35, .50, .15) the *original* prospect. Now let's substitute the risky prospect (.75, 0, .25) for the $6000 prize in the original prospect, thereby creating a compound prospect. Notice that only the $10,000 and $1000 prizes are possible in this compound prospect. What is the probability of the $10,000 prize in this compound prospect? In the compound prospect, we can think of two routes to the $10,000 prize — the *direct route* described in the original prospect, and the *indirect route* created by the substitution. The probability of getting $10,000 by the direct route is just .35 — the probability of the $10,000 prize in the original prospect. The probability of getting $10,000 by the indirect route is the product of two probabilities: the probability of the $6000 prize in the original prospect, which we can regard as the probability of substitution, times the probability of the $10,000 prize in the risky substitute prospect, or .5 times .75. Hence, in this compound prospect, the probability of the $10,000 prize is

$$.35 + .5 \times .75 = .725$$

Similarly, in the compound prospect, there is a direct and an indirect route to the $1000 prize. By the direct route, the probability is .15. The probability of getting $1000 by the indirect route is the product of two probabilities: the probability of the $6000 prize in the original prospect, or the probability of substitution, times the probability of the $1000 prize in the risky substitute prospect, or .5 times .25. Hence, in this compound prospect, the probability of the $1000 prize is

$$.15 + .5 \times .25 = .275$$

Thus, the compound prospect can be written as (.725, 0, .275).

To see what the substitution assumption is all about, let's ask how Jack in Problem 6.5 would rank the original prospect and the compound prospect. Will he prefer the original prospect (.35, .50, .15) or the compound prospect (.725, 0, .275) we just created? Because the value of e^* for Jack is .75, we know that he is indifferent between $6000 and the substitute prospect (.75, 0, .25). Because we created the compound prospect from the original prospect by substituting (.75, 0, .25) for the $6000 prize, it seems reasonable to assume that Jack will also be indifferent between the original prospect and the compound prospect. Indeed, the substitution assumption says that, in Jack's eyes, this compound prospect is equivalent to the original prospect. (Do you think that Jane would be indifferent between the original and compound prospects, or would she prefer the original prospect?)

ASSUMPTION: Substitution

Given any original prospect (p_1, p_2, p_3) and the number e^* for any individual, by substituting $(e^*, 0, 1 - e^*)$ for the $6000 prize, we create the compound prospect $[p_1 + p_2e^*, 0, p_2 + p_3(1 - e^*)]$. We assume that the individual is indifferent between the original and the compound prospects.

Let's distinguish two separate aspects of this assumption. The first seems reasonable enough: if individuals can do the required compound probability calculations effortlessly, then we assume that their preferences will satisfy this assumption. The second is that individuals can actually do the requisite calculations without great difficulty: they understand the laws of compound probability, and they can make calculations accordingly. Although some people have learned to do such calculations easily, many of us have fairly limited computational abilities. This suggests that the substitution assumption is problematical. To test your facility with such calculations, try the following problem.

PROBLEM 6.6

Recall from Problem 6.5 that Jack is indifferent between $6000 and a lottery that pays $10,000 with probability .75 and $1000 with probability .25. Show that for Jack, the following indifference statements are implied by the substitution assumption:

$$(1/3, 1/3, 1/3) \text{ I } (7/12, 0, 5/12)$$

and

$$(1/2, 1/4, 1/4) \text{ I } (11/16, 0, 5/16)$$

The Ordering Assumption

The **ordering assumption** concerns the way individuals order their preferences over prospects having the *same two outcomes* but *different probabilities.* Let's look at the two prospects (.26, 0, .74) and (.25, 0, .75). It seems reasonable to assume that the first prospect will be preferred to the second one, because the probability of winning the preferred $10,000 prize is higher with the first one.

ASSUMPTION: Ordering

Given two prospects that involve the same two outcomes and different probabilities, the preferred prospect is the one that offers the higher probability of winning the preferred outcome.

Constructing the Utility Function

Now we can construct an expected-utility function that will assign a utility number to each of the three outcomes: $10,000, $6000, $1000. We'll begin by assigning the utility number 1 to $10,000 and the utility number 0 to $1000. Thus,

$$U(10,000) = 1 \qquad U(1000) = 0$$

Next, we need to assign a utility number to $6000. As you'll see, only one number will work.

From the continuity assumption, we know that there is a risky prospect $(e^*, 0, 1 - e^*)$ that—in any given individual's eyes—is equivalent to the assured prospect offering $6000 with probability 1. In other words, for any individual there is a number e^*, greater than 0 and less than 1, such that

$$(0, 1, 0) \text{ I } (e^*, 0, 1 - e^*)$$

If the expected utility result is to hold, the expected utility of the assured prospect (0, 1, 0) must be equal to the expected utility of the equivalent risky prospect $(e^*, 0, 1 - e^*)$. The expected utility of the assured prospect is just $U(6000)$ because the probability of $6000 is 1 for this prospect. The expected utility of the equivalent risky prospect is $e^*U(10,000) + (1 - e^*)U(1000)$, or simply e^*, because $U(10,000)$ was assigned the number 1 and $U(1000)$ was assigned the number 0. But because the two expected utilities must be identical,

$$U(6000) = e^*$$

Given that $U(10,000) = 1$ and $U(1000) = 0$, no other number will do. The utility function is then

$$U(10,000) = 1, \ U(6000) = e^*, \ U(1000) = 0$$

To be sure that you know how this utility function has been constructed, try the following problem.[3]

PROBLEM 6.7

Using the information from Problem 6.5, construct a utility function for Jack.

The Expected-Utility Theorem

We can now summarize what the expected utility theorem tells us when all seven assumptions hold and when the utility function has been constructed in the way described above.

If an individual prefers one prospect to another, then the preferred prospect will have a larger expected utility. Furthermore, if an individual is indifferent between two prospects, then the two prospects will have the same expected utility.

To see just how powerful this result actually is, notice that if we have just one piece of information for any individual, we can predict that individual's choice in any situation where the prizes are $10,000, $6000, or $1000—assuming, of course, that the individual's preferences satisfy our seven assumptions. That crucial piece of information is e^*, the probability that makes the individual indifferent between $6000 and the risky prospect $(e^*, 0, 1 - e^*)$. The number e^* gives us this powerful predictive capacity because it allows us to construct the individual's utility function and therefore to calculate expected utilities for any pros-

---

[3] More generally, given any two numbers a and b with $a > b$, we could let $U(10,000) = a$ and $U(1000) = b$. We would then have to assign a utility number to $6000 as follows:

$$U(6000) = ae^* + b(1 - e^*)$$

Since the numbers a and b are arbitrary except for order, we clearly do not have a cardinal measure of utility.

pect involving these three prizes. The following problem will reinforce your understanding of this surprising result.

PROBLEM 6.8

Use the utility function you constructed in the previous problem to find Jack's preference ordering for the following prospects: (1/2, 1/4, 1/4); (1/3, 1/3, 1/3); (0, 1, 0); (7/12, 0, 5/12); (1/4, 1/2, 1/4); (3/4, 0, 1/4).

The predictive power of the theory of expected utility means that it is relatively easy to generate experimental evidence to test the theory. In fact, a great deal of experimental testing of the theory has already been done. One of the more interesting results of this research is evidence that, in certain situations, the theory is inadequate. In fact, a great deal of recent work attempts to modify the theory so that it does work in these problematical situations. Machina's 1987 article surveys this empirical evidence and the efforts to modify the theory.

6.3 Generalizing the Expected-Utility Theorem

Obviously, expected-utility theory is not restricted to prospects with the three prizes of $10,000, $6000, and $1000. Any three money prizes would do. Indeed, prizes other than money prizes are perfectly possible. For example, the prizes might be cars, houses, training programs, consumption bundles, or virtually anything else that individuals value. The expected-utility approach, therefore, is not limited to financial risk; it can be applied to a whole spectrum of individual choices involving risk.

We can also extend the theorem from the three-outcome case to prospects with any number of possible outcomes. For each additional outcome, we simply need to generate an additional utility number. Suppose, for example, that we added the possibility of

a $3000 prize to the three prizes we've been considering, and suppose, too, that Jack is indifferent between this $3000 prize and a lottery offering $10,000 with probability .4 and $1000 with probability .6. To extend Jack's utility function, we would assign the utility number .4 to $3000. Jack's utility function would then be $U(10,000) = 1$, $U(6000) = .75$, $U(3000) = .4$, and $U(1000) = 0$. Using this utility function, we could then predict what his choice would be in any situation in which prospects offer these four prizes.

In some important circumstances, however, the expected utility approach is not applicable, and in others it cannot be applied without reinterpreting the notion of probability.

State-Dependent Preferences

The expected-utility theorem cannot be applied when a person's preferences depend on which outcome, or "state of the world," actually turns up. We have implicitly assumed that an individual's preference ordering over prospects is independent of the outcome that actually occurs. In many cases, this assumption is appropriate. For example, if I win the Irish Sweepstakes, my preferences over consumption bundles will not change.

Sometimes, however, preferences are *state-dependent.* Imagine how the preferences of a childless couple hoping to adopt a baby might differ over items such as strollers, baby foods, and child-care services. In this case, preferences depend on whether an agency selects the couple to be adoptive parents. Whenever you venture out into rush-hour traffic, you risk being injured in an accident. If you were disabled, your consumption preferences would change — perhaps dramatically. When preferences are state-dependent, the expected-utility approach to risky choice making is not appropriate.

Subjective Probabilities

We've been using coin-tossing games as illustrations of risky situations for two reasons. First, these games are clearly risky because their outcomes are random events. Second, in these games, the probability of any outcome is objectively known. Yet, expected-utility theory is sometimes applied to risky situations in which the probability of any outcome is not objectively known. And it is often applied to situations that involve not risk, but **imperfect information** — that is, to situations in which the outcome is certain but unknown. The key to applying expected-utility theory in these latter two cases is to use **subjective probabilities.**

First, let's look at buying gum from a vending machine as a risky situation in which the probability of any outcome is not objectively known, and then reconsider it as a situation involving imperfect information. We'll see how the expected-utility approach can be applied to both cases with the use of subjective probabilities. Each time I drop 50 cents into a vending machine to get some gum, I think that there is some probability that the gum won't drop. This is a genuinely risky event — because the outcome is genuinely random — if, for instance, the machine is built so that it releases gum with probability 19/20 and does not release it with probability 1/20. My problem is that there is an objective probability that I won't get the gum — but I don't know what it is.

How do I make rational decisions in this case? Perhaps I could attach a subjective probability to the nonappearance of the gum, based on past experience with this machine or others like it. In this case, the expected-utility approach is applicable — if probabilities are reinterpreted as subjective probabilities.

But what if the outcome is not risky but certain? In other words, what if the vending machine is in one of the two states: working order or out-of-order. In this case, the prob-

lem is an informational one: I simply don't know whether the machine is functioning or not. How do I make rational decisions under imperfect information? Perhaps by forming a subjective probability about the state of the machine, again based on past experience with this or similar machines. Here, the expected-utility approach is applicable — if probabilities are interpreted as subjective probabilities.

From the vending-machine user's point of view, then, there is no difference between genuine risk, where outcomes are random, and imperfect information, where outcomes are certain but information is lacking. The outcome is treated as probabilistic in either case.

In fact, many choices include both risk and imperfect information. Enrolling in a premed curriculum in anticipation of being among the 3 out of every 10 applicants accepted by medical schools involves genuine risk, if selection procedures by admission officers are random — if candidates are chosen by throwing the names of acceptable applicants into a hat and drawing out the "winners." Enrolling also involves imperfect information if students who just don't have the ability necessary to meet medical school admissions standards nevertheless decide to take premed. The outcome is certain, but these students don't know it.

Whatever the nature of the choice — a genuinely risky problem, an informational problem, or both — we can still analyze it using the expected-utility approach, if we are willing to reinterpret the probabilities as subjective probabilities. The real issue is whether people actually do view outcomes in a choice situation as probabilistic.

6.4 Attitudes Toward Risk

What psychological attitudes do individuals have toward risk? Attitudes are diverse: some people are perfectly willing to invest in highly speculative penny stocks, for example, or in a resort development in the heart of the Amazon jungle, whereas others are unwilling to undertake any venture more risky than opening a savings account. A convenient way to think about this variation in attitudes toward risk is to view individual preferences as falling into one of three categories: *risk-averse, risk-neutral, or risk-inclined.*

Let's concentrate in this section on attitudes toward financial risk. We'll express utility as a function of dollars or wealth w and write an individual's utility as

$$u = U(w)$$

To see exactly what these three attitudes toward risk entail, we'll consider the following prospect:

$$(p, 1 - p: w_1, w_2)$$

where p is the probability of getting outcome w_1, and $1 - p$ is the probability of getting outcome w_2. In this notation for prospects, the first probability (p) pertains to the first outcome (w_1), and the second probability $(1 - p)$ to the second outcome (w_2). For convenience, we'll suppose that w_1 exceeds w_2.

Let's consider one individual's attitude. Suppose that this person — let's call him Jimmy — has initial wealth of w_0. If Jimmy holds the prospect described above, his wealth will be $w_0 + w_1$ with probability p and $w_0 + w_2$ with probability $(1 - p)$, and his expected utility will be

$$pU(w_0 + w_1) + (1 - p)U(w_0 + w_2)$$

The expected (monetary) value of this prospect, w_e, is just

$$w_e = pw_1 + (1 - p)w_2$$

If Jimmy held an assured prospect that offered w_e with probability 1, his expected utility would be

$$U(w_0 + w_e)$$

Now we'll offer Jimmy the choice between these two prospects. Keep in mind that both prospects offer identical expected monetary values — $w_e = pw_1 + (1 - p)w_2$ — but one is risky and the other assured.

We'll call Jimmy **risk-neutral** if the two prospects are equally attractive to him. That is, Jimmy is risk-neutral if

$$pU(w_0 + w_1) + (1 - p)U(w_0 + w_2)$$
$$= U(w_0 + w_e)$$

We'll call him **risk-averse** if the assured prospect is preferred. That is, Jimmy is risk-averse if

$$U(w_0 + w_e) > pU(w_0 + w_1)$$
$$+ (1 - p)U(w_0 + w_2)$$

Finally, Jimmy is **risk-inclined** if he prefers the risky prospect. That is, Jimmy is risk-inclined if

$$pU(w_0 + w_1) + (1 - p)U(w_0 + w_2)$$
$$> U(w_0 + w_e)$$

The following problem will help you to understand these important distinctions.

PROBLEM 6.9

Melvin's utility function is $U(w) = w^{1/2}$, Jane's is $U(w) = w$, and Baby Doe's is $U(w) = w^2$. All three have the same initial wealth — $w_0 = 0$. That is, they are all broke. Consider the risky prospect $(1/4, 3/4: 100, 0)$ — a prospect that offers \$100 with probability 1/4 and \$0 with probability 3/4. The expected (monetary) value of this prospect is \$25 — that is, $w_e = 25$. Show that, if given a choice between \$25 and the risky prospect $(1/4, 3/4: 100, 0)$, Melvin prefers the assured \$25, Jane is indifferent between the two, and Baby Doe prefers the risky prospect. Now quickly sketch these utility functions. Notice the differences in the curves associated with these risk-averse, risk-neutral, and risk-inclined preferences.

We can determine from the shape of the utility function — that is, from the way that the slope of the function changes as wealth

(a)

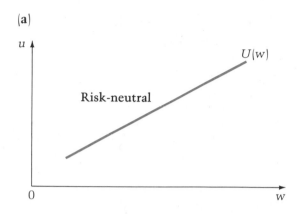

(b)

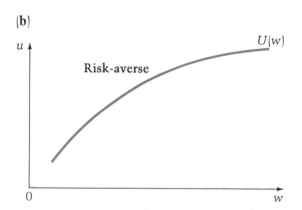

(c)

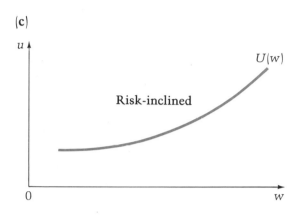

FIGURE 6.1   Preferences toward risk.

In (a), the slope of $U(w)$ is constant, reflecting constant marginal utility of wealth and risk-neutral preferences. In (b), the slope of $U(w)$ decreases as w increases, reflecting diminishing marginal utility of wealth and risk-averse preferences. In (c), the slope of $U(w)$ increases as w increases, reflecting increasing marginal utility of wealth and risk-inclined preferences.

w increases—which of the three cases we are considering. The utility function in Figure 6.1a represents the preferences of someone who is risk-neutral. As wealth w increases, utility increases at a constant rate: the slope of the utility function is *constant*. We can interpret the slope of the utility function as **marginal utility of wealth** because its slope is simply the rate at which utility increases as wealth increases. We then see that risk neutrality is associated with constant marginal utility of wealth.

By comparison, in the risk-averse case in Figure 6.1b, the slope of the utility function *decreases* as wealth increases, and in the risk-inclined case in Figure 6.1c, the slope *increases* as wealth increases. Risk aversion is thus associated with diminishing marginal utility of wealth and risk inclina-

tion with increasing marginal utility of wealth.[4]

Now, let's justify the taxonomy in Figure 6.1 by examining in detail the risk-averse case. In Figure 6.2, Jimmy's utility function is like the one in Figure 6.1b. We'll show that, given a choice between a risky prospect and an assured prospect with the same expected (monetary) value, Jimmy will prefer the assured prospect. We'll show that

$$U(w_0 + w_e) > pU(w_0 + w_1)$$
$$+ (1 - p)U(w_0 + w_2)$$

---

[4] We can use calculus to define marginal utility of wealth, $MU(w)$:

$$MU(w) = U'(w)$$

Then, $U''(w) = 0$ implies risk neutrality, $U''(w) < 0$ implies risk aversion, and $U''(w) > 0$ implies risk inclination.

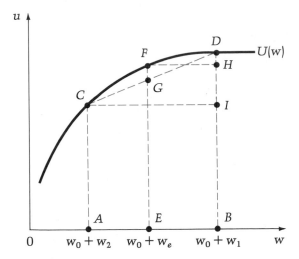

FIGURE 6.2   Risk aversion.

By construction, $w_0 + w_e = p(w_0 + w_1) + (1 - p)(w_0 + w_2)$. The utility of $w_0 + w_e$ is distance EF. The expected utility $pU(w_0 + w_1) + (1 - p)U(w_0 + w_2)$ is distance EG. Since the individual is risk-averse, EF exceeds EG.

when Jimmy's utility function exhibits diminishing marginal utility of wealth. As we proceed, we'll also be creating important tools to use in the applications that follow.

In Figure 6.2, point A on the w axis corresponds to wealth $w_0 + w_2$ and point B to wealth $w_0 + w_1$. The point $w_0 + w_e$ at E clearly lies somewhere between points A and B. Exactly where it lies depends on the value of p. As p goes from 0 to 1, $w_0 + w_e$ goes from point A to point B. If p is zero, $w_0 + w_e$ is coincident with point A: if p is $1/4$, it is one-fourth of the distance between A and B, and so on. Because we have assumed in constructing Figure 6.2 that p is equal to $1/2$, E is exactly half the distance from A to B. To find $U(w_0 + w_e)$ in Figure 6.2, simply move vertically up from point E to the utility function at point F. Thus, $U(w_0 + w_e)$ is the distance EF in the diagram.

Now we need to find Jimmy's expected utility for the risky prospect. To identify $pU(w_0 + w_1) + (1 - p)U(w_0 + w_2)$, construct the dashed line connecting points C and D in Figure 6.2, and then move vertically up from point E to point G on this dashed line. The distance EG is Jimmy's expected utility of this risky prospect. Why? Just as $w_0 + w_e$ moves from point A to point B as p moves from 0 to 1, so too, the expected utility of the risky prospect moves along the dashed line from point C to point D. In the case illustrated in this figure (p equal to $1/2$), the expected utility is halfway along this dashed line, directly above point E. Notice that distance EF exceeds distance EG or, equivalently, that

$$U(w_0 + w_e) > pU(w_0 + w_1) + (1 - p)U(w_0 + w_2)$$

We have shown, then, that the preferences drawn in Figure 6.2 are risk-averse.

Do risk-averse preferences characterize your own behavior? Recall your answer to Problem 6.1, where you considered the choice between the risky prospect $(1/2, 1/2 : 2000000, 0)$ and the assured prospect A. We asked you to write down the value of A that would make you indifferent between these two prospects. If that value is less than a million dollars, you are risk-averse.

Let's now turn to the risk-neutral case. If the utility function in Figure 6.2 had been linear, the dashed line CD would have been coincident with the utility function, and the points F and G would therefore have been coincident. In this case, the individual would have been indifferent between the two prospects: he or she would be risk-neutral.

PROBLEM 6.10

Use a graphic argument, similar to the one above, to show that a risk-inclined person will prefer the risky prospect to the assured prospect.

6.5 Shedding Risk

A common institution among people who fish for sport is a share-the-bounty convention. At the end of an outing, members of a fishing party usually have a tacit understanding that anyone who catches a trophy fish will take that fish home. Otherwise, the group divides the catch equally, without regard to who actually caught which fish. We can view this institution as a form of insurance against the embarrassment of being "skunked" — coming home empty-handed. Such forms of insurance are usually called risk pooling arrangements.

Another example is a business merger in which three weavers pool their resources to set up a retail shop, The Run of the Mill, and each agrees to draw out a certain percentage of the profit. Other examples of risk pooling include the understanding among nineteenth-century American pioneers that if one family lost a home to fire, the whole community would pitch in to help them rebuild and the tradition among the Inuit in the North American Arctic of sharing their food equally, even in times of famine.

Risk Pooling

In this section, we'll use our analytical tools to develop an understanding of **risk pooling** and of the preferences that make such an institution attractive. We'll begin by considering two householders, Abe and Martha, who face identical but independent risks — the risk that their houses will burn — and ask if there is any institution they can create that will reduce the burden of risk.

Imagine that the probability that either Abe or Martha will experience a fire is p. Further, suppose that the loss associated with a fire is L dollars. In the absence of a risk-pooling agreement, Abe's expected utility is just

$$pU(w_0 - L) + (1 - p)U(w_0)$$

where w_0 is his initial wealth. Abe's house will burn with probability p. If it does, Abe's wealth will be $w_0 - L$, and his utility will be $U(w_0 - L)$. On the other hand, the probability that his house will not burn is $1 - p$. Abe's wealth will then be w_0, and his utility will be $U(w_0)$. (In what follows, we'll concentrate on Abe, but it should be clear that the same analysis applies to Martha.)

Let's now suppose that Abe and Martha agree to pool their risks; that is, they agree to share any loss due to fire. We now have three relevant events: both houses burn; one house burns; neither house burns. Because the probabilities of fire are independent, the probability that both will burn is p^2, the product of the two independent probabilities that either house burns. If both houses do burn, Abe will incur a loss of L. Similarly, the probability that neither burns is $(1 - p)^2$. In this event, Abe experiences no loss. Finally, the probability that exactly one house burns is $2p(1 - p)$. In this event, Abe incurs a loss equal to $L/2$. (To calculate this probability, notice that the probability that Abe's house burns and Martha's does not is $p(1 - p)$. Similarly, the probability that Martha's burns and Abe's does not is also $p(1 - p)$. Thus, the probability that exactly one house burns is $2p(1 - p)$.) Abe's expected utility associated with this risk-pooling agreement is then

$$p^2U(w_0 - L) + 2p(1 - p)U\left(w_0 - \frac{L}{2}\right) + (1 - p)^2U(w_0)$$

When does this risk-pooling agreement actually enhance Abe's expected utility? More precisely, when is

$$p^2U(w_0 - L) + 2p(1 - p)U\left(w_0 - \frac{L}{2}\right) + (1 - p)^2U(w_0) > pU(w_0 - L) + (1 - p)U(w_0)$$

Or, by rewriting the expression, when is

$$2p(1-p)U\left(w_0 - \frac{L}{2}\right) > p(1-p)U(w_0 - L)$$
$$+ p(1-p)U(w_0)$$

Finally, dividing by $2p(1-p)$, when is

$$U(w_0 - L/2) > \frac{U(w_0 - L) + U(w_0)}{2}$$

We can use the graphic tools created in the previous section to find the answer. Figure 6.3 illustrates a risk-averse utility function: $U(w_0 - L/2)$ is distance EG: $U(w_0 - L)$ is distance AC: $U(w_0)$ is distance BD. To find $[U(w_0 - L) + U(w_0)]/2$, draw the dashed line from C to D and move to the midpoint of this line segment. Point F directly above point E is the midpoint, and $[U(w_0 - L) + U(w_0)]/2$ is equal to distance EF. Since EF is less than EG, we have discovered that Abe prefers the risk-pooling agreement to going

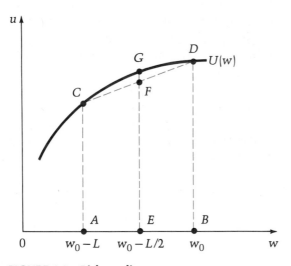

FIGURE 6.3   Risk pooling.

Loss L occurs with probability p, and the expected utility of bearing the risk personally is therefore $pU(w_0 - L) + (1 - p)U(w_0)$. By pooling risks with another person, the individual's expected utility is $p^2U(w_0 - L) + 2p(1 - p)U[w_0 - (L/2)] + (1 - p)^2U(w_0)$. The second expected utility is larger than the first if $U[(w_0 - (L/2)]$ exceeds $[U(w_0 - L) + U(w_0)]/2$. But $U[w_0 - (L/2)]$ is distance EG, and $[U(w_0 - L) + U(w_0)]/2$ is distance EF. A risk-averse individual therefore prefers to pool risks.

it alone, because he is risk-averse. Similarly, if Martha is risk-averse, she too will prefer the risk-pooling agreement.

By using the appropriately shaped utility functions, you can check to see that a risk-inclined householder prefers to go it alone and that a risk-neutral householder is indifferent between the two arrangements.

An important point emerges from this exercise. When householders are risk-averse, they have clear incentives to create institutions allowing them to share, or pool, their risks. The risk-pooling institution we have considered does nothing to alter the physical environment; it does nothing to reduce the incidence of fire. Yet it does increase the expected utility of the householders in the pool.

PROBLEM 6.11

Consider two identical steelhead fishers with utility functions $u = x^{1/2}$, where x is the number of fish. Graph this utility function and convince yourself that it represents risk-averse preferences. Assuming that the probability that either will catch one fish is $1/10$ and that it is impossible that one fisher can catch two fish, show that if they agree to pool their risks, both will be better off than if they refuse to divide the catch.

In pioneer societies, risk-pooling arrangements such as the community agreement to rebuild homes destroyed by fire were commonly informal arrangements. Such informal risk-pooling arrangements persist today among members of extended families or close-knit communities. In most modern societies, however, the functions these informal institutions used to perform have been taken over to a large extent by insurance markets. Let's look more closely at the market for insurance.

The Demand for Insurance

Using the risk-of-fire problem and once again assuming risk-averse preferences, we can identify Abe's expected utility in the absence of fire insurance in Figure 6.4. Simply move vertically up from point E on the horizontal axis — where wealth is equal to $p(w_0 - L) + (1 - p)w_0$, or simply $w_0 - pL$ — to the dashed line CD. Abe's expected utility in the absence of fire insurance is the distance EF; that is,

$$EF = pU(w_0 - L) + (1 - p)U(w_0)$$

Next, we want to identify the **certainty equivalent** of this risky prospect: the assured prospect, w_{ce}, such that the householder would be indifferent between the assured prospect and the risky one. Algebraically, the certainty equivalent w_{ce} satisfies the following equation:

$$U(w_{ce}) = pU(w_0 - L) + (1 - p)U(w_0)$$

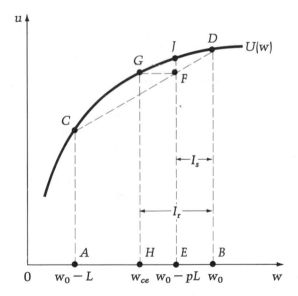

FIGURE 6.4   The demand for insurance.

Loss L occurs with probability p. If the individual does not insure, expected utility is $pU(w_0 - L) + (1 - p)U(w_0)$, which is equal to distance EF. Wealth w_{ce} with no risk yields the same utility since $HG = EF$. Therefore, w_{ce} is the certainty equivalent of the risky prospect: $(p, 1 - p: w_0, w_0 - L)$. Accordingly, the individual would pay up to I_r for full insurance coverage against loss L.

To identify w_{ce} in Figure 6.4, first move horizontally from point F to point G on the utility function and then vertically down to point H on the wealth axis. If Abe has this assured prospect, his expected utility will be HG. The length of line segment HG is equal to EF, the expected utility of the risky prospect that Abe has in the absence of insurance. Therefore, w_{ce} is the certainty equivalent of the risky prospect.

You already have some experience with certainty equivalents. In Problem 6.1, you wrote down your own certainty equivalent of the prospect $(1/2, 1/2: 2000000, 0)$, and in Problem 6.3, you calculated Chauncey's certainty equivalent of Risk. This is exactly the same kind of calculation.

Now let's consider an insurance policy offering full coverage; that is, one that will reimburse Abe for the full amount of the loss in the event of fire. Such a policy pays Abe L in the event of fire and, of course, nothing if no fire occurs. What is Abe's **reservation price** for such a policy? In other words, what is the *maximum amount* he is willing to pay to buy the policy rather than to bear personally the risk of fire?

Let I be the price that Abe would have to pay for the policy. If Abe buys the policy, his wealth level is assured: he bears no risk. That wealth level is just $w_0 - I$, and the expected utility associated with it is $U(w_0 - I)$. Abe's reservation price I_r then satisfies

$$U(w_0 - I_r) = pU(w_0 - L) + (1 - p)U(w_0)$$

Why? Because if I (the actual price of the insurance) is less than I_r, then Abe's (expected) utility is larger if he buys the policy than it is if he doesn't. Using what we have learned from our diagrammatic analysis, we see that I_r satisfies

$$U(w_0 - I_r) = EF = EG = U(w_{ce})$$

In other words, if Abe does pay I_r for full coverage, he will obtain the certainty equivalent of the risky prospect of personally bearing the risk of fire. This expression tells us that $w_0 - I_r$ is equal to w_{ce}, which implies that

$$I_r = w_0 - w_{ce}$$

Returning to Figure 6.4, I_r is distance HB along the wealth axis. We have thus characterized Abe's demand for full coverage: if $I < I_r$, he will buy full coverage, and if $I > I_r$, he won't.

The Supply of Insurance

Now that we know something about the demand for insurance, let's turn to the supply side of the question. Will insurance firms be willing to offer full coverage on terms attractive to the buyer? That is, is there a viable market for insurance? Let's begin by making the not-so-satisfactory assumption that insurance companies are risk-neutral. (We'll return later to a more satisfactory discussion of risk bearing by insurance companies.)

On the assumption that insurance companies are risk-neutral, what is the lowest price at which a risk-neutral firm will offer full coverage? The answer to this question is a reservation supply price, denoted by I_s. Because the firm is by definition risk-neutral, it will simply compare expected (monetary) values in deciding whether to offer insurance. Ignoring for simplicity any costs it incurs in writing and administering a policy, the firm will pay out $\$L$ with probability p and $\$0$ with probability $(1 - p)$. Its expected costs are therefore just $\$pL$. Its revenue from selling a policy is $\$I$, and it will write the policy if $\$I$ exceeds $\$pL$. Its reservation price is therefore

$$I_s = pL$$

or distance EB in Figure 6.4.

In this case, there is a viable market for insurance because the reservation supply price is less than the reservation demand price:

$$I_s < I_r$$

At any price I greater than I_s and less than I_r, both parties to the transaction gain from it. If we make the standard competitive assumption that many insurance firms compete to write insurance policies, we can conclude that price will be driven down to I_s.[5] In this case, Abe trades his risky prospect for the assured prospect $w_0 - pL$, and his utility is then $U(w_0 - pL)$, or the distance EJ in Figure 6.4. Abe's utility gain from the transaction is therefore FJ.

This result is really quite startling. In this market equilibrium, Abe's expected wealth is identical to his expected wealth in the absence of an insurance policy — yet he bears no risk. In terms of expected income forgone, the price of insurance is zero, yet the householder clearly benefits since all the risk associated with the probability of a fire is gone. We've learned, then, that the simple act of risk pooling uses no real resources but creates real value.

As we noted earlier, the analysis is based on the assumption that insurance firms are risk-neutral. There is, however, a sense in which insurance firms' attitudes toward risk are irrelevant to our analysis. If insurance companies sell a large number of such policies, they are effectively pooling a large number of independent risks of fire. A fundamental result in statistics, called the law of large numbers, then implies that such companies can be quite accurate in projecting their costs. The larger the number of policies they sell, the more accurate are their cost calculations. As the number of policies they sell gets very large, the risk that each firm bears gets very small. Effectively, such firms bear very little risk, and their attitudes toward risk are therefore not of material interest.

---

[5] To find the competitive equilibrium, we have invoked the fact that profit is zero in a competitive equilibrium, a result that you probably encountered in earlier course work in economics. We'll develop this result in Chapter 10.

PROBLEM 6.12

Show that the reservation price for full coverage of a risk-inclined householder is less than pL. This result implies that, for such householders, $I_r < I_s$. Thus, there is no price at which this householder and a risk-neutral insurance company could engage in a mutually beneficial transfer of risk.

Risk Spreading

We have seen that insurance is simply a market mechanism for risk pooling and that it is potentially valuable to risk-averse individuals. The other side of this coin is a phenomenon called **risk spreading.** To see what's involved, imagine that you hold some indivisible and risky asset — a promising 2-year-old race horse, for example. Clearly, risks are entailed in holding this asset. The horse's promise may not materialize: it may break a leg; it may be kidnapped for ransom and disappear; it may fail as a stud horse. In this circumstance, someone who is risk-averse might prefer to spread the risk rather than remain the sole owner of the asset.

A prime example of such an asset is Devil's Bag. As a 2-year-old, this horse was thought to be the latest and greatest American wonder. Its owner chose to sell it to a syndicate — a group of joint shareholders, each of whom owns a fraction of the horse — for $36 million, rather than to bear the risk alone. A syndicate is therefore a risk-spreading institution. In fact, the owner was wise to think that owning Devil's Bag was a risky business and to choose to spread that risk. The racehorse didn't pan out and was retired as a 3-year-old.

Syndicating a racehorse is only one illustration of risk spreading: the common device in which a risky, indivisible asset is spread over more than one holder. The joint-venture companies that sponsored voyages of discovery (or perhaps, plunder) by men like Sir Francis Drake are illustrations of risk spreading from an earlier time.

Today, joint-stock companies spread the risks of a firm among the firm's stockholders. The following problem conveys the basic insight of risk spreading: risk-averse individuals may prefer holding some part of a risky asset to holding the entire asset.

PROBLEM 6.13

Patricia's utility function is $U(w) = w^{1/2}$, and her initial wealth is 100, $w_0 = 100$. For a price of 100, she can buy an asset that will yield $10,000$ with probability $1/20$ and 0 with probability $19/20$. Show that she won't buy this asset alone but will join a syndicate with 10 equal partners.

The Case for Risk Aversion

Risk aversion has attracted so much theoretical attention because it is thought to be the usual, or most representative, attitude toward risk. This view is supported by abundant examples of risk-averse behavior. Most people choose to insure against various kinds of losses; even the fabulously wealthy are not the sole owners of Kentucky Derby contenders like Easy Goer and Sunday Silence; the joint-stock company is a dominant form of business enterprise. So, too, an ever-increasing number of U.S. firms are teaming up with foreign competitors in joint-venture arrangements. One of the motivating forces behind these joint ventures is that they lower the risk associated with high-tech product development, which almost invariably carries a multimillion dollar price tag. For instance, the arch rivals Texas Instruments and Hitachi recently joined forces to develop a 16-megabit dynamic RAM chip for the computer market because, as one TI executive put it, "We both needed a partner to minimize our risks." The ubiquity of these risk-pooling and risk-spreading arrangements is fairly convincing evidence that most individuals are risk-averse.

6.6 Some Issues in the Economics of Information

Young job seekers often complain that they could do jobs they have had no experience with, if only they were given the chance. Implicit in the statement are two presumptions: (1) that the young person in question could indeed do the job; and (2) that he or she can't successfully convey this fact to the prospective employer. As a result, the employer — who perhaps uses on-the-job experience as the criterion for separating good prospective workers from bad ones — is unwilling to hire the inexperienced youth. The key element in this case is clearly a problem in communicating relevant information.

A similar phenomenon arises in the market for car insurance. If a driver is under age 25, particularly if that driver is also male and single, his rates for collision insurance can be astronomical. These rates reflect the fact that, on average, drivers in this category have significantly worse accident records than do other drivers.

Not all young, single males are bad drivers, and some are very good. If we presume that the good drivers know that they are good, they face a problem analogous to that of young job searchers: they can't convey this information to insurance companies. Instead, their options are limited to either paying outrageous rates or going without collision insurance.

The Economics of Information: A Model

In this section, we'll develop a very simple model that lets us explore some problems in the economics of information. This model is an extension of the one in the preceding section. In this extended model, we'll make three special assumptions: (1) individuals are not homogeneous with respect to the risk that they will actually incur a loss; (2)

they cannot communicate information about themselves costlessly to others (especially to insurance firms); and (3) each individual is completely informed about the risks he or she faces. Our intention here is to capture the essence of situations in which there is **asymmetric information**: situations in which individuals know more about themselves than others do.

To incorporate heterogeneity in the simplest possible way, we'll assume that there are two groups of risk-averse individuals, differing in only one respect: the probability that they will incur some loss L. Let p^1 be the probability of loss for the low-risk group and p^2 the probability of loss for the high-risk group. Thus, p^1 is less than p^2. We'll examine the market for insurance against this loss L and will consider only insurance policies offering full coverage.

We'll begin by deriving in Figure 6.5 the reservation prices I_r^1 — for a member of the low-risk group — and I_r^2 — for a member of the high-risk group. Notice that in the figure, we have assumed that everyone in the two groups has identical preferences and initial wealth w_0. The only difference between the two groups is the probability of incurring the loss L. Thus I_r^1 is smaller than I_r^2. If insurance companies can identify without cost which risk group any individual belongs to, two types of policies will be written in a competitive market equilibrium: one for the low-risk group and the other for the high-risk group. If we again ignore the costs of writing insurance policies, their competitive prices will be $p^1 L$ and $p^2 L$ in Figure 6.5. When obtaining information about group identity is costless, then, the analysis is a simple generalization of what we have already discovered.

Adverse Selection

Let's suppose that individuals know their own probability of loss but that insurance companies have no way to freely acquire

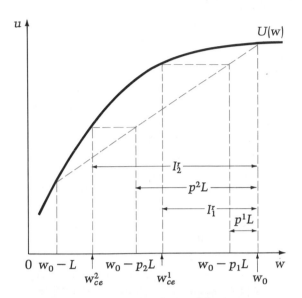

FIGURE 6.5 More on the demand for insurance.

Individuals in low-risk and high-risk groups incur loss L with probabilities p_1 and p_2, respectively, and they have identical utility functions and initial wealth w_0. For the low-risk group, w_{ce}^1 is the certainty equivalent of the risky prospect and I_1^r the reservation price for insurance offering full coverage against loss L. Similarly, for the high-risk group, w_{ce}^2 is the certainty equivalent and I_2^r the reservation price.

writing and administering policies, the market price for this policy will be determined by the *relative sizes of the two groups*. Let s be the proportion of low-risk individuals in the population; $1 - s$ is therefore the proportion of high-risk individuals. The probability that a randomly selected individual will incur loss L is then $sp^1 + (1 - s)p^2$. If they all buy insurance, the market price I' will satisfy

$$I' = L[sp^1 + (1 - s)p^2]$$

From this equation, we see that

$$p^1L < I' < p^2L$$

In other words, low-risk individuals pay more than they would have if information on the risk group had been freely available, and high-risk individuals pay less. In a sense, then, low-risk individuals subsidize the insurance purchases of high-risk individuals in this equilibrium.

Low-risk individuals will buy the policy, however, only if I' is less than (or equal to) the reservation price I_r^1. Because p^2L exceeds I_r^1 in Figure 6.5, I' is not necessarily less than I_r^1. If the proportion of high-risk individuals $(1 - s)$ is large enough, the price I' will exceed I_r^1. Low-risk individuals will therefore refuse to buy the policy, and the market price will not be I'. Instead, the resulting competitive equilibrium will be one in which only high-risk individuals buy insurance, and the price they pay will be p^2L.

This is a case of **market failure**: a failure that arises because information with respect to risk — though available to individuals — is not communicable. As we saw in the previous section, insurance markets perform a valuable function: with perfect information, such markets allow individuals to shed all risk at no cost to themselves (in terms of expected monetary wealth). When information is not communicable, however, the insurance market may fail, in the sense that low-risk individuals personally bear the risk of loss.

that information. In addition, let's suppose that firms can't generate, and individuals can't provide, convincing evidence of the probabilities of loss. (Simply claiming to be in the low-risk group wouldn't do, for instance, since all self-interested individuals — whether or not they were in fact in the low-risk group — might easily make similar claims.) We'll continue to restrict our attention to policies offering full coverage.[6]

What will happen in this extreme circumstance? The market will offer only one policy. Again assuming a competitive insurance market and ignoring firms' costs of

---

[6] See Rothschild and Stiglitz (1976) for a more complete analysis of insurance and asymmetric information.

This market failure arises from a phenomenon called **adverse selection**. When insurance companies cannot identify individual risk categories, they are forced to offer a single policy — one that is obviously more attractive to high-risk than to low-risk individuals. In fact, if some low-risk individuals choose not to insure, rates climb; that rate hike then drives even more low-risk individuals out of the market, causing rates to go even higher and forcing even more low-risk individuals out of the market. In our two-risk-group model, all the low-risk individuals are driven from the market — an extreme form of adverse selection.

The Lemons Principle

The phenomenon of adverse selection has a more colorful tag, attributable to George Akerlof (1970). Akerlof was concerned with the market for lemons — the kind you drive, not the kind for making lemonade. Akerlof asked, in essence, why the market price of a new car drops by $1500 or more the instant the proud owner drives it off the lot.

To understand his explanation, imagine that there are only two types of used cars: "lemons" and "jewels." Imagine, too, that ascertaining whether a particular used car is a lemon or a jewel is prohibitively costly for a potential buyer — but that car sellers do know. Imagine further that all car owners who want to sell their cars actually put them on the market.

The price of used cars will then reflect the mix of lemons and jewels offered for sale. We'll assume that buyers form subjective probabilities based on the relative proportions of lemons and jewels offered for sale. The owner of a jewel will then be unable to sell it at a price that reflects its true value, because the owner can't effectively communicate the car's true worth. (How many lemon owners will honestly say that their car is a lemon?)

Some owners who want to sell their jewels at a "fair" price may decide not to sell at the market price. The proportion of lemons on the market then increases, further depressing the market price and perhaps inducing other owners of jewels to withdraw their cars from the market. In the eventual equilibrium, some owners of jewels — unwilling to accept significantly less than the car's true value — choose not to sell at the market price. If all such owners make this choice, there will be a market for lemons but none for jewels.

In this situation of asymmetric information, lemons drive jewels (some or all of them) out of the market — a phenomenon that we might call *the lemons principle*.

PROBLEM 6.14

Suppose that, with perfect information, the market value of a jewel is $2400 and the market value of a lemon is $1200. Assume that, in the absence of perfect information, the market price of a car will be $s\$2400 + (1-s)\$1200$, where s is the proportion of jewels on the market. There are three groups of potential sellers. There are 200 owners of jewels whose reservation prices are $2000, 400 owners of jewels whose reservation prices are $1600, and 400 owners of lemons whose reservation prices are less than $1200. Show that the cars in the last two groups, but not those in the first group, will be sold. What is the market failure in this case?

Signaling and Screening

The problem that runs throughout this section is that people suffer real economic consequences because they are unable to communicate relevant information. But what if an individual can figure out a way to convey that information?[7]

Let's return to the insurance example and suppose now that, at a cost, low-risk

---

[7] Interested readers are referred to the insightful and remarkably readable book by Spence (1974).

individuals can signal their identity. How might they do this? In the market for automobile collision insurance, for instance, we can think of low-risk individuals as careful drivers and high-risk individuals as careless drivers. One obvious signal a careful driver can produce is a certificate from a reputable driver-education program, because good drivers will pass the course but bad drivers won't. Here we somewhat unrealistically ignore the possibility that the training actually changes the probability of an accident; we are assuming instead that such training simply certifies the driver as belonging to the low-risk group. If acquiring the certificate is not too expensive and if everyone acknowledges the information provided by the certificate, then regardless of what the equilibrium would be in the absence of this informational signal, good drivers will acquire it — and the market equilibrium will shift accordingly.

$(1 - s)$ is higher; when the discrepancy between probabilities of loss $(p^2 - p^1)$ is greater; and when the loss itself (L) is larger.

Suppose that C is small enough that low-risk drivers have an incentive to acquire the signal. The market equilibrium will then offer two policies at prices p^1L and p^2L; all drivers will buy insurance; and, of course, low-risk drivers will spend resources on signal acquisition.

In this case, signal acquisition, which uses real resources, simply performs a distributional task. It allows low-risk drivers to recover some — but not all — of the subsidy they would otherwise be forced to pay to high-risk drivers. They can't recover the entire subsidy because they have to spend resources acquiring the signal. In this case, the signaling is "unproductive," because everyone was already insuring.

Unproductive Signaling

Suppose that in the absence of such a signal, the equilibrium is one in which all individuals fully insure at the previously calculated equilibrium price:

$$I' = sp^1L + (1 - s)p^2L$$

If a low-risk driver could acquire the signal — the certificate in this case — then he or she could buy car insurance at the competitive price for low-risk drivers, p^1L. Notice that p^1L is less than I'. Letting C be the cost of acquiring good driver certification, the low-risk individual will do so if

$$p^1L + C < I' \quad \text{or if} \quad C < I' - p^1L$$

Using the definition of I', this condition can be rewritten as

$$C < L(1 - s)(p^2 - p^1)$$

This condition is more likely to hold (given C) when the proportion of high-risk drivers

Productive Signaling

The preceding example illustrates unproductive signaling. Now suppose that, in the absence of signaling, the equilibrium is one in which only high-risk drivers insure. In this case, low-risk drivers will acquire the signal if

$$C + p^1L < I_r^1$$

where I_r^1 is the low-risk drivers' reservation price for full coverage. If they do acquire the signal (if C is small enough), a market will form, and they will buy insurance at price p^1L. In this example of productive signaling, the signaling facilitates the formation of a new market in which individuals can shed risk that they otherwise would have borne themselves in the absence of a signal.

So far, we've focused on signaling by individuals. The other side of the coin is screening by firms. In the signaling equilibria we identified, firms used the signal (in this example, the certificate) to screen individuals. To return to our inexperienced job searcher, we see that employers sometimes use experience (and, of course, references) to screen applicants: job experience is a signal. Frustratingly, this screening technique has a catch-22. If all employers use such a screening technique, it may be impossible for the inexperienced worker to break into the market. In times of high unemployment, for example, employers may have no incentive to experiment with other screening techniques.

College Degrees As Signals

Once we grasp the basic insights of signaling-screening equilibria, we can look at familiar events from a new perspective. For example, these ideas suggest the possibility that a major function of higher education is to provide the relatively gifted with a means of signaling their abilities to the world. A degree from Harvard or Stanford or Oxford or Queen's may be valuable partly because it is seen as a signal of the degree holder's ability. The following problem, adapted from Stiglitz (1975), will allow you to explore this possibility in a very simple model.

P R O B L E M 6.15

Imagine a world peopled by superior and inferior workers: a superior worker is worth $50 per hour to any employer, and an inferior worker is worth only $20 per hour. These people work for exactly 10 hours, and then retire. Let s be the proportion of superior workers, and $1 - s$ the proportion of inferior workers. What will the common wage be if the superior workers do not signal their ability? Assume that in the labor-market equilibrium, workers are paid their expected worth. Now suppose that a degree costs superior workers $200 and that it is simply impossible for an inferior worker to get one. For what values of s will superior workers acquire a degree to signal their superior productivity?

Summary

In this chapter, we extended the theory of consumer behavior to situations involving risk and then used this expanded theory to examine a variety of problems in which either risk or imperfect information plays a central role. We began with an empirical paradox: decision makers usually do not make choices based on the relative expected (monetary) values of different risky outcomes. Instead, it seems plausible that they base their choices on the expected utility of the various prospects. We then detailed a set of assumptions that allowed us to convert this expected-utility hypothesis into an expected-utility theorem. If satisfied, these assumptions guarantee that individuals will base their choices on the expected utilities associated with those prospects.

In applying the expected-utility theory, we identified three potential psychological attitudes toward risk: risk aversion, risk neutrality, and risk inclination. Risk aversion accounts for a wide range of risk-pooling and risk-spreading institutions and is thought to be the prevailing attitude toward risk. Two important risk-related institutions are markets for insurance (risk pooling) and joint-stock companies (risk spreading).

We then turned to problems in the economics of information, focusing on the problem of asymmetric information as we examined (among other issues) Akerlof's lemons principle and the closely related phenomena of signaling and screening.

Exercises

1 Guy Rogers reveals the following piece of information regarding his preferences for risky prospects with prizes of $20, $12, and $0:

(0, 1, 0: 20, 12, 0) **I** (.7, 0, .3: 20, 12, 0)

a Explain in words the meaning of this preference statement.

b Assuming that Guy satisfies the expected utility assumptions, find a utility function that represents Guy's preferences for prospects with these three prizes.

c Is Guy risk-averse, risk-neutral, or risk-inclined? Explain.

d Compute Guy's expected utility for the following prospects:

Prospect A   (.6, 0, .4: 20, 12, 0)

Prospect B   (.4, .2, .4: 20, 12, 0)

Prospect C   (0, 1, 0: 20, 12, 0)

Prospect D   (.3, .4, .3: 20, 12, 0)

Prospect E   (.5, .2, .3: 20, 12, 0)

e What is Guy's preference ordering for these prospects?

2 Julie says that she is indifferent between (1) a lottery that pays either $100 or $10 with equal probability and (2) $50 with certainty. Which lottery will Julie choose in each of the following situations?

a (1/4, 3/4: 100, 10) or (1/2, 1/2: 50, 10)

b (3/4, 1/4: 100, 10) or (9/10, 1/10: 50, 10)

c (1/2, 1/2: 100, 10) or (2/6, 1/6, 1/6: 100, 50, 10)

3 Consider the following prospects, which offer prizes $10, $5, and $1.

Prospect A   (1/3, 1/3, 1/3: 10, 5, 1)

Prospect B   (1/2, 0, 1/2: 10, 5, 1)

Prospect C   (0, 3/4, 1/4,: 10, 5, 1)

a Let $U(10) = 1$ and $U(1) = 0$, and then find $U(5)$ for a risk-neutral person.

b Show that "C preferred to A preferred to B" is consistent with expected-utility theory. Is this preference ordering associated with risk aversion, risk inclination, or risk neutrality?

c Show that "B preferred to A preferred to C" is consistent with expected-utility theory. Is this preference ordering associated with risk aversion, risk inclination, or risk neutrality?

d Show that "C preferred to B preferred to

A" is inconsistent with expected-utility theory.

4 Consider the following game. Daniel offers to toss a coin until one head appears, and he promises to pay you 2^n dollars, where n is the toss on which the first head appears. If it appears on the first toss, you get $2; if on the second, $4; if on the third, $8; and so on. What is the maximum amount you would pay to play the game? What is the expected value of this game? This is the exercise that led Daniel Bernoulli to propose the expected-utility hypothesis.

5 Farmer Jane has to decide whether or not to fertilize her field. The decision is a difficult one, because her profit depends not only on her decision with respect to fertilizer, but also on whether it rains or not. Her profit w in each of the four possible cases is given below:

	Do not fertilize	Fertilize
Rain	$w = \$16$	$w = \$25$
No rain	$w = \$9$	$w = \$0$

Suppose that the probability of rain is 1/2. Will Jane fertilize her field if her utility function is $U(w) = w^{1/2}$? If it is $U(w) = w$? If it is $U(w) = w^2$?

6 Mike is going to Lake Tahoe and plans to take $2500. With probability 1/2, he will lose $1600 on his way to Tahoe. Thus, he'll spend $2500 in Tahoe if he is lucky and only $900 if he is unlucky. His utility from the trip is given by the following function:

$$U(E) = E^{1/2}$$

where E is the amount of money he spends in Tahoe.

a What is Mike's expected utility from the trip?

b Suppose Mike can buy an insurance policy that will cover the entire $1600 loss. Will he buy it if its price is $1000? $900? $800?

c What is Mike's reservation price for this insurance policy?

d What is the competitive equilibrium price of the policy if insurance companies have perfect information and incur no transaction costs?

7 Kevin is also going to Tahoe with $2500, has the same utility function as does Mike, but is more careful with his money than is Mike — Kevin will lose $1600 with probability 1/4.

a What is Kevin's reservation price for the insurance policy offering full coverage against the $1600 loss?

b Suppose now that there are many people like Mike, and many like Kevin, and that insurance companies can't tell which people are careless with their money ($p = 1/2$) and which are careful with their money ($p = 1/4$). Suppose too that the insurance market is competitive, that insurance companies incur no transactions costs, and that the only policy offered is the full-coverage policy. Carefully describe the competitive equilibrium when half the people are like Mike ($p = 1/2$) and half like Kevin ($p = 1/4$). When one-eighth are like Mike and seven-eighths like Kevin.

8 Some states have recently made it illegal to discriminate on the basis of sex and age in the sale of automobile insurance. Insurance firms must offer the same price to all residents of these states, regardless of age or sex. (An older friend is waiting for the day when the same sort of laws prohibit such discrimination in the sale of life insurance.) Could this sort of legislation be a source of market failure?

9 Given the utility function, $U(w) = 20 - 600/w$, suppose that initial wealth is zero ($w_0 = 0$) and that there are three prospects: (1/2, 1/2: 40, 40), (1/2, 1/2: 50, 30), and (1/2, 1/2: 60, 20). Notice that the expected (monetary) value of each of these prospects is 40. Show that the first is preferred to the second and the second to the third. Now, sketch this utility function and convince yourself that it represents risk-averse preferences. This problem illustrates the following proposition: given a choice between two risky prospects with the same expected values and the same probabilities but with different outcomes, a risk-averse person

will choose the prospect with the smaller spread in outcomes, and a risk-inclined person will choose the prospect with the larger spread in outcomes.

10 In bygone days, bank customers joined a lineup in front of a particular teller to transact their business at the bank. More recently, most banks have established a single lineup in which the customer at the head of the line goes to the next available teller. Using the hypothesis that bank patrons are risk-averse, discuss why banks have adopted this new system. Begin by assuming that when a risk-averse customer, Mr. Q, walks into the bank, two tellers and two customers are already in the bank and another customer is coming through the door behind him. Which lineup system would Mr. Q. prefer?

11 Ms. Q, whose $1000 wealth is invested in a riskless asset, has been offered the chance to buy a firm that produces snake oil. The price of the firm is $500. The Federal Drug Administration is reviewing the snake oil with an eye to banning its sale. She believes that with probability 1/2 the snake oil will be banned and the business will then be worthless and that with probability 1/2 it will be approved and the business will then be worth $2500. Her utility function is $\ln(w)$, the natural logarithm of her wealth w. Will she buy the business?

12 This problem concerns a puzzle raised by individuals who simultaneously insure and gamble. This behavior is puzzling because risk-averse preferences induce people to insure but not to gamble, and risk-inclined preferences induce them to gamble but not to insure. In this problem, you can rediscover a very famous explanation of this puzzle suggested by Friedman and Savage (1948). Mr. Inflection's utility function is

$$U(w) = w^{1/2} \quad \text{if } w \le 1$$

and

$$U(w) = w^2 \quad \text{if } w > 1$$

a What is Mr. Inflection's attitude toward risk?

b Let Inflection's initial wealth be equal to 1, $w_0 = 1$, and suppose that he will incur a loss $L = 1/2$ with probability $p = 1/20$ and that he can insure against this loss for a price p times L, or $1/40$. Suppose, too, that he can buy a lottery ticket that will pay $J = 1$ with probability $q = 1/1000$ (and will otherwise pay nothing) for a price equal to q times J, or $1/1000$. Inflection has four options: to buy insurance; to buy the lottery ticket; to buy both; or to buy neither. Rank the four options. In particular, show that he will buy both.

c In 25 words or less, what is the explanation of Mr. Inflection's curious behavior?

*13 Lucky Pierre is a risk-averse prospector who has struck it rich. He has $\$W$ worth of gold—his only wealth—safely stashed away on his claim. He wants to get his gold from his claim to the big city where he hopes to spend it. His friend Wells Fargo will transport the gold for him free of charge. With probability p, all the gold on any trip will be stolen; with probability $(1 - p)$, none of it will be stolen. Show that Lucky's expected utility is larger if half the gold is transferred in each of two trips than if all the gold is transferred in a single trip.

*14 On a popular TV game show, contestants are sometimes given the chance to choose the prize behind one of three curtains. Typically, a handsome prize (a new car, for example) is behind one curtain, and a booby prize (perhaps a year's supply of moustache wax or kitty litter) is behind each of the other two curtains. Knowing that there is one "good" prize and two "bad" ones, but not knowing what is behind any particular curtain, the contestant chooses a curtain. The host then opens one of the two curtains not chosen by the contestant. *Invariably*, a booby prize appears behind the opened curtain. The host then asks the contestant if he or she wants to switch choice of curtains. Get a friend to act as host, making sure that he or she always opens a curtain to reveal a booby prize, and try the switching strategy

20 times and the no-switching strategy 20 times. Based on your experience, which seems to be the better strategy? Can you show that the switching strategy produces the new car with probability 2/3 and that the no-switching strategy produces it with probability 1/3?

*15 Arlene and Bob inhabit a very boring economy in which the only scarce goods are two apples. Currently, Arlene has one apple and Bob has the other. They are trying to figure out whether they should just eat their apples or use them to do some gambling. The gamble they have in mind will result in one of them having both apples. Specifically, with probability p, Arlene will get both apples and Bob none, and with probability $1 - p$, Bob will get both and Arlene none.

a When is there a value of p such that both will prefer the gamble to eating their apples? Hint: Arlene's preferences can be captured by the following utility function: $U^A(2) = 1$, $U^A(1) = A$, $U^A(0) = 0$, where A is a number between 0 and 1; similarly, Bob's preferences can be captured by the following utility function: $U^B(2) = 1$, $U^B(1) = B$, $U^B(0) = 0$, where B is a number between 0 and 1.

b Are the following statements true or false? (1) "If both Arlene and Bob are risk-inclined, they will gamble instead of just eating their apples." (2) "If either Arlene or Bob is risk-averse, they will not gamble."

*16 Construct a graphic proof of the proposition stated in Exercise 9.

References

Akerlof, G. (1970), "The Market for 'Lemons': Quality, Uncertainty and the Market Mechanisms," *Quarterly Journal of Economics*, **84**:488–500.

Bernoulli, D. (1954), "Exposition of a New Theory on the Measurement of Risk," *Econometrica*, **22**:23–36.

Friedman, M., and L. J. Savage (1948), "The Utility Analysis of Choices Involving Risk," *Journal of Political Economy*, **56**:279–304.

Luce, R., and H. Raiffa (1957), *Games and Decisions*, New York: Wiley.

Machina, M. J. (1987), "Expected Utility Hypothesis," in *The New Palgrave*, J. Eotwell, M. Milgate, and P. Newman (eds.), London: Macmillan, pp. 232–238.

Rothschild, M., and J. E. Stiglitz (1976), "Equilibrium in Competitive Insurance Markets: An Eassy on the Economics of Imperfect Information," *Quarterly Journal of Economics*, **90**:630–649.

Spence, A. M. (1974), *Market Signaling: Information Transfer in Hiring and Related Screening Processes*, Cambridge, Mass.: Harvard University Press.

Stiglitz, J. E. (1975), "The Theory of 'Screening,' Education, and the Distribution of Income," *American Economic Review*, **65**:283–300.

von Neumann, J., and O. Morgenstern (1944), *The Theory of Games and Economic Behavior*, Princeton: Princeton University Press.

The Firm

The next three chapters focus on firms whose function is to transform the natural resources owned and supplied by individuals into the goods and services those individuals demand. Because these firms are entities created by and for human beings, the natural questions — given the infinitely many ways to organize economic activity — are: Why do firms come into being? Why do they take the particular organizational forms that we see? From the perspective of economic theory, this issue is new territory. Our treatment of the firm in Chapter 7 will be exploratory rather than authoritative. We'll see how firms resolve the contradiction between collective interests and individual self-interest through their organizational forms and ask why multiperson firms exist.

In Chapters 8 and 9, we'll take a more standard approach by viewing the firm as an organization described by its production function (by the terms on which it can transform inputs into outputs) and motivated by its desire to maximize profit. In Chapter 8, we'll construct the theory of production when only one input is variable, and then we'll build the corresponding theory of cost. In Chapter 9, we'll extend the theory of production and of cost to the more realistic environment of many variable inputs, drawing heavily on the techniques developed in the parallel but simpler exercise presented in Chapter 8.

*7

THE THEORY OF THE FIRM

In this chapter, we'll deal with some of the questions that arise when we analyze the firm. Because we'll be covering relatively new territory, our approach will be exploratory and suggestive. You should consider this material as work in progress rather than as traditional, firmly rooted, and widely accepted theory. Although modern treatment of the theory of the firm is attracting more and more attention, it is still pioneering work. We intend in this chapter to give an overview of the research to date and to provide guidelines for further exploration.

With this chapter, we'll make the leap from the theory of demand to the theory of supply. In the theory of demand, we focused on the behavior of individual consumers. In the theory of supply, we'll be looking instead at the behavior of firms.

7.1 The Standard Conception of the Firm

From the perspective of traditional economics, a firm is an entity that buys factors of production, or **inputs,** and transforms them into goods or services, or **outputs,** for sale. In a sawmill, for example, logs, labor, and saws are all inputs, and lumber is the output. If we suppose that a firm makes only one product, we can describe the firm's abil-ity to transform inputs into output by a **production function.** A production function might tell us, for example, that given 11 cubic yards of cedar, a 36-inch circular saw, and 12 hours of labor, a lumber company can produce 810 lineal feet of 4-by-4 lumber. We'll spend a great deal of time defining and exploring the production function in the next two chapters. For now, an intuitive notion of what the term means is sufficient.

In the traditional theory of supply, the firm plays a role closely analogous to the role played by the individual in the theory of demand. In the theory of demand, individuals are described by utility functions; they are motivated by the desire to maximize utility; and they are constrained by the terms on which they can buy goods and services and can sell labor and other resources. Correspondingly, in the traditional theory of supply, firms are described by production functions; they are motivated by the desire to maximize profit; and they are constrained by the terms on which they can buy inputs and can sell goods or services.

The power of this approach to the theory of supply derives in large part from the relatively simple model of the firm it assumes. In the traditional approach, the firm is a given, or predetermined entity, that is fully described by its production function: inputs go in at one end of the production process, they are transformed by the firm, and they emerge at the other end as output. A problem with this model, however, is that firms, unlike individuals in consumer theory, are not natural entities. Instead, they are owned by individuals and are usually created to serve the interests of those owners.

Once we pause to look inside the firm rather than to view it from the outside as a predetermined entity—as a sort of black box into which we cannot see—many intriguing questions emerge that simply would not arise in the traditional view of the firm. Among these are questions about the internal organization of firms and about the forces that both bring firms into existence and limit their size.

7.2 Organizational Forms and Questions in a Theory of the Firm

In this section, we'll raise some of the questions that the modern theory of the firm addresses and suggest a general approach to answering them. We can start by reexamining what the term **firm** means. Of course, a firm can range in size from one coconut-milk peddler on the beach or a mom-and-pop grocery around the corner to IT&T or General Motors Corporation. At least as significant as the variation in the size of firms is the variation in their organizational structure. The mom-and-pop grocery and GM differ not only in size but also in organization. (How would you quickly characterize the differences in organizational structure?)

Three Structures of the Firm

One way to get a useful overview of this vast diversity of organizational forms is to consider the relationship between the owner-

ship and the management, or control, of different firms. If we isolate this aspect of the firm, we discover that firms generally take one of three possible forms: the owner-managed firm, the partnership, and the publicly held firm.

The most common form is the owner-managed firm. In such a firm, one person owns the firm and also makes the important managerial decisions. Economists often use the term **residual claimant** for the person or persons who have claim to the profit of a firm. In the **owner-managed firm,** the owner-manager is the sole residual claimant. The window cleaning company owned and operated by Will Seymore is one example of an owner-managed firm. The economics consulting firm run by Marvin Shaffer is another. Both are cases of owner-managed firms because the person who makes the managerial decisions that affect the firm's profit is the same person who lays claim to that profit. In fact, if you think of all the firms that you have contact with in a week, many or even most will be owner-managed.

The second important organizational form is the **partnership.** In this case, there is no single owner, or residual claimant, and no single manager. Instead, the ownership and management functions of the firm are jointly shared by two or more people who work in the firm. Law and accounting firms are commonly organized as partnerships. Many small businesses, such as restaurants, gas stations, meat markets, and clothing goods stores, are often owned and operated by two or more business partners, all of whom work in the business, share in the managerial functions, and receive some share of the firm's profits.

If we rank organizational structures by the dollar volume of business, the third organizational form—the **publicly held firm**—must be considered the predominant form. In a publicly held firm, ownership is spread over many individuals, none of whom owns a significant portion of the firm. Consequently, ownership is almost totally separated from management or control.[1]

Most of the firms on the Fortune 500 list fit this category. Their owners are their shareholders — all those who hold some of the firm's common stock. The firms themselves, however, are actually run by professional managers who are essentially employees (even though they, too, may hold some of their firm's common stock). These managers are supervised by a board of directors that represents the firm's many shareholders.

Although individual shareholders may lay claim to some portion of the firm's profits, they play no significant role in the day-to-day management of the firm. Conversely, the firm's managers can claim relatively little of the firm's profits, even though they are responsible for making the decisions that affect the firm's operation.[2]

Although we can loosely identify three basic organizational structures, the significant point is that the patterns of ownership and control — the organizational forms laid

out in the firm's organization chart — are extremely diverse. Indeed, if we look more deeply into the firm, we see even more organizational diversity. For example, think of the many ways in which workers in a firm are compensated for their labor. Some get hourly wages, some get salaries, and others get piece rates. Compensation can also take other forms: for example, stock options and profit-sharing arrangements for managers and, in some cases, for all employees; Christmas bonuses or productivity-determined bonuses; and all sorts of perquisites ("perks"), ranging from a key to the executive washroom to personal use of the company car or even the corporate airplane.

For example, a rapidly expanding chain of Italian fast-food outlets, Sbarro, awards its productive managers up to 15% of a restaurant's net profits. Pepsi-Co gives its top 550 managers first-class air travel, luxury hotels on the road, a company car every 2 years or $11,000 every year, and annual salary bonuses of 25% to 50%; it gives all its employees access to a gym with a masseuse and a 150-acre sculpture garden as well as unlimited free Pepsi at work. Genentech, the company that engineered the blood-clot-dissolving drug Activase, offered each of its employees options on 100 shares of stock when the company was given the official green light to market its new product by the Food and Drug Administration. Inco Ltd. of Sudbury, Ontario, pays its mine workers individual bonuses for increased productivity in constructing underground supports (with unfortunate results, as we'll see).

Think, too, of the diversity of institutional arrangements governing job security. In many firms, seniority determines an employee's job security. The longer an employee has been with a firm, the more secure is his or her position. In other workplaces — in the construction industry, for example — workers are typically hired on a

---

[1] There are really three types of corporations: public, private, and governmental. The common stock of public corporations — the dominant form — is traded on organized markets such as the New York Stock Exchange, whereas the common stock of private corporations is not. Because we are concerned with private economic activity, government corporations are not a subject of our analysis.

[2] These distinctions concern the relationship between ownership and control in firms, not the legal status of firms. By *partnerships*, then, we mean firms characterized by a small number of residual claimants, each of whom exercises some managerial control. By *publicly held firms*, we mean not corporations but rather firms characterized by what Berle and Means (1935) call "divorce of ownership from control," because ownership is dispersed among a large number of people.

short-term basis and have virtually no job security. In some firms, management is constrained in deciding who is to be terminated by an elaborate set of quasi-judicial procedures. In others, management has nearly a free hand in deciding who is to be dismissed and what are acceptable grounds for dismissal.

Once we think in more detail about just what a firm is, we see that the term covers a colossal variety of institutional arrangements. The task of a modern theory of the firm — given this perspective from within the black box — is to create a systematic way in which to understand the diversity of the entity that we call "the firm." Therefore, a theory of the firm must help us to understand why firms exist and what determines both their size and their particular organizational structures.

A Puzzle: Cooperation from Noncooperative Behavior

At the heart of modern theories of the firm lies a puzzle. If we view the firm from the outside and ignore the details of its operation, we see the firm to be an enterprise fundamentally characterized by cooperation. Two lumberjacks using a double-handled saw work together to produce lumber for sale. Four employees of a small moving company cooperate to get the furniture out of the customer's apartment and into the van. Partners in a law firm specializing in criminal cases may jointly prepare and argue the cases; they may divide the cases between them, each preparing and arguing some of them; or one partner may research all the cases and the other argue them. But, whatever their arrangement, the services their firm provides depend on the partners' joint, or cooperative, effort. In short, the success of any firm ultimately depends on the cooperative efforts of its workers.

Once we abandon this external perspective and look inside the firm, however, a different picture emerges. When we venture into the firm we see only individuals: owners, managers, secretaries, supervisors, assemblers, receptionists, janitors, sales personnel, and cashiers. What motivates all these individuals? As economists, we assume that they are pursuing their own self-interest. But once we realize that the individuals who compose the firm are motivated by self-interest, a puzzle emerges. We know that the firm's success in achieving its collective objectives depends on the cooperative effort of the people involved in the productive process. Yet these people are motivated not by collective but by private objectives.

We must wonder, then, how and to what extent the self-interested individuals within the firm actually work to promote the interests of the firm as a whole. Do lumberjacks ever slack off when they are working or spend more time than necessary sharpening the saw? Do the moving company's workers ever take extended coffee breaks or pocket one of the customer's possessions? Does a lawyer ever take office supplies for private use or fail to put in the time needed to track down a key witness? Do assembly-line workers ever call in sick when they simply want a day off or deliberately assemble a product improperly?

Such common industrial ailments as slacking off at work, malingering, theft, and sabotage suggest that the behavior of individuals sometimes does frustrate and even undermine the collective interests of the firm as a whole. For example, a recent study of phone calls made by employees from the workplace found that about 33% of all such calls were personal rather than work-related, costing large companies as much as $1 million per year. In Britain, the former chairman of Guinness has been charged with stealing Guinness funds in connection with a multimillion dollar scandal. Using this internal perspective, we can rephrase our question: How can the firm secure the cooperation of its employees? The following problems will help to get you into the spirit of this inquiry.

PROBLEM 7.1

Life insurance salespeople are sometimes paid a large bonus for selling a new policy. For example, a salesperson might receive $1500 today for selling a new policy whose annual premium is only $1000. Of course, the purchaser has the option of canceling the policy at the end of any year. Given this scheme, how does the self-interest of an unscrupulous salesperson diverge from the insurance company's interest?

PROBLEM 7.2

A stock option allows its holder to buy stock from the firm at a specified price during a specified time period. Suppose that company X's stock is selling today for $10 a share and that the board of directors is thinking of giving Margaret, the CEO, the following stock option: she can buy up to 10,000 shares at $10 per share any time during the next 3 years. If you were a shareholder of this company, would you be in favor of giving the president this stock option? Why or why not?

A Key to the Puzzle: Institutions

As you probably realized from Problems 7.1 and 7.2, the key to answering the question "How can the firm secure the cooperation of its employees?" lies in the amazing diversity of institutions, or organizational forms, that firms exhibit. The central hypothesis of modern theories of the firm is that the institutional structure of a given firm is the structure that best harmonizes the self-interest of individuals within that firm with the wider collective interest of the firm itself. The important point is this: the way in which a firm is internally organized will depend on its objectives. For example, a garment manufacturer's institutional arrange-

ments will be different, depending on whether its goal is to make thousands of cheap dresses or a few hundred very expensive dresses.

Think of a particular dress manufacturer's decision about whether to pay sewing-machine operators an hourly wage or by piece rate. If the company decides on a piece rate (a fixed sum for each dress), what behavior can it anticipate from its employees? Under this arrangement, operators will try to increase their rate of production by sewing more quickly and paying less attention to detail, because their take-home pay will be larger.

In this case, then, a piece rate may induce the individual workers to produce relatively low-quality dresses at a relatively high rate. Thus, if the dress manufacturer is in the low-quality, high-volume segment of the garment industry, paying by piece rate serves to harmonize the self-interest of the individual operators with the dress manufacturer's objective. However, if the manufacturer produces an expensive line of dresses in which meticulous attention to detail counts, paying individual workers by piece rate might frustrate the firm's goals. A firm that sells in the high-quality segment of the industry, then, would be working against its own best interests by choosing piece-rate payments. We would therefore expect to see such a firm pay its operators an hourly wage.

All institutional arrangements can be analyzed in terms of how nearly they achieve congruity between individual self-interest and the collective interests of the firm. The work habits of individual sewing-machine operators will vary, for instance, depending on the circumstances in which they can be dismissed or suspended; on how often their work is monitored; and on benefit packages and bonus structures.

First Choice Haircutters is a firm that specializes in $10 haircuts. Because its success depends on high volume, all its haircutters receive both a share of the firm's profits and personal-productivity bonuses on a biweekly basis. These institutional arrangements encourage them to do what is in the best interest of the firm itself: to clip as many heads as possible in a given amount of time. As you saw in answering Problem 7.2, stock options encourage executives to be good managers by allowing them to capture some of the profit their good management creates.

The behavior of the individuals who make up a firm is moderated by the firm's organizational form — by its institutions. To repeat, the central hypothesis of the modern theory of the firm is that the organizational forms that we encounter every day are the ones that achieve the closest possible identity between the objectives of the individuals inside the firm and those of the firm as a whole.

Does cooperation actually arise from noncooperative behavior? We have already seen that people in the workplace sometimes frustrate the interests of the firm as a whole. Problem 7.1, for example, was inspired by a recent scandal in the sale of life insurance in Ontario, where insurance salespeople behaved in the unscrupulous way you may have imagined in answering that problem. Inco's productivity bonuses — characteristic of incentives used throughout much of the hard-rock mining industry — have recently sparked a controversy over underground safety. Some miners intentionally shorten the bolts that are critical for underground support because they can install almost three times as many shorter bolts during an 8-hour shift and thus almost triple their bonuses. If we suppose that incidents of this kind are not uncommon — that institutional arrangements resolve the potential conflicts of interest within the firm only imperfectly — then another puzzle arises. Why do we ever

see firms that involve more than one person?

A Second Puzzle: The Existence of Multiperson Firms

Let's look at achieving cooperation inside the firm from a different slant: if securing the cooperation of individual workers inside a firm is such a tricky business, why bother creating firms of more than one person? In the one-person, owner-managed firm, the firm is the individual; its collective goals are therefore identical to the individual's self-interested ones. Because owner-managers of one-person operations need not devise clever institutions to secure their own cooperative behavior, no organizational issues arise. Given that such difficult organizational issues inevitably crop up when more than one person works in a particular firm, why do multiperson firms exist? And what determines their size once they come into being?

7.3 The Basic Organizational Issues

A complete theory of the firm explaining such organizational questions doesn't yet exist. However, we can articulate the basic issues and illustrate some of the important research results to date. As we pursue this question, we'll draw heavily on the work of some pioneering economists. (All the research we'll be citing is relatively nontechnical and accessible to intermediate students. If you find the issues raised in this chapter interesting, do consult these sources for further reading.) Let's begin with a situation in which we would never expect to see more than one person in a firm. This exercise will help you to understand why multiperson firms create organizational dilemmas.

The One-Person Firm

In our neighborhood on the third Saturday of every month, the tinker's bell reminds us to bring out our dull knives to be sharpened — at a price, of course. The tinker, who we'll call Robert, combines his capital equipment (a cart, foot-powered grinding wheel, and brass bell); his skill; and, most important of all, his own effort, to sharpen the knives that are brought to him.

How much effort Robert puts in — and effort is the touchstone in this analysis — is entirely up to Robert. He can work at his wheel either quickly or slowly; he can spend time making small talk or not; he can walk along the sidewalk briskly or at a more leisurely pace; he can work from morning till night or put in only a few hours each day; he can be out on the streets 7 days a week or only on weekends. In short, Robert has a great deal of latitude in the effort he exerts.

We will limit our analysis to how much effort Robert chooses to expend and will therefore ignore other choices he might face, such as using an electrically powered grinding wheel instead of a foot-powered one; a siren instead of a bell; or a station wagon instead of a cart. In this very simple model, then, effort alone determines the tinker's output. If we assume that the number of knives the tinker actually sharpens in any period is proportional to the effort he expends and that he charges everyone the same price per knife, then the income his business generates in a period will be directly proportional to the effort he puts into it. For simplicity, we'll assume that each unit of effort generates \$1 of income. That is,

$$y_R = e_R$$

where y_R is Robert's income and e_R is his effort. Because this income-effort relationship tells us the terms on which Robert can convert his effort into command over goods — that is, into income — it effectively de-scribes the technology of tinkering for Robert.

How much effort will he actually choose to expend? To find the answer, we need to know what Robert's preferences are. Using the composite-commodity theorem from Section 4.13, we can capture his preferences in a utility function in which his utility is a function of the effort he expends, e_R, and the income he earns, y_R:

$$u_R = U(e_R, y_R)$$

We'll assume that income is a "good" (as y_R increases, u_R increases) but that effort is a "bad" (as e_R increases, u_R decreases). Therefore, his utility increases in any movement vertically upward in Figure 7.1 because his income (a good) increases, and it decreases in any movement horizontally to the right because effort (a bad) increases.

Because income is a good and effort a bad, the indifference curves in Figure 7.1 are upward sloping. If Robert increases his effort by one unit beginning at point C, for example, his utility decreases because effort is a bad. To get back to the original indifference curve, I_2, his income must be increased by DE in Figure 7.1. The first characteristic of these indifference curves, then, is that they are upward sloping.

We'll also assume that the larger the initial level of effort, the greater the increase in income necessary to compensate for a unit increase in effort. In other words, the more effort that Robert is already putting into his business, the greater must be the increase in his income to compensate for yet more effort on his part. Then, because effort at point F in Figure 7.1 exceeds effort at point C, distance GH exceeds distance DE. The second characteristic of any indifference curve, then, is that its slope increases from left to right.

Seeing how the one-person firm operates is now a simple matter. Robert will choose the amount of effort e_R that maxi-

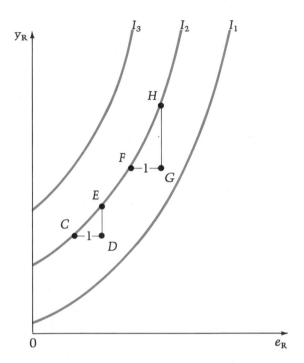

FIGURE 7.1 Preferences over effort and income.

Robert's utility increases as income y_R increases and decreases as effort e_R increases. His indifference curves are therefore positively sloped, and he prefers bundles on indifference curve I_3 to bundles on I_2 to bundles on I_1. His MRS of income for effort increases as e_R increases, and the slope of any indifference curve therefore increases from left to right.

rate of substitution of income for effort (MRS), is equal to 1, the rate at which additional effort generates additional income.

A Two-Person Alternative

What would be the comparable equilibrium if Robert were in a partnership with another tinker? By comparing the one-tinker and two-tinker firms, we can (1) identify an awkward organizational issue that arises in the two-tinker firm, and (2) see why the one-person firm, at least in this simple model, is the preferred organizational form and therefore the one we'd expect to see.

To make these points in the simplest possible way, we'll consider the case in which two tinkers — we'll call them Robert and Virginia — with identical preferences and identical technologies join together to form one firm. We are therefore assuming

mizes his utility $U(e_R, y_R)$, knowing that income y_R is proportional to effort: $y_R = e_R$. He must therefore choose a point on the line $y_R = e_R$ in Figure 7.2. The solution to Robert's choice problem, and therefore the equilibrium for the one-tinker firm, is at point W, where Robert exerts e^* units of effort and earns income y^* — an amount equal to e^*. Given the constraint that income equals effort, the equilibrium for the one-tinker firm is (e^*, y^*) at point W, because this point is associated with the highest attainable indifference curve. Notice that at W, the slope of the indifference curve, or the marginal

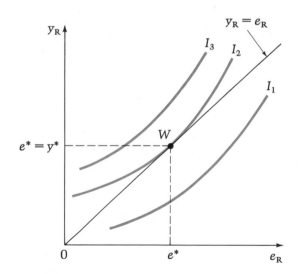

FIGURE 7.2 The one-person firm.

In the one-person firm, one unit of effort produces \$1. Robert's problem, therefore, is to choose e_R and y_R to maximize utility, subject to the constraint that $y_R = e_R$. The problem is solved by finding the point where an indifference curve is tangent to the line $y_R = e_R$. The solution is e^* units of effort and $y^* = e^*$ income.

that the indifference curves in Figures 7.1 and 7.2 describe Virginia's preferences as well as Robert's, and that a unit of her effort produces $1 of income, just as a unit of his effort does.

The technological constraint faced by the two-tinker firm is that the sum of their incomes must equal the effort that they jointly expend:

$$y_R + y_V = e_R + e_V$$

where y_R and e_R are Robert's income and effort, and y_V and e_V are Virginia's.

We'll determine these four quantities — effort and income for Robert and Virginia — in the context of a partnership form of organization. Let's suppose that Robert and Virginia are *equal partners* — that is, that each receives exactly half of their combined earnings. Every day, then, Robert and Virginia make their rounds, putting their effort into sharpening knives. At the end of the day they meet, pool their earnings, and divide them in half.

What will be the equilibrium in this two-person partnership? In other words, what effort will each put into the business and how much income will each get out of it? We'll use the notion of *Nash equilibrium* from Chapter 2 to find out. We'll suppose that Robert chooses his own effort to maximize his own utility, *taking Virginia's effort as given*, and that Virginia chooses her effort, *taking Robert's effort as a given*. (You may want to reread the discussion of Nash equilibrium in Section 2.7 before proceeding.) Furthermore, we'll look for an equilibrium in which Robert and Virginia expend the same effort and enjoy the same income; that is, we'll look for a *symmetric equilibrium*. We can find such an equilibrium because Robert and Virginia have identical preferences and are equally productive.

Notice that in this partnership, the aggregate income of the firm is equal to $(e_R + e_V)$, and Robert's share is exactly half that amount. Therefore, his income is deter-

mined by the following income – effort relationship:

$$y_R = \frac{e_R + e_V}{2}$$

Of course, Virginia's income is determined in exactly the same way.

Since their preferences and technologies are identical, we know from our analysis of the single-person firm that by working alone, each partner could have achieved point W in Figure 7.2. Can they manage the same result in their partnership? To find out, let's suppose that initially both tinkers put out e^* units of effort. Assuming that Virginia continues to expend e^*, let's see whether or not Robert will continue to expend e^* as well.

When e_V is equal to e^*, Robert's own effort generates the income

$$y_R = \frac{e_R + e^*}{2}$$

Given this income-effort relationship, Robert's private problem is to choose e_R so as to maximize his own utility.

In Figure 7.3, we've drawn this income-effort relationship — the solid line $y_R = (e_R + e^*)/2$. We have also included the analogous income-effort relationship for the one-tinker firm from Figure 7.2 — the dashed line $y_R = e_R$. The dashed line allows us to identify the equilibrium for the one-tinker firm, which is (e^*, y^*) at point W. Notice that the two lines intersect at W. In other words, given that Virginia puts out e^* units of effort, if Robert also put out e^* units of effort, his income would again be y^*.

Yet we know from Figure 7.3 that Robert will choose point D rather than point W. In other words, even if Virginia puts out e^* units of effort, Robert himself will decide to put out less effort. Because Robert and Virginia have identical preferences, we also know that if for some reason Robert were to put out e^* units of effort, Virginia would decide to put out less. In sum, neither Robert nor Virginia can achieve point W in their partnership: the partnership fails to achieve the equilibrium of the one-tinker firm.

Why does Robert expend less effort once he enters into a partnership with Virginia (who, we assume, still puts e^* effort into the business)? Notice that as Robert reduces his effort by one unit, the *total income* of the firm declines by \$1, but his *personal income* declines by only \$0.50. As a result, Robert will choose the combination of effort and income at D, where his MRS is equal to the rate at which his own effort increases his own income.

The Partnership Equilibrium

How much effort will the tinkers actually put into the partnership? In any symmetric equilibrium, both Robert and Virginia will supply the same effort and earn the same income — whatever that equilibrium may

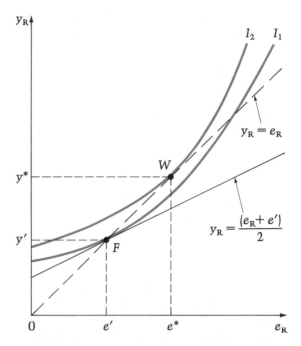

FIGURE 7.4 The partnership equilibrium.

In the partnership equilibrium, Robert (or Virginia) supplies e' units of effort, earns income y', and attains indifference curve I_1. This equilibrium is clearly Pareto-dominated by the one-person firm where Robert (or Virginia) supplies e^* units of effort, earns income y^*, and attains indifference curve I_2.

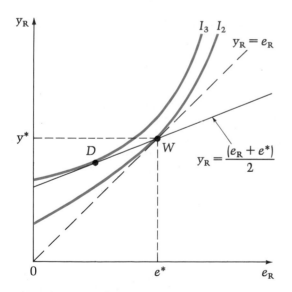

FIGURE 7.3 Shirking in a partnership.

Point W is the solution to Robert's problem in the one-person firm. Is this solution possible in the partnership? If Virginia supplies e^*, then Robert's income-effort relationship is $y_R = (e_R + e^*)/2$, and he will choose point D. Point W is therefore impossible in the partnership.

be. But this implies that at the equilibrium, Robert's income will be equal to the effort he supplies, since one unit of effort creates \$1 of income. In other words, we know that the equilibrium will lie on the dashed line $y_R = e_R$ in Figure 7.4. Furthermore, because each will choose the level of effort that maximizes private utility and because the slope of the income-effort relationship is $\frac{1}{2}$ for each of them, *MRS at the equilibrium will be* $\frac{1}{2}$. Therefore, the equilibrium will be at point F in Figure 7.4 on the line $y_R = e_R$ where MRS is equal to $\frac{1}{2}$.[3]

---

[3] It is possible that there is more than one point on the line $y_R = e_R$ at which MRS is equal to $\frac{1}{2}$. In this case, there are multiple equilibria in the partnership model. For simplicity, we ignore this possibility.

Notice that point W in Figure 7.4 once again represents the equilibrium for the one-tinker firm. By comparing points W and F, we can see that both Robert and Virginia are worse off in the partnership than if each worked in a one-person firm. Why? Because in this partnership, the pursuit of private self-interest by the two tinkers frustrates their collective interest. If, starting at the partnership equilibrium, the two partners were to simultaneously increase their effort, their personal incomes would increase by \$1 for each additional unit of effort — and they would obviously be better off. For example, Robert would move upward and to the right from F along the line $y_R = e_R$ in Figure 7.4. The difficulty with their partnership is this: at point F, neither Robert nor Virginia has a *private incentive* to put out more effort, because each receives only half the income generated by an additional unit of personal effort. That is, the partnership fails to create the right private incentives because neither Robert nor Virginia can capture the whole of the added output that their personal effort creates.

Notice the key role that residual claimancy plays as an incentive in this analysis. In both cases, an added unit of effort creates \$1 of income. In the partnership equilibrium, however, each tinker's MRS is equal to $\frac{1}{2}$ because each claims only half of the added income generated by personal effort. By contrast, in the equilibrium of the one-person firm, each tinker's MRS is equal to 1 because each claims the full income created by additional effort. In either case, the tinker's right as a residual claimant dictates the choice of effort he or she puts into the firm.

In using the concept of Nash equilibrium to analyze the partnership, we've assumed that Robert and Virginia are not honorable enough simply to agree to the equilibrium at point W in Figure 7.4 and to stick to their bargain by expending e^* effort apiece. This honorable solution is certainly

a possibility, particularly in the two-partner case. In Problem 7.3, however, you'll have a chance to see why honor might get stretched too thin when a larger number of partners is involved.

The fundamental point is that Robert and Virginia can't improve on the single-person equilibrium. They have nothing to gain, and — as our analysis reveals — may well have something to lose by forming a partnership. The partnership arrangement potentially involves a real cost to the two partners, and the magnitude of this cost increases as the number of tinkers in the partnership grows.

PROBLEM 7.3

Suppose that three individuals are in a partnership, that all three have identical preferences and technologies, and that each partner receives one-third of the total income from the firm. Construct a diagram analogous to Figure 7.4 and identify the equilibria for the one-person firm and for the two- and three-person partnerships. What is the fate of this type of partnership as the number of partners grows larger?

The two-tinker firm is preferable only if some real advantage is associated with it — for example, if a unit of effort produced more income in a partnership than it does in a one-person firm. We'll extend our model to incorporate this possibility in the next section. As it stands, however, there is no such advantage and therefore no reason for anything other than a one-person firm to exist: multiperson firms offer nothing but troublesome institutional dilemmas to resolve.

Pareto Optimality and Choice of Institutions

We can use the one- and two-tinker models to articulate more clearly the basic hypothesis of modern theories of the firm: the institutions that we actually see are the ones that most nearly harmonize the private interest of individuals with the collective interest of the firm as a whole. The hypothesis is based on the Pareto criterion and on the supposition that the Nash equilibrium associated with any organizational form correctly describes the positions that individuals would attain given that institution. Because our two tinkers are both better off in the Nash equilibrium of one-person firms than they are in the Nash equilibrium of the partnership, the one-person firm is the Pareto-preferred organizational form.

Modern theories of the firm assume, quite reasonably, that when individuals choose between organizational forms, they will choose the Pareto-preferred one. For example, this assumption implies that Robert and Virginia will choose to work in one-person firms rather than in a partnership. If the comparison is extended to all organizational forms, modern theories of the firm suppose that a Pareto-optimal organizational form will be chosen. An organizational form is Pareto-optimal if there is no other organizational form that will leave all parties at least as well off and at least one party better off.

7.4 Team Production and the Modern Theory of the Firm

If multiperson firms create nothing but trouble, why do we encounter so many larger firms in everyday economic life? Multiperson firms come into being only when the advantages that accrue to size outweigh the disadvantages created by organizational difficulties. One such advantage arises from the gains in productivity associated with team production. **Team production** refers to the arrangement in which two or more workers accomplish a productive task through their joint, or team, effort. The idea of team production is simply a varia-

tion on the old adage, "Many hands make light work." In team production, the hypothesis is that many hands do more work. In many circumstances, team production is potentially more productive than isolated production, in which laborers work alone. The higher productivity of team production may therefore account for the existence of multiperson firms.

We'll begin this section, then, by exploring the productivity gains associated with team production. We'll see that when these gains are large enough, the partnership form of organization is Pareto-preferred to the one-person firm. We'll then introduce and analyze another organizational form— *the owner-managed team*—and determine the circumstances in which each of the three organizational forms—the one-person firm, the partnership, and the owner-managed team—is Pareto-preferred to the other two.

In their pioneering work, Alchian and Demsetz (1972) used the example of workers loading boxes onto a truck to illustrate the productive potential of teams. Imagine two identical workers—each hired for 1 day only—loading boxes. For the moment, let's fix the effort expended by each worker over the day and compare the output when each laborer works in isolation with the output when the two work as a team.

First, suppose each worker expends his or her fixed effort in loading boxes alone. Let x be the aggregate number of boxes loaded. Then, suppose they work together, lifting one box from opposite sides and expending their fixed effort as a team. Let y be the aggregate number of boxes the team loads. Alchian and Demsetz argue that if the boxes are large and awkward or if they are heavy, y will exceed x. In this case, production in teams is potentially more productive than production in isolation. It is even possible—if the boxes are heavy enough that one worker cannot lift them but not too heavy for two to lift—that x is zero and y is positive. In this case, production in teams is infinitely more productive than production in isolation.

We can identify a whole array of jobs in which team production is economic. In a large number of carpentering tasks — siding or drywalling a house, for example — two pairs of hands are almost essential. Surveying is another productive activity in which two people working together as a team are vastly more productive than they would be if they worked in isolation.

In creating our own model of team production, we'll follow Alchain and Demsetz's lead by looking at the task of loading boxes onto a truck. We'll suppose that workers receive a fixed price for each box they load and that the number of boxes loaded is proportional to effort. We can then describe the technology by a proportional relationship between income and effort. When the task is done by individuals working in isolation, we'll suppose that each unit of effort produces $1 of income, and when individuals work in two-person teams, we'll suppose that each unit of effort produces $B of income. Team production is then more productive than isolated production when $B > 1$. In this section, we'll assume that B is greater than 1 — that is, we'll only look at the case in which team production is more productive than isolated production.

Organizing Team Production

The potentially superior productivity of teamwork provides an incentive to organize economic activity into multiperson firms. Yet will this potential be realized in a multiperson firm? If it is, which organizational form should we expect such team production to take — a partnership or an owner-managed team?

To find out, let's return to our two workers, Robert and Virginia, and continue to assume that they have identical prefer-

ences. We know exactly what will happen if they choose the isolated production technique. They will form two one-person firms, and each worker will attain point W in Figure 7.2. But if they instead decide to work as a team, which multiperson firm will they pick — a partnership or an owner-managed team? And under what circumstances will they be better off using the technology of team production rather than the technology of isolated production?

Given our assumptions, the aggregate income of the team is proportional to their aggregate effort:

$$y_R + y_V = B(e_R + e_V)$$

Notice that if one team worker decides not to put out any effort, a minor difficulty arises with this description of the team technology. For example, suppose that Virginia decides not to work, and that e_V is therefore equal to zero. This means that Robert is left loading boxes by himself. In this case, Robert's effort actually produces only $1 rather than $B per unit. To remedy this difficulty, we'll assume that the factor of proportionality for team production is B if both e_R and e_V are strictly positive, but is only 1 if either e_R or e_V is zero. That is,

$$y_R + y_V = \begin{cases} B(e_R + e_V) & \text{if } e_R > 0 \text{ and } e_V > 0 \\ e_R + e_V & \text{if } e_R = 0 \text{ or } e_V = 0 \end{cases}$$

Partnership with Team Production

We already know from the two-tinker model what the equilibrium will be if the team is organized as a partnership. In Figure 7.5, Robert will pick point C on the line $y_R = Be_R$ where his MRS is equal to $B/2$ since, in the partnership, an additional unit of his effort increases his income by $B/2$. (Of course, Virginia will also pick a point analogous to point C.) In the following problem, you can show that the partnership is Pareto-

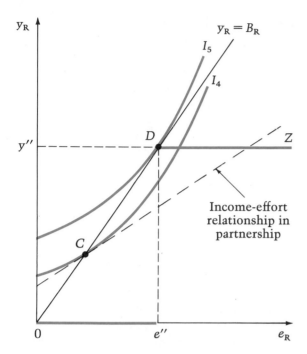

FIGURE 7.5   The owner-managed firm.

Both the owner-manager and the employee can attain point D. First, suppose that Robert is the employee and Virginia the owner-manager. As the employee, Robert's income-effort relationship is composed of two segments—$0e''$ and DZ—and to maximize utility, Robert will supply e'' and earn y''. Now, suppose that Robert is instead the owner-manager and Virginia the employee. Because he must now pay Virginia y'', and because Virginia will supply e'' effort, Robert's income-effort relationship is $y_R = B(e_R + e'') - y''$. But $y'' = Be''$, and this income-effort relationship reduces to $y_R = Be_R$. Hence, as owner-manager, Robert also chooses to supply e'' and earns y''.

preferred to the one-person firm if B is sufficiently large—that is, if the productivity gain associated with team production is sufficiently large.

PROBLEM 7.4

Begin by constructing the income-effort relationship for a worker loading boxes alone, and identify the equilibrium for the one-person firm. On the same diagram, identify the point that corresponds to the equilibrium for the partnership at point C

in Figure 7.5. In doing so, choose the value of B so that the equilibria of the partnership and the one-person firm are on the same indifference curve. Which organizational form is Pareto-preferred for larger values of B? For smaller values?

The Owner-Managed Team

If Robert and Virginia could overcome the difficulty inherent in this partnership equilibrium, however, they could do even better. Specifically, Robert could attain point D in Figure 7.5, where his effort is e'' and his income y''—a point clearly preferable to point C. Is there an organizational arrangement that would allow Robert to attain point D (and Virginia to attain the analagous point)? Yes, if it's not too costly to write contracts or to *monitor*—that is, to observe and verify—the effort of a teammate.

For the moment, let's assume that contracting and monitoring costs are nonexistent. (Later, we'll extend the model to include these costs.) Now suppose that Virginia becomes the team's owner-manager and that she offers to employ Robert under the terms of this contract:

Robert will receive an income of y'' from Virginia if he supplies e'' or more units of effort. If Robert fails to do so, he will receive no income.

If Robert agrees to these terms, the contract is enforceable, because we have assumed that his effort can be monitored without cost. There are two aspects to enforceability. First, enforceability means that if Robert fails to supply at least e'' units, Virginia can demonstrate without cost to some court that he did not meet the contractual conditions, and she will not have to pay him y''. On the other hand, it means that if Robert does supply at least e'' units of effort and Virginia fails to meet her end of the deal, then Robert can demonstrate without cost that he has met the contractual conditions, and he can force Virginia to pay him y''.

Let's show that this contract allows both parties to attain (e'', y'') at point D in Figure 7.5. It's a simple exercise for Robert. In Figure 7.5, Robert's income-effort relationship is composed of two thick horizontal line segments. The first is segment $0e''$ of the line $y_R = 0$ (the e_R axis), because he receives nothing if he doesn't supply e'' units of effort. The second is segment DZ of the line $y = y''$, because he receives y'' if he supplies at least e'' units. To maximize his own utility, Robert will therefore choose point D on this income-effort relationship where he supplies e'' units of effort and receives y'' in income.

Now let's turn to Virginia. As the owner-manager, she is the exclusive residual claimant for the firm. This means that her income is the amount remaining after Robert has supplied e'' and been paid y''. Accordingly, her income-effort relationship is

$$y_V = B(e'' + e_V) - y''$$

Because y'' is equal to Be'', however, Virginia's income-effort relationship can be rewritten as

$$y_V = Be_V$$

Given this income-effort relationship and preferences identical to Robert's, we know that to maximize her own utility, Virginia will choose a point analogous to point D in Figure 7.5 where she, too, supplies e'' units of effort and receives y'' as income. (If you do not understand this result, simply relabel Figure 7.5 by replacing e_R with e_V and y_R with y_V.)

The owner-managed team thus allows both team workers to attain the effort-income combination (e'', y'') — a combination that is clearly Pareto-preferred to the combination attainable in a partnership. In the following problem, you can show that the owner-managed team is also Pareto-preferred to the one-person firm.

PROBLEM 7.5

Draw a diagram in which you identify the point that corresponds to the equilibrium for an owner-managed team at point D in Figure 7.5. On the same diagram, construct the income-effort relationship for a one-person firm and identify the equilibrium. Notice that the owner-managed team is Pareto-preferred to the one-person firm.

Contracting and Monitoring Costs and the Owner-Managed Firm

We have discovered that when it costs nothing for a firm to enter into contracts with its employees or to monitor their performance, the owner-managed team is Pareto-preferred to both the single-person firm and the partnership. However, entering into such contracts is seldom free of cost. Even an unwritten agreement — the proverbial handshake — costs the parties to the agreement time and effort. Written contracts are even more expensive because somebody (or several somebodies) must draw them up, type them out, duplicate copies, send the copies to the contracting parties, and so on.

Monitoring workers can also be an expensive business. For example, it costs money — sometimes a great deal of money — to take a case through the courts if an employee does not meet the terms of a contract. It often costs money, too, just to find out whether the terms of a contract have been met. Think of the problem faced by a university president in deciding if some professor has actually fulfilled his or her contractual obligations. How can the president monitor classroom performance without spending money on regular in-class supervision, student achievement tests, and other assessment methods?

Other types of employee monitoring also can be expensive. For example, more and more businesses of all sizes are investing in costly telecommunications monitoring to generate data used to prod workers into higher productivity and to trap workers who abuse the phone system. Depending on the design of a company's telecommunications system, it can cost up to $100,000 to install call-accounting systems used to monitor and report on workers' use of company phones. So, too, Alchian and Demsetz (1972) argue that the cost of supervision in the legal profession is extremely high. For example, if a law firm supervisor wants to determine whether one of its lawyers has adequately prepared a case, he or she may have to replicate the whole of the employee's work. In such cases, the owner-manager's advantage in being the single residual claimant may well be outweighed by the cost disadvantage of monitoring employees.

Let's extend our model to include the costs associated with entering into contracts with employees and monitoring employee productivity. Notice that these costs arise only in the owner-managed team, since neither contracting or monitoring is necessary to enforce the equilibrium in either the partnership or the one-person firm.

What is the symmetric equilibrium of the owner-managed team in the presence of these contracting and monitoring costs — or **monitoring costs**, for short? To find out, let's begin by identifying the highest indifference curve Robert can attain if he has to pay for *half* the monitoring costs, denoted by M, but can keep *all* the income generated by his own effort. His income-effort relationship is then

$$y_R = Be_R - \frac{M}{2}$$

Given this relationship, the highest indifference curve that Robert can attain is the combination of e' units of effort and an income of y' at point V in Figure 7.6.

The following contract will allow both Robert and Virginia to attain the income-effort combination at point V in Figure 7.6:

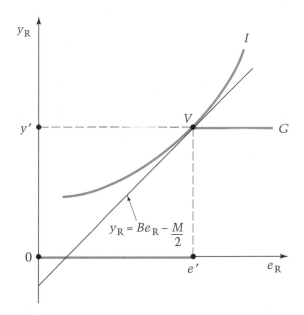

FIGURE 7.6   The owner-managed firm with monitoring costs.

The owner-managed firm's monitoring costs are M. As the employee, Robert's income-effort relationship is composed of two horizontal segments — $0e'$ and VG — and as the owner-manager, his income-effort relationship is $y_R = Be_R - M/2$. In either case, he supplies e' units of effort and earns income y'.

Virginia will pay Robert y' on the condition that Robert agrees to supply e' or more units of effort; if Robert fails to do so, he'll receive no income.

To see why, simply adapt the argument used to find the initial equilibrium for the owner-managed team. The following problem will get you started.

PROBLEM 7.6

Given this contract, what is Robert's income-effort relationship? What is Virginia's?

To reinforce your understanding of the role of monitoring costs, try the following problem.

1 First construct a diagram in which you identify the equilibrium of the one-person firm. Then find values for B and M such that the one-person firm and the owner-managed team are equally attractive.

2 Beginning at this position, if you increase M by a small amount, which of the two organizational forms is now Pareto-preferred?

3 Beginning again at the initial position, if you now increase B by a small amount, which is Pareto-preferred?

7.5 Finding a Pareto-Preferred Organizational Form

We now have a moderately complex model with three possible organizational forms: (1) the single-person firm using the isolated technology and (2) the partnership or (3) the owner-managed team using the team technology. Because each organizational form has its advantages and disadvantages, choosing the right one can be a complicated and interesting problem. As you'll soon see, depending on the circumstances, any one of the three organizational forms we've considered can be Pareto-preferred to the other two. Before we begin, however, let's recap the advantages and disadvantages of the three types of firms.

A single-person firm cannot take advantage of the potentially greater productivity associated with team production, but it can make the best of its less productive technology because it has no trouble harmonizing the self-interest of its single worker and the interest of the firm as a whole. They are one and the same. A partnership can take advantage of the productivity gains associated with team production, but it cannot make the best use of its more productive technology because the private self-interest of the individual partners is at odds with the collective interest of the partnership as a

whole. Then which of these two firms is preferable? It all depends on whether, in a given industry, the productivity advantage associated with teamwork, B, is large or small. If B is small, then a single-person firm will be Pareto-preferred. If B is large, then a partnership will be Pareto-preferred.

What about an owner-managed team? Like a partnership, it can take advantage of the greater productivity associated with team production. In fact, if monitoring costs, M, are small, it can take much better advantage of those productivity gains than the partnership can and will be Pareto-preferred to both a partnership and a single-person firm. If M is large, however, a partnership or a single-person firm — or both — will be Pareto-preferred to an owner-managed team.

Clearly, which organizational form will be Pareto-preferred in any given circumstance will depend on the specific values of the parameters B and M. If B is large and M is small, the owner-managed team will be Pareto-preferred. On the other hand, if B is small and M large, the one-person firm will be Pareto-preferred. And if both B and M are large, the partnership will be Pareto-preferred.

In fact, we can be very precise about these comparisons. In Figure 7.7, we've indicated the portions of the parameter space in which each of the three organizational forms is Pareto-preferred. In the dark green area, it is the partnership. In the light green area, it is the owner-managed firm. And in the unshaded area, it is the single-person firm. (To make the analysis complete, we have also allowed B to be less than 1 in Figure 7.7. When this is the case, team production is less productive than is production in isolation.)

Let's look more closely at Figure 7.7 — in particular, at lines AA', CC', and DD'. (Lines CC' and DD' are not necessarily straight, but it is convenient to draw them as

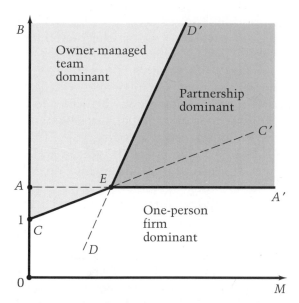

FIGURE 7.7 Pareto-preferred organizational forms.

In the dark green portion of the figure, the partnership is the Pareto-preferred form of organization; in the light green portion of the figure, the owner-managed team is the Pareto-preferred form of organization; in the unshaded portion of the figure, the one-person firm is the Pareto-preferred form of organization.

one-person firm; below CC', the reverse is true. This line has two special features. First, the point $M = 0$ and $B = 1$ is on the line CC'. When $B = 1$, the two technologies are equally productive, and since $M = 0$, both the owner-managed team and the one-person firm exploit their respective technologies equally effectively. Second, the line CC' is upward sloping. Beginning at any point on the line, as M increases, the one-person firm becomes more attractive than the owner-managed team, and to make them equally attractive once again, B must increase. This simply reflects what you learned in answering Problem 7.7.

On the line DD', the partnership and the owner-managed teams are equally attractive. Above DD', the owner-managed team is Pareto-preferred to the partnership; below DD', the reverse is true. DD' has three special features. First, it must pass through point E. Why? Because point E is on both AA' and CC', we know that all three organizational forms are equally attractive at point E, and DD' must therefore pass through it. Second, above its intersection with the line AA', DD' lies above EC'. Why? In the area above EA' and below EC', the partnership is Pareto-preferred to the one-person firm, and the one-person firm is Pareto-preferred to the owner-managed team. Hence, the partnership is Parcto-preferred to the owner-managed team in this area, and DD' therefore cannot enter it. Rather, it must lie above EC', as drawn. Third, below its intersection with the line AA', DD' lies below CE. Why? In the area above CE and below AE, the owner-managed firm is Pareto-preferred to the one-person firm, and the one-person firm is Pareto-preferred to the partnership. Hence, the owner-managed team is Pareto-preferred to the partnership in this area, and DD' therefore cannot enter it. Rather, it must lie below CE, as drawn.

Figure 7.7 is essentially a metaphor for the modern approach to the theory of the

if they were.) Notice that along each of these lines, two organizational forms are equally attractive. Each line therefore separates the parameter space into two regions. In one of the two regions, one of two organizational forms is Pareto-preferred, and in the other region, the reverse is true.

For example, on the horizontal line AA', the partnership and the one-person firm are equally attractive. Above AA', the partnership is Pareto-preferred to the one-person firm; below AA', the reverse is true. The line AA' simply reflects what you learned in Problem 7.4.

Similarly, on the line CC', the one-person firm and the owner-managed team are equally attractive. Above CC', the owner-managed team is Pareto-preferred to the firm: it conveys both how complex the problem of choosing an appropriate organizational form can be and how a modern economist approaches the solution to that problem. That approach is to assume that in any particular circumstance, the Pareto-preferred organizational form will be chosen. For example, the one-person firm is attractive because the owner of the one-person firm doesn't have to ask: How can I secure my own cooperation? But it is also unattractive because the firm size is limited to a single person — and therefore it can't tap into any productivity gains associated with team production. As a result, we would expect to see single-person firms in circumstances where gains from team production are small or nonexistent and where achieving cooperation is difficult.

7.6 Specialization and the Division of Labor

We have seen how team production is a potential source of productive advantages. In this section, we'll explore specialization and the division of labor. Adam Smith was the first to identify these twin phenomena as important sources of the productivity advantages that give rise to the "wealth of nations." (Indeed, most economists date the year of birth of economics as 1776 — the year in which Smith's *Inquiry Into the Nature and Causes of the Wealth of Nations* was first published.) In the opening few pages of *Wealth of Nations*, Smith argues that the greatest improvement in the productive powers of labor stems from the effects of the division of labor: the breaking up of the productive process into a series of smaller specialized tasks, each performed again and again by a single person.

Smith's fundamental insight is that a group of workers is potentially more productive with the **division of labor**, when an entire production process is divided into a series of separate tasks so that individual workers can **specialize** in one or a few of those tasks. In Smith's illustration — the eighteenth-century pin factory — labor is vastly more productive in the presence of the division of labor and of specialization.

We find a modern counterpart of the pin factory under any of the golden arches spread around the globe: in any McDonald's restaurant, the task of making and selling a Big Mac is divided into a number of separate operations. Among these tasks are taking the customer's order; cooking the meat patty; putting it in a bun; adding the lettuce, onion, cheese, pickle, and special sauce; boxing it up; conveying the box to the front counter; bagging it; handing it to the customer; pushing the Big Mac button on the cash register; taking the customer's cash; making change; and trying to sell an apple pie as well. No single person ever does all or even most of these jobs. Instead, each McDonald's employee specializes in just one or a few of them. In some outlets, specialization is so extreme that the person who rings up an order is different from the one who takes the customer's money and counts out the change.

According to Smith, three factors explain the increased productivity that arises from specialization and the division of labor. First, specialized workers become more productive simply as a result of practice and repetition. With practice, McDonald's employees who box the burgers get to be very fast at it. The longer people spend at one task — *learning by doing* — the more proficient they become.

Second, by specializing in one or a few tasks, workers don't lose time moving from one task to another. A firm therefore can economize on aggregate *setup costs* — the costs of getting ready to do each task — by having each worker perform one or a few rather than all jobs. Think how much time would be lost if each McDonald's order taker had to walk into the kitchen first to place and then to pick up each order.

Third, Smith argued that specialization encourages *technical progress*. People who concentrate on a small number of tasks are likely to discover more efficient ways to perform them. For example, workers who specialize in a task may be able to design tools and machines to make the work even more efficient. In many McDonald's outlets, for instance, standard cash registers have been replaced by simpler, more specialized ones, in which each key is a pictograph representing one of the items for sale. (Could it be that some clever employee devised this labor-saving cash register?) To see the productivity implications of setup costs, try the following problem.

PROBLEM 7.8

Suppose some manufacturing process involves two separate stages and that the setup times for each stage are 60 and 120 minutes, respectively. It takes 60 minutes for a worker to get ready for stage 1 and 120 minutes to get ready for stage 2. Suppose that the worker, having expended the setup time, takes 10 minutes in each stage to process 1 unit of output. Show that 1 worker could produce 15 units in 8 hours; that 2 workers, each working for 8 hours, could produce 36 units; and that 13 workers, each working for 8 hours, could produce 252 units. Given 13 workers, how many should specialize in stage 1 and how many in stage 2? Notice that the productivity per worker increases from 15 to 18 to 19.4 units per worker.

Team production and specialized production share one important feature: because both are potentially more productive, both may account for the existence of firms. (Whether the full potential of that specialization is realized, however, depends once again on how successfully a firm's organizational arrangements harmonize the self-interest of individual workers with the firm's collective goals.) However, team produc-

tion and specialization differ in one crucial respect: the team-production process does not take place as a series of specialized activities, each carried out by a single worker. Two important observations follow from this difference.

First, in specialized production, the task of determining whether a worker is carrying his or her own load is usually fairly simple. In a sequential production process, we can watch the semifinished good as it passes from hand to hand: we can inspect the frozen hamburger patties before they're put on the grill and after they've been cooked; check the Big Macs in their buns for the seven essential ingredients; and watch as they are placed on the racks by the checkout area. As a result, if something goes amiss, we can assess fairly accurately and relatively costlessly just which worker has let the firm down.

In team production, however, it may be harder to assess how much effort an individual worker puts into the job. Alchian and Demsetz have suggested that in team production, clues to each worker's effort are sometimes available. These might include how rapidly a man loading boxes moves to the next piece to be loaded, how many cigarette breaks he takes, and whether the box he carries with a coworker tilts downward toward his side. Such clues notwithstanding, all that we can observe for certain is the output produced by the team as a whole. We can't see the number of boxes that I lifted, or that you lifted, but only the number that we lifted together.

Second, in specialized production, all stages of the production process need not be carried out by a single firm. For instance, McDonald's frozen hamburger patties and its sesame-seed buns are both made by other firms; the sesame seeds on top of the buns and the beef that goes into making the meat patties are produced by still other firms. Thus, some segments of the Big Mac production process are carried out in-house and others are carried out in other firms.

By contrast, team production must always be carried out within the confines of a single firm because it cannot be divided into a series of segmented tasks. A large, heavy box is indivisible: I cannot first lift and load "my half" of it and then move on while you lift and load "your half."

Issues in Specialized Production

Specialized production — because it differs in essential ways from team production — raises distinctive issues. In particular, specialization permits the choice between coordinating all stages of the process in-house or coordinating some stages in-house and others through markets. We can see both arrangements in the world around us. For instance, the Croissant Palace bakes and sells its croissants on the premises, but it relies on another firm to produce its dough. A canola oil refinery may buy its canola seeds in the marketplace and have the seed oil extracted by another firm specializing in crushing and extraction, but may carry out the oil refining and product packaging processes in-house. The steel and glass used by Diamond-Star Motors Corporation, a new joint venture between Mitsubishi Motor Corporation and Chrysler Corporation, will be supplied by facilities owned by Mitsubishi, but other components such as engine mounts, bumpers, and shock absorbers will be supplied by outside firms. Campbell Soup Company in Canada gets its mushrooms and poultry from its own farms, but it buys the English muffins and precooked fried eggs in its Swanson's frozen breakfasts from outside suppliers.

Transactions Costs

What determines whether all stages of specialized production will take place within a single firm or will be coordinated by markets? The answer is actually a theory of firm size. It tells us, for example, what factors encourage Pillsbury to buy raw wheat and process its own flour or to buy flour from another firm; or it tells us what factors encourage Campbell Soup Company to produce and process its own fried eggs or to buy precooked fried eggs from another firm.

We already know that coordinating production inside a multiperson firm presents problems that can be difficult and expensive to resolve. If there were no costs associated with coordinating production through markets, we would expect to see a series of small firms interacting in markets for semifinished goods. However, market transactions do entail costs. The transactions costs of coordinating production through markets include the costs of writing and enforcing contracts between firms, the costs of keeping accurate records of transactions, and the time cost of exchanging money for goods.

Ronald Coase (1937) pioneered a general approach that has been used to determine whether specific production activities will take place inside a multiperson firm or through markets. Coase argued that the choice will depend on the relative costs of the two options. To simplify his argument, a firm will expand to the point at which the organizational cost of adding another function in-house is just equal to the transaction cost of coordinating that function through the marketplace.

Although we can't set out Coase's analysis in detail, we'll draw a fundamental distinction between two kinds of partly finished goods — generic and specific — that serve as inputs in other production processes, and we'll examine the transactions costs associated with each.[4]

---

[4] Williamson (1985) is the most comprehensive guide to literature on transactions-costs economics.

Generic Inputs

Think of the relationship between a baking company that makes bread from flour (and other essential ingredients) and a flour manufacturer that makes flour from wheat. We can imagine that a particular baking company might mill its own flour. If the flour it produces in-house is identical to the flour produced elsewhere, the company will be indifferent between using its own flour and using flour produced by a dozen other millers.

As Gertrude Stein might have said, "Flour is flour is flour." Because flour is a **generic input** — different sources of it are interchangeable — we can imagine a flour market composed of many suppliers (millers) and many demanders (a multitude of other baking companies, large and small, for example). In such a market, we can use Coase's hypothesis to separate the activities coordinated in-house from those coordinated through markets by comparing their respective costs.

Specific Inputs

In some production processes, however, inputs are not generic but specific. For example, N C Machine, a tool-and-die shop in Wichita, has manufactured a styrofoam container for a McDonald's hamburger, the handle for a Sears Craftsman wrench, and the plastic holder for a Toyota auto seat belt. Dowty Canada Ltd. builds the nose-wheel and main landing gear for Lockheed's P-7A airplane. Eagle Wings Industries will make bumpers for Diamond Star. A small Toronto supplier makes Campbell's fried eggs. These are **specific inputs** because they are of no use to any firm except the one they are intended for. A plastic holder for a Toyota auto seat belt, for instance, is of no use to anyone but Toyota.

When an input is highly specific, then, there cannot be a market for that input in the ordinary sense of the word. There might be more than one supplier, but there will be precisely one demander. (More than one firm might make the K-car chassis, for example, but only Chrysler Corporation will buy it.) Furthermore, no supplier will produce firm-specific, partly finished goods simply on speculation that the lone demander will buy them. The demander and its supplier(s) will invariably come to a detailed contractual agreement before any partly finished goods are produced. For example, Campbell Soup Company went through long, delicate negotiations before its fried-egg supplier agreed to buy the equipment it needed to begin producing fried eggs. And such agreements are costly.

Let's see what sort of issues specific inputs raise and why costly agreements are necessary if one firm is to produce a specific input for another. Specifically, let's suppose that I want to manufacture a one-of-a-kind customized car for someone whose tastes are so peculiar that the car will be worthless to anyone else. Suppose too that we have a verbal agreement in which you agree to make the auto body for me and I agree to pay you $100,000 for it. If you do produce the body to my specifications, will I actually pay you the promised price on delivery day? If I'm honest and if I can, I will. But if I'm less than honest, I may try to take advantage of you. Ignoring the scrap value of the body, you are now holding an auto body that has value to me alone. Suppose I offered you half the amount we had agreed upon? If I could convince you that I wouldn't offer more, you'd accept. In fact, you'd accept any positive price rather than keep the body yourself. By producing a highly specific input, then, you have put yourself into a very shaky bargaining position.

On the other hand, I may have put myself into an equally awkward position. If I don't have time to get the auto body elsewhere, you may be able to extract more than $100,000 from me. Suppose that I've incurred $100,000 in additional costs and that using the body you've made, I can immediately sell the car for $250,000. Suppose, too, that if I don't deliver the finished product immediately, the deal is off and I'll be left with an unmarketable car. What is the maximum I would pay for the body? It is virtually $250,000 — and if you were unscrupulous, you'd ask for that amount. Clearly, if you and I are to transact, we must have some form of contractual protection, and that protection will be costly. If it's too costly, our market arrangement simply will not be viable — and all production will be done in-house.

Any specific input raises this sort of issue. The consequence is that costly contractual arrangements must be entered into whenever one firm acquires a specific input from another. There is therefore a bias toward in-house production of specific inputs.

Specific Capital Assets

An equally important problem for suppliers of specialized parts is that they must often buy expensive single-purpose equipment. The dies used to stamp a specific auto body, for example, are extremely expensive and have only one use. Campbell's fried-egg supplier invested in expensive equipment to produce an input that only Campbell demands — fried eggs of very specific color, shape, and thickness. Again, suppliers will need to protect themselves against the potential for unscrupulous dealing created by these specific capital assets, and such protection may be expensive.

The problems associated with specific inputs and specific capital assets are common in all kinds of production processes. They almost invariably arise whenever one firm subcontracts work to another. A drywaller who subcontracts with a general contractor, for example, clearly faces these problems because the finished walls are specific to the building. An accounting firm may have difficulties if it puts effort and money into designing a specific bookkeeping system for a particular firm. A computer-parts manufacturing company may have problems if it produces components specific to a particular firm's computer. (Can you think of other examples?) These transactions almost invariably mean that the demander and the supplier must agree to mutually protective measures — and these measures cost something.

PROBLEM 7.9
The law sometimes attempts to facilitate contracting in the presence of specificity. For example, a Mechanic's Lien Act, on the books in virtually all jurisdictions in North America, permits building tradespeople to register a lien against the real property they are working on. The lien prevents the sale of the property until the tradesperson's bill has been paid. Is such legislation in the self-interest of property owners as well as tradespeople?

Specificity and the Coordination of Economic Activity

Let's summarize the implications of specificity. On one hand, firms have an incentive to decentralize their activity; that is, to buy partly finished goods as inputs, because they can thereby avoid the difficulties associated with harmonizing the interests of individuals within the firm. On the other hand, firms have a disincentive to buy specific inputs from other firms, because these inputs are associated with what we might call **contracting costs**. Whether we'll find decentralization (that is, coordination of economic activity by markets) or centralization (that is, coordination of economic activity within firms) depends on whether or not the advantages of decentralization outweigh the resulting contracting costs. Remember, too, that even when the activity is coordinated in the marketplace, a market for a specific input is not a "market" in the ordinary sense of the word. It is instead a hybrid of the in-house and market systems of coordination.

Summary

This exploration of the organization of the firm has been tentative rather than definitive. We wanted to provide you with a sampling of the kinds of intriguing (and sometimes difficult) questions that arise once we look inside the firm itself and to suggest how contemporary researchers in the area are attempting to analyze these questions.

We began with the observation that coordinating economic activity within firms is problematical. The basic problem — from the firm's point of view — is how to secure the cooperation of its members in achieving the firm's collective objectives. (How can a Macy's department store, for instance, control theft by its employees?) Broadly speaking, the answer lies in designing organizational forms that harmonize or identify as closely as possible the collective interests of the firm with the self-interest of the individuals within it.

We then developed a model in which we could explore this problem more fully. We looked at three organizational forms — a one-person firm using isolated production, a partnership using team production, and an owner-managed team using team production — in a range of environments described by two parameters — M the cost of monitoring and B the productivity of effort in team production. To illustrate the economist's approach to the theory of the firm, we used the Pareto criterion to choose among the three forms. If B is large and M is small, the owner-managed team is Pareto-preferred. If B is small and M is large, the one-person firm is Pareto-preferred. And if both B and M are large, the partnership is Pareto-preferred.

When we considered specialized production, we saw that the problem of harmonizing incentives also determines whether certain productive activities will be coordinated in-house or in the marketplace by means of transactions among vertically interrelated firms, or by a hybrid of the two. The theory of the firm is thus a part of a more general theory of the organization of economic activity as a whole.

We discovered, too, that incentive problems are extraordinarily diverse: different problems require different solutions. Given so many different incentive problems and so many different solutions in terms of organizational form, the range of economic questions yet unexplored is enormous. The theory of the firm and the broader theory of economic organization are both wide open to further analysis.

Exercises

1 In this problem, we'll use the following utility function to illustrate the possible equilibrium organizational structures explored in Sections 7.3 through 7.5.

$$U(e, y) = 8 \left(y - \frac{e^2}{2} \right)$$

With this utility function, MRS or the slope of an indifference curve is equal to e:

$$\text{MRS} = e$$

In the two-person team, each unit of effort produces $\$B$ of income, and in the one-person firm, each unit of effort produces $\$1$ of income.

a Draw two indifference curves.

b Derive the following results for the one-person firm:

utility-maximizing quantity of effort $= 1$

utility-maximizing income $= 1$

maximized utility $= 4$

Hints: At the utility-maximizing equilibrium, the slope of the income-effort relationship is equal to MRS; to compute maximized utility, evaluate $U(e, y)$ at the utility-maximizing values of effort and income.

c Derive the following results for the two-person partnership:

utility-maximizing quantity of effort $= \dfrac{B}{2}$

utility-maximizing income $= \dfrac{B^2}{2}$

maximized utility $= 3B^2$

Hint: The slope of the income-effort relationship for the partnership is $B/2$.

d Derive the following results for the owner-managed team:

utility-maximizing quantity of effort $= B$

utility-maximizing income $= B^2 - \dfrac{M}{2}$

maximized utility $= 4B^2 - 4M$

Hint: Both the manager and the employee in effect each pay half of the monitoring cost M.

e Use the maximized-utility results from above to construct a diagram with M on the horizontal axis and B^2 on the vertical axis, in which you identify values of M and B^2 such that (1) the one-person firm Pareto-dominates the other firms, (2) the owner-managed firm Pareto-dominates, and (3) the partnership Pareto-dominates. Hint: Begin by finding values of M and B^2 such that maximized utility is the same for the one-person firm and the partnership, for the one-person firm and the owner-managed firm, and for the partnership and the owner-managed firm.

2 Brothers Brett and Bart had a very strange argument—each claimed that his horse was slower than his brother's. To resolve their argument, they agreed to bet $100 on the outcome of a quarter-mile race. At the appointed hour, Brett mounted his horse and Bart mounted his, and when the starter's gun fired, nothing happened—whereupon a bystander, wise in the ways of economic incen-tives, whispered something to the brothers. In a matter of seconds, the question of which horse was the slower was resolved to the satis-faction of Brett and Bart. What did the wise bystander suggest?

3 Any homeowner will tell you that getting home repairs done satisfactorily by outside tradespeople is a tough job. The problem is one of asymmetric information: although in-dividual tradespeople know whether they are skilled and reliable, it is difficult for the homeowner to know. We pay $50 per year to belong to a homeowners' club that (1) refers us to tradespeople and (2) checks back to see that we are happy with their work. Our checks for repairs are written to the home-owners' club, which then pays the tradesper-son a specified percentage of the total bill. Is this sort of organization likely to solve the homeowner's asymmetric information prob-lem? If you were the manager of the home-owners' club, how would you operate the club? In particular, how would you use the information provided by the club members? If you were a homeowner, what sort of man-agement scheme would induce you to join the club? If you were a competent tradesperson, would you work for the club? What quality of work would you provide for club members?

4 Restaurants such as McDonald's and Burger King are typically run as franchises. The par-ent company (McDonald's of America, for ex-ample) teaches the franchisee how to run the establishment (in the case of McDonald's, at an institution called "Hamburger Univer-sity") and then allows the franchisee to use the product trademark (the golden arches, for example) and to buy specialized packaging materials and ingredients. The terms of the typical franchise contract require the franchi-see to pay an initial lump sum and a percent-age of its gross revenues to the parent firm. The parent company can and does inspect the franchisee's operation and records from time to time. If the operation is not up to the stan-dards of cleanliness and product quality spec-ified in the contract, the parent company can unilaterally revoke the franchise. In addition, the franchisee must be the exclusive or sole

owner of the restaurant and must agree to work full-time in the restaurant. The parent company typically agrees not to franchise another restaurant within a specified radius, say 10 miles. This type of contract raises a number of interesting questions. Why does the parent company choose to sell franchises instead of hamburgers? Why does the parent company insist on exclusive ownership of the franchised restaurant? Why does the parent company inspect the operations of its franchisees? Claim: a sensible franchisee would refuse to buy a franchise unless it knew that all other franchise contracts could and would be revoked if they failed to meet the parent company's standards. Do you agree? Why or why not? Why does one franchisee care about the way in which others run their restaurants? Why does the parent firm agree to the restriction that it cannot sell other franchises within a specified radius of existing franchises?

5   Success in the textbook market requires three things: a good book, the author's responsibility; an attractive book, the designer's responsibility; and an effective sales effort, the responsibility of the sales staff. The author typically is paid a royalty for each book sold, equal to something like 15% of the wholesale price of the book; the designer typically is a salaried member of the publisher's staff; and individual salespersons often receive a percentage commission on the sales they make. How do these compensation arrangements influence the incentives of the affected parties? Why are designers paid a salary instead of a commission? Why don't publishers pay authors a fixed sum to produce books? Why are commissions so often used in sales in preference to, or in addition to, salaries?

6   A home computer called the Orange is produced by combining a 256K chip with specialized equipment designed exclusively for it. Many firms produce identical chips, but only Firm O produces the specialized equipment. The market price for a chip is X; the cost to Firm O of producing the specialized equipment is Y; and the market price for the Orange computer is Z, which exceeds $X + Y$. The Orange computer can be produced and

marketed in one of three possible ways. Firm O can buy the chips and then assemble and sell Oranges. Some chip manufacturer can buy the specialized equipment from Firm O and assemble and sell Oranges. Some third firm can buy both the chips and the specialized equipment produced by Firm O and assemble and sell Oranges. Which of these organizational forms would you expect to see and why?

7   IBM buys many of the specialized parts for its IBM computers from other firms. So, too, General Motors buys many of the specialized parts for its cars and trucks from other companies. Buying a particular specialized part from two or more different firms is common practice for the purchasing firm. Why would a firm like IBM or GM insist on having multiple suppliers for each of its specialized parts?

8   In jobs characterized by a considerable amount of learning by doing, a long-time employee is more valuable to the firm simply because he or she is familiar with the ins and outs of the firm's operation. We can think of this learning as *firm-specific human capital*: "firm-specific" because the learning is valuable only to the particular firm and "human capital" because it is embedded in individual people. For example, a student who works in a summer resort may take anywhere from a day to a week to be able to do the job without asking a lot of questions that use up both the student's and the supervisor's time. A common practice in the resort business is to pay a substantial bonus to students who stay for the entire season and to refuse to rehire students who quit before the end of the season. Why do resorts use these compensation and hiring schemes? More generally, in occupations characterized by considerable firm-specific human capital, wages tend to increase with seniority, and firms sometimes establish nonvested pension plans that pay the employee a pension only if he or she stays with the firm for some specified length of time. What purpose do such compensation schemes serve for the firm?

9   Imagine an extreme case of firm-specific human capital. It takes a new employee one

period to learn a job. During that period, he or she is completely unproductive. Having mastered the job in the first period, the employee is productive in the second period. There are only two periods. All potential employees can earn wage w' in some other job in each period. Assuming that the rate of interest is zero, the firm must choose a wage rate for period 1, w_1, and for period 2, w_2, such that

$$w_1 + w_2 \geq 2w'$$

It could choose $w_1 + w_2 > 2w'$, of course, but will not do so. Why not? Will it ever choose $w_1 > w'$ and $w_2 < w'$? Is there any advantage to the firm in choosing $w_2 > w'$ and $w_1 < w'$? Suppose that there are two types of potential employees: the first type is going off to college after one period and the second type is not. Assuming that the firm cannot identify who is college-bound and who isn't, show that it should choose $w_1 < w'$ and $w_2 > w'$.

References

Alchian, A., and H. Demsetz (1972), "Production, Information Costs, and Economic Organization," *American Economic Review*, **62**:777–795.

Berle, A., and G. C. Means (1935), *The Modern Corporation and Private Property*, New York: Macmillan.

Coase, R. (1937), "The Nature of the Firm," *Economica*, **4**:386–405.

Smith, A. (1937), *The Wealth of Nations*, the Cannan Ed., New York: Random House, The Modern Library.

Williamson, O. (1985), *The Economic Institutions of Capitalism: Firms, Markets, Relational Contracting*, New York: Free Press.

8

PRODUCTION AND COST: ONE VARIABLE INPUT

Consumer theory, which helped us to understand the decisions of individual consumers in the marketplace, is complemented by another branch of microeconomics, the theory of the firm. We are now setting out on an extended journey as we create the tools needed to analyze the decisions of individual firms.[1] We can use these tools to answer several important questions: How will a firm decide which industry to enter in the first place? How does a firm decide how much to produce of whatever goods and services it sells? What inputs will a firm buy to make its products and how much of each will it buy? How much will it charge for its products? Finding ways to answer these questions will occupy us in Chapters 8 through 13. Along the way, we'll see that these tools can be applied to a number of interesting problems outside the confines of the theory of the firm.

The material is arranged in a sequence of steps, with each section building on the foundations laid in its predecessors. If you follow through the next few chapters slowly and carefully, checking your understanding at each step, you'll arrive at the end with a solid grounding in production, cost, and supply analysis — a grounding that will allow you to think clearly about a whole range of important and interesting economic problems.

In Section 8.1, we'll define and illustrate the concept of a production function. In Section 8.2, we'll define a number of cost-minimization problems, ranging from the long run down to the shortest possible short run. In Section 8.3, we'll explore the production function when quantities of all inputs but one are held constant. In Section 8.4, we'll develop the theory of cost when only one input is variable. In Section 8.5, we'll digress to apply the tools of short-run production and cost to an all-too-familiar traffic congestion problem.

8.1 The Production Function

Economists think of the firm as an organization that buys inputs and then transforms them into marketable goods or services.

---

[1] The classic presentations of most of the material in the next three chapters are in Hicks (1939) and Samuelson (1947).

186 — The Firm

This abstraction allows us to see the features common to all firms —from coconut-milk peddlers to IT&T. Imagine a popsicle manufacturing company that buys inputs such as sugar, sticks, packaging materials, natural and artificial flavoring, molds, labor, and refrigeration and then processes them to make popsicles of various flavors. If we suppose for simplicity that each firm produces only one good (say, grape popsicles), we can imagine a function that tells us what quantity of that good the firm can produce from any bundle of inputs. Thus, a grape-popsicle production function might tell us that if we had 24 hours of labor, 50 pounds of sugar, 1 gallon of grape flavoring, 20 gallons of water, 2 kilowatt-hours of electricity, and 10 standard popsicle molds, we could produce 500 dozen grape popsicles.

Defining the Production Function

In Chapter 7, we promised to expand on this intuitive definition of a **production function**. Let's begin by considering some product, which we'll call good Y, made from two inputs, which we'll call input 1 and input 2. We'll denote the *quantity* of good Y by y, the *quantities* of inputs 1 and 2 by z_1 and z_2, and an **input bundle** by (z_1, z_2). Thus, the input bundle (10, 97) is composed of 10 units of input 1 and 97 units of input 2. For simplicity, we will be concentrating on the two-input case.

Imagine combining the two inputs to produce good Y. Of course, these inputs can be combined by using any of a number of technologies, some of which may be more productive than others. For example, if the input bundle is composed of 1 acre of Kansas wheatland (input 1) and 100 pounds of wheat seed (input 2), these inputs can be combined in many different ways to produce wheat (good Y). The entire acre can be uniformly seeded at a rate of 100 pounds of seed per acre; $\frac{1}{3}$ of an acre can be seeded at a rate of 300 pounds per acre; and the

seed can be sown at any depth. We'll assume that among these possible technologies, one is **technically efficient**; that is, it maximizes the quantity of output that can be produced from a particular bundle of inputs. The technically efficient technology is used to define the production function, $F(z_1, z_2)$. Thus, the production function

$$y = F(z_1, z_2)$$

tells us the maximum quantity of good Y that can be produced from any input bundle (z_1, z_2).

We can describe a firm by this production function if we assume that the technically efficient production process is both known and used. In so doing, we are making the sweeping assumption that the firm has resolved complex informational, organizational, incentive, and engineering problems. For example, we're assuming that the Kansas farmer knows the technology that will yield the most output of wheat from 1 acre of land and 100 pounds of seed. Yet this is not always the case. For instance, when Millar Western Pulp Ltd. decided to go into pulp and paper production, it opted for the environmentally cleaner but more energy-intensive chemothermomechanical pulp mill technology used extensively in Europe and Scandinavia rather than the standard chemical technology common in North American pulp mills. Yet the company made its decision without knowing for certain which technology was in fact technically efficient. To help you understand just what a production function is, we'll begin by looking at two types of production functions— fixed and variable proportions —and by illustrating both types with examples drawn from everyday life.

A Fixed-Proportions Production Function

In the **fixed-proportions production function**, the ratio in which the inputs are used never varies. We need one nut and one bolt to make one fastener; one right shoe and one left shoe to make a pair of shoes; one piano and one pianist to make music.

However, the fixed proportion need not be a 1-to-1 ratio. For example, 6 ounces of apple juice and 4 ounces of cranberry juice are needed to make a perfect cranapple cocktail. This recipe gives rise to the following fixed-proportions production function:

$$y = \min\left(\frac{z_1}{6}, \frac{z_2}{4}\right)$$

where y is the number of cranapple cocktails, z_1 is ounces of apple juice, and z_2 is ounces of cranberry juice. In fact, as you'll see in the following problem, the recipe for any food or drink gives rise to a fixed-proportions production function.

PROBLEM 8.1

A good recipe for seviche calls for 16 ounces of red snapper fillet, 3 ounces of lime juice, 1 ounce of coriander, and 8 ounces of Bermuda onion.

1 If a restaurant has on hand 32 ounces of snapper, 9 ounces of lime juice, 5 ounces of coriander, and 48 ounces of onion, what is the maximum quantity of seviche the restaurant can make?

2 What is the production function for seviche?

These production functions are useful as illustrations not only because they are so simple, but also because they are economically important. For example, fixed-proportions production functions (also known as *Leontief production functions* in this context) are the basis of input-output analysis, a tool widely used for economic planning.

Variable-Proportions Production Functions

In most production functions, however, the proportions of the inputs can be varied. In **variable-proportions production functions,** increased amounts of one input can be substituted for decreased amounts of another.

For example, let's imagine a fictional firm — Mr. Tipple's Courier Service — that produces the output courier services, measured in miles. Tipple owns a truck around which he has built his courier service. In addition to the truck itself, he uses two inputs: a driver's time (input 1) and gasoline (input 2). Tipple can combine time and gasoline in varying proportions to produce the courier services he provides. For example, if he instructs his employee to drive at 70 miles per hour (mph), he needs to use less time and more gas to produce each mile of courier services than if he instructs his employee to drive at 40 mph.

Let's suppose that Tipple has an input bundle composed of z_1 hours of a driver's time and z_2 gallons of gasoline. The maximum number of miles of courier services, y, that he can produce given z_1 hours of time is determined by how fast the truck is driven. Letting s denote speed in mph, we see that

$$y \leq sz_1$$

For example, if z_1 is 10 and s is 50, a driver can't go more than 500 miles.

To determine how many miles z_2 gallons of gas will produce at speed s, we need the technological relationship between miles per gallon (mpg) and speed. For Tipple's truck, mpg is inversely proportional to s, and the factor of proportionality is 1200. That is,

$$\text{mpg} = \frac{1200}{s}$$

For example, if the truck is driven at 40 mph, it gets 30 mpg, and if it's driven at 60 mph, it gets 20 mpg. This relationship between mpg and s tells us that

$$y \leq \frac{1200z_2}{s}$$

For instance, if the truck is driven at 60 mph, it is impossible to go more than 100 miles on 5 gallons of gas.

Given the constraints embodied in these two inequalities, we can find the production function for Tipple's Courier Service by choosing speed s to maximize distance y. The two inequalities are plotted in Figure 8.1 for fixed values of z_1 and z_2. The solution to this maximization problem must be *on or below* both of these lines. The light green area represents all combinations of s and y that satisfy both constraints by requiring no more than z_1 hours of time or z_2 gallons of gas. In this light green area, s^* — the speed that maximizes distance y — is determined by the point at which the two constraints intersect. As you can easily determine, the speed that maximizes y is just

$$s^* = \left(\frac{1200z_2}{z_1}\right)^{1/2}$$

and the distance traveled y^* is

$$y^* = (1200z_1z_2)^{1/2}$$

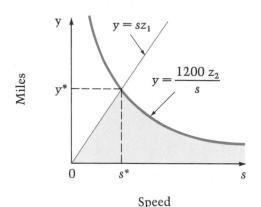

FIGURE 8.1   Finding a production function.

Given z_1 hours of a driver's time, the car cannot be driven more than sz_1 miles. Hence, $y \le sz_1$. Given z_2 gallons of gasoline, the car cannot be driven more than $1200z_2/s$ miles. Hence, $y \le 1200z_2/s$. To find the production function, choose s to maximize y, subject to these two constraints. Both constraints are satisfied only in the green area. The solution is to drive at speed s^*, which means that the car can be driven y^* miles.

To underscore the fact that this is the production function, we can rewrite this result as

$$F(z_1, z_2) = (1200z_1z_2)^{1/2}$$

How do we know that this is the production function? Because it tells us the maximum number of miles that any input bundle composed of time and gasoline will produce. Furthermore, we have also identified the technologically efficient method for combining any bundle of time and gasoline. Driving the truck at speed s^* will make the most of any such input bundle.

PROBLEM 8.2

Suppose that Tipple has an input bundle composed of 10 hours and 30 gallons of gas. What is the maximum number of miles his truck can be driven? What speed is required to achieve this result? Given the same input bundle, how far can the truck be driven at 40 mph? At 80 mph?

This production function is an illustration of the historically important **Cobb–Douglas production function.** The general form of this function in the two-input case is

$$y = Az_1^a z_2^b$$

where A, a, and b are positive constants. Cobb and Douglas (who later became a U.S. senator from Illinois) used this form to estimate a relationship between national product and the aggregate inputs of labor and capital (1948).

8.2   The Short- and Long-Run Cost-Minimization Problems

Before we explore the production function, we'll put it in perspective by seeing just how it fits into the standard theory of the firm. We'll assume that the firm's objective is to maximize its profit. A firm's profit is simply its revenue from selling its product minus the cost of producing that product. Although we'll defer analysis of the firm's revenue until later chapters, in this chapter and the next we'll focus on the firm's costs. We begin that analysis with an important observation: *profit maximization implies cost minimization.* A profit-maximizing firm will produce its output at minimum cost.

The Long-Run Cost-Minimization Problem

Let's begin with the problem of **long-run cost minimization.** By the long run, we mean a planning horizon long enough that a firm can vary all its inputs. In the two-input case, the long run is the planning horizon in which the firm can choose quantities of both inputs 1 and 2. Let's suppose that a particular firm wants to produce y units of output per period. It will minimize its cost by finding the least expensive input bundle that will produce y units of output. If the prices of its inputs are w_1 and w_2, then the cost of any input bundle the firm buys is simply the sum of the amounts spent on inputs 1 and 2, or

$$w_1 z_1 + w_2 z_2$$

The firm's long-run cost-minimizing problem, then, is to choose the input quantities z_1 and z_2 that will minimize its total costs, subject to the constraint that it can actually produce y units of output. Symbolically, we can write the long-run cost-minimization problem as

minimize $w_1 z_1 + w_2 z_2$
by choice of z_1 and z_2
subject to the constraint $y = F(z_1, z_2)$

Input Prices

Remember that the cost-minimization problem is formulated in terms of one period. Therefore, we are considering input quantities and prices in terms of one period

— and this can be a subtle qualifier. No real problem is associated with hired inputs, such as labor, or rented inputs, such as temporary office space. If the period is a year and if input 1 is unskilled labor, for instance, then z_1 is the number of worker-years (say, 507) and w_1 is an unskilled worker's annual wage (say, $20,000).

But some confusion is possible if capital inputs such as trucks or buildings are bought rather than rented, because these inputs deliver services for a period considerably longer than 1 year. How can we calculate annual input prices for such inputs?

To find out, let's focus on the case in which a firm buys a truck for P. We can think of P as the purchase price of the truck. For simplicity, let's suppose that the truck lasts for exactly D years, that it has no scrap value at the end of D years, and that it requires no maintenance. The cost of the services of one truck for the next D years is therefore simply the purchase price P, which is payable today. The question we must answer is this: What is the equivalent annual rental price, w_1? That is, what is the rental price w_1 that would make the firm indifferent between renting a truck and buying one?

We'll use the arithmetic of present value from Section 5.8 to answer this question. If the firm pays w_1 to rent a truck at the beginning of each of D periods, the present value of its rental payments will be

$$PV = w_1 + \frac{w_1}{1 + i} + \frac{w_1}{(1 + i)^2}$$
$$+ \cdots + \frac{w_1}{(1 + i)^{D-1}}$$

where i is the annual interest rate. We can use this expression to rephrase our question: What is the value of w_1 such that PV is equal to the purchase price of the truck P? Setting the expression for PV equal to P and solving for w_1, we obtain

$$w_1 = \frac{P}{\left[1 + \dfrac{1}{1+i} + \cdots + \dfrac{1}{(1+i)^{D-1}} \right]}$$

The price w_1 is an **equivalent rental price** for the truck because if the firm wants to acquire the services of a truck for D years, it will be indifferent between buying a truck for $\$P$ and renting one at the annual rental price w_1.

In deriving various cost functions, we will always use rental prices for capital inputs such as trucks. If the firm actually rents the input, we can simply use the actual rental price. If it buys the capital input, however, we will use the equivalent rental price.

PROBLEM 8.3

Gadgets Incorporated buys a machine that lasts for exactly 3 years, requires no maintenance, and has no scrap value. Its purchase price is $331. If the annual interest rate is 10%, what is the equivalent annual rental rate?

Short-Run Cost-Minimization Problems

As we have seen, a firm's long-run planning horizon is long enough that it can vary the quantities of all its inputs. Yet firms are not always in this fortunate position of complete flexibility. If Ford Motor Company wants to produce more Mustangs this year, its options are distinctly limited. It can run its assembly lines around the clock by hiring and training more workers, and it may be able to accelerate the assembly process itself, provided that its body-stamping plants, engine plants, and other facilities can put out enough parts. However, it doesn't have the necessary lead time in the space of a year to create new assembly lines (or body-stamping or engine plants).

If the firm's planning horizon is such that the firm can vary some, but not all, of its inputs, it faces the problem of **short-run cost minimization.** There are many short runs corresponding to planning horizons in which the firm can vary the quantity of just one, just two, or just three inputs, and so on. Each of these planning horizons defines its own short-run cost-minimization problem.

In the two-input case, if the quantity of input 2 is fixed, we have a short run in which input 1 is the only variable input. The short-run cost-minimization problem is then to choose z_1 to minimize the cost of producing y units of output. We'll consider this short-run cost-minimization problem later in this chapter, and we'll take up long-run cost minimization in the next chapter. But first we must see what the production function looks like when the quantity of one input is fixed.

8.3 Production: One Variable Input

We know what a production function is, what two simple production functions look like, and where the production function fits into the firm's profit and cost calculations. The next step is to ask: What happens to output as we vary the quantity of one input, holding the quantities of all other inputs fixed? For example, how does the Kansas farmer's wheat harvest change if we vary the quantity of wheat seed, holding the quantities of land and all other inputs fixed?

Total Product

By fixing, or holding constant, the quantity of all inputs except one, we can write the production function as a function of one variable — the quantity of the single variable input. Written this way, the production function is called the **total product function.** It tells us what the output — or total product — will be for any quantity of the variable input (given the fixed quantities of the other inputs). To see how a total product function is derived from a production function, let's look at the case in which there are only two inputs. If we fix z_2 at 105 units, then the total product function, denoted by $TP(z_1)$, is defined as follows:

$$TP(z_1) = F(z_1, 105)$$

In other words, the total product function $TP(z_1)$ is derived from the production function simply by fixing the value of z_2 in the production function $F(z_1, z_2)$.

PROBLEM 8.4

We have already derived the following production function for Tipple's Courier Service:

$$F(z_1, z_2) = (1200z_1z_2)^{1/2}$$

Find the total product function when z_2 is 12; when z_2 is 27. Graph these total product functions with z_1 on the horizontal axis and y on the vertical axis.

In Figure 8.2, we have drawn the standard or prototypical total product function. The quantity of the variable input z_1 is plotted on the horizontal axis, and output y is on the vertical axis. Notice that the slope of this total product function—which indicates the rate at which output changes as z_1 increases—is different at different values of z_1. For instance, the slope is relatively large near point G, while it is relatively small near the origin and near point C. This rate of change has a special name and a special role in the theory of the firm.

Marginal Product

The rate at which output changes as the quantity of the variable input increases (given fixed quantities of all other inputs) is called the **marginal product** of the input and is denoted by $MP(z_1)$.[2] Because this rate of change is just the slope of the total product function, we see that

DEFINITION

$$MP(z_1) = \text{slope of } TP(z_1)$$

In Figure 8.2, if you consider the curve that includes the dashed segment CD rather than the solid segment CE, you will perhaps recognize it from an introductory economics course. You have probably noticed, too, that the general shape of this curve is different from the total product functions you graphed in Problem 8.4. In a moment, we'll look more closely at the reasons for constructing the standard total product function in this way and consider, too, alternative stylized functions.

Notice that because the slope of the dashed-line segment CD in Figure 8.2 is negative, marginal product is also negative when z_1 exceeds 17. In this region, more of

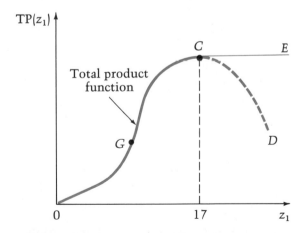

FIGURE 8.2 A total product function.

The curve $0CE$ is the standard stylization of a total product function. It gives us the maximum quantity of y that can be produced for any given quantity of input 1.

---

[2] In mathematical terms,

$$MP(z_1, z_2) = F_1(z_1, z_2)$$

where $F_1(\cdot)$ is the partial derivative of $F(\cdot)$ with respect to z_1.

the variable input actually reduces the total product. In the language of production functions, cows and common pasture can be combined to produce milk, but too many cows on the pastureland can cause milk production to decrease. (In fact, most of the common-property problems listed in Section 5.6 illustrate this problem.)

Although these possibilities are real, they are not consistent with our definition of a production function — if we assume that firms have the option of using all or part of any input bundle. Because a production function gives the maximum output producible from any bundle of inputs, if the firm in Figure 8.2 has more than 17 units of input 1, it will decide to use precisely 17 units of input 1 and no more. In other words, if too many cooks spoil the broth, some of the cooks will be kept out of the kitchen.

The assumption above is sometimes called the **free-disposal assumption.** (In the common-property problem, there is no central authority — that is, no firm — to keep the counterproductive cows off the common pasture.) Taken together, the definitions of the production function and the free-disposal assumption imply that marginal product cannot be negative — that is, CE rather than CD is the relevant total product function when z_1 exceeds 17.

Now let's consider a related question: Can the marginal products of all inputs simultaneously be zero? Imagine that input 1 is farm labor (measured in worker-hours), input 2 is a strawberry patch (measured in acres), and good Y is strawberries (measured in pints). If the input of land is fixed at 1 acre and if units of farm labor are continually added to it, eventually the point of maximum total product, corresponding to point C in Figure 8.2, will be reached. As more labor is added to the 1-acre patch beyond that point, an excess of farm labor will occur, and its marginal product will be zero.

Now, what is the marginal product of land when the marginal product of labor is zero? (Notice that in posing this question, we are assuming that farm labor is now the fixed input and the size of the strawberry patch is the variable input.) If another acre of land is brought into production and the excess farm labor is used to cultivate it, more pints of strawberries will be produced. In other words, when the marginal product of farm labor is zero, the marginal product of land is positive. More generally, although the marginal product of one input may be zero, the marginal products of all inputs cannot simultaneously be zero:

Given the free-disposal assumption, the marginal product of any input is always greater than or equal to zero; furthermore, for any input bundle, the marginal product of at least one input is positive.

The total product function from Figure 8.2 is plotted in Figure 8.3a. The associated marginal product function $MP(z_1)$ is plotted in Figure 8.3b. Notice that as z_1 increases, the slope of $TP(z_1)$, and therefore marginal product, increases until z_1 is equal to 10. The slope of $TP(z_1)$ and therefore marginal product, then decreases until z_1 is equal to 17. Finally, both the slope of $TP(z_1)$ and marginal product are zero when z_1 exceeds 17. Because marginal product begins to decline at 10, this point is called the point of **diminishing marginal productivity.** The fundamental assumption in production theory is that such a point of diminishing marginal productivity always exists.

Diminishing Marginal Productivity

The idea of diminishing marginal productivity is not only significant in the theory of production but also fundamental to the history of economic thought. Reverend Thomas Malthus, a prominent English

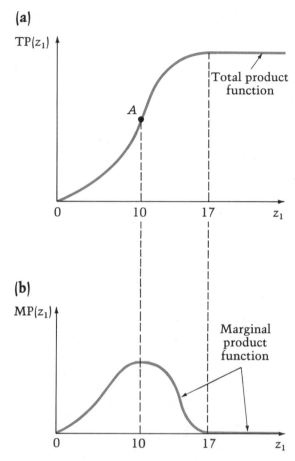

(a)

TP(z_1)

Total product
function

A

0   10   17 z_1

(b)

MP(z_1)

Marginal
product
function

0   10   17 z_1

FIGURE 8.3 From total product to marginal product.

The marginal product associated with any value of z_1 is the slope of the total product function at that value of z_1. For $z_1 < 10$, marginal product increases as z_1 increases because the total product function gets steeper as z_1 gets larger. For $z_1 > 10$, marginal product decreases as z_1 increases because the total product function gets flatter as z_1 gets larger. For $z_1 > 17$, marginal product is zero because the slope of the total product function is zero.

economist of the early nineteenth century, was the first to formulate the hypothesis of diminishing marginal productivity. He observed that in response to population pressure, new land was continually being opened for cultivation. He argued that if the converse of diminishing marginal productivity—increasing marginal productiv-

ity—were true, added labor would be more productive on cultivated than on virgin land. If that were the case, we would have no economic incentive to bring raw land under cultivation. From this argument and from the fact that new land was brought under the plow as the population grew, he concluded that labor devoted to food production necessarily brings diminishing marginal product. The following assumption, linked historically with Malthus's name, reflects his argument that at some point marginal product will begin to diminish.

ASSUMPTION: Diminishing Marginal Product

Suppose that the quantities of all inputs except one—say, input 1—are fixed. There is a quantity of input 1—say, z_1''—such that whenever z_1 exceeds z_1'', the marginal product of input 1 decreases as z_1 increases.[3]

Notice that in Figure 8.3b, marginal product not only diminishes when z_1 exceeds 10 but also increases when z_1 is less than 10. The Malthusian hypothesis of a declining marginal product is a fundamental assumption in production theory, and the empirical evidence that supports it is strong. But an initially increasing marginal product is neither an inevitable feature of the world nor guaranteed by our assumptions. Whether marginal product does or does not initially increase in a particular production process is an empirical question. The stylized total product function in Figure 8.3 therefore represents only one possibility.

---

[3] Diminishing marginal product is an assumption about a second partial derivative of the production function. For $z_1 > z_1''$, we assume that the partial derivative of marginal product with respect to z_1 is negative. That is,

$$MP'(z_1) = F_{11}(z_1, z_2) < 0 \qquad \text{for } z_1 > z_1''$$

where $F_{11}(\cdot)$ is the second partial derivative of $F(\cdot)$ with respect to z_1.

At least two alternative stylizations of the total product function are useful and interesting. One such possibility, illustrated in Figure 8.4, is that marginal productivity may be initially constant rather than increasing. (Notice that the linear segment of $TP(z_1)$ in Figure 8.4*a* is associated with a constant marginal product in Figure 8.4*b*.)

In the third stylization, the total product function exhibits diminishing marginal productivity from the outset. In this case,

(a)

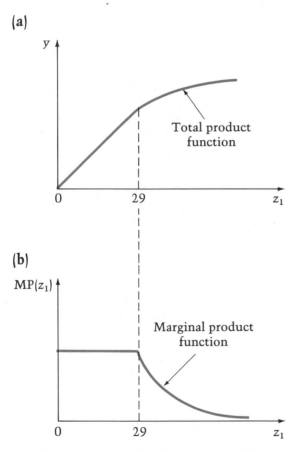

(b)

FIGURE 8.4   From total product to marginal product: another illustration.

The slope of the total product function in (a) is constant for $z_1 < 29$; marginal product in (b) is therefore constant for $z_1 < 29$. For $z_1 > 29$, the slope of the total product function gets smaller as z_1 gets larger; marginal product therefore decreases as z_1 increases for $z_1 > 29$.

the first unit of the variable input contributes most to total product, and each successive unit contributes less than the one preceding it. A total product function exhibiting diminishing marginal product throughout looks like the ones you constructed in answering Problem 8.4. The slopes of those total product functions became progressively smaller as z_1 increased, reflecting diminishing marginal productivity of the variable input for all values of z_1.

These alternative stylizations of the total product function are conceivable and relevant. However, $TP(z_1)$ is usually drawn to indicate that as the quantity of the variable input increases, the marginal product rises at first and only later begins to diminish. The rationale is that increasing the amount of the variable input at first increases the productivity of all the units of that input. Imagine the kitchen of a major metropolitan hotel. The dinner shift begins with only a few kitchen workers, but as more and more help is added, the number of dinners the kitchen can produce increases at a rapid rate. Why? One reason is that the workers can specialize. Some only prepare vegetables; others only make sauces; still others wash dishes. Another reason is that the kitchen can be organized more efficiently. For example, the workers can all save steps (and thereby spend more time at their individual tasks) by preparing food at more compact and specialized work stations. At some point, however, the gains from a more efficient division of labor and organizational structure begin to diminish. Beyond this point of diminishing marginal product, $TP(z_1)$ gets progressively flatter as z_1 increases. As even more help is added to our hotel kitchen, food production continues to increase, but at a declining rate until, perhaps, marginal product finally reaches zero.

Although this rationale seems most convincing when the variable input is labor, whether any particular production process does or does not exhibit initially increasing marginal product is a question we can answer only by empirical investigation. For this reason, it is useful to have all three of the stylized total product functions at your fingertips. In the following problem, you can discover yet another possibility.

PROBLEM 8.5

We can think of producing fasteners (good Y) by combining nuts (input 1) and bolts (input 2). If z_2 is fixed at 10 units ($z_2 = 10$), the total product function is

$$TP(z_1) = \begin{cases} z_1 & \text{if } z_1 \leq 10 \\ 10 & \text{if } z_1 > 10 \end{cases}$$

In one diagram, carefully graph this total product function. In another diagram directly below the first, graph the associated marginal product function.

Average Product

Like marginal product, **average product** is a way of looking at how output varies with changes in the quantity of the variable input. It is just the total product divided by the quantity of the variable input; that is, average product is the product per unit of the variable input. The average product of input 1, $AP(z_1)$, is therefore

DEFINITION

$$AP(z_1) = \frac{TP(z_1)}{z_1}$$

To reinforce your understanding of average product, try the following problem.

PROBLEM 8.6

In the production function for Tipple's Courier Service, suppose that z_2 is 12. Then, from Problem 8.4, the total product function is

$$TP(z_1) = 120(z_1)^{1/2}$$

Find the average product function.

Let's see how to derive the average product function from the total product function in Figure 8.5, so that we can compare the marginal and average products of input 1, $MP(z_1)$ and $AP(z_1)$. First, choose any point on the total product function and, from the origin, draw a ray that passes through that point. The slope of this ray is equal to average product at the point at which the ray intersects the total product function. At point A, for instance, the average product is the slope of the ray $0A$. Why? The slope of the ray is equal to distance DA divided by distance $0D$. But DA is the total product at point A, and $0D$ is equal to quantity of input 1 at A. Therefore, the slope of the ray $0A$ is the total product divided by the quantity of input 1, or the average product. Similarly, the slope of the ray $0B$ is the average product at point B.

Let's now compare $MP(z_1)$ and $AP(z_1)$. At point A in Figure 8.5, for instance, $MP(z_1)$

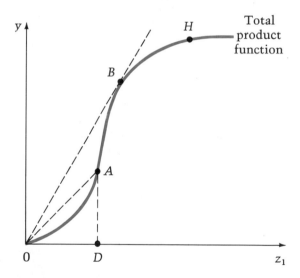

FIGURE 8.5 From total product to average product.

Average product at point A is the slope of the dashed line $0A$ because DA is total product and $0D$ is quantity of input 1. Similarly, average product at point B is the slope of the dashed line $0B$. Notice that average product is a maximum at point B.

exceeds AP(z_1). At point H, however, AP(z_1) exceeds MP(z_1). To see why, simply construct the line tangent to the total product function at point A and notice that the slope of the tangent line, which is marginal product at point A, exceeds the slope of the ray through point A. The opposite is true at point H.

Point B is of special interest. At this point, average product and marginal product are identical because the ray through the origin to point B is tangent to TP(z_1) at B. It is also a point of special interest for another reason: average product is at a maximum at B. To see why B is the point of maximum average product, try drawing another ray through the origin that intersects or is tangent to the total product function and that is steeper than $0B$. It can't be done.

We have drawn the standard stylization of the total product function in Figure 8.6a and both of the derived measures of productivity — average and marginal product — in Figure 8.6b. This diagram presents some important qualitative relationships between marginal product and average product. Although these relationships can be expressed in a variety of ways, the following observations offer perhaps the most insight:[4]

1 When marginal product is greater than average product, average product is increasing.

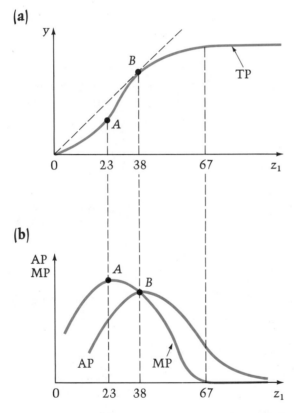

FIGURE 8.6 Comparing the average and marginal product functions.

In (b), we have derived AP and MP associated with TP in (a). Three values of z_1 — 23, 38, and 67 — are noteworthy: (1) MP is rising or falling as z_1 is less than or greater than 23, and MP attains its maximum value at $z_1 = 23$; (2) AP is rising or falling as z_1 is less or greater than 38, AP attains its maximum value at $z_1 = 38$, MP is equal to AP at $z_1 = 38$, and MP is greater or less than AP as z_1 is less or greater than 38; (3) MP is zero when z_1 exceeds 67.

[4] Because we'll encounter these sorts of relationships at several points in this and the following chapters, it is useful to explore them more carefully. Consider any function $f(x)$ with domain $x > 0$ and the implied "marginal" function

$$M(x) = M'(x)$$

and "average" function

$$A(x) = \frac{f(x)}{x}$$

Differentiating $A(z)$, we have

$$A'(x) = \frac{xf'(x) - f(x)}{x^2}$$

or, equivalently,

$$A'(x) = \frac{f'(x) - f(x)/x}{x}$$

But this can be written as

$$A'(x) = \frac{M(x) - A(x)}{x}$$

Therefore $A(x)$ is increasing, decreasing, or stationary as $M(x)$ is greater than, less than, or equal to $A(x)$.

2 When marginal product is less than average product, average product is decreasing.

3 When marginal product is equal to average product, average product is neither increasing nor decreasing; it is constant.

A simple analogy may help you to see the common sense of these relationships. Imagine a kindergarten room. If the average weight of the assembled children is a (for average pounds) and if another small person whose weight is m (for marginal pounds) joins the group, what will happen to the average weight of a child now in the schoolroom? If m exceeds a, the average weight of a child in the now larger group will rise; if m is less than a, it will fall; if m is equal to a, it will not change.

As you'll discover in Problem 8.7, these curves will be different for different stylizations of the total product function.

PROBLEM 8.7

Construct a total product function like the one in Figure 8.4a. Below the graph of the total product function, derive the corresponding average and marginal product functions. Compare these curves with those in Figures 8.6a and 8.6b. Check to see that the curves you have drawn are consistent with observations 1, 2, and 3 concerning the relationships between average and marginal products.

8.4 Costs of Production: One Variable Input

Now let's consider the short-run cost-minimization problem that arises when just one input is allowed to vary. If input 2 is the fixed input and input 1 the variable input, then the cost-minimization problem can be stated as

minimize $w_1 z_1$ by choice of z_1

subject to the constraint $y = \text{TP}(z_1)$

That is, choose z_1 to minimize the expenditure on the variable input $(w_1 z_1)$, subject to the constraint that the firm produces y units of output $[y = \text{TP}(z_1)]$.

Because this problem is so simple, we can learn in the space of a few pages everything there is to know about how various cost functions inherit the properties of their corresponding total product functions. This elementary grounding in the relationship between production functions and the cost of production will be very useful in the next chapter, where we'll reconsider production and cost in more complex, realistic cases, in which more than one input is variable.

We'll begin with the variable cost function, define average variable cost and short-run marginal cost, explore the fixed cost of production, and conclude with definitions of short-run total cost and short-run average cost.

The Variable Cost Function Illustrated

Once we know what quantity of output a particular firm wants to produce, we can discover from the total product function the *minimum quantity* of the variable input required to produce that output. This minimum quantity is the solution to our simple cost-minimization problem. We can then determine what the *minimum variable cost* of the output will be by multiplying this quantity by the price of the input w_1. We'll assume throughout that the firm can buy any amount of the variable input at a fixed price w_1 per unit. We can thus derive from the total product function the **variable cost function,** written as VC(y).

DEFINITION

VC(y) = the minimum variable cost of producing y units of good Y

Let's use Tipple's Courier Service to develop an algebraic illustration. Suppose that Tipple has just 12 gallons of gas on hand and that he can't buy any more in this period. In this case, gasoline is the fixed input and his driver's time is the variable input. From Problem 8.4, the total product function is

$$TP(z_1) = 120(z_1)^{1/2}$$

where z_1 is hours of time. Since this function describes the relationship between miles driven (y) and time (z_1), we have

$$y = 120(z_1)^{1/2}$$

For example, if Tipple wants the truck driven 240 miles, the minimum amount of a driver's time that he needs is 4 hours. Although a driver could take more than 4 hours to drive 240 miles on 12 gallons of gas, 4 hours is the minimum time required. Letting w_1 denote the hourly wage of Tipple's driver, we see that $4w_1$ is the variable cost of driving 240 miles, or $VC(240) = 4w_1$. Similarly, if Tipple wants the truck driven 360 miles, he needs 9 hours. In this case, we see that $VC(360) = 9w_1$.

More generally, if we invert the total product function by solving for z_1 in terms of y, we have the minimum time needed to drive the truck y miles. If we let z_1^* represent this minimum time, we have

$$z_1^* = \frac{y^2}{(14,400)}$$

Now, simply by multiplying by w_1 we have the variable cost function for Tipple's Courier Service when he has 12 gallons of gas:

$$VC(y) = \frac{w_1 y^2}{(14,400)}$$

This gives us the minimum cost of driving the truck y miles when Tipple pays his driver w_1 per hour and has just 12 gallons of gas on hand.

PROBLEM 8.8

Suppose that Tipple has 27 gallons of gasoline on hand. First find z_1^*, the minimum number of hours needed to drive y miles. Then find the corresponding variable cost function, $VC(y)$.

Deriving the Variable Cost Function

To this point, we have explored two variable cost functions for Tipple's Courier Service. Now we will develop a graphic technique that can be applied to any cost-minimization problem when only one input is variable. The series of four interlinked diagrams in Figure 8.7 shows just how the variable cost function $VC(y)$ can be derived from the total product function $TP(z_1)$ and the cost of input 1, w_1. We have plotted the standard total product function in Figure 8.7a, and we have then used the diagrams in Figure 8.7b and 8.7c to derive the variable cost function in Figure 8.7d.

Let's see how that derivation is accomplished. Suppose that the firm wanted to produce 768 units of good Y. Consulting $TP(z_1)$ in Figure 8.7a, we see that 16 units of input 1 is the least costly way of doing so because 16 is the smallest quantity of input 1 that will produce 768. From the ray in Figure 8.7b, we see that 16 units of input 1 will cost $16w_1$. Because the minimum cost of producing 768 units of Y is $16w_1$, $(768, 16w_1)$ is one point on the variable cost function $VC(y)$ in Figure 8.7d.

To identify this point in Figure 8.7d, we have (horizontally) projected the cost $16w_1$ from Figure 8.7b into Figure 8.7d; using the 45-degree line in Figure 8.7c, we have also projected output 768 from Figure 8.7a into Figure 8.7d. The intersection of these two projections at $(768, 16w_1)$ in Figure 8.7d is one point on $VC(y)$. All other points on $VC(y)$ have been constructed in the corresponding way. For example because 22 units of input 1 are needed to produce 2971 units of good Y, $(2971, 22w_1)$ is another point on $VC(y)$.[5]

---

[5] What we accomplish in Figure 8.7 is, in essence, the inversion of the function $y = TP(z_1)$. Write the inverse of this function as $z_1 = H(y)$. This function tells how much z_1 is required to produce any given y. The variable cost function is then just $w_1 \times H(y)$:

$$VC(y) = w_1 H(y)$$

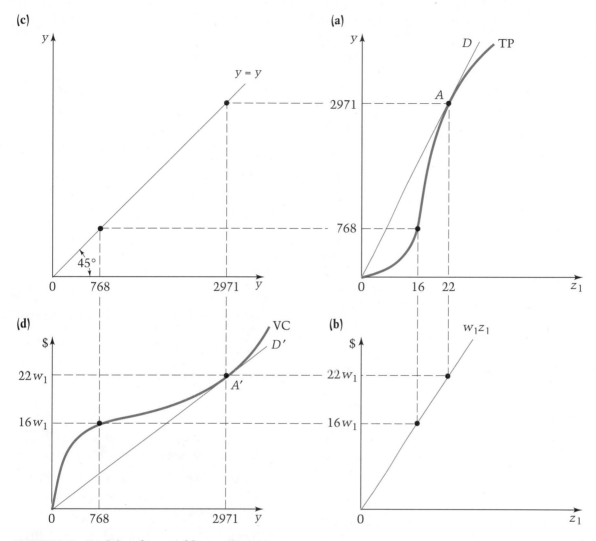

FIGURE 8.7   Deriving the variable cost function.

VC in (d) is derived from TP in (a). From (a), we see that $z_1 = 16$ is necessary to produce output $y = 768$; from (b), we see that 16 units of input 1 cost $16w_1$. Projecting $y = 768$ into (d), through the 45° line in (c), and projecting $16w_1$ into (d), we have one point on VC, the point $(768, 16w_1)$.

Average Variable Cost and Short-Run Marginal Cost

We defined the concepts of average product and marginal product when we looked at the total product function. Now we'll define the corresponding concepts of average variable cost and short-run marginal cost in relation to the variable cost function. Although their labels are a bit of a mouthful, the concepts themselves are straightforward. As you might have guessed, **average variable cost**, written AVC(y), is just the variable cost per unit of output.

DEFINITION

$$\mathbf{AVC}(y) = \frac{\mathbf{VC}(y)}{y}$$

The **short-run marginal cost**, SMC(y), as you might also have guessed, is the rate at which cost increases in the short run as output increases. Because the only variable cost in the short run is the cost associated with the variable input, the short-run marginal cost of output is simply the slope of the variable cost function:[6]

DEFINITION

SMC(y) = slope of VC(y)

In Figure 8.8, we have illustrated the graphic techniques used to derive the average variable cost and the short-run marginal cost. We have constructed the ray through the origin to point A on VC(y) and the line TT that is tangent to VC(y) at point A. Because the slope of the ray is average variable cost at A and the slope of the tangent line is marginal cost at A, we see that AVC(y) is less than MC(y) at point A.

We can use these graphic techniques to derive and to compare the average variable cost and short-run marginal cost functions implied by any variable cost function. The variable cost function VC(y) from Figure 8.7d is reproduced in Figure 8.9a. The average variable cost function AVC(y) and the short-run marginal cost function SMC(y) derived from VC(y) are shown in Figure 8.9b. You need to understand why both curves in Figure 8.9b are U-shaped and why they intersect at output level 2971. If you are unsure, pick up a pencil and paper and derive SMC(y) and AVC(y) from VC(y), using the technique described in Figure 8.8.

What does Figure 8.9 tell us about the relationship between average variable cost and short-run marginal cost? We see three perhaps familiar relationships.

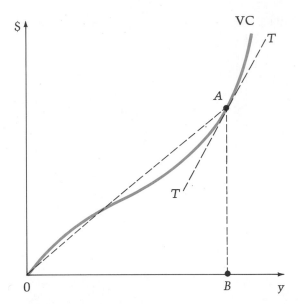

FIGURE 8.8   Deriving short-run average and marginal cost.

SAC at point A is equal to the slope of the dashed line 0A. SMC at point A is the slope of TT. At point A, SAC is less than SMC.

1 When SMC(y) lies below AVC(y), AVC(y) is decreasing as y increases.

2 When SMC(y) is equal to AVC(y), AVC(y) is neither increasing nor decreasing: its slope is zero.

3 When SMC(y) lies above AVC(y), AVC(y) increases as y increases.[7]

These relationships follow from the same arithmetic truisms that predict your grade point average: if your grades this term are lower than your previous average, your average will fall; if they are the same, your average will remain the same; if they are higher, your average will go up.

[6] Mathematically, we see that SMC(y) is simply the derivative of VC(y):

$$SMC(y) = VC'(y)$$

[7] These results are another application of the general relationship between averages and marginals developed in footnote 4.

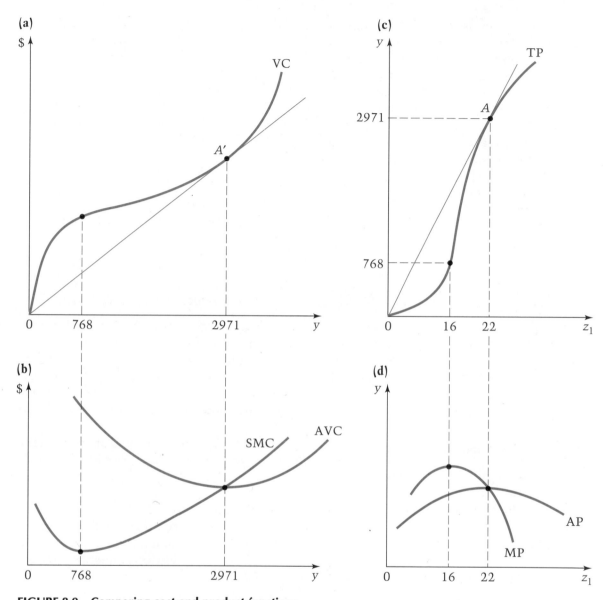

FIGURE 8.9   Comparing cost and product functions.

In (b), we've derived SMC and AVC from VC in (a). The slope of VC is smallest at $y = 768$; therefore, SMC attains its minimum value at $y = 768$. At $y = 2971$, the ray $0A'$ is tangent to VC; therefore, SMC is equal to AVC, and AVC attains its minimum value at $y = 2971$. Similarly, in (d), we have derived MP and AP from TP in (c). In comparing (b) and (d), notice that SMC and AVC are inverted images of MP and AP.

In Figure 8.9c, we've reproduced the standard total product function $TP(z_1)$ from Figure 8.7a, and in Figure 8.9d, we've derived the related marginal product and average product functions $MP(z_1)$ and $AP(z_1)$. In Figure 8.9d, marginal product is at its peak when the quantity of the variable input is 16 or when the output is 768, and it diminishes thereafter. Correspondingly, in Figure 8.9b, short-run marginal cost is at its lowest point when the output is 768, and it increases thereafter. Increasing short-run marginal cost, then, seems to be a direct implication of diminishing marginal product. Similarly, decreasing short-run marginal cost seems to be a direct implication of increasing marginal product. It is almost as if we could generate the marginal cost curve in Figure 8.9*b* by standing the marginal product curve in Figure 8.9*d* on its head.

The average product and average variable cost curves in Figures 8.9*b* and 8.9*d* show the same kind of strikingly similar, but inverse, relationship. At input levels below 22 (or output levels below 2971), average product is increasing and average variable cost is decreasing. At input levels above 22 (or output levels above 2971), average product is falling and average variable cost is rising. Once again, we could almost generate the average variable cost function by turning the average product function upside down.

Average Product and Average Cost

Doing two simple algebraic exercises will help you to see why these relationships hold. We'll look at an arbitrary point on the total product function:

$$y' = TP(z_1')$$

Average product at this point is just the output $TP(z_1')$ divided by the quantity of the variable input z_1':

$$AP(z_1') = \frac{TP(z_1')}{z_1'}$$

Average variable cost at this point is just the expenditure on input 1 divided by the output:

$$AVC(y') = \frac{w_1 z_1'}{TP(z_1')}$$

We can rewrite this expression as

$$AVC(y') = \frac{w_1}{\left[\dfrac{TP(z_1')}{z_1'}\right]}$$

But the denominator here is just average product. Thus, average variable cost is equal to the price of the variable input divided by the average product:

$$AVC(y') = \frac{w_1}{AP(z_1')}$$

In this sense, the average variable cost function is the average product function stood on its head.

Marginal Product and Marginal Cost

Let's turn now to the relationship between the marginal product function and the short-run marginal cost function. Again, imagine choosing some arbitrary level of the variable input z_1' and then increasing that level by some very small amount Δz_1. The corresponding increase in the variable cost Δc will be just the additional quantity of the input multiplied by the price of the input:

$$\Delta c = w_1 \Delta z_1$$

The amount by which output increases, Δy, will be (approximately) the marginal product of the variable input at level z_1' multiplied by the additional quantity of the variable input:

$$\Delta y = MP(z_1')\Delta z_1$$

By definition, short-run marginal cost is simply the rate of increase of variable cost as output increases; that is, it is approximately $\Delta c/\Delta y$. Substituting the results from above,

$$SMC(y') = \frac{w_1 \Delta z_1}{MP(z_1')\Delta z_1}$$

Canceling Δz_1, we see that the short-run marginal cost at output y' is simply the price of the variable input divided by the marginal product of the variable input at level z_1':

$$\text{SMC}(y') = \frac{w_1}{\text{MP}(z_1')}$$

Short-run marginal cost is therefore marginal product stood on its head.[8]

Fixed Cost

By specifying the price of the variable input w_1, we have been able to derive from the total product function the associated variable cost function. But what about the cost associated with the fixed input? The cost of the fixed input, which is called a **fixed cost**, is simply the price of the input times its quantity.

DEFINITION

$$\text{FC} = w_2 z_2$$

where z_2 is quantity of the fixed input.

We can express fixed costs on a per-unit basis by dividing the fixed cost by output. This is called the **average fixed cost** of production, denoted by AFC(y).

DEFINITION

$$\text{AFC}(y) = \frac{\text{FC}}{y}$$

---

[8] We noted in footnote 5 that

$$\text{VC}(y) = w_1 H(y)$$

where $H(y)$ is the inverse of $y = \text{TP}(z_1)$. Differentiating this expression, we see that

$$\text{SMC}(y) = w_1 H'(y)$$

But $H'(y)$ is $1/[\text{TP}'(z_1)]$, or $1/[\text{MP}(z_1)]$. Hence,

$$\text{SMC}(y) = \frac{w_1}{\text{MP}(z_1)}$$

To understand the relationship implied by this statement, try the following problem.

PROBLEM 8.9

Plot the horizontal line *FC* on a graph in which y is on the horizontal axis and dollars are on the vertical axis. Now graph AFC(y). What happens to AFC(y) as y gets arbitrarily large? As y gets arbitrarily small?

Short-Run Total Cost and Short-Run Average Cost

The **short-run total cost** of output, written STC(y), can be calculated simply by adding up the variable cost and the fixed cost.

DEFINITION

$$\text{STC}(y) = \text{VC}(y) + \text{FC}$$

PROBLEM 8.10

SMC(y) is defined as the slope of VC(y). Show that SMC(y) is also equal to the slope of STC(y). In other words, show that for any value of y, the slope of STC(y) is equal to the slope of VC(y).

Short-run total cost can also be expressed on a per-unit basis, called **short-run average cost** and written SAC(y), by dividing the short-run cost by the number of units of output.

DEFINITION

$$\text{SAC}(y) = \frac{\text{STC}(y)}{y}$$

Or, equivalently, short-run average cost can be calculated by adding together the average variable cost and the average fixed cost:

$$\text{SAC}(y) = \text{AVC}(y) + \text{AFC}(y)$$

We've illustrated all of these cost functions in Figure 8.10. We have drawn FC, STC(y), and VC(y) in Figure 8.10*a* and

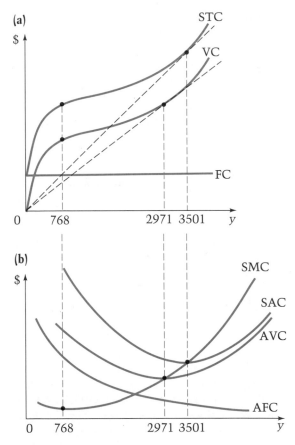

(a)

(b)

FIGURE 8.10   Seven cost functions.

In (a), STC is derived from VC by adding FC. Each of the cost functions in (b) can be derived from the cost functions in (a): AFC = FC/y, AVC = VC/y, and SAC = STC/y. Finally, SMC = slope of VC, and SMC = slope of STC.

AFC(y), AVC(y), SAC(y), and SMC(y) in Figure 8.10b.

Because SMC(y) is the marginal function associated with STC(y) and because SAC(y) is the average function associated with STC(y), we immediately know a great deal about the relationship between SMC(y) and SAC(y). SAC(y) is increasing or decreasing as SMC(y) lies above or below it, and the slope of SAC(y) is zero when SMC(y) is equal to SAC(y).

*8.5   An Application to Traffic Congestion

Let's use these tools to do some vicarious problem solving, just as we did in Chapter 5. The number of cars entering and leaving any major city in North America has grown dramatically over the past three decades. Bumper-to-bumper traffic as cars inch their way into the city at the start of a working day is a frustrating fact of everyday life for millions of commuters. Although the problem of traffic congestion doesn't involve a firm, we'll see that the production and cost concepts developed in this chapter will allow us to generate some interesting insights into this troubling problem. In addition, we'll see that much of what we learn about the congestion problem can be fruitfully applied to the firm.

A Model of Congestion

We will look at a highly stylized model of traffic congestion. Although it has few, if any, real counterparts, it nevertheless captures some of the important features of all real congestion problems. Imagine a suburb called Surrey that is connected to the nearby city of Wetvan by two roads — Route 1 and Route 2. Imagine, too, that every weekday morning 5000 residents of Surrey hop into their cars and drive to work in Wetvan and that every evening they get back in their cars and return to Surrey. We want answers to these questions: What principles determine how many commuters will choose each route? What are the costs of commuting for the Surrey commuters? Do these commuters make the most effective use of the two roads that connect their town to the big city?

We'll focus on the morning rush hour (the evening rush hour presents very similar problems). In addition, we will ignore the money that these commuters spend on gasoline and cars so that we can isolate the *time costs* of commuting. By focusing on time costs, we can create a simple model that will provide the answers to questions we just posed. These answers—and the way in which we discover them—will provide us with an entry into the more complex problems that real situations present.

To begin our analysis, we need to know about the technology of traffic on the two roads. Because an individual commuter is concerned about how long it takes him or her to make the trip, we must look at the technology from the commuter's perspective. As you undoubtedly know, commuting time on most roads depends on traffic density. If a small number of commuters pick a particular road, the trip takes a relatively short time. As more and more cars converge on a road, however, traffic begins to build up until, beyond some point, the larger the number of commuters, the longer it takes each commuter to get to work.

The precise relationship between commuting time and numbers of commuters on Route 1 is presented in Figure 8.11. The time per commuter is measured on the vertical axis and the number of commuters using Route 1, N_1, is measured on the horizontal axis. Notice that Route 1 is congestion-free when N_1 is less than 1200 and that when fewer than 1200 commuters take this route, each commuter spends 18 minutes traveling from Surrey to Wetvan. When more than 1200 commuters use Route 1, however, each commuter spends more than 18 minutes traveling to Wetvan, and the commuting time increases as N_1 increases. For example, if 3600 commuters use Route 1, the time per commuter rises to 30 minutes. And if 6000 commuters use it, the time per commuter is almost 47 minutes — more than double the time the trip takes when Route 1 is congestion-free.

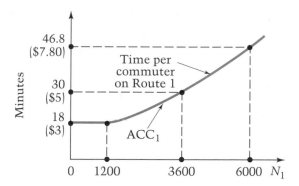

FIGURE 8.11   The costs of commuting.

If fewer than 1200 commuters use Route 1, commuting time per commuter is 18 minutes and there is no congestion. In contrast, if more than 1200 commuters use Route 1, time per commuter increases as the number of commuters increases, reflecting increasing congestion on the route. Since commuters value their time at $10 per hour, we can translate the time costs of commuting into money costs. For example, if 3600 commuters use the route, the money cost is $5 per commuter, equal to half an hour (30 minutes) times $10 per hour. ACC_1 gives the average cost per commuter on Route 1.

We are assuming that any commuter's commuting time on Route 1 is determined exclusively by the number of commuters using the route on that particular day. As a result, on any given day, every commuter on Route 1 spends the same amount of time commuting. We are ignoring a number of the features of real commuting situations so that we can concentrate on the relationship between traffic density and commuting time. For example, the very real possibility that a commuter who gets up early can reduce his or her commuting time by hitting the road while most other commuters are still in bed does not arise in this model.

Figure 8.11 presents what we can regard as the time cost per commuter on Route 1 as a function of the number of commuters using the route, N_1. For many purposes, it is useful to express this time cost in monetary terms. To do so, however, we need to know the value that commuters place on their time. From Section 5.5, we know that in some circumstances it makes sense to use the wage rate as the value of time. So we'll assume that the hourly wage rate of these commuters is $10. An 18-minute commute then costs $3 — since 18 minutes is three-tenths of an hour — and a 60-minute commute costs $10. On the vertical axis in Figure 8.11, we've attached alternative labels to convert the time cost per commuter into a dollar cost per commuter.

Notice that the dollar cost per commuter is, in effect, an average cost function, where the output is the number of trips to Wetvan from Surrey N_1, and the total cost is the total value of the time spent by the N_1 Surrey commuters in traveling to Wetvan. Therefore, we have attached an alternative label to the curve in Figure 8.11: ACC_1, for *average commuting cost* on Route 1. These costs are not borne by some firm, but rather by the commuters of Surrey. When we regard the relationship in Figure 8.11 as an average cost function, we are implicitly raising a number of questions. Among them is this one: What are the corresponding total and marginal cost functions?

In Figure 8.12, we've drawn the *total commuting cost* function associated with average commuting cost on Route 1 and labeled it TCC_1. (To derive this total cost function, notice that the total commuting cost is equal to the number of commuters N_1 multiplied by the average commuting cost ACC_1.) When N_1 is less than 1200, TCC_1 rises at a constant rate because Route 1 is congestion-free. When N_1 exceeds 1200, however, the ever-increasing congestion from that point on means that TCC_1 rises at an ever-increasing rate. For any point such as point A on TCC_1, the average commuter cost ACC_1 is equal to the slope of the ray from the origin to A, and what we'll call the *marginal commuter cost* — or MCC_1 — is equal to the slope of TCC_1. MCC_1 exceeds ACC_1 at point A because TCC_1 is steeper than the ray $0A$ at this point.

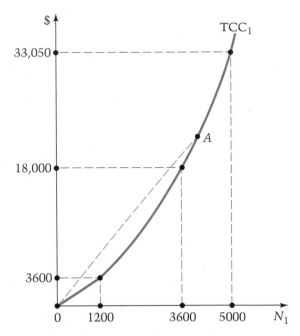

FIGURE 8.12 Total commuting costs.

TCC_1 gives the total commuting costs on Route 1. Notice that marginal commuting costs — equal to the slope of TCC_1 — are greater than average commuting costs — equal to TCC_1/N_1 — when the number of commuters exceeds 1200.

More generally, if N_1 exceeds 1200, then MCC_1 exceeds ACC_1. This result follows from the fact that Route 1 is subject to congestion when N_1 exceeds 1200. As we'll soon see, the fact that MCC_1 exceeds ACC_1 can have unfortunate consequences.

Because it is not subject to congestion, commuting on Route 2 is easy to model. A Surrey commuter on Route 2 will arrive in Wetvan in 30 minutes, *regardless of how many other commuters are also using this route*. In other words, Route 2 is slow but sure. No matter whether just 1 or all 5000 commuters choose this route, each commuter will spend 30 minutes getting to Wetvan. The average cost of the 30-minute commute on Route 2 is $5 — since the hourly wage rate is $10 and the trip takes half an hour, or $ACC_2 = \$5$. The total commuting cost on Route 2 is then $N_2 \times \$5$, or

$TCC_2 = 5N_2$. And finally, the marginal commuting cost is also \$5, or $MCC_2 = 5$.

To keep the model simple, we included a route that is always congestion-free—even though we recognize that virtually all real-world roads are subject to congestion. As you will see, however, we can discover the basic principles governing how commuters actually choose to distribute themselves over different routes as well as how they should distribute themselves to minimize the aggregate commuting costs.

Equilibrium in the Congestion Model

Now let's see what determines how many of Surrey's commuters will choose Route 1 and how many will choose Route 2. We will assume that every commuter in this model wants to minimize the time spent commuting—or, equivalently, the cost of commuting. Because each commuter is free to choose either route, the average commuting cost in equilibrium must be the same on both routes. Why? Suppose that on Monday, 1200 commuters choose Route 1 and 3800 choose Route 2. Then the average commuting costs on Route 1, ACC_1, on Monday are only \$3 but the average commuting costs on Route 2, ACC_2, are \$5. Some of the commuters who took Route 2 on Monday will then decide to switch to Route 1 on Tuesday. As a result, ACC_1 will increase on Tuesday. This process will end only when enough commuters have switched from Route 2 to Route 1 that ACC_1 is equal to ACC_2:

In equilibrium, the cost per commuter will be the same on both routes: $ACC_1 = ACC_2$.

Because ACC_2 is always \$5, we know that in equilibrium, N_1 must have adjusted so that ACC_1 is also equal to \$5. Because $ACC_1 = \$5$ when $N_1 = 3600$ in Figure 8.11, we know that in equilibrium, 3600 com-

muters will use Route 1, and the remainder of the 5000 commuters, or 1400 commuters, will use Route 2.

PROBLEM 8.11

What will the equilibrium allocation be if there are 6000 commuters? If there are 4000 commuters? If there are 3000 commuters?

A Suboptimal Equilibrium

Are these Surrey commuters making effective use of their roads? To find out, let's turn to Figure 8.13a, where we have plotted both TCC_1 and TCC_2. Notice that TCC_1 has been plotted relative to 0_1 in the standard way, and the values for N_1, written below the horizontal axis, increase from left to right beginning at 0_1. However, TCC_2 has been plotted relative to the second origin at 0_2, and the values for N_2, written above the horizontal axis, increase from right to left, beginning at 0_2. The distance from 0_1 to 0_2 is exactly 5000, reflecting the fact that 5000 Surrey commuters travel to Wetvan. Therefore, any point along the horizontal axis in Figure 8.13a corresponds to an allocation of commuters to the two routes. For example, at the equilibrium allocation, 3600 commuters take Route 1 and 1400 take Route 2.

Let's consider a particular allocation of commuters to the two routes—say, the allocation at point A. Notice that distance AC is the total cost of commuting on Route 1, TCC_1, and distance AB is the total cost of commuting on Route 2, TCC_2. Adding up the two distances gives us distance AD, the total cost of commuting for this allocation. Using this method, we have computed the total commuting cost for all possible allocations and have labeled the resulting curve TCC. Notice that TCC is smallest when 2000 commuters take Route 1 and 3000 take Route 2. The total commuting costs associated with this allocation are just \$21,800. By contrast, at the equilibrium al-

(a)

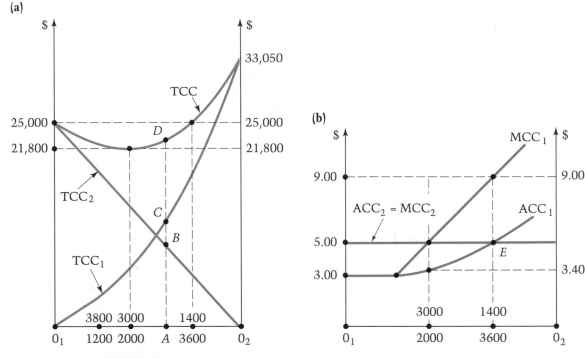

(b)

FIGURE 8.13 The allocation of commuters to routes.

In (a), total commuting costs on Route 1 and Route 2, TCC_1 and TCC_2, are plotted relative to 0_1 and 0_2, respectively. Since any point on the horizontal axis corresponds to an allocation of commuters to routes, we get total commuting costs for any allocation by vertically summing TCC_1 and TCC_2 to get TCC. Total commuting costs TCC are minimized when 2000 commuters are allocated to Route 1 and 3000 to

Route 2. In (b), we see that marginal commuting costs on the two routes — MCC_1 and MCC_2 — are equal when TCC is a minimum. Further, if commuters have common access to the two routes, average commuting costs on the two routes — ACC_1 and ACC_2 — are equalized in the equilibrium at E. The equilibrium allocation is 3600 commuters to Route 1 and 1400 to Route 2.

location (where 3600 take Route 1 and 1400 take Route 2), the total commuting costs are $25,000 — a significantly larger amount. In terms of total commuting costs, then, the equilibrium allocation is not very attractive. In fact, notice that if all 5000 commuters traveled along Route 2, the total commuting costs would likewise be $25,000. In this equilibrium, then, it is as if Route 1 simply did not exist.

Using the cost-benefit criterion, we then see that the Surrey commuters are not making effective use of their roads. Why not? According to the cost-benefit criterion,

one allocation is preferred to another if it is associated with smaller total commuting costs. Because the total commuting costs are smallest when 2000 commuters use Route 1 and 3000 use Route 2, this allocation is cost-benefit-optimal.

To understand these results, let's turn to Figure 8.13b. We have drawn the two sets of average and marginal cost curves and identified the equilibrium at point E at the intersection of ACC_1 and ACC_2. Why is the equilibrium at point E? Notice that to the right of point E the average cost of commuting is higher on Route 1 and that to the left it is higher on Route 2. Therefore, if the allocation of commuters were at any point other than E, some commuters would have a private incentive to switch routes. We know, then, that any such point could not be the equilibrium allocation.

Cost-Benefit Optimality

The marginal commuting cost curves reveal why the equilibrium is suboptimal and why total commuting costs are minimized when 2000 commuters use Route 1 and 3000 use Route 2. On either route, the marginal commuting cost is the rate at which total commuting costs on that route increase as the number of commuters increases — that is, the marginal commuting cost is the slope of the corresponding total commuting cost curve. Beginning at the equilibrium allocation, let's ask: What happens to the total commuting costs if we force one commuter off Route 1 and onto Route 2? Since MCC_1 is \$9, TCC_1 will decrease by (approximately) \$9, and since MCC_2 is \$5, TCC_2 will increase by \$5. Thus, total commuting costs TCC will decrease by approximately \$4. More generally, beginning at any point where MCC_1 is not equal to MCC_2, TCC can be reduced by shifting a commuter from the route where marginal cost is larger to the route where marginal cost is smaller. Therefore, we know that total commuting costs are smallest at the allocation where the marginal costs of commuting on the two routes are identical. The allocation where $MCC_1 = MCC_2$ in Figure 8.13a (and where TCC is lowest in Figure 8.13a) is at $N_1 = 2000$ and $N_2 = 3000$:

To minimize total commuting costs TCC, allocate commuters to the two routes so that $MCC_1 = MCC_2$.

We can now see why the self-interested decisions of individual commuters lead to a nonoptimal equilibrium. Because Route 2 is not subject to congestion, MCC_2 is always equal to ACC_2. This means that when an additional commuter chooses this route, that choice does not affect the costs borne by the other commuters on Route 2. The additional commuter personally bears all of the added commuting costs associated with the choice of Route 2. On the other hand, when N_1 exceeds 1200 on Route 1, an additional commuter adds to the congestion, and MCC_1 therefore exceeds ACC_1. In this situation, the addition of another commuter increases the total commuting costs by MCC_1, which exceeds ACC_1. Yet that additional commuter privately bears only the cost ACC_1. All the other commuters on Route 1 bear the remainder of the cost, $MCC_1 - ACC_2$. This means that beginning at the optimal allocation, a commuter presently using Route 2 can expect to reduce his or her private commuting costs by \$1.60 (\$5.00 − \$3.40) by shifting from Route 2 to Route 1. The optimal allocation is therefore not an equilibrium. Indeed, as long as ACC_2 exceeds ACC_1, commuters will shift from Route 2 to Route 1. The resulting equilibrium is *suboptimal* because the commuters switching from Route 2 to Route 1 impose costs on all the commuters already using Route 1.[9]

More generally, we know that the equilibrium will be at the point where ACC_1 is equal to ACC_2, because only at this point will it be in the private self-interest of all commuters to stick with the routes they have chosen. On the other hand, we know that the cost-benefit-optimal equilibrium will be at the point where MCC_1 is equal to MCC_2. Yet because Route 1 is subject to congestion, ACC_1 is less than MCC_1, and the equilibrium will not be optimal.

---

[9] This congestion problem is one example of an externality. The general issues raised by externalities are addressed in Chapter 17.

PROBLEM 8.12

What is the optimal allocation if there are 6000 commuters? If there are 3000 commuters? If there are 1000 commuters?

The Optimal Toll

The suboptimal equilibrium in this model arises from the assumption that commuters have unrestricted, or common, access to a road that is subject to congestion. Taking this perspective, you can see that the traffic congestion problem is yet another type of *common-property problem.* Like some of the other common-property problems we've encountered, solutions are possible. For example, one solution is to charge a toll on Route 1. What toll can be levied on Route 1 that will be large enough that commuters on Route 2 have no incentive to switch to Route 1 at the optimal allocation, when 3000 commuters use Route 2 and 2000 commuters use Route 1? From Figure 8.13*b*, it appears that a toll equal to $1.60 ($5.00 − $3.40) should do the job.

To see if it does, let's suppose that 2000 commuters are using Route 1 and 3000 commuters are using Route 2 and then impose the $1.60 toll. Does any commuter have a private incentive to switch routes? The costs borne by any commuter on Route 1 can be calculated by adding up the value of time spent commuting on Route 1 ($3.40) and the toll ($1.60) — a total of $5; the costs borne by any commuter on Route 2 are equal to the value of time spent commuting on Route 2 — also a total of $5. Because no commuter gains anything by switching routes — the costs are $5 on either route — we know that the model is in equilibrium at the optimal allocation. What happens to the revenue raised by the toll? Although it could be used in any number of ways, it is simplest to imagine that the revenue will be paid out as a lump-sum subsidy to the 5000 Surrey commuters.

Congestion and Diminishing Marginal Product

On Route 1, the input called "commuters' time" is used to produce an output called "trips to Wetvan." Notice from this perspective that TCC_1 is just a variable cost function. What is the associated total product function that translates the input "commuters' time" into the output "trips to Wetvan"? To find out, we could begin with the variable cost function TCC_1 and derive the total product function by reversing the procedure used in Figure 8.7. Yet without doing so, we can readily see two important properties of that total product function. First, it exhibits a constant marginal product for any amount of time less than 18 minutes per commuter. Second, it exhibits a diminishing marginal product for any amount of time greater than 18 minutes per commuter. Therefore, it has the same general shape as the total product function in Figure 8.4*a*. Of course, the point at which marginal product begins to diminish is just the point at which additional commuters begin to create congestion; in other words, *congestion* is a specialized name for *diminishing marginal product* on a road. Although Malthus never encountered the sort of congestion problem we're looking at, he certainly would have recognized it as a case of diminishing marginal product.

---

*8.6 Cost Minimization in a Multiplant Firm

Now that we recognize that TCC_1 and TCC_2 are variable cost functions, we can reinterpret what we learned about congestion from Figure 8.13*a* to discover something about **multiplant firms.** Let's reinterpret TCC_1 and TCC_2 in Figure 8.13*a* as the variable cost functions associated with two factories, or plants, owned by a single firm and MCC_1 and MCC_2 in Figure 8.13*b* as the corresponding short-run marginal cost functions. The length of the axis connecting 0_1 and 0_2 can be reinterpreted as a fixed output of 5000 units that this particular firm wants to produce. The firm's problem is to allocate the 5000 units of output to its two plants so as to minimize its total variable cost.

Given this reinterpretation, the TCC curve in Figure 8.13*a* tells us the firm's total variable cost for any allocation of the fixed output to the two plants. We can see that the firm's cost-minimization problem is solved by allocating 2000 units to the first plant and 3000 to the second plant. More important, we have found the rule that governs the cost-minimizing allocation to the two plants. The firm will allocate the fixed output so that short-run marginal cost is the same in both plants:

To minimize the total variable cost of producing a given output in two or more plants, allocate output to the plants so that short-run marginal cost is the same in all plants.

Summary

In Section 8.1 of this chapter, we defined a production function and provided illustrations of it. In Section 8.2, we defined the long-run cost-minimization problem and then observed that there are many short-run cost-minimization problems, depending on the firm's time horizon and the number of variable inputs over that time horizon. The simplest of these is the time horizon in which only one input is variable.

In Section 8.3, we began our exploration of the production function by fixing the quantity of all inputs but one, input 1, thereby defining the total product function $TP(z_1)$. We then defined the concepts of marginal product and average product:

$$MP(z_1) = \text{slope of } TP(z_1)$$

$$AP(z_1) = \frac{TP(z_1)}{z_1}$$

The most important assumption regarding $TP(z_1)$ is the assumption of diminishing marginal product: beyond some quantity of input 1, the slope of $TP(z_1)$ begins to get smaller, or marginal product diminishes. We then discovered some important interrelations between $MP(z_1)$ and $AP(z_1)$: $AP(z_1)$ is rising or falling as $MP(z_1)$ is greater or less than $AP(z_1)$.

In Section 8.4, we learned virtually everything there is to know about costs in the simple one-variable-input case. Indeed, we developed a total of seven cost concepts, beginning with the variable cost function $VC(y)$:

$$VC(y) = \text{minimum expenditure on the}$$
$$\text{variable input necessary to}$$
$$\text{produce } y \text{ units of output}$$

The expenditure on the fixed input, or the fixed cost FC, is held constant by definition and is therefore unrelated to the quantity of output.

All the other cost functions can be constructed from these two. First, by adding them together, we can define the short-run total cost function, $STC(y)$:

$$STC(y) = VC(y) + FC$$

Associated with each of these is an average function, which is derived simply by dividing by the quantity of output:

$$AVC(y) = \frac{VC(y)}{y}$$

$$SAC(y) = \frac{STC(y)}{y}$$

$$AFC(y) = \frac{FC}{y}$$

The *average fixed cost* function $AFC(y)$ is negatively sloped and asymptotic to both axes (that is, as y goes to zero, $AFC(y)$ goes to infinity, and as y goes to infinity, $AFC(y)$ goes to zero). In the standard case, both average variable cost AVC(y) and short-run average cost SAC(y) are U-shaped, and SAC(y) lies above AVC(y). Indeed, we can generate SAC(y) from AVC(y) by adding (vertically) AFC(y) to AVC(y):

$$SAC(y) = AVC(y) + AFC(y)$$

The most interesting cost concept is short-run marginal cost: the rate at which cost increases as output increases, or the added cost required to produce an added unit of output. SMC(y) can be derived from either VC(y) or STC(y) as follows:

$$SMC(y) = \text{slope of } VC(y) = \text{slope of } STC(y)$$

We also developed some important interrelationships: SMC(y) intersects AVC(y) at the point where AVC(y) attains its minimum value. To the left of this point, where SMC(y) is less than AVC(y), AVC(y) is falling; to the right of this point, where SMC(y) exceeds AVC(y), AVC(y) is rising. The interrelationships between SMC(y) and SAC(y) are qualitatively the same as those between SMC(y) and AVC(y).

Finally, in Section 8.5, we considered a traffic congestion problem. We discovered that to minimize total commuting costs, commuters traveling on two different routes should be allocated so that the marginal commuting costs on the two routes are identical. We also discovered that when commuters have unrestricted access to all routes, the equilibrium will be suboptimal because average commuting costs are equalized in equilibrium. We then saw how to find a toll that would shift the equilibrium to the optimum. Finally, we reinterpreted these results in the context of a multiplant firm that wanted to produce a fixed output at minimum variable cost. We saw that to minimize its variable cost, the firm must allocate its output so that the short-run marginal costs in all its plants are identical.

Exercises

In Exercises 1, 2, and 3, y is quantity of output and z is quantity of the variable input. In all three exercises, the total product function has the standard shape illustrated in Figure 8.3.

1 Suppose that the following statement is true: "When z increases from 10 to 11, average product increases from 45 to 48." Indicate whether each of the following statements is true, false, or uncertain; explain your answers.
   a Output y is 450 when z is 10.
   b When y is 450, SMC is upward sloping.
   c When y is 450, AVC is downward sloping.
   d When y is 450, SAC is downward sloping.
   e When z is 10, MP is upward sloping.
   f When z is 10, MP exceeds 45.
   g When y is 450, SMC is less than AVC.
   h When y is 450, SMC is less than SAC.
   i SAC is greater when y is 450 than it is when y is 528.

2 Suppose that the following statement is true: "When y is 300, SMC is $75, SAC is $65, and AP is 30." Indicate whether each of the following statements is true, false, or uncertain; explain your answers.
   a When y is 300, z is 10.
   b When z is 10, MP is less than 30.
   c When y is 300, AVC exceeds SMC.
   d The point of diminishing returns to the variable input occurs where z is greater than 10.
   e The price of the variable input is less than $2000.
   f The price of the variable input is greater than $500.
   g VC at y equal to 300 is less than $20,000.

3 Suppose that the following statement is true: "When y is 100 units, SMC is $100, SMC is upward sloping, MP is 10, and AP is 20." Indicate whether each of the following statements is true, false, or uncertain; explain your answers.
   a The price of the variable input is $1000.
   b The price of the fixed input is $1000.
   c When z is 10, MP is downward sloping.

d When y is 100, AVC is less than SMC.
e When y is 100, AVC is $50.
f When y is 100, SAC is upward sloping.
g When y is 100, SAC is greater than $49.

4 A firm buys trucks for $10,000 and uses them for 5 years. What is the *equivalent annual rental price* of the services of a truck for 1 year,
a If the scrap value of the truck is $0 and the annual interest rate is 0%?
b If the scrap value of the truck is $0 and the annual interest rate is 10%?
c If the scrap value of the truck is $5000 and the annual interest rate is 0%?
d If the scrap value of the truck is $5000 and the annual interest rate is 15%?

5 We all know that the more insulation a building has, the cheaper it is to cool or heat the building. Let T' denote the ambient temperature inside a building and T'' the ambient temperature outside. Suppose that the fuel consumption z_1 necessary to maintain a constant temperature differential D is inversely proportional to the amount of insulation z_2 and directly proportional to the square of the temperature differential. That is, suppose that

$$z_1 = \frac{D^2}{z_2}$$

a What is the good that is being produced, and what is its production function?
b Suppose that $z_2 = 1$, T'' is 50° F and $w_1 = \$2$. What expenditure on fuel is necessary to maintain a temperature of 70°F inside the building? How much more would it cost to maintain this temperature if T'' was 30°?
c Now suppose that $z_2 = 2$ and repeat these calculations.

6 Given the production function

$$y = \min(z_1, z_2)$$

first derive and plot $TP(z_1)$, $MP(z_1)$, and $AP(z_1)$, supposing that the quantity of input 2 is fixed at 100 units. Then, supposing that w_1 and w_2 are both $1, derive all seven cost functions and plot them in a graph analogous to Figure 8.10.

7 Consider the following production function:

$$y = (z_1)^{1/3}(z_2)^{2/3}$$

Input prices are $w_1 = \$2$ and $w_2 = \$3$.
a Suppose that z_2 is fixed at 1 unit: $z_2 = 1$. Derive the total product function, the variable cost function, the average variable cost function, and the short-run total cost function. Hint: To find the variable cost function, first observe that y^3 units of z_1 are needed to produce y units of output when $z_2 = 1$, and then compute the cost of y^3 units of input 1.
b Now suppose that z_2 is fixed at 8 units and repeat the same exercises.
c Using the cost functions from a and b, compute and compare the variable and short-run total cost of producing 1, 2, 3, and 4 units of output.

8 A firm owns two plants that produce the same good. The marginal cost functions for the two plants are

$$SMC_1 = 10y_1$$
$$SMC_2 = 5y_2$$

where y_1 and y_2 are quantities of output produced in each plant.
a If the firm wants to produce 15 units of output at minimum cost, how much should it produce in each plant?
b Now consider an arbitrary quantity of output y. To minimize costs, what fraction of the total output should the firm produce in each plant?

9 If a firm has two plants and can vary just one input, to minimize cost it should allocate output to the plants so that the marginal product of the variable input is the same in the two plants. Explain.

*10 Hank works for his dad, producing widgits by tending his dad's magic widgit maker. (His dad doesn't allow anyone else to even touch the magic machine.) For every hour he tends the machine, Hank produces 10 widgits. His dad pays Hank $10 per hour for the first 8 hours in any day, $20 per hour for the next 8 hours, and $40 per hour for the last 8 hours of the day.

a Find VC, AVC, and SMC.

b Now suppose that Hank's dad can sell each widget for $2.50 and that he wants to maximize his profit. How many widgits should he ask Hank to produce, and how many hours per day will Hank have to work?

*11 On the island of Molo there is a lovely lake that produces fish according to the following total product function:

$$y = 1000z^{1/2}$$

where y is the daily fish take and z is the number of fishers on the lake. The corresponding marginal and average product functions are

$$MP(z) = \frac{500}{z^{1/2}}$$

$$AP(z) = \frac{1000}{z^{1/2}}$$

At the end of the day, each fisher on the lake has the average product, $1000/z^{1/2}$ fish, in his or her creel; hence, the harvest of fish from the lake is equitably distributed among the fishers. Molo fishers can also fish in the ocean, where they catch 100 fish per fisher, regardless of the number of fishers. There are 150 fishers on the island.

a What are the total, marginal, and average product functions for the ocean fishery?

b Currently, 100 fishers fish on the lake and 50 fish in the ocean. Verify that all 150 fishers have 100 fish at the end of each day and that the total harvest is 15,000 fish per day.

c If all 150 fishers fished in the ocean, what would the total harvest be? Given the allocation in **b**, what is the net value of the lake fishery to the fishers of Molo?

d What allocation of fishers maximizes the total harvest?

e Given the optimal allocation from **d**, what is the total harvest of the fishers of Molo? What is the net value of the lake fishery with this allocation?

f Can you devise an institution that would produce the optimal allocation of fishers? Is there a property-rights solution to this problem?

g You've encountered these kinds of problems in Chapters 2 and 5. What is the generic name for these problems?

References

Douglas, P. H. (1948), "Are There Laws of Production?" *American Economic Review*, **67**:297 – 308.

Hicks, J. R. (1939), *Value and Capital*, London: The Clarendon Press.

Samuelson, P. A. (1947), *Foundations of Economic Analysis*, Cambridge, Mass.: Harvard University Press.

9

PRODUCTION AND COST: MANY VARIABLE INPUTS

In Chapter 8, we concentrated on the simple case in which only one input was variable, to develop a basic understanding of production and cost. In this chapter, we'll use that understanding to explore cost and production in the more complicated, realistic environment in which more than one input is variable. In most real situations, firms do have the flexibility to vary more than one input during the relevant period. For example, if the Denver and Rio Grande Western Railroad wants to increase the amount of coal it hauls out of western Colorado, it usually can acquire new rolling stock and hire more train crews within a 6-month time frame. If it wants to double its existing track, it can acquire the additional quantities of inputs such as tracks, ties, and signaling equipment, but it needs a lead time significantly longer than 6 months. If it wants to add whole new lines, it can again alter the quantities of the inputs it uses, but it needs an even longer lead time. You will have a good understanding of these more realistic cases once we extend our original theory of cost and production to the case in which two inputs can be varied.

In Section 9.1, we'll look at how one input can be substituted for another, given a fixed quantity of output, and in Section 9.2, we'll use this understanding to put the long-run cost-minimization problem in perspective. In Section 9.3, we'll view cost minimization from a more analytical perspective as we develop graphic techniques to solve more complex cost-minimization problems. In Section 9.4, we'll explore several important comparative statics results, and in Sections 9.5 and 9.6, we'll focus on homothetic production functions as we analyze the relationship between costs of production and economies of scale. In Section 9.7, we'll look closely at some relationships between long-run and short-run costs of production, and in Section 9.8, we'll develop a rudimentary theory of market structure.

9.1 Isoquants and Input Substitution

In Chapter 8, we defined the production function, $y = F(z_1, z_2)$, and began to explore it by fixing the quantity of one input to define the total product function. This allowed us to see how output changed as quantity of the variable input changed. In this section, we'll resume our exploration of the production function by fixing the quantity of output. This procedure allows us to investigate **input substitution** — that is, how one input can be substituted for another. Our goal is to understand the many ways in which a fixed quantity of output can be produced.

An **isoquant** is a curve composed of all the input bundles that will produce some fixed quantity of output. Isoquants are to production theory what indifference curves are to consumer theory. Just as indifference curves in consumer theory represent all the consumption bundles that a person ranks as equally attractive, an isoquant in production theory represents all the input bundles that can produce the same quantity of output.

To get a sense of what isoquants are, let's return to Tipple's production function for courier services,

$$y = (1200z_1 z_2)^{1/2}$$

Recall that y is the quantity of courier services measured in miles, z_1 is hours of a driver's time, and z_2 is gallons of gas. By fixing y, we define an isoquant. For example, suppose we fix y at 120 miles. Then, setting y equal to 120 in the expression above gives us the following algebraic description of the isoquant:

$$120 = (1200z_1 z_2)^{1/2}$$

Now, squaring both sides of this expression and dividing by 1200 gives us a simpler expression for the isoquant:

$$12 = z_1 z_2$$

This expression tells us that any input bundle such that the product of z_1 and z_2 is 12 will produce 120 miles of courier services. For example, the input bundle might be composed of 2 hours of a driver's time

and 6 gallons of gasoline, or 3 hours of a driver's time and 4 gallons of gasoline, or 4 hours of a driver's time and 3 gallons of gasoline. In Figure 9.1, we have constructed both this isoquant and the isoquant for 240 miles. (As you can verify, the 240-mile isoquant can be described by the following equation: $48 = z_1 z_2$.)

Notice that both isoquants in Figure 9.1 are smooth and that their slope decreases from left to right. But do all isoquants look like this? Are other general shapes possible? Try the following problem to find out.

PROBLEM 9.1

1 John Henry's Iron Works uses a furnace and fuel to produce heat. The furnace can use either coal or wood as a fuel. One ton of coal produces 5 thermal units. (TUs) of heat, and one ton of wood produces 2 TUs. Given the furnace, the production function for heat is

$$y = 5z_1 + 2z_2$$

where y is TUs of heat, z_1 is tons of coal, and z_2 is tons of wood. Construct the isoquant for 20 TUs.

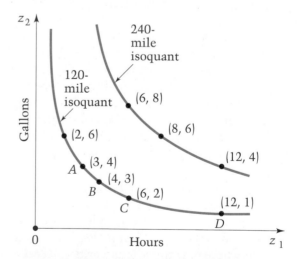

FIGURE 9.1 Isoquants for courier services.

All the bundles of hours and time on the 120-mile isoquant will produce 120 miles of courier services, and all the bundles on the 240-mile isoquant will produce 240 miles of courier services.

2 The standard bartender's recipe for rum-and-Coke calls for 2 ounces of rum and 6 ounces of Coke. The implied production function is

$$y = \min\left(\frac{z_1}{2}, \frac{z_2}{6}\right)$$

where y is number of drinks, z_1 is ounces of rum, and z_2 is ounces of Coke. Construct the isoquant for two drinks.

Just as any indifference map is filled with indifference curves, any isoquant map is filled with isoquants. And just as the farther an indifference curve is from the origin, the higher its utility number, so, too, the farther an isoquant is from the origin, the higher the level of output associated with it.

But what can we learn from the shapes of isoquants? As you discovered in Problem 9.1, they may take different forms. What is the economic meaning of the differences between the isoquants in Figures 9.2a and 9.2b, for example? (These are the isoquants you constructed in Problem 9.1.) Notice that the shape of each is distinctive. In Figure 9.2a, the slope of the isoquant is constant throughout. In Figure 9.2b, on the isoquant, the slope is infinite above the kink and zero to the right of the kink. At the kink itself, the isoquant has no well-defined slope. What does the slope of an isoquant tell us? And what is the significance of the fact that the isoquant in Figure 9.2b is kinked?

Marginal Rate of Technical Substitution

The absolute value of the slope of an isoquant is called the **marginal rate of technical substitution** (MRTS). The term deliberately echoes another familiar one from consumer theory, the **marginal rate of substitution** (MRS). In consumption theory, we used MRS to measure the rate at which one good could be substituted for another, holding

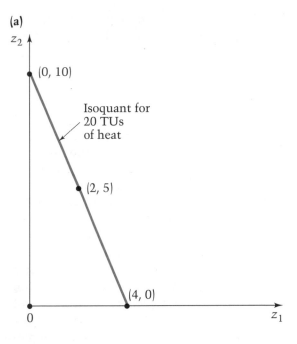

(a)

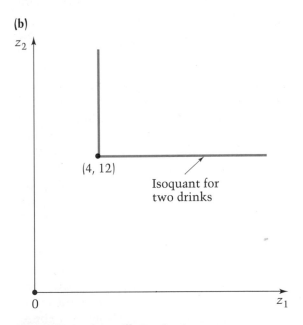

(b)

FIGURE 9.2 Some illustrative isoquants.

In (a), where inputs 1 and 2 are perfect substitutes, any bundle on the isoquant will produce 20 TUs (thermal units) of heat. In (b), where inputs 1 and 2 are perfect complements, any bundle on the isoquant will produce two drinks.

utility constant. In production theory, we will use MRTS to measure the rate at which one input can be substituted for the other, holding output constant.

Perfect Complements

We can now see the significance of not being able to determine the slope of the isoquant at the kink in Figure 9.2*b*. In this **fixed-proportions production function,** more of one input cannot be substituted for less of the other. In mixing standard rum-and-Cokes, more Coke is not a substitute for less rum: if a bartender has only 4 ounces of rum, he or she can't make more than 2 rum-and-cokes no matter how much Coke is on hand. So, too, in producing fasteners from nuts and bolts, more bolts cannot be substituted for fewer nuts. When inputs are **perfect complements,** substitution is impossible, and the marginal rate of technical substitution cannot be defined.

If the isoquants are like those in Figures 9.1 and 9.2*a*, however, input 2 (or input 1) can be substituted for input 1 (or input 2). To understand why MRTS measures the rate at which one input can be substituted for another, we'll use a procedure identical to the one used in discussing MRS in Section 3.5. Beginning at point A on the isoquant in Figure 9.3, suppose that the quantity of input 1 is reduced by some amount Δz_1. By increasing the quantity of input 2 by Δz_2, we return to the original isoquant at point B. Thus, Δz_2 substitutes for Δz_1. Dividing Δz_2 by Δz_1 gives us a measure of the *rate* at which input 2 must be substituted for input 1 to hold output constant. That is, the *nonmarginal* rate of technical substitution is equal to $\Delta z_2/\Delta z_1$. This rate is just -1 times the slope of the dashed line segment AB in Figure 9.3 (or the absolute value of this slope).

To determine the *marginal* rate of technical substitution, we simply let Δz_1 become

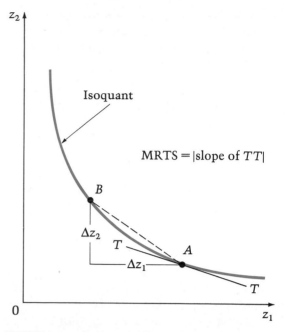

FIGURE 9.3   The marginal rate of technical substitution.

Beginning at point A, if we reduce the quantity of input 1 by Δz_1, we must increase the quantity of input 2 by Δz_2 to get back to the isoquant. The (nonmarginal) rate of technical substitution is therefore $\Delta z_2/\Delta z_1$, or -1 times the slope of the dashed line BA. To find the marginal rate of technical substitution, MRTS, let Δz_1 approach zero. As it does, the rate of substitution approaches -1 times the slope of the tangent line TT, which is MRTS at point A.

progressively smaller until point B approaches point A in Figure 9.3. As we let Δz_1 become arbitrarily small, $\Delta z_2/\Delta z_1$ will approach -1 times the slope of the tangent line TT in Figure 9.3. In other words, the MRTS at any point is just -1 times the slope of the isoquant at that point.

DEFINITION

$MRTS(z_1, z_2)$
$$= -[\text{slope of the isoquant at } (z_1, z_2)]$$

MRTS as a Ratio of Marginal Products

Figure 9.3 is also useful in establishing an important relationship between MRTS and the marginal products of the two inputs.

The marginal rate of technical substitution of input 2 for input 1 is equal to the marginal product of input 1 divided by the marginal product of input 2.

To understand why this is true, notice first that when the quantity of input 1 is decreased by Δz_1, the change in total output is (approximately) the marginal product of input 1 multiplied by the quantity change:

$$\Delta y = MP_1 \Delta z_1$$

Since Δz_2 compensates for this reduction in z_1, it must produce an identical change in output, Δy. Thus,

$$\Delta y = MP_2 \Delta z_2$$

Of course, MRTS is approximately Δz_2 divided by Δz_1. Solving the first of these approximations for Δz_1 and the second for Δz_2 and then forming the substitution ratio $\Delta z_2/\Delta z_1$ yields

$$MRTS = \left(\frac{\Delta y}{MP_2}\right) \Big/ \left(\frac{\Delta y}{MP_1}\right)$$

Canceling the Δy terms, this expression reduces to

$$MRTS = \frac{MP_1}{MP_2}$$

In other words, the MRTS is equal to the marginal product of input 1 divided by the marginal product of input 2.[1]

In the following problem, you can use this result to show that isoquants are downward sloping when both marginal products are positive.

PROBLEM 9.2

Using the assumption that marginal products are positive and the fact that the MRTS can be expressed as a ratio of marginal products, show that isoquants cannot have a positive slope.

In the following problem, you can check your understanding of MRTS by using it in some numerical calculations.

PROBLEM 9.3

In Problem 9.1, you constructed the following isoquant for heat produced from coal (input 1) and wood (input 2) as fuels:

$$20 = 5z_1 + 2z_2$$

Now determine the MRTS of wood for coal for all points along this isoquant.

---

[1] We can use the implicit function theorem to express MRTS in terms of the partial derivatives of $F(\,\cdot\,)$. The isoquant for y' units of output can be written as

$$y' = F(z_1, z_2)$$

where y' is fixed and z_1 and z_2 are free to vary. Since the isoquant defines z_2 as an implicit function of z_1, we can use the implicit function theorem to express this isoquant as

$$z_2 = g(z_1)$$

MRTS is, of course, just $-g'(z_1)$, where $g'(z_1)$ is the derivative of $g(z_1)$. Combining these equations, we have the following identity

$$y' = F[z_1, g(z_1)]$$

Differentiating the identity with respect to z_1 gives us

$$F_1[z_1, g(z_1)] + g'(z_1)F_2[z_1, g(z_1)] = 0$$

where $F_1(\,\cdot\,)$ and $F_2(\,\cdot\,)$ denote the partial derivatives of $F(\,\cdot\,)$ with respect to z_1 and z_2. The partial derivative $F_i(\,\cdot\,)$ is, of course, the marginal product of input i. Rearranging this equation, we get

$$-g'(z_1) = \frac{F_1(z_1, z_2)}{F_2(z_1, z_2)}$$

But the left side of this equation is just MRTS. Hence,

$$MRTS\,(z_1, z_2) = \frac{F_1(z_1, z_2)}{F_2(z_1, z_2)}$$

Thus, for example, for the production function $F(z_1, z_2) = z_1 z_2$, $MRTS(z_1, z_2) = z_2/z_1$.

Perfect Substitutes

You saw in Problem 9.3 that in John Henry's Iron Works, wood can be substituted for coal in the production of heat at a constant rate, 5/2. For example, if the quantity of coal is reduced by 2 tons, then the quantity of wood must be increased by 5 tons (2 tons times 5/2) to maintain heat output. Or, if the product is denim jeans, and if input 1 is cotton thread and input 2 is polyester thread, polyester thread can be substituted for cotton thread at the constant rate 1/1. In any production process in which MRTS is a constant, one of the inputs can always be substituted for the other on fixed terms, and the two inputs are **perfect substitutes.**

You are now familiar with the two extreme cases of input substitutability — perfect complements and perfect substitutes. Yet most interesting economic cases fall somewhere in between: one input can be substituted for the other, but the MRTS is not a constant. This intermediate case is represented by the isoquants for Tipple's Courier Service in Figure 9.1.

Diminishing Marginal Rate of Technical Substitution

In these intermediate cases, where isoquants are convex as in Figure 9.1, it becomes progressively more difficult to substitute one input for the other. To see why, let's substitute input 1 for input 2 on the 120-mile isoquant in Figure 9.1. In the move from A to B, 1 added hour of time substitutes for 1 less gallon of gas, while in the move from B to C, 2 added hours are needed to substitute for 1 less gallon, and in the move from C to D, 6 added hours are needed to substitute for 1 less gallon. This diminishing capacity to substitute one input for another accords with our intuition. Notice, too, that it means that MRTS gets smaller and smaller, or diminishes, from left to right along an isoquant. A diminishing MRTS is an assumption that is commonly adopted in production theory.

ASSUMPTION: Diminishing Marginal Rate of Technical Substitution

Moving from left to right on any isoquant, MRTS(z_1, z_2) decreases as z_1 increases.

In the following analysis, we will be setting aside this assumption whenever we use the case of perfect substitutes or perfect complements for illustration. Now let's use what we've learned about isoquants to solve the cost-minimizing problem when both inputs in the two-input case are allowed to vary.

9.2 The Cost-Minimization Problem: A Perspective

Before plunging into a detailed analysis of cost minimization, we need to define the long-run cost-minimization problem and then use the solution — a system of input demand functions that identifies the least costly input bundle for any level of output — to form the **cost function.** This cost function identifies the minimum cost of producing any level of output in the long run. It will play a central role in later chapters where we analyze the profit-maximizing decisions of firms. We'll conclude this section by finding the input demand and cost functions for a particularly simple production function so that you can see in a more tangible way just what these functions are and do. In subsequent sections, we'll look at the cost-minimization problem from a more analytical perspective.

As we saw in Section 8.4, the long-run cost-minimization problem is

minimize $w_1z_1 + w_2z_2$

by choice of z_1 and z_2

subject to the constraint $y = F(z_1, z_2)$

Before we can think of solving this problem, we must distinguish between the variables that are being chosen, or determined (the endogenous variables), and the variables that are givens (the exogenous variables).

In this problem, the endogenous variables are the quantities of the two inputs z_1 and z_2. The exogenous variables are the prices of the two inputs w_1 and w_2 and the level of output y. The input prices are, we assume, genuinely outside the firm's control; from the firm's point of view, they are fixed. The fact that output is exogenous in this problem simply reflects the fact that we are analyzing the firm's problem in stages. In the next stage (considered in later chapters), we'll use the cost function developed here in combination with revenue considerations to analyze the firm's choice of output. For now, however, the level of output is fixed by assumption.

Conditional Input Demand Functions

The solution to the cost-minimization problem gives us the cost-minimizing values of the endogenous variables, written as z_1^* and z_2^*, as functions of the exogenous variables y, w_1, and w_2. These functions are simply the rules prescribing the quantity of each input that minimizes the cost of producing y units of output when the prices of the inputs are w_1 and w_2. Because the quantity demanded of each input is so clearly dependent, or conditional, on the level of output y, these input demand functions are usually called **conditional input demand functions.**

The Cost Function

Once we know these demand functions, determining the **cost function** is a simple accounting step. This function—written $TC(y, w_1, w_2)$ to remind you that the total cost of production depends on the quantity of output and on the prices of the inputs—

is just the sum of the quantities demanded of the inputs multiplied by the respective prices of those inputs.

DEFINITION

$$TC(y, w_1, w_2) = w_1 z_1^* + w_2 z_2^*$$

Some Illustrations

To help you understand just what the terms *conditional input demand functions* and *cost function* mean, we'll derive them for the standard rum-and-Coke production function introduced in Problem 9.1. We've chosen this simple example because we can readily identify the cost-minimizing input bundles. The production function is

$$y = \min\left(\frac{z_1}{2}, \frac{z_2}{6}\right)$$

where y is number of drinks, z_1 is ounces of rum, and z_2 is ounces of Coke.

To minimize costs for this fixed-proportions production function, for every drink, simply use 2 ounces of rum and 6 ounces of Coke. If y is 2, use exactly 4 ounces of rum and 12 ounces of Coke; if y is 7, use exactly 14 ounces of rum and 42 ounces of Coke; and so on. More generally, the following rules tell us how much rum and how much Coke a bartender needs to mix y standard rum-and-Cokes:

$$z_1^* = 2y$$
$$z_2^* = 6y$$

These are the conditional input demand functions for this production function. Because the input proportions are fixed in this production function, the conditional input demand functions do not depend on prices of the inputs: if we want 5 standard rum-and-Cokes, we need 10 ounces of rum regardless of how expensive rum may be or how inexpensive Coke may be.

When we move from the conditional input demand functions to the cost function, however, input prices necessarily enter the picture, because the total cost is calculated by multiplying the price of each input by quantity demanded and then totaling the results. The cost function for rum-and-Cokes is

$$TC(y, z_1, z_2) = 2w_1 y + 6w_2 y$$

where w_1 is the price of an ounce of rum and w_2 is the price of an ounce of Coke.

In the following problem, you can find conditional input demand functions and a cost function for another simple case.

PROBLEM 9.4

From Problem 9.1, we know that in John Henry's Iron Works, heat is produced from coal and wood according to the following production function:

$$y = 5z_1 + 2z_2$$

Find the conditional input demand functions and the cost function for this production function. Begin by assuming that $2w_1 < 5w_2$ and show that John Henry should buy only coal to minimize his costs; then show that he needs $y/5$ tons of coal to produce y TUs of heat; then calculate the cost of producing y TUs of heat using coal as the only input. Now suppose that $2w_1 > 5w_2$. Which input should John Henry use? How much of it does he need to produce y TUs of heat? How much must he spend to produce y TUs of heat?

9.3 Solving Cost-Minimization Problems

To solve more complex cost-minimization problems, we can use graphic techniques like those we used to solve the consumer's utility-maximization problem in Section 4.5.

Feasible Input Bundles

If we want to produce y units of output, the set of **feasible input bundles** is composed of all the input bundles that will produce at

least y units of output. In Figure 9.4, we have again used Tipple's Courier Service as an illustration. The green area is the set of bundles of time and gasoline that will allow Tipple to produce at least 120 miles of courier service. Therefore, it is the set of feasible input bundles for output equal to 120, because Tipple can produce 120 miles with any input bundle in that area, but he can't produce 120 miles with any input bundle outside the green area. More generally, the set of feasible input bundles associated with

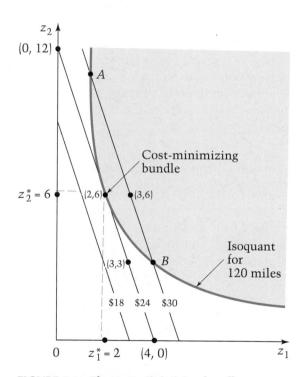

FIGURE 9.4   The cost-minimizing bundle.

Bundles in the green area on and above the isoquant are feasible bundles for 120 miles of output because they will produce 120 miles of courier services. All bundles on the lowest isocost line cost \$18, all bundles on the intermediate isocost line cost \$24, and all bundles on the highest isocost line cost \$30. The least expensive bundle that will produce 120 miles is bundle (2, 6), which costs \$24. Notice that the \$24 isocost line is tangent to the isoquant at the cost-minimizing bundle (2, 6). Alternatively, MRTS is equal to w_1/w_2 at the cost-minimizing bundle.

any isoquant is composed of all the input bundles on or above the isoquant.

Even though a firm can choose any of the feasible input bundles to produce the requisite quantity of output, we will assume that it will choose the least expensive one. The firm's problem then is to find the least expensive input bundle that is feasible.

Isocost Lines

If an hour of a driver's time costs $6 (if $w_1 = \$6$) and a gallon of gas costs $2 ($w_2 = \$2$), which input bundles will cost Tipple exactly $24? As you can easily verify, all the following input bundles cost $24: (4, 0), (0, 12), (2, 6), (3, 3). Indeed, any input bundle on the line

$$24 = 6z_1 + 2z_2$$

costs exactly $24. This line is an **isocost line** because all the input bundles on it cost the same amount, $24. In Figure 9.4, we have constructed this isocost line and two others associated with $18 and $30. Notice that the more expensive an input bundle is, the farther it is from the origin.

More generally, if the total amount to be spent on an input bundle is fixed at, say, c, then the following is a general expression for an isocost line:

DEFINITION
$$c = w_1z_1 + w_2z_2$$

Any input bundle that lies on this line costs exactly c.

PROBLEM 9.5
Consider the general expression for an isocost line set out above. What is the slope of an isocost line? What is the opportunity cost of input 1 in terms of input 2? Where does the isocost line intersect the z_1 axis? The z_2 axis?

We now have the tools necessary to solve the firm's cost-minimizing problem. In solving that problem, we will limit our attention to the case in which isoquants are smooth and convex and the quantity of both inputs in the cost-minimizing input bundle is positive. As you know from Chapter 4, this type of solution is called an **interior solution**.

Characterizing Interior Solutions

In Figure 9.4, we have solved Tipple's cost-minimizing problem, assuming that he wants to produce 120 miles of courier services and that the price of a driver's time is $6 per hour and the price of gas is $2 per gallon. We've constructed the 120-mile isoquant for the courier service and three isocost lines associated with $18, $24, and $30. As you know, the higher the expenditure associated with an isocost line, the farther it is from the origin — that is, the $30 isocost line is farther from the origin than the $24 isocost line, which is farther from the origin than the $18 isocost line.

Because Tipple wants to minimize his costs, his objective is to be on the isocost line associated with the smallest possible total expenditure. In other words, he wants to be on the isocost line closest to the origin. Of the three isocost lines in Figure 9.4, the $18 line is obviously the most preferred. However, no input bundles on the $18 isocost line will actually produce an output of 120 miles. Therefore, Tipple is constrained to choose an input bundle on an isocost line that is either *on or above* the 120-mile isoquant.

From Figure 9.4, we see that the input bundle (2, 6) — a combination of 2 hours of time and 6 gallons of gas — is the least costly input bundle that will produce 120 miles when w_1 is $6 and w_2 is $2. To minimize costs, then, Tipple should purchase input bundle (2, 6), which costs him $24. In this case, the minimum cost of producing 120 miles of courier services is $24. Of course, Tipple's cost-minimization problem is interesting only in that it illustrates the general principles of cost minimization. What are those principles?

The First Principle of Cost Minimization

First, suppose that a firm wants to produce a given output y. We know that the cost-minimizing input bundle (z_1^*, z_2^*) will lie on the isoquant associated with y units of output.

First Principle of Cost Minimization:

$$y = F(z_1^*, z_2^*)$$

Even though the requisite output can also be produced by any of the feasible input bundles above the isoquant, for any such input bundle there are cheaper input bundles on the isoquant. For example, input bundle $(3, 6)$ in Figure 9.4 allows Tipple to produce 120 miles, but there are any number of cheaper input bundles on the isoquant — all those on the 120-mile isoquant between points A and B. The first principle of cost minimization, then, is that the cost-minimizing input bundle is *on the isoquant.*

The Second Principle of Cost Minimization

We can also deduce the second principle of cost minimization from Tipple's problem. At the cost-minimizing input bundle in Figure 9.4 the isoquant is tangent to the isocost line. This is the second principle of cost minimization. We can express this principle in a slightly different way. Since the slope of the isoquant is $-\text{MRTS}(z_1, z_2)$ and, from Problem 9.5, the slope of the isocost line is $-w_1/w_2$, MRTS is equal to w_1/w_2 at the cost-minimizing bundle.

Second Principle of Cost Minimization:

$$\text{MRTS}(z_1^*, z_2^*) = w_1/w_2$$

These two principles characterize, or determine, the cost-minimizing input bundle

when isoquants are smooth and convex and when the solution is interior.[2]

Understanding the Second Principle

We can provide a more intuitive understanding of the second principle by making use of the fact that MRTS is the ratio of MP_1 to MP_2. The second principle can then be written as

$$\frac{\text{MP}_1}{\text{MP}_2} = \frac{w_1}{w_2}$$

Manipulating this expression yields

$$\frac{\text{MP}_1}{w_1} = \frac{\text{MP}_2}{w_2}$$

In other words, at the cost-minimizing input bundle, the marginal product per dollar for input 1, MP_1/w_1, is equal to the marginal product per dollar for input 2, MP_2/w_2. To see why, let's consider some other input bundle on the isoquant where the marginal product per dollar of input 1 is less than the marginal product per dollar of

---

[2] We can use the method of Lagrange to obtain this characterization. The Lagrangian function is

$$L(z_1, z_2, \lambda) = w_1 z_1 + w_2 z_2 + \lambda[y - F(z_1, z_2)]$$

Setting the partial derivatives of $L(\,\cdot\,)$ with respect to $z_1, z_2,$ and λ equal to zero, we obtain

$$w_1 - \lambda^* F_1(z_1^*, z_2^*) = 0$$
$$w_2 - \lambda^* F_2(z_1^*, z_2^*) = 0$$
$$y - F(z_1^*, z_2^*) = 0$$

The third condition is, of course, the first principle of cost minimization. Combining the first two conditions to eliminate λ^* yields

$$\frac{F_1(z_1^*, z_2^*)}{F_2(z_1^*, z_2^*)} = \frac{w_1}{w_2}$$

But from footnote 1, the left side is $\text{MRTS}(z_1^*, z_2^*)$, and we then have the second principle of cost minimization:

$$\text{MRTS}(z_1^*, z_2^*) = \frac{w_1}{w_2}$$

input 2. Specifically, let's suppose that MP_2 is 6 and w_2 is \$2 and that MP_1 is 2 and w_1 is \$1. Then

$$\frac{MP_1}{w_1} = \frac{2}{1} < \frac{6}{2} = \frac{MP_2}{w_2}$$

MP_1/w_1 is therefore less than MP_2/w_2. If we then decrease the quantity of input 1 by 1 unit, output will fall by approximately 2 units because MP_1 is 2. To compensate for this decrease in output, we must increase the quantity of input 2. By how much? By approximately $\frac{1}{3}$ of a unit because MP_2 is 6. What has happened to costs in this exercise? Because w_1 is \$1, as we decreased the quantity of input 1 by 1 unit, cost decreased by \$1. Because w_2 is \$2, as we increased the quantity of input 2 by $\frac{1}{3}$ of a unit, the cost increased by \$2/3 ($\frac{1}{3}$ times \$2). The net change in cost is $(-\$1 + \$2/3)$ or $-\$1/3$. Thus, by substituting input 2 for input 1, we were able to reduce the cost by one-third of a dollar, while maintaining the output. More generally, if MP_1/w_1 is less than MP_2/w_2, the input bundle cannot be the cost-minimizing input bundle because cost can be reduced and output maintained by substituting input 2 for input 1.

The Many-Input Case

Using this line of reasoning, we can easily generalize the second principle of cost minimization to the case in which there are many inputs: *To minimize costs, the marginal product per dollar must be identical for all inputs.* The first principle is also easily generalized: *When there are many inputs, the cost-minimizing input bundle will be on the appropriate isoquant.*

An Illustration

Now let's use the production function for Tipple's Courier Service to provide a concrete illustration of what we mean when we say that these two principles characterize, or determine the solution to, the cost-minimizing problem. The production function is

$$y = (1200z_1z_2)^{1/2}$$

The MRTS for this production function is given by the following equation:[3]

$$MRTS(z_1, z_2) = \frac{z_2}{z_1}$$

Do not be concerned if you don't understand how we found this function. Simply concentrate on what it tells us. At any input bundle, MRTS is the quantity of input 2 divided by the quantity of input 1. For example, MRTS is 3 at input bundle $(2, 6)$, and MRTS is $\frac{1}{3}$ at input bundle $(6, 2)$.

The first principle of cost minimization in the context of Tipple's Courier Service then gives us

$$y = (1200z_1^*z_2^*)^{1/2}$$

And the second principle of cost minimization in the context of Tipple's Courier Service then gives us

$$\frac{z_2^*}{z_1^*} = \frac{w_1}{w_2}$$

We now have two equations in two unknowns, z_1^* and z_2^*, and we can solve these equations for the conditional input demand functions

$$z_1^* = y \left[\frac{w_2}{1200w_1} \right]^{1/2}$$

$$z_2^* = y \left[\frac{w_1}{1200w_2} \right]^{1/2}$$

---

[3] The partial derivative of output with respect to z_1, or the marginal product of input 1, is $[(1200z_2)/(2z_1)]^{1/2}$. Similarly, the marginal product of input 2 is $[(1200z_1)/(2z_2)]^{1/2}$. Dividing the marginal product of input 1 by the marginal product of input 2 yields z_2/z_1, the marginal rate of technical substitution for Tipple's Courier Service.

Notice that z_1^* increases as w_2 increases and decreases as w_1 increases, and that z_2^* increases as w_1 increases and decreases as w_2 increases. That is, as our intuition suggests, the cost-minimizing quantity of either input is positively related to the price of the other input and negatively related to its own price. Notice, too, that both z_1^* and z_2^* increase as y increases — that is, the cost-minimizing quantities of both inputs increase as the quantity of output increases. This result is also in accord with our intuition.

If we now multiply z_1^* by w_1 and z_2^* by w_2 and add the results, we will have the cost function for Tipple's Courier Service:

$$TC(y, w_1, w_2) = y\left(\frac{w_1 w_2}{300}\right)^{1/2}$$

Notice that cost increases as output increases and as either input price increases. Like the other comparative statics results we've seen, these, too, are intuitive. In subsequent sections, we'll see which of these are and are not general results. But first, try the following problem.

PROBLEM 9.6

1 First solve the two simultaneous equations above to verify that the expressions we have written down are indeed the conditional input demand functions for this production function.

2 If $w_1 = \$6$ and $w_2 = \$2$, what is the cost-minimizing input bundle for 120 miles and what is the total cost? For 240 miles? For 360 miles?

3 Now suppose that input prices double so that $w_1 = \$12$ and $w_2 = \$4$. Show that the cost-minimizing input bundle for 120 miles is the same as it was in part 2 and that total cost is double what it was in part 2.

9.4 Comparative Statics Analysis

In this section, we'll establish an obvious but important comparative statics result: when the price of an input (of which a posi-

tive quantity is demanded) increases, the cost of producing a fixed quantity of output increases. This result is essential to our treatment of the theory of perfect competition in the next chapter. We'll also be posing some comparative statics problems for you to solve and exploring some comparative statics questions concerning changes in the level of output.

Long-Run Costs and Input Prices

The cost function for Tipple's Courier Service has the property that the minimum cost of producing any quantity of output increases when the price of an input increases. We want to show that this is a general result —one that is always true. Specifically, we want to derive the following result:

If the price of an input increases and if the quantity demanded of that input is positive, then the minimum cost of producing any given level of output increases.

Suppose that, initially, input prices are w_1' and w_2' and that the price of input 1 subsequently increases to w_1''. We want to show that the minimum cost of producing the output level y' in Figure 9.5 goes up. From the figure, we see that the initial cost-minimizing input bundle is (z_1', z_2') and the subsequent cost-minimizing input bundle is (z_1'', z_2''). We therefore want to show that

$$w_1'' z_1'' + w_2' z_2'' > w_1' z_1' + w_2' z_2'$$

We can begin by comparing the relative cost of the two input bundles (z_1'', z_2'') and (z_1', z_2') in Figure 9.5 before the price hike. Even at the original input prices w_1' and w_2', we know that (z_1'', z_2'') is the more expensive input bundle because it lies above the initial isocost line $c' = w_1' z_1' + w_2' z_2'$. This merely reflects the fact that the cost-minimizing input bundle at the initial prices is (z_1', z_2').

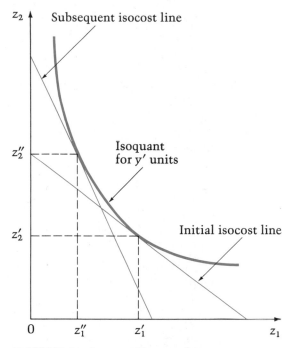

FIGURE 9.5   Costs and input prices.

Given initial input prices, the cost-minimizing bundle is (z_1', z_2'). After the price of input 1 increases, the subsequent cost-minimizing bundle is (z_1'', z_2''). At both the initial and the subsequent prices, the cost of (z_1'', z_2'') exceeds the cost of (z_1', z_2') at the initial input prices. This reflects the fact that when the price of an input increases, the minimum cost of producing a given level of output increases (assuming, of course, that the firm actually buys some of the input).

The following statement is therefore true:

$$w_1' z_1'' + w_2' z_2'' > w_1' z_1' + w_2' z_2'$$

Once the price of input 1 does increase from w_1' to w_1'', the new input bundle (z_1'', z_2'') is even more expensive than it was at the original input prices. That is,

$$w_1'' z_1'' + w_2' z_2'' > w_1' z_1'' + w_2' z_2''$$

By using these two inequalities, we obtain the result we want:

$$w_1'' z_1'' + w_2' z_2'' > w_1' z_1' + w_2' z_2'$$

The minimum cost of producing y thus increases as the price of input 1 increases.

Another intuitive feature of Tipple's Courier Service is that the cost-minimizing quantity of an input decreases when the price of the input increases. This is consistent with the following general result:

If the price of an input increases, the cost-minimizing quantity of that input does not increase.

PROBLEM 9.7

Prove this result. You can simply adapt the argument from Section 4.10 that we used to show that the substitution effect is nonpositive.

In Problem 9.6, you saw that when input prices doubled, Tipple's cost-minimizing input bundle for 120 miles did not change and the minimum cost of producing 120 miles doubled. This, too, is a general result:

If the prices of both inputs double, the cost-minimizing input bundle for any level of output does not change, and the minimum cost of producing any level of output doubles.

PROBLEM 9.8

Prove this result by showing that if an input bundle satisfies the two equations that characterize the cost-minimizing input bundle for input prices w_1 and w_2, then the same input bundle satisfies the two equations for input prices $2w_1$ and $2w_2$.

Input Substitution

The insight you gained in answering Problem 9.7 is one of the most important in economics. As the price of any input increases relative to other input prices, the firm will substitute away from the relatively more expensive input. This insight is important for the simple reason that most nonecomists overlook or underestimate this substitution response.

The Portuguese cod-fishing fleet in the harbor at St. Johns, Newfoundland, in 1970 provides a dramatic illustration of input substitution. The fleet consisted of some sailing ships, each carrying many dinghies, some fishers (one for each dinghy), fishing lines (two for each fisher), and a cook-captain. Each fisher set out in a dinghy with two fishing lines every day to jig for cod by hand while the cook-captain tended the ship and cooked dinner. An American or Canadian fishing fleet would never have operated this way. Americans and Canadians caught cod using electronic fish-locating gear, expensive nets set and pulled with powerful winches, fast boats (compared with the Portuguese fleet), and relatively few fishers. How are we to understand these differences? Because the fishers' wage—relative to the prices of boats, nets, winches, and fish-finding gear—was much lower in Portugal than in North America, the Portuguese used labor-intensive means of harvesting fish.

Traveling can offer many international examples of input substitution. In India, you may see large water-diversion systems and canals dug by hand and the dirt carried away in baskets because human labor is relatively cheap. Shrimp-packing industries are situated on either side of the Mexico-United States border along the Gulf of Mexico. In Texas the industry is capital-intensive, and in Mexico it is labor-intensive.

Many domestic examples of input substitution regularly appear in the headlines as well. For instance, increases in the price of oil in the 1970s resulted in a massive, economywide substitution away from oil and from energy in general. So, too, sudden spirals in metal prices can also trigger input substitution. For example, U.S. beverage-can makers started a serious search for alternative materials when aluminum-can sheet prices jumped by 10% in January 1988.

Most manufacturers picked sheet steel because it was selling at 15% less per pound than sheet aluminum.

Long-Run Costs and the Quantity of Output

Let's move now to comparative questions concerning changes in the cost-minimizing input bundle associated with changes in output, holding all input prices constant. Notice that line EE in Figure 9.6 runs through each of the three isoquants at the cost-minimizing input bundle. We call this line an **output-expansion path** because it connects the cost-minimizing input bundles that are generated as output is increased or expanded. Because input prices are held

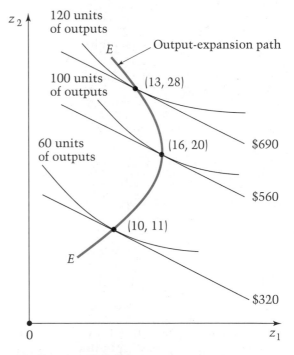

FIGURE 9.6   The output-expansion path.

The line EE is called an output-expansion path because it passes through the cost-minimizing bundles that are generated as output increases, holding input prices constant. Input 2 is a normal input for all values of y, whereas input 1 is an inferior input for output levels larger than 100 and a normal input for output levels less than 100.

constant in this comparative exercise—w_1 is \$10 and w_2 is \$20—the isocost lines in Figure 9.6 are parallel.

The output-expansion path in the theory of the firm is analogous to the income-consumption path in consumer theory. We can therefore draw on consumer theory for analogies as we classify and compare types of inputs. An input is said to be a **normal input** if the quantity demanded increases as output increases; it is an **inferior input** if quantity demanded decreases as output increases. In Figure 9.6, input 2 is a normal input—at least in the range of output levels represented in the figure—because as output increases, so does the quantity demanded of input 2. On the other hand, input 1 is a normal input at output levels up to 100. At levels beyond 100, however, input 1 is an inferior input because as output increases beyond 100, the quantity demanded of input 1 decreases.

P R O B L E M 9.9

We have already derived the following conditional input demand functions for Tipple's Courier Service:

$$z_1^* = y\left(\frac{w_2}{1200 w_1}\right)^{1/2}$$

$$z_2^* = y\left(\frac{w_1}{1200 w_2}\right)^{1/2}$$

Is a driver's time, input 1, a normal or an inferior input? What about gasoline, input 2? What is the output-expansion path when $w_1 = w_2$?

Notice that Figure 9.6 determines two factors for every quantity of output: it tells us which input bundle is least expensive and how much it costs. In Figure 9.6, for example, the cost-minimizing input bundle associated with 100 units of output is (16, 20) and the cost of the input bundle is \$560—that is, \$560 is the minimum cost of producing 100 units of output when the input prices are \$10 and \$20.

In principle, then, Figure 9.6 allows us to construct the cost function $\text{TC}(y, w_1, w_2)$. However, this diagrammatic tool does not yield a clear understanding of the relationship between costs of production and economies of scale. Because this relationship is an important one, we will use a different graphic technique.

Homothetic Production Functions

We will explore this important relationship by adapting the graphic technique we used in Section 8.4 to derive the variable cost function from the total product function. To adapt this tool, however, we must restrict our attention to a certain class of production functions known as **homothetic production functions**. For a homothetic production function, MRTS is constant along any ray through the origin in (z_1, z_2) space. Hence, the output-expansion path of a homothetic production function does not look like the one in Figure 9.6. Rather, it is a ray through the origin.[4]

We can turn again to Tipple's Courier Service for insight, since that production function is homothetic. Recall that MRTS for the courier service is just z_2/z_1. The second principle of cost minimization—MRTS equal to w_1/w_2—for this production function then yields the following relationship:

$$\frac{z_2^*}{z_1^*} = \frac{w_1}{w_2}$$

But this can be rewritten as

$$z_2^* = \left(\frac{w_1}{w_2}\right) z_1^*$$

---

[4] A differentiable production function is homothetic if $\text{MRTS}(z_1, z_2)$ can be written as a function of z_2/z_1. This property ensures that $\text{MRTS}(z_1, z_2)$ is constant along any ray through the origin and that expansion paths are therefore rays through the origin.

which is just a ray through the origin with slope w_1/w_2. Thus, from the second principle of cost minimization, we see that all cost-minimizing input bundles lie on this ray or, alternatively, that the firm's output-expansion path is the ray through the origin with slope w_1/w_2. When w_1 is $6 and w_2 is $2, for example, the output-expansion path is just $z_2 = 3z_1$. This output-expansion path is illustrated in Figure 9.7. A more general understanding can be drawn from this result:

When the production function is homothetic, the output-expansion path is a ray through the origin, and the second principle of cost minimization determines which ray is the output-expansion path.

PROBLEM 9.10

Suppose that Tipple must pay $10 per hour for labor and $1 per gallon for gasoline ($w_1 = $10 and

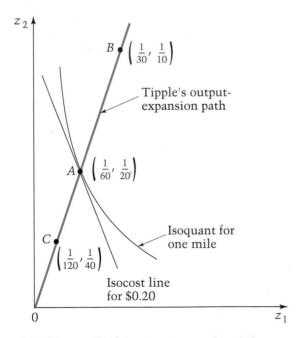

FIGURE 9.7   Tipple's output-expansion path.

Given that w_1 is $6 and w_2 is $2, Tipple's output-expansion path is $0CAB$. The expansion path is a ray through the origin because Tipple's production function is homothetic.

$w_2 = $1). Use the second principle to find the output-expansion path.**

PROBLEM 9.11

Can either input 1 or input 2 be an inferior input when the production function is homothetic?

In the next two sections, we will look more closely at homothetic production functions, but first we need to consider returns to scale.

9.5   Returns to Scale

Since his output-expansion path is a ray through the origin, as Tipple produces more and more output, he will increase the quantity of both inputs but will hold the ratio z_1/z_2 fixed. That is, given fixed input prices, to produce more output, Tipple changes the scale of production but not the mix of inputs. In this section, we'll explore what economists call **returns to scale** — that is, the way in which output changes as the scale of production changes. Although the techniques we will use can be applied to all production functions, we'll limit our discussion to homothetic production functions in most of what follows.

An Illustration

First, let's see exactly how output responds to changes in scale in the context of Tipple's Courier Service. We'll suppose that w_1 is $6 and w_2 is $2. Then, from the second principle of cost minimization, we see that the output-expansion path is

$$z_2 = 3z_1$$

Now let's find the input bundle that minimizes the cost of producing 1 mile. This bundle must lie on the output-expansion path and, in addition, must produce one unit of output. Therefore, it must satisfy the following expression:

$$1 = (1200z_1z_2)^{1/2}$$

Using these two equations, we can find the cost-minimizing input bundle for 1 mile. As you can verify, it is $(1/60, 1/20)$. In other words, 1 minute of a driver's time and $\frac{1}{20}$ of a gallon of gas is the least costly bundle that will produce 1 mile. This input bundle and the entire output-expansion path are illustrated in Figure 9.7.

Scale of Production

Now, suppose that we multiply the quantities of both inputs in this input bundle by a **scale factor** s. The scale factor is simply a positive number that defines new input bundles of the form $(s/60, s/20)$. Notice that any positive value of s gives us an input bundle on the output-expansion path. For instance, when s is equal to 1, the input bundle is the original one, $(1/60, 1/20)$, located at point A in Figure 9.7. When s is $1/2$, the input bundle is $(1/120, 1/40)$ at point C. When s is 2, it is $(1/30, 1/10)$ at point B; and so on. Since each of these input bundles lies on Tipple's output-expansion path, the scale factor s is a parameter, or measuring stick, that determines the scale of production along the output-expansion path.

Output as a Function of Scale

Now that we have a convenient yardstick — the scale factor s — we want to know how the output of Tipple's Courier Service changes as we increase or decrease s. To find out, we will form a new function by substituting $s/60$ for z_1 and $s/20$ for z_2 in the original production function to get a new function, $Y(s)$.

$$Y(s) = \left[1200 \left(\frac{s}{60} \right) \left(\frac{s}{20} \right) \right]^{1/2}$$

Or, simplifying,

$$Y(s) = s$$

In other words, output y is equal to scale factor s. Let's verify that this representation of Tipple's production function gives us sensible results. We discovered above that the cost-minimizing input bundle for 120 miles is $(2, 6)$. $Y(s) = s$ tells us that $s = 120$ will produce 120 miles at minimum cost. Are these results compatible? Yes; since $s = 1$ corresponds to input bundle $(1/60, 1/20)$, then $s = 120$ corresponds to input bundle $(120/60, 120/20)$ or to $(2, 6)$.

When w_1 is \$6 and w_2 is \$2, $Y(s) = s$ tells us that output is equal to scale along Tipple's output-expansion path. To reinforce your understanding of the procedure we used to find the function $Y(s)$, try the following problem.

PROBLEM 9.12

Suppose that w_1 and w_2 are both equal to \$5.

1   **What is the output-expansion path for Tipple's Courier Service?**

2   **What input bundle minimizes the cost of 1 mile of service?**

3   **What is the function $Y(s)$ along this output-expansion path?**

Now let's generalize the procedure for expressing output as a function of scale along any output-expansion path for any homothetic production function.

1   First find the bundle that minimizes the cost of producing one unit of output. Denote this bundle by

$$(z_1'', z_2'')$$

2   Then substitute sz_1'' for z_1 and sz_2'' for z_2 in the production function to get

$$Y(s) = F(sz_1'', sz_2'')$$

Since this function gives us output as a function of scale s, we can write

$$y = Y(s)$$

Notice that when s is equal to 1, so, too, is output; that is, $1 = Y(1)$ since $1 = F(sz_1'', sz_2'')$.

Scale Elasticity of Output

Returns to scale are concerned with the way in which output responds to changes in scale. This suggests that we should use the concept of *elasticity*, introduced in Section 4.12, to measure returns to scale. We'll use Figure 9.8 to develop this measure, called the **scale elasticity of output.** Output y is on the vertical axis and scale s is on the horizontal axis. The function we've plotted is another example of $Y(s)$. In this case, the slope of $Y(s)$ decreases as s increases. First, notice

that the *arc scale elasticity of output*, over arc AB of $Y(s)$, is

$$\left[\frac{\Delta y/y'}{\Delta s/s'}\right]$$

This is just the proportionate change in output divided by the proportionate change in scale. It can be rewritten as

$$\left[\frac{\Delta y/\Delta s}{y'/s'}\right]$$

We can find the more useful *point scale elasticity of output*, written as e by letting Δs approach zero. As Δs approaches zero, $\Delta y/\Delta s$ approaches the slope of the tangent line TT.[5] Thus,

DEFINITION

$$e = \frac{\text{slope of tangent line}}{[y'/s']}$$

Notice that the denominator in this expression is simply the slope of the ray from the origin to point A on $Y(s)$. That is, y'/s' is equal to the slope of ray $0A$ in the figure. Thus, we can write

$$e = \frac{\text{slope of tangent line}}{\text{slope of ray}}$$

At point A, the slope of the ray is greater than the slope of the tangent line and e is

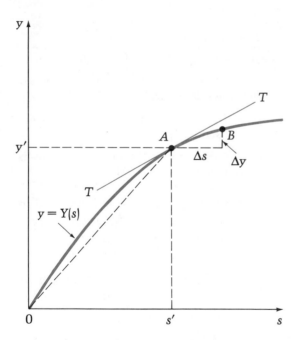

FIGURE 9.8 **Scale elasticity of output.**
The arc scale elasticity of output at point A is $(\Delta y/y')/(\Delta s/s') = (\Delta y/\Delta s)/(y'/s')$. As Δs approaches zero, $\Delta y/\Delta s$ approaches the slope of TT, and we have the point scale elasticity of output: $e = (\text{slope of } TT)/(y'/s') = (\text{slope of } TT)/(\text{slope of } 0A)$. At point A, e is less than 1 since $0A$ is steeper than TT, which means that there are decreasing returns to scale at A.

---

[5] Point scale elasticity of output is just

$$e = \lim_{\Delta s \to 0} \left[\frac{\Delta y/\Delta s}{y/s}\right]$$

which reduces to

$$e = \frac{Y'(s)}{(y/s)}$$

or

$$e = \frac{sY'(s)}{y}$$

As you may want to verify, for the following Cobb-Douglas production function

$$F(z_1, z_2) = z_1^a z_2^b$$

we have $Y(s) = s^{(a+b)}$, and the scale elasticity of output is just $a + b$.

therefore less than 1. This reflects the fact that the proportionate increase in output near point A is less than the proportionate increase in the scale of production. As you can verify, for the function $Y(s)$ depicted in Figure 9.8, e is everywhere less than 1. As we'll see, this reflects the fact that this function exhibits universal decreasing returns to scale.

Defining Returns to Scale

When e is less than 1, production is subject to *decreasing* returns to scale. When e is equal to 1, production is subject to *constant* returns to scale. When e is greater than 1, production is subject to *increasing* returns to scale. As you'll see in the following problem, in Tipple's Courier Service, e is always 1.[6]

PROBLEM 9.13

Consider the following possibilities for $Y(s)$:

$$Y(s) = s \qquad Y(s) = s^{1/2} \qquad Y(s) = s^2$$

The first of these represents Tipple's Courier Service. Graph each of these functions and show that the first exhibits universal constant returns to scale, the second universal decreasing returns to scale, and the third universal increasing returns to scale.

---

[6] Returns to scale for homogeneous production functions deserve special attention. A production function is homogeneous of degree $a > 0$ if

$$F(sz_1, sz_2) = s^a F(z_1, z_2) \text{ for all } s > 0$$

For a homogeneous production, the function $Y(s)$ is then

$$Y(s) = s^a$$

For this function,

$$e = a$$

Hence, for a homogeneous production function there are decreasing, constant, or increasing returns to scale as the degree of homogeneity is less than, equal to, or greater than 1.

The Standard Stylization

The standard stylization of $Y(s)$ is illustrated in Figure 9.9. Notice that it is very much like the standard stylization of the total product function from Chapter 8. In Problem 9.14, you can show that this stylization exhibits increasing returns to scale for output less than y' (or for scale less than s'), constant returns to scale for output equal to y' (or scale equal to s'), and decreasing returns to scale for output greater than y' (or scale greater than s').

PROBLEM 9.14

1 Show that $e = 1$ when $s = s'$, $e > 1$ when $s < s'$, and $e < 1$ when $s > s'$.

2 If you divide the output $Y(s)$ by the scale of production s, you have a measure of *average input productivity*. This measure corresponds to the measure of average product associated with the total product function. Show that $[Y(s)]/s$ increases as scale increases up to s', is

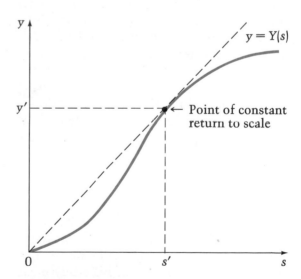

FIGURE 9.9 The standard case of returns to scale.
The standard stylization of $Y(s)$ is illustrated in this figure. Here $Y(s)$ exhibits increasing returns to scale for scale less than s' (or output less than y'), constant returns to scale at scale s' (or output y'), and decreasing returns to scale for scale greater than s' (or output greater than y').

at a maximum when scale is equal to s', and decrease as scale increases when scale exceeds s'.

Part 2 of this problem gives us another perspective on returns to scale. When there are increasing returns to scale, average input productivity increases as scale increases; when there are decreasing returns to scale, average input productivity decreases as scale increases.

Factors Determining Returns to Scale

In constructing the function $Y(s)$ when there are many inputs, we can obviously fix the quantities of some inputs and vary the scale on which we use the remaining variable inputs. In these cases, the kind of reasoning outlined in Section 8.3 leads to the standard stylization of $Y(s)$ in Figure 9.9. In the pure long-run case, where all the firm's inputs are variable, we might reasonably expect to see constant returns to scale throughout. For instance, if a firm decided to triple all its inputs, we would expect its output to triple. Of course, this is exactly what happens in Tipple's Courier Service. Indeed, many manufacturing industries that economists study — including the garment, textile, metal, and pulp and paper industries — seem to exhibit constant returns to scale at the scales of production at which the firms actually operate.

However, the relationship between scale of production and output in the long run is not necessarily so simple. Recall our discussion of Adam Smith in Chapter 7. Smith was the first to consider which factors might induce either increasing or decreasing returns to scale. From his study of an English pin factory, Smith reasoned that as the scale of pin production expanded, the output of pins should increase more than proportionally, because specialization of labor would create efficiencies in production. On the other hand, modern theories of the firm suggest that as the scale of production expands, output might increase less than proportionally because of inefficiencies arising from organizational difficulties. For instance, there might be so many managers that the firm could be effectively run only by adding a whole new layer of management to oversee the original group of managers.

We must determine empirically which of these two tendencies — one resulting in increasing returns to scale and the other in decreasing returns to scale — predominates in any particular production process (and at what scales of production each predominates). However, we can assume that the advantages from specialization predominate at low levels of output and that organizational difficulties predominate at high levels. For this reason, economists use the mixed case in Figure 9.9 as the standard case when more than one input is variable.

9.6 Returns to Scale and Costs of Production

Let's turn now to the relationship between costs of production and returns to scale. We were able to use the graphic technique in Figure 8.7 to derive the variable cost function from the total product function because, in the short-run cost-minimization problem, only one variable, z_1, is endogenous. Similarly, when the production function is homothetic, we can easily reduce the long-run cost-minimization problem to a choice of one variable — the scale factor s. This allows us to use the same graphic technique to see how returns to scale influence costs of production.

Simplifying the Cost-Minimization Problem

Tipple's Courier Service again provides a convenient illustration. When w_1 is $6 and w_2 is $2, we know a number of useful facts about this firm. The firm's output-expansion path is $z_2 = 3z_1$. The input bundle $(1/60, 1/20)$ is the cost-minimizing input bundle for 1 mile of service. All input bundles on the output-expansion path can be written in terms of scale as $(s/60, s/20)$. The production function can also be written in terms of scale, $Y(s) = s$.

To reduce Tipple's cost-minimization problem to a choice of s, we need to express costs along the output-expansion path in terms of s. Notice that the cost of input bundle $(1/60, 1/20)$ is $0.20 (since $6/60 + $2/20 = $2/10 = $0.20). It therefore costs Tipple $0.20 to produce 1 mile of service. Next, notice that the cost of bundle $(s/60, s/20)$ is just s times $0.20, since this bundle contains s times as much of each input as does bundle $(1/60, 1/20)$. When s is 60, for example, the input bundle contains 1 hour of a driver's time and 3 gallons of gas, and we can calculate its cost in two ways: $12 = 60 \times $0.20, or $12 = 1 \times $6 + 3 \times $2.

Now we can write Tipple's long-run cost-minimization problem as a choice of scale s. The bundle associated with scale s costs $0.20s$, and it produces $y = s$ miles of service. Hence, Tipple's problem is to

minimize $.20s$ by choice of s

subject to the constraint $y = s$

This problem is so simple that we don't need to use the graphic techniques from Chapter 8 to solve it. To minimize the cost of producing y miles, Tipple should choose s equal to y—that is, $s^* = y$. The minimum cost of producing y miles is then $.20y$. Thus, we can write

$$TC(y) = .20y$$

This is Tipple's cost function when w_1 is $6 and w_2 is $2. For example, 120 miles will cost Tipple $24, 240 miles will cost him $48, and 360 miles will cost him $72. Notice that these results replicate your answers to Problem 9.6.

Now let's describe how to achieve this simplification for any homothetic production function. (The first two steps are from the previous section.)

1 First find the input bundle that minimizes the cost of producing 1 unit of output. Denote this input bundle by (z_1'', z_2'').

2 Then substitute sz_1'' for z_1 and sz_2'' for z_2 in the production function to get

$$Y(s) = F(sz_1'', sz_2'')$$

3 Then calculate the cost c'' of the input bundle (z_1'', z_2''):

$$c'' = w_1 z_1'' + w_2 z_2''$$

4 Then write the cost-minimization problem as follows:

minimize sc'' by choice of s

subject to the constraint $y = Y(s)$

In this problem, sc'' is the cost of buying the input bundle (sz_1'', sz_2''), $Y(s)$ is the quantity of output that the input bundle will produce, and y is the given quantity of output that the firm wants to produce. In this problem, we can think of (z_1'', z_2'') as a "packet" of inputs and c'' as the price per packet. The cost-minimization problem is then to choose the number of packets s to minimize total cost sc'' subject to producing quantity y.

Before turning to a graphic solution of this problem, you can test your understanding by trying the following problem.

PROBLEM 9.15

1 Suppose that $c'' = 5$ and that $Y(s) = s^2$. Show that $TC(y) = 5y^{1/2}$.

2 Now suppose that $c'' = 7$ and that $Y(s) = s^{1/2}$. What is $TC(y)$ in this case?

Deriving the Cost Function

The long-run cost-minimization problem in item 4 above has the same form as the one in Section 8.4, where we derived the variable cost function from the total product function. There we wanted to minimize $w_1 z_1$, and here we want to minimize sc''. There we chose z_1, and here we are choosing s. There the constraint was $y = TP(z_1)$, and here it is $y = Y(s)$.

Because the form of the two problems is identical, we can adapt the graphic technique from Section 8.4 to analyze the relationship between production and costs in the long run. The function $Y(s)$ in Figure 9.10a is the standard stylization. It exhibits

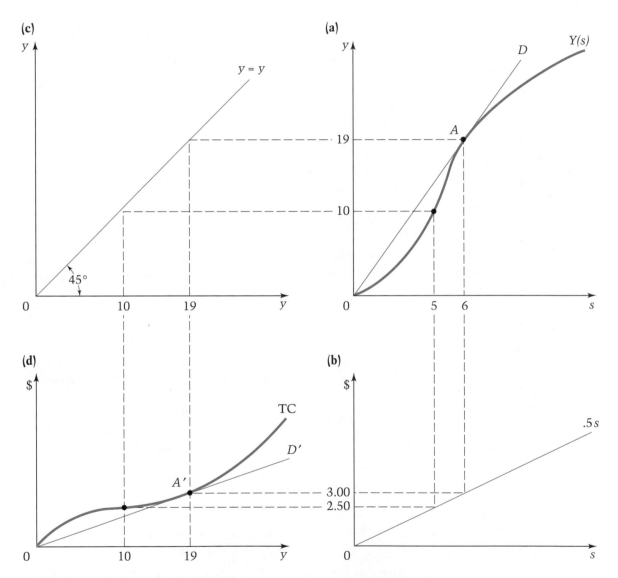

FIGURE 9.10   Deriving the cost function.

The figure illustrates the derivation of TC in (d) from $Y(s)$ in (a). From (a), we see that scale $s = 5$ is necessary to produce output $y = 10$, and from (b), we see that it costs \$2.50 to produce at scale

$s = 5$. Projecting $y = 10$ into (d) via the 45° line in (c) and projecting \$2.50 into (d), we have one point on TC, the point (10, 2.50).

initial increasing returns to scale and subsequent decreasing returns to scale. The single point of constant returns to scale is at point A where y is 19 and s is 6. The line $.5s$ in Figure 9.10*b* is the cost of buying the input bundle associated with the scale s, since we've assumed that the bundle associated with s equal to 1 costs $0.50; that is, $c'' = \$0.50$ in Figure 9.10. The 45° line in Figure 9.10*c* allows us to project values of y from Figure 9.10*a* into Figure 9.10*d*.

You can derive the function TC by following the steps outlined in Section 8.4. TC is, of course, just the cost function. For simplicity, we have suppressed the input prices in writing TC.

Two points of comparison between $Y(s)$ in Figure 9.10*a* and TC in Figure 9.10*d* deserve special attention. Notice that because ray $0D$ in Figure 9.10*a* is tangent to $Y(s)$ at point A, this is the single point of constant returns to scale. Correspondingly, ray $0D'$ in Figure 9.10*d* is tangent to TC at the same level of output, 19 units, at point A'. Notice too that the slope of $Y(s)$ is a maximum at 10 units of output. Correspondingly, the slope of TC is a minimum at this level of output.

Average and Marginal Cost in the Long Run

Before you can fully appreciate the significance of these observations, we need the concepts of long-run average cost LAC(y) and long-run marginal cost LMC(y). They are defined in the predictable ways.

DEFINITION

$$LAC(y) = \frac{TC(y)}{y}$$

DEFINITION

$$LMC(y) = \text{slope of } TC(y)$$

Again using techniques from Chapter 8, we have derived the functions LAC and LMC in Figure 9.11 from the cost function

TC in Figure 9.10. Notice that LAC is at a minimum at output level $y = 19$. We can infer from this, and from what we already know about this output level, the following important implications of increasing and decreasing returns to scale:

With increasing returns to scale, the average cost of producing a unit of output decreases as more output is produced.

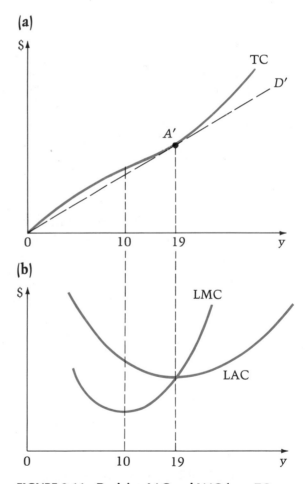

(a)

(b)

FIGURE 9.11   Deriving LAC and LMC from TC.
At $y = 19$, the ray $0D'$ is tangent to TC; therefore, LMC is equal to LAC when $y = 19$. Further, LAC attains its minimum value at $y = 19$. The slope of TC is smallest at $y = 10$, and LMC therefore attains its minimim value at $y = 10$.

With decreasing returns to scale, the average cost of producing a unit of output increases as more output is produced.

These functions also exhibit the relationships between marginals and averages familiar from Chapter 8:

When LMC lies below LAC, LAC is decreasing; when LMC lies above LAC, LAC is increasing; LMC intersects LAC where LAC is a minimum.

We can reinterpret these relationships in a more meaningful way:

With increasing returns to scale, long-run marginal cost is less than long-run average cost; with decreasing returns to scale, long-run marginal cost exceeds long-run average cost; and with constant returns to scale, long-run marginal cost equals long-run average cost.

The form that each of these cost functions takes depends on the form of the production function $Y(s)$. We need to consider three additional possibilities—the three "pure" cases representing *universally constant, universally decreasing,* or *universally increasing returns to scale.* These three pure cases and their implied cost functions are illustrated in Figure 9.12. Tipple's Courier Service is an example of universal constant returns to scale, and you encountered the two other possibilities in Problems 9.13 and 9.15.

9.7 Comparing Long-Run and Short-Run Costs

One final topic remains: identifying the relationships between long-run and short-run costs of production. Although only one long run exists, many short runs are possible, depending on the number of inputs that are variable. To further complicate matters, each of these short runs can have any number of cost functions, depending on the quantities of the fixed inputs. We can learn most of what there is to know about the relationship between short- and long-run costs, however, by limiting our discussion to the two-input case.

All the relationships between long-run and short-run costs spring from two basic relationships between the one long-run cost function and any of the short-run cost functions. The long-run cost of production is less than or equal to the short-run cost of production for all levels of output:

$$TC(y) \le STC(y) \qquad \text{for all values of } y$$

In addition, the long- and short-run costs of production are identical at one level of output:

$$TC(y) = STC(y) \qquad \text{for one value of } y$$

These two assertions are illustrated in Figure 9.13. $STC(y)$ lies above $TC(y)$ at all values of y other than $y = 100$, where $TC(y) = STC(y)$. How do we know that these assertions are true?

Suppose, for example, that the input bundle (10, 35) is cost-minimizing for 100 units of output. Then the long-run minimum cost of 100 units of output can be easily calculated:

$$TC(100) = 10w_1 + 35w_2$$

Now let's fix the quantity of input 2 at 35, thereby defining a total product function. What will be the minimum cost of producing 100 units of output in this particular short run with this total product function? Clearly, 10 units of input 1 are cost-minimizing in this short run. In turn, this implies that

$$STC(100) = 10w_1 + 35w_2$$

(a) Constant returns to scale

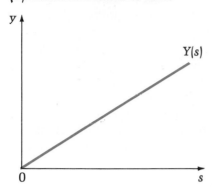 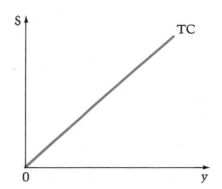

(b) Decreasing returns to scale

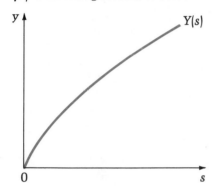 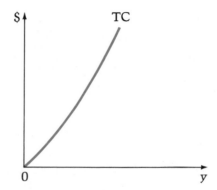

(c) Increasing returns to scale

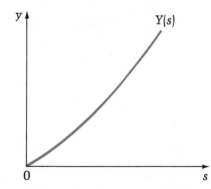 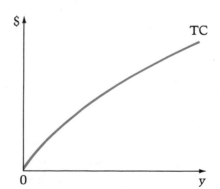

FIGURE 9.12   Returns to scale and the cost function.

If the production function shows constant returns to scale, as in (a), then TC is a ray through the origin. If the production function shows decreasing returns to scale, as in (b), then TC is convex from above. If the production function shows increasing returns to scale, as in (c), then TC is concave from above.

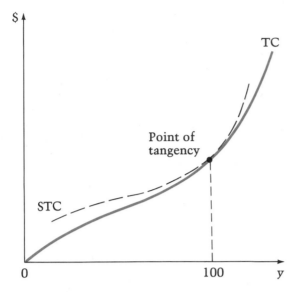

FIGURE 9.13   Comparing TC and STC.

STC is a short-run cost function. When $y = 100$, STC = TC, and the two functions are tangent at $y = 100$. For all other values of y, STC exceeds TC.

In other words, the minimum cost of producing 100 units of output is identical in this particular short run and in the long run. Thus, the two cost functions have one point in common. For any other level of output, the cost of production in the short run cannot be less than in the long run. Why not? Because the firm has more flexibility in the long run, it can choose the quantities of all its inputs in the long run, but it cannot do so in the short run. (Except in odd cases, the short-run cost of production will exceed the long-run cost of production for any output level other than 100. This standard case is presented in Figure 9.13.)

We can draw a number of implications from this standard case. The long-run cost function in Figure 9.14a is derived from a production function characterized by increasing returns to scale up to 78 units of output and by decreasing returns to scale thereafter. Figure 9.14a also includes two short-run cost functions STC_1 and STC_2.

STC_1 is tangent to TC at 45 units of output where there are increasing returns to scale. And STC_2 is tangent to TC at 93 units of output where there are decreasing returns to scale. The corresponding average and marginal cost functions are presented in Figure 9.14b.

Let's concentrate first on the relationship between the two short-run average cost functions and the long-run average cost

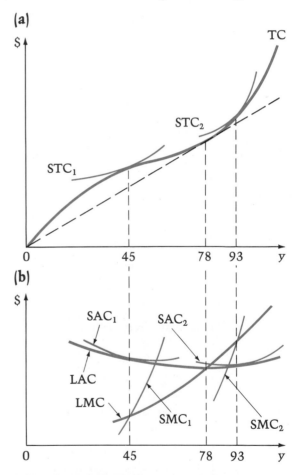

FIGURE 9.14   Relationships between long-run and short-run cost functions.

Here we see the relationships between various long- and short-run cost functions. STC_1 is tangent to TC at $y = 45$. Hence, at $y = 45$, SMC_1 is equal to LMC, and SAC_1 is tangent to LAC. Similarly, STC_2 is tangent to TC at $y = 93$. Hence, at $y = 93$, SMC_2 is equal to LMC, and SAC_2 is tangent to LAC.

function. SAC_1 is tanget to LAC when y is equal to 45, the output at which STC_1 is tangent to TC. At all other output levels, SAC_1 lies above LAC. Similarly, SAC_2 is tangent to LAC at 93 units of output and lies above it elsewhere.

Now let's turn to the relationships between the two short-run marginal cost functions and the long-run marginal cost function. Notice that at output 45, SMC_1 is equal to LMC and that at output 93, SMC_2 is equal to LMC. To understand why these relationships must hold, look for a moment at SMC_1 and LMC. Each is just the *slope* of the corresponding total cost function. Because the two total cost functions are tangent at output level 45, they have the same slope at this point. Notice, too, that both SMC_1 and SMC_2 intersect LMC from below.

Finally, notice the following relationships: the output at which SAC_1 attains its minimum value is greater than 45, and the output at which SAC_2 attains its minimum value is less than 93. These relationships are a bit surprising. The first implies that to produce 45 units of output at minimum cost in the long run, in the corresponding short run, the firm will be producing at a point where SAC_1 is still decreasing. Conversely, the second implies that to produce 93 at minimum cost in the long run, in the corresponding short run, the firm must be producing at a point where SAC_2 is increasing.

How can we understand these results? Let's look more closely at 45 units of output. LMC is less than LAC at this level of output, and LAC therefore must be falling at 45. Since STC_1 is tangent to TC at 45, SMC_1 must also be less than SAC_1 at 45. Hence, SAC_1 must also be falling at 45. You may want to construct an analogous argument to explain why SAC_2 must be increasing at 93 units.

Because these relationships can be slippery and practice is needed to master them, do try your hand at the following problem.

PROBLEM 9.16
Consider a cost function like the one in Figure 9.12a, which has been derived from a production function characterized by constant returns to scale throughout. Construct a diagram analogous to Figure 9.14.

9.8 A Theory of Market Structure

In Chapter 7, we posed a fundamental economic question: Why do firms exist at all? We approached this question from an organizational point of view. We can now use the insights from Chapter 9 to tackle that question from another perspective. Using the different average cost functions that we've encountered in this chapter, we can sketch out a rudimentary but insightful *theory of market structure*, a theory we can use to predict whether or not firms come into existence and how many firms will establish themselves in a particular market.

To articulate this theory, we'll use the four stylized long-run average cost functions in Figure 9.15. Let's begin with the case of **universal decreasing returns to scale** in Figure 9.15a. Because long-run average cost is everywhere increasing, size is obviously associated with a cost penalty. The bigger the output of a firm, the more costly the good or service is to produce. In fact, goods and services will not be supplied in this case by firms at all — at least not by firms as we know them. Why? Suppose a firm tries to serve more than one buyer. To cover its costs, its price will have to be no smaller than its average cost. But because potential buyers can produce the good or service for themselves at a lower average cost, they will not pay the higher price needed to cover the firm's costs. We don't know of any firms selling toothbrushing services, for example, because it is cheaper for us to brush our own teeth. We can think of the case of decreasing returns to scale as a case of "household production": produc-

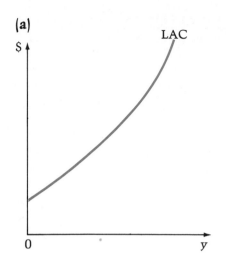

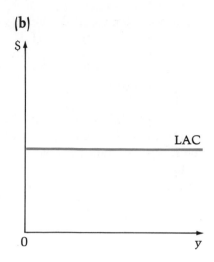

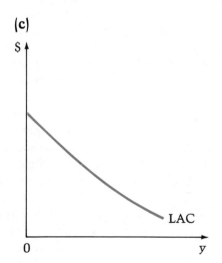

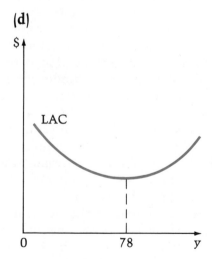

FIGURE 9.15   A cost-based theory of market structure.

With decreasing returns to scale, as in (a), LAC is everywhere upward-sloping. Thus, a cost penalty is associated with large size, and we expect this sort of good to be produced on the smallest possible scale. With constant returns to scale, as in (b), neither a cost penalty nor a cost advantage is associated with size, and this sort of good could be produced on any scale. With increasing returns to scale, as in (c), a cost advantage is associated with size, and this sort of good will be produced by one or a few firms. In the mixed case, as in (d), the initial increasing returns to scale guarantee that production will be done by firms. Whether it will be done by a few relatively large firms or by many relatively small firms depends on the output level at which LAC attains its minimum value.

tion will be conducted on the smallest possible scale.

What about the case of **universal constant returns to scale** in Figure 9.15*b*? When returns to scale are constant throughout, size is not associated with a cost penalty; however, nothing is gained by being large. If a firm were to come into existence, it could not sell its output at a price greater than its average cost of production. If it tried to sell at a higher price, its potential customers would simply make the good in their own backyards. When returns to scale are everywhere constant, firms have no compelling reason to exist.

In the remaining two cases in Figure 9.15, firms will come into being. Because both cases are characterized by ranges of output over which there are **increasing returns to scale,** the potential do-it-yourselfer in these cases must labor under the cost disadvantage associated with a relatively small scale of production.

Only in these two cases, then, do firms serve an economic purpose. When long-run average cost of production is everywhere downward-sloping, as in Figure 9.15*c*, there are increasing returns to scale at all levels of output: in this case, a cost advantage is always associated with a still larger output. As we'll discover in Chapter 11, in this circumstance, a small number of relatively large firms will supply the good or service in question. Public utilities such as electricity and telephone service are industries in which being big pays off. We have an important understanding, then, of the elementary force that generates *monopolies* or *oligopolies.*

We know that a U-shaped average cost curve reflects initial increasing and subsequent decreasing returns to scale, as in Figure 9.15*d*. Broadly speaking, two possible market structures arise in this case. If the output level at which LAC(*y*) attains its minimum value (78 units in Figure 9.14*d*) is

relatively large we again expect to see monopoly or oligopoly. On the other hand, if the output level at which the long-run average cost curve attains its minimum value is relatively small, then a large number of relatively small firms will supply the good or service. The initial increasing returns to scale guarantee that production will be done by firms, and the subsequent decreasing returns to scale guarantee that a large number of firms will do the job. Since there will be a large number of competing firms in this case, the market structure is *competitive.*

In this section, we have laid the groundwork for understanding market structure. The chapter as a whole has extended our understanding of how production functions —and their offspring, cost functions— provide the foundation for a theory of economic behavior of firms. In the following chapter, we'll take a closer look at competitive markets typified by a relatively large number of firms. And in subsequent chapters, we'll turn to markets typified by relatively few firms.

Summary

This chapter continued the exploration of a firm's production function begun in Chapter 8 by extending the analysis to cases in which more than one input is variable. We drew on correspondences between consumer theory and the theory of the firm as we looked at isoquants (analogous to indifference curves), defined the marginal rate of technical substitution (analogous to the marginal rate of substitution in consumption), and discussed the assumption of a diminishing marginal rate of technical substitution.

Turning from the theory of production to the theory of cost and drawing on our experience with utility-maximization problems, we solved the firm's cost-minimization problem by identifying the input bundle on the isoquant where the marginal rate of technical substitution is equal to w_1 divided by w_2, or where the marginal product per dollar is identical for all the inputs in the input bundle.

We then took up several comparative statics exercises. One of the resulting propositions — that firms substitute away from inputs as they become relatively more expensive — is extremely useful in understanding economic reality. For instance, it explains why a car that gets 50 mpg was not on the market until OPEC engineered worldwide increases in the price of oil, and why gold and silver are never used in household wiring even though they are both superior electrical conductors.

We then turned to the important relationship between returns to scale and costs of production. We restricted our attention to homothetic production functions and used the general concept of elasticity to define returns to scale. We saw that as output increased, the average cost of production increased, decreased, or remained unchanged as returns to scale were decreasing, increasing, or constant.

We then compared costs in the short run and the long run. All the comparisons were driven by two fundamental points: the short-run cost function STC is tangent to the long-run cost function TC at one point, and STC lies above TC at all other points. Finally, we presented a cost-based theory of market structure that prepares the way for the analysis in Part Four.

Exercises

1 Suppose that the following is true:

"A cost-minimizing firm, faced with constant input prices, recently increased the quantity of each of its inputs by 10%. As a result, its output increased from 100 units to 120 units. For this firm, the function $Y(s)$ is the standard case illustrated in Figure 9.9."

Indicate whether each of the following statements is true, false, or uncertain, and explain your answer.
a When y is 100, there are increasing returns to scale.
b The firm's production function is not homothetic.
c When y is 100, LAC is downward sloping.
d When y is 100, LMC exceeds LAC.
e When y is 100, LMC is downward sloping.
f If the firm had increased the quantity of each input by 5%, output would have increased from 100 to 110 units.

2 Suppose that the following is true:

"When $w_1 = w_2 = \$10$, the cost-minimizing bundle for 100 units of output is $z_1 = z_2 = 20$. When $w_1 = \$8$ and $w_2 = \$10$, the cost-minimizing bundle for 110 units of output is $z_1 = 28$ and $z_2 = 19$."

Indicate whether each of the following statements is true, false, or uncertain, and explain your answer.
a When $w_1 = w_2 = \$10$, LAC for $y = 100$ is $4.
b Input 2 is an inferior input.
c Input 1 is a normal input.
d The firm's expansion path is downward sloping.
e The production function is not homothetic.
f When $w_1 = w_2 = \$5$, LAC for $y = 100$ is $2.
g When $w_1 = \$16$ and $w_2 = \$20$, the minimum cost of producing $y = 110$ is $828.
h When $w_1 = \$8$ and $w_2 = \$10$, the minimum cost of producing $y = 100$ is no greater than $360.
i The bundle with 22 units of both inputs will not produce $y = 110$.
j When $w_1 = \$20$ and $w_2 = \$20$, the minimum cost of producing $y = 110$ is no greater than $940.

3 Indicate whether the following statements are true, false, or uncertain, and explain your answer.
a Increasing returns to scale and diminishing marginal product are incompatible.

b When the firm's expansion path has a negative slope, input 2 is inferior.

c When the firm's expansion path has a negative slope, both inputs are inferior.

d A cost-minimizing firm would never use an input bundle where the isoquant was upward sloping.

e At Fomoco, the marginal products of inputs 1 and 2 are 5 and 10, respectively, and their prices are $30 and $15; hence, Fomoco is using a cost-minimizing input bundle.

f The production function $F(z_1, z_2) = \min(z_1, 2z_2)$ is homothetic.

4 Indicate whether each of the following statements is "possibly true" or "certainly false," and explain your answer.

a The cost-minimizing bundle for $y = 50$ is $z_1 = 10$ and $z_2 = 40$ when $w_1 = w_2$, and it is $z_1 = 12$ and $z_2 = 37$ when $w_1 = \$20$ and $w_2 = \$15$.

b The cost-minimizing bundle for $y = 50$ is $z_1 = 10$ and $z_2 = 40$ when $w_1 = w_2$, and it is $z_1 = 7$ and $z_2 = 42$ when $w_1 = \$20$ and $w_2 = \$15$.

c The cost-minimizing bundle for $y = 50$ is $z_1 = 10$ and $z_2 = 40$ when $w_1 = w_2$, and it is $z_1 = 6$ and $z_2 = 45$ when $w_1 = \$20$ and $w_2 = \$15$.

5 Kim runs a very interesting business—she buys pizzas from one of two parlors in her town and then delivers them. It takes her 20 minutes to deliver one pizza. If she buys pizzas from Sorento's Pizza Parlor, she pays w_1 for a box with one pizza in it, and if she buys them from Pizza 222, she pays w_2 for a box with two pizzas in it. Show that her cost function is

$$TC(y, w_1, w_2, w_3) = y\left[\frac{w_3}{3} + \min\left(w_1, \frac{w_2}{2}\right)\right]$$

where w_3 is the value of an hour of Kim's time.

6 Jeff runs a roadside stand in which he sells soft drinks. One of his creations, Razapple Juice, is concocted by mixing raspberry juice with apple juice. Long experience has taught Jeff that he must use at least 30% apple juice and at least 30% raspberry juice when mix-

ing a batch of Razapple. If he doesn't, his customers demand a refund, claiming that the mix is not Razapple, and if he does, they are perfectly satisfied with the product.

a Considering only the costs associated with buying apple and raspberry juice, what is the minimum cost of producing a gallon of Razapple Juice when raspberry juice costs $10 per gallon and apple juice costs $20 per gallon? When raspberry juice costs $20 per gallon and apple juice costs $10 per gallon? When raspberry juice costs $10 per gallon and apple juice costs $10 per gallon?

b Construct the isoquant for 1 gallon of Razapple Juice. For y gallons of Razapple Juice.

c Find the cost-minimizing bundle for y gallons of Razapple Juice when the price of a gallon of apple juice is less than the price of a gallon of raspberry juice. When the price of a gallon of apple juice is greater than the price of a gallon of raspberry juice.

d Find the cost function for Razapple Juice.

7 A young entrepreneur, Liz, is considering going into the lawn-mowing business for the summer. Since she can work as many hours as she chooses in the family business at w_1 per hour, her time is worth w_1 per hour. The price per gallon of the gasoline that she needs to buy for her lawn mower is w_2. She can rent a mower that cuts a 12-inch swath and uses $\frac{1}{3}$ of a gallon of gas per hour for w_3 per hour. Using this mower, she can cut 10,000 square feet of lawn in an hour. For convenience, we'll let 10,000 square feet be the unit in which we measure output. She can rent a larger mower, for w_4 per hour, that uses 1 gallon of gas per hour and cuts 3 units of lawn per hour.

a Find the production functions for the smaller and the larger mowers. Note that each production function has three inputs: hours of Liz's time, gallons of gas, and hours of the smaller or the larger mower.

b Derive the conditional input demand functions and the cost functions.

c Show that using the smaller mower is a cheaper way to cut grass if $2w_1 < w_4 -$

$3w_3$. Why is this result independent of the price of gasoline?

d How large must be the price she gets for cutting a unit of lawn to induce her to choose to cut grass rather than to work in the family business?

8 The following is a general case of the Cobb-Douglas production function:

$$F(z_1, z_2) = z_1^a z_2^b$$

where a and b are positive constants. The marginal rate of technical substitution for this production function is

$$\text{MRTS}(z_1, z_2) = \left(\frac{az_2}{bz_1}\right)$$

a What do the first and second principles of cost minimization imply about the cost-minimizing input bundle for this production function?

b Let $a = \frac{1}{3}$ and $b = \frac{2}{3}$, and then find the conditional input demand functions, the cost function, and the average cost function.

c Let $a = \frac{3}{4}$ and $b = \frac{3}{4}$, and repeat these exercises.

*9 Draw an isoquant that is concave (as opposed to convex) to the origin. Show that a cost-minimizing firm will never choose an input bundle with a positive quantity of both inputs. More generally, show that a cost-minimizing firm will never choose an input bundle with a positive quantity of both inputs on a concave portion of an isoquant.

*10 Consider the following production functions:

$$F(z_1, z_2) = [(z_1)^2 + (z_2)^2]^{1/2}$$

$$F(z_1, z_2) = z_1 + z_2$$

a On one diagram, draw the isoquants associated with one unit of output, paying special attention to the points where the isoquants intersect the axes.

b Now suppose that $w_1 < w_2$, and find the cost-minimizing bundles on each isoquant. Then find the cost-minimizing bundles when $w_1 > w_2$.

c Find the cost functions associated with these production functions.

d "The concave portion of any isoquant is economically irrelevant." Do you agree?

IV

Goods Markets

In Part Four, we'll combine the theories of consumer choice and of the firm into a larger picture of the interaction of consumers and firms in markets for goods. Our objective is to learn about the forces that determine equilibrium price and quantity in any goods market and about the properties of equilibrium in goods markets.

We'll take up competitive markets in Chapter 10, monopoly in Chapter 11, oligopoly in markets for homogeneous goods in Chapter 12; and oligopoly in markets for differentiated goods in Chapter 13.

In Chapters 10 and 11, we focus on efficiency. We'll see that competitive markets are efficient while monopoly markets are not, and we'll carefully analyze a number of institutions designed to rectify the inefficiency of monopoly. In Chapter 12, we grapple with one of the toughest questions in economics: What is the appropriate model of oligopoly? In Chapter 13, we focus on product design and niche marketing as the key decisions of the modern firm.

10

THE THEORY OF PERFECT COMPETITION

At the end of the last chapter, we noted that one type of market structure, perfect competition—is characterized by a large number of relatively small firms. In this chapter, we'll explore **perfect competition** in detail and define the kinds of markets to which the model of perfect competition applies. Much of the theory of perfect competition was developed by Alfred Marshall, a turn-of-the-century British economist. The classic reference is Book V of Marshall's *Principles of Economics* (1920).

The questions we'll be asking fall into two categories: conceptual and technical. Sections 10.1 and 10.2 focus on conceptual issues: What is a competitive equilibrium? What are its properties? In what circumstances is the model of perfect competition appropriate? To isolate these conceptual issues from technical ones, we'll take them up in the restricted context of a simple **exchange economy** in which goods are exchanged, but not produced.

Sections 10.3 through 10.8 address technical issues: Where do the demand and supply functions used to identify a competitive equilibrium come from? How does short-run equilibrium differ from long-run equi-

librium? We'll raise these issues in the wider context of an economy characterized by both **production and exchange.**

Finally, in Section 10.7 where we discuss rent control, we will consider what happens when competitive markets are fettered by price controls.

10.1   A Competitive Model of Exchange

By creating an extremely simple competitive model, we can highlight the essential features of competitive market transactions in the ordinary world. In the interest of simplicity, we'll set aside production questions until Section 10.3. In this elementary market, then, goods are exchanged but not produced.

The goods in our simple competitive model are five tickets to a rock concert and the participants are 10 students. Assuming that each student wants only one ticket to the concert, we can completely describe the preferences of a student by a **reservation price.** If the student has no ticket, what is the maximum price he or she will pay to buy one? Or, if the student has a ticket, what is the minimum price he or she will accept for it?

In either case, the answer is the student's reservation price. For simplicity, we'll suppose that potential buyers are male and potential sellers are female. On the buyer's side, we'll assume that a male student will buy a ticket at his reservation price. If a male student is offered one at a price greater than his reservation price, he won't buy it. But if the price is less than or equal to his reservation price, he will. On the seller's side, if a female student is offered a price higher than her reservation price, she will sell her ticket. But if the price is less than or equal to her reservation price, she won't.

We can then describe the preferences of these 10 students by 10 reservation prices, R_A through R_J, which we'll list in descending order. For simplicity, we'll suppose that the highest reservation price is $100 and that reservation prices fall by $10 increments as we move down the list. Thus,

$$R_A = \$100, R_B = \$90, \ldots, R_J = \$10$$

Imagine that each of the five female students has a ticket and that none of the five male students can buy a ticket elsewhere. Because all 10 students would like to attend the concert and only five tickets are available, they can potentially enter into market exchanges among themselves. Which five students will ultimately hold the concert tickets and at what price will the tickets be exchanged?

Suppose that the five tickets are initially allocated to the five students whose reservation prices are $R_B = \$90$, $R_C = \$80$, $R_F = \$50$, $R_H = \$30$, and $R_I = \$20$. We'll give these students feminine names that begin with the identifying reservation price subscript. Betty is the student whose reservation price is R_B, Cathy is the one whose reservation price is R_C, and so on. These students are the potential suppliers of tickets. The male students without tickets — the potential demanders — are those whose reservation prices are $R_A = \$100$, $R_D = \$70$, $R_E = \$60$, $R_G = \$40$, and $R_J = \$10$. We'll give these students masculine names in exactly the same way.

Market Demand

We know the individual demand functions of each male student. For example, Dan will demand one ticket at any price less than or equal to $70 and no ticket at any higher price. We can use individual demand information of this kind to construct a **market demand function** that gives the total number of tickets demanded by the five male students at any given price. First, let's consider relatively high prices. Because Alan's reservation price, $R_A = \$100$, is the highest of the five demanders, we know that if the price of a ticket exceeds $100, the group of five demanders will demand zero tickets. At slightly lower prices — prices below $R_A = \$100$ but above $R_D = \$70$ — Alan will demand a ticket, but neither Dan nor any of the remaining three demanders will. At such moderately high prices, then, the market demand is one ticket. At any price less than $R_D = \$70$ but greater than $R_E = \$60$, Alan and Dan will demand tickets, but Earl and the remaining two demanders will not. At any price in this range, then, the market demand is two tickets. By simply repeating this procedure, we can construct the entire market demand function for the group of five demanders.

That market demand function is plotted in Figure 10.1a, where p is price and y is quantity. The six vertical line segments labeled dd represent the market demand function. (The horizontal dashed lines have been added to give the demand function visual integration.) To read from Figure 10.1a the quantity demanded at any given price, first locate the price on the vertical axis, move horizontally to the demand function, and

---

(a) Demand for tickets   **(b)** Supply of tickets

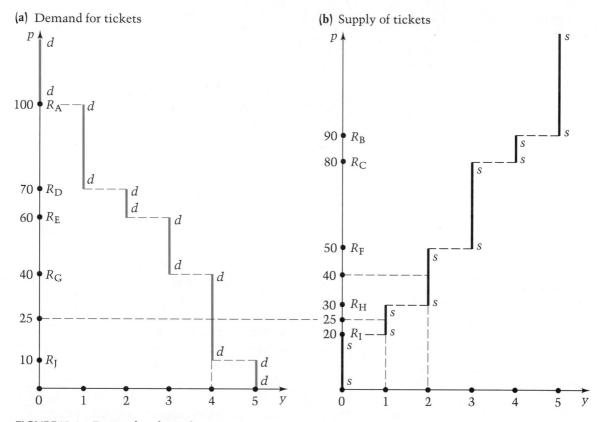

FIGURE 10.1   Demand and supply.

A student without a ticket will (will not) demand one if price p is less than or equal to (greater than) his reservation price. In (a), we have constructed the market demand function implied by the five reservation prices of students without tickets: $100, $70, $60, $40, and $10.

A student with a ticket will (will not) sell it if price exceeds (is less than) her reservation price. In (b), we have constructed the market supply function implied by the five reservation prices of students with tickets: $20, $30, $50, $80, and $90.

then move vertically downward to identify quantity demanded on the horizontal axis. For instance, at a price of $25, the quantity demanded is four.

Market Supply

Now let's construct a **market supply function.** Whether or not the suppliers — the five female students who have tickets — will be willing to sell their tickets is determined by their individual reservation prices. For instance, Cathy will offer her ticket for sale at any price greater than

$R_C = 80, but she'll keep it at any price less than or equal to $80. Using this kind of information, we can construct the market supply function just as we constructed the market demand function by asking who will and who won't supply a ticket at any given price.

The market supply function in Figure 10.1b is composed of six vertical segments labeled ss and connected by dashed lines. Figure 10.1b is read in exactly the same way as Figure 10.1a. If the price of a ticket exceeds the highest reservation price among the suppliers, $R_B = 90, for instance, all five ticket holders will offer a ticket for sale. At prices above $90, then, five tickets will be supplied. If the price is $40 in Figure 10.1*b*, Helen and Irene will each supply a ticket because $40 exceeds their reservation prices ($30 and $20), but the remaining three suppliers will not because $40 is less than their reservation prices ($50, $80, and $90). At the price $40, then, two tickets will be supplied.

The Walrasian Auctioneer

Now that both the market supply and the market demand functions are in place, how many tickets will ultimately be exchanged and at what price? In other words, what will be the equilibrium in this market for concert tickets? To find out, we'll use an auctioneer who acts as a *price setter* in the market. Because Leon Walras, a nineteenth-century French economist, invented this process to study competitive equilibrium, the auctioneer is called the **Walrasian auctioneer.**

In a competitive market, since all participants take price as given, none of the participants is a price setter. To study competitive equilibrium, therefore, it is useful to introduce a price setter, the Walrasian auctioneer. As you know, most real markets don't have a price-setting auctioneer. Hence you should regard the auctioneer as simply a useful device for studying competitive equilibrium.

The Walrasian auctioneer begins by announcing a price for a ticket. Each demander then writes "X" on a slip of paper if he is willing to buy a ticket at that price and "O" if he isn't. At the same time, each supplier writes down "Y" if she is willing to sell a ticket at that price and "O" if she isn't.

The auctioneer then collects the slips from all 10 students and compares the number of X's — quantity demanded at the announced price — and the number of Y's — quantity supplied at the announced price. If

quantity demanded at the announced price exceeds quantity supplied — if there is **excess demand** — the auctioneer then announces a higher price and repeats the procedure. If, instead, quantity supplied exceeds quantity demanded — if there is **excess supply** — the auctioneer then announces a lower price and repeats the procedure.

If the auctioneer announces the price $25 in Figure 10.1, for example, Alan, Dan, Earl, and George will mark down X's, but only Irene will write down a Y. Because there is excess demand, the auctioneer will announce a higher price and proceed to tabulate the results at that new and higher price. If the auctioneer announces the price $95 in Figure 10.1, for example, only Alan will be willing to buy a ticket, but all five ticket holders will be willing to sell one. Because there is excess supply, the auctioneer will announce a new, lower price and again tabulate the results.

The auction ends, and the market is in **competitive equilibrium,** only when quantity demanded is equal to quantity supplied. When this happens, the auctioneer collects money from each demander willing to buy at the announced price, gives the appropriate amount of money to each of the sellers, and transfers the tickets from sellers to buyers.

Competitive Equilibrium

How many tickets will be exchanged once this point of equilibrium has been reached, and what will the competitive equilibrium price be? In Figure 10.2, both the demand and supply functions have been plotted in one diagram. The demand function is labeled *DD* and the supply function *SS*. From Figure 10.2, we see that the auction will end only when the auctioneer announces a price that lies somewhere in the interval $50 to $60. At higher prices, there is excess supply; at lower prices, excess demand. At any price

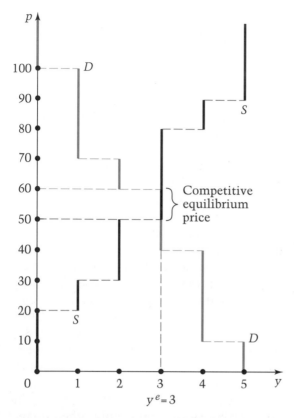

FIGURE 10.2 Competitive equilibrium in an exchange economy.

A competitive equilibrium price is a price such that quantity supplied is equal to quantity demanded. The functions labeled SS and DD are the supply and demand functions from Figure 10.1. Any price p^e greater than $50 and less than or equal to $60 is a competitive equilibrium price. The competitive equilibrium quantity is $y^e = 3$.

in this interval, however, three tickets will be demanded and three supplied.

Any point at which quantity demanded is equal to quantity supplied is a competitive equilibrium. In this case, there are many competitive equilibrium prices. Denoting an equilibrium price by p^e, we see that $\$50 \le p^e < \$60$. (We have included the weak inequality sign because we have assumed that at a price equal to $50, Earl, whose reservation price is $50, will buy a ticket.) Denoting an equilibrium quantity

by y^e, we see that in each of these competitive equilibria $y^e = 3$; that is, three tickets are exchanged.

This market-clearing process thus determines both equilibrium price and quantity. In our ticket model, although the equilibrium quantity is unique, the equilibrium price is not: the auction will stop when the auctioneer announces any price between $50 and $60. The equilibrium price that actually emerges from the auction will depend on the precise rules used by the auctioneer. Yet, equilibrium price and quantity are simply by-products of a more fundamental process in this competitive market: the allocation of tickets and of wealth to students. By allocation, we mean two things: (1) which students finally do and do not have a ticket to the concert, and (2) how much money is in each student's pocket at the end of the process. The competitive equilibrium therefore determines how both tickets and wealth (or command over all other goods) are allocated to students.

Pareto Optimality, or Efficiency

One feature of the **competitive equilibrium allocation** in this market deserves careful attention. The students with the five highest reservation prices, R_A through R_E, have tickets, and the five students with the lower reservation prices, R_F through R_J, do not; that is, the five students who value the tickets most highly are the ones who have them. An implication of this feature is that no further exchange of tickets for money between any two of the ten students can keep both students as well off and make at least one of them better off. Why is this true?

The highest reservation price among those without tickets is Fran's, $R_F = \$50$, and the lowest among those with tickets is Earl's, $R_E = \$60$. Since R_E exceeds R_F, there is no sum of money that Fran will be willing to offer Earl for a ticket and that Earl will also be willing to accept. We've then established an interesting result: the competitive equilibrium allocation is Pareto-optimal, since no student can be made better off while leaving the other students at least as well off. This illustrates an important, even fundamental, result:

Provided that certain conditions are met, a competitive equilibrium allocation is Pareto-optimal, or efficient.

We will consider the conditions under which competitive equilibrium is Pareto-optimal at various points in this and subsequent chapters.

The Role of Initial Allocation

What would happen with a different initial allocation? Would the equilibrium price and quantity also be different? Would the tickets still be allocated to those with the highest reservation prices? Would the equilibrium allocation again be Pareto-optimal? To find out, try the following problem.

PROBLEM 10.1

Suppose that the students who were given the tickets in the initial allocation were those with the reservation prices $100, $90, $70, $40, and $10. Construct a diagram analogous to Figure 10.2. What is the range of equilibrium prices and the equilibrium quantity in this case? What is the allocation of tickets in this competitive equilibrium? Identify the students who are better off and those who are worse off in the new equilibrium than in the original equilibrium.

This problem illustrates some important points about this particular economy. First, the competitive equilibrium quantity depends on the **initial allocation**. In the case analyzed in the text, the quantity exchanged in the competitive equilibrium was 3, but in Problem 10.1 — where the initial allocation of tickets to students was different — the

quantity exchanged was 2. To cite another example of the dependence of equilibrium quantity on the initial allocation, if tickets were initially given to the students with the five highest reservation prices, equilibrium quantity would be zero. Why? Second, a student is better off when he or she initially has a ticket. Third, although equilibrium quantity and the welfare of individual students depend on the initial allocation, the competitive equilibrium allocation is always the same. In the competitive equilibrium, the tickets go to the five students, male or female, with the five highest reservation prices.

The Function of Price

Finally, notice that the range of competitive equilibrium prices does not depend on the initial allocation in this model. This reflects the fact that price is a signal that serves to allocate tickets to the students who place the highest value on them. The artifice of a Walrasian auctioneer highlights the allocational role of price, since each demander responds to the announced price by indicating whether he wants to buy a ticket at that price and each supplier responds by indicating whether she wants to sell her ticket at that price. Thus, we see the fundamental role that price plays in an unfettered market economy — that is, in an economy free of impediments to the voluntary exchange of goods or services between suppliers and demanders:

In a market economy, prices are the signals that guide and direct allocation.

In our ticket model, price performs this allocative function well, since the equilibrium is Pareto-optimal.

As we'll see in subsequent chapters, the Pareto optimality of competitive equilibrium is a result that requires careful qualification and interpretation. For example, in

Chapter 17, we'll look at some important qualifications under the general heading of *externalities.* In the meantime, you can discover the general nature of such qualifications in the following problem.

PROBLEM 10.2

Consider a ticket model with just four people and two tickets. Harry and Sarah have ordinary reservation prices, each equal to $10. However, because Jane and Bob are "going steady," their reservation prices are more complex. If Jane has a ticket, then Bob's reservation price is $20; if she doesn't, his reservation price is $0. Similarly, if Bob has a ticket, Jane's reservation price is $20; if he doesn't, her reservation price is $0. Show that there are two competitive equilibrium allocations. In one allocation, the price is less than or equal to $10, and Harry and Sarah have the tickets. In the other, the price is greater than $10 and less than $20, and Jane and Bob have the tickets. Show that the first of these allocations is not Pareto-optimal.

A competitive market system of allocation is appealing to many economists (and noneconomists) because the gains from trade are fully realized in competitive equilibrium. In our exchange model, gains from trade were possible in the initial allocation of tickets, but were fully realized in the competitive equilibrium allocation.

Notice, however, that the initial allocation is not unlike the distribution of inherited wealth and abilities in the real world. Each of us must play life's game with the "tickets" allocated at birth, including inherited wealth and talent. Some of us are lucky and others unlucky, just as five of the students were fortunate and five unfortunate in the initial allocation of concert tickets. And what one ends up with in the competitive equilibrium depends on what one begins with. In Problem 10.1, you discovered the unsurprising but important result that students were better off when they were given tickets in the initial allocation than when they were not.

The larger implication is that a competitive equilibrium is incapable of redressing initial inequalities. It merely provides a means for realizing the full potential of gains from trade, given the initial allocation. As we'll see in the last section of this chapter where we consider rent control, impediments are sometimes placed on the market system of allocation in order to redistribute income. Not surprisingly, the consequences for allocation are adverse. Rent control thus illustrates the potential for conflict between equity and allocational efficiency.

10.2 Potential Difficulties with the Competitive Model

Our ticket model is founded on two crucial assumptions that are analytical trouble spots. Because these two troublesome assumptions are at the core of all models of perfect competition, we'll look at both very carefully. Later in the chapter, we'll consider the additional assumptions that come into play in a competitive model once production is introduced.

Price Taking or Price Manipulating

First, let's consider the assumption, implicit in these models, that all the students behaved as if they were price takers. We assumed that in responding to the auctioneer's announced price, the students simply consulted their preferences and honestly reported the action that was in their own self-interest at the announced price.

Yet any of these students might have misrepresented their preferences in an attempt to influence the market-clearing price in a personally favorable direction. Indeed, we can easily identify real-world situations in which demanders or suppliers intentionally misrepresent their positions. In the residential real estate market, for instance, homeowners regularly quote to agents or to prospective buyers a selling price higher than their real reservation price in an attempt to increase the price at which the house is finally sold.

Their behavior indicates that they do not see themselves as mere price takers, unable to affect the market price of a good. On the other side of the real estate coin, potential home buyers typically negotiate by underrepresenting their real reservation price for buying a home in an attempt to lower the price at which the house is sold. Again, these potential home buyers do not see themselves as price takers.

Individuals do have the incentive and, as we'll see, some power to manipulate prices. Suppose that nine students in our ticket model are ingenuous souls who view themselves as price takers but that one student is a fox among the chickens: a price manipulator. Now, suppose that the manipulator is a supplier, Fran. How can she increase the market-clearing price? By responding to the auctioneer's announced prices as if her reservation price were higher than $R_F = \$50$, or, loosely speaking, by reporting a false reservation price R_F' higher than $50. Will her manipulative behavior pay off? Suppose that her false reservation price R_F' is $55, less than Earl's reservation price, $R_E = \$60$, but greater than her true reservation price, $R_F = \$50$. Fran's price manipulation in this case gives rise to a (false) supply function that shifts from two to three tickets at $55 rather than at $50. As you can easily verify, the range of market-clearing prices is now reduced from the interval $50 to $60 to the interval $55 to $60. In this instance, Fran's deliberate misrepresentation works to her advantage (and, incidentally, to the advantage of Helen and Irene as well) because the market-clearing price may increase but will not decrease as a result of her manipulations.

What will happen if Fran decides to report an even higher false reservation price, $65, which is larger than $R_E = \$60$ but less than $R_D = \$70$? Now the (false) supply function, $S'S'$ in Figure 10.3, shifts from two to three tickets at $65. In this situation, the auction will not close at a competitive equilibrium price. Instead, as the figure reveals, the market-clearing price will be in the interval $60 to $65, and only two units will be

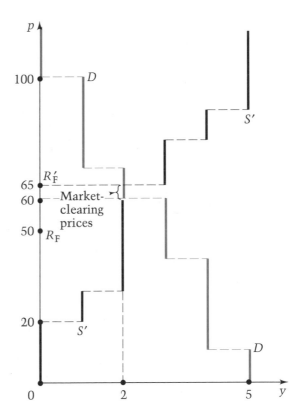

FIGURE 10.3   Price manipulation.

From Figure 10.2, we know that any price between $50, Fran's reservation price, and $60 is a competitive equilibrium price. Suppose that Fran attempts to manipulate price by acting as if her reservation price were $65. If no one else attempts to manipulate price, the market-clearing price will lie between $60 and $65, and Fran's price manipulation will have worked to her own disadvantage since she will not sell her ticket.

traded. Alan and Dan will each buy a ticket, and Helen and Irene will each sell one. In this case, Fran's misrepresentation works to her disadvantage, since she ends up keeping a ticket she otherwise would have sold.

If she doesn't overdo it, then, Fran can manipulate the price of the tickets to her own advantage by misrepresenting her true position — and she may be tempted to do so. Of course, any of the demanders or suppliers could choose to play the role of the fox among the chickens. If one of the demanders — say, Earl — is the price manipulator instead of Fran, and if the nine other students all represented their positions honestly, he could reduce the range of market-clearing prices from the interval $50 to $60 to the interval $50 to $52 by reporting the false reservation price $R_E' = \$52$. If Earl is the only price manipulator, reporting $R_E' = \$52$ would clearly be in his own best interest.

PROBLEM 10.3
Suppose that Earl chose to report an even lower false reservation price, $R_E' = \$45$. What would be the range of market-clearing prices? How many tickets would be traded? Who would gain and who would lose as a result of this misrepresentation?

Why would any of the students then choose to be chickens (or price takers) rather than foxes (or price manipulators)? By misrepresenting their true reservation prices rather than reporting them honestly, all the students could potentially manipulate the market-clearing price to their own advantage. Yet if any of them chose to do so, the result might or might not be a competitive equilibrium. And, of course, the manipulator might or might not gain from the misrepresentation. The assumption of price-taking behavior is necessary because if students reported false reservation prices, the outcome might not be a competitive equilibrium.

Large Numbers and Price-Taking Behavior

One way out of this dilemma is to restrict our model to situations in which there are large numbers of both demanders and suppliers, none of whom demands or supplies a significant percentage of the quantity traded in a competitive equilibrium. In this case, it's reasonable to suppose that the gaps between reservation prices will be small. As a result, since no individual can significantly affect the market-clearing price by misrepresenting his or her true position, no individual has any incentive to try to manipulate price. If out of 100,000 wheat farmers, one farmer chooses to report a false reservation price, for instance, the likely consequences are that price will not be significantly affected, and the lone manipulator will end up holding wheat that he or she would have preferred to sell at the equilibrium price.

Given large numbers of insignificant buyers and sellers, then, the competitive model is appropriate because all potential participants in the process of market exchange will see themselves as price takers rather than price manipulators. For this reason, economists typically assume large numbers of insignificant buyers and sellers in setting out a model of perfect competition.

Price Making: The Walrasian Auctioneer

We have now come to acceptable terms with one problematic assumption only to be confronted by another, more difficult one. In our simple model, we invoked the convenient artifice of a Walrasian auctioneer, who announced a price, adjusted the price up or down in response to excess demand or to excess supply, and cleared the market only at the equilibrium price, where quantity demanded was equal to quantity supplied. This artifice functions like the dramatic device of the deus ex machina, the god who brings a play to a harmonious conclusion by sorting out the muddled affairs of mere human beings.

Yet in the real world, there are only a few markets—the London Bullion Exchange is one—that have an auctioneer who follows market-clearing rules such as those outlined in the ticket model. If we drop this assumption of a godlike auctioneer who brings about the competitive equilibrium, what is left? Where does the competitive equilibrium price come from?

In most real transactions, the price maker is the supplier or the demander (or both). In the market for groceries, for example, a Safeway outlet sets the prices, and grocery shoppers take them (or leave them). A tuna cannery sets the price it will pay for tuna, and a tuna fisher either sells the catch to the cannery or goes elsewhere. A ticket scalper at a major league ballpark quotes a price; a potential ticket buyer rejects it and offers another; the scalper rejects the buyer's price and makes another. The process continues until either the two strike a bargain or the potential buyer goes off to find another scalper.

In all these cases, price makers are constrained by the prices their competitors offer, because their potential customers (or suppliers) typically have the option of approaching someone else. Safeway cannot set prices higher than those that their customers think they can get at the A&P, for example, without losing potential buyers to the A&P. The point remains, however, the individual suppliers or demanders are the price makers in most actual market transactions, transactions that are characterized by the process of offer and counteroffer.

Once we eliminate the assumption of the auctioneer, does any other assumption guarantee that a competitive equilibrium will result from the more characteristic real-world process of offer and counteroffer?

Perfect Information

Economists sometimes invoke the assumption of **perfect information** to fill the void created by the exodus of the auctioneer. The argument is that if all buyers and sellers are sufficiently well informed, then the process of offer and counteroffer will result in a competitive equilibrium price. Suppose that all the participants in the process of exchange set prices: buyers make bids to buy and sellers make offers to sell. Suppose, too, that every buyer knows the offer prices of all sellers and that every seller knows the bid prices of all buyers. All the buyers will approach the seller with the lowest offer price, who then raises it. Conversely, all the sellers will approach the buyer with the highest bid price, who then lowers it. This process continues until all the bid and offer prices converge to the same price.

Will that common price, the price at the point of convergence, necessarily be a competitive equilibrium price? If it were not, there would be either excess demand or excess supply. If there were excess demand, then some buyer or buyers, unable to buy anything at the common price, would raise their bid prices, and sellers would respond by raising their offer prices. At a common price, then, there can be neither excess demand nor excess supply. But this means that the common price that emerges from this process of offer and counteroffer in the presence of perfect information must be a competitive equilibrium price.

The bedrock assumptions of the theory of competitive markets are thus the assumptions of large numbers (or of price taking) and of perfect information. Nevertheless, economists have achieved no unanimous agreement about whether either or both assumptions are necessary. The debate centers on whether or not a competitive equilibrium will result from voluntary market exchange even in the absence of large numbers of inconsequential buyers and sellers or of perfect information.

Robustness of the Competitive Model

Essentially, the issue is one of the robustness of the model when either one or both of these assumptions is not satisfied. As we noted in Chapter 1, however, testing the robustness of an economic model can be very difficult because economics is not a laboratory science. Nevertheless, within the last three decades, some economists have conducted laboratory experiments that do bear directly on these two assumptions.

In the laboratory design, experimenters induce real people to exhibit specified reservation demand and supply prices for some artificial commodity chosen by the researchers. These kinds of experiments test the robustness of the competitive model. First, the typically small number of suppliers and demanders in the laboratory fails to meet the criterion of large numbers (or price taking). Second, the very limited information made available to each of these suppliers and demanders fails to satisfy the criterion of perfect information. Because the demand and supply functions are known to the experimenter, the equilibrium price and quantity predicted by a competitive model can be calculated and then compared with the results from the laboratory market. Furthermore, by using alternative trading institutions — the sets of rules governing the trading activity of the subjects — experimental economists can examine the robustness of the competitive model under a range of such institutions.

To what extent are the experimental results consistent with the predictions of the model of perfect competition? In summarizing the results from approximately 175 experiments, Vernon Smith (1982) concludes that they converge with astonishing

speed to the competitive equilibrium. These experiments and others like them suggest that neither of the two assumptions is necessary for the model of perfect competition to provide a close approximation of what takes place in real markets.

10.3 The Assumptions of Perfect Competition

Having looked at perfect competition in a simple exchange economy, we can now present a comparatively more complex treatment of the theory in markets where firms produce the goods demanded by consumers. We will begin by setting out the traditional assumptions on which the theory is built. The first two assumptions are now familiar; the other two are new.

ASSUMPTION: Large Numbers
No individual demander buys and no individual supplier produces a significant proportion of the total output.

As we have seen, this assumption implies that all demanders and suppliers will be price takers.

We've already considered the role of perfect information in a simplified market environment in which goods are bought and sold but not made. Here, we'll broaden the assumption somewhat to apply to more complex market environments in which goods are also produced.

ASSUMPTION: Perfect Information
All participants have perfect knowledge of all relevant prices and of all relevant technological information.

This assumption means, on one hand, that firms know the prices of all the goods they could possibly produce, the technology for producing those goods, and the prices at which they could buy the required inputs. It means, on the other hand, that all individuals know both the prices at which they can buy all goods and the prices at which they can sell their resources in general and their labor in particular.

The third assumption concerns the nature of the products made for sale in a competitive market.

ASSUMPTION: Product Homogeneity

In any given market, the products of all firms are identical.

This assumption limits the applicability of the competitive model to markets in which the products made by competing firms are virtually the same, or homogeneous. It rules out the application of the model to markets in which products are significantly differentiated, or heterogeneous. The model applies to the market for corn, for instance, because the corn produced by thousands of farmers in the American Midwest is virtually indistinguishable. But it does not apply to the automotive industry, for example, because no two firms make cars or trucks that are identical.

The fourth assumption concerns the possibility of switching resources from one use to another.

ASSUMPTION: Perfect Mobility of Resources

All inputs are perfectly mobile.

If firms can freely allocate resources to different uses, they are then able both to expand (or to contract) their scale of production in a particular market and to enter (or to leave) the industry itself. As we'll see later on in the chapter, this flexibility plays an important role in the theory of perfect competition.

We can use these four assumptions as the foundation on which to build the theory of perfect competition in the short run and in the long run.

10.4 Short-Run Competitive Equilibrium

Because firms cannot change the quantities of their fixed inputs in the short run, we know that, by definition, new firms cannot enter the industry. By contrast, in the long run, they can enter and exit the industry, and the characterization of the **long-run competitive equilibrium** thus will differ from the **short-run competitive equilibrium**.

Graphically, a competitive equilibrium is determined by the intersection of a market demand function and a market supply function. In Figure 10.4, the equilibrium price is p^e and the equilibrium quantity y^e. (In contrast to our ticket model, the equilibrium price in Figure 10.4 is unique.) Our primary analytical tasks are to see how the market demand function DD and the market supply function SS in Figure 10.4 are actually constructed.

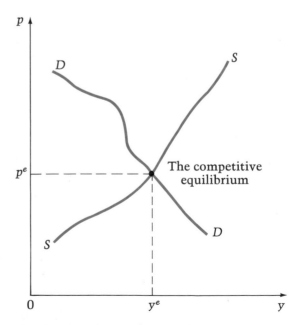

FIGURE 10.4 Competitive equilibrium.

The competitive equilibrium is at the intersection of the demand *(DD)* and the supply *(SS)* functions, where y^e is demanded and supplied at price p^e.

Aggregating Demand

We'll examine the market demand function first. We have assumed that all demanders are price takers, and in Chapter 4 we used the same price-taking assumption to derive individual demand functions. To find the market demand function for any particular good, we need a way to add up, or *aggregate*, those individual demand functions.

Figure 10.5 illustrates the process of aggregation for two demanders. The individual demand functions for good Y are labeled AA' and BB', and the green line labeled BCD represents the aggregation of these two individual demand functions, or the market demand curve when there are just two consumers in the market. This market demand curve is constructed by choosing a price, finding the quantities of good Y demanded by each of the individuals at that price, summing the quantities to locate one point on

the aggregate demand function, and then repeating the process for all other possible prices. When the price is $4, for instance, the buyer whose demand function is AA' will demand 5 units; the buyer whose demand function is BB' will demand 11 units; and their aggregate demand is 16 units. The point (16, 4), therefore, is one point on the market demand function.[1]

PROBLEM 10.4

Why is the aggregate demand function coincident with BB' when price exceeds $12 in Figure 10.5? What is distance OD in Figure 10.5?

PROBLEM 10.5

Suppose there are 1000 individuals with the following demand function for good Y

Quantity demanded $= 1 - .001p$

Show that the market demand function is $y = 1000 - p$, or that the (inverse) market demand function is $p = 1000 - y$.

The Profit Function

The first step in creating a short-run market supply function is to determine the short-run supply function of an individual firm. What exactly is a short-run supply function? Just as an individual consumer's demand

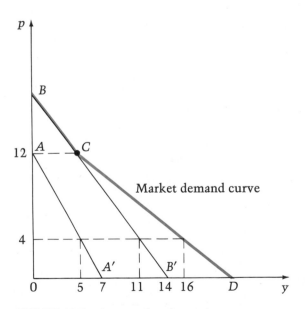

FIGURE 10.5   Aggregating demand.

The individual demand functions are AA' and BB', and the aggregate demand function is BCD. When price is $4, one individual demands 5 units and the other 11. Together they demand 16 units, and (16, 4) is therefore one point on the market demand function.

[1] Let's consider an algebraic example. Suppose the two individual demand functions are

$$p_1 = \frac{1}{y_1} \quad \text{for the first individual}$$
$$p_2 = \frac{10}{y_2} \quad \text{for the second individual}$$

The aggregation question is this: Given a common price, say $p = p_1 = p_2$, what is the aggregate quantity demanded? To answer the question, we first write y_1 and y_2 as functions of the common price p (that is, $y_1 = 1/p$, $y_2 = 10/p$) and then add to obtain

$$y_1 + y_2 = \frac{1}{p} + \frac{10}{p} = \frac{11}{p}$$

In aggregating the supply functions of individual firms, the same procedure is necessary. Since we are interested in obtaining the aggregate quantity supplied at any price, we must write the quantity supplied by any firm as a function of the common price before adding.

function for good Y tells how much the consumer will demand at any given price p, so the individual firm's **short-run supply function** for good Y tells us how much the firm will supply at any given price p. How do we find the firm's short-run supply function? Just as we found the consumer's demand function by solving the consumer's utility-maximizing problem, so we will find the firm's supply function by solving its profit-maximizing problem.

A firm's profit is simply the firm's revenue less its cost:

$$\text{profit} = \text{revenue} - \text{cost}$$

Since the competitive firm is a price taker, its revenue is just price multiplied by the quantity produced, or py. It is convenient to call this expression the competitive firm's **total revenue function,** $\text{TR}(y)$. Thus, $\text{TR}(y) = py$.

In the short run, the competitive firm's cost is given by the short-run cost function $\text{STC}(y)$ from Chapter 8. We can therefore express the firm's profit as a function of its output y in the following way:

$$\pi(y) = \text{TR}(y) - \text{STC}(y)$$

We'll call $\pi(y)$ the firm's **profit function** because this function gives us the firm's profit as a function of its output y.

Notice that profit depends on both price p and output y. But, since the competitive firm is a price taker, price is an exogenous variable—one that the firm cannot choose. It can choose its own output, however, and y is therefore the endogenous variable in this profit-maximizing problem. The problem we want to solve is then

$$\text{maximize profit } \pi(y)$$
$$\text{by choice of output } y$$

The solution to this problem will give us the profit-maximizing output, which we'll denote by y^*, as a function of the exogenous variable p. This function is called the firm's **short-run supply function.**

The Profit-Maximizing Output Level

In Figure 10.6a, the firm's total revenue function is the line py, and its short-run cost function is the curve STC. Because p is fixed, the total revenue function is a straight line whose slope is p: each additional unit of output adds p to the firm's total revenue. The short-run cost function is the standard stylization from Section 8.4.

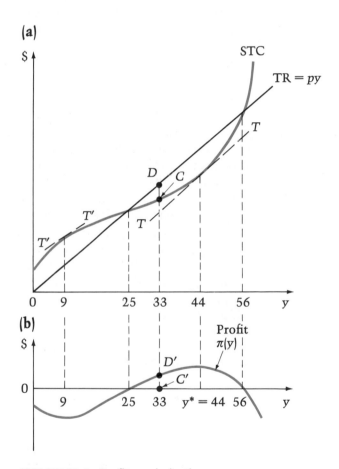

FIGURE 10.6   Profit maximization.

In (a), we have drawn the short-run total cost function STC and the total revenue function TR. Subtracting STC from TR, we derive the profit function $\pi(y)$ in (b). Profit is maximized at $y^* = 44$, where the slope of the profit function is zero. But the slope of the profit function is just p, the slope of TR, minus SMC, the slope of STC. Therefore, at y^*, SMC = p. That is, when profit is maximized, SMC is equal to p.

The profit function $\pi(y)$ in Figure 10.6*b* is derived from the two functions in Figure 10.6*a* by subtracting cost STC(y) from revenue py for every value of y. For example, when output is 33, profit is the distance *CD* in Figure 10.6*a*. Therefore, the distance *C'D'* in Figure 10.6*b* is equal to the distance *CD* in Figure 10.6*a*. Notice, too, that in Figure 10.6*a*, revenue is equal to cost at two levels of output — at 25 and at 56 — and so in Figure 10.6*b*, profit is equal to zero at these output levels. Finally, notice that profit is negative when output is less than 25 or when it is greater than 56.

The profit-maximizing output in Figure 10.6 is clearly $y^* = 44$. What can we say about this level of output that will help us to identify the firm's profit-maximizing rule and, therefore, its supply function? The crucial observation is that the slope of the profit function is zero at $y^* = 44$ or, putting the same observation differently, that the rate of change of profit with respect to output is zero at the point where profit is a maximum. Why must this be true at the point of maximum profit? If the slope of the profit function is positive (as it is to the left of 44 units of output in Figure 10.6*b*), the firm can increase profit by increasing output. Conversely, if the slope of $\pi(y)$ is negative (as it is to the right of 44 units of output), the firm can increase profit by decreasing output. We can state this result as follows:

The rate of change of profit with respect to output is zero at the point where profit is a maximum.

But the rate of change of profit with respect to output is simply the rate of change of total revenue with respect to output minus the rate of change of cost with respect to output. The rate of change of cost with respect to output is just short-run marginal cost SMC(y). The rate of change of total revenue with respect to output — or **marginal revenue** (MR) — is equal to the slope of the

total revenue function. For a price-taking firm, this slope is constant and equal to price p, since each unit of output contributes p to the firm's revenue. That is, for a competitive firm, marginal revenue is equal to price: MR = p.

To maximize profit, therefore, the firm will choose a level of output at which SMC(y) is equal to MR, which itself is equal to price p. Thus, we can infer that

$$\text{SMC}(y^*) = \text{MR} = p$$

To understand this result, let's return to Figure 10.6*a*. Line *TT*, which is tangent to SC(y) at $y^* = 44$, has the same slope as the total revenue function. This means that SMC is equal to MR at 44 units of output. As a result, the slope of the profit function is zero at $y^* = 44$.

We seem to have found a simple rule of thumb for the profit-maximizing firm:

Produce the level of output at which marginal revenue (or price) is equal to marginal cost.

This rule obviously requires qualification, because SMC is equal to MR at two levels of output in Figure 10.6 — at 44 units, where profit is a maximum, and at 9 units, where profit is a minimum. And as we will see, the firm's profit-maximizing rule requires yet another qualification.

The Short-Run Supply Function

Although the diagrammatic apparatus in Figure 10.6 is fine for finding the profit-maximizing output for one price, it is not well suited to finding the profit-maximizing output for many different prices. This means that we need a different apparatus to find the firm's supply function. The "marginal revenue equals marginal cost" rule suggests that we use a framework that includes MR and SMC. In Figure 10.7, we have also included the average variable cost

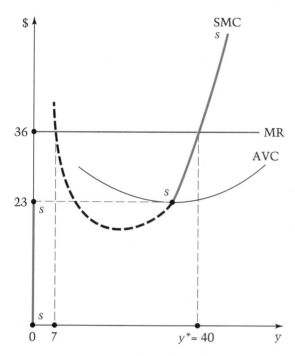

FIGURE 10.7 The competitive firm's supply function.

The competitive firm's supply function is composed of the two segments labeled *ss*. When *p* is less than $23, the minimum value of AVC, the firm supplies nothing because it can't cover the variable costs associated with any positive quantity. When *p* exceeds $23, the firm chooses the level of output where *p* = SMC. If *p* = $36, for example, the firm supplies *y** = 40. Thus, the second segment of the firm's supply function is SMC above the point where SMC intersects AVC.

function AVC(*y*) to capture the second qualification. We'll show that the firm's short-run supply function is composed of the two segments labeled *ss* in Figure 10.7.

What is the profit-maximizing output when price is $36 in Figure 10.7? The horizontal line running through $36 and labeled MR is marginal revenue when price is $36, since marginal revenue is equal to price. Notice that marginal cost is equal to marginal revenue, or SMC = MR, at two levels

of output: 7 and 40. Our experience with the previous figure suggests that one of these maximizes profit and the other minimizes it. Which is which?

Profit is a maximum at 40 units because SMC(*y*) intersects MR from below. To see why, suppose that the firm is producing 40 units. What will happen to its profit if it produces an additional unit? The added cost of the extra unit is given by SMC and the added revenue by MR. Because SMC exceeds MR to the right of 40 units, the added unit of output adds more to cost than to revenue, and profit falls. Beginning again at 40, what will happen to the firm's profit if it produces one less unit of output? The reduction in revenue is given by MR and the reduction in cost by SMC. Since MR exceeds SMC to the left of 40 units, the drop in revenue exceeds the drop in cost, and profit falls once again. Profit is therefore a maximum at 40 units.

On the other hand, profit is a minimum at 7 units because SMC intersects MR from above. To see why, let's suppose that the firm is producing 7 units. What will happen to its profit if it produces an additional unit? The added cost of the extra unit is given by SMC, and the added revenue by MR. Because SMC is less than MR to the right of 7 units, the rise in cost resulting from an additional unit of output is less than the rise in revenue, and profit increases. Beginning again at 7 units, what will happen to the firm's profit if it produces one less unit of output? The reduction in revenue is given by MR and the reduction in cost by SMC. Since MR is less than SMC to the left of 7 units, the drop in revenue is less than the drop in cost, and profit increases once again. Profit is therefore a minimum at 7 units.

These results suggest a rule that can be used to identify the profit-maximizing output for any price: move horizontally from price to the rising portion of SMC and then vertically down to the quantity axis. The firm's supply function therefore seems to be the rising, or positively sloped, portion of SMC.

With the addition of one more qualification, it is. Notice that in Figure 10.7, average variable cost is never less than $23 since the minimum value of AVC is $23. This means that at any price less than $23, the firm cannot cover its variable costs of production if it produces a positive quantity of output. Because it can avoid these variable costs of production altogether by shutting down production, when price is less than $23, the firm will maximize profit by producing nothing at all. The firm's supply curve in Figure 10.7 is then composed of the two segments labeled *ss*.

These results are easily generalized:

When price is less than the minimum value of AVC, there is no level of output at which the firm can cover its variable costs of production, and it will therefore produce nothing.

When price is greater than the minimum value of AVC, the firm's supply function is the rising portion of SMC that lies above AVC.[2]

Now let's find a way to represent the firm's profit using a similar figure. Profit is simply total revenue py^* minus short-run total cost STC (y^*). STC(y^*) is equal to output multiplied by short-run average cost, or

y^*SAC(y^*). The firm's profit can therefore be expressed as

$$\pi(y^*) = y^*[p - \text{SAC}(y^*)]$$

By adding SAC to the figure, we can identify the firm's profit as well as its supply function. In Figure 10.8, we have added SAC and identified the firm's profit when p is $36 by the green rectangle. The vertical side of the profit rectangle is price minus short-run average cost, $p - \text{SAC}$. The horizontal side is the profit-maximizing output y^*. The area of the profit rectangle is then $y^*(p - \text{SAC})$, or the firm's profit.

PROBLEM 10.6

Make your own diagram of Figure 10.8, and suppose that p is $24. In your diagram, identify the quantity that the firm will supply at this price. Notice that short-run average cost at this level of output is greater than $p = $24, so the firm's profit is negative. Construct a rectangle in your diagram with area equal to the firm's negative profit. Why would a firm ever produce a positive output when it makes a negative profit by doing so?

Aggregating Short-Run Supply

It is now a simple matter to calculate the short-run market supply function by aggregating the short-run supply functions of all firms in the market. To illustrate the aggregation procedure, we have constructed in

[2] The firm's supply function is derived by solving its profit-maximization problem: maximize $\pi(y)$ by choice of y. Differential calculus tells us two useful things about the profit-maximizing value of y, y^*, in the event that $y^* > 0$.

1 If $\pi(y)$ is differentiable, then $\pi'(y^*) = 0$. That is, a necessary condition for $y^* > 0$ to be the profit-maximizing value of y is that $\pi'(y)$ be equal to zero at y^*.

2 If $\pi'(y^*) = 0$ and $\pi''(y^*) < 0$, then $\pi(y)$ attains a (local) maximum at y^*; that is, $\pi'(y^*) = 0$ and $\pi''(y^*) < 0$ are sufficient conditions for $\pi(y)$ to attain a (local) maximum at y^*.

These two statements allow us to find the firm's

supply function. Application of the first yields

$$p - \text{STC}'(y^*) = 0$$

or

$$p = \text{MC}(y^*)$$

because STC$'(y)$ is MC(y). The second statement is satisfied at y^* if STC$''(y^*) > 0$ or, equivalently, if MC$'(y^*) > 0$. MC$'(y^*) > 0$ simply means that the marginal cost function is rising at y^*. That is, $\pi''(y^*) < 0$ tells us that only the *rising portion* of the marginal cost function is relevant. Of course, y^* will be zero if p is less than the minimum value of AVC(y), because in this case there is no positive output that will allow the firm to recover its variable costs.

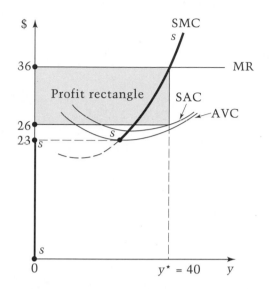

FIGURE 10.8   The profit rectangle.

When $p = \$36$, the firm supplies $y^* = 40$. Total revenue is therefore $36 times 40. SAC is $26 when output is 40, so that the firm's total costs are $26 times 40; therefore, its profit is ($36 − $26) times 40, equal to the area of the profit rectangle.

Figure 10.9 the market supply function for a case in which two firms are in a market. One firm's supply function is represented by the two segments $0A$ and BC, the other firm's by the two segments $0A'$ and $B'C'$. The aggregate, or market supply function, is composed of the three segments labeled SS in Figure 10.9. In the following problem, you can check your understanding of this aggregation procedure.

P R O B L E M   10.7

Suppose that 100 firms — each with the following short-run supply function for good Y — are in a particular market:

$$\text{quantity supplied} = .01p$$

Show that the market supply function is

$$y = p$$

Short-Run Competitive Equilibrium

We can now identify the short-run competitive equilibrium by finding the price at which quantity demanded equals quantity supplied. This equilibrium is represented in Figure 10.10b by the intersection of the market supply and market demand functions at point (y^e, p^e). The competitive equilibrium price is p^e, and the quantity exchanged at this price is y^e. The position of a representative firm in this market is illustrated in Figure 10.10a. Because the scales on the two (vertical) price axes are identical, we can project the market price p^e from Figure 10.10b into Figure 10.10a. The scales on the two (horizontal) quantity axes are not

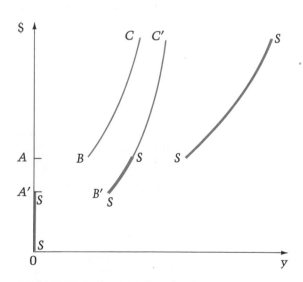

FIGURE 10.9   Aggregating supply.

The aggregation of supply is analogous to the aggregation of demand. The supply function for one firm is composed of segments $0A$ and BC; the supply function for the other is composed of segments $0A'$ and $B'C'$. The aggregate supply function is composed of the three segments labeled SS.

(a)

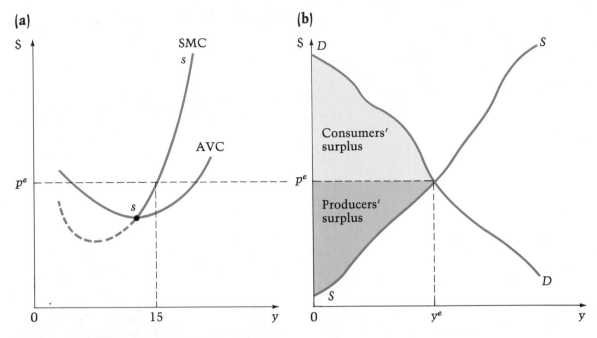

(b)

FIGURE 10.10   Short-run competitive equilibrium.

In (b), the competitive equilibrium price is p^e and quantity is y^e. In (a), the representative firm supplies 15 units at the equilibrium price p^e. The light green area in (b) is aggregate consumers' surplus, and the dark green area is aggregate producers' surplus. In the competitive equilibrium, the sum of consumers' surplus and producers' surplus is maximized, and in this cost-benefit sense, the competitive equilibrium is optimal.

the same because the representative firm's output, 15 units, is only a small fraction of the total market output y^e. To get some feel-ing for short-run competitive equilibrium, try the following comparative statics exer-cise.[3]

---

[3] We can use differential calculus to see the precise nature of this sort of comparative statics question. For example, suppose that we are interested in the effect that a change in the price of mangoes p_M will have on the equilibrium price of apples p_A. Write the demand for apples as

$$y = D(p_A, p_M)$$

to reflect the possibility that the demand for apples is affected by the price of mangoes. Because different soil conditions and climates are needed to produce mangoes and apples, the supply of apples will not de-pend on the price of mangoes; so we write the supply of apples as

$$y = S(p_A)$$

In equilibrium, we have

$$D(p_A^e, p_M) = S(p_A^e)$$

where p_A^e is the equilibrium price of apples. Now, totally differentiate this equilibrium condition to obtain

$$D_2(p_A^e, p_M)dp_M = [S'(p_A^e) - D_1(p_A^e, p_M)]dp_A^e$$

and solve for dp_A^e/dp_M: the rate of change of the equilibrium price of apples with respect to the price of mangoes:

$$\frac{dp_A^e}{dp_M} = \frac{D_2(p_A^e, p_M)}{[S'(p_A^e) - D_1(p_A^e, p_M)]}$$

The denominator on the right is ordinarily positive since $S'(p_A)$ is likely to be positive and $D_1(p_A, p_M)$ negative. Therefore, the sign of dp_A^e/dp_M turns on the sign of $D_2(p_A, p_M)$. For example, if apples and mangoes are substitutes, then $D_2(p_A, p_M) > 0$ and therefore $dp_A^e/dp_M > 0$. Chapters 9 and 10 of Samuelson (1947) are devoted to the method of comparative statics analysis in economics.

PROBLEM 10.8

Suppose that firms are forced to pay an excise tax of $10 per unit on every unit they sell. Show that this tax shifts each firm's supply curve vertically upward by $10. What happens to the market supply curve? If the demand curve is vertical — if demand is perfectly price inelastic — what happens to equilibrium price when this tax is imposed? If the demand curve is not perfectly price inelastic, show that the price increases will be less than $10.

10.5 Efficiency of the Short-Run Competitive Equilibrium

At the beginning of this chapter, we saw that the competitive equilibrium of the exchange economy model was Pareto-optimal, or efficient. Is the equilibrium in Figure 10.10 similarly efficient? Because every firm in this competitive equilibrium is producing at the point where price equals short-run marginal cost, none can sell an additional unit of output at a price that will cover the short-run marginal cost of producing that additional unit. Remember, too, that the short-run marginal cost of a unit of output is just the market value of the variable inputs needed to produce the unit. If we think of firms in the short run as trading variable inputs (processed into good Y) for consumers' dollars, we recognize that the potential gains from trade are fully realized in this equilibrium. Once the competitive equilibrium is attained, it is impossible to sell an additional unit of output at a price that will cover the market value of the added resources needed to produce it. In this sense, the short-run competitive equilibrium is efficient.

Having an economic measure of the gains from trade is useful in many circumstances. (We will be using such a measure in this and subsequent chapters.) In Figure 10.10, we can identify gains to both consumers and firms. The aggregate measures of these gains are known, respectively, as consumers' surplus — indicated by the light green area of Figure 10.10*b* — and producers' surplus — indicated by the dark green area. But where do these measures come from and what do they mean?

We introduced the notion of one consumers' surplus in Section 5.2. (You may want to review that discussion briefly.) Consumers' surplus in competitive equilibrium is just the sum of the surplus enjoyed by all consumers at the competitive equilibrium price. As we noted in Section 5.2, however, consumer surplus is a theoretically well-grounded benefit measure only in the special case in which the consumers' indifference curves are vertically parallel — the case in which quantity demanded of Y is *unresponsive* to the consumer's income. If the indifference maps of all consumers are characterized by such parallel indifference curves, then CS can be used without hesitation as a measure of aggregate consumer benefit. If consumer demand for Y is responsive to income, we can use CS as long as we recognize that it is just a rough-and-ready approximation of consumer's benefits.

Producer's surplus is a measure of benefits to the owners of firms. The measure of benefit to any one owner would seem to be a profit measure. In the short run, the appropriate measure is revenue minus variable cost since the firm's fixed cost is just that — fixed. We can identify producers' surplus by calculating aggregate revenue minus aggregate variable cost. Aggregate revenue is the rectangle in Figure 10.10*b* with sides p^e and y^e. Since the supply curve is the marginal cost of output, aggregate variable cost is the area under the supply curve *SS* from the origin to y^e. Thus, producers' surplus, calculated by subtracting aggregate variable cost from aggregate revenue, is indicated by the dark green area in Figure 10.10*b*. The sum of consumers' and producers' surplus, called **total surplus,** is a measure of the aggregate gains from trade realized in this market.

PROBLEM 10.9

In Problems 10.5 and 10.7, you found the following market demand and supply functions

$$\text{market demand} = 1000 - p$$

$$\text{market supply} = p$$

First, find the competitive equilibrium and draw a diagram to illustrate it. Then compute consumers' and producers' surplus in this equilibrium. (Remember that the area of a triangle is $\frac{1}{2}$ its base times its height.)

Because the aggregation procedures used to define these measures of benefit are simply to add up the benefits accruing to all individuals without any regard to the distribution of those benefits, they are *cost-benefit* measures of benefit. Wherever we use them, then, we are implicitly invoking the controversial assumption discussed in Section 1.5, that a dollar of benefit is a dollar of benefit — regardless of who gets it.

10.6 Long-Run Competitive Equilibrium

Although new firms cannot enter or leave the industry in the short run, they can in the long run. In the long-run analysis, then, we need to distinguish between established firms (those already in the market) and potential firms or entrants (those not yet in existence). If the market is house painting, for instance, the established firms are the commercial house painters currently in business. The potential entrants are house-painting firms that have not yet been established, firms that are just twinkles in some entrepreneurial student's eye, for example.

No-Exit, No-Entry, and Long-Run Equilibrium

There are two obvious requirements, or conditions, of long-run equilibrium:

1 **No-exit condition:** In long-run equilibrium, no established firm wants to exit the industry.

2 **No-entry condition:** In long-run equilibrium, no potential firm wants to enter the industry.

The no-exit condition implies that the long-run equilibrium price p^e must be high enough that each established firm makes at least zero profit. The no-entry condition implies that p^e must be low enough that no potential entrant could earn positive profit.

As we'll see, these two conditions tell us a great deal about long-run competitive equilibrium. But first, let's note the economic role of profit as a signal guiding the allocation of resources in the long run. In effect, positive profit is a signal that induces entry, or the allocation of additional resources to the industry. On the other hand, negative profit is a signal that induces exit, or the allocation of fewer resources to the industry.

Two factors determine the menu of long-run production choices open to established firms: the long-run average cost function LAC and the possibility of exiting the industry. (We'll use the U-shaped stylization of LAC in Figure 10.11 throughout the analysis, even though other stylizations are possible.) Established firms can decide to produce at any point on LAC in Figure 10.11, or they can decide to exit — to buy no inputs. The choices open to entrants are much the same. They can enter the market by producing at some point on LAC, or they can stay out of the industry.

To talk more easily about the position of any particular firm in the long-run competitive equilibrium, we need some terminological shorthand. We'll call the level of output at which long-run average cost attains its minimum value the **efficient scale of production**. In Figure 10.11, the efficient scale of production is y' units of output. And we'll call the average cost at the efficient scale of production the **minimum average cost**. In Figure 10.11, minimum average cost is c'.

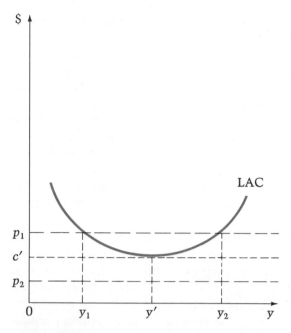

FIGURE 10.11 Exit, entry, and long-run competitive equilibrium.

In long-run competitive equilibrium, price must be such that no established firm wants to exit (the no-exit condition) and no potential firm wants to enter (the no-entry condition). The no-exit condition is violated for any price less than c', the minimum average cost. At price p_2, for example, established firms take losses and therefore will exit in the long run. The no-entry condition is violated for any price larger than c'. At price p_1, for example, any quantity larger than y_1 and less than y_2 offers positive profit, and new firms will enter. The only price that satisifes both conditions is c'. That is, the long-run competitive equilibrium price p^e is equal to the minimum average cost c'.

Price Equal to Minimum Average Cost

The no-exit and no-entry conditions imply that the long-run competitive equilibrium price is equal to the minimum average cost. To see why, suppose the price were higher than c' — say, p_1 in Figure 10.11. Because p_1 exceeds LAC for any level of output larger than y_1 but smaller than y_2, potential entrants anticipate making a positive profit at any such level of output. In the long run,

then, new firms will enter the industry when price is p_1. That is, because the no-entry condition is not satisfied, price p_1 cannot be the long-run equilibrium price. Because an analogous argument applies to any other price higher than c', we see the following:

The no-entry condition implies that the long-run equilibrium price cannot exceed the minimum average cost.

Now suppose that the price were less than c' — say, p_2 — in Figure 10.11. Because LAC now exceeds p_2 at all levels of output, all established firms will be incurring losses. In the long run, then, profit-maximizing firms will leave the industry. That is, because the no-exit condition is not satisfied, p_2 cannot be the long-run equilibrium price. Because an analogous argument applies to any other price less than c', we see the following:

The no-exit condition implies that the long-run equilibrium price cannot be less than the minimum average cost.

Since p^e cannot exceed c', nor be less than c', it must equal c'. That is,

In long-run equilibrium, price is equal to the minimum average cost.

The Individual Firm in Long-Run Equilibrium

Knowing that price equals minimum average cost, we also know the position of every firm in the long-run equilibrium. In Figure 10.12, y' is the only output level at which an established firm can cover its cost of production when price is equal to c'. To avoid losses at the equilibrium price, each must be producing at the efficient scale of production, y'. This, in turn, means that each firm will be on the short-run average cost function SAC tangent to LAC at y' in Figure

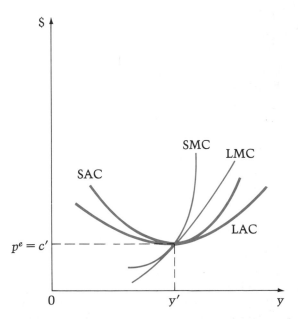

FIGURE 10.12 The firm in long-run competitive equilibrium.

In long-run competitive equilibrium, each firm produces at the efficient scale of production y', and price is equal to the minimum average cost c'. As a consequence $p^e = c' = LAC = LMC = SMC = SAC$.

10.12. From the relationship between marginals and averages developed in Chapters 8 and 9, we also know that both long-run and short-run marginal cost functions will pass through the point (y', c').

We can summarize these results by the following series of equalities. In long-run equilibrium, marginal revenue is equal to price, which is equal to the minimum average cost of production, which in turn is equal to long-run average cost, short-run average cost, long-run marginal cost, and short-run marginal cost:

$$MR = p^e = LAC(y') = SAC(y')$$
$$= LMC(y') = SMC(y')$$

Long-Run Supply Function

We can use the properties of equilibrium to develop what is called the **long-run supply function** (LRS). The long-run competitive equilibrium is then determined by the intersection of LRS and the demand function. We'll consider three cases: industries characterized by constant costs, by increasing costs, and by decreasing costs. In the short run, we assumed that all input prices were constant. As we derive LRS, we will incorporate changes in input prices that arise as industry output expands or contracts. It is these changes in input prices that determine whether any particular industry is a constant-cost, increasing-cost, or decreasing-cost industry.

As the aggregate output of a certain industry expands or contracts, the aggregate quantities of the inputs used in that industry will correspondingly expand or contract. If egg production goes up, for instance, the amounts of hens, chicken coops, and chicken feed required by egg producers will also go up. And as input requirements increase, the price of any particular input will either remain constant, increase, or decrease. These three possibilities determine the three cases of constant-cost, increasing-cost, and decreasing-cost industries.

LRS: The Constant-Cost Case

In the constant-cost case, as the aggregate quantity produced changes, the prices of all inputs remain constant. Because in the constant-cost case the prices of all inputs are independent of aggregate industry output, the various cost functions for individual firms will not change as industry output changes. In particular, neither the efficient scale of production nor the minimum average cost will change as aggregate industry output expands or contracts. The position of a representative firm in long-run equilibrium will always be exactly as pictured in Figure 10.12, and the long-run competitive equilibrium price will always be c'. This means that LRS must be a horizontal line through c', as in Figure 10.13, because this is the only possible shape such that any market demand function will intersect LRS at price c'. If the market demand function in Figure 10.13 is DD, for instance, the long-run equilibrium quantity will be y_1; if it is $D'D'$, the long-run equilibrium quantity will be y_2. In both cases, the long-run equilibrium price is c'.

A Dynamic Story

If market demand changes, how will an industry characterized by constant costs move from one long-run equilibrium to another in response to that change? Let's suppose that the industry is initially in the long-run equilibrium at point E in Figure 10.14b. The representative firm in Figure 10.14a is producing y' units of output in response to the initial long-run equilibrium price of c'.

In Figure 10.14b, the short-run supply function SS is the aggregation of SMC over all firms in the industry; that is, SS is the short-run supply function in the initial

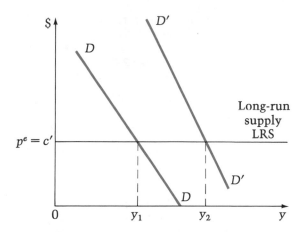

FIGURE 10.13   LRS in the constant-cost case.

In the constant-cost case, the minimum average cost c' is independent of the industry's aggregate output, and the long-run supply function LRS is therefore the horizontal line through c'. In response to a shift in demand from DD to $D'D'$, output in long-run competitive equilibrium increases from y_1 to y_2, but equilibrium price does not change.

equilibrium. Then for n identical firms, the aggregate output in the initial equilibrium at E is ny'.

Suppose that the demand function now shifts from DD to $D'D'$ in Figure 10.14b because one of the exogenous variables has changed. For example, it might shift because the price of a substitute has risen or because the price of a complement has fallen. In the short run, the price of the good will increase to p'', and each established firm will expand its output to the point where short-run marginal cost equals price p''. In other words, each firm will produce y'' in Figure 10.14a, and their aggregate output will be ny'' in Figure 10.14b. Because in the short run p'' exceeds SAC, each firm will be earning a profit. Further, because p'' exceeds LMC, established firms have a long-run incentive to further expand their output. Given the price p'', in the long run they would choose the output level where long-run marginal cost equals p''. More important, because p'' exceeds c', the shift in demand will also spur new firms to enter the industry.

The supply response to this shift in demand is then twofold: established firms expand their production, and new firms enter the industry. However, as established firms expand and as new firms enter, the short-run supply function shifts to the right, and the short-run equilibrium price drops. We have not shown this short-run market supply function or the short-run equilibrium associated with it because as long as the price exceeds minimum average cost c', new entrants can still earn a profit and so will enter the industry. This entry will continue until the price is driven back down to c'.

When price is again equal to c', the only level of output that does not create losses for the representative firm is once again y'. In the new long-run equilibrium, each firm will again produce output y' at long-run average cost equal to c'. If n' is the new and larger number of firms in the new long-run

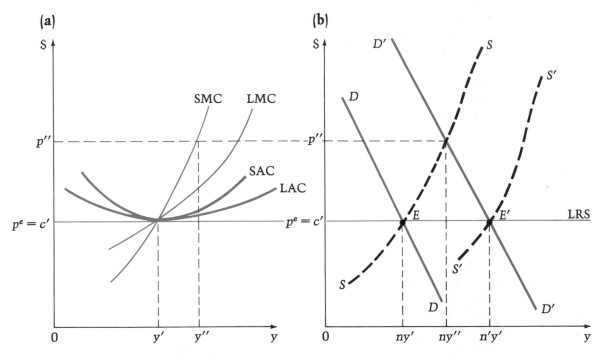

FIGURE 10.14   Pseudodynamics in the constant-cost case.

The initial demand function in (b) is DD, and the equilibrium is therefore at E. SS is the short-run market supply function in the initial equilibrium. The representative firm in (a) produces y′, and the n firms in the industry produce aggregate output equal to ny′. The demand function now shifts to D′D′, producing the short-run equilibrium price p″. At this price, each firm produces y″, and aggregate output is ny″ in the short-run equilibrium. Because p″ exceeds c′, new firms will enter the industry. This process of long-run adjustment through entry will continue until there are n′ firms each producing y′, so that price is driven back down to c′. In the new long-run equilibrium at E′, the short-run supply function is S′S′.

equilibrium at E′, the aggregate output will be n′y′. The short-run supply function at the new long-run equilibrium S′S′ in Figure 10.14b will then be the aggregation over n′ firms of the short-run marginal cost function SMC in Figure 10.14a.

The Inadequacy of the Dynamic Story

Our account of the adjustment from one long-run equilibrium to another contains some serious deficiencies. In both the initial and the subsequent long-run equilibria, each firm is in the position shown in Figure 10.12. Yet during the adjustment process, price is obviously not equal to c′. If firms took these transient nonequilibrium prices as given and if they expected them to be maintained, their long-run decisions would lead them to produce at a point where long-run marginal cost is equal to the nonequilibrium price. Of course, as the price changes, these firms would discover that they had made the wrong long-run decision.

This scenario suggests that if firms have any foresight, they will realize that these nonequilibrium prices will not be maintained indefinitely and therefore will decide against basing their long-run decisions on these prices. To analyze their decisions in this case, we would need a theory of how firms form their expectations about the path of future prices when the industry is in disequilibrium. But since we have no such theory, we have no adequate theory of decision making in disequilibrium. We have only a theory of equilibrium, not a theory of the dynamics of market adjustment as an industry shifts from one long-run equilibrium to another.[4]

LRS: The Increasing-Cost Case

In many industries, as the marketwide output expands and as the quantities of inputs demanded therefore increase, the prices of some or all of those inputs will also increase. Where inputs are natural resources, this input-price response is almost universally true. Mining firms that supply ore, for example, naturally exploit the richest and most accessible ore bodies first. As more ore is demanded, they move on to poorer, less accessible ore bodies. As they do so, the cost per unit of ore rises.

In industries where inputs are characterized by increasing costs, what will the long-run supply curve look like? As aggregate industry output increases and as the prices of at least some inputs also increase, the minimum average cost of production must rise. Therefore, as industrywide output increases, the long-run equilibrium price — which is equal to the minimum average cost of production — must also increase. This means that the LRS must be upward sloping.

The increasing-cost case is illustrated in Figure 10.15. Given the demand function DD, the long-run equilibrium price is p_1 and

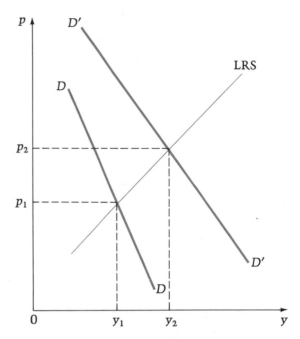

FIGURE 10.15   LRS in the increasing-cost case.

In the increasing-cost case, efficient average cost increases as industry output increases. Thus, LRS is upward sloping in the increasing-cost case. In response to a shift of the demand function from DD to $D'D'$, output in long-run equilibrium increases from y_1 to y_2, and equilibrium price increases from p_1 (the minimum average cost in the initial equilibrium) to p_2 (the minimum average cost in the subsequent equilibrium).

quantity is y_1. Given $D'D'$, the long-run equilibrium price is p_2 and quantity is y_2.

Although we can't discuss the process of adjustment rigorously, we can consider a mock dynamic exercise similar to that considered for the constant-cost case. The exercise allows us to identify some of the forces at play in the adjustment process and to compare the size of a representative firm in the initial and the subsequent equilibria.

Suppose that at an initial equilibrium, each of n firms supplies y' units of output at a long-run equilibrium price equal to the initial minimum average cost of production c'. The position of a typical firm is presented in

---

[4] Frisch (1936) provides an interesting discussion of the very troublesome problem of choice in disequilibrium.

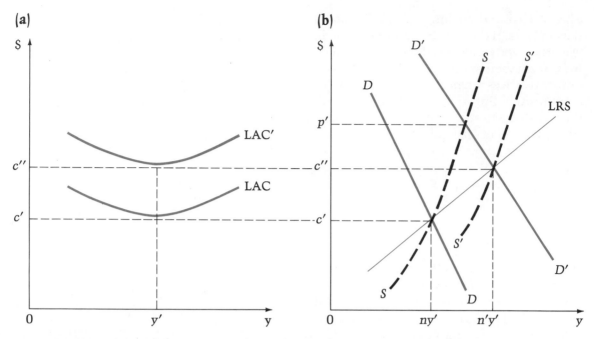

FIGURE 10.16   Pseudodynamics in the increasing-cost case.

Given the demand function *DD*, price in the initial equilibrium is *c'*, each firm produces *y'*, and aggregate output is *ny'*. When demand shifts to *D'D'*, the short-run equilibrium price is *p'*. At this price, new firms will enter and established firms may expand. As this process of industry expansion occurs, input prices are pushed up, shifting up the long-run average cost function. In the new long-run equilibrium, the long-run average cost function has shifted up to LAC', and price has been driven to *c''*, the minimum average cost in this long-run equilibrium.

Figure 10.16*a*. The aggregate quantity *ny'* supplied by these *n* firms at price *c'* is one point on the long-run market supply function, and *SS* is the initial short-run supply function. What will happen if demand now shifts from *DD* to *D'D'*? The price of the good will initially rise and, just as in the constant-cost case, the firms in the market will earn profit. In the short run, established firms will again respond by expanding output. This profit also acts as a spur to potential entrants, and new firms will enter the market.

As a result, the industry as a whole will demand more inputs and, by definition, the price of some inputs will increase. As input prices increase, each firm's cost of produc- tion will also increase. In particular, the ef- ficient cost of production will increase, and each firm's long-run average cost function will therefore shift upward. Suppose for the moment that in the long run the efficient scale of production does not change. That is, suppose that LAC shifts directly upward, as illustrated in Figure 10.16*a*, rather than up- ward and to the left or to the right. Because of the upward shift in each firm's LAC, the quantity of output produced by each firm in the new long-run equilibrium will still be equal to *y'*, but the equilibrium price will equal the new — and higher — minimum average cost *c''*.

In response to this shift in demand, the number of firms increases from *n* to *n'*, the long-run equilibrium price of the good increases from c' to c'', and the marketwide output increases from ny' to $n'y'$. The quantity $n'y'$ at price c'' in Figure 10.16b, therefore, is another point on the long-run market supply function, labeled LRS.

Because we assumed that the efficient scale of production y' did not change, the increase in industrywide output in the long run was necessarily achieved by new firms entering the industry. But if the efficient scale of production had increased — if LAC had shifted up and to the right — the story would have been different. For example, the increase in efficient scale might have been so large that no new entry was required. Indeed, the number of firms actually might have decreased as industry output expanded. On the other hand, if the efficient scale had decreased — that is, if LAC had shifted up and to the left — the number of firms required in the new equilibrium would be larger than n'.

LRS: The Decreasing-Cost Case

It is also possible that the prices of some inputs might decrease as industry demand for them increases. Although examples of such inputs are not easy to find and the decreasing-cost case is rare, we'll quickly consider this possibility. As you can easily verify, if the prices of some or all inputs decrease (and if the prices of the remaining inputs are constant) as the aggregate quantity of inputs demanded increases, the LRS will be downward sloping.

10.7 Comparative Statics

When we characterized industries as belonging to one of three categories — constant costs, increasing costs, or decreasing costs — and saw how firms in each category moved from one long-run equilibrium to another in response to shifts in market demand, we accomplished two related tasks. We created both a theory of equilibrium price and quantity and a theory of the allocation of resources to markets. Let's take some time to put these results into perspective by considering some comparative statics exercises. Let's consider what happens to equilibrium price and quantity when market demand shifts and when market supply shifts. (You should be able to verify the following results by constructing the relevant demand and supply diagrams.)

The market demand function for a good can shift for any number of reasons. Tastes may change, causing a shift in market demand. For example, in the 1970s, there was apparently no demand for the New Wave paraphernalia that became popular in the 1980s. So, too, the price of either a substitute or a complement for the good may change, causing the market demand for that good to shift accordingly. If the price of a substitute for good Y goes up, then the market demand function for good Y will shift upward and to the right. For example, if coffee becomes more expensive, the demand for tea will shift upward and to the right. If the price of a complement goes up, the opposite will occur. For example, if a ski-lift ticket becomes more costly, the demand for ski rentals will shift down and to the left.

Suppose that for some reason the demand function for good Y does shift up and to the right. In all three cases — constant costs, increasing costs, and decreasing costs — both short-run equilibrium price and quantity will increase. In the constant-cost case, however, the long-run equilibrium quantity will increase, but long-run equilibrium price will remain unchanged. In the increasing-cost case, both long-run equilibrium price and quantity will increase. In the decreasing-cost case, long-run equilibrium price will decrease, but long-run equilibrium quantity will increase.

Let's turn now to changes in market supply. Again, a number of factors can cause a shift in the market supply function. Technological change—the development of more efficient production processes, for example—can cause shifts in market supply functions, as can changes in the prices of inputs. If the price of a variable input goes up, both the short-run and the long-run market supply functions will shift upward and to the left. For instance, the dramatic increases in the price of crude oil in the 1970s caused a shift in the supply functions for a whole range of plastic products, including plastic cups, because crude oil is an essential input in the production of many plastics. Suppose, then, that either the short-run or the long-run market supply function does shift up and to the left: in any of the three cases, the equilibrium price will increase and the equilibrium quantity will decrease.

As we saw earlier, these kinds of price and quantity responses to changes in market demand and market supply are merely symptomatic of a more fundamental market process: the competitive allocation of resources. We'll examine this topic more closely in Chapter 15. For now, we'll simply highlight the role that competitive markets play by contrasting the competitive equilibrium to the outcome that results when an impediment to market exchange is imposed. By a *market impediment*, we mean anything that alters the ability of suppliers and demanders to voluntarily exchange goods or services free of institutional interference. The classic example of such an impediment is rent control.

*10.8 Rent Control

We began this chapter with a model in which goods were exchanged, but not produced. The central message emerging from that model was that prices serve an important role as signals that guide the allocation of goods to their most productive uses. Specifically, we saw that the allocation of goods associated with the competitive equilibrium price is Pareto-optimal. We will close the chapter by viewing allocation from a different perspective, as we explore a case in which prices are not allowed to perform their allocative function.

We'll look at a case in which a **price ceiling** is imposed in a competitive market. Specifically, we'll think of a market for rental housing and we'll call the price ceiling rent control. Our model will capture important features of actual rental housing markets that have rent control. It will not be directly applicable to any of them, however, because any real market is characterized by significant variation among rental units. For example, some units are detached houses, others are duplexes, and still others are apartments in very large complexes. Some units have a superb view or access to recreational facilities, and others offer almost no amenities. By contrast, in this model, we will assume that all rental units are identical.

In addition, real rent-control laws vary widely from one jurisdiction to another. In some jurisdictions, rent-control legislation has almost no real impact on rental prices, while in others the ceiling on rental prices is substantially below the competitive equilibrium price and is strictly enforced. In some jurisdictions, rent control applies to all rental units, while in others it applies only to older units. Rent-control laws are often complex and sometimes involve an elaborate enforcement mechanism. Under some legislation, controls are placed on the rental price itself, whereas under other legislation, controls are placed on the rate of increase in rental prices. By contrast, in this model, rent control is just a rent ceiling, and—although we will consider some enforcement issues—the model itself does not provide for an enforcement mechanism.

The Model

In any month, there are 1000 demanders of rental units in this model. We will call the demanders renters, the rental units apartments, the renters who are looking for an apartment searchers, and the renters who occupy an apartment tenants. Each renter's demand can be described by a reservation price, and, as we learned in Section 10.1, the market demand curve is then composed of 1000 vertical segments. For simplicity, we have approximated this segmented curve in Figure 10.17 by a smooth market demand curve.

Because real rental markets cater to the housing needs of people such as students who move frequently, turnover is an important feature of any such market. To capture turnover in this model, we'll assume that each month 2% of the 1000 renters leave this market and are replaced by other renters with identical reservation prices. As a result, the market demand curve remains the same, but the population of renters changes from month to month as renters enter and leave the market.

Like the market demand curve, the long-run supply curve is composed of a large number of vertical segments reflecting a reservation supply price for each apartment. (Below we will consider more carefully the factors that determine reservation supply price.) Once again, we have approximated this segmented curve in Figure 10.17 by a smooth long-run supply curve.

Since the decisions to replace and maintain rental units are important in real rental markets, we will assume that apartments last for a finite period of time and that they require periodic maintenance. Specifically, we'll adopt the following assumptions. Each apartment is owned by one landlord and accommodates one renter. Maintenance entails the expenditure of $50 per month. Each new apartment lasts for 120 months (10 years) if it is maintained every month. If

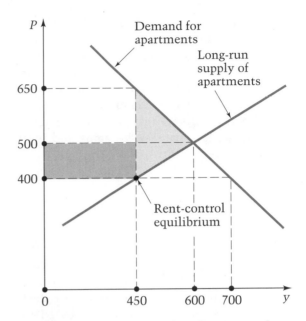

FIGURE 10.17 **The economics of rent control.**

In the absence of rent control, the equilibrium price and quantity would be $p^e = \$500$ and $y^e = 600$ apartments. Relative to this competitive equilibrium, the rent-control equilibrium — in which the price ceiling is $400 and quantity of rental housing supplied is 450 apartments — has several properties. The dark green area represents surplus that is apparently transferred from landlords to tenants. The light green area represents the surplus that is destroyed (or the potential gains from trade that are not realized). At the $400 price ceiling, there is excess demand for 250 apartments (700 − 450). Because this rental price cannot increase, this excess demand will result in phenomena such as excessive search costs and under-the-table deals.

maintenance is not done in a given month, the apartment becomes uninhabitable. In any event, it becomes uninhabitable after 120 months.

In a competitive equilibrium, it makes no difference who actually pays the monthly maintenance. If the tenant pays the maintenance cost, the equilibrium rental price for an apartment is lower by $50 than if the landlord pays. For simplicity, we'll assume that the landlord pays for maintenance.

Let's suppose that this market is initially in the long-run equilibrium shown in Figure 10.17, where the rental rate is $500 per month and 600 apartments are supplied. Now suppose that a rent ceiling of $400 per month is imposed in this market. What are the effects of this rental ceiling in the short run? In the long run? Who gains and who loses from rent control?

Apparent Effects of Rent Control

Assuming that this price ceiling is enforced, its impact seems to be straightforward. There is an apparent *distributional effect*, since each tenant seems to be better off by $100 per month and the owner of each apartment seems to be worse off by $100. When the $400 ceiling is imposed, then, income or surplus is transferred from landlords to tenants. And there are apparently no *short-run allocational effects*, since the initial allocation is Pareto-optimal, and no tenant has an incentive to move once the rental price falls to $400 per month. Yet the actual distributional and allocational effects may not be so clear-cut as the model initially suggests. Let's see what we might be overlooking.

Short-Run Effects

We can begin by looking at the allocation of the 600 existing apartments. To capture one important feature of real rental markets, we assumed a 2% turnover rate in this market. As some renters move on and others replace them, on average 12 apartments are vacated and reallocated to new tenants in each month. The question we want to answer is this: What principles govern this reallocation of apartments? If the landlord gets only $400 per month, then price no longer guides allocation, because in Figure 10.17 there is excess demand at the $400 rental rate. Seven hundred renters want an apartment, but

only 600 can be accommodated in the 600 existing apartments. If price does not perform the allocational role, what does?

Let's suppose for a moment that the addresses of all vacant apartments are published in the local newspaper and that the first searcher to get to a vacant apartment rents it. On average, 12 apartments will be vacated in each month, and a large number of searchers will be trying to rent them. If the *effective price* of an apartment were only $400 per month on average, more than 100 searchers would be apartment hunting; however, as we'll see, the effective price will actually be more than $400. Rent control then creates a game, apartment hunting, played each month by a large number of searchers trying to rent just 12 apartments. It is this game that replaces price as the allocative mechanism.

If you've ever hunted for an apartment in a tight rental market, you'll know how this game played. The minute the local paper hits the streets, searchers grab one from the nearest paper box, thumb through the "for rent" section of the classified ads, and then speed off to the nearest advertised vacancy, hoping to be the first on the scene. Any more leisurely strategy is bound to fail when excess demand is significant at the rent-controlled price. Of course, the success rate will be small, meaning that a searcher who is new to the market must expect to spend a great deal of time and energy before finally finding an apartment. The costs of this search activity — gas, time, and wear and tear on the car and nerves — mean that the effective price of an apartment will be considerably more than the $400 paid to the landlord each month.

Looked at from another perspective, these search costs mean that some of the surplus available from the original 600 apartments is destroyed in the game of apartment hunting, which replaces price as the allocative mechanism under rent control. That is, attempting to use a rent ceiling to transfer surplus from landlords to tenants creates forces that tend to destroy some of that surplus. Because effective rent control confers a valuable monthly bonus on tenants, searchers willingly expend time, energy, and money to get access to this bonus, thereby dissipating its value.

The situation is closely analogous to the problem of allocating racquetball courts on a first come, first served basis in Section 5.6. In both cases, real resources are used to achieve an allocation that could have been achieved at lower cost by a price mechanism. We can draw a general conclusion from this result:

The real costs of allocating a fixed quantity of some good or service are higher when a nonprice allocative mechanism is substituted for a price mechanism.

The next question is this: Who gets the vacant apartments? We can't be exactly sure, since blind chance plays an important role in determining who gets to a vacant apartment first. But we can be sure about one thing: almost certainly, some renters with reservation prices lower than $500 will be lucky enough to get apartments. For example, in the very first month after rent control comes into force, most of the searchers will have reservation prices less than $500. Why? Therefore, we must expect these searchers to get most of the vacant apartments in that first month.

So far we've assumed that landlords advertise vacant apartments and rent to the first searcher who shows up. In reality, the landlord may not be willing to rent to the first searcher. Because there is excess demand, the landlord can afford to pick and choose among searchers based on his or her personal likes and dislikes. It is also possible, and even likely, that if excess demand is large enough, vacant apartments won't be advertised at all. The landlord (or the last tenant) may already know one or more

searchers and may find it attractive to rely on these informal contacts rather than to deal with the large numbers of searchers who will respond to a formal ad.

Thus blind chance, the personal preferences of landlords, and personal contacts will all play some role in reallocating apartments as they become vacant. As a consequence, the allocation of apartments will not be Pareto-optimal because the 600 available apartments will not be allocated to the 600 renters with reservation prices greater than or equal to the long-run equilibrium price of $500. Instead, some of the 100 renters with reservation prices between $400 and $500 will inevitably manage to rent apartments because they are lucky enough to spot an ad first, or because some landlord likes their looks, or because they know the vacating tenant. Again, we can draw a general conclusion:

When the allocation of a fixed quantity of some good or service is not guided by price signals, the allocation need not be Pareto-optimal.

To this point, we have implicitly assumed that the tenant pays and the landlord receives just $400 per month for any apartment. Even the most casual observation of real markets with rent control reveals that more money is likely to change hands. In New York, "key money" means a bribe that a searcher pays a landlord for the privilege of signing an initial lease. In Toronto, a "sublet fee" means a bribe that a searcher pays a tenant to sublet a rent-controlled apartment. These bribes are so much a part of apartment hunting that often no attempt is made to be discreet about them. For example, the following advertisement appeared on a bulletin board in a convenience store located in a large rent-controlled apartment complex: "Wanted: one-bedroom apartment. Willing to pay $500 sublet fee."

Rent control may also be circumvented in more subtle ways. In this model, maintenance is the landlord's responsibility. Given the excess demand caused by rent control, the landlord has an incentive to pass the $50 per month maintenance cost to the tenant, while maintaining the rent-controlled price of $400. And the landlord can always find a tenant willing to pay the additional $50. If it is possible to do so, then, landlords will shift maintenance responsibilities to tenants. Alternatively, the landlord may be able to tie the lease of the apartment to the lease of furniture — charging just $400 to rent the apartment while overcharging for the furniture — thereby increasing the effective rental rate for the apartment.

These are just a few of the many possibilities for circumventing the intent of rent control. These can be thought of as informal and incomplete price mechanisms that emerge to fill the void created when the real price mechanism is suspended. They clearly work to reduce the extent of income redistribution and to increase the price of rent-controlled accommodations. The final conclusion to be drawn from the analysis of the short run is this:

The actual extent of redistribution of income from landlords to tenants will be less than it initially appears to be.

Long-Run Effects

Before we can consider the effects of rent control in the long run, we need to think about what the *long-run reservation supply price* for an apartment actually means. Once an apartment becomes uninhabitable at the end of 120 months, the landlord faces a long-run investment decision: whether to build a new apartment or to convert the land to its next best use. For example, let's suppose that it will cost some landlord $60,000 to rebuild the apartment and that the landlord's next best option is to sell the land to a 7-Eleven convenience store for $50,000. The landlord's reservation supply price is a monthly rental price for the apartment such that he or she is indifferent between rebuilding the apartment and selling the land to 7-Eleven. If the rental price is p per month, the landlord's net monthly return is $(p-50)$, since maintenance is the landlord's responsibility. The reservation supply price is then the value of p such that the discounted present value of the net monthly return over 120 months, less the $60,000 rebuilding cost, is just equal to the $50,000 that 7-Eleven is willing to pay for the property. If the real rental rate is larger than this value, then the landlord will rebuild the apartment; if it is less than this value, he or she will sell the land to 7-Eleven.

To the extent that rent control reduces the net monthly return of landlords, the supply of apartments in the long run will diminish as some landlords decide to convert their land to alternative uses at the end of the 120 months. If we suppose for purposes of illustration that the $400 rent ceiling is effective, then we see from Figure 10.17 that just 450 apartments will be supplied in the long run. Thus, 150 potential landlords and potential tenants will be frozen out of the market by rent control. The surplus that is destroyed as a result is represented by the triangular green area in Figure 10.17. Notice, too, that in the long run, apartment hunting becomes a grim affair. Again assuming a turnover rate of 2% per month, many searchers will be looking and only nine apartments will be vacant each month.

Although we have learned that in the long run, the supply of rental housing will shrink under rent-control legislation, it is entirely possible that a significant drop in the supply might take place within a much shorter time span. For instance, one obvious response that landlords can and do make to rent control is to convert their rental units to owner-occupied units, which they then sell off to individual buyers. In particular, renters in apartments and townhouses can often be evicted; their vacated apartments can then be converted into condo units and sold within a matter of months. Not surprisingly, in many rent-controlled jurisdictions, it is illegal to convert apartments into condominiums. Indeed, in some places it is illegal to demolish rental accommodation.

Let's briefly summarize what we have learned about the potential effects of rent control in this model. Some tenants will clearly be better off under rent control. In particular, tenants who occupy apartments when rent-control legislation is imposed will benefit. All landlords will be worse off, and some will be induced to convert their land to alternative uses, thereby reducing the supply of apartments. As a consequence of that reduced supply, some renters will be worse off. Under rent control, the ways in which available apartments are allocated both impose costs on searchers — thereby increasing the effective price of rental housing — and produce an allocation that is not Pareto-optimal.

Rent control is just one example of a market impediment. In the following problem, you can explore some implications of another impediment — a **price floor**.

PROBLEM 10.10

Suppose that a government agency tries to support the price of a commodity by offering to buy it at a price higher than its competitive equilibrium price. Identify the surplus destroyed by this policy and the implications for the public purse.

Summary

A market demand function tells us the aggregate quantity of a good demanded by all consumers at any given price, and a market supply function tells us the aggregate quantity supplied by all suppliers at any given price. A competitive equilibrium price — determined by the intersection of market demand and market supply functions — is the price at which the quantity demanded exactly equals the quantity supplied. Although both a price and a quantity are determined in any competitive equilibrium, both are symptomatic of the more fundamental function served by any market: the allocation of goods to individual consumers.

We began the chapter with an elementary exchange-economy model that allowed us to concentrate on the properties of a competitive market allocation and examine two crucial (and problematical) assumptions of the competitive model. The most important property is that the allocation of goods in competitive equilibrium is Pareto-optimal: all the gains from trade are realized in the competitive equilibrium. However, this result requires careful qualification — a task we'll take up in the context of general equilibrium in Chapters 15 and 17.

We used the device of the Walrasian auctioneer to find the competitive equilibrium in this exchange economy. In so doing, we implicitly assumed that all the economic actors behaved as price takers in responding to the prices announced by the auctioneer. This price-taking assumption raised an important conceptual difficulty: In what circumstances will individuals act as price takers rather than price manipulators? We found that individuals act as price takers when there are large numbers of insignificant buyers and sellers. This is the basis of the large-numbers, or price-taking, assumption, which is included in most models of perfect competition.

The presence of the Walrasian auctioneer raises yet another conceptual problem: In the absence of this device, is the competitive model still applicable? We found that it does apply if all buyers and sellers are perfectly informed. This is the basis of the perfect-information assumption, which models of perfect competition also include. These two conditions are really sufficient conditions for the applicability of the competitive model: if a market is characterized by large numbers and by perfect information, then the competitive model applies.

Because the world so rarely conforms to these two conditions, we are naturally led to ask if something less will do. This is the question at the heart of a great deal of recent work in experimental economics. The results to date suggest that less may well do: the competitive model seems to yield fairly good predictions when numbers are small and information quite imperfect.

When we replaced the exchange model with a more complex competitive model incorporating both production and exchange, the supply function became more complicated. We discovered that (with suitable qualifications) a firm's marginal cost function is its short-run supply function. Then, by aggregating short-run supply functions over firms and demand functions over individuals, we were able to identify the short-run competitive equilibrium.

In the long run, the competitive model is driven by exit and entry. Taken together, these two processes imply that in long-run equilibrium, each firm will operate at the minimum point on its long-run average cost function and that price, marginal revenue, long-run average cost, short-run average cost, long-run marginal cost, and short-run marginal cost will be identical.

The long-run competitive equilibrium is determined by the intersection of the long-run supply function and the market demand function. The slope of a long-run supply function depends on the nature of the response of input prices to an industry's demand for those inputs. It may be upward sloping, flat, or downward sloping, depending on whether the industry is characterized by increasing costs, constant costs, or decreasing costs.

Because in any competitive equilibrium with production, the competitive price is equal to the short-run marginal cost of each firm (and in any long-run equilibrium, price is equal to long-run marginal cost), no further gains from trade are possible. No customer is willing to pay what it costs any firm to produce an additional unit of output. This result, which we'll examine in more depth in Chapter 15, is a reflection of the Pareto optimality or efficiency of competitive equilibrium.

We closed the chapter by considering a model of rent control — a common institution that results in a noncompetitive equilibrium. The detailed analysis of this noncompetitive equilibrium allowed us to put the allocative function of competitive prices in perspective. Of course, allocation is not the only function served by prices. They also determine the distribution of income. And rent control is just one of many noncompetitive institutions — including agricultural price supports, quotas, and minimum wages — that are intended to redistribute income or wealth. The appeal of all such institutions lies largely in their redistributionary impact. Yet they all result in an equilibrium that is not Pareto-optimal. The rent-control case thus serves to highlight a troubling issue in economics: the tension that often arises between the objectives of economic efficiency, or Pareto optimality, and distributional equity. In Chapter 16, we'll analyze this problem of efficiency versus equity in more detail.

Exercises

1 Indicate whether each of the following statements is true, false, or uncertain, and explain your answer.
   a In the short run, a competitive firm would never produce where AVC is downward sloping.
   b A competitive firm in long-run equilibrium in an increasing-cost industry will produce at a point where LAC is rising.
   c If LAC is U-shaped, the number of firms in a constant-cost industry will decrease in response to a decrease in demand.

d In the short run, a competitive firm would never produce where SAC is downward sloping and AVC is upward sloping.

e If a competitive firm is currently producing where SAC is upward sloping, then other firms will enter the industry.

f If LAC is U-shaped, the number of firms in an increasing-cost industry will increase in response to an increase in demand.

g A competitive firm in long-run equilibrium in a constant-cost industry will produce at a point where LAC is a minimum.

h In the short run, a competitive firm would never produce where SMC is downward sloping.

i A competitive firm in long-run equilibrium in a decreasing-cost industry will produce at a point where SMC exceeds LMC.

j If a competitive firm is currently producing where SAC is downward sloping, then no other firms will enter the industry.

k In long-run competitive equilibrium, all firms produce at a point where there are constant returns to scale in production.

l If a competitive firm in short-run equilibrium is currently making zero profit, then no other firms will enter the industry.

2 Gismos are produced in a constant-cost industry by firms that have a U-shaped LAC. Minimum average cost is $2 and the efficient scale of production is 50 gismos. The demand for gismos is

$$p = 12 - .001y$$

where p is price and y is quantity of gismos.

a In the long run, what are the equilibrium price and quantity of gismos? How many firms will produce gismos, and how much will each produce in equilibrium? What profit will each firm earn in equilibrium?

b Now suppose the demand for gismos changes to

$$p = 16 - .001y$$

Now what are the equilibrium price and quantity of gismos? How many firms will produce gismos, and how much will each produce in equilibrium?

c Suppose now that the government imposes an excise tax equal to $1 per gismo and that demand is as specified in b. What effect will this tax have on long-run equilibrium price and quantity? What can you say about the short-run effects of this tax, relative to its long-run effects?

d Now suppose that the market for gismos is initially in the long-run equilibrium you described in part a and that demand again shifts as in part b. What could you say about the new long-run equilibrium if the gismo industry was an increasing-cost industry instead of a constant-cost industry?

3 The government of Tasmann is thinking about paying every milk producer a $100,000 annual subsidy. Supposing that milk production is a constant-cost industry in Tasmann and that milk producers have U-shaped average cost curves, what effect will this subsidy have (1) on the long-run equilibrium price and quantity of milk, (2) on the quantity of milk produced by each firm, and (3) on the number of firms producing milk?

4 The government of Xanadu is going to impose one of two taxes on the widgit industry, a perfectly competitive, constant-cost industry, in which firms have U-shaped average cost curves. One tax is a $2 per unit excise tax on widgits, and the other is a $1000 lump-sum tax on each firm in the industry. The Secretary of Commerce has determined that the two taxes will raise the same tax revenue from each firm in the long-run equilibrium associated with each tax.

a Which tax will widgit consumers prefer?

b What effect will the excise tax have on output per firm? What effect will the lump-sum tax have on output per firm?

5 The strawberry industry is perfectly competitive, and the cost function of a typical firm is

$$TC(y) = 100 + y^2$$

where y is crates of berries per day. The corresponding marginal cost function is

$$LMC(y) = 2y$$

What is LAC(y)? What is the efficient scale of production? Hint: LMC intersects LAC at the efficient scale of production. What is the minimum average cost? What is the long-run equilibrium price of strawberries?

6   In Chapter 9, we derived the following cost function for Tipple's Courier Service

$$TC(y, w_1, w_2) = y\left(\frac{w_1 w_2}{300}\right)^{1/2}$$

This cost function is associated with the following constant-returns-to-scale production function,

$$y = (1200z_1 z_2)^{1/2}$$

The associated average and marginal cost functions are

$$LMC(y) = LAC(y) = \left(\frac{w_1 w_2}{300}\right)^{1/2}$$

Given these cost functions, what is the long-run competitive equilibrium price? Claim: The number and sizes of firms in long-run competitive equilibrium are indeterminate even though long-run equilibrium price and quantity are perfectly well defined. Explain. What accounts for these curious results?

7   Firm F's short-run cost function is

$$STC(y) = 30y + y^2 + 400$$

and its short-run marginal cost function is

$$SMC(y) = 30 + 2y$$

a   If $p = \$50$, how much will this firm produce? What will its profit be? Is $p = \$50$ a long-run equilibrium price?
b   What is this firm's short-run supply function? Graph the supply function.
c   Find the price at which this firm would earn zero profit in the short run. Is this price a long-run equilibrium price?

8   Consider an industry in which there are 10 identical firms and 1000 identical demanders. Each demander has the following demand function:

$$y = 1 - .005p$$

Each firm has the following short-run cost function:

$$STC(y) = 10y + y^2$$

The associated marginal cost function is

$$SMC(y) = 10 + 2y$$

a   What is the market demand function?
b   What is one firm's supply function?
c   What is the market supply function?
d   Construct a graph illustrating one firm's supply function, the market supply function, and the market demand function. What are short-run equilibrium price and quantity?
e   Suppose that firms must pay an excise tax equal to $10 per unit of output. Show that a firm's marginal cost function inclusive of the excise tax is

$$SMC(y) = 20 + 2y$$

Given the $10 excise tax, what is the market supply function, and what is the equilibrium price?
f   Compare the price increase associated with the excise tax with the tax itself. Why did price rise by less than the $10 tax?

*9   Governmentally imposed output restrictions of one form or another are notoriously popular with farmers. In Canada, for example, egg producers have lobbied successfully for quotas on egg production. Suppose that egg production is a constant-cost industry initially in long-run competitive equilibrium, that LAC is U-shaped, and that each farmer currently produces 5000 eggs per day. Now suppose that each farmer is given a quota allowing the farmer to produce up to 4000 eggs per day, and the quotas can be bought and sold.
a   What impact will this quota system have on the price of eggs in the short run and in the long run?
b   What impact will it have on the number of eggs produced by a typical firm in the short run and the long run?
c   What impact will it have on the number of firms in the long run?
d   What will be the price of the quota (or the right to produce an egg) in the long run? Hint: You will need to use the tools developed in Section 5.8.
e   Who benefits and who is harmed by this quota system? In particular, do future

egg farmers benefit from this quota system?

f What sort of enforcement problems do you think the quota system might raise?

g Will this quota system be more attractive to established egg farmers when the demand for eggs is inelastic with respect to price or when the demand is elastic with respect to price?

*10 The production of gasoline in the United States is an increasing-cost industry because the price of crude oil increases as gasoline producers demand more of it. Suppose that the supply of crude oil to the United States from the Middle East is cut off. What impact will this have on LRS for gasoline? On the equilibrium price and quantity of gasoline in the U.S. market? In response to this disruption in the supply of crude oil, imagine that an effective ceiling is imposed on the price of gasoline. Write a short essay on the probable impacts of the price ceiling. Address the following questions. How will the available supply of gasoline be allocated? Will the allocation be Pareto-optimal? Will the allocation process

needlessly use real resources? Will a black market for gasoline emerge? Relative to the free-market equilibrium, who will benefit from the price ceiling and who will be hurt by it? What sorts of enforcement issues are likely to arise?

References

Frisch, R. (1936), "On the Notion of Equilibrium and Disequilibrium," *Review of Economic Studies*, **3**:100–105.

Joyce, P. (1984), "The Walrasian Tâtonnement Mechanism and Information," *Rand Journal*, **15**:416–425.

Marshall, A. (1920), *Principles of Economics*, 8th ed., New York: Macmillan.

Samuelson, P. A. (1947), *Foundations of Economic Analysis*, Cambridge, Mass.: Harvard University Press.

Smith, V. (1982), "Markets as Economizers of Information: Experimental Examination of the 'Hayek Hypothesis,'" *Economic Inquiry*, **20**:165–179.

11

MONOPOLY

Now we turn from the competitive market to its extreme opposite: monopoly. Imaginatively, this is a shift from the New York Stock Exchange (a market characterized by many buyers and sellers) to local telephone service (a market served by a single firm). We'll begin by defining monopoly and analyzing how a monopolist chooses price and quantity, and we'll discover that the monopoly equilibrium is not Pareto-optimal. Next we'll identify the sources of monopoly power and consider a number of public policy responses to monopoly. Then we'll look at several kinds of price discrimination — the extremely clever pricing strategies monopolists can and do use. Finally, we'll look in some detail at the issues raised by patent policy.

11.1 Monopoly Defined

A firm is a **monopoly** if no other firm produces either the same good or a close substitute for it. This definition of monopoly is unavoidably ambiguous because we can't define "close substitute" with perfect precision. For example, we might decide to call General Motors (GM) a monopolist in Corvettes because only GM makes Chevrolet Corvettes. But are any (or all) of the sports cars produced by Jaguar, BMW, Mercedes-Benz, or Nissan — the Jaguar XJ6, the BMW 325i, the Mercedes-Benz 300E, or the Nissan Infiniti Q45 — close substitutes for a Corvette? So, too, the Detroit Tigers are the only major-league baseball team in Detroit. But are the Tigers a monopolist in the Detroit market? Or are either (or both) of Detroit's other major-league football or basketball teams — the Lions or the Pistons — close substitutes? Or is a television all-sports network a close substitute? Whether either GM or the Detroit Tigers is technically a monopolist is unclear.

Telephone service is a less ambiguous case. In most communities, only one firm provides local services. We can imagine substitutes for the telephone service — carrier pigeons, smoke signals, or the government mail service — but none of these seems similar enough to phone service to be a close substitute.

How can we be certain that a conceivable substitute is a close substitute? This question has been the central issue in several antitrust cases in the United States. In the famous "cellophane case," for example, Du Pont was charged with monopolizing the production of cellophane. In defense against the charge, Du Pont argued successfully that its market was not the market for cellophane, but the broader market for flexible packaging materials. The defense supported this argument by demonstrating a high **cross-price elasticity of demand** between cellophane and other flexible packaging materials.

One way to systematically distinguish substitutes that are "close enough," then, is to ask whether a change in the price of any substitute substantially changes the demand for the good or service in question. This is simply a cross-price elasticity measure of the demand for one good (cellophane, for example) to a change in the price of another good (waxed paper, for example.)[1] If none of the cross-price elasticities is large, then none of the potential substitutes is close enough. The firm can then be regarded as a monopoly.

Why is this qualification about close substitutes so important? Suppose that two firms produce two distinct products but that these products are close substitutes. For example, the New York City Opera and the Metropolitan Opera Company offer similar kinds of musical entertainment to New Yorkers. How much profit each company makes depends both on its own pricing decision and on its competitor's pricing decision. When the Met thinks about cutting its price, for example, it must also anticipate the New York City Opera's reaction to the price cut. The Met's profit from any price cut depends on whether or not the New York City Opera decides to lower its own price in response. In considering the pricing decisions of firms such as the Met or the New York City Opera, then, the presence of close substitutes necessarily muddies the waters because pricing decisions are *interdependent*. We'll look further at these complex pricing scenarios in the following two chapters on oligopoly. By contrast, a monopolist does not need to concern itself with how other firms will react to its decision. As a result, the theory of monopoly is considerably simpler than the theory of oligopoly.

11.2 The Monopolist's Profit-Maximizing Decisions

For the moment, let's suppose that we have successfully identified a monopolist. How will the monopolist decide what price to charge for its good and how many units to produce? Like the competitive firm's profit, the monopolist's profit is just its total revenue minus its total cost. We'll denote total cost as a function of output y by $TC(y)$ and total revenue as a function of output y by $TR(y)$.

The Profit-Maximizing Problem

The monopolist's profit $\pi(y)$ can then be written as a function of output y as follows:

$$\pi(y) = TR(y) - TC(y)$$

The monopolist's profit-maximizing problem, like the competitive firm's, is then to

maximize profit $\pi(y)$
by choice of output y

As you'll soon see, the monopolist—like the competitive firm—will choose the quantity of output at which *marginal revenue equals marginal cost*.

The Monopolist as Price Setter

Unlike the competitive firm, however, the monopolist is the only game in town. As a result, it not only chooses how many units will be produced and sold in the market, but also sets the market price for its good. Because its demand curve is also the market

---

[1] You may want to review the definition of cross-price elasticity in Section 4.12.

demand curve, price itself is a function of output:

$$p = D(y)$$

We'll quite reasonably suppose that the demand curve $D(y)$ is downward sloping — that is, as price drops, demand rises. Letting y^* represent the monopolist's profit-maximizing quantity, its profit-maximizing price is then given by the demand function; that is, $p^* = D(y^*)$.

11.3 The Monopolist's Revenue Functions

The fundamental difference between the profit-maximizing problem faced by the competitive firm and that faced by the monopolist lies in the difference between their total revenue functions. As we have seen, a competitive firm lacks the power to set market price. Because it is a price taker, its total revenue is just quantity multiplied by a *fixed price*, and as we saw in Chapter 10, its total revenue curve is just a ray through the origin. On the other hand, the monopolist sets the market price. As you will see, its total revenue curve is necessarily more complex.

Total Revenue

Just how is the monopolist's **total revenue** curve — and the associated marginal and average revenue curves — different from the competitive firm's? The monopolist's revenue is just price multiplied by quantity y. Because price as a function of y is $D(y)$, we can write the monopolist's total revenue function $TR(y)$ in the following way:

DEFINITION

$$TR(y) = yD(y)$$

Marginal Revenue

Marginal revenue $MR(y)$ is just the rate at which total revenue changes as y increases:

DEFINITION

$$MR(y) = \text{slope of } TR(y)$$

The contrasts between a competitive firm's and a monopolist's total revenue functions are mirrored in their marginal revenue functions. As you know, for a competitive firm, marginal revenue is equal to price. By contrast, for a monopolist, the following — and very important — statement characterizes the relationship between price and marginal revenue:

When the monopolist's output is positive, its marginal revenue is *less than* its price.

To see what this statement means, consider the illustration in Figure 11.1. Suppose that the monopolist is initially at point A, where it is selling 3 units at price $82. To sell one additional unit — or 4 units in total — it must lower its price from $82 to $76. Is the marginal revenue generated by selling the fourth unit less than the price of $76 at which it is sold? Notice that marginal revenue is (approximately) equal to the change in total revenue, $TR(4) - TR(3)$. Because $TR(4)$ is $304 ($4 \times 76) and $TR(3)$ is $246 ($3 \times 82), marginal revenue is only (approximately) $58. In this illustration, then, marginal revenue is less than price.

More generally, this illustration also lets us see why marginal revenue is less than price. We are assuming that the monopolist sells all units at the same price. For example, if it sells 3 units, all 3 will be sold at a price of $82. If it sells 4 units, all 4 will be sold at the lower price of $76. The marginal revenue of the fourth unit is less than its $76 price because — even though the fourth unit sells at $76 — the other three units *also* sell at $76 rather than at the higher price of $82. Thus, in increasing its production from 3 to 4 units, the monopolist's marginal revenue

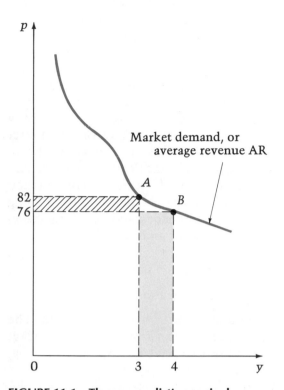

FIGURE 11.1   The monopolist's marginal revenue.

Beginning at point *A*, suppose that the monopolist drops price by just enough to sell one additional unit of output. The change in total revenue, which approximates marginal revenue, is the area of the green rectangle ($76) minus the area of the cross-hatched rectangle ($18).

is not $76. Instead, it is $76 minus an $18 reduction in revenue on the first three units, resulting from the fact that each is sold not at $82 but at $76. This $18 reduction is represented by the crosshatched area in Figure 11.1. In this illustration, then, marginal revenue is not $76, but instead $58 ($76 − $18).

Because to this point we have thought in terms of increasing quantity sold by one unit instead of increasing it by an arbitrarily small or infinitesimal amount, we found only an approximation of marginal revenue. However, this approximation enables us to understand the following precise definition of marginal revenue at a point *(y, p)* on the demand curve.

DEFINITION

$$MR(y) = p + y(\text{slope of the demand curve})$$

In other words, marginal revenue MR is equal to price *p* plus quantity *y* multiplied by the slope of the demand curve.[2]

In this expression, *p* captures the rate at which revenue increases as an infinitesimal additional amount is sold at price *p*. This term is analogous to the added revenue generated in Figure 11.1 when a fourth unit is sold at a price of $76. The rate at which price must be decreased in order to sell an infinitesimal additional amount is given by the slope of the demand curve. Of course, it is negative because the demand curve is downward sloping. Therefore, the second term — *y*(slope of the demand curve) — captures the rate at which revenue on the original *y* units drops as price is decreased to sell an infinitesimal additional amount. This second term is analogous to the reduction in the revenue from the original three units in Figure 11.1 when price is reduced from $82 to $76 to sell a fourth unit.

Average Revenue

Once we see that price can also be interpreted as **average revenue**, we can think about the relationship between price, or

---

[2] Letting $D(y)$ be the demand function, we have

$$TR(y) = yD(y)$$

Marginal revenue is, of course, just the derivative of $TR(y)$. Differentiating $TR(y)$, we have

$$MR(y) = D(y) + yD'(y)$$

which is clearly less than price as long as *y* is positive; that is,

$$D(y) + yD'(y) < D(y)$$

because $D'(y)$ is negative. Notice, too, that the demand and marginal revenue functions must intersect the price axis at the same point since, when *y* is zero, marginal revenue is equal to price.

average revenue, and marginal revenue in a different way. Average revenue AR(y) is just total revenue divided by quantity of output: AR$(y) = $ TR$(y)/y$. Since TR(y) is y multiplied by $D(y)$, we see that the average revenue function is just the market demand function $D(y)$:

DEFINITION

$$\text{AR}(y) = D(y)$$

We'll use the terms market demand function and average revenue function interchangeably in the rest of this chapter.

In Chapter 8, we learned that when the average product curve was downward sloping, marginal product was necessarily less than average product. Adapting this lesson, we see that *because the average revenue (or demand) curve is downward sloping, marginal revenue is less than average revenue (or price)*.

Marginal Revenue and the Price Elasticity of Demand

Economists sometimes find it convenient to express marginal revenue in terms of the **price elasticity of demand**, introduced in Section 4.12. Price elasticity of demand at a point (y, p) on the demand curve can be written as

$$\eta(y) = \frac{-p}{y(\text{slope of the demand curve})}$$

Combining this expression with the earlier expression for marginal revenue yields

$$\text{MR}(y) = p\left[1 - \frac{1}{\eta(y)}\right]$$

Notice that marginal revenue is positive if $\eta(y)$ exceeds 1 — that is, if demand is elastic with respect to price. It is negative if $\eta(y)$ is less than 1 — that is, if demand is inelastic with respect to price.

11.4 Linear Market Demand Function

So far, we have formed the total revenue function, defined marginal and average revenue, and discovered that marginal revenue is less than price, or average revenue, for any positive level of output. To give you a better sense of what these relationships mean, we'll explore in some detail the special (and simpler) case in which the market demand function is a straight line. We'll be using such linear market demand functions at several points in this and subsequent chapters.

The linear market demand function in Figure 11.2a can be written algebraically as

$$p = a - by$$

where a and b are positive constants. The total revenue function for this market demand function is y multiplied by $a - by$, or

$$\text{TR}(y) = ay - by^2$$

This total revenue function is plotted in Figure 11.2b and labeled TR.

Two features of this TR function are immediately apparent. First, when output is zero, total revenue must also be zero. Second, when output is equal to a/b, total revenue must again be zero because the quantity a/b can be sold only at a price equal to zero. Of course, for any quantity of output greater than zero and less than a/b, total revenue will be positive because price exceeds zero for any such quantity. In Figure 11.2b, total revenue increases as y increases until total revenue reaches a maximum at $a/2b$. Thereafter, as y increases, total revenue decreases until it is again zero at a/b.

The next step is to derive the marginal revenue function MR(y) from the total revenue function TR(y). Suppose that beginning at some value of y, output is expanded by a small amount Δy. Total revenue at the new output, $y + \Delta y$, will be

$$\text{TR}(y + \Delta y) = a(y + \Delta y) - b(y + \Delta y)^2$$

(a)

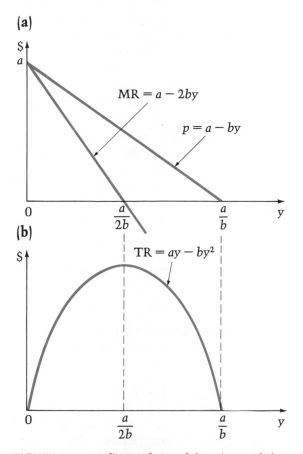

FIGURE 11.2   A linear demand function and the associated total and marginal revenue functions.

The linear demand function $p = a - by$ intersects the price axis in (a) at a and the quantity axis at a/b. The associated marginal revenue function MR is also linear. It, too, intersects the price axis at a, but is twice as steep as the demand function and therefore intersects the quantity axis at $a/2b$. Using the total revenue function TR in (b) and MR, we see that when marginal revenue is positive (negative), total revenue increases (decreases) as more output is sold and that when marginal revenue is zero, total revenue is at a maximum.

Subtracting TR(y) from TR$(y + \Delta y)$, the change in total revenue is then

$$\Delta y(a - 2by - b\Delta y)$$

To express this change in revenue as a *rate of change*, we must divide by Δy, which yields

$$a - 2by - b\Delta y$$

Now, as Δy approaches zero, the last term disappears. The result is the marginal revenue function associated with the linear market demand function:

$$\text{MR}(y) = a - 2by$$

This marginal revenue function is presented in Figure 11.2*a*. It intersects the vertical axis at a, just as the demand function does. But it is twice as steep as the market demand function. The market demand function intersects the quantity axis at a/b. Because the marginal revenue function is twice as steep, it intersects the quantity axis at $a/2b$.

Notice especially the following relationships between TR(y) and MR(y): (1) when the total revenue function is positively sloped, marginal revenue is positive; (2) when total revenue is a maximum, marginal revenue is zero; and (3) when the total revenue function is negatively sloped, marginal revenue is negative. In the following problem, you can establish similar relationships between marginal revenue and the price elasticity of demand.

PROBLEM 11.1

Using what you have just learned about the linear market demand curve and its marginal revenue curve, and the graphic techniques developed in Section 4.12 to measure price elasticity of demand, establish the following relationships: (1) when marginal revenue is positive, demand is elastic with respect to price; (2) when marginal revenue is negative, demand is inelastic with respect to price. You may want to begin by using a specific linear market demand function: $p = 100 - y$, for instance.

11.5   The Profit-Maximizing Rule

Let's turn now to the monopolist's profit-maximizing decision, which closely parallels the competitive firm's decision. Because the principles that guide the monopolist's choice in the short run and in the long run are virtually identical, we'll consider them together. The monopolist's cost function TC(y) can therefore be interpreted as either the long-run cost function or the short-run variable cost function. (We'll see below why we use the variable cost function in the short run.)

Figure 11.3a presents a monopolist's total revenue function, labeled TR, and its cost function, labeled TC. Where TC lies above TR at output levels less than 29 and greater than 95, profit is negative. Where

TC lies below TR at output levels between 29 and 95, however, profit is positive.

We have derived the corresponding profit function, labeled π, in Figure 11.3b by everywhere subtracting cost TC from revenue TR in Figure 11.3a. The profit-maximizing level of output, y*, is 71 units, where the slope of the profit function, or the rate of change of profit with respect to output, is zero. But the rate of change of profit with respect to output is simply the rate of change of revenue with respect to output (marginal revenue) minus the rate of change of cost with respect to output (marginal cost). Thus, the profit-maximizing level of output for the monopolist is one at which marginal revenue is equal to marginal cost:

At the profit-maximizing level of output y*, marginal revenue is equal to marginal cost.

Yet there is one difficulty with this profit-maximizing rule. The profit function in Figure 11.3 has a zero slope at two output levels, 11 and 71; marginal revenue is therefore equal to marginal cost at both points. Yet profit is clearly at a minimum rather than a maximum at 11 units.

We can both resolve this difficulty and better understand the economic sense underlying the monopolist's profit-maximizing decision by turning to Figure 11.4, where the average cost function AC and the marginal cost function MC associated with the cost function TC from Figure 11.3a have been plotted. In addition, the marginal revenue function MR and the market demand or average revenue function AR, associated with the total revenue function TR from Figure 11.3a, have also been plotted in Figure 11.4. We will focus on the four levels of output — 11, 29, 71, and 95 — that appear in both figures.

First, notice that in both figures, profit is equal to zero at two output levels — 29

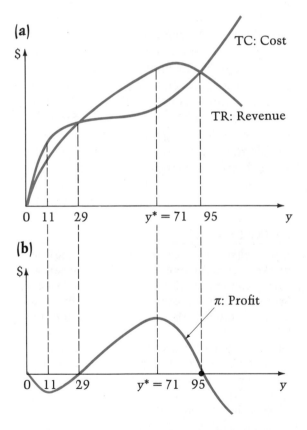

FIGURE 11.3   The monopolist's profit function.

In (a), we have constructed the monopolist's total revenue and cost functions, TR and TC. By subtracting TC from TR, we have generated the monopolist's profit function, π, in (b). Profit is maximized at y* = 71, where the slope of π is zero.

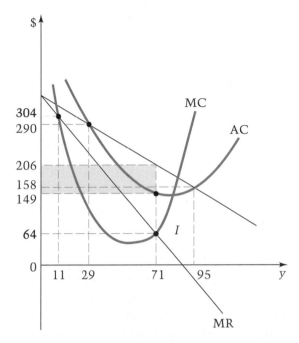

FIGURE 11.4   Maximizing the monopolist's profit.
To maximize profit, find the point where MC intersects MR from below, point *H* in the figure. To find the profit-maximizing output $y^* = 71$, drop vertically down to the quantity axis. To find the profit-maximizing price $p^* = \$206$, move vertically up from *H* to the demand curve and then horizontally over to the price axis. The monopolist's profit is the light green area.

and 95. In Figure 11.4, zero profit occurs where average revenue AR, or price, is equal to average cost AC:

$$AR = AC = \$290 \qquad \text{when } y = 29$$

and

$$AR = AC = \$158 \qquad \text{when } y = 95$$

Of course, profit is positive in the range of output between 29 and 95 because average revenue exceeds average cost. Conversely, it is negative at output levels less than 29 and greater than 95 because average cost exceeds average revenue.

Notice, too, that marginal revenue is equal to marginal cost at two levels of output — 11 and 71.

$$MR = MC = \$304 \qquad \text{when } y = 11$$

and

$$MR = MC = \$64 \qquad \text{when } y = 71$$

From Figure 11.3, we know that profit is a minimum at 11 and a maximum at $y^* = 71$. (From Figure 11.4, we see that the profit-maximizing price is $206.) To understand why profit is a maximum at one of these points in Figure 11.4 and a minimum at the other, we need to look more closely at the relationship between the marginal revenue and marginal cost functions.

Using only the information in Figure 11.4, how do we know that profit is a maximum at $y^* = 71$? First, let's suppose that the monopolist is initially producing $y^* = 71$ and ask: What will happen to its profit if it produces one more unit of output? The addition to its revenue is given by MR and the addition to its cost by MC. Because MC exceeds MR to the right of $y^* = 71$, the increase in its cost exceeds the increase in its revenue, and profit therefore falls as the monopolist produces one more unit. Now, beginning again at $y^* = 71$, let's ask: What will happen to its profit if the monopolist produces one less unit? The reduction in its revenue is given by MR and the reduction in its cost by MC. Because MR exceeds MC to the left of $y^* = 71$, the reduction in revenue exceeds the reduction in cost, and profit therefore falls as the monopolist produces one less unit. Since profit falls as the monopolist produces either more than or less than $y^* = 71$, profit is a maximum at $y^* = 71$.

We seem to have simply reestablished what we already knew — that profit is a maximum at $y^* = 71$. Yet we can use the analysis of Figure 11.4 to state the general conditions for identifying a point of maximum profit in any figure of this type. The first condition is, of course, that marginal revenue equals marginal cost at the profit-maximizing output y^*. The second condition is that marginal cost MC exceeds marginal revenue MR to the right of y^*, which guarantees that profit falls as the monopolist produces more than y^*. The third condition is that marginal revenue MR exceeds marginal cost MC to the left of y^*, which guarantees that profit falls as the monopolist produces less than y^*. We can telescope these three conditions into one: *profit is a maximum at the point where MC intersects MR from below.*

In the following problem, you can use the same kind of reasoning to show that profit is at a minimum when marginal cost intersects marginal revenue from above, as it does at 11 units of output in Figure 11.4.

PROBLEM 11.2

Show that profit is at a minimum when MR = MC and MC intersects MR from above.

One last detail requires attention. If the average cost function AC lies above the average revenue function AR, there is no positive output level at which the monopolist can cover its costs; therefore, it will shut down production. Because the monopolist's profit is *zero* if it produces nothing but is *negative* if it produces some output, it will produce nothing. This line of reasoning is obviously true if AC is the long-run average cost function, and it is also true in the short-run — if AC is the short-run average variable cost function. It is for this reason that we defined TC(y) at the outset of this section as *either* the long-run cost function *or* the short-run variable cost function. For simplicity, we will ignore this detail in most of what follows and focus instead on cases in which the monopolist does produce a positive amount of output.

Now let's carefully write down the monopolist's profit maximizing rule.[3]

To maximize profit, the monopolist will produce the output level y^* that meets the following conditions:

1 **MR is equal to MC at y^*.**

2 **For output levels larger than y^*, MC exceeds MR.**

3 **For output levels smaller than y^*, MR exceeds MC.**

Taking a more mechanical approach, we can easily see how to find the profit-maximizing solution in any situation like the case in Figure 11.4. First, find the point where MC intersects MR from below. To identify the profit-maximizing level of output, move vertically downward from the point of intersection to the horizontal axis. To identify the profit-maximizing price p^*, move vertically upward through the point of intersection to the average revenue AR curve and then horizontally over to the price axis. To identify the monopolist's profit (the light green area in Figure 11.4), construct the profit rectangle with one side equal to y^* and the other equal to $p^* - $ AC.

Finally, it's helpful to notice that the output level chosen by the monopolist is in the portion of the demand curve where de-

---

[3] All this can be said more simply using a little calculus. We know (1) that $\pi'(y^*) = 0$ is necessary for $y^* > 0$ to be a profit-maximizing level of y and (2) that $\pi'(y)$ attains a (local) maximum at y^* if, in addition, $\pi''(y^*) < 0$. By definition,

$$\pi(y) = TR(y) - TC(y)$$

Differentiating with respect to y and setting the result equal to zero, we obtain the following first-order condition for profit maximization:

$$MR(y^*) = MC(y^*)$$

The second-order condition, $\pi''(y^*) < 0$, is just

$$MR'(y^*) < MC'(y^*)$$

That is, the slope of the marginal revenue function is less than the slope of the marginal cost function at the profit-maximizing quantity.

mand is elastic with respect to price. As you showed in Problem 11.1, where demand is inelastic, marginal revenue is negative; however, marginal cost is positive—or at least not negative. It is therefore impossible for marginal revenue to equal marginal cost at an output level where demand is inelastic with respect to price. Thus, a profit-maximizing monopolist will choose to produce at an output level in the range where demand is elastic.

In the following problems, you will have the opportunity to practice finding the graphic solution to the monopolist's profit-maximizing problem and to review the crucial relationship between the MR and MC curves in determining the profit-maximizing output.

PROBLEM 11.3

Suppose that the average revenue function is

$$p = 10 - y$$

and that the cost function is

$$TC(y) = 4y$$

On one diagram, carefully construct the average revenue, marginal revenue, average cost, and marginal cost functions. Then show that y^* is 3 and p^* is 7. Construct the profit rectangle and show that profit is equal to 9.

PROBLEM 11.4

First, draw a linear AR curve, like the one in Problem 11.3, and the associated MR curve. Then draw a U-shaped MC curve that is tangent to the MR curve at one point and lies above it at all other levels of output. Beginning at the point where MR = MC, what happens to profit as the monopolist produces one more unit? One less unit? What is the profit-maximizing level of output?

11.6 The Inefficiency of Monopoly

Because in a competitive equilibrium each competitor's marginal cost is equal to equilibrium price, no firm can sell an additional unit of a good at a price that covers its additional cost of production. In other words, all the potential gains from trade are fully realized in competitive equilibrium. By contrast, all the gains from trade will not be fully realized in the monopoly equilibrium. Notice first that

In the monopoly equilibrium, marginal cost —which is equal to marginal revenue—is less than price because the marginal revenue function lies below the average revenue function.

Therefore, beginning at the profit-maximizing output, an additional unit could possibly be sold at a price that covers its marginal cost. (We will see soon why a monopolist may not be able to take advantage of this opportunity.) Therefore, the gains from trade are not fully exploited in monopoly equilibrium. For example, the profit-maximizing output in Figure 11.5 is $y^* = 6$, and the profit-maximizing price is $p^* = \$50$, which is greater than $MC^* = \$25$. Therefore, some potential gains from trade are not realized—and this is the fundamental difference between competitive and monopolistic markets.

The following thought experiment is designed to help you understand what it means to say that some potential gains from trade go unrealized in the monopoly solution. Let's begin by reinterpreting the average revenue, or market demand, function as the aggregation of individual reservation prices for one unit of the monopolist's good Y. (You encountered this type of demand curve in the discussion of the exchange model in Section 10.1. Although such a demand curve is actually a series of descending vertical segments rather than a smooth line, if the number of individual demanders is large enough, their aggregated demand function can be approximated by a smooth market demand function.) Imagine that a

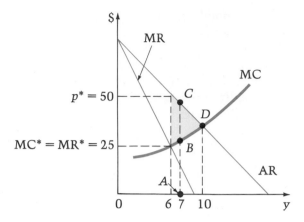

FIGURE 11.5 The inefficiency of monopoly.

Suppose the monopolist initially sells $y^* = 6$ at the profit-maximizing price $p^* = \$50$ and then decides to sell one more unit at a price greater than distance AB and less than distance AC. The buyer, who is willing to pay AC, and the monopolist, whose marginal cost is AB, are both better off, and none of the original buyers is worse off. Therefore, the monopoly equilibrium — selling $y^* = 6$ at price $p^* = 50$ — is not Pareto-optimal. The light green area — the potential surplus that is unrealized in the monopoly equilibrium — is a cost-benefit measure of the burden of monopoly.

monopolist first announces a "take it or leave it" price of $p^* = \$50$ and that all potential buyers take the monopolist's announcement at face value. The result is just the standard monopoly equilibrium in Figure 11.5: $y^* = 6$ units will be sold at price $p^* = \$50$. The monopolist then considers making and selling one additional unit. If it sells that unit at any price greater than distance AB but less than distance AC, both the monopolist and the purchaser of that additional unit will be better off — and no purchaser who bought the good at price p^* will be worse off. Therefore, we have discovered that *beginning at the monopoly equilibrium, the sale of the additional unit is Pareto-improving.* Or, to rephrase the result slightly, the gains from trade are not fully realized in the monopoly equilibrium.

Measuring the Burden of Monopoly

We can use the concept of **total surplus** to measure the potential gains from trade that are not realized at the monopoly equilibrium, or **the burden of monopoly.** In so doing, we're assuming that the demand function for good Y is independent of consumers' incomes. If we pursue this thought experiment to its logical conclusion by imagining that the monopolist continues to sell additional output one unit at a time — at a price greater than or equal to its marginal cost and less than or equal to the corresponding reservation price on the demand function — we see from Figure 11.5 that 10 units will eventually be sold. Relative to the monopoly equilibrium, the additional surplus realized is indicated by the light green area in Figure 11.5. This is a measure of the *burden of monopoly* — that is, the potential surplus that is unrealized at the monopoly equilibrium. Because these gains are not fully realized, monopoly is said to represent a **market failure.**

The Efficiency Criterion

This thought experiment also reveals that the gains from trade in Figure 11.5 do become fully realized when 10 units are produced and sold. More generally, it reveals the efficiency criterion for a market that is monopolized and, indeed, for markets in general:

Efficiency requires that the good be produced up to the point where price p is equal to marginal cost MC.

Inefficiency and Unrealized Profit

One final, important message comes out of this thought experiment:

The unrealized gains from trade in the monopoly equilibrium signal unrealized monopoly profit.

In other words, at the monopoly equilibrium, the monopolist has failed to extract the maximum profit possible. Indeed, the monopolist's strategy in this thought experiment of first announcing a "take it or leave it" price and later announcing a price reduction is a wily attempt to extract a profit greater than the one it makes in the monopoly equilibrium. In a market characterized by repeated sales over many periods, however, this strategy will not work. What eventually occurs is a slightly altered version of the story of the boy who cried wolf. Buyers with the higher reservation prices soon catch on to the monopolist's stratagem and withhold their demand at the original price in anticipation of being able to buy the good at a lower price in the future. Even though this particular pricing strategy cannot succeed for long, we should nevertheless recognize that a monopolist has a clear incentive to devise strategies that are more profitable and more complex than the simple MR equals MC strategy.

We'll look at such strategies in Section 11.5, under the general rubric of *price discrimination*. In the meantime, the following problem will help you to review the important points arising out of our thought experiment. Because we'll be returning to this problem at crucial places later in the chapter, it deserves your careful attention.

PROBLEM 11.5

Suppose that some book vendor can produce a book at a constant marginal cost of $8 and that 11 potential buyers have the following reservation prices: $55, $50, $45, . . ., $10, $5. Each will buy the book at any price less than or equal to his or her reservation price.

1 If the book vendor must announce a "take it or leave it" price, what price maximizes profit? What quantity will be sold, and what are the book vendor's profits? Are there unrealized gains from trade? Hint: The only prices you need to consider are the 11 reservation prices,

and you can calculate profit for each of these reservation prices.

2 Now suppose that the book vendor knows what each potential buyer's reservation price actually is and that those buyers are completely isolated from each other. The vendor can then set an individual price for each buyer. How many books will it sell? At what price will it sell each book? What are its profits? Show that this solution is Pareto-optimal, or efficient.

11.7 Sources of Monopoly

By now, you know what a monopoly is, how the profit-maximizing monopolist chooses price and quantity, and in what sense the monopoly equilibrium represents a market failure. But what forces bring a monopoly into being in the first place? And what are the possible policy responses to the market failure associated with monopoly? We'll look at each question in turn.

Although the sources of monopoly power are many and varied, we can classify monopolies under five categories: the franchise monopoly; the resource-based monopoly; the patent monopoly; the technological, or natural, monopoly; and what we might call the monopoly by good management.

Government Franchise Monopoly

One historic and contemporary source of monopoly power is the franchise. A **franchise monopoly** arises when a government grants the exclusive right to do business in a specified market to some individual or firm. A historic example is King George III's granting of the exclusive rights to the North American fur trade to the Hudson's Bay Company. A contemporary example is the granting of exclusive rights to broadcast at specified frequencies to radio and television stations. Broadcast franchises sometimes give rise to monopoly and more frequently to oligopoly.

Patent Monopoly

Another form of monopoly arising from governmental action in many countries is the **patent monopoly,** secured by either patent or copyright. In the United States, for example, authors and inventors are granted "the exclusive right to their respective writings and discoveries" under the U.S. Constitution. Patents in the United States are granted in most cases for a period of 17 years. Patent monopoly is a pervasive phenomenon in the prescription drug trade and has played a central role in a wide range of other industries as well, including the photocopying, computer, and telecommunications industries. Even the shoe industry was at one time significantly affected by patent monopoly.

Resource-Based Monopoly

Another source of monopoly power is the exclusive ownership of a natural resource essential in a particular production process. For example, owning one of the various hot springs scattered throughout Europe and North America conveys monopoly power to its owners in the local or regional markets for water spas. The Aluminum Company of America offered a more powerful example of a **resource-based monopoly** prior to the end of World War II. Alcoa was a virtual monopolist in primary aluminum production from its inception in the late nineteenth century until 1945; its monopoly position arose in part from its control of virtually all domestic sources of bauxite ore.

Technological (or Natural) Monopoly

In Section 9.8, we discussed market structure and argued that if the efficient scale of production in a given industry is large enough, we expect to see only one firm in the market. The source of monopolistic power in this case is technological, the by-product of significant economies of scale. A firm in this category is therefore called a technological, or **natural monopoly.** Because these firms experience declining average cost over a significant range of output, rival firms are unable to produce at these low costs and will fail.

Public utilities such as natural gas, electricity, and telephone services are classic illustrations of technological, or natural, monopolies. In all three cases, the economies of scale are driven by the distribution networks needed to deliver the good or the service to the point of use. We find other, less conspicuous natural monopolies in the many small towns of rural North America that have only one movie theater. Although the economies of scale in absolute terms are not large in this industry, they are nevertheless large relative to the demand generated by a population of 5000 or fewer. The local Odeon theater is to such a town what the Tigers baseball club is to Detroit.

Let's be more precise about what we mean by the term *natural monopoly.* We'll say that a firm is a natural monopolist if no other firm will enter the market when the monopolist produces the standard profit-maximizing output.[4] To use this definition, we need a theory of entry, since a firm is a natural monopolist only if no other firm will enter its market when it pursues the profit-maximizing strategy outlined in the previous section. We'll use a very simple theory of entry driven by one assumption — often called the **Sylos postulate,** after the Italian economist Paulo Sylos-Labini:

ASSUMPTION

In deciding whether to enter a market, a potential entrant takes the output of existing firms as given.

---

[4] The term *natural monopoly* is sometimes used in another way by economists. If LAC is everywhere downward sloping, then to minimize the total cost of industry output, all the output should be produced by just one firm. Hence, industries in which LAC is everywhere downward sloping are sometimes called natural monopolies.

Figure 11.6a presents the standard production and pricing decisions of a monopolist. It chooses to produce $y^* = 410$ and to sell each unit of output at a price of $p^* = \$48$. First, we will examine the case in which the firm presented in Figure 11.6a is a natural monopolist. Assuming that the potential entrant regards the monopolist's current output $y^* = 410$ as fixed, it will consult its own **residual demand function** in Figure

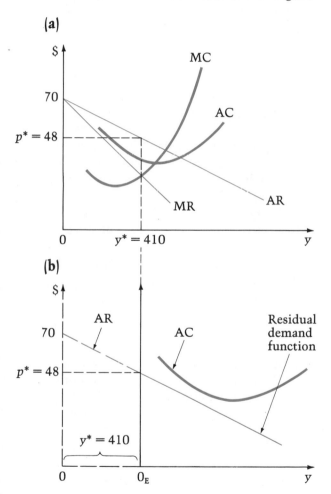

(a)

(b)

FIGURE 11.6   Natural monopoly.

In (a), the monopoly equilibrium is price $p^* = 48$ and quantity $y^* = 410$. If an entrant took the monopolists output $y^* = 410$ as fixed, it would perceive the residual demand function in (b). Since AC lies above the residual demand function, there is no quantity at which the entrant could make a profit, and the case is therefore one of natural monopoly.

11.6b to see if it can expect to cover its costs if it does enter. The demand function faced by the potential entrant is called residual because it represents that portion of the market demand that remains unsupplied by the monopolist. Thus, the origin of the residual demand function in Figure 11.6b, labeled 0_E, corresponds to the output level $y^* = 410$ in Figure 11.6a. The entrant's residual demand function intersects the entrant's price axis at $p^* = \$48$, which means that price will be no higher than $48 even if the entrant produces nothing. The entrant's average cost curve AC is also presented in Figure 11.6b and is plotted relative to the entrant's origin 0_E.

In general, whether the potential entrant can find a level of output that allows it to cover its cost will depend on the relationship between its average cost function and the residual demand function. Because AC lies everywhere above the residual demand function in the case illustrated in Figure 11.6b, the potential entrant will recognize that it cannot cover its production costs at any level of output, and it will decide against entry. The firm presented in Figure 11.6a is therefore a natural monopoly. In the following problem, you can construct the case in which there is no natural monopoly in the industry because the potential entrant does see a chance of becoming a viable competitor.

PROBLEM 11.6

In Figure 11.6a, the average revenue function intersects the price axis at $70. Construct a diagram identical to Figure 11.6a in all respects except one. Shift the average and marginal revenue functions up by $30. Then show that there is no natural monopoly in this case.

Monopoly by Good Management

Suppose that a monopolist finds itself in the position you considered in Problem 11.6. If it chooses price and quantity in the ordinary way, a second firm will enter — and the first firm therefore will *not* be a natural monopolist. Some obvious and intriguing questions beg to be answered in this case.

First, is there anything the monopolist could do to deter entry of a second firm? If so, would the monopolist find it profitable to deter entry? These are really oligopoly rather than monopoly questions because they involve the interaction between two firms: the established monopolist and a potential entrant. Although we won't consider them until the next chapter, we can preview the results by noting that in certain circumstances, the answer to both questions is yes. In these circumstances, there will be just one firm in the market, but that firm will not be a natural monopolist. Rather, this is a case of **monopoly by good management:** the firm is a monopolist because it manages its affairs with an eye to deterring entry.

In these circumstances, the monopolist will not simply produce the output where marginal revenue is equal to marginal cost. It will instead take a larger view of the profit-maximizing problem, by essentially redefining it as the problem of maximizing profit subject to the constraint that there be no entry. Ordinarily, to deter entry, the solution is to produce an output larger than the standard monopoly output. It is important to realize that this behavior can result in significantly less unrealized surplus than occurs in the ordinary monopoly equilibrium. That is, this behavior can dramatically reduce the burden of monopoly. Monopoly by good management is thus quite a different phenomenon from natural monopoly.

---

*11.8 Regulatory Responses to Monopoly

From whatever sources monopoly power may spring, its very existence poses two closely related problems that seem to demand some kind of governmental regulatory response. The first problem is that the potential gains from trade are not fully realized, because price exceeds marginal cost. The problem for governments is that in monopolized industries, the goods or services are underproduced. Governments then face an *efficiency dilemma:* Should they step in and attempt to induce greater production?

The second problem stems from the fact that price ordinarily exceeds average cost at the monopoly solution. As a result, monopolists may be able to make a supranormal profit — one above the normal or "fair" return on capital investment included among the costs in the cost function. Governments then face a *distributional dilemma.* Who should be the ultimate recipients of the supranormal profit — the owners of the monopoly or someone else? To complicate matters, the current owners of a monopoly may not be earning a supranormal profit. Suppose that the present owners bought the monopoly from its original owners. The selling price of such a firm will have included a "goodwill" element, which is, in effect, the discounted present value at the time of sale of all future monopoly profits. In this case, the current owners will be earning only a normal return on their investment. In this section, we'll largely ignore the distributional questions raised by monopoly and concentrate on the efficiency issue.

The particular governmental responses that will be effective depend on the source of the monopoly power. In resource-based monopolies, regulatory measures that promote competition as an alternative to monopoly are sometimes possible. In the other monopolies, however, competition is not a feasible alternative, and governments must look elsewhere for remedial measures.

Divestiture in a Resource-Based Monopoly

From an economic standpoint, regulating resource-based monopolies is a relatively easy task because eliminating monopoly power is both feasible and sensible. If exclusive ownership of a resource is the only source of monopoly power, a regulatory body can simply force the monopolist to sell off, or divest itself of, some portion of the essential resource. Such divestiture then makes competition a feasible market alternative to monopoly.

Responses to Patent Monopoly

Governments could apply a similar regulatory remedy to patent monopolies and simply wipe the right to patent inventions off the books; the monopoly power that patents convey would then be disposed of neatly. Yet patents serve a potentially useful economic purpose by stimulating the invention and development of new products and processes. From this perspective, eliminating patenting rights might not be sensible, because the economic benefit to customers of patented products might well outweigh the economic cost of monopolistically exploited innovations. As these observations suggest, patent policy is not a simple matter. Because the issues raised by patent policy are interesting, important, and illustrative of issues encountered in other policy settings, we'll devote the last section of this chapter to a detailed consideration of patent policy.

Responses to Natural Monopoly

Patent monopoly poses one set of issues for regulatory agencies. Natural monopoly presents quite a different set. Because a natural monopoly arises in response to a technological phenomenon—an efficient scale of production that is large relative to market demand—the industry simply cannot support a large number of competing firms:

Competition is not a feasible alternative to natural monopoly.

Governments have recognized that some industries—local telephone services, electricity, and other public utilities, for instance—are natural monopolies. They typically permit such industries to be monopolized but attempt to limit the monopolist to a "fair" rate of return on its investment. Fixing a precise dollar value on a "fair" rate of return is a serious accounting problem, and debate on this question periodically flares up between public utilities and regulatory agencies. Nevertheless, a "fair" rate of return is easy enough to define theoretically as a zero profit. Remember that a normal rate of return on investment forms a part of the costs included in the cost functions. We'll look at two regulatory mechanisms aimed at achieving a fair rate of return—average cost pricing and rate-of-return regulation. And we'll discover why each fails to achieve efficiency. We will close this discussion of the regulation of natural monopoly by considering an efficient mechanism.

Average Cost Pricing

In keeping with their objective of limiting monopolies to a fair, or normal, rate of return, regulatory agencies sometimes attempt to implement an **average-cost-pricing policy.** One major problem with this policy is that even though average cost pricing (if successful) does eliminate monopoly profit, it does not induce the monopolist to produce the efficient level of output. Figure 11.7a presents one such average-cost-pricing regulatory solution. In this case, the monopoly will, in effect, be ordered to produce 47 units of output and to set price equal to its average cost of $20. Yet, like the monopoly solution it is intended to replace, the regulatory solution at point A is inefficient. At point A, marginal cost of $30 exceeds price of $20. From the perspective of efficiency, the monopolist produces too much.

(a)

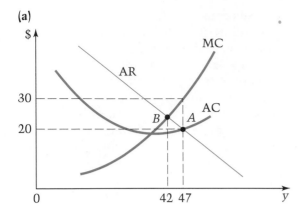

(b)

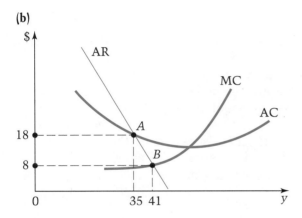

FIGURE 11.7   Average cost pricing.

In both (a) and (b), the monopolist is forced to operate where it makes no profit — where AC is equal to price. In (a), the resulting output $y = 47$ is larger than the output $y = 42$ where price is equal to MC, and average cost pricing induces the monopolist to produce too much output. In (b), the resulting output $y = 35$ is less than the output $y = 41$ where price is equal to MC, and average cost pricing induces the monopolist to produce too little output.

In this case, the efficient solution is instead at point B, where price equals marginal cost. In the case presented in Figure 11.7a, then, an average-cost-pricing regulatory scheme induces the monopolist to produce too much output.

Figure 11.7b presents another possibility. Although the regulatory solution is at point A, where price equals average cost, the efficient solution is instead at point B, where price equals marginal cost. In this case, the regulatory solution induces the monopolist to produce too little output relative to the efficient solution.

Average cost pricing not only fails to induce the monopolist to produce the efficient level of output, but also fails to provide the monopolist with an incentive to minimize its costs of production. This is an even more serious drawback. If the regulatory authority allows the monopoly to recover all its costs but never permits it to make a profit, why should the firm worry about keeping its costs as low as possible? The monopolist lacks any incentive to minimize its costs.

Rate-of-Return Regulation

Closely related to average cost pricing is the predominant form of regulation in the United States, **rate-of-return regulation**, which is aimed at limiting the rate of return a regulated natural monopoly can earn on its invested capital. Unfortunately, under this type of regulation, a natural monopolist will again fail to minimize its costs of production — in this instance, by choosing to use too much capital relative to the cost-minimizing input bundle. (See Averch and Johnson, 1961, on this point.) To understand why this distortion arises, let's consider a natural monopolist that is using just two inputs: capital owned by the firm, input 2, and some other input hired by the firm (say, labor), input 1. The monopolist's return on its capital is then its total revenue $TR(y)$ minus its expenditure on input 1, $w_1 z_1$:

$$\text{Return on capital} = TR(y) - w_1 z_1$$

Rate-of-return regulation, then, imposes the following constraint on the firm's behavior: it must choose output y and an input bundle (z_1, z_2) such that

$$TR(y) - w_1 z_1 \leq r z_2$$

where r is the allowed rate of return on capital and z_2 is the quantity of capital. Averch and Johnson argue that the sensible regulatory agency will choose an allowed rate of return r greater than the price of capital w_2, because if r is less than w_2, the monopolist will be forced out of business. And if r is equal to w_2, the monopolist will have no incentive to minimize its costs, just as it had no incentive to minimize costs in the case of average cost pricing. Therefore, we will assume that the allowed rate of return r is greater than the price of capital w_2.

Why will the monopolist use too much capital? We can develop an intuitive understanding by starting with an entirely imaginary form of regulation analogous to rate-of-return regulation. If the monopolist is told that its profit cannot exceed $1 per pound of jelly beans held in the firm's vault, then the firm will fill a huge vault with useless jelly beans because the amount of profit it can earn is constrained by the weight of the jelly beans in its vault. Under rate-of-return regulation, it is the quantity of capital instead of pounds of jelly beans that constrains the firm's ability to earn profit. We can see why by subtracting $w_2 z_2$ from both sides of the rate-of-return constraint:

$$TR(y) - w_1 z_1 - w_2 z_2 \leq (r - w_2) z_2$$

The expression on the left is just the firm's profit, and the entire inequality then means that the profit the firm is allowed to earn is constrained by the quantity of capital it has. As a result, rate-of-return regulation induces the regulated firm to use *too much capital* and *too little labor.*

Let us be more precise about the distortionary effect of rate-of-return regulation on the monopolist's choice of an input bundle. Suppose that the quantity of output produced by the monopolist, the prices of the two inputs, and the allowed rate of return on capital are all fixed. Specifically, suppose that output is 100, that the prices w_1 and w_2 are both $5, and that r is $8. We'll show that if the rate-of-return regulation is effective, the monopolist will produce 100 units of output using an input bundle that has too much capital and too little labor relative to the cost-minimizing input bundle.

Because output is fixed, price and therefore total revenue are also fixed. Again for convenience, suppose that price is $1.85 when the firm sells 100 units. Its total revenue is then $185. Since output and revenue are fixed, the monopolist's profit-maximizing problem is now reduced to choosing an input bundle that minimizes the cost of producing the fixed level of output, subject to the regulatory constraint:

minimize $5z_1 + 5z_2$ by choice of z_1 and z_2

subject to the constraint $100 = F(z_1, z_2)$

subject to the constraint $185 - 5z_1 \leq 8z_2$

The first constraint, $100 = F(z_1, z_2)$, is the standard constraint in all cost-minimization problems. The second constraint is the regulatory constraint. The monopolist then faces the standard cost-minimization problem from Section 9.3 — with the additional twist of a regulatory constraint.

If the allowed rate of return is large enough, the regulatory constraint is ineffective, and the solution to the problem is the standard cost-minimizing input bundle for 100 units of output. This case is uninteresting because rate-of-return regulation then has no effect; it fails to alter the monopolist's behavior.

The interesting case occurs when the regulatory constraint is effective, or binding. In Figure 11.8, the standard cost-minimizing input bundle is (10, 10) at point E, where the 100-unit isoquant is tangent to the dashed $100 isocost line. If the firm were to choose this input bundle, its profit would then be $85 ($185 − $100). The rub is that this input bundle fails to satisfy the regulatory constraint because 135 — i.e., $185 - (5 \times 10)$ — is greater than 80 (8×10). To satisfy the rate-of-return constraint,

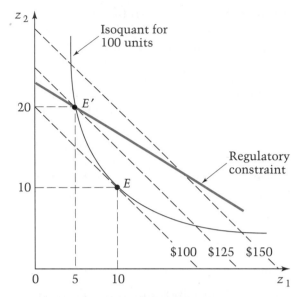

FIGURE 11.8   Rate-of-return regulation.

The rate-of-return-regulated monopolist will, we assume, produce 100 units of output, and its revenue is therefore fixed. Since revenue is fixed, to maximize its profit, it will minimize its cost, subject to two constraints: that it be on the isoquant for 100 units and that it be on or above the regulatory constraint. In the solution to this problem, the regulated monopolist uses the bundle at E', which costs \$125. In the absence of regulation, the monopolist would use the bundle at E, which costs only \$100.

the monopolist will instead choose an input bundle on or above the green regulatory constraint. As Figure 11.8 reveals, the cheapest input bundle on the 100-unit isoquant that satisfies that constraint is (5, 20) at E'. It is this input bundle that the monopolist will choose. Since this bundle is on the \$125 isocost line, the monopolist's profit under rate-of-return regulation is \$60 instead of \$85, and its costs are \$125 instead of \$100. More generally:

The rate-of-return regulated firm chooses an input bundle that is not cost minimizing, and it uses too much capital and too little labor relative to the cost-minimizing bundle.

Why is it a matter of social concern that the monopolist chooses an input bundle that is not cost minimizing? Suppose that demand for the monopolist's good is independent of income. Suppose, too, that the prices of the inputs are independent of the monopolist's demand for them. That is, regardless of how much or little the monopolist buys, the prices for the two inputs are always \$5. In this case, point E is clearly Pareto-preferred to point E'. The monopolist's customers are indifferent between the two points because they buy 100 units at \$1.85 per unit in either case. The owners of the inputs are also indifferent because they sell their inputs for \$5 in either case. But the monopolist is better off at point E because its profit is larger by \$25. Thus, rate-of-return regulation creates a social problem because it induces an inefficient equilibrium.

Efficient Regulatory Mechanisms

Given the difficulties with traditional regulatory policies, can we imagine any other regulatory schemes that might work better? The answer depends on how much information a regulating agency has at hand. For example, if it knows the relevant cost and demand functions in Figure 11.7a, it can simply order the monopolist to produce the efficient level of output at point B. If the relevant cost and demand functions are instead those in Figure 11.7b, the regulatory agency can also order the monopolist to produce the efficient level of output at point B. However, in this case, the monopolist will incur a loss because price is less than average cost at point B — and the agency must therefore provide a subsidy equivalent to the monopolist's loss.

Yet regulatory agencies are not likely to be so well informed about the relevant cost and demand functions. In particular, collecting all the necessary detail about a monopolist's costs of production might well be far too expensive an undertaking. Nevertheless, if a regulatory agency knows only the market demand function and nothing more, it can apply one regulatory mechanism (formulated by Loeb and Magat, 1979) that will induce a monopolist both to minimize costs and to produce the efficient level of output.

You actually discovered the crucial insight in Problem 11.5, where you found that if a monopolist can pick a unique price for each demander, it will choose a price equal to each demander's reservation price—as long as that reservation price exceeds the monopolist's marginal cost of production. To see how this insight can be translated into an efficient regulatory mechanism, let's return to the reservation-price demand function with n demanders and array the reservation prices of demanders from highest to lowest:

$$R_1 > R_2 > \cdots > R_n$$

Suppose that the regulatory authority —knowing these reservation prices— imposes the following subsidy scheme on the monopolist. If the monopolist sells m units at some price p, it will be given a subsidy equal to

$$R_1 + R_2 + \cdots + R_n - mp$$

The monopolist's total revenue from the sale of m units is now the sum of the revenue generated from sales and the subsidy paid by the regulatory authority. The sum is

$$R_1 + R_2 + \cdots + R_n$$

For example, suppose that the monopolist sells two units at a price equal to 10. The subsidy will be $R_1 + R_2 - 20$, and the revenue generated by the sale of two units will be 20. The sum of the subsidy and the sales revenue will then be $R_1 + R_2$.

Given this subsidy scheme, what will the monopolist decide to do? Suppose that it is currently selling m units at price R_m. Will

it choose to sell one additional unit? If so, it must lower its price to R_{m+1} and incur an additional cost equal to the marginal cost of the additional unit, $MC(m + 1)$. Under the subsidy scheme, the monopolist's revenue from the first m units is unchanged (despite the price drop) because the reduction in the sales revenue is exactly balanced by an increase in the subsidy. For instance, if the monopolist must cut its price by \$1 to sell an additional unit, the revenue from the sale of the first m units will decrease by m dollars, but the revenue from the subsidy on these units will increase by m dollars. Therefore, in deciding whether it should sell the additional unit, the monopolist will simply compare the price at which the additional unit can be sold, R_{m+1}, with the marginal cost of the additional unit, $MC(m + 1)$. If the reservation price exceeds (is less than) the marginal cost, it will decide in favor of (against) making and selling the additional unit.

If the profit-maximizing output under this subsidy scheme is m^*, then m^* will satisfy the following conditions:

$$MC(m^*) \leq R_{m^*}$$

and

$$MC(m^* + 1) > R_{m^*+1}$$

You discovered this type of solution when you answered Problem 11.5. You also found that this type of solution is efficient because all the gains from trade are realized as profit to the monopolist.

The regulatory agency might regard the outcome as unfortunate because it is the monopolist who receives all the gains from trade as profit. Yet, as you will see in the following problem, the agency could recover virtually all the monopolist's profit by coupling the subsidy scheme with an appropriate proportional tax on profit. As long as the monopolist is left with *some* profit, it will produce the efficient output.

PROBLEM 11.7

Suppose that a 10% tax is imposed on the monopolist's profit. Then the monopolist will choose output to maximize $.9\pi(y)$ instead of $\pi(y)$. Show that the profit-maximizing output is the same for both profit-maximizing problems.

Even though the regulatory agency has no information about the monopolist's costs, it still manages to provide the monopolist with an incentive both to minimize costs and to produce the efficient output. Can this subsidy scheme be applied to other demand conditions as well? Consider the demand curve in Figure 11.9. If the monop-

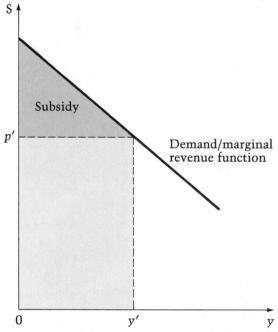

FIGURE 11.9   An efficient regulatory mechanism.

The regulator tells the monopolist that if the monopolist sells quantity y' at price p', the regulator will pay a subsidy equal to the consumers' surplus. The monopolist's total revenue is then the light green area, equal to $p'y'$, plus the dark green area, equal to the subsidy promised by the regulator. As a result, the monopolist's marginal revenue function is coincident with the demand curve. Under this subsidy scheme, a profit-maximizing monopolist will produce the output where its marginal cost function intersects the demand/marginal revenue function.

olist sells quantity y' at price p', its revenue is $p'y'$, or the light green portion of Figure 11.9. What happens if the regulatory agency tells the monopolist it will be given a subsidy equal to the dark green area in Figure 11.9 if it produces output y' and sells it at price p'? First, the introduction of the subsidy means that the monopolist's total revenue — which now includes both the revenue from sales and the subsidy from the government — is equal to the area under the demand curve from 0 to y' units of output. More to the point, when the monopolist now sells an additional unit under the subsidy regulation, the revenue from the original quantity sold remains unchanged. Thus, the price of that additional unit is now the monopolist's marginal revenue, and the market demand curve is then its marginal revenue curve. To maximize its profit, the monopolist will simply move to the point at which its marginal cost curve intersects the demand/marginal revenue curve. In other words, the monopolist will choose to produce the efficient level of output.[5]

---

[5] Given this sort of subsidy scheme, the firm's total revenue function is just

$$TR(y) = \int_0^y D(y)dy$$

or

$$TR(y) = H(y) - H(0)$$

where $H(\cdot)$ is the indefinite integral of $D(\cdot)$. Its profit function is then

$$\pi(y) = H(y) - H(0) - TC(y)$$

Differentiating with respect to y, we see that profit maximization requires that

$$H'(y^*) = TC'(y^*)$$

But $H'(y)$ is just $D(y)$, and $TC'(y)$ is just $MC(y)$. Therefore, at the profit-maximizing quantity,

$$D(y^*) = MC(y^*)$$

That is, the firm produces where the marginal cost function intersects the demand function. Notice, too, that virtually all the profit can be taxed away without reintroducing inefficiency, because the quantity that maximizes $\pi(y)$ also maximizes $(1 - t)\pi(y)$, where t is a tax rate greater than 0 and less than 1.

Franchise Monopoly

Finally, what are the possible government responses to franchise monopolies, such as the franchises for municipal garbage collection or city bus services? When such franchise monopolies are put out at tender and awarded to the highest bidder, we can often treat these cases as instances of natural monopoly. However, when political patronage rather than economic decision making determines the award of such franchises—be it the historical award of dominion over chunks of the New World or the more contemporary award of the rights to television broadcasting in Austin, Texas—economists have little to say.

11.9   Price Discrimination

The fact that price exceeds marginal cost at the standard monopoly solution is a symptom of the monopolist's failure to extract the maximum possible profit. An imaginative monopolist therefore will take dead aim on the as-yet-unrealized profit by trying to devise more sophisticated pricing schemes. Although sophisticated strategies aimed at extracting that unrealized profit may take many forms, the encompassing rubric for them all is *price discrimination.*

As you take a closer look at price discrimination, you'll recognize that this behavior is too pervasive to apply only to monopolists, given our restrictive definition of monopoly. Price-discriminating activities are attractive to any firm with some degree of market power—that is, to any firm with some ability to set its own price. What we say here about price discrimination will also apply to *oligopolies,* or markets dominated by a few firms. As you'll discover in the following two chapters, the theory of oligopoly is complicated enough in the absence of price discrimination. We'll therefore take up price discrimination in the relatively simpler context of monopoly.

Market Segmentation

All **price discrimination** schemes share an underlying strategy: to segment the market and to charge each segment a different price. You discovered the monopolist's ideal **market segmentation** scheme in the book vendor's pricing strategy in Problem 11.5. There, the monopolist appropriated all the surplus as profit by extracting from every consumer the largest sum of money each was willing to pay. Recall the conditions that made this most profitable strategy possible: the monopolist was able to isolate its potential customers from one another, and it knew the individual reservation prices of each customer. These conditions will rarely, if ever, be satisfied. Nevertheless, the market segmentation that makes this scheme effective can be realized and exploited to a lesser extent by other means.

Economists usually view cases of price discrimination as falling into three broad theoretical categories. The first category is **perfect price discrimination,** the "ideal" but effectively unrealizable case exemplified by the book vendor. The monopolist successfully extracts the maximum possible profit from each customer and therefore from the whole market.

The second category is **ordinary price discrimination.** This is the familiar case in which the monopolist identifies potential customers by groups and charges each group a separate price. For example, the pervasive phenomenon of charging different admission prices for groups called "seniors," "adults," "students," and "children" is one instance of ordinary price discrimination.

The third category, **block or multipart pricing,** is the case in which the monopolist charges different rates for different amounts, or "blocks," of a good or service. For instance, it is common practice to charge one rate for the first block of so many kilowatt-hours of electricity in a period and lower rates for subsequent blocks.

Perfect Price Discrimination

As you already know, perfect price discrimination means that the monopolist extracts the maximum possible profit from its market. The book vendor's problem illustrates the simplest type of perfect price discrimination because each customer demands only one unit of the product. In Section 5.4, which treated two-part tariffs, we outlined a general strategy for extracting maximum possible profit from one consumer when the monopolist knows that consumer's preferences. That strategy is to price the good at marginal cost and then charge an "entry fee" to extract maximum profit. We can view the solution to the book vendor's problem as an application of this more general result. The firm sells its book at marginal cost but adds to the price an "entry fee" equal to the customer's reservation price minus the marginal cost.

Although this theoretical case may have no precise real-world counterparts, it nevertheless throws light on the pricing strategies of firms such as Disneyland and Polaroid. Other examples include golf courses that charge a membership fee and green fees, car rental firms that charge a daily fee and a charge per mile, and telephone and cable TV companies that charge a hookup fee and a monthly rental fee. In the pure case (not necessarily found in these examples), the solution is efficient because the product is sold at marginal cost, and all the potential gains from trade are therefore realized.

Ordinary Price Discrimination

Now let's look at ordinary price discrimination by considering first the theory and then the circumstances in which this strategy is feasible. To keep matters simple, we'll ask how a monopolist sets price in a market divided into just two segments.

Let's begin with a simplifying assumption, which we will later change: the monopolist has produced a certain quantity of output — say, 44 units — and wants to maximize the profit from selling it. Its problem is to decide how much of the output to sell in each market segment and at what prices. Since the firm has 44 units to sell, we have assumed away all production questions and reduced the monopolist's problem to one of maximizing revenue.

The two panels in Figure 11.10 represent the two market segments. Suppose that the monopolist begins by considering selling 21 units in the first market segment and 23 in the second. At this allocation, the marginal revenue of $5 in the first market segment is less than the marginal revenue of $34 in the second segment. Beginning at this allocation, if the monopolist transfers 1 unit from the first market segment to the second, the reduction in revenue in the first segment (a drop of approximately $5) will be more than compensated by the increase in revenue in the second (an increase of approximately $34). More generally, the firm's revenue will increase as it transfers output from the market segment with the lower marginal revenue to the market segment with the higher marginal revenue:

To maximize revenue from the sale of a fixed quantity of output, allocate output so that marginal revenue is identical in all market segments.

In Figure 11.10, revenue is maximized when the monopolist allocates 14 units to the first market segment and 30 to the second, since marginal revenue is then $20 in each segment.

PROBLEM 11.8

As you know, if the monopolist presented in Figure 11.10 has 44 units of output, it will sell all 44 units. Suppose that it has 100 units. Will it sell all 100 units? How many units will it sell in each market segment? Is this result consistent with the rule for maximizing revenue?

(a) First market segment

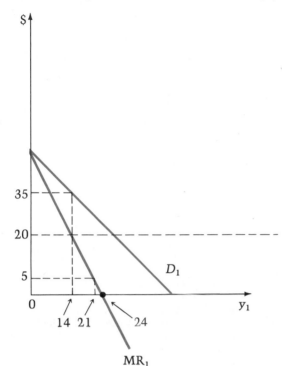

(b) Second market segment

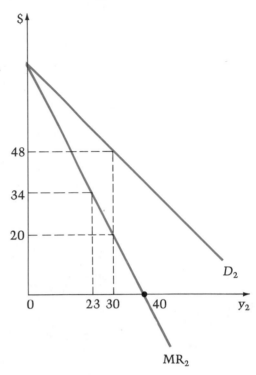

FIGURE 11.10 Price discrimination: equality of marginal revenue.

The monopolist has 44 units of output that it wants to allocate to the two market segments so as to maximize its revenue. To do so, it allocates the fixed quantity to the two market segments so that marginal revenue is identical in the two segments. The optimal allocation is 14 units to segment 1 and 30 to segment 2.

Let's expand the problem to include production. The monopolist's profit is then

$$\pi(y_1, y_2) = TR_1(y_1)$$
$$+ TR_2(y_2) - TC(y_1 + y_2)$$

where TR_1 and TR_2 are total revenue in the two market segments. The monopolist's problem is to choose the two outputs y_1 and y_2 so as to maximize its profit $\pi(y_1, y_2)$. This problem is considerably more complex than the standard monopoly problem. However, if we think of it in a different way, we can easily use familiar concepts to solve it. Let's think of the monopolist's decision as occurring in two stages. First, it chooses an aggregate output, and then it allocates that aggregate output to the two market segments. From what you just learned, you know that in the second stage the aggregate output will be allocated so that *marginal revenue is identical in the two market segments*. And from what you know from your initial encounter with monopoly, it makes sense that in the first stage, the monopolist will choose aggregate output so that *marginal cost is equal to aggregate marginal revenue*. But exactly what is aggregate marginal revenue?

To find out, let's turn to the aggregate marginal revenue curve presented in Figure 11.11*c*. It has been constructed by horizontally summing MR_1 and MR_2 from Figures 11.11*a* and 11.11*b*. To see its significance,

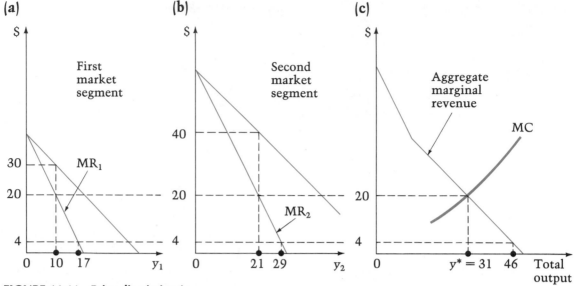

FIGURE 11.11   Price discrimination.

To find the profit-maximizing set of prices and quantities, first horizontally aggregate the marginal revenue functions in (a) and (b) to obtain the aggregate marginal revenue function in (c). Then find the aggregate profit-maximizing quantity, $y^* = 31$, where aggregate marginal revenue is equal to marginal cost. Finally, allocate the 31 units to the two market segments so as to equalize marginal revenue; that is, sell 10 units at price $30 in segment 1, and 21 units at price $40 in segment 2.

suppose that the monopolist produces 46 units and allocates 17 units to the first market segment and 29 to the second. As Figures 11.11a and 11.11b reveal, marginal revenue in each market segment is then $4. Therefore, this allocation—17 units to the first market segment and 29 to the second—maximizes the monopolist's revenue from the 46 units. As Figure 11.11c reveals, the monopolist's marginal revenue is also $4. That is, the aggregate marginal revenue curve in Figure 11.11c gives us the monopolist's marginal revenue when it allocates output to market segments to so as to maximize revenue. We can therefore use this curve—in conjunction with the marginal cost curve—to determine the monopolist's profit-maximizing aggregate output.

The profit-maximizing aggregate output is determined by the intersection of the aggregate marginal revenue and marginal cost curves at $y^* = 31$ units in Figure 11.11c. At this output level, aggregate marginal revenue and marginal cost are each $20. As Figure 11.11 reveals, the monopolist will then allocate $y_1^* = 10$ units to the first market segment and $y_2^* = 21$ to the second, and the corresponding profit-maximizing prices will be $p_1^* = \$30$ and $p_2^* = \$40$. We've learned the following:[6]

---

[6] We can use calculus to solve this profit-maximizing problem. The firm will choose y_1 and y_2 to maximize profit. Hence, the partial derivatives of the firm's profit function with respect to y_1 and y_2 must both be zero at the profit-maximizing solution. Differentiating the profit function first with respect to y_1 and then to y_2 and setting results equal to zero yields

$$MR_1(y_1^*) - TC'(y_1^* + y_2^*) = 0$$
$$MR_2(y_2^*) - TC'(y_1^* + y_2^*) = 0$$

But $TC'(\cdot)$ is just $MC(\cdot)$. Thus,

$$MR_1(y_1^*) = MR_2(y_2^*) = MC(y_1^* + y_2^*)$$

A profit-maximizing monopolist who is able to engage in ordinary price discrimination will choose an aggregate output where aggregate marginal revenue is equal to marginal cost, and it will allocate the profit-maximizing output so that marginal revenue is identical in all market segments.

To get a better sense of what actually determines relative prices in the two market segments, it is useful to characterize the solution in terms of the *price elasticities of demand* in the two market segments. As we saw in Section 11.5, marginal revenue at a point on any demand curve can be expressed in terms of the price elasticity of demand. Using this expression for marginal revenue — and keeping in mind that marginal revenue is the same in both segments — we see the following:

$$p_1^*\left[1 - \frac{1}{\eta_1(y_1^*)}\right] = p_2^*\left[1 - \frac{1}{\eta_2(y_2^*)}\right]$$

Now let's ask: What must be true if p_2^* is greater than p_1^*? From the equality above, the following must be true:

$$\left[1 - \frac{1}{\eta_1(y_1^*)}\right] > \left[1 - \frac{1}{\eta_2(y_2^*)}\right]$$

This inequality can be rewritten as

$$\eta_1(y_1^*) > \eta_2(y_2^*)$$

Therefore, p_2^* will exceed p_1^* if — at the equilibrium — price elasticity of demand in the second market segment is less than price elasticity of demand in the first. Or, putting the result differently:

Price is higher in the market segment with the lower price elasticity of demand.

This result makes good sense of ordinary observations. If one of your parents falls desperately ill in Orlando or if your branch plant in London is threatening to close, you'll catch the next flight out almost regardless of the fare. Your demand for air-

line travel is relatively price inelastic. By contrast, if you have decided to treat yourself to a holiday next spring but do not care if you go to Orlando or Mazatlan or London or Zermatt, you can pick and choose. Accordingly, your demand on any of these routes is relatively price elastic. Airline companies respond to these differing elasticities by discriminating — by charging the traveler who wants to depart tomorrow one price and the traveler who wants to depart sometime in the next month or two another, much lower price.

PROBLEM 11.9
Suppose that the firm in Figure 11.12 has monopoly power in the first market segment but none in the second. First, find the aggregate marginal revenue curve. Then solve the monopolist's profit-maximizing problem for the conditions presented in Figure 11.12.

Market Segmentation Revisited

To establish a successful scheme of ordinary price discrimination, the monopolist must be able to identify different price elasticities of demand and to segment its market accordingly by isolating one portion of the market from the other. One entrepreneurial activity called **arbitrage** undermines the monopolist's price-discriminatory objective of market segmentation. Arbitrage is buying a good in a low-priced market segment and reselling it in a high-priced segment. Where arbitrage can occur, market segmentation cannot be effectively achieved. In some markets, however, arbitrage is impossible; in others, unprofitable.

In a wide range of cases characterized by what we might call personal services, arbitrage is impossible. Although "seniors" get a discount on movie admission prices, for example, they cannot arbitrage in this market because they cannot transfer the good — a movie they have seen — to someone else. Similarly, children cannot arbitrage in

(a)

(b)

(c)

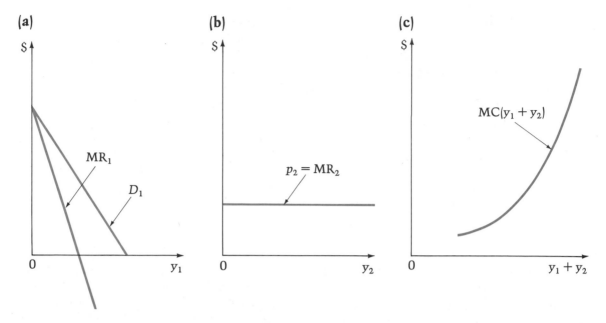

FIGURE 11.12   A price-discrimination problem.

the market for haircuts — even though they can buy them more cheaply than adults — because haircuts are not transferable. All sorts of personal services, from massage therapy and fitness classes to dental and medical services, are markets in which arbitrage cannot occur.

In other cases, arbitrage is possible but unprofitable. For example, the retail price of a new car in Detroit, Michigan, is sometimes lower than the price of the identical model in Provo, Utah. But, relative to the price differential, the cost of transporting a car from Detroit to Provo is high enough to discourage significant arbitrage. If the price differential is large enough, however, arbitrage will occur. Thus, the possibility of arbitrage limits the degree to which prices can diverge in the two markets. In general, where transaction costs — the costs of buying, selling, and transporting — are significant, arbitrage will be unprofitable.

In still other cases, arbitrage may be both possible and potentially profitable, but

the price discriminator may be able to subvert it effectively. A classic example is the case in which the duopolists Du Pont and Röhm and Haas sold the plastic molding powder methyl methacrylate to general industrial users for $0.85 per pound and to dental manufacturers for $22 per pound. When arbitragers began buying methyl methacrylate at the industrial price and reselling it to denture manufacturers at a price below $22 per pound, Röhm and Haas considered cutting the ground out from under the arbitragers by mixing arsenic with the plastic powder sold for industrial use so that it could not be used for denture work. Although the firm ultimately rejected the idea, it did circulate rumors suggesting that the industrial methyl methacrylate had been adulterated (Stocking and Watkins, 1946).

In cases where arbitrage is either impossible or not profitable, how can the monopolist achieve market segmentation? One method is to sort the individuals in different segments of the market by requiring them to identify themselves. For example, for "seniors" to receive lower prices on prescription drugs or movie tickets, they must somehow certify their age. Requiring direct identification is the most obvious way to isolate market segments from one another.

Another method is to rely on *self-selection*; that is, to induce individuals to sort themselves into the appropriate market niche voluntarily. The most conspicuous example is the two-segment market for airline travel. In the business-travel segment of the market, demand is likely to arise on relatively short notice and to be relatively price inelastic. In the holiday-travel segment, demand is usually anticipated well in advance and is likely to be relatively price elastic. A standard discriminatory mechanism is the "advanced booking discount," often hedged by such other restrictions as requiring the traveler to stay at least a week or to stay over at least one Saturday night. Because only holiday travelers are able to plan well ahead and stay for at least a week — and are therefore able to take advantage of the discount — the airline's customers reveal their identity as business people or vacationers simply by their response to its price structure.

Annual or semiannual department store sales are another rather puzzling feature of economic life that we can better understand in the context of price discrimination through self-selection. In these sales, the items are sold at prices substantially below their everyday prices, and the sales are often predictable events. The January white sales are a regular feature of the American department store landscape, for example. What is puzzling is how stores can still manage to sell a good portion of their merchandise at everyday prices. A form of market segmentation through self-selection is part of the answer. Going to these sales usually means putting up with crowds and long lines at the cash register. To some shoppers, the package of crowds and lower prices is

preferred to more elbow room and regular prices. To other shoppers, the opposite is true. Because the two kinds of shoppers select themselves by going to sales or staying away, the retailing strategy effectively segments the market. We can't regard this strategy as a pure form of ordinary price discrimination, however, because the cost of retailing during such sales, in which volume is considerably heavier, is lower than usual.

PROBLEM 11.10

Canadian Tire offers a 4% discount for cash payments. Instead of taking 4% off the total bill, however, the firm gives customers the equivalent in Canadian Tire money. This "money" then can be presented in lieu of cash the next time customers make a purchase at a Canadian Tire store. Can you identify the two forms of price discrimination through self-selection at work here?

Multipart or Block Pricing

Finally, let's consider *multipart or block pricing*. We will not attempt a complete or rigorous analysis of multipart pricing. Rather, we'll concentrate on understanding what it is, the circumstances in which it is feasible, and why it is even more profitable than ordinary price discrimination.

To understand multipart pricing we need the concept of a **price schedule.** You are already familiar with a one-part price schedule. When your grocer posts a sign indicating that the (single) price of mushrooms is $3 per pound, the price schedule that you face is a one-part price schedule since you can buy any quantity you want at a single price. A multipart price schedule associates different prices with different quantity blocks. For example, your grocer might post the following two-part price schedule for mushrooms: $3 per pound for the first 5 pounds and $2 per pound for each pound in excess of 5 pounds. In this case, if you buy 8 pounds, you'll pay $3 per pound for the first

5 pounds and $2 per pound for the next 3 pounds, for a total expenditure of $21. The following is a three-part price schedule: $3 per pound for the first 5 pounds, $2 per pound for the next 5 pounds, and $1 per pound for any amount greater than 10 pounds.

Now that you understand what a multi-part price schedule is, let us see why it is more profitable than ordinary price discrimination. Figure 11.13 presents two individual demand curves. The demand curve for Betty is on the right. The demand curve for Sam is on the left. For reasons that will soon be apparent, we will assume that Sam's demand curve is independent of his income. And to keep the analysis simple, we will also

assume that the monopoly supplier of this good incurs no costs in producing it and that Betty and Sam are its only customers. As a point of reference, we can identify what the monopolist's pricing strategy will be if it engages in ordinary price discrimination. Since the monopolist's marginal cost is 0, it will choose the point on each demand curve where marginal revenue is equal to 0. As you can easily verify, it will charge $12 per unit in the first market segment, and Betty will buy 5 units; it will charge $8 per unit in the second market segment, and Sam will buy 24 units. The monopolist's profit and revenue will then be $252.

To show that multipart pricing can be more profitable than ordinary price discrim-

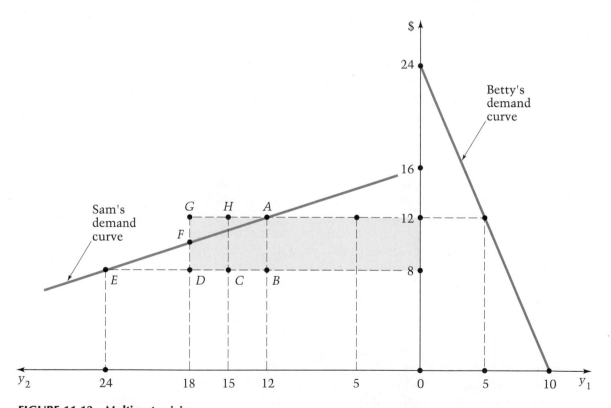

FIGURE 11.13   Multipart pricing.

With the multipart pricing scheme, the firm charges any consumer $12 for the first 18 units and the lower $8 price for any units in excess of

18. Betty buys 5 units at price $12 and none at price $8, while Sam buys 18 units at price $12 and 6 units at price $8.

ination, let's consider a two-part price schedule in which the monopolist charges a price of $12 per unit for the initial quantity block and a lower price of $8 per unit for each unit in excess of the initial block limit. The monopolist's problem is then to choose the block limit in the two-part price schedule — but not the two prices — that maximizes its profit. Clearly, the monopolist will choose a block limit of at least 12. What will happen if the monopolist actually set a block limit of 12 units? Both Betty and Sam would face this two-part price schedule: a price of $12 per unit for the first 12 units and a price of $8 for every unit in excess of 12. Given this price schedule, Betty will again buy 5 units at $12 per unit. On the other hand, Sam will again buy 24 units, but he will pay $12 instead of $8 for the first 12 units. Relative to the ordinary price discrimination case, then, the monopolist will sell exactly the same amount. Yet its revenue will rise by $48 since Sam will have paid an extra $4 per unit on the first 12 units. Its profit under this two-part price schedule is $300 rather than $252. Clearly, multipart pricing is more profitable than ordinary price discrimination.

Yet the monopolist can do even better by choosing a *larger* block limit. Suppose, for example, that it increases its block limit to 15. Once again, Betty will buy 5 units at $12 per unit. The interesting question concerns Sam, who has two courses of action open to him. He will either buy just 12 units at $12 per unit, ending up at point A on his demand curve, or he will buy the entire 15-unit block at the $12 price and an additional 9 units at the $8 price, ending up at point E on his demand curve.

To see which course of action Sam will choose, suppose that he is at point A in Figure 11.13, where he has bought just 12 units at $12 apiece. First, what would Sam be willing to pay for the privilege of buying additional units at the $8 price? Second,

what is the *implicit price* of this privilege under the 15-unit block limit?

To answer the first question, we note that Sam's demand curve is independent of his income; therefore, we can use the concept of consumer surplus to measure his willingness to pay for this privilege. Beginning at point A, if he could buy additional units at the $8 price, he would buy 12 more units (moving from point A to point E on his demand curve). The added consumer surplus would then be $24, equal to the area of triangle EBA in Figure 11.13. Therefore, Sam would be willing to pay up to $24 for this privilege.

Now for the second question. Under the 15-unit block limit, he must pay not $8 but $12 for the first three additional units (units 13, 14, and 15). The implicit price of the privilege is therefore $12. Because $12 is less than $24, he'll choose the option represented by point E, where he buys 15 units at $12 per unit and 9 more units at $8 per unit — and the monopolist's profit will therefore rise by an additional $12 to $312.

Which block limit *maximizes* the monopolist's profit? The monopolist will continue to increase the block limit until the implicit price of the privilege of buying additional units at the $8 price is equal to the $24 maximum price Sam is willing to pay for that privilege. The block limit that maximizes the firm's profit is therefore 18 units since the implicit price of the privilege is then $24, equal to $4 per unit multiplied by 6 units. Under this 18-unit block limit, the monopolist's profit is $324.

Our purpose is not to present a complete analysis of the monopolist's choice of a multipart price schedule, but to indicate how this pricing strategy works. As you have seen, a multipart pricing strategy can be significantly more profitable than ordinary price discrimination. And as you will discover in the following problem, the monopolist who institutes such a strategy will not simply mimic the prices it would otherwise have charged under ordinary price discrimination, as we have so far assumed.

PROBLEM 11.11

Notice that for every $1 drop in the price per unit, Sam buys 3 more units.

1 Consider a two-part price schedule with prices of $12 and $6. What block limit maximizes profit? Is the monopolist's profit larger than it is with the $12 and $8 prices and the 18-unit block limit? Is Sam any better off?
2 Consider a two-part price schedule with prices of $12 and $0. What block limit now maximizes profit? Is the monopolist's profit now larger than in part 1? Is Sam any better off?

You may be wondering why ordinary discrimination exists if multipart pricing is so much more profitable. The answer is that the monopolist must be able to meter or otherwise monitor the consumption of specific consumers like Betty and Sam. The reason your grocer does not post a multipart pricing schedule for mushrooms like the one in our example is that it can neither prevent arbitrage nor monitor the consumption of individual consumers. However, this kind of pricing scheme is common in the sale of electricity, natural gas, and water, because consumption is literally metered and arbitrage is costly. Cable television service is another, less obvious example of a market in which multipart pricing schemes are used. For example, Shaw Cable Company offers a limited number of television channels for $13.97 per month; a full range of television channels for $17.44; a full range of television channels plus one pay movie channel for $35.03; and a full range of television channels plus one pay movie and one pay family channel for $38.71. Another example is the common banking practice of charging a higher rate for cashing the first block of so many checks, a lower rate for the next block, and so on. Whenever it is feasible, then, monopolists do appear to use multipart pricing.

*11.10 Patent Policy

Seen in the framework of the static, unchanging economic world we have modeled so far in this chapter, monopoly is most striking for its allocative inefficiency. Yet the real economic world is not static and unchanging, but dynamic and ever-changing. As we now place monopoly within the very different framework of a dynamic model, it will undergo a striking metamorphosis. The lure of monopoly profit becomes the magnet that attracts new and better products into being, and monopolists become the providers of products of the future.

Let's step back from monopoly for a moment to appreciate just how rapidly the economic world is changing. First, try to think of 10 products available at the turn of the century that are still on the shelves today. (Once past Arm and Hammer baking soda, we found that it was no easy task.) Now try to list some of the products that are a familiar part of your landscape but that were unavailable, and perhaps even unimaginable, to a college student at the turn of the century. Your list can legitimately include almost any product in transportation or communication; any article of clothing made from a synthetic fabric; any item of frozen food in your local supermarket; all of your audio equipment, tapes, records, and compact discs; almost all prescription drugs; all computer products; and on and on. Now try to imagine the thousands of new products that are just coming onto the market. Here are but a few: a voice-synthesized electronic dictionary from Franklin Computer that will enunciate words as well as give their meanings; revolutionary new cameras from Sony and Canon that use erasable floppy disks instead of film; Squibb-Novo's NovolinPen, which makes taking insulin injections much simpler for diabetics; a lobster trap with a biodegradable door made of plastics, cobalt, starch, and a fatty acid that rots away, allowing the lobster to escape if the trap is lost; a powdered additive called Eubacteria that can turn cholesterol into a less harmful substance; and a miniature sewing machine that can be swallowed by patients and used to stitch internal tissues together without surgery.

In this dynamic context, monopoly is no longer just the source of a static inefficiency problem. In addition, it plays an important role in ensuring that bright, new ideas about potential goods and services are actually transformed into bright, new goods and services. For this reason, patent and copyright protection, which provide monopoly power over a specified period of time, play critical roles in promoting these transformations from idea to actuality.

As you know, patents provide exclusive rights to a new product, invention, or process for a specified period of time. Similarly, copyrights provide exclusive rights to art, music, or written material for a specified period of time. (We'll use the word *patent* to refer to both.) These exclusive, or monopoly, rights are an important policy tool for governments in virtually all market economies. (The framers of the U.S. Constitution thought patent policy important enough to enshrine in that document.) In this section, we will develop a model that will let you see why granting patents can make economic good sense—and see, too, some of the economic pitfalls associated with patents.

The Appropriability Problem

Let's begin by asking: What economic problem do patents solve? When Jonas Salk created the Salk vaccine, his invention conferred real benefits to society at large. Polio was virtually eliminated in developed countries by the early 1960s. So, too, thousands of other inventions—Bell's telephone, Land's camera, Mozart's music, Jobs and Wosniack's computer, Virginia Woolf's novels, Lear's jet, and so on—have created what we will call **social value**. We'll see below how to use the cost-benefit criterion to attach a dollar figure to the social value of an invention. For now, we can simply note that according to this criterion, a bright idea should be developed into a new product if the social value of the new product is greater than the development cost. But will a socially valuable invention always come into being? It is easy to see that if inventors were to bear all the development costs and reap all the benefits—thereby personally capturing, or *appropriating*, all the excess of social value over the cost of development associated with their inventions—every socially useful invention would be produced. Yet inventors are not able to appropriate all the social value created by their inventions. As a result, many potentially valuable ideas never appear as products on market shelves, because their inventors simply do not have the private incentive to pursue them. This is the **appropriability problem**.

A number of responses to the appropriability problem are possible. One response is to provide governmental assistance to alleviate the sometimes massive costs of research and product development (R&D). For example, to develop a new microeconomics textbook—to write and edit it, to have it reviewed and to respond to the reviews, to design the book and the graphs, to set the type—costs approximately $500,000. To put a new prescription drug on the market is significantly more expensive. R&D costs, the key to success in the drug industry, have jumped from an average of $55 million for each new medication in the 1970s to $125 million in 1990. Governments can and do subsidize new product development by providing a variety of support measures. For instance, scattered across the United States are more than 75 joint industry-government research consortiums that are developing generic technologies in everything from cement to semiconductors. Member companies can then hone those technologies for their own specific needs.

We will be focusing instead on another possible response: granting patents—which confer monopoly power, and therefore monopoly profit—to inventors, thereby increasing their private incentive to create new products. For example, the copyright on "Happy Birthday to You"—the four-line verse written by two Louisville teachers as a classroom greeting—generates about $1 million in royalties annually.

A Model of Inventions

Let's begin by supposing that a vast number of individuals or firms—for convenience, we'll call them all "developers"—have an equally vast stock of innovative ideas that can be developed into marketable products. Let's suppose, too, that it costs money—a good deal of money—to transform innovative ideas into marketable products. Of course, the magnitude of this **product development cost,** denoted by $D, will vary from one innovation to another.

Suppose, too, that the developer—once having invested in the R&D necessary to create a marketable product—can produce it at a constant marginal cost of $1 per unit, and that in each of a number of years, the market demand for its product is given by a linear market demand function like the one presented in Figure 11.14.[7] The green area in Figure 11.14 is the *annual profit* $M that a monopolist in this market could earn. (We'll consider only innovations for which $M is positive.) Like the development cost $D, the annual monopoly profit $M and the

---

[7] Throughout our discussion, we will assume that the demand functions for different products are independent of each other; that is, new products are neither substitutes nor complements for each other. Without this assumption, we could not use consumer surplus to measure the social value of a new product.

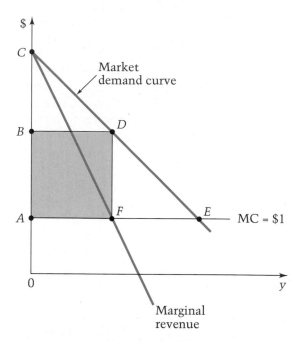

FIGURE 11.14   Patent protection.

Will this firm incur the costs necessary to develop its product? If it anticipates monopoly power—either because it will have patent protection or because other firms cannot imitate its product—it will earn annual profit equal to the area of the dark green rectangle. This profit is the inducement for the firm to develop its product. Since an effective patent allows the firm to earn this annual profit over the life of the patent, a patent enhances the firm's incentive to develop its product. If, instead, other firms can imitate its product and it has no patent protection, the equilibrium price will be $1 and the firm will earn zero annual profit. In this case, it has no incentive to develop its product.

precise shape of the demand curve will vary from one innovation to another.

Initially, the developer of this new product will be a monopolist, and the period over which it will remain the sole firm in its industry will be determined by what we'll call an *imitation lag L.* For example, when the IBM personal computer hit the market in 1981, its rival clone manufacturers were in hot pursuit less than a year later. In this case, then, the imitation lag L is a year's time. The imitation lag for a book is even shorter. Using modern reproduction techniques, book bootleggers can begin to market duplications of a newly released book in a matter of days. And as any experienced software pirate knows, the imitation lag for much computer software can be a matter of minutes.

In other cases, the lag time is apparently large. If Bill Cosby is right, Pepsi still has not figured out how to replicate Coke. Thus, we'll assume that the developer is the sole manufacturer of its product for a lag period of L, but that once the lag period L has elapsed, anyone else can also manufacture the developer's product at a marginal cost of $1. (Notice that we are implicitly supposing that imitators incur no development costs.) In the absence of patent protection, then, the developer is a monopolist until L has elapsed — at which point it becomes just another perfectly competitive producer. Clearly, if patent protection is to mean anything, it must extend this monopoly period beyond the L time periods attributable to imitation lag.

Finally, because patents obviously raise intertemporal issues, time considerations must be introduced. For simplicity, let's suppose that every product has a 40-year product cycle. Specifically, suppose that the market demand curve (illustrated in Figure 11.14) will be stable for 40 years, and thereafter it will, as it were, evaporate overnight. In addition, suppose that the entire stock of innovative ideas is in place at time-zero, that all decisions about product development are made at time-zero, and that product development itself requires no time. A patent policy will then shape developers' incentives at time-zero, thereby indirectly determining the products that will be marketed in this miniature economy across the whole 40-year time span.

In this model, then, each of the multitude of innovative ideas in the minds of developers can be described by its demand curve and three numbers: D, the sum of money needed to develop the idea into a marketable product; M the profit per year that a monopolist could earn by marketing the product; and L, the number of years before other firms can imitate the developed product.

We'll assume that each developer knows what these three numbers are and that no one else does. In what circumstances will a developer choose to transform an innovative idea into a marketable new product?

Product Development in the Absence of Patents

If no patent protection is in place, the developer will be a monopolist for L years — and will therefore earn monopoly profits of $M per year for L years. Once L years have elapsed, the developer's monopoly power will vanish. It will become just one more perfect competitor, selling its product at a price equal to the marginal cost of $1 and earning no profit.

In deciding whether to go ahead with its product development and marketing plans, a profit-maximizing developer will compare the present value of its monopoly profits with the development cost $D. For simplicity in calculating present values, let's suppose that the rate of interest is 0%. With this simplification, the present value of its annual monopoly profit $M over L years is just L multiplied by M, or $LM. A profit-maximizing developer will proceed with its plans only if $LM exceeds $D. Thus, if L is greater than D/M, the new product will be marketed, and if L is less than D/M, it will not.

We see, then, that in the absence of patents, some innovative ideas will be transformed into marketable goods, and others won't. In particular, if the imitation lag period L is small enough, no matter how socially valuable an idea might be, the developer has no private incentive to market it. For example, imagine that you have thought up a new computer game. You realize that once you have invested in the R&D necessary to develop a marketable product, your potential competitors can immediately copy and produce it at a constant marginal cost of $1. In this situation, L will certainly be less than D/M — and neither you nor anyone else will bother to invest in developing the computer game. In such cases, the appropriability problem becomes a serious consideration.

Since patents operate by extending the period of monopoly beyond the L years attributable to the imitation lag, the next question is this: What is the number of years of monopoly profit J such that the present value of the annual monopoly profit $M is just equal to the development cost $D? Since J satisfies $JM = D, we see that

$$J = \frac{D}{M}$$

If a developer could count on being a monopolist for J years, then it could just recover its R&D costs. Therefore, if its actual monopoly period I exceeds J, the developer will opt for creating its new product. We'll call J the just-sufficient monopoly period. For simplicity, we'll suppose that J is a shorter time period than a 40-year product cycle. (If it were a longer time period, the product would never come into being, because it would be obsolete before the developer could recover its R&D costs.)

The Effects of Patents

How will patent protection alter a developer's decision making? Any patent law can be completely described by T, the time period over which patent (or monopoly) rights are granted. For example, in the United States, the copyright period for works of art extends 50 years beyond the artist's time of death, and the standard patent period is 17 years. How any particular patent law will affect a developer's decision depends on the nature of the relationships among the patent period T, the imitation lag L, and the just-sufficient monopoly period J. Let's look at these relationships systematically:

1 If $T > J > L$, in the absence of patent protection, the potential new product will not be marketed because the just-sufficient period J is longer than the imitation lag period L. Under patent protection, however, it will be marketed, because the patent period T is indeed longer than the just-sufficient period J. In this case, then, a patent law solves the appropriability problem.

2 If $T > L > J$, the new product will be marketed even in the absence of patent protection because the imitation lag time L is longer than the just-sufficient period J. The patent period T simply extends the monopoly period from L years to T years. In this case, a patent law is not required to solve the appropriability problem, yet it does increase the developer's monopoly profit.

3 If $L > T > J$, the new product will be marketed because the imitation lag time L is longer than both the patent period T and the just-sufficient time J. In this case, the patent law is beside the point.

4 If $J > T$ and $J > L$, the potential new product will not be developed and marketed because the just-sufficient period J is longer than both the patent period T and the imitation lag time L. Once again, the patent law is beside the point.

Optimal Patent Policy

Now that we understand the possible effects of a patent in this model, let's turn to patent policy. Our first problem is to define the social value of a new product. If we suppose that the demand for these new products is independent of income, we can use the concepts of consumers' and producers' surplus to define social value.

For any new product in the marketplace, the equilibrium will be in one of two phases: either a monopoly equilibrium (where its developer is still protected from competition by imitation lag or by a patent) or a competitive equilibrium (where neither imitation lag nor a patent remains operative). In the monopoly phase, total surplus in each period is the trapezoidal area $ACDF$ in Figure 11.14. It is composed of producer's surplus (that is, the monopolist's profit), an amount equal to the area of rectangle $ABDF$, and consumers' surplus, an amount equal to the area of triangle BCD. In the competitive phase, total surplus in each period is the area of the triangle ACE. It is composed entirely of consumers' surplus. Notice that total annual surplus is thus larger in the competitive phase than in the monopoly phase by an amount equal to area of triangle DEF in Figure 11.14. This triangle simply reflects the static burden of monopoly. Of course, if the product is not developed and marketed, then total surplus is zero in each period.

In general, the cost-benefit criterion defines the social value of a new product as the discounted present value of the total annual surplus over the product's life. In the present context, the *social value of any new product* is then just the sum of total surplus in each period over all 40 periods.[8] In this model, the *social cost of any new product* is its R&D cost $$D$.

We will consider two cases in analyzing optimal patent policy. We'll begin by making the unrealistic assumption that a product-specific patent law can be devised for each possible new product. Then we will

drop this assumption as we take up the more realistic and challenging case in which one patent law applies across the board to all new products.

Given our assumptions, we know that each of the multitude of innovative ideas described in this model is socially desirable. Why? Recall that the just-sufficient time period J for each product is less than 40 years. Hence, the social value of each product exceeds its social cost—even when its developer is a monopolist over the entire 40-year product cycle. This means that if the patent period T is 40 years, every innovative idea will actually be translated into a marketable product, and both the developer and all the product's consumers will be better off. Of course, this does not mean that the optimal patent period is 40 years. It simply indicates that all the products in this model are socially desirable.

What is an optimal patent policy in this circumstance? It is one that maximizes a new product's social value less its social (or R&D) cost. Let's identify that optimal patent policy. First, consider a potential new product that will not come into existence unless it is patent-protected—that is, a potential product for which the just-sufficient period J is longer than the imitation lag time L. The patent period we choose must be long enough that its developer will have a profit incentive to bring the product to market—that is, the patent period T must be longer than or identical to the just-sufficient period J. Once we have hit this target, our objective then will be to *minimize the length of the monopoly phase*. Why? Because total surplus in each period in the monopoly phase is smaller than it is in the competitive phase. Therefore, when J is greater than L, the optimal patent period is $T^* = J$. Any shorter patent period would fail to provide the developer with a profit incentive. Any longer patent period would needlessly extend the monopoly period, thereby reducing total surplus for each additional year of mo-

---

[8] Here we are ignoring an important question: What is the appropriate social discount rate? This is an important and complex issue that we will not address.

nopoly by an amount equal to the area of triangle *DEF* in Figure 11.14.

Now let's take up the case of a product that will come into being even though it is not patent-protected — that is, a product for which the lag time *L* is longer than the just-sufficient period *J*. In this case, no patent is required. The developer already has all the profit incentive it needs to bring the product to market. And that's all there is to optimal patent policy-making — when we can tailor a product-specific patent period for each new product.

This seemingly easy answer has a fatal drawback. The policymaker doesn't have the information necessary to compute the just-sufficient monopoly period *J* for each product — information that is crucial in identifying the optimal patent period for that particular new product. This means that policymakers are inevitably forced to apply a single patent period to a whole host of products.

Let's assume that a single patent period covers all products. What is the optimal patent policy in this circumstance? To answer that question, we need to aggregate social value and social (or product development) costs over all products. We'll call the sum of social value over all products the *aggregate social value* and the sum of social cost over all products *aggregate social cost*.

The optimal patent policy maximizes aggregate social value less aggregate social cost.

Unfortunately, when one patent period applies to a multitude of innovations, policymakers are forced to confront a trade-off between creating the necessary incentives to encourage new product development and minimizing the static inefficiency of monopoly. Suppose, for example, that a policymaker is trying to choose between patent periods *T* of 10 or 15 years. If the policymaker opts for the shorter, 10-year period, some innovative ideas will be transformed into marketable products and others will not. Among the products that will remain undeveloped are some that would have come into being if *T* had instead been 15 years long. These would-be products are composed of all the innovative ideas for which the imitation lag *L* is shorter than the just-sufficient time period *J* and for which *J* is between 10 and 15 years. If the policymaker had instead fixed on the longer, 15-year patent period, these innovations would have come into being — and aggregate social value less aggregate social cost would have risen accordingly. The resulting influx of new products onto the market is directly attributable to the more attractive profit incentives stemming from the now-longer patent period.

Yet this gain is offset by a loss. If the policymaker settles on the longer, 15-year patent period, the monopoly period of some — but not all — of the products that would have been developed under the shorter patent period is needlessly extended. (If the imitation lag *L* is shorter than 10 years, then the needless extension of the monopoly period is 5 full years; if *L* is between 10 and 15 years, then the extension is 15 minus *L* years; and if *L* exceeds 15 years, then the monopoly period is unaffected by the increase in *T*.) The total social value from these products therefore drops under the longer patent period because, for each product, annual surplus in the now-extended monopoly phase is less than it is in the now-shortened competitive phase. This is the nature of the trade-off that policymakers must confront. How can they decide on the optimal patent policy?

To find out, let's consider a small, or marginal, increase in the patent period. A marginal increase in *T* will have two effects. On the one hand, because it will stimulate the development of additional new products, it will tend to increase aggregate social value less aggregate social cost. On the other hand, because it needlessly increases the monopoly period of some products that would have been brought to market in any case, it will tend to decrease aggregate social value less aggregate social cost. If we call the first effect the *marginal social benefit* of increasing the patent period, and the second effect the *marginal social cost* of increasing the patent period, we can neatly characterize the optimal patent policy:

At the optimal patent period, the marginal social benefit of increasing the patent period is equal to the marginal social cost.

Application of this rule is more difficult than our simple model suggests because policymakers will have a hard time obtaining all the necessary information. What is that information? It is a list of all the possible products and — for each product — the annual total surplus associated with that new product in both its monopoly and its competitive phases, the product developer's R&D costs and annual monopoly profit, and the imitation lag time. To even begin to approximate this type of information is a major undertaking. As a result, policymakers are typically forced to set patent policy under conditions of very imperfect information.

What have we learned? That monopoly profit — and therefore monopoly itself — can play a beneficial role in a dynamic economy by providing an incentive to new product development. We also learned that in creating patent law, the patent policymakers are invariably caught between a rock and a hard place. They must try to find the right balance in the inevitable trade-off between creating incentives for new product development and minimizing the static inefficiency associated with monopoly.

The policymakers' balancing act is made even trickier because it takes place in an environment characterized by very imperfect information. Trying to find the delicate balance between such trade-offs under

conditions of imperfect information is a difficulty that policymakers in general confront time and again. Thus, the principles and problems that arise in trying to set an optimal patent policy can serve as a metaphor for the more general principles and problems encountered in a wide spectrum of policy issues.

Summary

From a formal standpoint, what differentiates the monopolist's profit-maximizing problem from the perfect competitor's is that its revenue function is more complex because the monopolist is a price setter. Its marginal revenue function lies below the demand, or average revenue, function. As a result, at the monopolist's profit-maximizing solution — producing at the output level where marginal revenue equals marginal cost — price exceeds marginal cost.

Two important implications follow from this result. First, the monopoly solution is not Pareto-optimal; it is inefficient. Second, at the monopoly solution, the monopolist fails to extract the maximum possible profit. The first implication raises a normative question: What, if anything, should be done about monopoly? The second stimulates the monopolist to search for clever pricing strategies to extract more profit than under the ordinary, or "unimaginative," monopoly solution.

In considering the normative question, we argued that the proper policy response to monopoly depends on the source of monopoly power. If monopoly power springs from the ownership of some scarce resource, then competition — created by a governmental policy of divestiture — is a feasible alternative. If the source is a patent, the best response may be to do nothing. As we saw at the end of the chapter, patents are one response to the appropriability problem, and the static inefficiency of patent monopoly may then be viewed as the price paid for stimulating new product development. The critical question, then, is whether product development can be induced by other and better means than patent protection.

If monopoly power comes from economies of scale — and the monopoly is therefore a natural monopoly — the ideal regulatory response is to induce the monopolist (whether public or private) to behave efficiently. Unfortunately, neither average-cost-pricing nor rate-of-return regulations — both standard governmental responses — is entirely satisfactory because neither regulatory mechanism induces the monopolist to behave efficiently. As we saw, however, if the regulatory agency knows the monopolist's demand curve, it can devise an efficient regulatory mechanism.

In considering the monopolist's response to the "unimaginative" monopoly solution, we analyzed the more sophisticated strategies of price discrimination that are based on the monopolist's ability to segment its market. Two types of such market segmentation are common: direct identification (as in various discounts for senior citizens and students, for example) and self-selection (as in different fares for airline tickets, for example).

We considered three types of price discrimination: perfect price discrimination, ordinary price discrimination, and multipart pricing. Perfect price discrimination is not something we expect to see in the real world; however, this ideal case does let us see just how strong a monopolist's incentive to devise clever pricing strategies can be. Ordinary price discrimination is something we encounter almost every day of our lives, and it can take very subtle forms. Multipart pricing is more profitable than ordinary price discrimination, but, because it requires the monopolist to monitor the customer's consumption, it is not as common as ordinary price discrimination.

Exercises

1   The demand function for a very famous introductory economics textbook is

$$p = 100 - .005y$$

The publisher must pay $20 per book in printing and distribution costs and, in addition, it must pay the author a $20 royalty for each book sold.

a   Your job is to advise the publisher. What price will maximize the publisher's profit? How much profit will the publisher earn? How large will the author's royalty check be?

b   A consultant says that the publisher and the author have the wrong sort of agreement. He says that the author and the publisher should tear up their original agreement, in which the author gets $20 per book sold, and enter a profit-sharing agreement. He recommends that the author get 40% of the profit and the publisher 60%. What price should the publisher set with this profit-sharing agreement? Hint: is marginal cost $40 or only $20? Will both the author and the publisher prefer the profit-sharing agreement to their original agreement? Which agreement will the students who buy the textbook prefer?

c   Can you explain why the original royalty agreement is not economically sound?

2   In Montrose, there is just one movie theater. The price elasticity of demand for movies is 2 for adults, 4 for students, and 6 for children. Who will pay the highest price, and who will pay the lowest? If the children's price is $2, what are the other prices? What is the monopolist's marginal cost?

3   The demand for Wayless, a dietary supplement, is

$$p = 110 - y$$

and the cost function for any firm producing Wayless is

$$C(y) = 10y + F$$

where F is a fixed cost.

a   What is marginal cost? How much Wayless would a monopolist produce? What price would it charge? How much profit would it earn?

b If the monopolist did produce the profit-maximizing quantity you found in part **a**, show that an entrant's residual demand function would be

$$p_E = 60 - y_E$$

c What quantity would maximize an entrant's profit, given this residual demand function? What would price be? What would the entrant's profit be?

d For which of the following values of F is the market for Wayless a natural monopoly? $F = \$200$, $F = \$400$, $F = \$600$, $F = \$800$.

4 Warner-Lambert Company's patent on its anticholesterol drug Lopid expires soon. It is now lobbying the U.S. congress to extend the patent for 5 more years. If you were acting as an economic advisor to Congress, what advice would you offer? What are the implications for the price of Lopid? Is there an economic case for extending this patent? If there is an economic case for offering a patent before the drug is invented, is there a case for extending the patent period after it is invented?

5 Suppose a monopolist must pay an excise tax equal to t per unit sold—if it produces y units, it must pay ty in taxes. To the monopolist, these taxes are just another cost of production, so we can write the monopolist's profit function as

$$\pi(y) = yD(y) - ty - TC(y)$$

The monopolist's profit-maximizing rule is then

$$MR(y^*) = MC(y^*) + t$$

a Explain this rule.

b Now, suppose that the monopolist's demand curve is

$$p = 200 - 5y$$

and that the monopolist's marginal cost is $10 per unit. What are the profit-maximizing price and quantity and the monopolist's profit when t is $10? When t is $20? When t is $30? When t is $0?

6 The managers of Vancouver's Expo 1986 considered selling two types of admission

tickets: one for $20 and another for $100. The more expensive ticket would have allowed its holder to move to the head of the line into the Expo grounds. The Monterey Bay Aquarium in California uses a similar strategy. Customers who take out a year's membership are allowed to enter the aquarium at any time. Nonmembers must buy day passes good for the next available time slot—ordinarily an hour or two after they buy their tickets. Explain the conditions necessary for this sort of pricing strategy to be profitable.

7 In the book trade, it's common practice to publish a novel in hardcover and sell it for, say, $30 and then to bring out a paperback edition about 6 months later and sell it for, say $10. The motion picture industry uses a similar strategy. A good, new movie might be screened at first-run movie theaters for about 3 months. About the time the first run closes, the movie is typically available on videocassette. Explain these curious practices.

8 Price ceilings offer some interesting possibilities in monopoly markets. Consider the following demand function of some monopolist:

$$p = 200 - 2y$$

The monopolist's marginal cost is $80.

a What is MR? Carefully draw both the demand curve and the marginal revenue curve. What is the profit-maximizing price and quantity?

b Now suppose a price ceiling equal to $100 is imposed on the monopolist. Show that the monopolist's MR curve is now composed of two segments: MR is $100 for the first 50 units and is given by the original MR function for larger outputs. Draw this revised MR curve. Notice the gap or discontinuity in MR at $y = 50$.

c What is the profit-maximizing price and quantity when a $100 price ceiling is imposed? When a $160 price ceiling is imposed?

d What is the efficient level of output? Is there a price ceiling that will induce the monopolist to produce the efficient output?

9 Firm A has no costs of production and sells its product to just two buyers. Buyer 1's demand function is

$$p_1 = 90 - 10y_1$$

and Buyer 2's is

$$p_2 = 60 - 5y_2$$

a Assuming that the firm can engage in ordinary price discrimination, find the profit-maximizing prices. What is A's profit?

b Now, suppose that the monopolist can engage in multipart pricing. Find a two-part price schedule that generates more profit than the firm gets in part **a**. How much additional profit does it earn?

c Finally, suppose that the firm cannot price-discriminate. First find the firm's aggregate demand function. (It is composed of two linear segments, like the demand function in Figure 10.5.) Then find its marginal revenue function. (It is composed of two linear segments, with a gap or discontinuity.) Find its profit-maximizing price, and compute its profit.

*10 Suppose that the Nickel Company is the sole producer of nickel in a "small" country such as Canada. The demand function for nickel in Canada is

$$p = 100 - y$$

where y is tons of nickel sold in Canada. Outside Canada, the market for nickel is perfectly competitive, and nickel is priced at \$60 per ton. Canada sets a tariff on imported nickel equal to \$30 per ton. Show that Nickel Company's aggregate marginal revenue function is

$$MR(y) = 90 \quad \text{if } y \leq 10$$
$$MR(y) = 100 - 2y \quad \text{if } 10 < y \leq 20$$
$$MR(y) = 60 \quad \text{if } y > 20$$

Nickel Company's marginal cost function is

$$MC(y) = ay$$

a Suppose that $a = 2$. How much nickel will the company produce? How much will it sell in Canada and at what price? How much will it sell in the international market? What profit will Nickel Company earn?

b Now, suppose that $a = 14/3$ and repeat these exercises.

c Finally, suppose that $a = 30$, and repeat these exercises.

*11 Let's reconsider one aspect of the efficient regulatory solution in Section 11.8. We'll use the following demand function:

$$p = 160 - y$$

Recall that the subsidy associated with any quantity y was identical to consumers' surplus at y, which implies that the firm's marginal revenue function is identical to its demand function. First, compute the subsidy paid for an arbitrary quantity of output y. (Remember that the area of a triangle is $\frac{1}{2}$ its base times its height.) Then compute the firm's total revenue — including the subsidy — as a function of y. Finally, divide total revenue by y to get the average revenue function associated with this subsidy scheme. Then construct a diagram in which you identify the regulated firm's profit-maximizing output and use the average revenue function to identify its profit.

References

Averch, H., and L. L. Johnson (1961), "Behavior of the Firm Under Regulatory Constraint," *American Economic Review*, **52**:1052–1069.

Hansen, R. (1979), "The Pharmaceutical Development Process: Estimates of Development Times and the Effects of Proposed Regulatory Changes," in *Pharmaceutical Economics*, R. I. Chien (ed.), Lexington, Mass.: Lexington Books, pp. 151–187.

Loeb, M., and W. A. Magat (1979), "A Decentralized Method for Utility Regulation," *The Journal of Law and Economics*, **22**:339–404.

Stocking, G. W., and W. R. Mueller (1955), "The Cellophane Case and the New Competition," *American Economic Review*, **45**:29–63.

Stocking, G. W., and M. W. Watkins (1946), *Cartels in Action*, New York: Twentieth Century Fund, pp. 402–404.

*12

UNDIFFERENTIATED OLIGOPOLY

Two pieces of the theory of market structure are now in place: perfect competition and monopoly. What remains — the theory of **oligopoly,** or competition among the few — fits less tidily into an overall picture of market structure. Indeed, to speak of *the* theory of oligopoly, as if only one existed, is misleading. Unlike monopoly and perfect competition, oligopoly has no single theory. Instead, different models yield different insights into the conduct of real oligopolies.

Each of the models we'll consider reveals an important facet of oligopolistic behavior. For example, the Cournot model provides a solid understanding of how the number of firms in the market affects the price and the aggregate quantity of output in an oligopolistic setting. Indeed, this model encompasses the whole spectrum of market structures, ranging from monopoly to perfect competition. The Bertrand model helps to explain the factors that can lead to the price wars that sometimes break out between gas stations, grocery stores, and cigarette manufacturers — to name just a few. The collusive model highlights the incentive that motivates firms to collude. It helps to explain the existence of the OPEC cartel of petroleum-producing nations and the

"conferences" in ocean shipping, both of which are intended to facilitate collusive behavior. So, too, it accounts for the price-fixing activities occasionally encountered in a wide range of other industries, including cigarette manufacturers; baby-formula makers; ready-mix concrete suppliers; moving companies; meat packers; the potash, titanium, uranium, gypsum, cardboard, and paper bag industries; and even private colleges.

In the first half of the chapter, we'll explore models in which the number of oligopolists in an industry is fixed and determine what the equilibrium price and quantity will be in each model. We might think of these as models of the short run. In the second half, we'll shift our attention to models in which firms can enter an industry and determine how many firms we can expect to see — that is, we'll determine what the market structure will be. We might think of these as entry equilibrium models of the long run.

Our underlying aim is to give you an understanding of the theoretical problems that oligopoly poses and a sampling of the tactics oligopolists use to secure market power. In fact, strategic maneuvering is the name of the oligopolistic game. In an oligopolistic industry, the number of firms — two or more — is small enough that each has some, but not complete, market power. Oligopoly thus occupies a middle ground between perfect competition and monopoly: an oligopolist neither takes price as given nor independently sets industry price and quantity. Instead, an oligopolist's decisions are always made with one eye fixed on its competitors — either anticipating or responding to moves by its rivals in the industry as they all maneuver for a bigger chunk of the profit.

In this chapter, we'll look at oligopolistic industries in which products are undifferentiated, or homogeneous; in Chapter 13, we'll look at those oligopolistic industries in which products are differentiated, or heterogeneous. Some of the more notable oligopolistic industries characterized by homogeneous products are steel, crude oil, plywood, sugar, aluminum, and uranium. Ready-mix concrete in a regional market and pulp and paper products—including the paper in this book—are yet other examples of undifferentiated products.

12.1 Monopoly Equilibrium: A Point of Reference

We will be using a single set of demand and cost conditions throughout this chapter as we develop and examine a number of oligopoly models. Because we will want to compare the equilibrium of each of these models with the monopoly equilibrium, we will begin the chapter by setting out the demand and cost conditions and by computing the monopoly equilibrium.

You will be encountering the following linear market demand function throughout the chapter:

$$p = 100 - y$$

where p is price and y is aggregate, or industry, output. We'll also assume that each

firm in the industry can make the product at a constant marginal cost of $40 per unit. In the first half of the chapter, we'll assume, too, that no additional costs of production are relevant and that the oligopolists are existing, or established, firms. In the second half, we'll add the product development, or setup, costs that a potential firm will incur when it enters an industry.

We'll begin by computing the standard monopoly solution. It will serve as a benchmark for comparing the equilibria in a variety of oligopoly models. The standard graphic solution to the monopoly problem is presented in Figure 12.1. The monopolist will produce 30 units and sell them at a price of $70 per unit. It is useful to find the solution to the monopolist's problem using algebraic techniques as well. Recall that for linear market demand functions, the marginal revenue function and the market de-

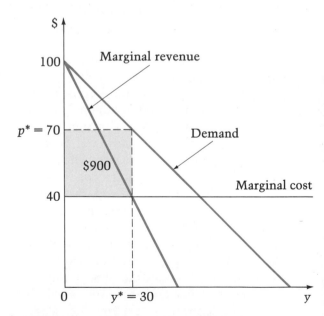

FIGURE 12.1   The monopoly equilibrium.

The monopoly equilibrium is to produce 30 units and to sell them at price $p^* = \$70$. The resulting monopoly profit is $900, equal to the green area.

mand function intersect the price axis at the same point and that the marginal revenue function is twice as steep. Therefore,

$$MR = 100 - 2y$$

To find the profit-maximizing output, simply identify the value of y, written as y^*, at which marginal revenue equals marginal cost, or \$40:

$$100 - 2y^* = 40$$

or

$$y^* = 30$$

Next, we can compute price at the profit-maximizing output level by using the market demand function:

$$p^* = 100 - y^*$$

or

$$p^* = 70$$

The monopolist's profit is then simply total revenue minus total cost:

$$\pi^* = p^*y^* - 40y^*$$

or

$$\pi^* = 900$$

The \$900 profit is represented graphically by the green area in Figure 12.1

12.2 Duopoly as a Prisoners' Dilemma

To better to understand the puzzles that arise in oligopolistic settings, we'll begin by considering a **duopoly**—an oligopoly in which just two firms are in an industry. In reality, each duopolist is free to produce whatever level of output it chooses. To simplify the problem, however, let's suppose that each duopolist will choose between a small quantity—say, 15 units—and a large quantity—say, 20 units. Notice that the smaller output of 15 units is exactly half the monopoly output of 30 units. Thus, if

the duopolists were to choose an output of 15 units apiece, their joint, or market, output would replicate the monopoly output of 30 units. We can infer that they if they did so, they would also maximize their joint, or total, profit.[1] Will the duopolists actually choose the strategies that lead to a replication of the monopoly profit? Or will their rivalry lead them to choose strategies that result in a joint, or total, profit smaller than the monopoly profit?

To answer this question, let's return to the concept of **Nash equilibrium** introduced in Chapter 2. That is, we'll assume that each duopolist chooses its quantity to maximize its private profit—taking its rival's choice of quantity as a given. We'll denote a duopolist's strategy of producing the smaller output of 15 units by S and its strategy of producing the larger output of 20 units by L. Because each duopolist will choose either S or L, four strategy combinations are possible in this duopoly game: both choose S; both choose L; the first duopolist chooses S, and the second, L; the first duopolist chooses L, and the second, S.

Now let's compute each duopolist's profit for each of these strategy combinations. If both choose S, price will be \$70 $(100 - 15 - 15)$, and profit per unit produced will be \$30 $(70 - 40)$. As a result, each duopolist's profit will be \$450 (15×30)— or *exactly half the monopoly profit*. By contrast, if both choose L, price will be \$60 $(100 - 20 - 20)$, and profit per unit produced will be \$20 $(60 - 40)$. As a result, each duopolist's profit will be \$400 (20×20)— or *less than half the monopoly profit*. If the first duopolist chooses S and the second L, price will be \$65 $(100 - 15 - 20)$, and profit per unit produced will be \$25 $(65 - 40)$. As a result, the first duopolist's profit will be \$375 (15×25) and the second's will be \$500 (20×25). Conversely, if the first duopolist

[1] This requires that the two firms have identical and constant marginal costs.

chooses L and the second S, the first duopolist's profit will be $500 and the second's $375.

The Duopoly Game in Matrix Form

We've incorporated this information in the *profit matrix* presented in Table 12.1. The first duopolist's strategies are represented along the left side of the matrix, and the second duopolist's along the top of the matrix. Each of the four cells in the matrix corresponds to one of the four possible strategy combinations. In any cell, the entry to the left is the first duopolist's profit; the entry to the right, the second duopolist's. If both choose S, each receives $450. If both choose L, each earns $400. If one chooses S and the other L, the duopolist that chooses S earns $375, and the one that chooses L earns $500.

If the second duopolist chooses L, what is the first duopolist's **best response?** It is also to choose L, because it earns $400 if it chooses L and only $375 if it chooses S. If the second duopolist chooses S, the first duopolist's best response is again L, because it earns $500 if it chooses L but only $450 if it chooses S. Thus, no matter which strategy the second duopolist pursues, the first duopolist's best response is to choose L. For this reason, L is said to be a **dominant strategy** for the first duopolist.

Because the second duopolist's options are exactly those of the first's, its best response is likewise to choose L—regardless of what the first duopolist chooses. That is, L is a dominant strategy for the second duopolist as well as for the first. Thus, the Nash-equilibrium strategy combination is

for each duopolist to choose L. In this equilibrium, each duopolist will produce 20 units and will realize a profit of $400. Yet, if they could only agree to restrict their individual outputs to 15 units apiece—that is, to **collude** successfully—each could earn $450.

The Oligopoly Problem

This simplified version of the duopoly game illustrates the fundamental quandary encountered by economic theorists in trying to model oligopoly—and by real oligopolists in trying to play real oligopoly games. As we just saw, the blind pursuit of self-interest leads to an equilibrium in which both oligopolists are worse off than they might otherwise be. This leads us to one important insight:

Oligopolists have a clear incentive to collude, or cooperate.

Yet we also discovered that if one duopolist were to cooperate by producing just 15 units, its rival's best response would be to produce 20 units. This leads us to the second, contradictory insight:

Oligopolists have a clear incentive to cheat on any collusive, or cooperative, agreement.

As we'll see in subsequent sections, these contrary forces arise in almost all oligopoly models. Interestingly, they also arise in many economic contexts outside of oligopoly and even outside of economics. When they arise in a matrix game characterized by two players and two strategies, the game is called a *prisoners' dilemma*.

The Prisoners' Dilemma

The matrix game in Table 12.1 is an illustration of one of the most famous and puzzling games in the entire field of game theory. The game and its title—the prisoners' dilemma

TABLE 12.1 Duopoly Profit Matrix

| | | Second duopolist's strategy | |
		S	L
First duopolist's strategy	S	450/450	375/500
	L	500/375	400/400

—were invented by A. W. Tucker.[2] In Tucker's original game, two criminal suspects — whom we will call Bonnie and Clyde — have been apprehended, but the district attorney (D. A.) doesn't have sufficient evidence to convict them. The D. A. offers the following deal to Bonnie. If she will provide evidence against Clyde — and if Clyde does not incriminate her — she will receive a 1-year sentence and Clyde a 10-year sentence; if, however, both provide evidence, each will receive a 5-year sentence; and if neither provides evidence, each will be convicted on a lesser charge and will receive a 2-year sentence. The D. A. offers the corresponding deal to Clyde.

This game has the same qualitative structure as the game in Table 12.1. Regardless of what the other prisoner does, the dominant strategy for Bonnie and for Clyde is to provide evidence. In the Nash equilibrium of the game, both testify against one another and both receive 5-year sentences. Yet if they had instead managed to collude successfully, both would have been sentenced to the lesser, 2-year jail terms.

P R O B L E M   12.1

Construct the payoff matrix for this game and verify that regardless of what the other prisoner does, the individually rational action for each prisoner is to provide evidence.

Common Property and the Prisoners' Dilemma

The prisoners' dilemma has become the generic name for any game with this qualitative structure. You have already explored another example of the game in the common-property fishery problem of Chapter 2. In that model, when fish tomorrow were common property, both individuals ate all their fish in the initial period instead of returning any to the river for harvesting in the

second period. As a result, the equilibrium was not Pareto-optimal. In Exercise 2 at the end of this chapter, you can show that the institution of common property creates a prisoners' dilemma.[3]

12.3   The Cournot Model of Oligopoly

Now that you have some feeling for the oligopoly problem, let's drop the restrictive assumption that the duopolists have a choice of only two levels of output and replace it with the assumption that they have a free choice of any level of output. You can now explore the oldest and in many ways the most interesting oligopoly model, attributable to the French economist Auguste Cournot and dating from 1838. Cournot noticed that only two French firms were producing mineral water for sale. He was intrigued by how these two firms would decide just how much to sell of the water that flowed from their mineral springs. In developing his model, he argued that each firm would choose the quantity that would maximize profit, taking the quantity marketed by its competitor as a given. Suppose that the second firm intended to sell 30 bottles of water. Cournot assumed that the first firm would take this quantity as given in deciding how many bottles it should sell.

The crucial features of the **Cournot model** are (1) that each firm chooses a quantity of output instead of a price and (2) that in choosing its output, each firm takes its rival's output as a given. In Cournot's model, then, the duopolists' strategies are their (independent) choices of the level of output to produce, denoted by y_1 and y_2. As in the matrix game in the previous section, the problem here is to identify the duopolists' equilibrium strategy combination.

---

[2] See Luce and Raiffa (1957), p. 94.

[3] Robert Axelrod's book *The Evolution of Cooperation* is a fascinating and very readable account of how people often manage to cooperate in playing repeated prisoners' dilemma problems.

Best-Response Functions

Let's return to the method used to analyze the matrix game, and begin to analyze Cournot's model by asking: What is the first firm's *best response*, taking its rival's output of y_2 units as given? Its market demand function is just

$$p_1 = (100 - y_2) - y_1$$

If the first firm produces nothing, the price will be $100 - y_2$; therefore, the intercept for the first firm's demand function is $100 - y_2$. We see, then, that the first firm's market demand function intersects the price axis in Figure 12.2 at $100 - y_2$ and that for every unit the first firm puts on the market, price drops by $1. (This is another example of a residual demand function, introduced in 11.7.)

Once we consider the first firm's market demand function in this light, it is clear that we can adapt the techniques used to

solve the monopolist's profit-maximizing problem to identify the first firm's best response. Notice that the first firm's marginal revenue function intersects the price axis at $100 - y_2$ and, as usual, is twice as steep as the market demand function:

$$MR_1 = (100 - y_2) - 2y_1$$

To maximize its profit, the first firm will choose the output level y_1^* at which marginal revenue equals marginal cost. In other words, y_1^* satisfies

$$(100 - y_2) - 2y_1^* = 40$$

or, solving this expression for y_1^*,

$$y_1^* = 30 - \frac{y_2}{2}$$

This equation answers our question. It gives us a rule for calculating the first firm's best response for any value of y_2. For example, if y_2 is zero, the first firm will maximize its profit by producing the monopoly output of 30 units [$30 - (0/2)$]. If y_2 is 10, it will maximize its profit by producing 25 units [$30 - (10/2)$], and so on. Because this rule tells us the first firm's best response to any quantity of output produced by it rival, it is called a **best-response function** (for obvious reasons, it is sometimes called a *reaction function* as well).

Because the second firm's marginal cost is also $40, its best response function is a twin to the first firm's:

$$y_2^* = 30 - \frac{y_1}{2}$$

The Cournot Equilibrium

Taken together, these two best-response functions can be used to find the equilibrium strategy combination for Cournot's model — or, more simply, the Cournot equilibrium. Both firms' best-response functions are presented in Figure 12.3, and the Cournot equilibrium is the point where

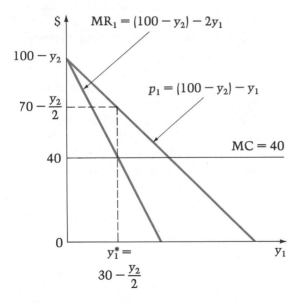

FIGURE 12.2 Finding a Cournot best-response function.

Given y_2, the first firm's demand function is $p_1 = (100 - y_2) - y_1$, and its marginal revenue function is $MR_1 = (100 - y_2) - 2y_1$. Its profit-maximizing output is y_1^*, equal to $30 - y_2/2$, since MR is equal to MC at this level of output.

the best-response functions intersect. In this equilibrium, each firm produces 20 units, price is $60 ($100 - 20 - 20$), profit per unit is $20 ($60 - 40$), and each firm's profit is $400 ($20 \times 20$).[4]

In what sense is this strategy combination an equilibrium? From the first firm's best-response function in Figure 12.3, we see that when its rival produces 20 units, the output that maximizes the first firm's profit is likewise 20 units. Similarly, from the second firm's best-response function, we see that when its rival produces 20 units, the output that maximizes the second firm's profit is also 20 units. At the Cournot equilibrium, then, neither firm can increase its profit by choosing some other output. Or, putting the same point in a slightly different way, given its rival's output, each firm's output is profit-maximizing.

These remarks indicate that the Cournot equilibrium is also a Nash equilibrium. That is, Cournot used precisely the same equilibrium concept more than 100 years before Nash articulated it. (To give Cournot due credit, some economists use the term

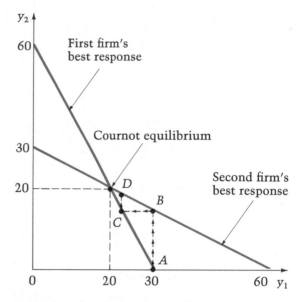

FIGURE 12.3 The Cournot equilibrium.

The Cournot equilibrium, in which each firm produces 20 units, is determined by the intersection of the two best-response functions.

Cournot–Nash equilibrium instead of Nash equilibrium.)

To find the Cournot equilibrium algebraically, we could solve the two best-response functions for the equilibrium values of y_1 and y_2. However, we can take an even simpler approach. Because the two best-response functions are symmetric, we know that both firms will produce the same quantity in equilibrium. This means that we can compute the equilibrium by setting both y_1^* and y_2 equal to y' in the first firm's best-response function, reflecting the fact that both will produce the same quantity y' in equilibrium. Then we can simply solve for y'. The resulting number $y' = 20$ is the quantity each will produce in the Cournot equilibrium.[5]

---

[4] More generally, we can write the duopolists' profit function as

$$\pi_1(y_1, y_2) = y_1 D(y_1 + y_2) - TC(y_1)$$

$$\pi_2(y_1, y_2) = y_2 D(y_1 + y_2) - TC(y_2)$$

where $D(\cdot)$ is the demand function and $TC(\cdot)$ the cost function. The first firm chooses a quantity y_1^*, where the partial derivative of $\pi_1(\cdot)$ with respect to y_1 is equal to zero:

$$\frac{\partial \pi_1(y_1^*, y_2)}{\partial y_1} = 0$$

Of course, this is an implicit expression for the first firm's best-response function because it determines the profit-maximizing quantity of y_1, y_1^*, for any value of y_2. Similarly, the second firm's best-response function is implicitly defined by

$$\frac{\partial \pi_2(y_1, y_2^*)}{\partial y_2} = 0$$

The Cournot equilibrium is then a pair of quantities (y_1^C, y_2^C) that satisfies both best-response functions.

[5] If the two firms had different marginal costs, the equilibrium would not be symmetric, and we could not use this approach to find equilibrium quantities.

Mock Dynamics in the Cournot Model

To understand more about the Cournot model, let's perform a somewhat artificial dynamic exercise. Imagine that in odd-numbered periods, the first firm chooses the quantity it will produce in that period and in the next. For example, the first firm chooses the output for periods 1 and 2 in period 1; for periods 3 and 4 in period 3; and so on. Imagine, too, that in even-numbered periods the second firm chooses the quantity it will produce in that period and the next. For example, the second firm chooses its output for periods 2 and 3 in period 2; for periods 4 and 5 in period 4; and so on. If the duopolists follow the maximizing rules in the Cournot model, how will production in this market evolve? In particular, will this dynamic model converge to the Cournot equilibrium?

Suppose that in period 1, the second firm is not yet in the market. The first firm — at this point a monopolist — will choose y_1 based on a y_2 equal to zero. That is, it will produce the monopoly output of 30 units in period 1, and the duopoly will therefore be at point A in Figure 12.3. Because we have assumed that the first firm will continue to produce the 30-unit output in the next period, the second firm will base its own production decision on a fixed output of 30 units for its rival when it enters the market in period 2. The second firm will then produce 15 units [30 − (30/2)] in period 2, and the duopoly will be at point B on the second firm's best-response function. In period 3, the first firm will now base its production decision on a fixed output of 15 units for its rival. It will produce 22.5 units [30 − (15/2)], and the duopoly will be at point C on the first firm's best-response function. In period 4, the second firm will produce 18.75 [30 − (22.5/2)], and the duopoly will be at point D. As you can see from Figure 12.3, the dynamic exercise is rapidly converging to the Cournot equilibrium.

The Cournot Model with Many Firms

What happens to the Cournot equilibrium as the number of firms in an industry expands? You can find the answer in the case of three firms in Problem 12.2.

PROBLEM 12.2

Assuming that three firms are in the industry, show that the first firm's best-response function, or profit-maximizing rule, is

$$y_1^* = 30 - \frac{(y_2 + y_3)}{2}$$

Then show that each of the three firms will produce 15 units in the Cournot equilibrium. Hint: Adapt the algebraic technique based on symmetry that we described for finding the duopoly equilibrium. Calculate each firm's profit in the three-firm Cournot equilibrium.

Let's quickly generalize what you discovered in this problem. If n firms are in the market, the demand and marginal revenue functions of the first firm will be

$$p_1 = (100 - y_2 - y_3 - \cdots - y_n) - y_1$$
$$MR_1 = (100 - y_2 - y_3 - \cdots - y_n) - 2y_1$$

Because the first firm will choose y_1 so that marginal revenue is equal to marginal cost, its best-response function is

$$y_1^* = 30 - \frac{(y_2 + y_3 + \cdots + y_n)}{2}$$

But because all other best-response functions are symmetric to this one, all n firms will produce the same output in the Cournot equilibrium. To discover the output of one firm in this equilibrium, set y_1^*, y_2, y_3, ..., y_n all equal to y' in the first firm's best-response function. Then solve for y' to obtain

$$y' = \frac{60}{n+1}$$

This is the output of one firm in the Cournot equilibrium when there are n firms in the market.

The Attractive Features of the Cournot Model

It is useful to compute the aggregate equilibrium output and price in the Cournot model with n firms.

$$\text{aggregate equilibrium output} = \frac{60n}{n+1}$$

$$\text{equilibrium price} = \frac{100}{n+1} + \frac{40n}{n+1}$$

These formulas yield a number of interesting insights into the Cournot model. First, as n increases, aggregate output increases and equilibrium price decreases. When n is 1, the aggregate output is the monopoly output of 30 units and price is \$70; when n is 2, aggregate output is 40 units and price is \$60; when n is 3, output is 45 and price is \$55; and so on. Second, as n increases without bound, the aggregate output approaches the competitive output, and the price approaches the competitive price. As you can verify, the competitive output is 60 units, and the competitive price is \$40. Notice that as n gets arbitrarily large, $n/(n+1)$ approaches 1. Therefore, in the Cournot equilibrium, aggregate output approaches 60 units, and equilibrium price approaches \$40.

Finally, notice that the Cournot model is appealing because it spans all possible market structures. When only one firm is in a market, the Cournot equilibrium is the monopoly equilibrium. As the number of firms increases, output likewise increases. As a result, price and aggregate oligopoly profit decrease. In the limit, when there are infinitely many firms, the Cournot model is effectively a perfectly competitive model, since price is equal to average cost and ag-

gregate profit vanishes. None of the other models we will consider has these intuitively appealing properties.

12.4 The Bertrand Model

Responding to Cournot's analysis of the duopoly problem, Joseph Bertrand argued that firms choose *price*—not quantity. The **Bertrand model** simply substitutes prices p_1 and p_2 for quantities y_1 and y_2 as the variables to be chosen. Thus, the Cournot and Bertrand equilibria are logical first cousins. Cournot identified the Nash equilibrium when the duopolists' strategic decisions centered on a choice of quantities, and Bertrand identified the Nash equilibrium when their strategic decisions centered instead on a choice of prices. What is the equilibrium strategy combination—or, more simply, the Bertrand equilibrium—when the duopolists choose prices instead of quantities?

Best-Response Functions

Once again, we can begin to analyze Bertrand's model by asking: What is the first firm's best response—taking its rival's price p_2 as given? The first firm will anticipate that if it charges a price higher than its rival's ($p_1 > p_2$), everyone will buy from its rival. If the first firm charges a price lower than its rival's ($p_1 < p_2$), however, everyone will buy from it. And if it charges a price equal to its rival's ($p_1 = p_2$), the duopolists will split the market. For convenience, let's assume that they split it in half. The resulting—somewhat peculiar—market demand function is

$$y_1 = 0 \qquad \text{if } p_1 > p_2$$
$$y_1 = 100 - p_1 \qquad \text{if } p_1 < p_2$$
$$y_1 = \frac{100 - p_1}{2} \qquad \text{if } p_1 = p_2$$

(Notice that in these equations, the roles of price and quantity have been inverted: quantity is now on the left and price on the right.)

Given this market demand function, what will the first firm's profit function look like? If p_1 is greater than p_2, the first firm attracts no business. That is, y_1 is equal to zero, and its profit is also zero:

$$\pi_1 = 0 \quad \text{if } p_1 > p_2$$

On the other hand, if p_1 is less than p_2, the first firm captures the whole market. That is, y_1 is $100 - p_1$, and its profit per unit is $p_1 - 40$. Therefore, its total profit is

$$\pi_1 = (p_1 - 40)(100 - p_1) \quad \text{if } p_1 < p_2$$

If p_1 is equal to p_2, however, the two firms evenly split the market; that is, y_1 is $(100 - p_1)/2$, and profit per unit is $p_1 - 40$. Therefore, the first firm's total profit is

$$\pi_1 = \frac{(p_1 - 40)(100 - p_1)}{2} \quad \text{if } p_1 = p_2$$

Given this profit function, we can determine what the first firm's best response will be. This is the question we must answer: Given p_2, what value of p_1 maximizes the first firm's profit? To find the answer, we need to consider four possible cases. Let's begin with the two easy cases. First, if its rival charges a price greater than the monopoly price of $70, the first firm can capture the whole market with a lower price, and its best response is obviously to charge the monopoly price of $70. Second, if its rival charges a price that is less than the $40 cost per unit produced, the first firm's best response is to charge any price greater than p_2. Why? Because by choosing this price, the first firm will attract no business and will therefore incur a zero profit — an outcome that is clearly better than incurring a negative profit by matching or undercutting its rival's price.

Now let's turn to the more interesting third case, where the second firm's price is

greater than the $40 cost per unit produced and less than or equal to the monopoly price of $70. The graph of the profit function for this case is presented in Figure 12.4. The first firm's price is on the horizontal axis and its profit on the vertical axis. The profit function is composed of three segments. First, if the first firm chooses a price lower than its rival's $(p_1 < p_2)$, as the first firm's price increases, its profit likewise increases. In this segment of the profit function, the profit-maximizing price is arbitrarily close

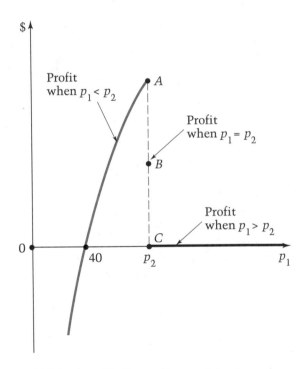

FIGURE 12.4 Finding a Bertrand best-response function.

The second firm's price is p_2, which we assume is less than the monopoly price. The first firm's profit function is composed of three segments. When $p_1 < p_2$, the first firm captures the entire market, and its profit increases as its price increases. When $p_1 = p_2$, the two firms split the total profit, equal to distance CA, each getting CB. When $p_1 > p_2$, the first firm's profit is zero because it sells nothing when its price exceeds the second firm's price. Given p_2, the first firm's profit-maximizing price, or best price response, is then a price just less than p_2.

to — but less than — p_2. Thus, when p_1 is less than p_2, the first firm's maximum profit is distance CA, and its best price is a price just less than p_2.[6] Second, if the first firm chooses a price equal to its rival's price ($p_1 = p_2$), its profit drops by a factor of one-half because it now evenly splits the profit with the second firm. The first firm's profit is therefore just half of the distance CA, or the distance CB. Third, if the first firm chooses a price greater than its rival's price ($p_1 > p_2$), its profit is zero. Graphically, the firm's zero profit is represented by the horizontal axis from point C onward to the right. What have we learned? When its rival's price is greater than the marginal cost of $40 and less than or equal to the monopoly price of $70, the firm's best response is to undercut its rival's price by just a hair's breadth.

Now let's take up the fourth case, where the second firm sets a price that is exactly equal to the marginal cost of $40 per unit. If the first firm sets a price lower than $40, it will incur a loss on every unit it sells, and its profit will therefore be negative. On the other hand, if it sets a price greater than or equal to $40, its profit will be equal to zero. Why? If it chooses any price above $40, its profit will be zero because it will attract no business. And if it chooses a price equal to $40, its profit will be zero because it will break even on every unit it sells. Because making a zero profit is better than making a negative profit, the first firm's best response is to charge any price greater than or equal to $40.

Let's summarize our results with respect to the first firm's best response to its rival's price. (The second firm's best-response function is obviously symmetric.)

1 p_1^* is $70   if $p_2 > 70$
2 p_1^* is any price greater than p_2 if $p_2 < 40$
3 p_1^* is just less than p_2 if $40 < p_2 \leq 70$
4 p_1^* is any price greater than or equal to p_2 if $p_2 = 40$

The Bertrand Equilibrium

What is the Bertrand equilibrium — that is, what is the strategy combination when firms choose prices? From **4**, we see that this strategy combination is one in which each duopolist chooses a price equal to $40. Why? If the second firm sets a price of $40, then **4** tells us that the first firm's best response is also to set a price of $40. (Do notice, however, that $p_1 = 40$ is not the only best response, since charging any price higher than $40 also results in zero profit.) Similarly, if the first firm sets a price of $40, then the second firm's best response is to set a price of $40. Therefore, the Bertrand equilibrium of $p_1 = 40$ and $p_2 = 40$ is a Nash equilibrium. Notice that in this equilibrium, each firm's profit is exactly zero.

Dynamics in the Bertrand Model

We can also see how the Bertrand equilibrium might come about by considering a dynamic exercise in which the duopolists alternately choose prices. The first firm will choose the monopoly price of $70. Its rival will then undercut the first firm by setting a price just less than $70. The first firm will respond with a still lower price. This pattern of successive price undercutting will stop only when both prices have been driven down to the Bertrand equilibrium price of $40.

As this dynamic scenario reveals, the Bertrand equilibrium is not altogether satis-

---

[6] Strictly speaking, the best price for the first firm is not well defined here since there is no largest price less than p_2. We will, however, ignore this point.

factory. First one firm shaves its price ever so slightly to undercut its rival, fully expecting to capture the whole market. Then its rival retaliates by shaving its price, again expecting to capture the entire market. They seesaw back and forth, each progressively undercutting the other in the expectation of capturing the entire market until, in the equilibrium, price is so low that each firm is indifferent to serving the market or abandoning it — since its profit is zero in either case.

Bertrand and Cournot Compared

Even though the Bertrand and Cournot models differ in just one respect — prices are chosen in Bertrand's model and quantities in Cournot's — the equilibria are strikingly different. By contrast to the Cournot equilibrium, the Bertrand equilibrium *does not change as the number of firms increases.* As long as at least two firms are in a particular industry, the Bertrand equilibrium is a price equal to marginal cost, and aggregate oligopoly profit is zero.

12.5 The Collusive Model of Oligopoly

Although intuitively appealing, the Cournot model may seem a bit naive. Its central assumption, after all, is that oligopolists choose their outputs independently, taking the output of rivals as given. And if the Cournot model is a bit naive, the Bertrand model seems extraordinarily so, in that by setting price independently, the oligopolists arrive at an equilibrium in which no one makes any profit whatsoever in a potentially lucrative market. Indeed, in a number of industries dominated by a few firms, *collusive* rather than *independent* behavior seems to be a fact of economic life. For example, the two U.S. companies that control 90% of the infant formula market, Ross Laboratories and Mead Johnson, have nearly always raised prices by about the

same amounts and at about the same times. The four ready-mix concrete firms in Toronto that control 92% of the industry have set uniform prices for concrete products for at least 5 years. Such uniform pricing in concrete products is also the norm for many other cities across North America. Even private colleges have recently come under investigation by the Justice Department because within groupings — the Ivy League schools and the Seven Sisters, for instance — yearly tuitions tend to be quite similar. In this section, we'll see what happens when oligopolists do decide to collude on a joint strategy. Then we'll compare that outcome with the monopoly equilibrium on one hand and with the Cournot and Bertrand equilibriums on the other.

We can begin with the simplest case of a duopoly. The best equilibrium that the duopolists can jointly come up with is one in which joint output, y_1 plus y_2, is equal to the monopoly output of 30 units. That is, since each firm's marginal cost is \$40, the two can jointly do no better than the monopoly equilibrium. They might agree, for example, to produce half the monopoly output (15 units) apiece. The price per unit will then be \$70, and each will earn half the monopoly profit, or \$450.

The Oligopoly Problem Revisited

By contrast, each duopolist in the Cournot equilibrium earns only \$400, or \$50 less than in the collusive equilibrium. This means that the Cournot equilibrium, although individually rational, is collectively irrational because each firm earns less profit than it could have earned in the collusive equilibrium. The primary objection to the Cournot model is that if firms do find themselves at the Cournot equilibrium, they have a clear incentive to attempt to form a collusive agreement.

These remarks are even more appropriate to the Bertrand model. Each duopolist in the Bertrand equilibrium earns exactly $0 profit, or $450 less than in the collusive equilibrium. Like the Cournot equilibrium, the Bertrand equilibrium is individually rational, but collectively irrational. As with the Cournot model, the primary objection to the Bertrand model is that if firms do find themselves at the Bertrand equilibrium, they have a clear incentive to collude. Does this mean that the collusive model makes better sense of oligopoly than do the Cournot and Bertrand models?

Not necessarily. To see why not, we'll focus on the Cournot model. Suppose that the two rivals agree to split the monopoly output evenly by producing 15 units apiece. Now, let's look at their private incentives to stick to the agreement or break it. Suppose that the first firm is convinced that its rival will abide by the agreement to produce just 15 units. By consulting the first firm's best-response function, we can infer that its private incentive is to respond by producing 22.5 units [30 − (15/2)]. If it actually were to break the agreement by producing 22.5 units — and if its rival kept to the agreement by producing only 15 units — then the total industry output would be 37.5 (22.5 + 15), and price would be $62.5 (100 − 37.5). The first firm's profit would be $506.25 [22.5 × (62.5 − 40)], and its rival's would be $337.50 [15 × (62.5 − 40)].

If the first firm could get away with this deceptive strategy, it would earn an additional $56.25 in profit (506.25 − 450) relative to the collusive equilibrium. Again relative to the collusive equilibrium, its rival would lose $82.50 (450 − 337.50) — a loss that exceeds the first firm's gain. Therefore, the collusive strategy is collectively rational because it maximizes joint profit, but it is individually irrational because each firm's private profit incentive urges it to depart from the collusive equilibrium.

We have once again encountered what we called the **oligopoly problem** in Section 12.2. On the one hand, if firms find them-

selves at a Cournot or a Bertrand equilibrium, they have a clear incentive to collude. On the other hand, if firms manage to forge a collusive agreement, there is a clear private incentive for each party to cheat on the collusive agreement.

The history of the OPEC cartel illustrates both sides of the problem. OPEC is a cartel of oil-exporting countries that operates by assigning export quotas to individual member countries in an attempt to reduce the supply of crude oil to the world market. At various times, particularly during the mid-1970s, the cartel has been successful in restricting supply and thereby raising prices. At other times, however, many OPEC member countries have cheated on their collusive agreement by exporting more than their allotted quotas. For instance, in the late 1980s, newspapers were full of reports about individual OPEC countries that were "keeping their spigots wide open" — that is, exceeding their quotas on the sale of crude oil in the international oil market. In fact, one news item in *Business Week* contained this report on the purpose of an emergency meeting called by the president of OPEC: "Item One on the agenda: Restoring discipline to the cartel, which is pumping far more than its daily quota of 126.6 million [barrels]" (*Business Week*, September 7, 1987, p. 24). As you'll discover in the following problem, in the Cournot model, the individual incentive to cheat on a collusive agreement increases as the number of parties to the agreement increases, which means that the larger the number of firms in an industry, the less likely is a collusive equilibrium. If the number of firms is large enough, some firm or firms will succumb to the temptation to cheat, thereby destroying the collusive agreement.

P R O B L E M 12.3

If three parties form a collusive agreement, the equilibrium is to allocate 10 units to each member at a profit of $300 per member. Show that if one party decides to cheat and the other two do not, the cheater will produce 20 units and enjoy a profit of $400. Therefore, the inducement to cheat is $100 when three firms form a collusive agreement, but only $56.25 when just two firms form the agreement. Now suppose that four firms are party to the agreement and that each firm is allocated 7.5 units. What is the inducement to cheat in this case?

The Collusive Model with Many Firms

What happens to the collusive equilibrium as the number of firms in the market expands? Nothing, except that more and more firms split a fixed-profit pie: aggregate output and aggregate profit do not change. Compare this property of the collusive model to the corresponding property in the Cournot model. In the Cournot model, as the number of firms expands, aggregate output increases and aggregate profit decreases. As the number of firms gets arbitrarily large, aggregate profit goes to zero.

The Electrical Equipment Price-Fixing Conspiracy

Let's look at another case that dramatizes the conflicting incentives that give rise to the oligopoly problem. We'll examine the behavior of various parties in the infamous electrical equipment price-fixing conspiracy of the 1950s. As we'll see, these electrical firms, having recognized the clear incentive to collude, produced elaborate price-fixing agreements — only to renege on them later.[7]

The conspiracy involved more than 20 producers of electrical equipment with annual sales of $1.5 billion. Company representatives met periodically to set prices on such standardized products as insulators. They also produced extraordinarily detailed — sometimes book-length — pric-

ing formulas for nonstandard or customized products such as turbine generators. And they devised an ingenious scheme, called the "phase of the moon," for fixing prices and sharing out the business in sealed-bid competitions. Under this scheme, the designated "winner" of the bid (whose identity changed every 2 weeks) submitted the bid decreed by the price-fixing formula, and all other bidders were supposed to submit higher bids.

Despite these elaborate agreements, the history of this conspiracy, like the recent history of OPEC, was a variant on the old theme that there is no honor among thieves. As one GE executive put it in explaining why his group left the conspiracy: "No one was living up to the agreement and we . . . were being made suckers. On every job someone would cut our throat; we lost confidence in the group."[8] Thus, the companies acted both on their mutually strong incentive to collude and on their own individually strong incentives to cheat on that collusive agreement later on.

12.6 Experimental Evidence

What are professional economists — and economics students — to make of such a profusion of oligopoly models, all yielding different equilibria? There is no answer that all or even most economists can agree on. Indeed, some evidence from experimental economics suggest that there can be no general oligopoly model applicable to all situations — at least, not unless the model takes into account the inclinations of the individual economic actors.[9]

Let's look briefly at a series of experiments that Fouraker and Siegal (1963) con-

---

[7] See Smith (1961) or Harling (1962) for detailed accounts of this saga of collusion and betrayal.

[8] Smith (1961), p. 172.

[9] See Plott (1982) for a careful and thorough review of experimental evidence on oligopoly problems.

ducted to test the duopoly equilibrium when two subjects, like the firms in the Cournot model, chose quantities. In the first set of 14 experiments, each subject was given a table specifying his or her individual payoffs (or profits) as functions of the quantities provided by the two players. The two subjects then played the "duopoly game" a number of times. In these experiments, each subject knew only the quantities that the other player had chosen in all previous periods—and, of course, his or her own quantities and profits. The equilibrium in the last period of this set of experiments closely approximated the Cournot equilibrium.

In a second set of 14 experiments, both subjects knew their own quantities and profits in all previous periods and those of the other player. Relative to the first set of experiments, they had additional information regarding the other player's profits. In about one-half of these experiments, the equilibrium in the last period closely approximated the Cournot equilibrium; in about one-third, it approximated the collusive equilibrium; and in about one-sixth, it approximated the competitive equilibrium.

In another series of experiments, the subjects were asked to choose price, not quantity. When both subjects knew only the price charged by the other subject in all previous periods, the best approximation was almost invariably the Bertrand equilibrium. When both subjects knew the other subject's profits in all periods as well, in nine cases the best approximation was the Bertrand equilibrium; in four, it was the collusive equilibrium; and in four, it was an intermediate equilibrium.

Taken together, these experiments suggest that no single model is applicable to all oligopoly situations. Perhaps the most economists can hope for is a selection of oligopoly models, each applicable to a particular range of economic circumstances.

12.7 Repeated Play, Supergames, and Richer Strategies

The oligopoly models we have been looking at do not capture one very important aspect of real-world oligopolies. Because the models are essentially static, or concerned with strategies and payoffs in just one period, they fail to capture the long-term dynamic interplay that characterizes most real-world oligopoly relationships. We have no adequate way to capture in these one-period models the phenomenon of what we might call "repeated play" of similar oligopoly games.

Once we recognize that oligopolists repeatedly play games of strategy and counterstrategy as they jockey for market power—often for extended periods of time—we can imagine that the strategies available to them are potentially far richer than our simpler static models suggest. We'll do an intuitive treatment of one strategic possibility developed by James Friedman (1971) that arises under repeated play.[10]

As you know, although collusive agreements are collectively more beneficial to oligopolists, the individual firms nevertheless have strong private incentives to try to grab a larger share of the market for themselves by cheating on the agreement. To induce all members of a collusive agreement to stick to the bargain, Friedman considered **punishment strategies** that oligopolists can devise for breaches of the collusive agreement.

These punishments must be both *severe* and *credible*. It is obvious that not all punishments satisfy both these criteria. Suppose, for example, that each duopolist threatens to murder the other if the other violates the agreement. In this case, the pun-

---

[10] See Friedman (1977) for an excellent treatment of the material outlined below.

ishment is severe enough to deter breach, but it is not credible because carrying it out would surely result in imprisonment or worse for the punisher. We'll say that a punishment strategy is credible if it is in the punisher's self-interest to carry out the punishment, once a breach of the agreement occurs.

Suppose that two firms play their duopoly game an infinite number of times, in what is sometimes called a **supergame**. Remember that in any particular period, the collusive solution for each is to produce 15 units, and the Cournot solution is for each to produce 20 units. The objective is to devise punishment strategies that will make the collusive solution of 15 units in each period not only the collectively rational but also the individually rational, or profit-maximizing, solution.

For a possible set of strategies, we'll consider the following variant on the fable of the donkey and the carrot and stick. The first firm's carrot is its promise to produce 15 units in any given period, provided that its rival has produced 15 units in all previous periods. Its stick is its threat to provide 20 units in all subsequent periods if it ever discovers that its rival has cheated on the agreement by producing more than 15 units. The second firm's strategy precisely parallels the first firm's. Having devised and announced these carrot-and-stick strategies to each other, the duopolists break off communication and go their separate ways.

Is the threatened punishment severe enough to encourage each duopolist to produce just 15 units in each period? Is it credible? To answer the first question, we need to compare a firm's maximum profit if it abides by the collusive agreement with its maximum profit if it breaches the agreement. Let's focus on the second firm's decision. Given the first firm's announced strategy, if the second firm produces 15 units in all periods, it will earn $450 in each period.

As we saw in the previous section, if it cheats on the agreement, the best it can do in the present period is to produce 22.5 units (the profit-maximizing quantity, given that the first firm produces 15 units). Its profit is then $506.25 in the present period. If the first firm then carries out its threat by raising its own output to 20 units in all subsequent periods, the best that the second firm can do thereafter is to produce 20 units in each period — thereby inducing the Cournot equilibrium — and its profit will then be $400 in every subsequent period. In contrast to the collusive solution, then, if the second firm breaches the collusive agreement, it gains $56.25 in the present period but loses $50 in all future periods. Whether the punishment is severe enough to be a deterrent then depends on the rate of interest. If a dollar today is not worth significantly more than a dollar tomorrow, then the punishment of losing $50 per period forever will be large enough to offset the temptation of gaining $56.25 today. In other words, unless the interest rate is extremely high, the punishment is severe enough to deter cheating.

The other question is whether the punishment is credible. That is, will it be in the first firm's self-interest to carry out its threat by actually producing 20 units in each future period if its rival breaches the collusive agreement? Let's begin with the second firm's strategy. Once it has cheated on the agreement, it will expect the first firm to carry out its threat to produce 20 units. In response, it will decide to produce 20 units as well. In this situation, what will the first firm's response be? Because it will expect the second firm to produce 20 units, the first firm will serve its own self-interest best by producing 20 units as well — thereby producing the Cournot equilibrium in all future periods. The punishment is therefore credible because the first firm will actually make good on its threat to up its own production when it discovers that its rival has cheated. Thus, if the collusive agreement is breached in some period, the announced punishment strategy will produce the Cournot equilibrium in every subsequent period.

We now know that if either firm breaches the collusive agreement to produce 15 units in each period, the duopolists will be locked into the Cournot solution for all future periods. If the interest rate is not too high, then neither firm will ever breach the agreement, and the punishment strategy does make the collectively rational solution individually rational as well.

Repeated oligopoly games open up many more questions and possibilities than our example suggests. We implicitly assumed, for example, that each firm could detect cheating by its rival(s). In an industry in which market demand is subject to significant random variation or in which the number of firms is comparatively large, detection will be a harder task. If detection is too difficult, the punishment strategy simply will not do the job.[11]

PROBLEM 12.4

Salop (1986) has identified an interesting punishment strategy in observing that in some industries, all the firms in the market agree to include in their contracts with buyers a most-favored-customer clause. The clause stipulates that if a firm sells the same product to another customer at a lower price within some specified period of time, then the original customer can claim a rebate equal to the price differential multiplied by the quantity purchased. Explain how such clauses — which are apparently in the individual customer's interest — can be used to support a collusive pricing agreement that is clearly not in the interest of consumers.

12.8 The Limit-Output Model

Because the number of firms has been exogenous, the models we have explored to this point serve only as an introduction to the important and intriguing topic of oligopoly. In the rest of this chapter, we will focus on the theory of oligopoly in the long run. In these models, the number of firms — or the **market structure** — is endogenous. The number of firms in any industry is determined by economic considerations, and in oligopolistic industries, as in competitive industries, the key process in determining the long-run equilibrium is the *possibility of entry*.

We'll explore the approach to endogenous market structure pioneered by Joe Bain (1956) and by Paolo Sylos-Labini (1961) in the mid-1950s; we'll look, too, at recent extensions of their approach.[12] Bain and Sylos-Labini were the first to recognize the critical role that entry plays in determining the structure of an oligopolistic industry. In particular, they addressed the key question: Under what conditions will a potential firm find it unprofitable to enter an oligopolistic market? The answer to this question is what we will call a **no-entry condition** — a condition that obviously must be satisfied in any long-run oligopoly equilibrium.

Modigliani formalized some of Bain's and Sylos-Labini's insights into what we'll call the **limit-output model,** more commonly called the **limit-price model.** In presenting the limit-output model in this section and recent refinements of it in the next, our objective is not to produce a rigorous general

---

[11] Stigler (1969) presents a thorough discussion of the conditions that are and are not conducive to effective collusion.

[12] The review article by Modigliani (1958) is an excellent introduction to the work of Bain and Sylos-Labini. You may want to consult Dixit (1980) and Eaton and Lipsey (1980) for extensions of the basic approach.

model, but to introduce you to useful ways of thinking about endogenous market structure in oligopolistic industries.

Barriers to Entry

We'll continue to use the market demand and cost functions from the first half of the chapter, with one important exception. Given the cost function we've been using, entry will continue until the competitive equilibrium prevails — until price is driven down to marginal cost, or $40. Therefore, the theory of market structure is interesting only when there is some barrier to the entry of new firms.

The natural barrier we'll be using is a **setup cost** (or product development cost) first introduced in the patent model in Section 11.10. Such costs are ubiquitous and can be very large indeed. As we mentioned in Chapter 11, a microeconomics textbook costs approximately $500,000 in R&D. Bringing a new prescription drug to the market now costs an average of $125 million for R&D. Polaroid spent $500 million on R&D to produce its SX-70 camera and film. And Airbus has chewed up $15 billion in development costs. Clearly, the need to incur such sizable setup costs can and does deter potential entrants.

In fact, deliberately incurring whopping setup costs can be seen as a strategic move to deter entry. For example, a public relations officer of Apple Inc., — the maker of the Macintosh family of computers — recently commented on Apple's decision to invest heavily in R&D as a means of discouraging cloning by rival manufacturers: "We've built a lot of custom chips, designed for us to specifically enhance the operation and function of [our] computers. That, in itself, creates a tremendous barrier to anyone who wants to copy the hardware because the investment in research, development and custom manufacturing is in the

millions and millions of dollars" (*The Financial Post*, May 29, 1989, p. S3).

Let's suppose that all firms must incur a setup, or product development, cost equal to $S. In any one period, the rate of interest will determine the fixed cost associated with the setup cost. Denoting the rate of interest by i, the fixed cost is

$$K = iS$$

Adding this fixed cost to previous costs yields the following cost function:

$$C(y) = K + 40y$$

The fixed cost associated with product development — or the **barrier to entry** — is captured in the first term on the right, K, and what we can now call the variable costs of production are captured in the second term, $40y$.

The Sylos Postulate

The key assumption in the limit-output model of market structure — sometimes called the Sylos postulate — is that any potential entrant takes the current industry-wide output as a given. For example, if the industry is producing 30 units at present, a potential entrant assumes that if it actually enters the industry, the established firms will continue to produce 30 units. This model is then an extension of the Cournot model, and we can use what we know about that model to develop the limit-output model.

The Inducement to Entry

If the fixed cost K is the barrier to entry in this model, what is the **inducement to entry?** It is the excess of revenue over variable costs that the entrant would earn if it did enter the market. To see what's involved in calculating the inducement to entry, let's suppose that the established firm or firms are currently producing 30 units, and then compute the excess of revenue over variable costs the entrant would earn if it were to enter the market. Figure 12.5 presents the market demand function, the entrant's residual demand function $(p_E = 70 - y_E)$, and the entrant's marginal revenue function $(MR_E = 70 - 2y_E)$ for this case. The entrant's demand and marginal revenue functions are plotted relative to the origin labeled 0_E, which is 30 units to the right of the origin labeled 0. If the entrant were to enter this market, it would produce 15 units, since its marginal revenue is equal to its marginal cost at this output level. If it did produce 15 units, price would be $55, its revenue would be $825 ($55 \times 15$), and its variable costs would be $600 ($40 \times 15$). In this case, then, the inducement to entry is

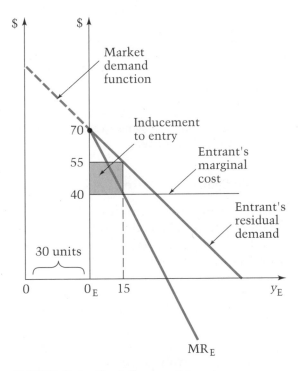

FIGURE 12.5   The inducement to entry.

Since the monopolist produces 30 units, the entrant perceives the residual demand curve in this figure. If it did enter, it would maximize profit by producing 15 units, and it would anticipate profit per period equal to the green area, which is the inducement to entry.

$225 ($825 - 600$), equal to the dark green area in Figure 12.5. Will a potential entrant actually enter this market, or will it stay out? If the barrier to entry $K is less than the inducement to entry—that is, if K is less than $255—it will enter. If K is greater than or equal to $225, it will stay out. (For simplicity, we are assuming that a potential entrant will not enter if it anticipates zero profit.)

What is the inducement to entry when established firms produce no output? Or 60 units? Or, more generally, y units? The first two questions are easily answered. If established firms produce nothing, the inducement to entry is $900—the excess of revenue over variable costs for a monopolist. If the established firms produce 60 units, the inducement is $0 because the entrant's residual demand curve is then $p_E = 40 - y_E$. As you can see, the inducement to entry shrinks as the output of established firms grows. The third question is harder and more interesting. From the Cournot model, we see that when established firms produce y units, the entrant's best response is

$$y_E^* = 30 - \frac{y}{2}$$

The entrant's residual demand function is just

$$p_E = (100 - y) - y_E$$

Using this demand function, we can compute the price that will prevail if the entrant produces y_E^* units:

$$p_E^* = (100 - y) - y_E^*$$

More important, we can compute p_E^* minus the $40 marginal cost. As you should verify,

$$p_E^* - 40 = 30 - \frac{y}{2}$$

The inducement to entry, $p_E^* \times (p_E^* - 40)$, is then

$$\text{inducement to entry} = \left(30 - \frac{y}{2}\right)^2$$

This expression gives us the excess of revenue over variable costs that an entrant would earn if established firms continued to produce y units after entry.

The Limit Output

Entry will occur if the inducement to entry exceeds K, but will not occur if it is less than or equal to K. We will call the smallest value of y such that no entry occurs the *limit output*. Alternatively, we can think of the limit output as the value of y such that the inducement to entry is equal to the barrier to entry. Letting y_L denote the limit output, we have

$$\left(30 - \frac{y_L}{2}\right)^2 = K$$

Or, solving for y_L

$$y_L = 60 - 2K^{1/2}$$

For instance, if K is $100, the limit output is 40 units; if K is $225, the limit output is 30; and so on. We can use the limit output to write the no-entry condition in a different way:

Entry will not occur if the output of established firms is greater than or equal to the limit output, y_L.

The *limit price* is just the price associated with the limit output, $100 - y_L$, or

$$p_L = 40 + 2K^{1/2}$$

The limit output and the limit price when K is 400 are presented in Figure 12.6. The limit output is 20, and the limit price $80. When established firms produce 20 units, the inducement to entry of $400 is identical to the barrier to entry K. Therefore, the entrant's average cost function is tangent to its residual demand function at point E. To check your understanding of the limit output, try the following problem.

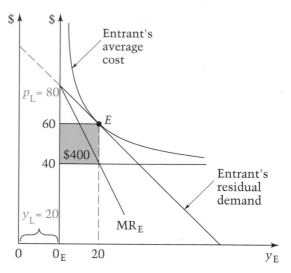

FIGURE 12.6 Identifying the limit price and limit output.

If established firms produce 20 units, the inducement to entry is $400, which is identical to the $K = \$400$ barrier to entry. Hence, 20 units is the limit output—$y_L = 20$—and $80 (equal to $100 - 20$) is the limit price—$p_L = 80$—when K is $400.

PROBLEM 12.5

Construct a diagram analogous to Figure 12.6 for the case in which K is $196.

Strategic Choice of Industry Output

Now let's shift our attention away from entrants and think about the no-entry condition from the perspective of established firms. First, how does the possibility of entry constrain established firms in their ability to earn profit? And how does the possibility of entry affect their strategic decision making—assuming that established firms know that a limit quantity and a limit price will effectively deter such entry? To simplify matters, let's suppose that there is just one established firm, or a *sitting monopolist*.

We already know precisely how the entrant will behave. If y is less than the limit output y_L, it will enter the industry; if y is greater than or equal to y_L, it will stay out. If we presume that the sitting monopolist can also calculate the limit output that precludes entry, y_L, how will it make use of this piece of information? We have calculated that if K is $225, then y_L is 30 units — and 30 units is the monopoly output. Thus, if the setup costs in this industry, K, are $225 or higher, the monopoly output of 30 units will successfully deter entry — and the sitting monopolist will remain the only firm in the market. Given the Sylos postulate, if the sitting monopolist is already producing 30 units, an entrant has no profit incentive to enter. When K is $225 or more, then the industry is a **natural monopoly.**

On the other hand, if K is less than $225, the ordinary monopoly output will not deter entry, because the limit output y_L is then larger than 30 units. What action will the sitting monopolist take in this case? It will produce exactly y_L units of output. Why? Because it has already incurred the setup cost, its objective now is to maximize the excess of its revenues over its variable costs, or what we'll call *gross profit;* that is, it wants to maximize $y(p - 40)$. If it deters entry by producing the limit output, its gross profit will be $y_L(p_L - 40)$. What would happen to the sitting monopolist's profit if it were to allow entry by producing less than the limit output y_L — say, y'. Because entrants would continue until price p' was less than or equal to p_L, its gross profit would then fall to $y'(p' - 40)$ — a sum obviously less than $y_L(p_L - 40)$ because y' is less than y_L and p' is no larger than p_L. Thus, the sitting monopolist will always choose to protect its own profitability by deterring entry in this model.

Notice that when K is less than $225, we have the case called **monopoly by good management** in Chapter 11. The efficiency implications of this kind of monopoly are very different from those we encountered in Chapter 11. First, to deter entry, the sitting monopolist produces more than the ordinary monopoly output. Second, because entry is costly — it uses real resources — other things being equal, it is wasteful to have more than one firm serving this market. Of course, other things are not necessarily equal: in particular, two firms might produce even more than y_L units of output. Whether the added output is worth the additional expense of the second firm's setup cost, however, is an open question. Indeed, it is entirely possible that the monopoly by good management equilibrium is the best of the free-market alternatives.

PROBLEM 12.6

In light of the limit-output model, try answering the following question: A monopolist will never operate in the inelastic portion of its demand curve. True or false? Explain.

Critique of the Model

The Sylos postulate — that entrants take the current industry output as given — is the Achilles heel of the limit-output model. A potential entrant's real concern is not with the present but with the future output of a sitting monopolist. When a sitting monopolist produces the limit output, its decision is intended as a credible warning to potential entrants that it will continue to produce the limit output in future periods. If entrants take the warning seriously, they will stay out of the market.

But is the threat credible? If entry does occur, will a sitting monopolist respond by continuing to produce the limit output? To answer this question, we need to look more closely at the underlying oligopoly model. The following approach to answering the credibility question raised by the limit-output model was pioneered by Michael Spence (1977).

12.9 Refinements of Limit Output

Let's suppose that the appropriate model of oligopoly is the Cournot model and that *every potential entrant knows that the Cournot model is appropriate*. Given n established firms, the entrant can now actually calculate what the industry equilibrium would be if it were to enter and, more to the point, what its own profit would be in that equilibrium.

Notice that this approach neatly finesses the credibility question. Since the entrant knows that the Cournot model is appropriate and can calculate the Cournot equilibrium that will prevail after entry, it knows exactly how much output established firms will actually produce if it does enter. As a result, the credibility question never arises. If established firms are going to produce more than the limit output if entry occurs, then the entrant can anticipate that maneuver correctly, and it will stay out. On the other hand, if established firms are going to produce less than the limit output, the entrant will once again anticipate that maneuver correctly, and it will enter. The potential weakness of this approach is that the Cournot model may not be appropriate. As long as it is, however, the entrant will be able to make the right calculations concerning the postentry output. Furthermore, as you will see in answering the exercises at the end of this section, if a different oligopoly model is appropriate, the same general method can be used to model the resulting market structure.

To see how this approach works, suppose that the industry is currently a monopoly. If entry occurs, the industry will then be a duopoly. Reinterpreting what we learned in Section 12.3, the excess of revenue over variable cost for the entrant—or the inducement to entry—is $400. Entry will therefore occur if this $400 inducement exceeds the fixed cost K—or the barrier to entry—but it will not occur if K exceeds $400.

This raises another question: How large must the fixed cost K be so that a third firm will not enter the market? In Problem 12.2, you identified the Cournot equilibrium with three firms: each firm produces 15 units and realizes a gross profit of $225. If at present only two firms are in the market, the inducement to entry is $225, and entry will therefore not occur if K is larger than $225. Thus, if K exceeds $225 and is less than $400, only two firms will be in this market. On the other hand, if K is less than $225, a third firm will enter. This raises yet another question: How large must K be so that a fourth firm will not enter? The answer to this question raises yet another, and so on.

We can answer this unending string of questions by performing a single general exercise. Suppose that n established firms are currently in the industry. What is the inducement to entry? Because the entrant will increase the number of firms to $n + 1$, we can simply reinterpret what we already know about the Cournot model to discover the answer. Each of the $n + 1$ firms will produce $60/(n + 2)$ units in the Cournot equilibrium. As you should verify, the price in this equilibrium minus the marginal cost of $40 is also $60/(n + 2)$. Therefore, when n firms are in the market, the inducement to entry is

$$\text{inducement to entry} = \left(\frac{60}{n + 2}\right)^2$$

The generalized no-entry condition is then

$$\left(\frac{60}{n + 1}\right)^2 \leq K$$

Given K, this condition determines the minimum number of firms that must serve this market if entry is to be unprofitable.

If we now suppose that firms enter the industry sequentially, we have a complete theory of market structure for this illustra-

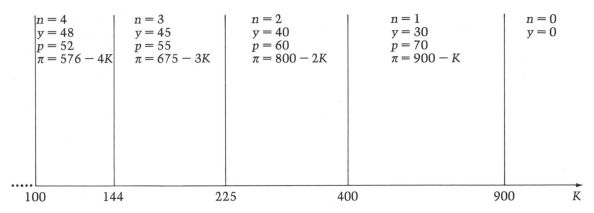

$n = 4$	$n = 3$	$n = 2$	$n = 1$	$n = 0$
$y = 48$	$y = 45$	$y = 40$	$y = 30$	$y = 0$
$p = 52$	$p = 55$	$p = 60$	$p = 70$	
$\pi = 576 - 4K$	$\pi = 675 - 3K$	$\pi = 800 - 2K$	$\pi = 900 - K$	

| 100 | 144 | 225 | 400 | 900 | K |

FIGURE 12.7   Cournot oligopoly and entry equilibrium.

The number of firms in entry equilibrium is inversely related to the magnitude of the product development cost, or the barrier to entry K. As K decreases, the number of firms and aggregate output increase, while price and profit decrease. When K is more than \$225 and less than \$400, for example, there are two firms, aggregate output is 40 units, price is \$60, and aggregate profit is $800 - 2K$.

tion. Given K, the number of firms in the industry will be the smallest value of n such that the generalized no-entry condition is satisfied. These results are presented in Figure 12.7, where K is measured along the horizontal axis. If K is greater than the gross profit of \$900 earned by a monopolist, the market is not a viable one: no firms will serve it. If K is greater than \$400 but less than \$900, the industry is a natural monopoly. A single firm will produce 30 units, sell them at a price equal to \$70, and earn \$900 minus K in profit. If K is greater than \$225 but less than \$400, a duopoly will serve the market. Aggregate output will be 40 units, price will be \$60, and aggregate profit will be \$800 minus $2K$. If K is greater than \$144 but less than \$225, three firms will be in the industry, and so on.

In this model, setup or product development costs K can be interpreted as a barrier to entry; K is the only factor that differentiates established firms from potential entrants. Because established firms have already incurred this cost, they view it as a sunk cost—a cost that has no bearing on their profit-maximizing decisions. Because potential entrants have not incurred this cost, however, they see it instead as an avoidable cost of production—a cost they will incur only if they opt for entry. When K is large, few firms will opt for entry; when it is small, many firms will opt for entry. The *magnitude of the barrier to entry therefore determines the market structure* in this simple model.

In a more elaborate model, however, demand conditions will also be factors in determining market structure. For example, if the market demand function is $p = 200 - y$ instead of the demand function used throughout this chapter, $p = 100 - y$, we would expect to see more firms in the industry for any given value of K. Further, as you will soon see, a setup or product development cost is not the only barrier to entry. We have used it simply to suggest the role that such barriers play in determining market structure. The precise effect of any particular entry barrier will vary.

As you'll discover in the following problems, once the possibility of entry is introduced into the simple oligopoly models of the first half of this chapter, these models appear in a new light. Recall that in the context of a fixed number of firms, the Bertrand model seemed absurd because the cutthroat competition that drives that model ensured that the outcome would be prices equal to marginal cost. When we couple the Bertrand model with entry, however, the result is instead universal monopoly. As long as K is positive, a second firm will never enter the market. By contrast, in the collusive model at the beginning of the chapter, gross profit was maximal for a fixed number of firms. When we couple the collusive model with entry, however, potential entrants find entry enticing. As a result, in the long run, firms continue to enter the market until, in equilibrium, gross profit is minimal.

PROBLEM 12.7

Suppose that cost and demand conditions are identical to those used throughout this chapter. Suppose, too, that the underlying oligopoly model is the Bertrand model and that, at present, a single established firm is in the market. This sitting monopolist is producing the monopoly output and earning the full monopoly profit. What is the inducement to entry? Show that as long as K is positive, an entrant who understands oligopoly pricing behavior in the Bertrand model will never enter.

PROBLEM 12.8

Now suppose that the underlying oligopoly model is the collusive model. Suppose, too, that the entrant sees that it will be admitted to the collusive club once it incurs the setup cost, thereby becoming an established firm. What is the inducement to enter? Show that the no-entry condition is

$$\frac{900}{n+1} \le K$$

Assuming that entry is sequential, compare industrywide profit in this model with industrywide profit in the Cournot model of long-run equilibrium when K is 400; when K is 100.

As you have just discovered, if a sitting monopolist in the Bertrand model can credibly threaten to pursue the postentry strategy of cutthroat competition implicit in that model, it can continue to monopolize its market regardless of how small K is. By contrast, if the established oligopolists in the collusive model anticipate that their collusive behavior will simply entice potential entrants to join the collusive club, their preentry incentive to act collusively will be seriously eroded.

What have we learned? First, setup costs differentiate the real economic position of established firms from the position of potential entrants. Therefore, such costs act as a barrier to entry. Second, the precise way in which this differentiation affects an entrant's anticipated profit—or the inducement to entry—depends on the nature of the oligopoly behavior subsequent to entry. Roughly speaking, the more aggressive oligopoly behavior is subsequent to entry, the more effective setup costs are as a barrier to entry. Conversely, the more cooperative oligopoly behavior is subsequent to entry, the less effective setup costs are as a barrier to entry.

Any firm's decision to incur the setup cost can be seen as a strategic decision to position itself as an established firm. It is strategic because it affects the incentives of other firms. In particular, if the firm does choose to position itself as an established firm, it effectively reduces the profit that subsequent firms can anticipate from the market.

This view of the decision to incur setup costs as a positioning strategy raises an important question. In what other ways can establish firms position themselves relative to potential entrants to manipulate those entrants' incentives? The recent literature on long-run equilibrium in oligopolies has examined a whole arsenal of such positioning strategies, including moves to acquire specialized and durable capital equipment, to create patents, to stockpile essential raw materials, to hold extensive inventory, and to spend money on advertising and product development.

12.10 Positioning and Reacting

Because the subject of oligopoly is complex and sometimes confusing, in closing we'll attempt to draw together insights from the entire chapter. In doing so, we will be drawing heavily on Spence (1981)—a source that provides an accessible, wide-ranging discussion of the issues raised in this chapter.

Any firm able to earn consistently high profit over a long period of time requires some form of protection from potential entrants. Yet the existence of such profit is clearly an enticement to potential entrants, which raises the question: What can protect a firm's profit from entry? The answer is, a combination of *structural features*, such as economies of scale and product development or setup costs, and of *actions designed to inhibit entry*. We have highlighted setup costs as a structural feature in this chapter. Their role in entry deterrence is straightforward: to entice entry, the potential entrant's market share must be large enough that the firm at least recovers its setup costs. The larger such setup costs are, the less attractive is the opportunity to enter. Thus, setup costs are one important barrier to entry and are therefore an important determinant of market structure. More generally, economies of scale are a barrier to entry.

Turning to the actions that established firms undertake in an attempt to inhibit entry, Spence distinguishes two separate but strategically interrelated sets of activities: positioning and reacting. **Positioning** is concerned with actions taken prior to entry. Accumulating inventory is one possible positioning strategy. Others include adver-

tising, acquiring capital or production capacity, and choosing product durability. (Selling durable products today, for example, allows an established firm to capture today's and tomorrow's market today—a strategy that will materially affect potential entrant's profitability.) **Reacting** refers to the actions of established firms subsequent to entry. An entry-deterring reaction discussed in this chapter is the threat to market a quantity at least as large as the limit output subsequent to entry.

Reacting and positioning are clearly substitutes in the sense that if the established firm can credibly threaten to be sufficiently aggressive subsequent to entry, it need not pursue any clever positioning strategy prior to entry. Recall, for example, what you learned from Problem 12.7. If firms behave in accordance with the Bertrand model, as long as K is positive, entry will never occur. Hence, an established firm might try to substitute the postentry threat of the ruthless price cutting imagined by Bertrand for the preentry positioning strategy of holding inventory. The difficulty is that this postentry threat may not be credible, because once entry does occur, the established firm would be cutting its own throat (as well as the entrant's) by driving price down to marginal cost.

Where reactive threats may not seem credible in themselves, they sometimes can be made more believable when coupled with a positioning strategy. By actually producing output prior to entry and holding it in inventory, for example, an established firm makes more credible its threat to market that output. By actually acquiring production capacity prior to entry, an established firm makes the threat to use that capacity subsequent to entry more believable, and so on.

Indeed, in a famous antitrust case, Alcoa was accused of effectively deterring competition by using excess capacity to make more credible its implicit threat to market the limit output if entry occurred. In making a judgment against Alcoa (1945), Judge Hand pointed to Alcoa's deliberate decisions to repeatedly build up its capacity as the market for aluminum expanded:

> It was not inevitable that it should always anticipate increases in the demand for ingot and be prepared to supply them. Nothing compelled it to keep doubling and redoubling its capacity before others entered the field. It insists that it never excluded rivals; but we can think of no more effective exclusion than progressively to embrace each new opportunity as it opened and to face every newcomer with new capacity already geared into a great organization, having the advantage of experience, trade connections and the elite of personnel.

In the so-called Cheerios case, the leading ready-to-eat cereal makers — Kellogg, General Mills, and Post — were similarly accused of strategically deterring entry, in their case by a strategy of brand proliferation. (We'll look at the "Cheerios case" in the next chapter.)

Summary

In the first part of this chapter, we limited our attention to a fixed number of firms and learned one relatively simple but basic lesson about oligopolistic interactions: there is a fundamental contradiction between what is privately rational (or profit-maximizing) and what is collectively rational. In any simple Nash equilibrium, firms have a clear incentive to collude. Yet each party to a collusive agreement has a private incentive to cheat by producing more than the agreed-upon output or by charging less than the agree-upon price. The prisoners' dilemma is the game that illustrates these conflicting forces most clearly. This contradiction arises in Cournot's model of oligopoly, where firms independently choose quantities, and in Bertrand's model, where firms independently choose prices. Evidence from experimental economics and from the history of real collusive agreements supports the view that oligopolists do recognize and act on these conflicting incentives at different times.

We saw, too, that Cournot's model responds in an appealing way to changes in the number of firms. When there is only one firm. Cournot's model is identical to the standard monopoly model. As the number of firms increases, aggregate output increases, and aggregate profit and price decrease. As the number of firms approaches infinity, Cournot's model converges to the competitive equilibrium. Thus, Cournot's model captures the entire range of market structures, from monopoly to perfect competition. Neither Bertrand's model nor the collusive model has these appealing properties. In Bertrand's model, price is equal to marginal cost whenever there are two or more firms. In the collusive model, price and aggregate output are always at the monopoly levels.

When we looked at supergames — those in which firms repeatedly play the same game — we saw that the set of possible strategies was much richer. In particular, in a supergame, firms can condition their current behavior on the past behavior of their rivals. This opens up the possibility of punishment strategies that can support collusive, or cooperative, behavior among oligopolists. Wherever these strategies are used, the fundamental contradiction between collective and private rationality is surmounted because the private incentives of oligopolists will lead them to produce the collusive output.

In the second part of the chapter, we arrived at several additional insights as we explored the theory of oligopoly in the long run, when firms are allowed to enter a market. We began with the limit-output model, in which established firms produce enough output (the limit output) that an entrant who takes the output of established firms as given will not enter. As we saw, the weakness of this model lies in the question of credibility: How believable is the threat by established firms to actually produce the limit output after entry occurs. To find a way around the credibility question, we coupled the Cournot model with the entry considerations of the limit-output model to produce a more adequate theory of market structure.

We closed the chapter by summing up the insights to be drawn from our foray into the fascinating but complicated world of oligopolistic decision making. It is fascinating because it is at heart a game of strategic maneuvering: a game of positioning and reacting. Yet it is precisely the business of anticipating and responding to strategic moves of rivals (present and potential) that makes oligopoly so difficult to model.

Exercises

1 In this problem, you'll be asked to adapt much of the analysis in this chapter to a model with different cost and demand conditions. The market demand function is

$$p = 460 - .5y$$

The constant marginal cost for all firms is $100.

a Find the monopoly output and price, and compute the monopolist's profit.

b Find the Cournot equilibrium output for each firm and the aggregate output and price in the Cournot equilibrium, and compute the equilibrium profit of a representative firm, when there are two firms in the market. When there are three firms in the market. When there are four firms in the market.

c Suppose that there are two firms in the market. What is the symmetric collusive equilibrium? How much profit does each

firm earn in this equilibrium? If one firm honors the collusive agreement, and the other violates the agreement, how much should the violator produce to maximize its profit? What is the magnitude of the inducement to violate the collusive agreement?

d Now suppose that there is a fixed cost in addition to the $100 marginal cost. If the fixed cost K is $3200, what is the limit output y_L? What is the limit price p_L? Supposing that the limit output effectively deters entry, what profit would a monopolist earn by using the limit-output strategy?

e Now suppose that K is $20,000 that all firms regard the Cournot model as the correct oligopoly model, and that entry is sequential. How many firms will enter the market? What profit will each firm earn?

f Now suppose that K is $20,000, that all firms regard the collusive model as the correct oligopoly model, and that entry is sequential. How many firms will enter the market? What profit will each firm earn?

g Finally, suppose that K is $20,000, that all firms regard the Bertrand model as the correct oligopoly model, and that entry is sequential. How many firms will enter the market? What profit will each firm earn?

2 In this problem, you can see that common property creates a prisoner's dilemma. Harry and Sally each have 90 fish in their pens, and their preferences are such that they prefer bundles, composed of fish consumed today and fish consumed tomorrow, with more total fish. That is, the total number of fish he (she) consumes over the two periods is what matters to Harry (Sally). Each can choose one of the following two strategies: E denotes the strategy of eating all 90 fish today, and R denotes the strategy of returning all 90 fish to the river. Each fish returned to the river today results in $\frac{5}{3}$ fish for consumption tomorrow. Under the common-property institution, Harry and Sally each take half of tomorrow's fish harvest. Construct a matrix analogous to Table 12.1 in which the entries are the total numbers of fish consumed by Harry and by Sally, and show that E is a dominant strategy for both Harry and Sally. Show, too, that they

would have been better off had they both chosen R instead of E. Suppose that they are operating under a private-property institution; repeat the exercise.

3 The daily demand for round-trip air travel between cities A and B is

$$p = 2000 - y$$

where y is the number of passengers. There is no demand for one-way travel. Each plane can carry up to 1000 passengers. The cost of flying a plane from A to B and back again is K, regardless of the number of passengers on the plane. Each firm owns only one plane. Suppose that there are a number of firms in this market and that they can collusively choose and enforce one price. What price will they choose? Suppose, too, that the price-setting club cannot keep other firms from entering the market; that is, free entry into the market (and the club) prevails. Find the number of firms and the number of seats that will be occupied in each plane in free-entry equilibrium when K is $600,000. When K is $300,000. When K is $150,000.

• 4 Two courier firms serve a market with the following demand function

$$p = 100 - y$$

where y is aggregate quantity, $y_1 + y_2$. Each firm has the following cost function:

$$C(y_i) = \frac{y_i^2}{2}$$

where y_i is firm i's output. The marginal cost function is

$$\mathbf{MC}(y_i) = y_i$$

a Given y_2, what is the first firm's demand function, and what is its marginal revenue function? Draw the first firm's demand, marginal revenue, and marginal cost functions on the same diagram. What is the first firm's best-response function? What is the second firm's best-response function?

b How much does each firm produce in the Cournot equilibrium? What is price in the Cournot equilibrium? How much profit does each firm earn in the Cournot equilibrium?

5 It is sometimes argued that advertising is a barrier to entry. Explain the circumstances in which a large expenditure on advertising by some firm in this year may be a barrier to entry for another firm next year.

6 At various times in its history, Dow Chemical, the dominant producer of magnesium in the United States, has held an entire year's production in inventory. Since it is costly to hold such inventories, the interesting question is: Why do it? Some economists have claimed that large inventories create a barrier to entry, and Dow may have held them to discourage entry. Explain how inventories might serve as a barrier to entry.

7 Firms 1 and 2 both produce gismos, but firm 1 does it at a lower cost than firm 2. Firm 1 has a constant marginal cost of $15, and firm 2 has a constant marginal cost of $30. The demand for gismos is

$$p = 120 - y$$

where y is aggregate output.

a Suppose that the firms choose quantities. Find both best-response functions. Remember, marginal costs are different, so the best-response functions will not be symmetric. Find the Cournot equilibrium quantities. Hint: Treat the best-response functions as two equations in two unknowns—the Cournot equilibrium quantities—and solve the equations for the unknown quantities. Compute each firm's profit in the Cournot equilibrium.

b Suppose that the firms choose prices instead of quantities and that prices must be announced in dollars and cents. Then $15.71, $45.95, and $39.00 are permissible prices, but $45.975 and $57.0067 are not. What are the Bertrand equilibrium prices? How much does each firm earn in the Bertrand equilibrium?

8 In many high-tech industries, there is considerable "learning by doing." In particular, in these industries, the marginal cost of production appears to be strongly influenced by cumulative past output—the more the firm has produced in the past, the lower its marginal cost of production in the present. Discuss the possible effects of learning by doing on market structure.

References

Axelrod, R. (1984), *The Evolution of Cooperation*, New York: Basic Books.

Bain, J. S. (1956), *Barriers to New Competition*, Cambridge, Mass.: Harvard University Press.

Dixit, A. (1980), "The Role of Investment in Entry-Deterrence," *Economic Journal*, **90**:95–106.

Eaton, B. C., and R. G. Lipsey (1980), "Exit Barriers Are Entry Barriers: The Durability of Capital as a Barrier to Entry," *Bell Journal of Economics*, **11**:721–729.

Fouraker, L., and S. Siegal (1963), *Bargaining Behavior*, New York: McGraw-Hill.

Friedman, J. (1977), *Oligopoly and the Theory of Games*, Amsterdam: North-Holland.

Herling, J. (1962). *The Great Price Conspiracy*, Washington, DC: Luce.

Luce, R. D., and H. Raiffa (1957), *Games and Decisions*, New York: Wiley.

Modigliani, F. (1958), "New Developments on the Oligopoly Front," *Journal of Political Economy*, **66**:215–232.

Plott, C. R. (1982), "Industrial Organization Theory and Experimental Economics," *Journal of Economic Literature*, **22**:1485–1527.

Salop, S. C. (1986), "Practices That (Credibly) Facilitate Oligopoly Co-ordination," in *New Developments in the Analysis of Market Structure*, J. E. Stiglitz and G. F. Mathewson (eds.), Cambridge, Mass. MIT Press, pp. 265–290.

Smith, R. A. (1962), "The Incredible Electrical Conspiracy," *Fortune*, April and May.

Spence, A. M. (1981), "Competition, Entry and Antitrust Policy," in *Strategy, Predation and Antitrust Analysis*, S. Salop (ed.), Federal Trade Commission.

———(1977), "Entry, Capacity, Investment, and Oligopolistic Pricing," *Bell Journal of Economics*, **8**:534–544.

Stigler, G. (1969), "A Theory of Oligopoly," *Journal of Political Economy*, **72**:44–61.

Sylos-Labini, P. (1962), *Oligopoly and Technical Progress*, Cambridge, Mass.: Harvard University Press.

United States v. Aluminum Company of America et al. (1945), 145 F.2d 416, 424.

*13

PRODUCT DIFFERENTIATION

The homogeneous, or undifferentiated, goods discussed in Chapter 12—for example, magnesium, coal, ready-mix concrete, plywood, petroleum, and paper—are typically used as inputs in making finished consumer goods. As we turn our attention to such consumer goods, we will confront markets that are startlingly different: in place of the earlier homogeneity is a sometimes overwhelming diversity. The products available to consumers in any product group—say, VCRs or microeconomic textbooks—are almost invariably heterogeneous, or differentiated.

Differentiated products are goods that, as a group, satisfy a particular need but differ in their individual specifications. For example, some 40 different brands of VCRs are available in about 150 models, at prices ranging from as little as $200 to as much as $1500. The array of what advertisers call "features" and economists call "product specifications," or "characteristics," is staggering and continues to grow. Prospective buyers can choose between Beta- or VHS-format machines in either portable or tabletop models, for example. They can also look for a host of additional features, including cable-ready equipment, multievent pro-

grammability, remote-control devices (attached or detached), high-fidelity stereo, or combinations of VCRs and video cameras. Although every model is a VCR, each is differentiated from other products in the same group by a distinguishing set of characteristics. Firms can also differentiate their products by variations in packaging, in servicing and warranty arrangements, and (as we saw in Chapter 1) in the firm's location. Everywhere we look, from answering services to zippers, we see product differentiation.

The fact of such heterogeneity in consumer goods arises in response to significant differences in consumer preferences —the basic stuff of consumer choice making, which we explored in Chapters 3 and 4. If individual consumers did not differ markedly in their tastes, firms would have no reason to differentiate products. In the absence of such variations in personal preferences, for instance, we might all choose the Eastman Kodak 8-millimeter video camera with a VCR. However, potential VCR buyers who do not see themselves as budding filmmakers welcome the range of alternative choices.

The same range of product choices, however, is not available to all consumers.

As we might expect, the availability of products differs markedly among economies. For example, an emigrant Polish actor once described how a friend newly arrived from Poland burst into tears when she saw all the different things for sale in an ordinary Swedish supermarket—things that were unavailable in her homeland. However, even within an advanced technological society, such as Sweden or the United States, the diversity of products or services available to particular consumers can still vary markedly. For example, one of the features that distinguishes life in large cities such as New York from life in small towns such as Montrose, Colorado, is the difference in the range of products and services available. On any given night, New Yorkers can choose to eat virtually any cuisine known to humankind and can pick an evening's entertainment from any number of plays, movies, or dance productions. Montrosers have only a handful of restaurants, one movie theater, and no resident drama or dance companies. This suggests that within a society, the greater the number of people who live in proximity, the larger the diversity of products in that locale.

This difference in the range of product diversity suggests that producers do encounter certain factors that limit product diversity. Those limits are product development or setup costs and increasing returns to scale. Setup costs can be sizable. For instance, Walt Disney Studios spends approximately $1 million every time it develops a new television show. These costs can be high enough to prohibit the development of a new product. So, too, the presence of economies of scale means that producers face a cost penalty for being small. A designer-label clothing store in Montrose, for instance, may not have a large enough clientele to make it a paying proposition. Two questions come naturally to mind: How many products will be available in a particular product group? What are the implications for individual consumers of such differences in availability?

If we choose to look at the flip side of product diversity—to see things from the entrepreneur's rather than the consumer's perspective—the question that arises is a separate but related one: What product (or line of products) should an entrepreneur produce? The answer is often some yet-unknown product. Indeed, the classic way for an entrepreneur to seize a share of a market is to introduce an innovative product. For example, the Filofax is a big, bulky address book, diary, and loose-leaf personal organizing system that has become an instant status symbol for globetrotting executives. Philip Morris Companies Inc., the biggest U.S. cigarette manufacturer, has launched Superslims, a cigarette that is said to emit 70% less smoke from the lighted end than most comparable brands. A new disposable diaper, which takes only 2 years to disintegrate in landfills, has been brought to market under a mouthful of a name: Chemical-Free TenderCare Biodegradable. MCA's LJN Toys has produced 164 talking baseball cards that have tiny vinyl records on the back for playing on a compact disc player. And Lick Your Chops is a new dog food that contains no preservatives, additives, salt, sugar, or artificial colors. Each of these products is carefully differentiated from other products in the same group.

Once we begin to talk about the development of newly differentiated products, we have crossed over from an economy characterized by a finite number of goods whose exact number and characteristics are *exogenous*, or given, to an economy in which the number and the characteristics of goods are instead *endogenous*, or to be determined. As we make this shift in our analysis, we see that the economy is now quite different, and we must therefore recreate the models we use to analyze it.

In this chapter, we'll introduce two different models, each intended to determine both the number of products available in a particular product group and the prices at which those differentiated products will be marketed. The second model also determines the characteristics of these products. Several features are common to both models: product differentiation is taken to be a response to the diversity of individual tastes, the amount of product diversity is limited by product development costs or by increasing returns to scale, and new and important normative issues concerning the efficient amount of product diversity are raised.

13.1 Chamberlin's Symmetrically Differentiated Products

The first model, Chamberlin's model of monopolistic competition, may already be familiar. This model focuses on product groups with a multiplicity of actual and potential products. For example, the product group of ready-to-eat breakfast cereals includes all the cereals presently marketed, such as Cheerios, Team, Corn Chex, Grapenuts Flakes, Rice Crispies, Alpha Bits, and Fruit & Fibre. The product group also includes all the unnamed, undeveloped, and unproduced cereals that have not yet appeared on supermarket shelves. The Chamberlin model is intended to determine how many of the products in this group will ultimately be produced and what the price of each product will be. We'll use this model to analyze the equilibrium that results both when the number of differentiated products in the market is small and when the number is large.

Before we move to the equilibrium analysis, let's scrutinize the crucial, simplifying assumption of Chamberlin's model: given any subset of products actually produced, *all demand functions are symmetric.* This **symmetry assumption** is the hallmark

of the Chamberlin view of product differentiation. As you'll discover later on, this assumption may not be appropriate for many product groups. Its limitations, in fact, motivated the development of the second model we'll explore in this chapter, which does not make the assumption of symmetry.

Assumption of Symmetry

To help you understand what the symmetry assumption means, we'll lay out a simple illustration inspired by Perloff and Salop (1985). To keep the illustration within manageable bounds, we'll assume that only four different products are technically possible in this particular product group: the products labeled A, B, C, and D. Notice that when there are four products, precisely 24 unique rankings of the four products, or 24 **preference orderings,** are possible. Hence, we'll assume that there are 24 different types of consumers. For simplicity, we'll also assume that there is just one consumer of each type (our analysis will require only that there be the same number of consumers of each type) and that the consumer buys just one unit of his or her most favored product in the group of products actually on the market. If only two of the four products are actually available, for example, each consumer will buy one unit of the product more preferred at the current prices.

When product prices are identical, each of the 24 consumers has a unique ranking (from most preferred to least preferred) of the four products. These 24 rankings are illustrated in Table 13.1. Consumer 1, for example, prefers A to B, B to C, and C to D.

The key property of the symmetry assumption concerns each consumer's second rather than first choice. The first six consumers in Table 13.1, for instance, all agree that A is the most preferred product, but they systematically disagree about which product is the best substitute for A. Because one-third of the consumers prefer B, one-

TABLE 13.1   Consumers' Preferences When All Products Are Available at a Common Price

Consumer	Preference Ordering	Consumer	Preference Ordering
1	ABCD	13	CABD
2	ABDC	14	CADB
3	ACBD	15	CBAD
4	ACDB	16	CBDA
5	ADBC	17	CDAB
6	ADCB	18	CDBA
7	BACD	19	DABC
8	BADC	20	DACB
9	BCAD	21	DBAC
10	BCDA	22	DBCA
11	BDAC	23	DCAB
12	BDCA	24	DCBA

third C, and one-third D, their second choices are evenly distributed over the other three products B, C, and D. In the same way, the second choices of those consumers whose first choices are instead B (or C or D) are evenly distributed over the remaining three products.

What will spur individual consumers to switch from their favorite product to one of the other three? A price differential that is "large enough." Let's assume that the consumer will decide to change from one brand to the next-preferred brand only if the price differential between adjacent products in a consumer's preference ordering is larger than e. Consumer 1 will buy B in preference to A, for instance, only if the difference between the two prices, $p_A - p_B$, is greater than e. He or she will buy C in preference to A if the difference between the two prices, $p_A - p_C$, is greater than $2e$. And he or she will buy D in preference to A if $p_A - p_D$ is greater than $3e$.

Symmetric Demand Functions

Given these consumers' preferences, what will the product demand functions be like with one, two, three, or four products on the market? First, suppose that only product A

is actually for sale. In this case, each of the 24 consumers will demand one unit of A regardless of its price tag. In other words, the demand function for A will be perfectly price-inelastic, or graphically vertical, at 24 units. The same result holds if the single available product is instead B or C or D.

What if two products are on the market? If the two available products are A and B and if the price of B is p', or $p_B = p'$, what is the demand function for A? As you can deduce from Table 13.1, when the price of A, p_A, is within e or p', then exactly half of the 24 consumers (those numbered 1, 2, 3, 4, 5, 6, 13, 14, 17, 19, 20, and 23) prefer A, and the quantity demanded of A at any price greater than $p' - e$ and less than $p' + e$ will be 12 units. In Figure 13.1a, then, one segment of the demand function for A is the vertical line segment labeled d directly above 12 units on the horizontal axis.

When p_A is greater than $p' + e$ (but less than $p' + 2e$), however, six customers (1, 2, 13, 17, 19, and 23 in Table 13.1) will switch from A to B. In Figure 13.1a, then, a second segment of the demand function for A is the vertical line segment labeled d immediately above 6 units. When p_A exceeds $p' + 2e$ (but is less than $p' + 3e$), four more customers (3, 5, 14, and 20) will switch from A to B, and a third segment of the demand function for A is then the vertical segment labeled d above 2 units. And when the price of A exceeds $p' + 3e$, the remaining two customers (4 and 6) will switch from A to B.

If we now decrease rather than increase p_A by increments of e, the pattern is reversed: as p_A drops below $p' - e$, six customers (7, 8, 15, 18, 21, and 24) switch from B to A; as p_A drops below $p' - 2e$, four more customers (9, 11, 16, and 22) switch to A; and as p_A drops below $p' - 3e$, the remaining two customers (10 and 12) switch to A.

Although we could derive the demand function for B in just the same way, we would be wasting our time. We can simply replace the label y_A by y_B in Figure 13.1a and

(a)

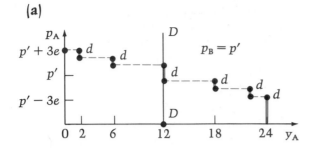

(b)

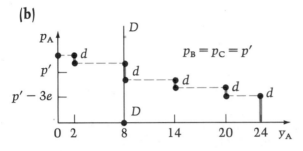

(c)

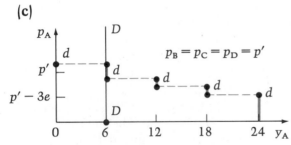

FIGURE 13.1 Chamberlin symmetric demand functions.

In (c), four products are produced. The line segments labeled *d* comprise the demand function for one product when the prices of the other three are held constant at *p'*. The line labeled *DD* gives the quantity demanded of any one of the four products when all four prices change in unison. In (a) and (b), the numbers of products are 2 and 3.

the label p_A by p_B — and voilà, the figure illustrates the demand function for B when the price of A is *p'*. Although the customers who switch as the price increases or decreases by increments of *e* are different, the resulting demand functions are nevertheless symmetric. Indeed, we could pick any pair of products, and the product names (and therefore the labels in Figure 13.1a)

would change, but the resulting demand functions would not. This property is what we mean, then, by symmetric demand functions.

In deriving the demand functions in Figure 13.1a, we held the price of product B constant and allowed the price of A to vary. We can also derive the demand functions for A and B when their prices move up and down in unison. If the prices of A and B are initially the same, and if these prices are increased or decreased in unison, customers will not switch brands. At any common price, 12 units of A and 12 of B will be demanded. The resulting demand function for A, for instance, is the function labeled *DD* in Figure 13.1a. More generally, the demand functions for any pair of products, when their prices are identical, are just like the *DD* function for A in Figure 13.1a.

What happens when not two, but three products are on the market — say A, B, and C? If these three products have a common price, they will split the market evenly, and the quantity demanded of each will therefore be 8. If their prices are then allowed to move up and down in unison, the demand function for each will be completely price inelastic at 8 units. For example, the demand function for A in this case is the function labeled *DD* in Figure 13.1b. What happens if the prices of two of the products — say, B and C — are fixed at a common value *p'*, but the price of the third — say, A — is allowed to vary? The resulting demand function for A is composed of the vertical segments again labeled *d* in Figure 13.1b, and the demand functions for B and C are symmetric to it. You can discover how these demand functions have been generated in the following problem.

PROBLEM 13.1

First, use Table 13.1 to identify which eight customers prefer good A when all three prices are identical — say, *p'*. Holding p_B and p_C equal to *p'*, as p_A rises above $p' + e$, A loses six customers.

Which six customers? Which three customers go to B and which three to C? As p_A drops below $p' - e$, A gains six customers. Which three does it gain from B and which three from C? Now fix p_A and p_C at p'. Identify the eight customers B attracts if p_B is also p'. As p_B drops below $p' - e$, which six does it gain?

Finally, what happens when all four products are on the market? By now, you can easily deduce the results presented in Figure 13.1c. Although this figure illustrates the two demand functions for A, once again the demand functions for the other three products are symmetric to A's.

If we take a slightly wider perspective and compare the demand functions in all three parts of Figure 13.1, we see that as the number of products in the market grows, the dd demand function for a representative product shifts down and to the left, and the DD function shifts to the left. Another thing we learn from these exercises is that if a new product, the nth product, is introduced — and if the new and the previously available products all sell at the same price — then the nth product will attract $1/n$ of all the customers from the product group. These customers will be drawn evenly from each of the products previously available. Entry of the new product thus diminishes demand equally for each of the goods already in the marketplace. In other words, this nth product is *equally differentiated* from all previously available products.

These results are clearly generated by the simplifying assumption of symmetric demand functions. Underlying this simplification is the notion that new goods compete with and are equally differentiated from all other goods currently available in the same product group. If the context is breakfast cereals, for example, it means that when Sugar Sweeties, a new breakfast cereal, hits the shelves, it draws an equal number of customers from former buyers of

Cheerios, Fruit Loops, Cocoa Puffs, All-Bran, and all the other brands currently available — if their prices are all the same. If we blindly apply the assumption to movie theaters, we conclude that if a new movie theater opens in the Bronx, it will draw away customers equally from other theaters in the Bronx, in Manhattan, in Westchester County, on Long Island, and even in Montrose, Colorado — if all charge the same admission price. You can see from this illustration that the symmetry assumption is not always applicable. We'll take a closer look at the limits of applicability of Chamberlin's model when we introduce the second model of product differentiation.

Before we use these kinds of symmetric demand functions to analyze the resulting short- and long-run equilibria, we need to make them both more realistic and more manageable. For the sake of realism, we'll assume that a consumer's demand for the chosen product is responsive to price: the higher the product's price, the smaller the quantity demanded. This means that the functions labeled DD in Figure 13.1 — those generated by changing all product prices in unison — will not be perfectly inelastic. Instead the functions will be downward sloping. For the sake of manageability, we'll also smooth out the discontinuities in the functions labeled dd in Figure 13.1 — discontinuities that arise as customers switch from one product to another.

These modifications are illustrated in Figure 13.2. The function labeled DD gives the quantity demanded of a representative product at any price common to all goods in the product group. By a representative product, we mean any one of a number of products in a group actually available in the marketplace. We have denoted the price of the representative product by p_R. The function labeled dd gives the quantity demanded of the representative product when the prices of all other products are equal to p'.

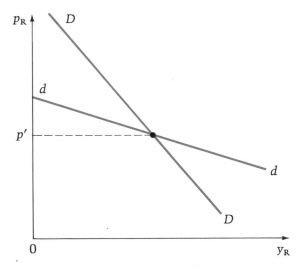

FIGURE 13.2   Smoothing the Chamberlin demand functions.

The demand function labeled dd gives the quantity demanded of a representative product as its price p_R changes, holding the prices of all other products fixed at p'. The function labeled DD gives quantity demanded of a representative product when the prices of all products move up or down in unison. The two demand functions intersect at price p'.

Notice that the function dd is flatter, or more elastic, than DD and that it intersects DD at the common price for all other products p'. It is more elastic because as the price of the representative product changes, while the prices of all other products remain constant, consumers switch brands. Consumers switch away from the representative product as p_R rises above p', and they switch to it as p_R drops below p'. It intersects DD when p_R is equal to p' because — as the symmetry assumption guarantees — when the prices of all the products are the same, the quantity demanded of each product will also be the same.

13.2   Chamberlin's Small-Numbers Case

In analyzing the equilibrium in the **small-numbers case**, there are few differentiated products, we'll limit our attention to the simplest case: the two-product, or duopoly, case. Back in the 1950s, American teenagers seemed to belong either to "Ford" or to "Chevy" families, and they regularly amused themselves by arguing about the relative merits of Chevys and Fords.

For illustrative purposes, let's think of the differentiated-product duopoly problem as the pricing problem Ford and Chevrolet face as each firm attempts to pry dedicated customers away from its competitor. We'll assume that the costs of production for Ford and for Chevrolet are identical and that their total cost function TC(y) is the sum of a fixed cost K and a constant marginal cost of production c multiplied by output y:

$$TC(y) = K + cy$$

Because product-development costs loom large in the automobile industry — Nissan recently spent $500 million to develop its European-style luxury sedan, the Infiniti Q-45, and GM expects to spend $5 billion to develop its Saturn subcompact — it is natural to think of K as a fixed cost associated with product development. For simplicity, we'll call K a product development cost.

The Nash Price Equilibrium

The first equilibrium we'll take up corresponds to the Bertrand equilibrium in Chapter 12, in which each firm chooses its price to maximize its own profit, taking the other firm's price as given. Because each firm acts independently rather than collusively in choosing its price, the equilibrium will be a Nash equilibrium.

What can we say about a firm's decision with respect to price? Because both firms' demand conditions and cost conditions are symmetric, we know that in equilibrium, the two will charge exactly the same price. What will that equilibrium price p^e be? The function labeled DD in Figure 13.3a is the

(a)

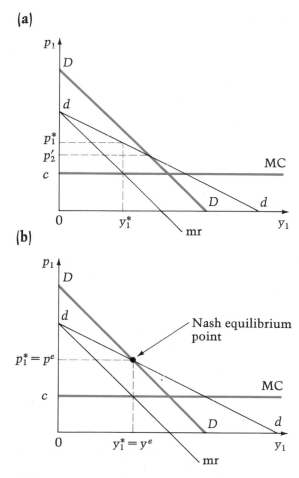

(b)

FIGURE 13.3   Finding the duopoly price equilibrium.

In (a), the second firm is charging price p_2'; therefore, DD and dd for the first firm intersect at price p_2'. Given p_2', the profit-maximizing price for the first firm is p_1^*. Since p_1^* is not equal to p_2', these prices are not Nash equilibrium prices. In (b) the second firm's price is p^e. Given this price, the profit-maximizing price for the first firm is $p_1^* = p^e$. Since the two prices are identical, we have found the Nash equilibrium price for this symmetric duopoly.

demand function for the first firm when the prices of the two firms are identical; the function labeled dd is its demand function when the second firm's price is p_2'. The DD and dd demand functions must therefore intersect when p_1 is equal to p_2'. Given

that the second firm's price is p_2', we can find the profit-maximizing price for the first firm, or the first firm's best price response, by finding the point where mr, the marginal revenue function associated with dd, intersects the marginal cost line MC in Figure 13.3a. This intersection determines price p_1^*, the first firm's best price response given that the second firm's price is p_2'.

Is p_1^* the Nash equilibrium price p^e? No — in equilibrium, both firms will charge the same price, and since p_1^* is not equal to p_2', we have not found the Nash equilibrium price. The Nash equilibrium price is the one identified as p^e in Figure 13.3b. Why? Suppose that the second firm is charging p^e. In this case, dd must intersect DD at p^e. Furthermore, mr is equal to MC when the first firm's price is p^e. Therefore, when the second firm charges p^e, the profit-maximizing price for the first firm is also p^e. This price is therefore the Nash equilibrium price.

The Collusive Price

What happens if the duopolists get together to establish price collusively instead of setting price independently? The collusive price, which maximizes the joint profit of the two firms, is p_1^* in Figure 13.4. To identify the collusive price p_1^*, we first construct the marginal revenue function associated with DD, labeled MR. This function gives the marginal revenue for both firms as their prices move up and down in unison. Because MR intersects MC at y_1^*, the collusive price is p_1^*.

The Oligopoly Problem Again

For the sake of comparison, the Nash equilibrium price p^e is also illustrated in Figure 13.4. Notice that in the Nash price equilibrium, MR is less than MC. Beginning at the Nash equilibrium at point E in Figure 13.4, imagine that both firms simultaneously in-

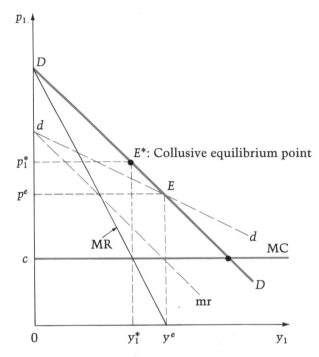

FIGURE 13.4   The oligopoly problem revisited.

The collusive price is p_1^* (because MR = MC at y_1^*), and the Nash equilibrium price is p^e (because mr = MC at y^e). Beginning at the Nash equilibrium at E, if both firms simultaneously increased their prices, they would move along DD toward E^*. As they did so, their profit would increase because MC > MR to the right of y_1^*. Therefore, the Nash equilibrium price, which is individually rational, is not collectively rational.

sive solution at E^*, each will have a private incentive to cheat on the collusive agreement by independently lowering the price of its product. You can demonstrate this in Problem 13.2.

PROBLEM 13.2

You'll need to construct the appropriate diagram very carefully. First, draw a linear DD function and its associated marginal revenue function. Remember that MR will be exactly twice as steep as DD. Then identify the collusive solution E^*. Now draw through E^* a linear dd function that is flatter than DD, and construct the associated mr function, again remembering that it is twice as steep as its demand function. Using these tools, find the price that maximizes one firm's profit when the other charges the collusive price. Show that it is lower than the collusive price.

crease price (and therefore decrease quantity). As they do so, traveling up DD from E toward E^*, the profit for each increases because MR is less than MC. This implies that the individually rational, or Nash equilibrium, price p^e is not collectively rational. We have encountered again one half of what we called the oligopoly problem in Chapter 12.

As you have probably anticipated, we'll also become reacquainted with the other half of the oligopoly problem. If the two firms somehow manage to reach the collu-

Once again, we are faced with the oligopoly problem — this time in the context of differentiated products: at the independently rational, or Nash equilibrium price, the duopolists have a profit incentive to collude; however, at the collectively rational, or collusive, equilibrium price, each duopolist has a profit incentive to cheat on the collusive agreement by independently lowering price.

Thus, in the cases of differentiated as well as undifferentiated products, punishment strategies (of the sort considered in Section 12.7) that eliminate the incentive to cheat on a collusive agreement may be attractive. Chamberlin (1933) argued, however, that such formal punishment strategies are not necessary when the number of firms is small enough. In fact, he even argued that explicit collusive agreements among oligopolists are superfluous:

> If each [oligopolist] seeks his maximum profit rationally and intelligently, he will realize that when there are only two or a few sellers his own move has a consider-

able effect upon his competitors, and that this makes it idle to suppose that they will accept without retaliation the losses he forces upon them. Since the result of a cut by any one is inevitably to decrease his own profits, no one will cut, and although the sellers are entirely independent, the equilibrium result is the same as though there were a monopolistic agreement between them. (p. 48)

As Chamberlin suggests, the very structure of the problem forces competitors to realize just how interdependent their fortunes are. If one firm cuts its price, another firm will follow suit. All parties will recognize that such a short-sighted pursuit of self-interest will drive down the price in Figure 13.4 from p_1^* to p^e, an outcome that benefits no one. Because they do recognize their interdependence, Chamberlin suggested competing firms are inevitably led to practice **tacit collusion**.

PROBLEM 13.3

You can adapt the model of oligopoly pricing, taken from Sweezy (1939), to develop Chamberlin's insight more formally. First, construct a diagram in which you identify the collusive price; then construct dd through the collusive solution; then construct mr, and suppose that all firms are charging the collusive price. To capture the spirit of Chamberlin's argument, suppose that each firm believes that all other firms will match any price reduction it initiates and not respond to any price increase. Given these beliefs about the price responses of other firms, MR is the appropriate marginal revenue function for price reductions, and mr is the appropriate one for price increases. Show that with these beliefs about the responses of competitors, no firm has a private incentive to change price.

Sweezy proposed this model as an explanation of observed price rigidity in actual oligopolized industries. For instance, until recent developments created a much more hostile economic environment, the six major U.S. cigarette companies coexisted in a cozily oligopolistic relationship, free of (heaven forbid) price wars.

Is either of the two solutions we have identified a long-run equilibrium? That is, will any other firm enter this product group? The answer depends once again on the magnitude of product development costs. If product development costs are large enough, they will act as a barrier to entry too formidable for an entrant to surmount profitably. In this case, the duopoly will be protected from competition by further rivals. For example, so far only NASA and Europe's Arianespace are competing in carrying commercial satellite payloads into space because developing the necessary facilities is a very expensive proposition.

If such development costs are too small to deter entry, however, we can expect to find large numbers of differentiated products in a given product group. One result of the court order breaking up American Telephone and Telegraph, for instance, is that its previously monopolized Yellow Pages came up for grabs. The barrier to entry is low because telephone companies are required in some states to sell listings at a nominal price and because establishing the requisite advertising network and printing facilities is not prohibitively expensive. Even the slogan "Let your fingers do the walking" is not copyrighted. As a result, regional telephone companies, established publishing houses, and newly formed companies have all scrambled to enter products in the telephone directories market.

13.3 Chamberlin's Large-Numbers Case

In the **large-numbers case**, where product groups are characterized by large numbers of symmetrically differentiated products, what will the resulting equilibrium look like? We can start by analyzing the price equilibrium when the number of products on the market is fixed. If we assume that each of these symmetrically differentiated products is made by a separate firm, then each firm will take the price of all other products as given when it decides on its own price. Why? We use the same reasoning here that we used to justify the price-taking assumption in perfect competition. Because a price change by one firm will have an insignificant effect on the demand for any other product in the group, the rival firms will not think of their individual pricing decisions as obviously interdependent, in the way that Chamberlin argued they were in the small-numbers case. Because firms in the large-numbers case make their pricing decisions independently and because they take their rivals' prices as given, the resulting equilibrium is a Nash price equilibrium.

Short-Run Price Equilibrium

Given that each firm regards the prices of all other products as fixed, the equilibrium price p^e must have the property that any one firm finds it profit-maximizing to charge p^e if all other firms are charging p^e. This property tells us both what *equilibrium price* means and how to find it.

To find the price equilibrium in this large-numbers case, we can simply adapt the argument used to find the Nash price equilibrium in the duopoly case. Let's see why the price p^e identified in Figure 13.5 is the equilibrium price. Because costs and demand functions are symmetric for all firms in the group, we can pick a representative firm, and then suppose that all other firms are charging p^e. The representative firm, whose price and quantity are denoted by p_R and y_R, will consider its demand function to be the one labeled dd in Figure 13.5. Given this demand function, the profit-maximizing price p_R^* is equal to p^e. Because all the other firms are in the identical position,

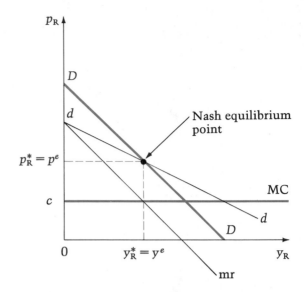

FIGURE 13.5 Price equilibrium in the large-numbers case.

All firms other than the representative firm, whose price and quantity are denoted by p_R and y_R, are charging price p^e. Therefore, DD and dd intersect at price p^e. The representative firm's profit-maximizing price is p^e (because mr = MC at this price). Thus, p^e is the equilibrium price for all firms, and each sells y^e at this price.

they too will choose price p^e (if all other firms have done so): p^e is therefore the Nash equilibrium price.

Long-Run Equilibrium

Let's turn from the short run to the long run. To find the long-run equilibrium with large numbers of differentiated products, we need to identify the condition that deters entry. The symmetry and large-numbers assumptions imply that an entrant will make a profit slightly smaller than the profit of a representative firm prior to its entry. This suggests that in the long-run equilibrium, firms will earn approximately zero profit. Why? Because if existing firms are earning a sizable profit, an entrant will anticipate making a healthy profit itself. Entry will continue until profit is driven down to ap-

(a)

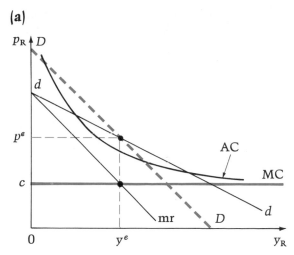

(b)

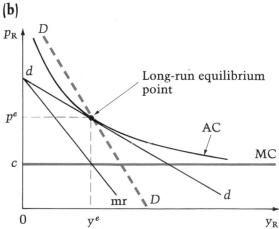

FIGURE 13.6   Long-run equilibrium in Chamberlin's large-numbers case.

In (a), the equilibrium price is p^e, and each firm sells y^e. Since p^e exceeds AC at y_e, all firms are earning positive profit. As a consequence, more firms enter, shifting both DD and dd to the left. In (b), just enough firms have entered that each firm is earning zero profit in the price equilibrium illustrated there. The no-entry condition is then satisfied, and (b) represents a long-run equilibrium.

proximately zero. The no-entry condition, then, is that each firm earns zero profit.

This long-run equilibrium is illustrated in Figure 13.6. The representative firm in Figure 13.6a is earning a significant profit

because the short-run equilibrium price p^e exceeds the long-run average cost at the short-run equilibrium output y^e—and new firms will enter. As entry occurs, both the DD and the dd functions will shift to the left. When each firm is earning zero profit, as in Figure 13.6b, entry will come to a halt. At the long-run equilibrium, the average cost function is tangent to the dd function. This means that price is equal to average cost at the equilibrium output—and the representative firm is earning zero profit.

Efficiency and the Chamberlin Model

In Chapter 11, you discovered that monopolies are inefficient because price exceeds marginal cost: the price consumers are willing to pay for additional units is higher than the marginal cost to the producer of making those units, but the extra units nevertheless go unproduced. Therefore, the potential gains from trade are not fully realized. The same sort of inefficiency arises in the Chamberlin model of differentiated products: as Figure 13.6 reveals, the equilibrium price of each product inevitably exceeds marginal cost at the equilibrium quantity.

Yet another sort of efficiency question, this one concerning the degree of product diversity emerges from the Chamberlin model: How can we determine the efficient number of products? We can provide a quick intuitive understanding of how this question is tackled by returning to the illustration of four possible products and 24 consumers. Using the cost-benefit criterion, we'll say that the amount of product diversity that maximizes total surplus is *cost-benefit efficient*, or *c.b. efficient*.

Suppose that only products A and B are actually on the market. Should a third product be introduced? To limit the issue to the amount of product diversity, we'll assume that (1) whether there are two products or three, the price of each product is nevertheless p', and (2) p' is not smaller than marginal cost c. If the third product, C, is put on the market, we know from Table 13.1 that it will attract the six buyers (13 through 18) who place C first in their preference rankings and also the two buyers (23 and 24) who rank the unavailable product D first and C second.

How much is it worth to each of these eight potential buyers to have the opportunity to buy C rather than A or B? In the absence of products C and D, consumer 13, whose preference ordering is CABD, buys A at price p'. We know, however, that because A is adjacent to C in that particular preference ordering, consumer 13 is actually willing to pay any sum up to $p' + e$ for product C. The opportunity to buy C at price p' is therefore worth e to consumer 13. Consumer 17, whose preference ordering is CDAB, will also buy A at price p' in the absence of products C and D. Yet consumer 17 is actually willing to pay up to $p' + 2e$ for C; the opportunity to buy C at price p' is therefore worth $2e$ to this particular buyer.

You can check to see that the result of aggregating all eight consumers' evaluations of the opportunity to buy C at price p' is $10e$. This sum is just another kind of consumers' surplus measure. What is the corresponding change in producers' surplus associated with the introduction of product C? Producer surplus drops by K when the third product is introduced, because total revenues are unchanged but total costs are increased by K. Does the increase in consumers' surplus exceed the decrease in producers' surplus? That is, does $10e$ exceed K? If it does, then a third product increases total surplus and should be introduced according to this cost-benefit criterion.

PROBLEM 13.4

Suppose that only one product is available. Show that the consumers' surplus associated with a second product in the illustration above is $20e$. Then show that if three products are available, the consumers' surplus associated with the fourth product is only $6e$. Next, suppose that K is equal to $8e$. What is the c.b.-efficient degree of product diversity?

Although determining the c.b.-efficient amount of product diversity can be a tough analytical nut to crack, this illustration should give you at least a sense of the approach. A related question concerns the relationship between the number of products produced in the long-run equilibrium and the c.b.-efficient number of products. Are there too many, too few, or just the right number of products in the long-run equilibrium? These issues are considered at length in Spence (1976) and in Dixit and Stiglitz (1977). They show that the number of products in the long-run equilibrium can be larger than, smaller than, or equal to the c.b.-efficient number of products. Therefore, in the Chamberlin model it is not necessarily the case that the number of products offered in equilibrium is the c.b.-efficient number.

13.4 Address Models of Monopolistic Competition

The linchpin of the Chamberlin model—the assumption of symmetry—implies that a product newly on the market will draw an equal number of buyers from all previously available products in its group. By this implication, competition is generalized: each product competes directly and equally with every other product. In many product groups, however, the assumption that competition is *localized* rather than *generalized* seems more nearly appropriate. If competition is localized, each product competes directly only with its "neighboring" products rather than with all other products in the same group. Competitors in the luxury car market, for instance, see themselves as positioning against specific neighboring competitors rather than against every product in the market. For example, Saab, Volvo, Audi, and a middle-of-the-line Mercedes-Benz go head-to-head in the $30,000 to $40,000 sticker-price range; Jaguar and Mercedes-Benz are mutual targets in the $40,000 to $75,000 range; and Ferrari, Aston Martin, and Rolls-Royce fight it out at price tags above $75,000. Cadillac and Lincoln compete against each other for older buyers; Honda, Toyota, and Nissan are all aiming at American buyers. In the computer printer market, Olympia bills its new Startype 130i printer as "The Competition" for IBM's Wheelwriter 6 printer. And in the frozen foods industry, Campbell Soup Company pegged McCain's Foods Ltd. as the competitor to beat in its bid for market share in microwavable breakfast foods. The Chamberlin model cannot accommodate such positioning strategies, which are aimed at capturing specific portions of a market rather than drawing equal portions from all competitors.

We'll create a model of localized rather than generalized competition by developing a model of geographic, or spatial, product differentiation — a model very much akin to the Hotelling model of Chapter 1. As we'll see, the presence of significant transportation costs for potential customers in this model implies that competition within the product group is localized. The model that captures such spatially localized competition is called an **address model** because products can be described by their locations or addresses in the space.

We can reinterpret this model as a more general model of product differentiation by thinking in terms of characteristics rather than geographical space. For example, if the amount of sugar is a crucial characteristic to breakfast-food buyers, the hypothetical new product Sugar Sweeties is not likely to draw the same number of customers from devotees of a sugar-free cereal, such as Shredded Wheat, as it draws from lovers of a cereal chockful of sugar, such as Marshmallow Krispies. Instead, Sugar Sweeties is likely to compete locally with the cereals that have just slightly more and slightly less sugar content. (Below we'll indicate more carefully how to reinterpret the model of spatial competition as a model of characteristic competition.) Either way we interpret the model, the product's address, or location, vis-à-vis its competitors is the factor that determines for any specified product which other products are and are not effective competitors.

A Model of Spatial Competition

To emphasize how this approach differs from Chamberlin's, we'll resort to another illustrative exercise. Because this is a model of spatial competition, we must naturally begin by choosing a geographical space. This time around, we'll imagine a large number of customers spread out evenly along the circumference of a circle, perhaps that of a volcanic island on which travel overland is impossible. (By using a circular model, we can avoid the problems encountered in Chapter 1 associated with boundaries of the market.)

Suppose for the moment that we have eight firms spaced at equal intervals along the circle, each retailing the same product — say, Polaroid film — and each charging the same price for the film. Their locations are indicated by the Roman numerals I through VIII in Figure 13.7. Since self-interested customers will choose to buy their film at the nearest store, each firm will attract the one-eighth of the customers who live closest to it. Once again, the crucial element here is not the first choice, but the second.

What will the island customers' second choices be? Each customer's second choice

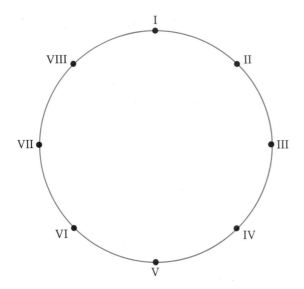

FIGURE 13.7   A circular model of spatial competition.

The market is the circle on which consumers live and around which they travel to buy their Polaroid film. The Roman numerals, which are evenly spaced around the circle, represent the locations of the eight film retailers.

will be the store immediately to the right or to the left of that consumer's first choice. Half the customers whose first choice is I will pick II as a second choice, for instance; half will pick VIII; and none will pick III, IV, V, VI, or VII. (Identify the half whose second choice is II and the half whose second choice is VIII.) Their second choices are clearly not evenly distributed over all the other firms. The same is true of those customers whose first choice is II. Half select I as a second choice, and half III. This view of differentiated products as competing locally rather than generally — a view that is reflected in the failure of second choices to be evenly distributed over all other firms — distinguishes the address model from the Chamberlin model. As you'll see, it also means that an entrant's demand function is not symmetric to the demand functions of

established firms. In terms of our illustration, it means that an entrant who sets up between any two of the eight film outlets will not draw customers equally from all eight stores. Instead, it will draw only from its two neighboring outlets, to the right and to the left.

Short-Run Price Equilibrium

Let's analyze the equilibrium that results from our alternative assumption about competition between differentiated products. We can begin by finding the price equilibrium when the number of firms is fixed. To simplify the analysis, we'll think of the customers as distributed evenly along the circumference of the circle at a density equal to one: there is one customer per unit of market length. We'll assume, too, that each customer demands one unit of the product, regardless of its price.

Because equilibrium prices depend on where each of the n firms is located, we need to specify their locations. If we assume that firms are evenly spaced throughout the market, we can then determine the short-run price equilibrium, as we did in the Chamberlin model, by examining the profit-maximizing decision of a representative firm. (Be aware, though, that firms need not be evenly spaced. Given different assumptions about the firms' locations, equilibria other than the one considered here are possible in this model.)

The length of the interval between any two of the firms, denoted by L, is just the circumference of the circle C divided by the number of firms n. Figure 13.8 illustrates the configuration of locations we have in mind: F denotes the location of a firm and L the distance between any pair of adjacent firms.

What will be the demand function for a representative firm? Figure 13.9 depicts a

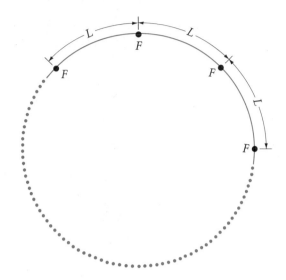

FIGURE 13.8   Locations on a circle.

Firms are located at equal intervals of length L along the circle. The Fs denote the locations of firms, and L is the distance between any pair of adjacent firms.

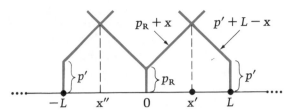

FIGURE 13.9   Market boundaries of a representative firm.

The representative firm is located at 0, and the two neighboring firms, each of which charges price p', are located at L and $-L$. The market boundaries between the representative firm and the firms at L and $-L$ are at x' and x'', respectively. The distance from x'' to x', which is the representative firm's market area, is equal to $2x'$. Because the density of customers is one and because each customer buys one unit of the good, quantity demanded from the representative firm is also equal to $2x'$.

segment of the circumference removed from the circle and straightened out. The representative firm is located at 0, and its neighboring firms are each located at a distance L from it: one to the left at $-L$ and one to the right at L. As in the Chamberlin model, we'll assume that all firms except the representative firm charge a common price p'. The price p' charged by each of the two neighboring firms and the price p_R charged by the representative firm are measured vertically in Figure 13.9.

Because the diagonal lines emanating from these prices represent the total price that the consumer must pay, including transportation costs, they can be regarded as **delivered price schedules.** Assuming that the cost of transportation is just 1 per unit of distance, the consumer's delivered price of buying the product from the representative firm and transporting it to point x' in the figure, for instance, is just the price of the product plus x', or $p_R + x'$. The delivered

price of buying it instead from the firm located at L and carrying it to point x' is $p + L - x'$. Point x' is important because it is the **market boundary** between the representative firm and the firm located at L. Customers to the left of x' will patronize the representative firm at 0, and those to the right will patronize the firm at L. In other words, x' satisfies the following equation:

$$p_R + x' = p' + L - x'$$

or solving for x',

$$x' = \frac{p' + L - p_R}{2}$$

As the representative firm lowers its price p_R, the market boundary x' moves to the right. As it increases p_R, the market boundary x' moves to the left.

The point x'' is the representative firm's market boundary on the other side. Because the firm at $-L$, like the firm at L, is

L units from the representative firm and charges price p', the intervals between 0 and x' and between 0 and x'' are necessarily the same length; the length of the representative firm's total market is therefore just $2x'$. Because we have assumed one customer per unit along the length of the market and because each customer buys only one unit of the product per period, the quantity demanded of the representative firm's product must also be $2x'$.[1] In other words, the representative firm's demand function is

$$y_R = p' + L - p_R = 2x'$$

We can rewrite this demand function with price on the left and quantity on the right:

$$p_R = p' + L - y_R$$

This function, labeled dd, and its associated marginal revenue function, labeled mr, are illustrated in Figure 13.10. Assuming that both neighboring firms charge p', we can now find the profit-maximizing output level and price for the representative firm. Because it will choose a point where marginal revenue is equal to marginal cost — and assuming once again a constant marginal cost equal to c — the profit-maximizing output level y_R^* will satisfy

$$p' + L - 2y_R^* = c$$

or, solving for y_R^*,

$$y_R^* = \frac{p' + L - c}{2}$$

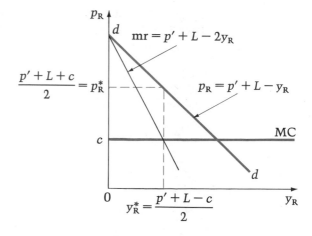

FIGURE 13.10   The profit-maximizing price.

Marginal revenue is equal to marginal cost at y_R^*, which is the representatives firm's profit-maximizing quantity. The corresponding price is p_R^*.

By combining this result and the demand function, we discover the profit-maximizing price:

$$p_R^* = \frac{p' + L + c}{2}$$

Knowing how the representative firm chooses price and quantity (given p') allows us to determine the equilibrium price. Because each firm is essentially in the same boat — each has the same marginal cost, and each has rival firms at a distance of L on either side — we know that in the equilibrium, all firms will charge the same price. Therefore, in this equation, if we set p_R^* and p' equal to p^e and then solve for p^e, we'll have the Nash equilibrium price when firms are located L units apart:[2]

$$p^e = L + c$$

---

[1] Notice that if p_R is sufficiently small, the representative firm's delivered price at L (and at $-L$) will be less than p'. In this case, the representative firm would wipe out its competitors. However, those competitors will not continue to charge price p'; they will lower their prices rather than sell nothing at all. For this reason, we'll assume that no firm entertains the possibility that it can charge a price so low that its neighbors sell nothing. Eaton and Lipsey (1978) discuss this problem in some detail.

[2] As in the models of oligopoly considered earlier, other types of pricing behavior are possible. Collusive pricing is one such possibility. To keep the analysis simple, we've chosen to ignore alternative strategies in this section.

We can combine this equation with the equation for the profit-maximizing quantity to find the equilibrium quantity y^e:

$$y^e = L$$

We can calculate the profit for a representative firm in this Nash equilibrium, π^e, by multiplying the equilibrium price less marginal cost by the equilibrium quantity and subtracting the product development cost K:

$$\pi^e = L^2 - K$$

Given the initial assumption that firms are evenly distributed, we have found the short-run equilibrium in this address model of spatially differentiated products. Notice that the profit of any firm increases as the distance L between firms increases. In the short run, then, the fewer the firms, the higher the profits.

Long-Run Equilibrium

What will the long-run equilibrium be in this model? That is, under what conditions will entrants decide not to enter the market? We can discover this no-entry condition by putting ourselves into the shoes of a potential entrant. What does this entrant see when it scans the market? It sees established firms that are located L units of distance from one another and are charging the same price, $p^e = L + c$.

Should we suppose that the entrant will take these locations and prices as given? The assumption of fixed locations seems reasonable enough: established firms have incurred a product development cost K by developing a specialized outlet for retailing a certain product (or products). They cannot change sites without incurring the product development cost anew. Because these product development costs are specific to a particular location, the assumption that the

entrant takes established firms' locations as given seems reasonable enough.

The assumption that it also takes their prices as fixed seems less reasonable because established firms will respond to entry by lowering their prices. When the Utah Pie Company began marketing frozen pies in the Salt Lake City area in 1957, for instance, its three principal rivals—the Carnation Company, Pet Milk, and Continental Baking—all responded by significantly lowering their prices. Although we'll make use of the price-taking assumption because it simplifies the analysis, be aware that the entrant will be overestimating the size of its potential profit by taking the prices of the established firms as given.

Once the entrant has surveyed the market, it must pick a spot for itself somewhere between two established firms. It can do no better than to choose a point midway between the two. The entrant, whose location is at 0 in Figure 13.11, therefore has a neighboring firm a distance $L/2$ to the right of it,

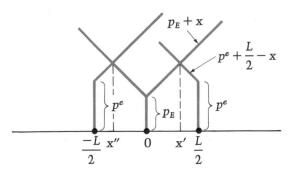

FIGURE 13.11   Entry in a spatial market.

Two established firms are located at $-L/2$ and $L/2$ each charging the equilibrium price p^e. The market boundaries between the entrant, who is located at 0 and charges p_E, and the established firms at $L/2$ and $-L/2$ are at x' and x'', respectively. The distance from x'' to x', which is the entrant's market area, is equal to $2x'$. Because the density of customers is one and because each customer buys one unit of the good, quantity demanded from the entrant is also equal to $2x'$.

and another a distance $L/2$ to the left of it. (Here we are arbitrarily choosing an origin to coincide with the entrant's location, just as we chose an origin in Figure 13.9 to coincide with the location of a representative firm.) As you'll find in the following problem, the entrant's demand function is

$$y_E = p^e + \frac{L}{2} - p_E$$

where y_E is the quantity demanded from the entrant and p_E is the entrant's price. Since p^e is equal to $L + c$, its demand function can be written as

$$y_E = \frac{3L}{2} + c - p_E$$

Its profit-maximizing quantity and price are

$$y_E^* = \frac{3L}{4}$$

$$p_E^* = c + \frac{3L}{4}$$

and its anticipated profit is

$$\pi_E^* = \frac{9L^2}{16} - K$$

PROBLEM 13.5

Verify these results. You'll need to adapt the procedures used to find the corresponding magnitudes for the representative firm in the short-run price equilibrium.

Whether the entrant actually enters hinges on the length of the interval L between the two established firms. The no-entry condition is that the potential entrant's profit π_E^* must be less than or equal to zero or, to put it in terms of L,

$$L \leq \frac{4K^{1/2}}{3}$$

If L satisfies this inequality, entry will not occur: this no-entry condition therefore determines the long-run equilibrium.

Profit in Long-Run Equilibrium

Notice that firms in the address model of product differentiation, unlike firms in the Chamberlin model, potentially can earn supranormal profit in the long-run equilibrium. To see how large that profit might be, suppose that L is as large as possible while still meeting the no-entry condition; that is, let L be equal to $4K^{1/2}/3$. As we saw earlier, the profit of a representative firm in equilibrium is

$$\pi^e = L^2 - K$$

With L equal to $4K^{1/2}/3$, its profit is

$$\pi^e = \frac{7K}{9}$$

This is a significant profit. If a potential entrant made the more realistic forecast that the established firms would respond to entry by lowering price, then the no-entry condition would permit even larger values of L—and correspondingly higher profits for the established firms.

We can extend our understanding of the relationship between the no-entry condition and established firms' profit potential in the long run by seeing what happens in this model when prices are fixed rather than determined by choice. For concreteness, we'll think about the sale of lottery tickets in our model. The growth of lotteries has been phenomenal because they offer governments a booming source of revenue. Lottery ticket agents must pay certain setup costs (including buying a license and often a specialized computer terminal), and all agents must sell the lottery tickets at the same price. In a given market for lottery tickets, what will the no-entry condition be, and what is the maximum profit an established lottery ticket agent can earn?

PROBLEM 13.6

Suppose that all lottery ticket agents—established firms and entrants alike—must charge

$5, a fixed price that exceeds their $4 marginal cost. Show first that the resulting no-entry condition is

$$L \leq 2K$$

and second that the maximum profit an established ticket agent can earn is therefore K.

An important lesson emerges from this address model of spatially differentiated products: in the long run, established firms can earn supranormal profits. This possibility arises because the demand conditions faced by an entrant in this model are very different from those that confront an entrant in the Chamberlin model. In Chamberlin's model, a direct result of the symmetry assumption is that an entrant (who charges the same price that established firms charge) will sell a quantity equal to $n/(n + 1)$ multiplied by the quantity sold by an established firm prior to entry. This means that when n is large, the entrant, simply by attracting a proportionate share of the total market, can sell a quantity virtually identical to that sold by an established firm prior to entry. The net effect is that each firm's profit in the long run is approximately zero.

In the address model, however, the entrant's position is markedly different from that of the established firms. Prior to entry, each established firm sells L units of output at the equilibrium price p^e. If an entrant chooses to market its product at the same price p^e, it will sell exactly half the amount sold by the established firms prior to entry. Why? Because the entrant entices away customers only from its two nearest rivals, not from the full spectrum of firms.

Where competition is localized, it is necessarily oligopolistic because any given firm competes only with two others. Yet as we move around the circular market, the identities of the oligopolists change. In this sense, the address model is characterized by what Kaldor (1935) called a series of "overlapping oligopolies."

Product Proliferation

Because garnering supranormal profit is a distinct possibility in address models of location and of product characteristics, established firms may be tempted to stake out a greater share of the market for themselves. One of the preemptive positioning strategies they might use is **product proliferation.**

In the spatially differentiated address model, the strategy might be to establish outlets at a number of locations to ward off potentially threatening competition by entrants. For instance, a local suntanning salon in Toronto has recently opened four new outlets within a radius of 2 miles. This proliferation of shops is a preemptive move to deflect other suntanning retailers from entering. McDonald's Restaurants seems to have pursued a similar strategy worldwide to deter entrance by other fast-food chains.

In the model of products differentiated by characteristics other than physical location, a firm might produce a range of differentiated products within a particular group, once again to lay claim to product "territory" that potential entrants might otherwise seize. As we mentioned in Chapter 12, in 1972 the U.S. Federal Trade Commission accused Kellogg, General Mills, General Foods, and Quaker Oats of producing a whole battery of differentiated breakfast cereals to preempt potential competition.[3] In a similar preemptive strategy of product proliferation, Star Micronics markets a range of ImagePower Printers, each specifically designed with an intended user in mind — banker, executive, student, editor, accountant, lawyer, engineer, and retailer. In the following problem, you have a chance to explore the basic relationship between strategic preemption and product proliferation.

---

[3] Schmalensee (1978) has developed an economic model of this case.

PROBLEM 13.7

From Problem 13.6, you are familiar with the features of a long-run equilibrium in our circular model when price is fixed. Suppose that you are the first to have stumbled onto this market with very lucrative potential. Suppose, too, that you realize that soon the rest of the world will find out about this market. What strategy would you pursue to maximize your profit?

Generalizing the Model

The address model of spatial competition captures an essential element of competition in many industries. Three crucial features characterize the model: (1) consumers of the industry's product are spread out over some physical space; (2) because transporting the product is costly, other things being equal, the consumer prefers the closest product; and (3) because of product development costs, the number of products is small relative to the number of consumers. Virtually all retail and service industries share these features, as do many markets for intermediate products. Thus, the address model can make sense of a range of products differentiated by their geographical locations.

The address model can also serve as a metaphor for differentiation among products that can be meaningfully described by their characteristics along some continuum other than geographical space. In our geographical example, each product was described by a single characteristic: its location along a one-dimensional continuum. We suggested earlier that breakfast cereals might possibly be described by another kind of characteristic: their locations along some one-dimensional "sugar content" continuum. It is more likely, however, that breakfast cereals — and most other differentiated products — are more meaningfully described by a number of such characteristics.

To describe a product group meaningfully means to write down all the characteristics that matter to consumers. Underlying this view of product differentiation, of course, is the idea that consumers' tastes are diverse. For example, think of the differences in taste among buyers of home computers. Many people are interested in home computers exclusively for their video-game capabilities; others for their word-processing capabilities; others for their accounting capabilities; and still others for some combination of two or more of these characteristics. To locate products in this group implies using not one but a number of characteristics in the address model. Lancaster (1979) presents the most thorough treatment of an address model in which goods are differentiated by characteristics.

Efficiency

In address models, as in the Chamberlin model, equilibrium price exceeds marginal cost. The result is once again the classic inefficiency that we associated earlier with monopoly. With address models, however, the issue of the efficient number of products arises as well.

Again using cost-benefit analysis, the c.b.-efficient number of differentiated products in our circular model is fairly easy to identify: we want to choose L to maximize total surplus. However, this is equivalent to choosing L to minimize the total cost of supplying the demand generated as each consumer buys one unit of the product per period.[4] The total cost of supplying the consumer demand is threefold: the marginal

---

[4] To understand this equivalence, first notice that the only effect of a price hike is to transfer surplus from consumers to firms because each consumer buys one unit regardless of price. We can therefore fix price and turn our attention to producers' and consumers' surplus. Producers' surplus at the fixed price is total revenue (a constant) less the total costs incurred by firms. Consumers' surplus at the fixed price increases or decreases as consumers' transportation costs decrease or increase. By adding up producers' and consumers' surplus, we find that total surplus is maximized by minimizing the total costs incurred by all producers and consumers.

cost per unit of product c, the transportation costs borne by consumers, and the product development costs K borne by firms.

What value of the interval between firms L will minimize these costs? We can leave the question of marginal cost aside because regardless of the size of L, the marginal cost required to produce each unit is inevitably incurred. Yet the other two costs — transportation costs and product development costs — do vary as L varies. As L increases, the average distance between each consumer and the nearest firm increases, and consumers' transportation costs therefore rise. Yet as L increases, the number of spatially differentiated products, or firms, decreases, and the product development costs of all firms taken together therefore drop.

The value of L that minimizes the cost of meeting each consumer's demand, therefore, is the value that meets the following criterion: the decrease in (total) product development costs (arising from a small increase in L) just balances the increase in (total) consumer transportation costs (arising from the same small increase in L). The precise value is $2K^{1/2}$.[5]

Product Diversity: Equilibrium Versus Cost-Benefit Efficiency

In this very simple address model, it's easy to compare the c.b.-efficient amount of product diversity with the amount of product diversity in the long-run equilibrium. Cost-benefit efficiency demands that the spacing between firms be $2K^{1/2}$, and long-run equilibrium demands that the spacing be less than or equal to $4K^{1/2}/3$. Because the former spacing exceeds the latter, there is too much product diversity in long-run equilibrium. In other words, if the c.b.-efficient spacing were imposed initially, entry would inevitably follow.

Given that there is always too much product diversity in the long-run equilibrium, which of the long-run equilibria is the most c.b. efficient? The one that maximizes the distance between firms. In other words, the most c.b. efficient of the long-run equilibria in this model is the one in which L is equal to $4K^{1/2}/3$. Notice, too, that this equilibrium is also the one in which the profits of established firms are maximized.

However, the particular c.b. efficiency result in this model — too much product diversity in the long-run equilibrium — is not a general result. We find some address models with too little and others with just the right amount of product diversity in the long-run equilibrium.[6]

Summary

In this chapter, we introduced two approaches to product differentiation. The first is the Chamberlin model, in which products are symmetric and the competition among them is generalized: each product competes with every other in the product group. The second is the address model, in which competition is localized: each product competes only with neighboring products in its product group.

A simple conceptual experiment is useful to identify the circumstances in which

---

[5] We need to use some calculus to derive this result. If C is the circumference of our circle, then C/L is the number of firms, and total product development costs are then just CK/L. Transport costs for one firm serving a market L units long are $L^2/4$, or the integral of transport costs over the firm's market. Total transport costs are then $L^2/4$ multiplied by the number of firms C/L, or $CL/4$. We then want to choose L to minimize

$$\frac{CK}{L} + \frac{CL}{4}$$

Differentiating with respect to L, setting the derivative equal to zero, and solving for L gives the cost-minimizing value: $2K^{1/2}$.

---

[6] See Eaton and Wooders (1985), for example.

one or the other model is applicable. Pick any product on the market and then imagine lowering its price. How will this price drop affect the demand for other products in the group? If the price reduction decreases the quantity demanded of all other products in the group, then competition is generalized —and the Chamberlin model apparently applies. On the other hand, if the price cut reduces the quantity demanded of only a small subset of products in the group, then competition is localized—and the address model appears to be the right one. The major analytical distinction between the two models is in how the no-entry condition is formulated.

Because competition is generalized in the Chamberlin model, the no-entry condition is that established firms must earn zero profit. Consider the fortune of an entrant— say, firm $n + 1$—if it charges the same price that established firms charged prior to its entry. Because competition is generalized, the entrant will sell $n/(n + 1)$ times the quantity sold by each established firm prior to entry. If n is large, then $n/(n + 1)$ is approximately 1, and the entrant will anticipate earning the same profit that each established firm earned prior to entry. Long-run equilibrium requires, then, that the established firms earn zero profit.

By contrast, because competition is localized in the address model, the no-entry condition is not that established firms earn zero profit. Again, consider the fortune of an entrant—firm $n + 1$—that charges the same price as established firms prior to entry. In the one-dimensional product continuum used as an illustration in this chapter, the entrant will anticipate selling substantially less than the quantity sold by established firms prior to entry because it will be competing with only two established firms—that is, competition is localized. In fact, if the demand of individual consumers is perfectly price inelastic, the entrant will

sell only half the quantity sold by established firms prior to its entry. Therefore, zero profit is not a condition of long-run equilibrium in address models.

In address models, the possibility of profit in long-run equilibrium suggests that product proliferation will be a profitable positioning strategy. In other words, by marketing a range of different products throughout the product spectrum, established firms will be able to capture this profit for themselves. Casual empiricism is certainly consistent with this insight. The Safeway grocery store chain and McDonald's Restaurants are conspicuous examples of firms that appear to have pursued a strategy of product proliferation very successfully.[7] You can undoubtedly identify other firms that are engaged in the same sort of behavior.

In both of these models, price exceeds marginal cost in equilibrium. This implies that the kind of inefficiency associated earlier with monopoly exists in markets for differentiated products as well. An additional interesting issue arises in these models concerning the c.b.-efficient number of differentiated products in a product group, where *c.b. efficient* means the number of differentiated products that maximizes total surplus. Knowing what c.b. efficiency means in this context, we then asked if there is an invisible hand at work in markets for differentiated goods: Does the long-run equilibrium actually provide the c.b.-efficient number of differentiated products? Unfortunately, the answer is no, or at least, not always. We found that we could not even determine in general whether there are too many, too few, or just the right number of products in long-run equilibrium.

---

[7] See West (1982) for a careful empirical analysis of this type of strategy in the supermarket industry.

Clearly, we have raised more questions in this chapter than we have answered: What is the appropriate model of product differentiation in any particular application? How can we tinker with the incentives of private firms to induce them to produce more c.b.-efficient solutions? For that matter, how can we recognize a c.b.-efficient number of differentiated products if we see it? By articulating these issues, we hope to put them on your agenda of interesting problems that need answers.

Exercises

1 In Myrtha Tidvale, everyone lives on Main Street, which is 10 miles long. There are 1000 people in this hamlet, uniformly spread up and down Main Street, and they each buy one ice cream cone every day from one of two stores located at either end of Main Street. These ice cream junkies ride their motor scooters to and from the store, and the motor scooters use $0.10 worth of gas per mile. Customers buy their cones from the store offering them the lowest delivered price (delivered price is the store's price plus the customer's expenditure on gas getting to and from the store.) Jones owns the store at the west end of Main Street, and Smith owns the store at the east end of Main Street.

a If both Jones and Smith charge $1 per cone, how many will each of them sell in a day? If Jones charges $1 per cone and Smith charges $1.40, how many cones will each sell in a day?

b If Jones charges $3 per cone, what price would enable Smith to sell 250 cones per day? 500 cones per day? 750 cones per day? 1000 cones per day?

c If Jones charges p_1 and Smith charges p_2, what is the location of the customer who is indifferent between going to Smith's or Jones' store? How many customers go to Smith's store and how many go to Jones' store? What are the two demand functions? Notice that they are symmetric: if you replace p_1 by p_2 and p_2 by p_1 in one demand function, you get the other.

d Rewrite Jones' demand function, isolating p_1 on the left side of the equal sign. What is Jones' marginal revenue function?

e The marginal cost of an ice cream cone to Smith and to Jones is $1. In addition, each of them pays the hamlet $800 per day for the right to sell ice cream to the citizens of Myrtha Tidvale. Adapt the method pictured in Figure 13.10 to find equilibrium prices, quantities sold, and profits.

f Llewelyn wants to open an ice cream store at the midpoint of Main Street. He, too, is willing to pay the hamlet $800 a day for the privilege. If Jones and Smith did not change their prices, what is the best price for Llewelyn to charge? How much profit would he earn?

g What do you think would happen if Llewelyn did open another store at the middle of Main Street? Would Jones or Smith change their prices or their locations? Would one or both leave the market?

References

Chamberlin, E. (1933), *The Theory of Monopolistic Competition*, Cambridge, Mass.: Harvard University Press.

Dixit, A., and J. Stiglitz (1977), "Monopolistic Competition and Optimum Product Diversity," *American Economic Review*, **67**:297–308.

Eaton, B. C., and R. G. Lipsey (1978), "Freedom of Entry and the Existence of Pure Profit," *Economic Journal*, **88**:455–469.

Eaton, B. C., and M. H. Wooders (1985), "Sophisticated Entry in a Model of Spatial Competition," *The Rand Journal of Economics*," **16**:282–297.

Kaldor, N. (1935), "Market Imperfection and Excess Capacity," *Economica*, **2**:35–50.

Lancaster, K. (1979), *Variety, Equity, and Efficiency: Product Variety in an Industrial Society*, New York: Columbia University Press.

Perloff, J. M., and S. C. Salop (1985), "Equilibrium with Product Differentiation," *Review of Economic Studies*, **52**:107–120.

Schmalensee, R. (1978), "Entry Deterrence in the Ready-to-Eat Breakfast Cereal Industry," *Bell Journal of Economics*, **9**:305–327.

Shaked, A., and J. Sutton (1983), "Natural Oligopolies," *Econometrica*, **51**:146–183.

Spence, A. M. (1976), "Product Selection, Fixed Costs, and Monopolistic Competition," *Review of Economic Studies*, **43**:217–235.

Sweezy, P. M. (1939), "Demand Under Conditions of Oligopoly," *Review of Economic Studies*, **36**:399–415.

West, D. S. (1981), "Testing for Market Preemption Using Sequential Location Data," *The Bell Journal of Economics*, **12**:129–143.

P A R T

V

Resource Markets and General Equilibrium

We'll begin the last section of the book with input markets. In Chapter 14, we'll take advantage of the analytical similarities between output-market and input-market analysis to treat perfectly competitive and monopsonistic input markets in the space of a single chapter. In Chapter 15, we'll carefully define efficiency in a general equilibrium framework and explore the conditions that ensure that the general competitive equilibrium is, and is not, efficient. In Chapter 16, we'll disrupt the harmonious vision of economic efficiency created in Chapter 15 as we introduce distribution and discover why many institutions that are intended to redistribute wealth are incompatible with economic efficiency. Finally, in Chapter 17, we'll take up the fascinating topics of externalities and their close relatives, public goods.

14

INPUT MARKETS AND THE ALLOCATION OF RESOURCES

All too easily, we can lose sight of the fact that economics is essentially concerned with the allocation of scarce resources to alternative uses. By glancing back over the preceding four chapters, we can highlight how that analysis was basically about the allocative process. After the review, we'll look at a model of equilibrium price and quantity in a perfectly competitive input market. As we analyze the resulting allocation, we deepen our understanding that competitive markets — unlike monopolistic or oligopolistic markets — successfully allocate resources to their most valuable uses. Next, we'll develop a model of equilibrium in a monopsony: an input market characterized by a single buyer. We'll discover that monopsony — like monopoly — is not consistent with efficiency. Then, we'll take up price discrimination in input markets. Finally, we'll move beyond analysis centered on identifying the equilibrium in a single period to consider the intertemporal allocation of natural resources.

14.1 A Retrospective and a Preview

In Chapter 10, we studied the concept of a scarce good by imagining an exchange economy with a limited number of rock concert tickets. Then we created a simple competitive model to analyze the allocation of tickets and money: how many tickets would be exchanged and at what price. As you discovered, the price of the tickets served as a signaling device; it guided the allocation of tickets and of money to the 10 students. We saw that the competitive equilibrium price and quantity were therefore indicative of the more basic process whereby certain people got scarce tickets and others got money (or command over other scarce goods).

We then extended this simple exchange model to include production. As we look back at the extended model of a perfectly competitive market in Chapter 10 and at the models of monopolistic and oligopolistic markets in Chapters 11, 12, and 13, we can loosely regard the function of firms as combining an assortment of scarce resources into a finished product and then offering the resulting resource "package" for sale. This vision of the role of firms allows us to see that the equilibrium price and quantity in any market for goods are indicative of a more fundamental allocative process in which scarce resources (packaged as finished goods) are traded by firms for consumers' dollars. For example, labor and iron ore, among other resources, are packaged as automobiles, toasters, and filing cabinets. These "processed resources" then end up in the garages, kitchens, and offices of the nation. In this sense, the price system serves to allocate resources to competing ends.

What we suppressed in our analysis was the allocative role played by the **resource,** or **input, markets.** The time has come to bring the input markets at the bottom of the circular-flow diagram of Figure 2.4 to center stage. For example, how does the input price of steel influence the amount of steel bought, processed, and sold by automobile, small-appliance, and office-equipment manufacturers?

Although input markets now come to the fore, output markets do not entirely disappear from view, because an input's value to any firm depends on the price that the firm can charge for its output. For example, demand for the epoxy resins used to make cars and pop cans depends on the output prices of goods in the auto and beverage industries. Like the output prices in goods markets, the input prices for natural resources and for various sorts of labor in resource markets signal where more resources are needed and from where they are to be drawn.

14.2 Perfectly Competitive Input Markets

Let's begin with a model of equilibrium price and quantity in a perfectly competitive input market: an input market characterized by many insignificant buyers and sellers. A perfectly competitive input market is characterized by firms that are price takers, in the sense that they fail to exercise any appreciable control over the price they pay for the input. For instance, if the input market for unskilled labor in the Albuquerque area is perfectly competitive, none of the many firms hiring unskilled labor can significantly affect the wage rate.

Notice that this definition says nothing about the position of firms in their output markets, where they may be either perfectly competitive or monopolistic. For example, a lettuce grower is a perfect competitor in both its input and output markets. On the other hand, a local telephone company is competitive in many of its input markets but monopolistic in its output market. We'll include both types of firms in our analysis.

What about the supply and demand functions in input markets? Notice that the term *input markets* includes both **primary input markets** (land, oil, and labor markets, for example) and **intermediate input markets** (iron ingot and hog belly markets, for example). We'll assume that in primary input markets the suppliers are individuals and that in intermediate input markets the suppliers are firms. Then the input supply functions in primary input markets (the market for unskilled labor, for example) reflect the utility-maximizing decisions of individuals, and in intermediate input markets (the iron ingot market, for instance), they reflect the profit-maximizing decisions of firms. We'll also assume that in all input markets the demanders are firms. We then know that the input demand functions will reflect the profit-maximizing decisions of firms.

Our primary task will be to derive these input supply and demand functions. Before launching into this task, however, we need to look quickly at the assumptions about competitive input markets. Not surprisingly, they closely parallel earlier assumptions about competitive output markets. In particular, the first two assumptions are familiar and important. The first is the assumption of large numbers, which guarantees that all demanders and all suppliers are price takers in the input market:

ASSUMPTION 1: Large Numbers

The number of input demanders (suppliers) is large enough and each demander (supplier) is small enough so that no individual buys (sells) a significant portion of the total quantity traded.

The second is the assumption of perfect information, which guarantees that all demanders and all suppliers are perfectly informed. The demanders (firms, in this case) know the prices of all inputs and outputs as well as the relevant production functions. The suppliers (individuals in primary input markets and firms in intermediate input markets) know the prices of all goods and, in particular, the prices of all relevant inputs.

ASSUMPTION 2: Perfect Information

All demanders and suppliers have perfect knowledge of the relevant prices, and all firms have perfect knowledge of the relevant production functions.

The third assumption is that inputs are homogeneous. This assumption rules out the case of differentiated inputs. For example, this means that one barrel of bunker-C oil can be substituted for any other barrel and that the labor of one systems analyst in the Atlanta labor market is indistinguishable from that of any other systems analyst.

ASSUMPTION 3: Input Homogeneity

In any input market, all units of the input are identical.

The last assumption is that inputs are perfectly mobile. This implies that all units of the same input will command the same price in competitive equilibrium. However,

as you'll discover in Section 14.8, this assumption is often not satisfied. For example, intermediate goods such as cement may not be easily transportable, and individual workers may not want to relocate. When resources are imperfectly mobile, the firms demanding these "immobile" inputs can exercise some control over input prices, and the result, known as monopsony, is something very much akin to monopoly in an output market. For example, a fish-processing plant located in an isolated coastal village will exercise some significant control over the wages it pays its workers.

ASSUMPTION 4: Perfect Mobility of Resources

All inputs are perfectly mobile.

These four assumptions are a sufficient set for the competitive model: when all four are satisfied, the perfectly competitive model can be applied without hesitation. But the four assumptions are not a necessary set: if one (or more) of the assumptions is not fulfilled, the model may or may not apply. The question in this case is whether the model is robust under changes in its assumptions. Does it continue to yield accurate predictions or not? Answers necessarily come from empirical and experimental testing. In fact, you know something about the robustness of this model from the experimental results summarized in Section 10.2, because they also apply to input markets.

14.3 The Supply of Inputs

We will begin the task of deriving input supply and demand functions with an analysis of the supply of inputs. As you will see, we will be able to take advantage of analytical similarities between output-market analysis and input-market analysis to treat supply decisions fairly quickly. As we noted, suppliers may be firms (in intermediate input markets) or individuals (in primary input markets). If the input supplier is a firm—say, a manufacturer of cold rolled steel—then the analysis of supply decisions in Chapter 10 is immediately applicable to input markets. In this case, we can think of firms as producing and supplying not a consumption good, but an intermediate input. It's as simple as that.

If the primary input supplier is an individual and if the primary input is a **nonexhaustible resource** such as land, we'll simply assume that the supply is perfectly inelastic with respect to input price: landowners simply offer their land at whatever price it will fetch in the market. By invoking this assumption, however, we are ignoring some important questions concerning the improvement of a resource. For instance, if a marshland needs to be drained before it can be used for farming, the supply will not be perfectly price inelastic because the price must be high enough to justify the expense of drainage.

If the primary input supplied by an individual is a **nonrenewable resource** such as oil, we'll again make the simplifying assumption that the supply is perfectly price inelastic. In so doing, we are setting aside the question of the time period in which the resource will be supplied. In other words, when we assume that supply is perfectly price inelastic, we are analyzing the *equilibrium within a single period*. In Section 14.10, we'll combine the results from this one-period analysis with an analysis of multiperiod, or intertemporal, supply to determine the *intertemporal equilibrium* in a nonrenewable resource market.

If the primary input is labor, we can use the analysis in Section 5.5 to determine the supply of labor. Remember that we used the composite commodity theorem to represent an individual's preferences by a utility function $U(x_1, x_2)$, where x_1 is quantity of leisure and x_2 is expenditure on consumption goods

or, more simply, income. Let's quickly review that analysis. The budget constraint is

$$x_2 = A + wh$$

where A is nonwork income, h is hours worked, and w is the wage rate. The time constraint is

$$x_1 + h = T$$

where T is total time available. The two constraints can be combined to produce the combined constraint

$$wx_1 + x_2 = A + wT$$

The utility-maximization problem is then to choose x_1 and x_2 to maximize $U(x_1, x_2)$, subject to the combined constraint.

The solution—illustrated in Figure 14.1—determines x_1^*, x_2^*, and h^*, the supply of labor. At the utility-maximizing solution, the marginal rate of substitution of in-

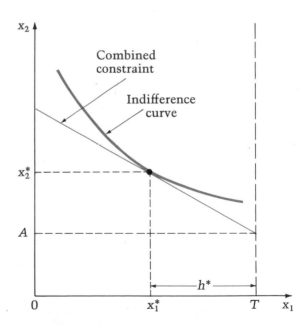

FIGURE 14.1   The demand for leisure and the supply of labor.

The utility-maximizing bundle of leisure and consumption is (x_1^*, x_2^*), which implies that the individual supplies h^* hours of labor.

come for leisure is equal to w. We'll use this formulation of labor supply, in which the hours of work supplied are a function of the wage rate w, throughout the chapter.

14.4   The Firm's Demand for One Variable Input

Now let's turn to the demand for inputs, beginning with the input demand function when only one input is variable — or what we'll call the **short-run input demand function**. Specifically, let's think of a firm — The Fish Company — that hires people to catch fish from The Fish Company's lake. We'll initially suppose that there is just one good in the economy — fish. In this case, The Fish Company's profit will be measured in fish and the workers will be paid in kind — that is, in fish instead of dollars. We'll denote the hourly wage rate by a, the number of fish a worker is paid for an hour of work. After we find the firm's demand for labor in this case, we can easily generalize results to the more realistic case in which workers are paid in money.

Input Demand in a One-Good Economy

Figure 14.2 presents The Fish Company's marginal product function MP(z) and its average product function AP(z), where z is hours of labor. Because the unit of measure on the vertical axis is units of fish, we can represent the wage rate a on this axis. We'll find The Fish Company's demand curve by answering the following question: Given any wage rate a, how many hours of labor will The Fish Company buy to maximize its profit?

As long as marginal product exceeds the wage rate, The Fish Company's profit increases as it hires more labor. To maximize its profit, The Fish Company will therefore hire labor up to the point at which marginal product is equal to the wage rate:

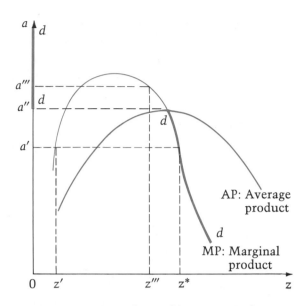

FIGURE 14.2   Input demand in a one-good economy.

When the wage rate a exceeds a'', The Fish Company demands no labor because AP is less than the wage for all values of z. When the wage rate is less than a'', The Fish Company's demand function is MP. For example, if $a = a'$, The Fish Company hires z^* hours of labor.

The marginal product function would appear to be the firm's demand curve.

With two qualifications, the marginal product function is the demand curve. To see the first qualification, suppose that the wage rate is a' in Figure 14.2 — a wage rate less than the maximum value of average product a''. Although marginal product equals a' at both z' and z^* hours of labor, the point of maximum profit is at z^* on the downward-sloping portion of the marginal product function, as you'll see in the following problem.

PROBLEM 14.1

Assuming that the wage rate is a', show that profit is maximal at z^*. To do so, imagine that the firm is currently hiring z^* hours of labor, and then show that profit falls as the firm hires both more labor and less labor. Now show that profit is minimal at z'.

The result from Problem 14.1 can be generalized:

For any wage less than the maximum value of average product, the firm's demand function is the downward-sloping portion of its marginal product function.

This segment of the marginal product function is labeled *dd* in Figure 14.2.

To see what the second qualification is, suppose the wage rate is a''' in Figure 14.2. As you will see in the following problem, to maximize its profit, The Fish Company decides not to hire any workers, since a''' exceeds the maximum value of average product, a'', in Figure 14.2.

PROBLEM 14.2

Given that the wage rate is a''' in Figure 14.2, if the company actually were to hire labor, it would hire z''' hours. On the other hand, if it hired no labor, its profit would be zero, since no fish would be caught and no wages paid. Show that the company's profit is larger if it hires no labor than if it hires z''' hours, or equivalently, that its profit is negative if it hires z''' hours of labor. Hint: The company's profit is just average product minus the wage rate multiplied by the number of hours.

The result from Problem 14.2 can also be generalized:

For any wage rate greater than the maximum value of average product, the firm maximizes profit by hiring no labor.

Thus, for wage rates greater than a'' in Figure 14.2, the company's demand function is the vertical axis, also labeled *dd*. At any of these wage rates, the firm will shut down. The Fish Company's demand for labor in this one-good economy is thus composed of the two segments labeled *dd* in Figure 14.2.

Marginal Revenue Product and Average Revenue Product

Because we do not live in a one-good world, where inputs are paid and profits are measured in kind, we need to generalize this simple example to a many-good framework, in which inputs are paid and profit is measured in money. The generalization is surprisingly simple. Because a firm's demand for the input Z is just the profit-maximizing quantity of Z, we know that its demand for Z is determined by identifying the quantity at which two rates of change are identical—the rates of change of cost and revenue with respect to the quantity of Z, denoted by z. If the money price of Z is w, then 1 additional unit of Z increases the firm's cost by w. In other words, w is the rate at which the firm's cost of production increases as z increases. This is half the information needed to determine the firm's demand for Z.

The other half is the rate at which its revenue increases as z increases. Suppose that the firm uses 1 additional unit of Z, which will produce additional output approximately equal to MP(z). When the additional output is sold, the change in the firm's revenue is the additional output MP(z) multiplied by marginal revenue in the firm's output market MR(y). The product of marginal revenue and marginal product is called the **marginal revenue product,** or MRP(z):

$$MRP(z) = MR(y)MP(z)$$

If MP(z) is 5 and MR(y) is \$10, for example, then MRP(z) is equal to \$50. MRP(z) is the rate at which the firm's revenue changes as z increases. Therefore, MRP(z) tells us the value to the firm of an additional unit of Z. (Even though y and z both appear on the right side of the equality sign, the marginal revenue product is written as a function of z alone because the quantity of output, y, is itself determined by z.)

We must also define **average revenue product** ARP(z): it is the price of the firm's output, p, multiplied by the average product of z, AP(z).

$$\text{ARP}(z) = p\text{AP}(z)$$

In the following problem, you can derive MRP(z) and ARP(z) from MP(z) and AP(z) for a firm that is a perfect competitor in both its input and output markets.

PROBLEM 14.3

First draw the standard stylizations of MP(z) and AP(z) illustrated in Figure 14.2. The units on the vertical axis are measures of output. (If Y is fish, the unit might be tons of fish.) Now change the label on the vertical axis from units of Y to units of money, or dollars. Suppose initially that p is \$1, and construct MRP(z) and ARP(z). Recall that for a perfect competitor in the output market, marginal revenue is equal to price. Next, suppose that p is \$2, and again construct MRP(z) and ARP(z).

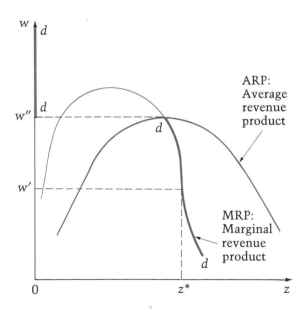

FIGURE 14.3 The firm's demand for one variable input.

If input price w exceeds w'', the firm demands nothing because the input price exceeds ARP for all z. If w is less than w'', the demand for z is MRP. For example, if $w = w'$, then the firm demands z^*.

The standard stylizations of MRP(z) and ARP(z) are illustrated in Figure 14.3. The firm's demand function for z is composed of the two segments labeled dd.

For input prices less than the maximum value of ARP, the demand function is the downward-sloping portion of MRP.

If the input price is w', for example, the firm will demand z^* units. You can easily establish this result by adapting your answer to Problem 14.1.[1] On the other hand:

For input prices greater than the maximum value of ARP, the firm will not demand any Z.

Why not? The firm's revenue is equal to zARP(z) and its short-run cost is wz. Its variable profit — its revenue minus its variable cost — is therefore just

$$z[\text{ARP}(z) - w]$$

At input prices higher than w'', w exceeds ARP(z) for all values of z. This means that if the firm were to buy a positive amount of Z, its variable profit would be negative. By contrast, if it buys no Z, its revenue, its vari-

---

[1] When there is just one variable input, the firm's profit function is $yD(y) - wz - \text{FC}$, where FC is the firm's fixed cost and $D(\cdot)$ is the firm's price as a function of quantity produced. Of course, $y = \text{TP}(z)$. Using this fact, we can write the firm's profit as a function of z:

$$\pi(z) = \text{TP}(z)D[\text{TP}(z)] - wz - \text{FC}$$

If z^*, the profit-maximizing quantity of Z, is positive, then $\pi'(z^*) = 0$, or

$$\text{MP}(z^*)\{D[\text{TP}(z^*)] + \text{TP}(z^*)D'[\text{TP}(z^*)]\} = w$$

since MP(z) = TP$'$(z). The expression in braces is marginal revenue at the profit-maximizing level of output, since

$$p + yD'(y) = D[\text{TP}(z)] + \text{TP}(z)D'[\text{TP}(z)]$$

But MP(z)MR(y) is just MRP(z), and we see that $\pi'(z^*) = 0$ implies that

$$\text{MRP}(z^*) = w$$

able cost, and its variable profit will all be zero. Therefore, when the wage rate exceeds w''', it will decide against buying any Z— that is, it will shut down. The firm's demand curve is then composed of the two segments labeled dd in Figure 14.3.

It is useful to highlight some qualitative properties of the firm's input demand function:

In response to an increase in the price of an input, a firm will not demand an increased quantity of the input. If the firm originally demanded a positive quantity of the input, the quantity demanded will decrease.

In short, we know that the firm's short-run demand function is downward sloping when only one input is variable: the lower the input price, the higher the quantity demanded.

We have now looked at the firm's short-run profit-maximizing decision in two ways. In Chapters 10 and 11, we concentrated on the firm's choice in the output market. Here, we have fixed our attention on the firm's choice in the input market. In the following two problems, you can show that the two short-run profit-maximizing rules are equivalent.

PROBLEM 14.4

In Section 10.4, you saw that if the firm produces a positive output, then $SMC = MR$. You just learned that if the firm buys a positive amount of the variable input, then $w = MRP$. From Section 8.4 you know that $SMC = w/MP$. Using this relationship, show that the two profit-maximizing rules are equivalent.

PROBLEM 14.5

You know from Section 10.4 that a perfectly competitive firm will produce no output if the output price p is less than the minimum value of AVC. You have just learned that if the input price w exceeds the maximum value of ARP, the same is true. Can you show why these statements are equivalent?

Value of the Marginal Product

Now let's turn to the question of efficiency in input markets. In thinking about how efficiently inputs are allocated in input markets, we'll ask: What is the value to consumers of an additional unit of an input used by a firm? For example, what is the value to consumers who buy Roquefort cheese of an additional gallon of sheep's milk used by some Roquefort cheese maker? Knowing that these consumers value the cheese, not sheep's milk, we can break this question into two parts: How much additional cheese can be made from 1 more gallon of milk? How much do the consumers value that additional amount of cheese? If Z is appropriately defined as sheep's milk, the answer to the first question is, of course, $MP(z)$. If p is the price of Roquefort, the answer to the second question is just $p \times MP(z)$. More generally, the **value of the marginal product** of Z to consumers, or $VMP(z)$, is output price multiplied by the marginal product of Z:

$$VMP(z) = pMP(z)$$

PROBLEM 14.6

First, show that if the firm is a perfect competitor in its output market, then $VMP = MRP$. Next, show that if the firm is instead of monopolist in its output market, then $VMP > MRP$.

$VMP(z)$ can be interpreted as the value to consumers of an additional unit of Z in a given production process. $MRP(z)$ is, of course, the value to a firm of an additional unit. From Problem 14.6, you know that if a firm is a perfect competitor in its output market, its valuation of an additional unit of Z is identical to consumers' valuation— that is, for such a firm, $VMP = MRP$. If the firm is a monopolist in its output market, however, its valuation of an additional unit is less than consumers' valuation—that is, for such a firm, $MRP < VMP$. As we'll see in

14.5 Input Demand with Many Variable Inputs

In the preceding section, we derived the firm's input demand function when only one input was variable. What will a firm's input demand function look like when more than one input is variable — say, when two inputs are variable? As in Chapter 9, the quantities of inputs 1 and 2 will be denoted by z_1 and z_2 and their respective input prices by w_1 and w_2. We can interpret the results in this case either as a short-run exercise in which only two of any number of inputs are variable or as a long-run exercise in which there are only two inputs. Here, we'll call it the long-run case, just for convenience.

We learned earlier that the short-run input demand function is downward sloping: the lower the input price, the higher the quantity demanded. In this section, we'll argue that the long-run demand function is also downward sloping, and we'll compare these two input demand functions. Our treatment will be intuitive and nonrigorous.

Downward-Sloping Long-Run Input Demand Curve

Firms have more flexibility in responding to an input-price change in the long run than in the short run. The added flexibility is reflected in two kinds of decisions the firm makes in response to an input-price change: it can change its mix of inputs by substituting toward the now relatively cheaper input, and it can alter its total output. Thus, we will decompose the firm's response to an input-price change into a **substitution effect** and an **output effect**. Then we'll argue that

both effects tend to produce a downward-sloping long-run input demand curve.

Let's first fix the price of both inputs at, say, $w_1 = \$15$ and $w_2 = \$12$ and then identify the initial long-run equilibrium. When a firm is in long-run equilibrium, its output — say, $y = 100$ units — is, by definition, produced at minimum cost. This means that the point of long-run equilibrium in Figure 14.4 is at E, where the steeper isocost line is tangent to the 100-unit isoquant. At input prices $w_1 = \$15$ and $w_2 = \$12$, then, this firm demands 15 units of input 1 and 30 units of input 2. Now, how will its demand for input 1 change if its price drops from $w_1 = \$15$ to $w_1 = \$10$?

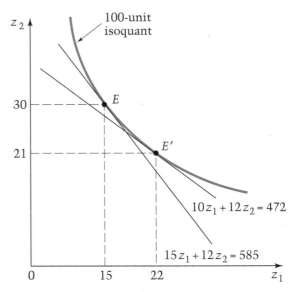

FIGURE 14.4 The substitution effect of an input price change.

At input prices $w_1 = \$15$ and $w_2 = \$12$, the cost-minimizing input bundle for 100 units of output is 15 units of input 1 and 30 units of input 2. Now suppose that w_1 drops from \$15 to \$10. To identify the substitution effect, hold output constant at $y = 100$, and find the cost-minimizing bundle for input prices $w_1 = \$10$ and $w_2 = \$12$. It is 22 units of input 1 and 21 units of input 2. We see that the substitution effect works to produce a downward-sloping input demand function — as the price of an input decreases, the firm demands more of it.

First, let's look at the substitution effect. If we imagine the firm continuing to produce 100 units of output after the price change, it would substitute toward the now-cheaper input 1, moving from E to E' on the 100-unit isoquant in Figure 14.4. The quantity demanded of input 1 would therefore rise from 15 units to 22 units. In this illustration, the substitution effect produces an *inverse relationship* between the quantity demanded of an input and its price. In Problem 9.7, you saw that this inverse relationship is generally true. The substitution effect therefore tends to produce a downward-sloping demand function. The cheaper input 1 becomes, the more of it the firm buys.[2]

Now let's turn to the output effect. When the input price changes, the firm alters its level of output because its total cost function is now different. We can easily see how the firm's cost function shifts. At the original input prices, the minimum cost of producing 100 units was $585—($15 × 15) + ($12 × 30)—while at the new input prices, it is only $472—($10 × 22) + ($12 × 21). The minimum cost of producing 100 units is less after the price decrease. By extension, the cost of producing any level of output has decreased. In this way, the firm's cost function has shifted downward. The output effect associated with the input price change is this: because the firm's total cost function has shifted downward, its choice of output—and its demand for input 1—will also change.

Just how is the shift in the firm's cost function reflected in its choice of output? If input 1 is a normal rather than an inferior input, the input-price reduction shifts downward not only the firm's total cost function but also its marginal cost function. (Do notice that we are only asserting this result, not proving it.) As a result, the firm will produce more output. Because input 1 is a normal input, the firm will demand even more input 1 as it produces more output. Therefore, the output effect reinforces the substitution effect in generating a downward-sloping demand function when input 1 is a normal input.

If input 1 is instead an inferior input, will the two effects still tend to produce a downward-sloping demand curve? The direction of the substitution effect is unchanged: the firm will substitute input 1 for input 2 as w_1 drops. Surprisingly, the direction of the output effect is also unchanged. A reduction in the price of an inferior input causes the marginal cost function to shift upward. (This result, which is not particularly intuitive, is asserted rather than proved.) As a result, the firm will produce less output and, because input 1 is an inferior input, it will demand more of that inferior input as its output decreases. Again, substitution and output effects complement each other in producing a downward-sloping demand function in the long run.

A Comparison of Long-Run and Short-Run Input Demand

If we compare the steepness of the long-run and the short-run demand functions, we discover that the long-run function is flatter than its short-run counterparts. The quantity response to an input-price decrease (or increase) is larger in the long run than in the short run.

The long-run input demand function in Figure 14.5 is labeled DD; the representative short-run function is labeled MRP. (We can identify any number of possible short-

[2] In Chapter 9, we analyzed the firm's *conditional input demand function*, which gives the quantity of the input in the cost-minimizing input bundle when output y is held constant. Since output is held constant, the conditional input demand function captures only the substitution effect. The long-run input demand function that we are now considering captures the *output effect* as well as the substitution effect.

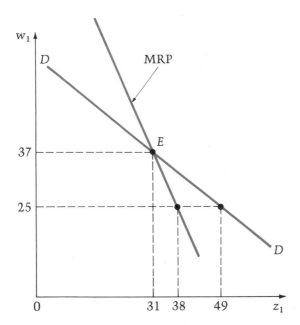

FIGURE 14.5 Comparing long- and short-run input demand functions.

DD is the long-run demand function for input 1, and MRP is a short-run input demand function. The two demand functions have one point in common, and MRP is steeper than *DD*.

run demand functions, depending on the quantity of the fixed input 2.) The long-run input demand function and any short-run demand function will have one point in common because a firm in long-run equilibrium is also in a particular short-run equilibrium. Accordingly, *DD* and MRP intersect at *E* in Figure 14.5.

However, *DD* is flatter than MRP, indicating that the response to an input-price change is greater in the long run. For instance, if the input price dropped from $37 to $25 in Figure 14.5, the firm's demand for the now less expensive input will rise from 31 to 38 in the short run, but it will rise from 31 to 49 in the long run.

The fact that *DD* is flatter than MRP is a general result. Intuitively, we can interpret this result as reflecting the firm's added flex-ibility associated with input substitution in the long run. In response to a decrease in the price of input 1, the firm can both change its level of output and substitute input 1 for input 2 in the long run, whereas it can only change its output in the short run. We have learned the following:

The response to an input price change in both the short and the long run is to demand more (less) of the input as its price falls (rises), and the response to any such price change is greater in the long run than in the short run.

14.6 Competitive Equilibrium in an Input Market

To analyze competitive equilibrium in an input market, we need to aggregate input demand and input supply. Aggregating input supply presents no special problems because it is accomplished by simply horizontally summing the supply functions of individual suppliers. However, because input prices and output prices are so clearly interdependent, the aggregation of input demand is slightly more complex.

Aggregating Input Demand

To see what's involved in aggregating input demand, let's suppose that all the firms that buy input Z are perfect competitors in their output markets (notice that we used "output markets," the plural). Many different output markets are necessarily a part of the analysis because a single input, such as sulfuric acid or unskilled labor, typically can be used in any number of production processes.

Because we assume that all firms are perfectly competitive in their output markets, when we derive the input demand functions of individual firms, we must hold output prices constant. From a wider perspective, however, we know that as the quantity demanded of an input changes, the quantities supplied in output markets will also change, and output prices will necessarily change as well. As we derive the **aggregate input demand function** (AID), we'll need to take these output price effects into account.

The derivation of AID when input Z is a normal input is presented in Figure 14.6. If the initial input price is $35, the initial equilibrium will be at point A. Corresponding to this equilibrium is a set of equilibrium prices in the relevant (perfectly competitive) output markets. If these output prices are held constant, the aggregate demand for input Z, labeled $D(z)$, can be derived by hori-

zontally summing the demand functions for all the firms that buy Z. Therefore, point A in Figure 14.6 is on both AID and $D(z)$.

Now suppose that the price of input Z falls from $35 to $26. If output prices did not change, the quantity demanded would then be 495, and the equilibrium would be at point C. Yet we know that firms in the aggregate will *produce more output* as they buy more of the now-cheaper input Z. As a result, output prices will drop, shifting aggregate input demand leftward from $D(z)$ to $D'(z)$ in Figure 14.6. Thus, at input price $26, the aggregate demand will not be 495 units but 370 units. Therefore, a second point on AID is point B. We have derived all other points on AID in precisely the same way. AID is therefore the aggregate quantity demanded of input Z when we take into account the output price changes resulting from an input price change.

Now let's consider input demanders that are monopolists in their output markets. Because monopolists are price setters rather than price takers, output-price changes are automatically included in the derivation of monopolists' demand functions. Therefore, their input demand functions do not shift as they produce more output in response to an input-price change. Suppose, for example, that *all* the firms demanding input Z are monopolists in their output markets. Then, in response to changes in input price, the input quantity demanded would be given by an unchanging input demand function $D(z)$, which would then be AID.

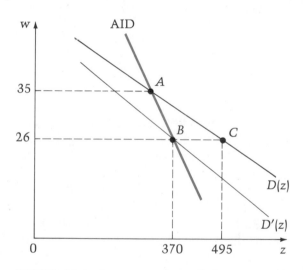

FIGURE 14.6 Aggregate demand for a normal input.

Given $w = \$35$, the initial equilibrium is at point A on AID, the aggregate input demand function, and on $D(z)$, the output-prices-constant horizontal aggregation of input demand functions. As w drops from $35 to $26, firms demand more of the input. If the prices of the products these firms produced did not change, the new equilibrium would be at C. But as firms demand more of the input and produce more output, the prices of their products will tend to fall, shifting $D(z)$ to $D'(z)$. Thus, point B is a second point on AID.

Equilibrium and the Allocation of Inputs

A long-run competitive equilibrium in the market for input Z is presented in Figure 14.7. The market demand and market supply functions, AID and SS, respectively, are shown in Figure 14.7c, and the competitive

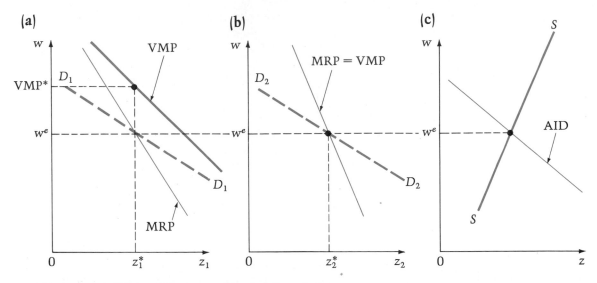

FIGURE 14.7   Equilibrium in a competitive input market.

In (c), we see that w^e is the equilibrium input price. In (b), we see that a firm that is perfectly competitive in its output market buys z_2^* of the input, where VMP and MRP are equal to the input price w^e. In (a), we see that a firm that is a monopolist in its output market buys z_1^* of the input, where MRP is equal to w^e and where VMP exceeds w^e.

equilibrium is identified in the familiar way: at the equilibrium price w^e, quantity supplied equals quantity demanded. The supply function SS is simply the horizontal aggregation of quantities supplied by all suppliers.

The position of a firm that is a perfect competitor in both its output market and the market for input Z is shown in Figure 14.7b. The position of a firm that is a monopolist in its output market and a perfect competitor in the input market for input Z is shown in Figure 14.7a. Recall that we can interpret MRP as the value to the firm itself of one more unit of input Z and VMP as the value to the firm's consumers of one more unit of input Z. We will use these interpretations in conjunction with Figure 14.7 to deepen our understanding of the inefficiency of monopoly and the efficiency of perfect competition.

Let's begin with the firm shown in Figure 14.7b. In long-run equilibrium, the firm is on both its long-run demand function D_2 and its short-run demand function MRP. Since the firm is a perfect competitor in its output market, MRP is coincident with VMP. Thus, beginning at the equilibrium position of the firm, we know that if the firm were to use one more unit of input Z, the increase in its cost of production w^e would exceed the values its consumers place on the added output VMP. In other words, if these consumers were allowed to make the firm's production decisions, they would decide against buying more than z_2^* units of input Z to produce additional output because the additional output that an additional unit of input Z would produce is not worth w^e to these consumers. This property reflects the efficiency of perfect competition.

Now consider the firm shown in Figure 14.7a. In equilibrium, the monopolist, like the competitive firm, is on both its long-run demand function D_1 and its short-run demand function MRP. Because this firm is a monopolist in its output market, MRP is less than VMP. Therefore, VMP exceeds w^e at the monopolist's point of equilibrium. If this firm's customers were put in charge, they would opt for buying more input Z because at z_1^* their valuation of the output produced by an additional unit of input Z, VMP* in Figure 14.7a, exceeds the equilibrium price of the additional unit w^e.

Although we'll examine these efficiency results in a rigorous and economy-wide context in Chapter 15, Figure 14.7 gives a clear understanding of the efficiency of perfect competitors and the inefficiency of monopolists. It's useful to summarize results so far:

In long-run equilibrium, a perfect competitor in both its output and its input markets will choose an input bundle such that, for each input,

$$w^e = \text{MRP}(z) = p\text{MP}(z) = \text{VMP}(z)$$

In long-run equilibrium, a firm that is a perfect competitor in its input markets, but a monopolist in its output market, will choose an input bundle such that, for each input,

$$w^e = \text{MRP}(z) = \text{MR}(y)\text{MP}(z)$$
$$< p\text{MP}(z) = \text{VMP}(z)$$

14.7 Monopsony in Input Markets

Let's now turn to a monopsonistic input market; that is, a market in which a monopsonist—like its logical cousin, the monopolist—is a price setter. The Harlem Globetrotters basketball team is a monopsonist in the market for show-biz basketball players. As far as basketball clubs that hire

entertainers rather than competitors are concerned, it is metaphorically the only game in town. Any company owning a "company town" is likewise a monopsonist in the local labor market because it, too, is the only game in town. A sugar refinery in an isolated, relatively small agricultural region is a monopsonist in the local sugar beet market for precisely the same reason. How will such a monopsonist choose input price and quantity? And what are the sources of a monopsonist's input market power? To determine how a monopsonist will set price and quantity in an input (or "factor") market, we need three new concepts: the firm's total factor cost TFC(z), its marginal factor cost MFC(z), and its average factor cost AFC(z).

Total Factor Cost

Let's denote the supply function for input input Z to some monopsonist by $S(z)$. The supply function gives us the input price w at which z units can be bought:

$$w = S(z)$$

We'll assume that the supply function is upward sloping: the larger the quantity of input Z the monopsonist wants to buy, the higher the input price it must offer. The monopsonist's **total factor cost** function TFC(z), illustrated in Figure 14.8a, is just z, the amount of the input it buys, multiplied by the input price $S(z)$:

$$\text{TFC}(z) = zS(z)$$

The related **marginal factor cost** function MFC(z) and the **average factor cost** function AFC(z) are presented in Figure 14.8b. Marginal factor cost is just the rate of change of TFC(z) with respect to z or, more simply, the slope of the total factor cost function:

$$\text{MFC}(z) = \text{slope of TFC}(z)$$

(a)

(b)

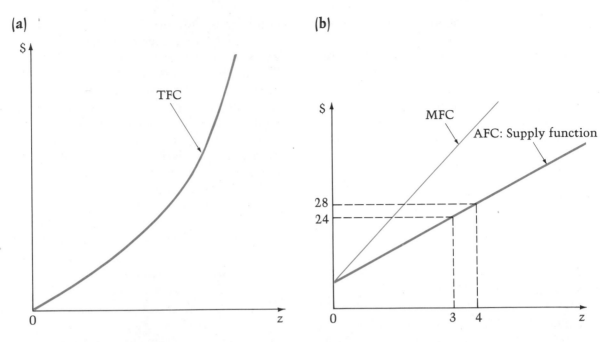

FIGURE 14.8   Total, marginal, and average factor cost functions.

AFC, which is equal to TFC/z, is also the input supply function. MFC is the slope of TFC.

Because the input supply function is upward sloping, MFC lies above AFC.

Average factor cost is just total factor cost divided by z. Because TFC(z) is $zS(z)$, however, we know that the average factor cost function is the supply function:

$$\text{AFC}(z) = S(z)$$

Notice that when z is positive, MFC(z) lies above AFC(z), and that marginal factor cost therefore exceeds the input price w.

Marginal Factor Cost

This result is a general one: as long as the supply function is upward sloping, the marginal factor cost function lies above the input supply function. More to the point:

For a monopsonist, marginal factor cost MFC exceeds input price w.

To see why, suppose that in some period, the firm in Figure 14.8b buys 3 units of input Z at a price of $24. If it decides in the next period to buy 4 units instead, it will have to pay the higher price of $28 for all 4 units. (Notice that the firm pays the same price for each unit in any period.) The resulting change in total factor cost is therefore $40 = $28 + (3 \times $4)$. The first term ($28) is the payment for the additional unit itself. The second term $(3 \times $4)$ is the increase in the expenditure on the original 3 units. The presence of the second term means that the resulting change in total factor cost exceeds the price paid for the last unit.

The general expression for marginal factor cost is

$$\text{MFC}(z) = w + z[\text{slope of } S(z)]$$

The first term in this expression is the expenditure on the marginal unit; the second is the increase in the expenditure on the original z units. Because the slope of $S(z)$ is positive, the second term is also positive, which means that MFC(z) exceeds w.[3]

This result is analogous to our discovery in Section 11.3 that a monopolist's marginal revenue function lies below its demand function. As we'll see, the resulting efficiency implications are also analogous.

PROBLEM 14.7

Suppose that the supply function is

$$w = 1 + z$$

Show that

$$MFC(z) = 1 + 2z$$

Hint: First calculate TFC$(z + \Delta z)$ and TFC(z). Then subtract TFC(z) from TFC$(z + \Delta z)$ to get the change in TFC associated with buying Δz additional units of input z. Then divide the result by Δz to express the change in total factor cost on a per-unit basis. Finally, to get MFC, see what happens as Δz approaches 0.

More generally, if the supply function is linear,

$$w = a + bz \qquad \text{where } a > 0 \text{ and } b > 0$$

then MFC is

$$MFC(z) = a + 2bz$$

---

[3] Total factor cost is

$$TFC(z) = zS(z)$$

Marginal factor cost is the derivative of TFC(z). Hence,

$$MFC(z) = S(z) + zS'(z)$$

which can be written as

$$MFC(z) = w + zS'(z)$$

because $w = S(z)$. Since $S'(z) > 0$ for a monopsonist, it is clear that when $z > 0$, MFC$(z) > w$ for a monopsonist. In contrast, MFC$(z) = w$ for a competitor, since the supply curve for a perfect competitor is horizontal.

The Short-Run Monopsony Equilibrium

We can learn the essential features of monopsony equilibrium by concentrating on the monopsonist's short-run decisions. Let's assume, for illustrative purposes, that the monopsonist is one of the major oil companies and that input Z is the labor services of petroleum engineers. Figure 14.9 presents the oil company's MRP, MFC, and supply function when the quantities of all inputs except input Z (engineering services) are fixed. On the one hand, MRP is the value to the oil company of employing an additional unit of engineering labor because it is the rate at which the company's revenue increases as z increases. On the other hand, MFC is the cost to the company of each additional unit of engineering labor because it is the rate at which its expenditure on labor increases as z increases.

The monopsonist's profit-maximizing rule is to employ input Z up to the point at which MFC equals MRP at z^* units in Figure 14.9. Why? As it moves to the right of z^* by

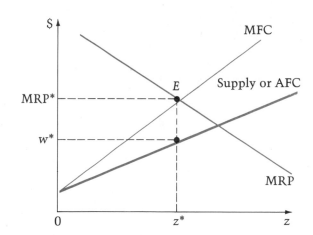

FIGURE 14.9 A monopsonist's profit-maximizing decision.

A profit-maximizing monopsonist employs any input up to the point where MFC is equal to MRP. Thus, the monopsonist employs z^* units of the input at price w^*. Notice that w^* is less than MRP*.

hiring more engineers, the oil company's profit decreases because MFC(z) exceeds MRP(z). As it moves to the left of z^* by hiring fewer engineers, profit once again decreases because the rate of decrease of its costs MFC is less than the rate of decrease of its revenues MRP.

The monopsonist maximizes profit by choosing the quantity of an input where marginal factor cost is equal to marginal revenue product: MFC(z^*) = MRP(z^*).

It is useful to describe mechanically the monopsonist's profit-maximizing rule: to find the profit-maximizing level of the input z^*, first identify the intersection of MFC and MRP—point E in Figure 14.9. Then move vertically down to the z axis to find the profit-maximizing quantity of input Z, or z^*. To find the associated wage rate w^*, move vertically up from z^*, not to MRP, but instead to AFC, and then horizontally to the vertical axis.

The following problems will reinforce your understanding of monopsony.

PROBLEM 14.8

Suppose that

$$MRP(z) = 10 - z$$

and that the supply function is

$$w = 1 + z$$

Show that $z^* = 3$ and $w^* = 4$. Carefully construct a diagram illustrating this solution.

PROBLEM 14.9

Ten suppliers of coal are spread out along a railroad line at 50, 150, 250, . . ., 950 miles from the origin in Figure 14.10. The lone demander is located at the origin. Each supplier will supply 1 ton if the price offered by the demander minus the transport costs incurred by the supplier is greater than or equal to $100. It costs $0.10 to transport 1 ton of coal 1 mile. Derive the supply function faced by the demander. If the demander's MRP is $200 per ton, show that it will buy 5 tons at $145 per ton.

As we saw in Section 14.4, a firm that is competitive in its input markets buys an input up to the point where the wage rate is equal to MRP. Of course, for such a competitive firm, the wage rate is its marginal factor cost because it can hire all the labor it wants at the competitive wage rate.

The general profit-maximizing rule in an input market is to hire an input up to the point where marginal factor cost is equal to marginal revenue product. For a perfect competitor in the input market,

$$MRP(z^*) = MFC(z^*) = w$$

For a monopsonist,

$$MRP(z^*) = MFC(z^*) > w$$

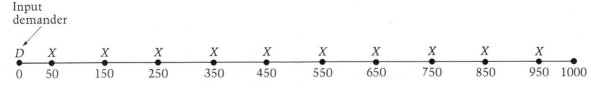

FIGURE 14.10 Monopsony in a spatial resource market.

A railroad line runs from 0 to 1000. A coal demander is located at 0, and suppliers are located at the points 50, 150, . . ., 950, denoted by Xs. As long as it is costly to transport coal, the demander has monopsony power. To get more coal, the demander must offer a higher price.

The Inefficiency of Monopsony

Now let's see why monopsony, like monopoly, is inefficient. We can eliminate any market failure arising from the monopsonist's output market by assuming that the firm is a perfect competitor in its output market. In this case, the value to consumers of the monopsonist's use of an additional unit of input Z, or VMP(z), is equal to MRP(z).

Suppose that the monopsonist in Figure 14.11 follows its maximizing rule by buying z^* at price w^* in a certain period. Now imagine that it "reopens" the market, as it considers buying more labor without increasing the wage rate of the workers it has already hired. Can the monopsonist improve its position by buying more of input Z? (Notice that this hypothetical experiment corresponds to the exercise used to demonstrate

monopoly inefficiency in Section 11.6.) The answer is yes. If the firm buys 1 more unit of labor at any price less that w'', its profit will increase. Furthermore, the supplier of the additional unit of labor will happily provide it at any price greater than w'. Because at any price less than w'' and greater than w' both the monopsonist and the labor supplier are better off, and because no one else is worse off, the original equilibrium clearly was not Pareto-optimal, or efficient. Furthermore, we can see from this exercise that in the original equilibrium, the monopsonist fails to extract the maximum possible profit.

The monopsonistic equilibrium identified by picking the point at which MFC intersects MRP is "uninventive" in very much the same way that the monopolistic equilibrium identified by picking the point at which MR = MC is unimaginative. The inventive monopsonist, like the imaginative monopolist who resorts to price discrimination to reap more of its potential harvest of profit, will therefore search for some sort of discriminatory solution. You can discover the theory of the perfectly discriminating monopsonist in the following problem. We'll consider monopsonistic discrimination more carefully in Section 14.9.

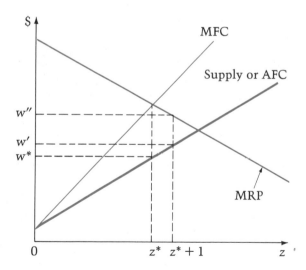

FIGURE 14.11   The inefficiency of monopsony.

To see the inefficiency of the monopsony equilibrium, let the monopsonist buy z^* units at price w^*. The supplier of unit $z^* + 1$ would happily sell it at any price larger than w', and the firm would happily buy it at any price less than w''. Because any price greater than w' and less than w'' would make both the monopsonist and the supplier better off and would leave the suppliers of the original z^* units no worse off, the monopsony equilibrium is inefficient.

PROBLEM 14.10

Suppose that the setup is exactly as it was in the previous problem: a demander of coal is at one end of a railroad line, and the suppliers are spread out along the line, as indicated in Figure 14.10. In contrast to that problem, however, suppose that the demander buys the coal from each supplier at the minehead and bears the transport cost itself. How much will it buy and how much will it pay for each ton? Hint: Think back to the perfectly discriminating book vendor in Problem 11.5.

14.8   Sources of Monopsony Power

The telltale sign of a monopsony power is an upward-sloping supply function to the individual firm. The extent of monopsony power is determined by the responsiveness of quantity supplied to changes in input price. Let's see what we can discover about one important source of monopsony power by considering the labor supply response to a salary reduction. Imagine that Bloomingdale's department store in New York cuts its security officers' salaries and that the Bell Laboratories in New Jersey cuts its computer scientists' salaries. How might the supply responses in these two cases differ?

Let's skip over each employee's labor/leisure choice by supposing that the job entails a fixed work week. The supply behavior of every employee can then be described by his or her reservation salary, the lowest possible dollar figure at which the employee will continue to work for the firm. Of course, these reservation salaries will vary from employee to employee, because each places different valuations on such factors as personal relationships developed on the job, the company's location, and working hours. We can array these different reservation prices from lowest to highest and then use familiar techniques to construct the supply function of current employees presented in Figure 14.12. If Bloomingdale's (or Bell Labs) is now paying its employees a salary of w'', we know that salary must be higher than the highest reservation salary of its current employees.

What happens if Bloomingdale's (or Bell Labs) decides to cut its security officers' (computer scientists') salary to, say, w' in Figure 14.12? Every employee whose reservation salary is above the new salary—three employees in this example—will then quit.

What determines exactly how high (or low) any individual's reservation salary will actually be? Perhaps the most important factor is the availability and the salaries of alternative jobs. Because security officers at Bloomingdale's are likely to find comparable jobs in the immediate area without too

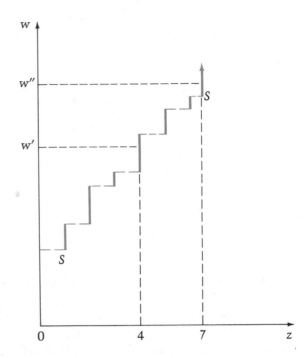

FIGURE 14.12 Monopsony and reservation supply prices.

Given employees' reservation supply prices, we construct the supply function by arraying reservation prices from lowest to highest and then aggregating in the familiar way. A firm has some monopsony power with respect to its current employees if, in response to a wage reduction, they do not all quit.

much trouble, we can reasonably expect that most of their reservation salaries will be close to the initial salary w''. If Bloomingdale's cuts into their salaries by very much, the security officers will go elsewhere. In this case, the supply response to a relatively small salary reduction will presumably be large, and we might think of Bloomingdale's as a perfect competitor in the market for security officers.

By contrast, the computer-science researchers at Bell Labs are much less likely to find similar research jobs within easy commuting distance. For Bell researchers, a job change will probably entail moving and all the consequent social and economic disruption that moving implies. Even if these researchers are willing to look for nonresearch jobs in the immediate area, a career change is likely to bring a significant salary cut. Because major relocation costs or salary reductions are distinct possibilities, the supply response to a significant cut in Bell researchers' salaries will presumably be relatively small. In other words, Bell Labs differs from Bloomingdale's in having some significant monopsony power with respect to its employees.

Immobility

The general lesson that emerges from this labor-supply discussion and from the earlier coal-supply problems is that immobility of inputs can be an important source of monopsony power. The difficulty for Bell Labs' computer scientists is that they are not perfectly mobile: changing jobs is likely to be costly, and the more costly it is, the less mobile a Bell employee is. Therefore, Bell Labs' monopsony power arises from its employees' immobility. The difficulty for the coal suppliers is that coal is not perfectly mobile: transporting coal from the mine to the place where it is needed is expensive. The farther it must be shipped, the more expensive it will be. Therefore coal demanders' monopsony power springs from the immobility of coal.

In both cases, the resource immobility is primarily due to locational considerations familiar from the address models of Chapters 1 and 13. If all the economic activity in the world were concentrated at a single point—which we might call the economist's black hole—this sort of monopsony power could not arise. Because economic activity does not take place at a single point, however, monopsony power is an important feature of the resource market landscape. Locational issues are therefore at least as important in input markets as in output markets.

Monopoly and Specialized Inputs

For more than 40 years, the Harlem Globetrotters have provided a unique brand of entertainment for children of all ages. As we saw in Section 14.7, the Globetrotters illustrate another (but less central) source of monopsony power: the demand by a monopolist for a specialized input. This organization—a virtual monopolist in show biz basketball—demands a specialized input: the "showboat" basketball player. Organizations such as the NBA clubs also demand the services of skilled basketball players, but they look for quite different skills. Because only the Globetrotters' organization wants players who specialize in entertainment, the club is a monopsonist in the market for show business players.

So, too, Dow Chemical—a virtual monopolist in primary magnesium production in the United States—demands the specialized input magnesium chloride: a salt with no other important chemical use. Because Dow is the only significant demander, it is also a virtual monopsonist in the magnesium chloride input market.

*14.9 Monopsonistic Price Discrimination

Let's turn to price discrimination in a monopsonistic market. Knowing how to solve the book vendor's dilemma in Problem 11.5 was the key to solving the coal buyer's dilemma in Problem 14.10 because perfect price discrimination is so similar in monopoly and monopsony. In this section, we'll again exploit the similarity between monopolistic and monopsonistic price discrimination as we do a quick treatment of **ordinary monopsonistic price discrimination.**

Suppose that a monopsonist can buy input Z from two identifiable groups of suppliers—say, labor from women and men or from whites and nonwhites. Suppose, too, that the supply functions of these groups are different. How will a profit-maximizing monopsonist exploit this chance to price discriminate? Let's defer the firm's profit-maximizing problem until we have answered a simpler question: What combination of labor from the first group, z_1, and the second group, z_2, will minimize the cost of hiring a fixed amount of labor, say z'?

Recall that we used a similar strategy to solve the monopolist's price-discrimination problem in Section 11.5. We can make use of the correspondence with the monopolist's revenue-maximizing rule for allocating a fixed quantity of output in a two-segment goods market to find the monopsonist's cost-minimizing rule for acquiring inputs in a two-segment labor market. The monopsonist in Figure 14.13 will choose z_1 and z_2 so that $MFC(z_1)$ and $MFC(z_2)$ are equal and so that the sum of z_1 and z_2 is z'. At the solution presented in Figure 14.13, the monopsonist buys z_1^* from the first group at the price w_1^*, and z_2^* from the second group at the price w_2^*. We can see why this is the cost-minimizing solution by considering a departure from it. If the monopsonist were to buy 1 unit less from the first group and 1 unit more from the second, for example, its cost would increase because MFC at $z_1^* - 1$ in the first market (equal to AB in Figure 14.13a) is less than MFC at $z_2^* + 1$ units in the second market (equal to $A'B'$ in Figure 14.13b).

Again exploiting the obvious correspondence with the discriminating monop-

(a) First market segment   **(b)** Second market segment

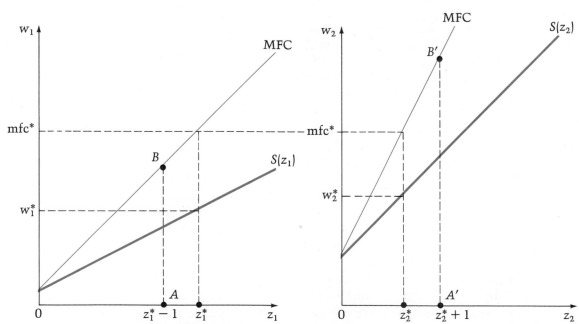

FIGURE 14.13   Discriminatory hiring to minimize costs.

To minimize the cost of buying z' units of the input from two market segments, the firm chooses the two quantities so that $z_1 + z_2 = z'$ and so that MFC is identical in the two market segments. It buys z_1^* and z_2^*. The price paid in the first market segment is w_1^*, which is less than the price paid in the second, w_2^*.

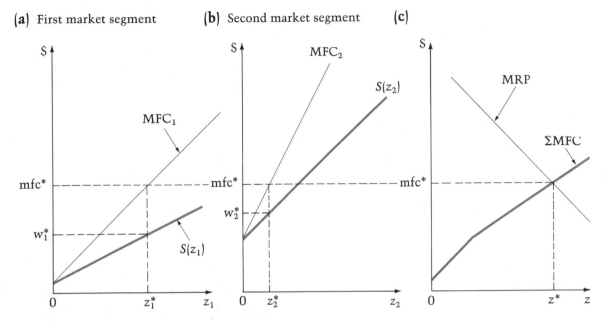

(a) First market segment   **(b)** Second market segment   **(c)**

FIGURE 14.14   Discriminatory hiring to maximize profit.

To find the profit-maximizing solution, horizontally aggregate MFC_1 and MFC_2 to obtain ΣMFC in (c). The profit-maximizing quantity z^* is the quantity such that ΣMFC is equal to MRP. Allocate the z^* units to the two market segments so as to equalize MFC in the two segments. That is, buy z_1^* in the first market segment and z_2^* in the second.

olist's profit-maximizing rule, we have solved the discriminating monopsonist's profit-maximizing problem in Figure 14.14. The two marginal factor cost functions in Figures 14.14*a* and 14.14*b* have been horizontally summed to obtain the function labeled ΣMFC in Figure 14.14*c*, which gives the marginal cost of input Z when the monopsonist follows its cost-minimizing rule. To maximize its profit, the monopsonist will buy input Z up to the point where its marginal factor cost function intersects its marginal revenue product function at z^* units in Figure 14.14*c*. We can identify the corresponding prices and quantities in the component submarkets simply by projecting mfc* from Figure 14.14*c* into Figures 14.14*a* and 14.14*b*.

In discussing monopoly price discrimination in goods markets, we discovered that the possibility of arbitrage significantly limited the monopolist's ability to price discriminate. For example, if the price of a new car in Vancouver exceeds the price of the same model in Seattle by more than the combined costs of transportation and import duty (soon to be eliminated), arbitragers will begin buying cars in Seattle and selling them in Vancouver. Yet we also found that when the goods are personal services, arbitrage is not possible: parents cannot have their kids buy haircuts for them at the children's price, for example. So, too, when the inputs in resource markets are labor services, arbitrage is once again impossible because employment contracts involve the employer and specific employees: women cannot have men obtain employment for them at the male worker's wage rate. Because arbitrage is difficult in labor markets, we might expect to see significant monopsonistic discrimination.

Certain conditions must prevail, however, before monopsonistic discrimination in labor markets can occur. First, the market must be characterized by monopsony power; second, the degree of monopsony power must be different for identifiable groups of workers within that market. Although we will not examine this sort of discrimination in any detail, we can outline the important questions to be asked. First, is the labor market characterized by significant job immobility? For example, are accountants or hair stylists fairly immobile? Second, is one segment of the labor force significantly less mobile than another? For example, are female accountants or hair stylists less mobile than their male counterparts? If the answer to both questions is affirmative and if the less mobile group is paid less, we can tentatively ascribe that differential in wage rates to ordinary monopsonistic discrimination.

The whole question of discrimination is a hotly debated issue as well as a complex economic problem. Comparable pay for comparable work and affirmative action programs for identifiable minorities are just two of the many policy issues related to labor market discrimination that regularly appear in the headlines. Many theoretical approaches have been proposed to explain this important and difficult problem. For example, Gary Becker (1958) has presented an interesting theory of discrimination that is based not on profit maximization, but on employers' utility maximization. If you are intrigued by other ways to model labor market discrimination, Kenneth Arrow (1972) provides an accessible and stimulating discussion of a number of theoretical approaches.

*14.10 Markets for Nonrenewable Resources

In discussing nonrenewable resources such as oil, coal, and iron ore, we simply assumed that the supply of those resources was perfectly inelastic with respect to price within any period. However, the old aphorism, "Oil in the ground is like money in the bank," reminds us of an important intertemporal question: When will oil in the ground be pumped, sold, and turned into money in the bank? This kind of supply decision clearly depends on the prices that suppliers anticipate today, tomorrow, and the day after, for the simple reason that the oil that is not supplied today can be supplied tomorrow.

Because time is an important element in such markets, we'll develop a two-period model for any nonrenewable natural resource in fixed supply — oil, for example. Even by using just two time periods, we can learn the basic principles that guide the intertemporal allocation of nonrenewable resources. We'll start by analyzing the supply behavior of individual owners of oil and then combine these results with the tools developed earlier in the chapter to determine the intertemporal equilibrium: the price and the allocation of oil to each of the two periods.

Individual Supply Behavior

Let's begin with the supply decision of an individual, Bagwell, who owns 10,000 barrels of crude oil. For simplicity, we'll assume that Bagwell incurs no cost in pumping and selling his oil and that oil is his only source of income. Suppose, too, that there are only two periods in this economy and that Bagwell must therefore decide how much of his 10,000 barrels of oil to supply in period 1, z_1, and how much in period 2, z_2.

We'll assume, as always, that Bagwell is motivated by utility maximization. If he has the opportunity to borrow against future income for current consumption and to save current income for future consumption at a common rate of interest i, then his utility-maximizing problem can be separated into two parts. In the first part of the problem, he chooses z_1 and z_2 to maximize the present value of his wealth. In the second part, he allocates the resulting wealth to consumption goods over the two periods to maximize his utility. It is the first part of the problem that concerns us here, because it is the choice to maximize present value that determines how much oil Bagwell will supply in each period.

The Separation Theorem

The fact that Bagwell's utility-maximizing decision can be separated into these two parts is sometimes called **the separation theorem**. In effect, we discovered this theorem in our discussion of present value and intertemporal choice in Section 5.8, where the individual chose the inheritance bundle associated with the larger present value.

Bagwell's problem is similar. He will choose z_1 and z_2 to maximize the present value of his wealth PVW. The present value of his wealth is

$$PVW = w_1 z_1 + \frac{w_2 z_2}{1 + i}$$

where i is the interest rate and w_1 and w_2 are the prices of oil in periods 1 and 2. Of course, since Bagwell has just 10,000 barrels of oil,

$$z_2 = 10000 - z_1$$

If we then substitute this expression for z_2 in the expression for the present value of Bagwell's wealth, we get

$$PVW = \frac{10000 w_2}{1 + i} + z_1\left(w_1 - \frac{w_2}{1 + i}\right)$$

The first term is Bagwell's wealth if he sells all of his oil in period 2. The second term is

the crucial one: it is the rate of change of Bagwell's wealth as he sells 1 more unit of oil in period 1 and therefore 1 less unit in period 2. If this term is positive—that is, if w_1 exceeds $w_2/(1 + i)$—then wealth increases as z_1 increases (and z_2 correspondingly decreases). Therefore, Bagwell will sell all 10,000 barrels of his oil in period 1 and none of it in period 2 if w_1 exceeds $w_2/(1 + i)$.

To understand this result, suppose that Bagwell initially sells only 9000 barrels in period 1. The increase in Bagwell's wealth from selling 1 more unit of oil in period 1 is w_1, and the decrease in his wealth from selling 1 less unit in period 2 is $w_2/(1 + i)$. If w_1 exceeds $w_2/(1 + i)$, the net change in wealth, $w_1 - w_2/(1 + i)$, is positive. Therefore, Bagwell will sell his whole supply of oil in period 1.

This sort of reasoning also reveals that if w_1 is less than $w_2/(1 + i)$, he will sell all his oil in period 2. Finally, if w_1 is equal to $w_2/(1 + i)$, Bagwell's wealth is independent of how much oil he sells in each period. The rules we have just derived for Bagwell describe the supply behavior of any owner of oil. Let's record them for future use.

If $w_1 > w_2/(1 + i)$, all oil is sold in period 1.

If $w_1 < w_2/(1 + i)$, all oil is sold in period 2.

If $w_1 = w_2/(1 + i)$, some oil may be sold in each period.

Hotelling's Law

Now that we know the supply response of any individual to any pair of prices for oil in the two periods, we can combine this knowledge with the tools developed earlier in the chapter to determine the competitive equilibrium allocation of a fixed supply of oil and the equilibrium prices in the two periods. So that we can concentrate on the competitive equilibrium in the resource market, we'll assume that each of a great many people owns a small portion of a fixed supply of oil, denoted by z'. Quantities allocated to the two periods will be denoted by z_1 and z_2. We'll show that in the normal case, competitive equilibrium prices will satisfy Hotelling's law.

We expect that under normal circumstances, some portion of the oil will be sold in the first period and some in the second; that is, in the normal case, both z_1 and z_2 will be positive. If this is so, then the following relationship between w_1 and w_2 must hold:

$$w_1 = \frac{w_2}{1+i}$$

If w_1 were less than $w_2/(1+i)$, for instance, then no one would supply any oil in period 1, and if w_1 were larger than $w_2/(1+i)$, then no one would supply any in period 2. By rewriting our equation as

$$w_2 = w_1(1+i)$$

we can see that the price of oil rises from one period to the next at the rate of interest. This result is **Hotelling's law.**

Determining the Competitive Equilibrium

We can now use the four-quadrant diagram in Figure 14.15 to find equilibrium prices and the equilibrium allocation. Notice that all four quadrants share a common origin at the center of Figure 14.15, labeled 0, and that the arrows at the ends of the axes indicate the direction in which the given price or quantity is increasing.

Hotelling's law tells us that the pair of equilibrium prices in periods 1 and 2, (w_1^e, w_2^e), will lie on the line $w_2 = (1+i)w_1$ in quadrant I. But which point on the line represents the equilibrium-price pair, and what is the corresponding allocation of oil to the two periods?

We can find out by using the ordinary tools of input supply and demand to derive a locus of market-clearing prices. Any point

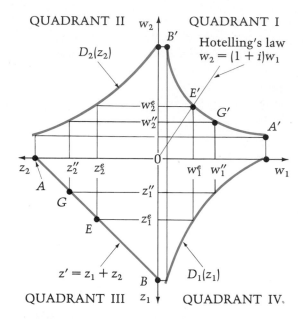

FIGURE 14.15   Intertemporal allocation of a nonrenewable natural resource.

The line $0E'$ in quadrant I captures Hotelling's law. We therefore know that the equilibrium prices for oil in the two periods will lie on $0E'$. To discover which point on the line represents the equilibrium-price pair, we have derived the locus of market-clearing prices in quadrant I: $B'E'G'A'$. The demand functions for periods 1 and 2 are constructed in quadrants IV and II, and the line $AGEB$ in quadrant III represents all possible allocations of the fixed supply of oil to the two periods. Suppose that (z_1'', z_2'') at point G in quadrant III is the allocation. The market-clearing prices from quadrants IV and II are (w_1'', w_2''). Projecting those prices into quadrant I, we have point G' on the locus of market-clearing prices. The pair of prices (w_1^e, w_2^e) is the equilibrium pair because it is consistent with Hotelling's law (it lies on $0E'$) and because it lies on the locus of market-clearing prices (on $B'E'G'A'$).

on the line $z' = z_1 + z_2$ in quadrant III is a possible allocation of the fixed supply to the two periods. By choosing any one of those allocations — say, (z_1'', z_2'') at point G in quadrant III — we can identify the corresponding pair of market-clearing prices by referring to the demand functions in quadrants II and IV. The allocation at G gives rise to point G' on the locus of market-clearing prices in quadrant I, for instance, because the competitive equilibrium price in period 1 is w_1'' when z_1'' units are supplied and because the competitive equilibrium price in period 2 is w_2'' when z_2'' units are supplied. The entire locus of market-clearing prices —the line $B'E'G'A'$ in quadrant I—has been derived with this technique. (On this locus, the price pairs at points B', E', and A' correspond, respectively, to the allocations labeled B, E, and A in quadrant III.)

The equilibrium-price pair (w_1^e, w_2^e) is determined by the intersection of the line $w_2 = (1 + i)w_1$, which captures Hotelling's law, and the locus of market-clearing prices at point E' in quadrant I. The corresponding equilibrium allocation (z_1^e, z_2^e) is at point E in quadrant III. Why? Notice first that because (w_1^e, w_2^e) is on the locus of market-clearing prices, quantity demanded is equal to z_1^e in period 1 and z_2^e in period 2. Notice, too, that because the price combination (w_1^e, w_2^e) is on the line $w_2 = (1 + i)w_1$, the allocation (z_1^e, z_2^e) is consistent with the supply behavior of individual owners of oil.

Let's see why other price combinations cannot be equilibrium prices. At the prices (w_1'', w_2'') at point G', for instance, all the suppliers will want to sell all their oil in period 1 because w_1 exceeds $w_2(1 + i)$. Therefore, the corresponding allocation (z_1'', z_2'') at point G in quadrant III, in which z_2'' is positive, will not be forthcoming. To sharpen your understanding of this model, try the comparative statics exercises in the following problem.

PROBLEM 14.11

Suppose that the interest rate increases. Show that z_1^e increases; z_2^e decreases; w_1^e decreases; and w_2^e increases.

We've learned from this exercise that given a fixed supply of a nonrenewable resource, the price that governs the intertemporal allocation of the fixed supply to

different time periods is the rate of interest. Thus, a drop in the interest rate serves to reallocate resource use from the present to the future. More generally, we've learned that the rate of interest is a key price governing the intertemporal allocation of resources.

Summary

This chapter has focused on one of the fundamental problems in economics: the allocation of resources. The results from the first nine sections are summarized in Figure 14.16, where four types of firms are characterized according to their status as either monopolists or perfect competitors in their

INPUT MARKET

	Competitive	Monopsonistic
Competitive	$w^e = \text{MFC} = \text{MRP} = \text{VMP}$ I Efficient allocation	$w^e < \text{MFC} = \text{MRP} = \text{VMP}$ II Inefficient allocation
Monopolistic	$w^e = \text{MFC} = \text{MRP} < \text{VMP}$ III Inefficient allocation	$w^e < \text{MFC} = \text{MRP} < \text{VMP}$ IV Inefficient allocation

OUTPUT MARKET (left axis)

FIGURE 14.16 Resource allocation summarized.

In all four cases, MFC = MRP, reflecting the profit-maximization hypothesis. In quadrant I, $w^e = \text{VMP}$, which reflects the efficiency of competitive markets. In quadrant II, $w^e < \text{VMP}$ because the input market is monopsonistic. In quadrant III, $w^e < \text{VMP}$ because the output market is monopolistic. Finally, in quadrant IV, $w^e < \text{VMP}$ because both the input and the output markets are imperfect.

output markets, and as either monopsonists or perfect competitors in an input market. We learned that in long-run equilibrium, any profit-maximizing firm uses an input up to the point where MRP equals MFC. Thus, MRP = MFC in each cell of Figure 14.16.

From the perspective of resource allocation, the important differences among firms stem from the following relationships. When a firm is a monopolist in its output market, VMP (value of the marginal product) exceeds MRP because a monopolist's price is greater than its marginal revenue. When a firm is a perfect competitor in its output market, VMP equals MRP because the firm's marginal revenue equals its output price. When a firm is a monopsonist in an input market, MFC (marginal factor cost) exceeds w^e (the equilibrium wage rate). When a firm is a perfect competitor in an input market, MFC equals w^e. These differences arise because perfect competitors are price takers and monopolists and monopsonists are price setters.

The value that consumers place on an additional unit of any input used by a firm is VMP. To find out whether too little of an input is allocated to any firm in equilibrium, we can simply ask if VMP exceeds w^e. If so, then too little of the input is allocated to the firm. In Figure 14.16, VMP does exceed w^e in three of the four types of firms: II, III, and IV. In cell II, $w^e <$ MFC because this type of firm has monopsony power; in cell III, MRP < VMP because this type of firm has monopoly power; and in cell IV, $w^e <$ MFC and MRP < VMP because this type of firm has both monopoly and monopsony power. Only the type of firm in cell I — where $w^e =$ VMP, the case of the perfect competitor in both markets — is consistent with Pareto optimality. We'll extend this partial equilibrium analysis of allocational efficiency (and inefficiency) in Chapter 15, when we examine allocation in a general equilibrium framework.

In considering the intertemporal allocation of a fixed supply of a nonrenewable natural resource in the last section of the chapter, we discovered Hotelling's law: if a positive quantity of the resource is to be supplied in all periods, then the price of the resource must rise from each period to the next at the rate of interest. We then combined this result with the tools developed in earlier sections to identify the intertemporal competitive equilibrium.

Exercises

1 If all input and output markets are competitive, then all inputs are allocated to their most productive uses in competitive equilibrium. Explain. If some input and/or output market is imperfectly competitive, however, then inputs are not allocated to their most valuable uses. Explain.

2 The City Council of Podunk has given Walley the exclusive right to sell Coke at local baseball games. The operation is very simple. Walley buys Coke from the local Coke distributor (who lives next door to Walley) for $0.40 per can and takes his supply of Coke to the ballpark in his picnic cooler. Anyone wanting to buy a Coke walks down to Walley's seat behind home plate and buys it. Since Walley would go to the ballgames even if he didn't have the Coke franchise, his only cost in the short run is the $0.40 per can that he pays to buy the Coke. The demand for Coke at a typical ballgame is

$$p = 1.60 - .01y$$

For example, he could sell 100 cans for $0.60 per can, or 150 cans for $0.10 per can.

a First, let's focus on the output market. What is Walley's marginal revenue function and what is his marginal cost? What is his profit-maximizing level of output? How much profit does he earn? Construct a graph to illustrate Walley's situation in the output market.

b Now let's focus on the input market. What is the one costly input? What is the marginal revenue product function? What is the input demand function? How much of the input does Walley buy? If the distributor charged $0.60 per can, how much would he buy? Construct a graph to illustrate Walley's situation in the input market.

3 Suppose that a firm that is a perfect competitor in its output market can vary only input Z in the short run and that

$$AP(z) = 100 - z$$

and

$$MP(z) = 100 - 2z$$

a Suppose that the price of the firm's product is $10. What are the firm's marginal and average revenue product functions? What is the firm's short-run demand function for input Z? How much input Z will the firm use when its price is $40? When its price is $60?

b Show that the results in part a are consistent with the profit-maximizing rule in the firm's output market: produce the level of output where SMC is equal to output price.

c What is the firm's short-run demand function for input Z when the price of the firm's product is $25? How much input Z will the firm now use when the input price is $40? When the input price is $60?

4 Many countries, states, and provinces have passed "equal pay for equal work" legislation, which is intended to discourage discrimination by forcing firms to pay the same wage to all employees who do the same job. Some jurisdictions have gone even further by passing "equal pay for work of equal value" legislation, which is intended to force firms to pay the same wage to all employees whose work is of equal value, regardless of the job.

a Using the model of monopsony discrimination developed in this chapter, discuss the implications of equal pay for equal work.

b Using the productivity concepts developed in this chapter, discuss the difficulties involved in implementing "equal pay for work of equal value."

c Would either kind of legislation serve a useful economic purpose if all labor markets were competitive?

5 Consider a firm in which each unit of labor produces 1 unit of output that can be sold for $100. The firm faces two different supply functions from groups 1 and 2. The supply functions for the two groups are

$$w_1 = 10 + z_1$$

$$w_2 = z_2$$

where w_1 and w_2 are wage rates and z_1 and z_2 are quantities of labor supplied.

a Assuming that the firm can discriminate, find the firm's profit-maximizing solution and calculate its profit. What wage is paid in each market, and how much labor is hired in each market?

b Assuming that the firm cannot discriminate, first find its aggregate supply function, and then find the firm's profit-maximizing solution and calculate its profit.

c Compare your results from parts a and b. In particular, determine who is better off in a and who is better off in b.

6 Consider a world with only two types of workers, A and B. For example, type A might be blacks (or men) and type B whites (or women). Assume that types A and B both prefer to work with others of their own type. Show that this sort of bigotry is likely to produce firms in which all workers are of the same type. Will it produce wage differentials?

7 Suppose that the demand function for some nonrenewable resource is

$$w_1 = 200 - 2z_1$$

in period 1 and

$$w_2 = 200 - 2z_2$$

in period 2. There are 100 units of the resource to be allocated for use in the two periods, and the interest rate is 50%. Find the competitive equilibrium prices in periods 1 and 2 and the competitive equilibrium allocation to the two periods.

*8 In this chapter, we ignored the possibility of oligopsony: the case in which more than one firm has some monopsony power in the same input market. We can alter Problem 14.9 to construct a very simple model of oligopsony to convey the flavor of such problems. We'll suppose that there are two demanders on the railroad—one at mile 0 and the other at mile 975—and we'll suppose that the demanders bear the costs of transport. For each demander, marginal revenue product is $200 per ton of coal; otherwise, the setup is as specified in Problem 14.9.

a   Construct a table in which you identify the maximum price each of the demanders would pay each of the suppliers for the supplier's ton of coal. For each supplier, note which demander is willing to pay the higher price.

b   Now consider the "game" between the two demanders as they vie to buy the coal offered by the supplier at mile 500. Suppose that prices must be announced in dollars and cents—$130.75 is a permissible price, but $130.753 is not. Show that the Nash equilibrium price offers are $150.00 for the firm located at mile 0 and $150.01 for the supplier located at mile 975. The supplier, of course, sells the ton of coal to the buyer offering the higher price. (You may want to review Bertrand's oligopoly model, discussed in Section 12.4.)

c   Now find the Nash equilibrium prices offered to the nine other suppliers, and compute each demander's profit.

d   Finally, compare the prices that the suppliers receive in this oligopsony with the prices they received in Problem 14.10.

*9   In this exercise, you can explore what is called a bilateral monopoly. Firm A is the only demander of input Z, and its marginal revenue product function is

$$MRP(z) = 200 - 2z$$

Firm B is the only supplier of input Z, and its reservation price for each unit of input Z, $R(z)$, is

$$R(z) = z$$

You can think of $R(z)$ as firm B's marginal cost of producing input Z.

a   Suppose first that firm A can choose a price w and that firm B then decides how much input Z to sell to A at the price A chooses. What price maximizes A's profit, and what quantity will B sell to A?

b   Now reverse the exercise. Suppose that B can choose a price and that A then decides how much to sell at B's chosen price. What price maximizes B's profit, and what quantity will A buy at this price?

c   Finally, suppose that firm C were to buy both firms A and B. How much input Z would firm C produce?

*10   The Fraser River Valley is the "breadbasket" of British Columbia. The agriculture in the valley uses relatively little labor, except at harvest time. Much of the harvest labor is supplied by recent immigrants to Canada who live about 40 miles away in Vancouver, who have little or no facility in English, and who do not own cars. The market in harvest labor is mediated by labor brokers. A labor broker typically owns a truck for transporting laborers and speaks both English and the laborers' language. The broker buys labor at one price w_1 and sells it to farmers at a higher price w_2. Assume that the demand for farm labor from a particular broker is linear and downward sloping, that the supply of labor is linear and upward sloping, and that all of the broker's costs are fixed, or independent of the quantity of labor bought and sold. Find the values of w_1 and w_2 and the quantity of labor bought and sold that maximize the labor broker's profit.

References

Arrow, K. (1972), "Models of Job Discrimination," in *Racial Discrimination in Economic Life*, A. H. Pascal (ed.), Lexington, Mass.: D.C. Heath, pp. 83–102.

Becker, G. (1957), *The Economics of Discrimination*, Chicago: University of Chicago Press.

15

EFFICIENCY AND THE ALLOCATION OF RESOURCES: A GENERAL EQUILIBRIUM APPROACH

Two problems are basic to all economic analysis. The first problem is **allocation**: How does an economic system allocate scarce resources to competing uses? More specifically, using the Pareto criterion as the evaluative yardstick, when does a market system successfully direct resources to alternative uses? The second problem is **distribution**: How are wealth and income, or command over goods and services, distributed among the individual members of society? More specifically, what criterion should we use to evaluate distribution, and if we judge redistribution as socially desirable, what institutions are effective in moving an economy from one economic state to another, more "distributionally acceptable" state?

The distribution problem will occupy us in Chapter 16. In this chapter, we'll take up the allocation question as we finally fit all the analytical pieces of earlier chapters into one large picture of efficiency in an economywide context. We are now widening our perspective from the earlier **partial equilibrium** framework, characterized by a market-by-market analysis, to a **general equilibrium** framework, in which we simultaneously consider all markets in the economy.

At every turn, we'll be drawing on what we learned in earlier chapters. This chapter will serve both to integrate much of what we've learned so far and to review that material. If at any point you are uncertain of that earlier material, briefly review it before proceeding.

A recurring theme in economics concerns the extent to which the interactions of self-interested individuals yield results that are in some sense socially desirable. Adam Smith, the father of the doctrine of "natural identity of interests," argued that each individual, in pursuing his or her own self-interest, would be lead as by an "unseen hand" to undertake activities that ultimately contributed to the welfare of society as a whole. As George Stigler has noted, Smith's doctrine of the natural identity of interests is "not really a doctrine at all: it is a problem."[1] Smith's doctrine raises this question: What kinds of social arrangements promote an identity between public and private interests? In this chapter, we'll rise to the challenge posed by Smith's doctrine as we look for a set of institutions consistent with the natural identity of interests. We'll discover that when certain restrictive conditions are satisfied, the institutions of perfect competition promote efficiency, or Pareto optimality.

15.1 The General Equilibrium Perspective on Efficiency

To an economist, the overriding purpose of the economic system is to transform the scarce resources held by individuals into consumption goods that benefit those same individuals. Individual people are therefore the leading actors in the economic drama. From them (and from nature) comes the wherewithal to produce goods, and goods are produced for their benefit. In this larger, general equilibrium drama, then, firms are the bit players. Their only role is to facilitate the process of transforming resources into consumption goods. Questions of efficiency are therefore concerned not with the profit of firms, but exclusively with the well-being of individual people.

Using the Pareto criterion, we then see that the general equilibrium of an economy is efficient if no person can be made better off without making another person worse off.

We'll begin our analysis by focusing on a simple economy in which goods are exchanged and consumed but not produced. We'll discover exactly what efficiency means in this exchange economy, and then we'll show that general competitive equilibrium is efficient if certain conditions are satisfied. We'll then introduce production into the model and generalize the understanding developed in the exchange economy context.[2]

15.2 Efficiency in an Exchange Economy

In the next two sections, we'll look at an economy in which goods are traded and consumed, but not produced. Since goods are exchanged but not produced, the model is called an **exchange economy.** In this section, we'll discover how to determine which allocations of available goods to individual consumers are Pareto-optimal. In the next section, we'll create competitive markets in which the goods can be traded, find the competitive equilibrium, and consider two results or theorems that are the cornerstones of what is called welfare economics.

Pareto-Optimal Allocations

Imagine, then, two people—Marvin and Shelly—on some isolated island where there are 102 units of good 1 and 66 units of good 2. We can use a box diagram to describe all possible allocations of goods in this island exchange economy. The dimensions of the box diagram in Figure 15.1 reflect the available quantities of goods 1 and 2: the horizontal sides are 102 units long because there are 102 units of good 1 in this economy; the vertical sides are 66 units long because there are 66 units of good 2 in this economy. Possible consumption bundles for Shelly, or possible allocations of goods to

[1] See Stigler's (1957) introductory remarks. His *Selections from The Wealth of Nations* is an excellent introduction to Smith's great work.

[2] Walras (1874, 1977) is the founder of general equilibrium theory. Jaffe (1954) is the English translator. Arrow and Hahn (1971) present a comprehensive treatment of general equilibrium theory and (in Chapter 1) an interesting history of it.

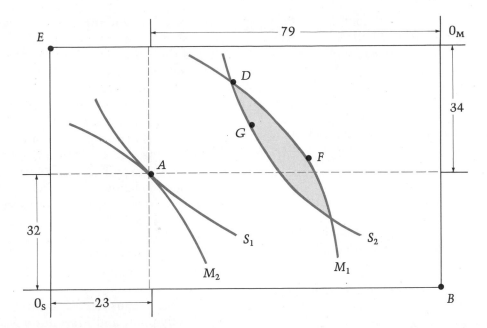

FIGURE 15.1   The Edgeworth box diagram.

Shelly's consumption bundles and indifference curves are plotted relative to 0_S; Marvin's, relative to 0_M. Because Shelly's and Marvin's indifference curves are tangent at allocation A, the allocation is Pareto-optimal. In contrast, because Shelly's and Marvin's indifference curves intersect at allocation D, the allocation is not Pareto-optimal: allocations in the green lens-shaped area are Pareto-preferred to allocation D.

Shelly, are plotted relative to the origin 0_S at the lower left-hand corner of the box. Possible allocations of goods to Marvin are plotted relative to the origin 0_M at the upper right-hand corner of the box diagram.

The important thing to recognize is that any point in the box is an allocation of the available quantities of the two goods to Marvin and to Shelly. Conversely, any allocation of the 102 units of good 1 and 66 units of good 2 to Marvin and Shelly is described by some point in the box.

PROBLEM 15.1

How much of each good does Marvin have, and how much does Shelly have at each of the following points in Figures 15.1? Point A; Marvin's origin 0_M; point B. Suppose that all 66 units of good 2 are allocated to Shelly and all 102 units of good 1 to Marvin—what point in Figure 15.1 describes this allocation?

The Edgeworth Box Diagram

Notice too that we can plot Shelly's and Marvin's indifference curves in the box diagram. When we include indifference curves, the diagram is called an **Edgeworth box** diagram, after F. Y. Edgeworth, a late nineteenth-century British economist who was the first to use this sort of diagram. Since Shelly's indifference curves, labeled S_1 and S_2, are plotted relative to the origin 0_S, they have the familiar convex-to-the-origin shape. In contrast, Marvin's indifference curves, labeled M_1 and M_2, seem strange. They are, in fact, also standard convex-to-the-origin indifference curves, but they seem strange because they are plotted relative to Marvin's origin 0_M. To see that they are convex to Marvin's origin, pick your book up and reorient it so that 0_M is at the lower left-hand corner of the box. Marvin's indifference curves will then have the familiar shape, while Shelly's will seem strange. To be sure that you understand the Edgeworth box diagram, try the following problem.

PROBLEM 15.2

What is Shelly's preference ordering of the four allocations A, D, G, and F in Figure 15.1? What is Marvin's?

Preference Assumptions

To keep our discussion as simple as possible, we'll use four assumptions about preferences throughout the chapter:

1 Indifference curves are convex to the appropriate origin.

2 Indifference curves are smooth.

3 Both goods are essential for all consumers.

4 The only variables that affect an individual's economic well-being are the quantities of the two goods consumed by that individual.

In Problem 15.3, you'll have a chance to discover for yourself the role played by the convexity assumption. The second assumption allows us to use the marginal rate of substitution MRS in analyzing Pareto optimality, and the third allows us to concentrate on allocations in the interior of the Edgeworth box. (See Section 3.5 for the definition of MRS, and Section 4.5 for a discussion of essential and inessential goods.)

The fourth assumption rules out externalities involving consumption — in essence, it means that the only things individuals care about are their own consumption bundles. In Chapter 17, which focuses on externalities, we'll see that consumption externalities raise some very interesting and tough questions.

Now let's look at some specific allocations and ask if they are Pareto-optimal. (Be-

fore you go on, you may want to review the discussion of Pareto optimality in Section 1.5.) Is the allocation at D in Figure 15.1, which puts Shelly on indifference curve S_2 and Marvin on indifference curve M_1, Pareto-optimal? It is, if there are no other allocations that make one of them better off while leaving the other at least as well off. Shelly prefers any allocation above and to the right of S_2 to point D, and Marvin prefers any allocation below and to the left of M_1 to point D. Therefore, any allocation in the green area above S_2 and below M_1 is preferred by both Marvin and Shelly to D; that is, any allocation in the green area Pareto-dominates D. Therefore, point D is not Pareto-optimal.

Now let's consider allocation A, which puts Shelly on S_1 and Marvin on M_2. Take your pencil and first shade in the allocations above and to the right of S_1 which make Shelly better off than she is at A, and then shade in the allocations on M_2, or below and to the left of M_2, which make Marvin no worse off than he is at A. Since these two shaded areas have no points in common, it is impossible to make Shelly better off without making Marvin worse off. Similarly, given the allocation at A, it is impossible to make Marvin better off without making Shelly worse off. Therefore, allocation A is Pareto-optimal.

What distinguishes allocation D from allocation A is that indifference curve M_1 intersects or crosses indifference curve S_2 at D, while indifference curve M_2 is tangent to indifference curve S_1 at A. As you can easily verify, any allocation in the interior of an Edgeworth box where two indifference curves intersect is not Pareto-optimal. Furthermore, the following is true:

When indifference curves are smooth and convex, if the indifference curves through a point in an Edgeworth box are tangent, then that point is a Pareto-optimal allocation.

PROBLEM 15.3

In an Edgeworth box, construct an indifference curve for Shelly that has a concave portion in the middle. Now construct an indifference curve for Marvin, convex to Marvin's origin, that is tangent to Shelly's indifference curve at one point and intersects her indifference curve at two other points. Show that the point of tangency is not a Pareto-optimal allocation, and identify the allocations that Pareto-dominate it.

Notice that at the Pareto-optimal allocation A in Figure 15.1, the marginal rate of substitution MRS is identical for Marvin and Shelly. This follows from the definition of MRS—the absolute value of the slope of the indifference curve—and the fact that the indifference curves S_1 and M_2 are tangent at A. This observation allows us to restate our understanding of Pareto optimality in an exchange economy: *Given convex indifference curves, if MRS at some allocation is identical for Marvin and Shelly, then that allocation is Pareto optimal.*

Efficiency in Consumption

More generally, let's see what we can say about Pareto optimality, or efficiency, in an exchange economy composed of many people. Suppose that we have an exchange economy with many individuals and, for purposes of argument, that MRS at the current allocation is identical for all individuals. We could isolate any two individuals—consumption bundles in hand—to form an exchange economy very much like the one pictured in Figure 15.1. In that two-person exchange economy, the initial allocation would be Pareto-optimal since MRS is identical for the two individuals. Therefore, if MRS is identical for all individuals in a many-person exchange economy, there are no bilateral trades that are Pareto-improving. Although we will not attempt a proof, there are also no multilateral trades that are Pareto-improving. Therefore, we have the following general result:

CONDITION: Efficiency in Consumption

Given the assumptions we have made, an allocation of goods is Pareto-optimal in a many-person exchange economy if MRS is identical for all individuals.[3]

The Contract Curve

Given our assumptions, we know that any point in an Edgeworth box where the indifference curves of the two individuals are tangent is a Pareto-optimal allocation. By finding all the points in the Edgeworth box where the indifference curves are tangent,

---

[3] We can use the technique of constrained maximization to show this result. Pick any two consumers with utility functions $U^1(x_1^1, x_2^1)$ and $U^2(x_1^2, x_2^2)$, and any bundle of the two goods to be allocated to the two individuals—say, the bundle (x_1', x_2'). If we fix the utility level of the first individual at, say, u^1, then efficiency in consumption—Pareto optimality—clearly demands that we allocate the available bundle of goods to the two individuals so as to maximize $U^2(x_1^2, x_2^2)$, subject to the constraint that $u^1 = U^1(x_1^1, x_2^1)$. This is a standard constrained-maximization problem, and we will show that its solution implies that MRS is identical for the two consumers. The Lagrangian is

$$L(x_1^2, x_2^2, \lambda) = U^2(x_1^2, x_2^2) - \lambda[u^1 - U^1(x_1' - x_1^2, x_2' - x_2^2)]$$

where (x_1^2, x_2^2) is the second individual's consumption bundle and $(x_1' - x_1^2, x_2' - x_2^2)$ is the first individual's bundle. Setting the partial derivatives of $L(\cdot)$ with respect to x_1^2 and x_2^2 equal to zero, we have

$$U_1^2(x_1^2, x_2^2) - \lambda U_1^1(x_1' - x_1^2, x_2' - x_2^2) = 0$$
$$U_2^2(x_1^2, x_2^2) - \lambda U_2^1(x_1' - x_1^2, x_2' - x_2^2) = 0$$

Manipulating these two expressions, we have

$$\lambda = \frac{U_1^2(x_1^2, x_2^2)}{U_1^1(x_1' - x_1^2, x_2' - x_2^2)}$$
$$= \frac{U_2^2(x_1^2, x_2^2)}{U_2^1(x_1' - x_1^2, x_2' - x_2^2)}$$

This result implies equality of the marginal rates of substitution:

$$\frac{U_1^2(x_1^2, x_2^2)}{U_2^2(x_1^2, x_2^2)}$$
$$= \frac{U_1^1(x_1' - x_1^2, x_2' - x_2^2)}{U_2^1(x_1' - x_1^2, x_2' - x_2^2)}$$

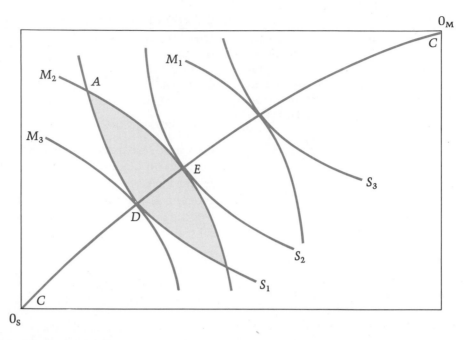

FIGURE 15.2   The contract curve.

The contract curve *CC* passes through the points of tangency of Marvin's and Shelly's indifference curves. Allocations on the contract curve are Pareto-optimal, and allocations off it are not. For example, the green area represents the set of allocations that are Pareto-improving relative to allocation *A*.

we can describe the entire set of Pareto-optimal allocations. This set, called the **contract curve,** is the line connecting all these points of tangency.

Line *CC* in Figure 15.2 is the contract curve for Marvin and Shelly. Even though we have drawn only three indifference curves for each, the box is filled with indifference curves. At any point on *CC*, two indifference curves, one for Marvin and one for Shelly, are tangent.

Let's see why this set of allocations is called the contract curve. Any allocation that is not on *CC* — point *A*, for example — is not Pareto-optimal. If Marvin and Shelly are initially at point *A*, any point in the green area on or above S_1 and on or below M_2 Pareto-dominates *A*. In other words, mutually beneficial exchanges relative to point *A* are available to them. Segment *DE* of *CC*

represents the set of Pareto-optimal allocations that Pareto-dominate allocation *A*.[4]

Imagine that Marvin and Shelly agree to an exchange that moves them from point *A* to some point in the green region. If that agreement, or contract, moves them to a point that is not on *DE*, then both have an incentive to recontract for another mutually beneficial exchange. Because their recontracting activity will end only when they have achieved an allocation on *DE*, the set of Pareto-optimal allocations is called the **contract curve.** Once on the contract curve, there is no further exchange to which both Marvin and Shelly would willingly agree.

[4] The set of Pareto-optimal allocations that Pareto-dominate an allocation like *A* in Figure 15.2 is called the *core*. Hence, relative to initial allocation *A*, segment *DE* of the contract curve is the core.

15.3 Competitive Equilibrium in an Exchange Economy

Now let's give Marvin and Shelly an initial endowment of goods at some point in their Edgeworth box, create markets in which they can buy and sell goods 1 and 2, and give them a Walrasian auctioneer to help them find the competitive equilibrium. (Recall that we introduced a Walrasian auctioneer to coordinate trading in the ticket model in Section 10.1.) We'll suppose that Shelly's initial allocation is 22 units of good 1 and 56 units of good 2 and that Marvin's allocation is 80 units of good 1 and 10 units of good 2.

Budget Lines in an Exchange Economy

The first thing to note about an exchange economy is that the prices of goods not only determine what consumption bundles an individual can buy, given his or her income, but also determine what income itself is. Suppose, for example, that the auctioneer announced the following prices: $p_1 = \$2$, and $p_2 = \$1$. Then Shelly's income is, in effect, equal to $\$100 - (\$2 \times 22) + (\$1 \times 56)$ — since she could generate this amount of income by selling her initial endowment of 22 units of good 1 and 56 units of good 2. Given these prices, her budget line is

$$2x_1^S + x_2^S = 100$$

More generally, for arbitrary prices p_1 and p_2, we have

Shelly's income $= 22p_1 + 56p_2$

since she has 22 units of good 1 and 56 units of good 2. Shelly's budget line is then

$$p_1x_1^S + p_2x_2^S = 22p_1 + 56p_2$$

The second thing to notice about an exchange economy with two goods is that there is really only one price to be determined in equilibrium: the price of good 1 relative to good 2, or the relative price of good 1. Notice that Shelly's budget line always passes through her initial endowment; that is, the consumption bundle (22 units of good 1, 56 units of good 2) is always on Shelly's budget line. The budget line will be steep if p_1 is large relative to p_2, and it will be flat if p_1 is small relative to p_2, but it will always pass through her initial endowment of 22 units of good 1 and 56 units of good 2. Therefore, the price of good 1 relative to the price of good 2 — or the ratio of p_1 to p_2, or the relative price of good 1 — is what really matters to Shelly. From her point of view, $(p_1 = \$2, p_2 = \$1)$, $(p_1 = \$4, p_2 = \$2)$, and $(p_1 = \$6, p_2 = \$3)$ are equivalent since all three price pairs imply a budget line through her initial endowment, with slope equal to -2, and a relative price of good 1 equal to 2. Similarly, Marvin's only concern is the price of good 1 relative to the price of good 2.

We can simplify our analysis of an exchange economy by fixing the price of good 2 at $1. When we set $p_2 = \$1$, then p_1 becomes the relative price of good 1. With this **price normalization**, Shelly's budget line becomes[5]

$$p_1x_1^S + x_2^S = 22p_1 + 56$$

In Figure 15.3, we have illustrated Shelly's budget line for three different values of p_1. Notice that as p_1 changes, her budget line swivels around her initial endowment — 22 units of good 1 and 56 units of good 2. Given this price normalization, Marvin's budget line is

$$p_1x_1^M + x_2^M = 80p_1 + 10$$

since he has 80 units of good 1 and 10 units of good 2.

Finding the Competitive Equilibrium

To find the competitive equilibrium, we'll use the device of a Walrasian auctioneer, who will begin the process by announcing a

---

[5] We are free to choose any price normalization. Another commonly used normalization is $p_2 = 1 - p_1$.

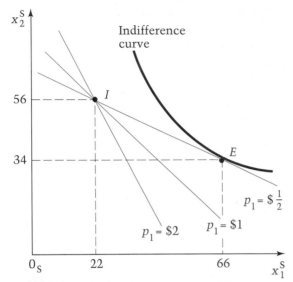

FIGURE 15.3   Budget lines in an exchange economy.

Shelly's initial endowment is point I. As relative price p_1 changes, her budget line swivels about I, her initial allocation. This reflects the fact that she can always afford her initial endowment. Given p_1 equal to $\$\frac{1}{2}$, Shelly's utility-maximizing consumption bundle is E.

relative price p_1. Marvin and Shelly could respond to the auctioneer by announcing a *net demand*, or supply, for each good. For example, if the auctioneer announced $p_1 = \$\frac{1}{2}$, we see from Figure 15.3 that Shelly could respond with a *net demand* for good 1 equal to 44 units — since she wants to consume 66 units of good 1 and has 22 — and a *net supply* of good 2 equal to 22 units — since she has 56 units of good 2 but wants to consume only 34.

Alternatively, Marvin and Shelly could respond to the auctioneer by reporting their *gross supply* of each good and their *gross demand* for each good. In the preceding example, if the auctioneer announced $p_1 = \$\frac{1}{2}$, Shelly would respond by offering to supply 22 units of good 1 and 56 units of good 2 — her entire endowment of each good — and to demand 66 units of good 1 and 34 units of good 2.

In either case, at the utility-maximizing bundle, Shelly's MRS will be equal to the announced price p_1, since p_1 is the relative price of good 1. Similarly, at his utility-maximizing bundle, Marvin's MRS will be equal to the announced price p_1. (You may want to review Section 4.5 on the individual's utility-maximizing problem.)

For clarity, we'll suppose that Marvin and Shelly respond by reporting their gross supply of each good and their gross demand for each good. To find the competitive equilibrium, the auctioneer begins by announcing a price p_1. Given that price, Marvin and Shelly then report to the auctioneer the gross *quantity supplied* of each good and the gross *quantity demanded* of each good. The auctioneer first adds their responses to get *aggregate supply* and *aggregate demand*, and then compares aggregate supply and aggregate demand for each good.

1   If aggregate demand is not equal to aggregate supply for both goods, no trading takes place. Instead, the auctioneer announces another price, and the process is repeated.

2   If, for both goods, aggregate demand is equal to aggregate supply, the announced relative price is a competitive equilibrium price, goods are traded, and the auction stops. In the resulting **competitive equilibrium allocation**, both individuals get the gross demands announced to the auctioneer.

As we'll see, the auctioneer can focus on just one market because when aggregate demand is equal to aggregate supply in one market, aggregate demand is equal to aggregate supply in the other as well. To see this result, suppose the auctioneer has found some price p_1^e such that aggregate demand for good 1 is equal to aggregate supply of good 1. Then, since aggregate supply of good 1 is

102 units, Shelly's demand for good 1, x_1^S, plus Marvin's demand for good 1, x_1^M, must satisfy

$$x_1^S + x_1^M = 102$$

To see that aggregate demand for good 2 is also equal to its aggregate supply (66 units), let's first add Marvin's and Shelly's budget lines to get the following equation:

$$p_1(x_1^S + x_1^M) + (x_2^S + x_2^M) = 102\,p_1 + 66$$

When price is equal to p_1^e, demand is equal to supply of good 1, or $x_1^S + x_1^M = 102$; therefore, the first terms on the left and right cancel, and this combined budget constraint reduces to

$$x_2^S + x_2^M = 66$$

Recalling that the aggregate supply of good 2 is 66 units, we see that the demand for good 2 is equal to its supply. This result is known as **Walras' law**:[6]

If at price p_1^e demand is equal to supply in one market, then demand is equal to supply in the other market as well, and p_1^e is therefore a competitive equilibrium price.

We can use the Edgeworth box diagram to illustrate the competitive equilibrium of our two-person exchange economy. In Figure 15.4, the initial endowment is at point A. E^* is the competitive equilibrium allocation, and the green line is a common budget line whose slope reflects the competitive equilibrium price. Relative to Shelly's origin 0_S, the green line can be seen as Shelly's budget line, and relative to Marvin's origin 0_M, it can be seen as Marvin's budget line.

The utility-maximizing bundles are both at point E^*, which is the competitive equilibrium allocation in this exchange economy.

PROBLEM 15.4

In this competitive equilibrium, Shelly is a net demander of one good and Marvin a net supplier of that good. What is the good, and what is her net demand and his net supply? Similarly, Marvin is a net demander of one good and Shelly a net supplier of that good. What is the good, and what is his net demand and her net supply? What trade will implement the competitive equilibrium allocation?

Notice that the competitive equilibrium allocation is on the contract curve in the diagram. This is a general and important result, so let's take time to examine it. In responding to the auctioneer, Shelly and Marvin solve a standard utility-maximizing problem. They each find a bundle where MRS is equal to the announced relative price p_1. That is, every time they respond to the auctioneer, they each plan to consume a bundle where MRS is equal to the price p_1 announced by the auctioneer. They cannot, and therefore do not, implement these consumption plans until they are mutually consistent, or until aggregate demand is equal to aggregate supply in both markets — that is, until the auctioneer has announced the equilibrium price. At the equilibrium price, their consumption plans are consistent; therefore, trades are made to implement the competitive equilibrium allocation where MRS is equal to the equilibrium price p_1^e for each of them. Shelly's MRS is therefore identical to Marvin's, which means that the equilibrium allocation is on the contract curve, or is Pareto-optimal.

The First Theorem of Welfare Economics

In a many-person exchange economy, we get an analogous result. In the competitive

---

[6] More generally, when there are n markets in a general equilibrium model, Walras' law says that if demand is equal to supply in $n-1$ markets, then demand is equal to supply in the nth as well.

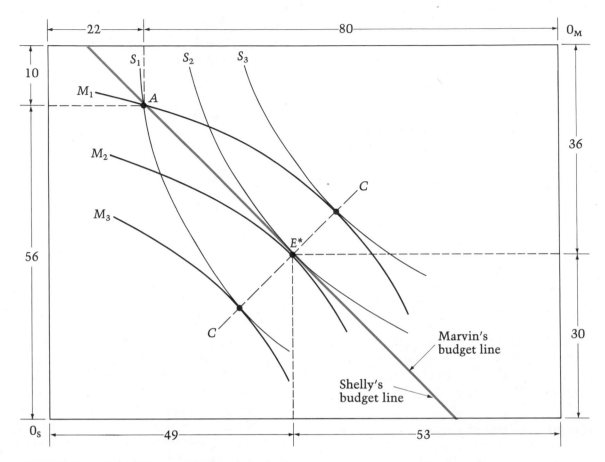

FIGURE 15.4 Competitive equilibrium in an exchange economy.

The initial allocation is at point A. Given the announced (relative) price, the line AE^* can be seen as both Shelly's budget line and as Marvin's budget line. Since both Shelly and Marvin choose the allocation at E^*, the announced relative price is a competitive equilibrium price, and E^* is the competitive equilibrium allocation. Since E^* is on the contract curve CC, the competitive equilibrium is Pareto-optimal.

equilibrium of such an economy, each person consumes a bundle where MRS is equal to the equilibrium relative price for good 1. Therefore, MRS is identical for all consumers, and the competitive equilibrium allocation is Pareto-optimal. We then have what is called the **first theorem of welfare economics:**

Given the assumptions we have made, the competitive equilibrium allocation of a many-person exchange economy is Pareto-optimal.

This theorem says, in effect, that the gains from trade are exhausted in competitive equilibrium.[7]

---

[7] Given the assumptions we have made, it is entirely possible that there are many competitive equilibria. If there are many equilibria, the first theorem says that they are all Pareto-optimal. You can easily construct an Edgeworth box with two competitive equilibria. Begin by drawing two budget lines through the same initial endowment, and then construct indifference curves so that there is a competitive equilibrium on both budget lines.

The Second Theorem of Welfare Economics

Of course, any allocation on the contract curve is Pareto-optimal. The second theorem of welfare economics concerns a way of attaining any of these Pareto-optimal allocations. Suppose that we have identified some Pareto-optimal allocation that we would like to implement. The second theorem tells us first to redistribute the initial endowment and then to rely on competitive markets to achieve Pareto optimality.

To see how this works, let's reinterpret Figure 15.4 by supposing that the initial endowment is at 0_M, where Shelly owns everything. Suppose too that we have somehow identified E^* as the Pareto-optimal allocation that we would like to implement. How can we achieve it? We do so by first redistributing the initial endowment to attain an endowment anywhere on the green budget line in Figure 15.4, and then using a competitive market to attain the desired Pareto-optimal allocation at E^*. In particular, we could transfer 80 units of good 1 and 10 units of good 2 from Shelly to Marvin to attain the endowment at point A, confident in the knowledge that this endowment will produce the desired Pareto-optimal allocation at E^*. (After all, we initially found the equilibrium at E^* by supposing that the allocation was A.) A little thought should convince you that any allocation on the green line, including E^* itself, will produce E^* as the competitive equilibrium allocation. Thus we have the **second theorem of welfare economics:**

If preferences satisfy the assumptions we have made, given any Pareto-optimal allocation POA, there is an initial allocation IA such that, given initial allocation IA, the competitive equilibrium allocation is POA.

Let's introduce production into our model and see how these theorems can be extended. After we've achieved this exten-sion, we'll try to put these results in perspective.

15.4 Efficiency in a General Equilibrium Model with Production

We'll suppose that there are a fixed number of firms that produce good 1 and a fixed number that produce good 2. Therefore, firms do not enter or exit in this general equilibrium model; they simply choose how much to produce. We'll suppose too that there are a fixed number of individuals in the economy and that their preferences satisfy the assumptions laid out in the previous section.

We'll suppose that all firms that produce the same good have the same constant-returns-to-scale production function. To produce their goods, firms use two *primary inputs*, input 1 and input 2. We'll assume that there is a fixed supply of each input. Hence, quantity supplied is not responsive to input price.

Production Assumptions

To keep our discussion as simple as possible, we'll use a number of assumptions about production or technology throughout the chapter. We'll assume that

1 Isoquants are convex.

2 Isoquants are smooth.

3 Both inputs are essential in the production of both goods.

4 Production functions exhibit constant returns to scale.

5 Production involves no externalities.

The first assumption is standard. The second assumption implies that the marginal rate of technical substitution MRTS is well defined, and the third that all firms will use a positive quantity of both inputs. We'll explain the role of the fourth assumption when we define the marginal rate of transformation. In Chapter 17, we'll see how production externalities, such as air and water pollution, which are ruled out by our fifth assumption, fit into the analysis.

Efficiency in General Equilibrium with Production

Before plunging into the analysis, a short discussion of how we will approach efficiency in this general equilibrium model is useful. Given the assumptions we have made, three conditions are *necessary* and *sufficient* to achieve efficiency in our model. One familiar condition concerns efficiency in consumption; a second, similar condition concerns efficiency in production; and the third condition concerns efficiency of product mix. When we say that these three conditions are *necessary* for efficiency in general equilibrium, we mean that if any of them is not satisfied, then the allocation of resources is not Pareto-optimal. When we say that these three conditions are *sufficient* for efficiency in general equilibrium, we mean that if all of them are satisfied, then the allocation of resources is Pareto-optimal. In discussing these conditions, we'll focus almost exclusively on showing that they are necessary conditions. Hence, our discussion is somewhat incomplete.

Efficiency in Consumption

Efficiency in consumption requires only that the allocation of the goods that are actually produced to the individual consumers in the economy be Pareto-optimal. Therefore, the condition for efficiency in consumption for an exchange economy is directly applicable to an economy with production.

C O N D I T I O N: Efficiency in Consumption

The allocation of the goods actually produced is Pareto-optimal if MRS is identical for all individuals.

Production Possibilities Frontier

From Section 2.2, you are familiar with the concept of a **production possibilities frontier.** In Figure 15.5, we've measured the quantity of good 1 on the horizontal axis and the quantity of good 2 on the vertical axis. Given the fixed supplies of the two primary inputs, any combination of goods on or below PP can be produced, and any combination above PP cannot be produced. For example, the combinations at points A, B, and C in Figure 15.5 could be produced, and the combination at point D could not.

An obvious efficiency requirement is that the combination of good 1 and good 2 actually produced must be on PP rather than below it. Point B, for example, is inconsistent with efficiency. By moving upward and to the right from point B, the output of each good increases. And by giving each person

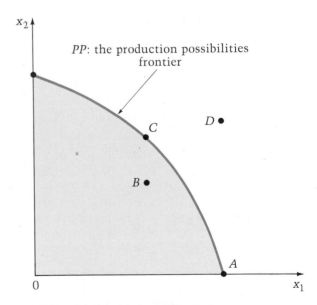

FIGURE 15.5   The production possibilities set.

The production possibilities set, represented by the green area, is the set of consumption goods that the economy could produce. The bundles at points A, B, and C can be produced, whereas the bundle at D cannot be. The boundary of the production possibilities set PP is the production possibilities frontier.

some share of that increased output, everyone can be made better off. Point B is therefore inconsistent with efficiency: if the economy was at point B, Pareto-improving moves would be possible. The second efficiency condition in general equilibrium, called **efficiency in production,** is that the combination of goods actually produced must be on the production possibilities frontier.

Efficiency in Production

An economy could become "stuck" at an inefficient point such as B in Figure 15.5 in two ways. If any inputs are unemployed, then the economy is inevitably inside PP. We'll ignore the possibility of unemployed inputs in what follows. There is, however, a more subtle way in which the economy could end up at a point such as B. To understand this more subtle source of inefficiency, we'll adapt the Edgeworth box analysis to a new purpose.

Suppose that MRTS is different for some pair of firms, given their current input bundles. (See Section 9.1 for the definition of MRTS.) Both firms might be producing the same good, or they might be producing different goods. We'll show that, because MRTS is not identical for the two firms, the output of both firms can be increased by reallocating inputs and therefore that the current allocation of inputs to firms is not efficient.

For concreteness, suppose that MRTS for the first firm exceeds MRTS for the second and that the first firm currently has 7 units of input 1 and 17 units of input 2, while the second firm currently has 18 units of input 1 and 3 units of input 2. Now let's put these firms in an Edgeworth box diagram, as illustrated in Figure 15.6. The dimensions of the box are determined by the total quantities of inputs 1 and 2 in the two input bundles—its horizontal sides are therefore 25 units long, and its vertical sides

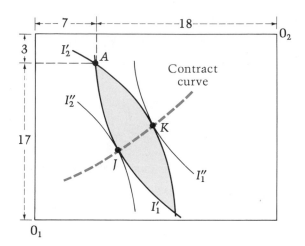

FIGURE 15.6   An Edgeworth box for production.

Here we consider the allocation of a fixed quantity of two inputs to two firms. The first firm's input bundle and isoquants are measured relative to 0_1, and the second firm's relative to 0_2. An allocation such as A, which is not on the contract curve, is inefficient. The green area is the set of allocations that allow both firms to produce more than they do at A. Allocations such as J and K, where MRTS is identical for the two firms, are on the contract curve. Efficiency in production demands that MRTS be identical for all firms.

are 20 units long. The first firm's isoquants, I_1' and I_1'', are plotted relative to 0_1; the second firm's, I_2' and I_2'', relative to 0_2. The current allocation of inputs to the two firms is A in Figure 15.6, where MRTS is larger for the first firm than for the second. The first firm is currently on isoquant I_1' and the second is on I_2'. Notice that any reallocation of inputs in the interior of the green area allows both firms to produce more. Hence, input allocation A is not efficient.

Let's see what these reallocations mean in terms of Figure 15.5. If one firm produces good 1 and the other good 2, then any reallocation from A to the interior of the green area in Figure 15.6 moves the economy pictured in Figure 15.5 in a northeasterly direction from a point such as B. If both firms in Figure 15.6 produce the same good—say, good 2—then the movement in Figure 15.5

is due north. If the initial allocation had been on the contract curve in Figure 15.6 — that is, if MRTS had been identical for the two firms — then increasing the output of one firm would have meant decreasing the output of the other firm. MRTS therefore must be identical for all firms if the allocation of inputs is to be efficient.

C O N D I T I O N: Efficiency in Production

Efficiency in general equilibrium requires that MRTS be identical for all firms.[8]

Keep in mind why this is a condition of efficiency. If the condition were not satisfied, we could increase the output of one good while maintaining output of the other, which would allow us to make some consumers better off while leaving all others no worse off.

P R O B L E M 15.5

Suppose that MRTS for all producers of good 1 exceeds MRTS for all producers of good 2. What sort of reallocation of inputs is necessary to achieve efficiency in production? Is it possible to achieve efficiency in production while holding the output of good 1 constant?

Notice that each of these efficiency conditions concerns one side of the economy in isolation from the other. The first proposition concerns consumption and the second concerns production. The third con-

dition for efficiency in general equilibrium concerns the interface between consumption and production and is called **efficiency of product mix**.

To see the nature of the product-mix problem, suppose that good 1 is food and good 2 shelter and that 99.9% of all inputs go to the production of one good — say, shelter. If MRS is identical for all consumers, the economy will be efficient in consumption. If all firms have the identical MRTS, the economy will be efficient in production. But because we humans cannot live by shelter alone, the right product mix has not been produced; that is, there is more to Pareto optimality in an entire economy than efficiency in production and efficiency in consumption. Before we can confront the product-mix problem head on, we need to understand a bit more about the production possibilities frontier.

The Marginal Rate of Transformation

The absolute value of the slope of the production possibilities frontier at any point is called the **marginal rate of transformation** at that point and is denoted by MRT.

$$MRT = |\text{slope of PP}|$$

MRT is the opportunity cost for the economy as a whole of a bit more of good 1 in terms of good 2. In Figure 15.7, for example, the absolute value of the slope of the tangent line TT is the rate at which production of good 2 must be decreased as production of good 1 is increased when the economy is at point C.

P R O B L E M 15.6

Approximately how much of good 2 must be given up to get an additional unit of good 1 if MRT is 2? If MRT is $\frac{1}{5}$? Approximately how much of good 1 must be given up to get an additional unit of good 2 if MRT is 3? If MRT is $\frac{1}{3}$?

---

[8] The calculus argument in footnote 3 is easily adapted to show that efficiency in production requires that MRTS be identical for all firms. Pick any two firms with production functions $F^1(z_1^1, z_2^1)$ and $F^2(z_1^2, z_2^2)$, and any bundle of the two inputs to be allocated to the two firms — say, the bundle (z_1', z_2'). If we fix the output of the first firm at, say, x^1, then efficiency in production clearly demands that we allocate the available bundle of inputs to the two firms so as to maximize $F^2(z_1^2, z_2^2)$, subject to the constraint that $x^1 = F^1(z_1^1, z_2^1)$. From this point, the argument exactly parallels that in footnote 3.

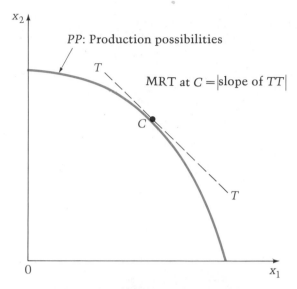

FIGURE 15.7 The marginal rate of transformation.

The marginal rate of transformation at a point on PP is the absolute value of the slope of PP at the point. MRT at point C, for example, is the absolute value of the slope of TT. MRT measures the opportunity cost of a bit more good 1 in terms of quantity of good 2 foregone.

We have assumed in this section that all firms experience constant returns to scale in production. This assumption guarantees that PP will not be convex to the origin. (We will, in fact, draw PP as concave to the origin, as illustrated in Figure 15.7.) Hence, in moving from left to right along PP in Figures 15.7 and 15.8, the opportunity cost of each additional unit of good 1 in terms of foregone good 2 is progressively larger; that is, MRT gets progressively larger. If there were significant increasing returns to scale in the production of good 1, MRT could decrease in moving from left to right along PP.

We can express MRT in terms of the marginal product of input 1 for a representative producer of good 1, MP_1^1, and the marginal product of input 1 for a representative producer of good 2, MP_1^2. (Keep in mind that because the economy is assumed to be on its PP, MRTS is identical for all firms.) To see

how this is accomplished, suppose that we wanted to produce a bit more good 1 — say, Δx_1. We can do it by transferring a bit of input 1 — say, Δz_1 — from the representative producer of good 2 to the representative producer of good 1. The necessary transfer of input 1, Δz_1, (approximately) satisfies

$$\Delta x_1 = \Delta z_1 MP_1^1$$

This implies that Δx_2, the decrease in production of good 2, is (approximately)

$$\Delta x_2 = \Delta z_1 MP_1^2$$

Dividing Δx_2 by Δx_1 gives us the absolute value of the slope of PP, or MRT:

$$MRT = \frac{MP_1^2}{MP_1^1}$$

You may be wondering why we couldn't achieve this increase in the production of good 1 by transferring input 2 instead of input 1 or by transferring a little of both input 2 and input 1. The answer is that we could. Suppose that we had transferred input 2 instead of input 1: by replicating the argument of the previous paragraph, we would conclude that

$$MRT = \frac{MP_2^2}{MP_2^1}$$

where MP_2^2 is the marginal product of input 2 for the producer of good 2 and MP_2^1 is the marginal product of input 2 for the producer of good 1.

If MRT is to be meaningful in either of these expressions, the expressions must be equivalent. Let's see that they are equivalent. Since we have efficiency in production, we know that MRTS is identical for producers of good 1 and good 2:

$$MRTS_1 = MRTS_2$$

From Section 9.1, we know that any firm's MRTS is equal to the ratio of the marginal product of input 1 to the marginal product of input 2 in that firm. By combining this information with the previous expression, we see that

$$\frac{MP_1^1}{MP_2^1} = \frac{MP_1^2}{MP_2^2}$$

or that

$$\frac{MP_2^2}{MP_2^1} = \frac{MP_1^2}{MP_1^1}$$

The two measures of MRT are therefore equivalent.[9]

Thus, the marginal rate of transformation can be expressed in terms of marginal products in two different but equivalent ways:

$$MRT = \frac{MP_1^2}{MP_1^1} = \frac{MP_2^2}{MP_2^1}$$

These results will be quite useful in subsequent sections.

PROBLEM 15.7

Suppose that MRTS $= \frac{1}{2}$ for all firms, that $MP_1^1 = 1$, and that $MP_2^2 = 2$. What is MRT?

Efficiency in Product Mix

We can now return to the problem of efficiency in product mix. Imagine that we have

---

[9] Suppose that we transfer a small amount of each input from the production of good 2 to the production of good 1. We want to show that this exercise yields an equivalent measure for MRT. To get Δx_1 additional units of good 1, we require

$$\Delta x_1 = \Delta z_1 MP_1^1 + \Delta z_2 MP_2^1$$

which means that the reduction in output of good 2 is

$$\Delta x_2 = \Delta z_1 MP_1^2 + \Delta z_2 MP_2^2$$

Dividing Δx_2 by Δx_1 and rearranging, we get

$$MRT = \frac{MP_1^2(\Delta z_1 + \Delta z_2 MP_2^2/MP_1^2)}{MP_1^1(\Delta z_1 + \Delta z_2 MP_2^1/MP_1^1)}$$

But, as we have just seen, when the economy is on its PP, MP_2^2/MP_1^2 is equal to MP_2^1/MP_1^1. Hence,

$$MRT = \frac{MP_1^2}{MP_1^1}$$

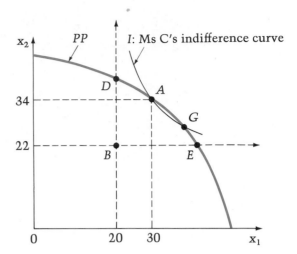

FIGURE 15.8   Efficiency in product mix.

Point A is the initial position in the economy, and Ms. C initially has 10 units of good 1 and 12 of good 2. Now let her choose a point on PP, constraining her to leave all other consumers in their original positions. To leave them in their original positions, she must make 20 units of good 1 and 22 units of good 2 available to them. Therefore, we can regard B as Ms. C's origin and segment DE of PP (relative to this origin) as the consumption choices open to her. She will choose some point other than A because her indifference curve through A intersects PP. The initial position is therefore not Pareto-optimal. Pareto optimality requires that her indifference curve be tangent to PP, or that her MRS be equal to the economy's MRT.

picked an arbitrary person, Ms. C, and devised a mechanism (1) that allows her to control the allocation of resources in the whole economy by choosing a point on PP, and (2) that constrains her to leave everyone else in his or her initial position. Imagine, too, that the economy Ms. C is about to take charge of is initially at some point on PP — say, at point A in Figure 15.8 — where 30 units of good 1 and 34 units of good 2 are being produced. Imagine too that Ms. C's current consumption bundle contains 10 units of good 1 and 12 of good 2. Taken together, the remaining individuals in this economy therefore have 20 units of good 1 $(30 - 10)$ and 22 units of good 2 $(34 - 12)$.

We'll show that if this economy is efficient, then Ms. C's MRS must be equal to the economy's MRT. To do so, we'll suppose that her MRS is not equal to, but instead exceeds, MRT, and then show that when she takes over, she can make herself better off without making anyone else worse off.

Now let's put Ms. C in charge of this economy and allow her to choose a point on *PP* that is in her own self-interest. She is, of course, constrained to keep all other consumers in their original positions. In Figure 15.8, we see how this constraint works. Point *A* represents the original position for the economy: 30 units of good 1 and 34 of good 2. If we subtract Ms. C's consumption bundle from point *A*, we get point *B* in Figure 15.8, 20 units of good 1 and 22 of good 2. This point represents the initial consumption of everyone else in the economy — recall that Ms. C is constrained to make this combination available to them. This implies that she cannot choose any point on *PP* to the left of point *D* or to the right of point *E*, but she can choose any point on segment *DE* of *PP*.

Analyzing Ms. C's problem of choosing a point on segment *DE* is now a simple matter. We can regard point *B* as an origin for her private consumption bundle. Segment *DE* of *PP*, relative to the origin at *B*, then represents the consumption choices open to her. To analyze her choice, we simply plot her indifference map relative to the origin at *B* in Figure 15.8. Remember that we assumed that her MRS exceeds MRT at point *A*. She is therefore initially on an indifference curve, such as *I* in Figure 15.8, that is steeper than *PP* at point *A*. She will obviously choose some point on *PP* that is to the right of *A* and to the left of *G*, a point where some indifference curve not drawn in the diagram is tangent to *PP*. When she does, she is better off, and every one else is just as well off. Therefore, if her MRS (or any consumer's MRS) is not equal to MRT, the allocation of resources to the production of good 1 and good 2 is inefficient.

CONDITION: Efficiency in Product Mix

Efficiency, or Pareto optimality, in general equilibrium requires that each consumer's MRS be identical to the economy's MRT.

Notice how we have approached each of these efficiency conditions. We have shown that when any of them is not satisfied, a Pareto-improving move is possible and the allocation is therefore inefficient. In other words, we have shown that each of these three conditions is *necessary* for an efficient allocation of resources. Although we will not show it, these three conditions are also *sufficient:* if they are satisfied, then the allocation is efficient. These three conditions thus tell us clearly what *efficiency* means in our general equilibrium model.

PROBLEM 15.8

Suppose that MRT exceeds each consumer's MRS. To achieve efficiency in product mix, must the economy be producing more or less of good 1?

15.5 Efficiency and Competitive General Equilibrium

What institutions and circumstances are and are not conducive to efficiency? We'll begin this inquiry by restating the first theorem of welfare economics and then showing that it is true in this general equilibrium model with production.

PROPOSITION: First Theorem of Welfare Economics

Given the assumptions we have made, the competitive equilibrium of this general equilibrium model with production is efficient.

The first theorem emphasizes the power of self-interest in directing the allocation of resources. In the perfectly competitive setting envisioned in the theorem, the pursuit of self-interest allows the collectivity of individuals to extract all the gains possible from their economic union. The theorem is, in essence, the embodiment of Smith's doctrine of the natural identity of interests, discussed at the beginning of this chapter.

We can be confident that the theorem is true if we can assure ourselves that an economy in competitive general equilibrium is efficient in production, in consumption, and in product mix. We will not consider how competitive equilibrium is attained in the model. Rather, we will suppose that we have competitive equilibrium prices for goods 1 and 2 and for inputs 1 and 2; that is, prices such that aggregate demand is equal to aggregate supply for both goods and both inputs. Then we'll use our understanding of consumer and producer behavior to show that the three conditions for efficiency are fulfilled.

Let p_1^e and p_2^e denote the competitive equilibrium prices for goods 1 and 2, and let w_1^e and w_2^e denote the competitive equilibrium prices for inputs 1 and 2. You can easily see that an economy in this competitive equilibrium is efficient in production and in consumption. From Section 9.3, we know that each firm chooses an input bundle at which its MRTS is equal to w_1^e/w_2^e. MRTS is therefore identical for all firms, and the economy is efficient in production. Similarly, from Section 4.5, we know that each consumer chooses a consumption bundle at which MRS is equal to p_1^e/p_2^e. MRS is therefore identical for all consumers, and the economy is efficient in consumption.[10]

Showing that an economy in competitive general equilibrium is also efficient in product mix is only slightly more compli-

cated. To do so, we need to use what we know from Section 14.6 about a profit-maximizing firm that is a perfect competitor in its input markets and in its output market. Figure 15.9 illustrates the position of two representative producers—one of good 1 and the other of good 2—in the market for input 1. The producer of good 1 uses 35 units of input 1 at the equilibrium price w_1^e, and the producer of good 2 uses 30 units. Both firms are in long-run equilibrium and therefore in short-run equilibrium as well. Accordingly,

$$w_1^e = p_1^e MP_1^1 = p_2^e MP_1^2$$

Rearranging, we have

$$\frac{p_1^e}{p_2^e} = \frac{MP_1^2}{MP_1^1}$$

As we showed in Section 15.4, the right side of this expression is just the economy's MRT. Because every consumer chooses a bundle at which his or her MRS is equal to the left side, p_1^e/p_2^e, we see that every consumer's MRS is equal to the economy's MRT; that is,

MRS = MRT for every consumer

Therefore, the economy produces an efficient product mix.

Although we will not consider it in great detail, the second theorem of welfare economics also holds in our model of general equilibrium with production. Recall that the second theorem concerns a two-stage procedure for attaining any Pareto-optimal allocation. In the exchange economy, the first stage of this procedure involves the redistribution of goods. In the current model with production, individuals are endowed not with goods but with inputs, which they sell in input markets to earn the incomes that they spend on goods. Therefore, in this model, the second theorem relies on the redistribution of the ownership of inputs—instead of the redistribution of goods—in effect, to redistribute purchas-

---

[10] Since there are only three independent relative prices in this model, we could eliminate one price by choosing a convenient normalization. We could, for example, set p_2 equal to 1.

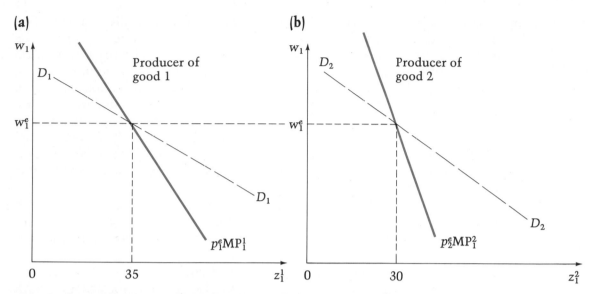

FIGURE 15.9   Efficiency in product mix for general competitive equilibrium.

In competitive equilibrium, we see that any producer of good 1 uses input 1 up to the point where $w_1^e = p_1^e MP_1^1$, and any producer of good 2 uses input 1 up to the point where $w_1^e = p_2^e MP_1^2$. Therefore, $p_1^e/p_2^e = MP_1^2/MP_1^1$. But the right side of the equality is, by definition, MRT. Every consumer chooses a consumption bundle such that $MRS = p_1^e/p_2^e$. Therefore, MRT = MRS for every consumer, and the economy exhibits efficiency in product mix in competitive equilibrium.

ing power. For example, a redistribution of labor (or land), as opposed to some consumption good, might be required to achieve the given Pareto optimum as a competitive equilibrium.

Suppose then that we have identified an efficient allocation of goods that we would like to achieve. In the background there is, of course, a corresponding allocation of inputs to firms, but we are interested here in the allocation of goods to individuals. The second theorem is concerned with a two-stage procedure to achieve this allocation. In the first stage, the ownership of inputs is reallocated among individuals. In the second stage, the theorem tells us to rely on competitive markets to achieve efficiency.

P R O P O S I T I O N: Second Theorem of Welfare Economics

With the assumptions we have made, given any Pareto-optimal allocation of goods POA that is attainable in the model, there is a distribution of ownership of inputs DOI such that POA is the competitive equilibrium allocation associated with DOI.

The beauty of the second theorem is the neat separation of distribution and efficiency that it envisages. In effect, the second theorem tells us: *to achieve equity, redistribute the ownership of inputs; to achieve efficiency, use competitive markets.*

A moment's reflection will reveal that the redistribution envisaged in the second theorem involves lump-sum taxes for some individuals and lump-sum subsidies for others. What is being redistributed in a lump-sum fashion is, of course, the ownership of inputs, not money. As we saw in a partial equilibrium context in Section 5.1, these lump-sum taxes and subsidies have some very attractive features. The second theorem reveals the source of their beauty

—lump-sum taxes and subsidies do not interfere with the allocative function that competitive markets do so well, whereas other forms of tax and subsidy do. (We'll see this difference clearly in our discussion of the redistribution of income in Chapter 16.)

As we also saw in Section 5.1, it's almost impossible to find a lump-sum tax or subsidy in the real world. It's clear, then, that the second theorem does not dominate the thinking of the people who design taxes. Why not? Some economists argue that such taxes and subsidies are a near impossibility. This seems to be true in regard to the labor of individuals, which, from the point of view of generating income, is the dominant input owned by most people. In a democratic society, it is extremely difficult to imagine significant lump-sum taxes on the labor of individuals. The real message of the second theorem, then, is that redistribution almost inevitably involves a potentially serious conflict between equity and efficiency.[11]

15.6 Sources of Inefficiency

What can go wrong? What produces an inefficient allocation of resources? Although there are many sources of inefficiency, we'll look at just two of the major ones in this section: monopoly and taxation.

The Inefficiency of Monopoly

We can begin with monopoly. Suppose that there is only one producer of good 1 and that all other markets are perfectly competitive. To see why resources are inefficiently allocated in general equilibrium, let p_1^e, p_2^e, w_1^e, and w_2^e again represent general equilibrium

[11] The first essay in Koopmans' (1957) book is an excellent exposition of the relationship between efficiency and competitive equilibrium.

prices. The equilibrium price of good 1—p_1^e—is, of course, a monopoly price. The first two efficiency conditions still hold: because all firms face the same input prices, each chooses an input bundle at which MRTS is equal to w_1^e/w_2^e. Similarly, because all consumers face the same product prices, each chooses a bundle at which MRS is equal to p_1^e/p_2^e. The economy is therefore efficient in production and in consumption in this general equilibrium.

The monopoly inefficiency arises from a distortion of product mix. This becomes apparent when considering the positions of the monopoly producer of good 1 and of any producer of good 2 in an input market. In the market for input 1, for example, both firms use the input up to the point at which marginal revenue product is equal to the price of the input:

$$w_1^e = \mathrm{MRP}_1^1 = \mathrm{MRP}_1^2$$

where MRP_1^1 and MRP_1^2 are the respective marginal revenue products of input 1 for the monopolist and the representative producer of good 2. But MRP_1^1 is equal to $\mathrm{MR}_1\mathrm{MP}_1^1$, where MR_1 is the monopolist's marginal revenue in its output market, and MRP_1^2 is equal to $p_2^e\mathrm{MP}_1^2$. Therefore,

$$w_1^e = \mathrm{MR}_1\mathrm{MP}_1^1 = p_2^e\mathrm{MP}_1^2$$

Furthermore, as we discovered in Section 11.6, MR_1 is less than p_1 because a monopolist is producing good 1; that is, a profit-maximizing monopolist always produces at a point where its marginal revenue is less than its price. Combining this knowledge with knowledge from the input market, we see that

$$\frac{p_1^e}{p_2^e} > \frac{\mathrm{MP}_1^2}{\mathrm{MP}_1^1}$$

However, the right side of this expression is MRT, and the left side is equal to each consumer's MRS. Each consumer's MRS therefore exceeds the economy's MRT:

MRS > MRT for all consumers

In the presence of monopoly, then, the product mix is wrong; accordingly, the allocation of resources is inefficient:

If we have only one producer of good 1 and if all other markets are perfectly competitive, resources will be inefficiently allocated in general equilibrium.

These inefficiencies arise not just in the case of a monopolist, but in any case in which there is market power — any case in which the firm's demand curve is downward sloping. In the following problem, you can see more clearly the distortions associated with market power.

PROBLEM 15.9

Taking the general equilibrium in the presence of a monopoly producer as an initial condition, construct a diagram in which you show (1) that Ms. C could make herself better off, and no one else worse off, if she could directly control the allocation of resources, and (2) that the monopolist produces too little.

PROBLEM 15.10

Show that if the monopolist engages in ordinary price discrimination, the economy is inefficient not just in product mix, but also in consumption.

Taxation and Efficiency

Taxes not only are painful but also are a source of inefficiency in the allocation of resources. Now that you have some facility in determining whether a particular general equilibrium is efficient, you can discover in Problem 15.10 some inefficiencies associated with taxes.

PROBLEM 15.11

Suppose that some government authority imposes a tax equal to t on the sale of each unit of good 2 but not on the sale of good 1. Assuming that all markets are competitive, show that competitive general equilibrium in the presence of this tax is inconsistent with efficiency. Hint: The product mix is not efficient. Is too little or too much of good 2 produced in equilibrium? Now suppose instead that a subsidy is imposed on the consumption of good 2 and repeat the exercise.

Summary

In this chapter, we have drawn together, in a more rigorous general equilibrium framework, much of what we have already learned about economic efficiency and about the conditions that interfere with it or promote it. In this general equilibrium context, the allocation of resources is *efficient* when no changes of any sort will make some person better off without making someone else worse off.

This correct but imprecise definition of economic efficiency is equivalent to the following precise statement: given the assumptions we made in this chapter, an economy is efficient if (1) MRTS is identical for all producers, (2) MRS is identical for all consumers, and (3) the common MRS is equal to the economy's MRT. These three conditions concern efficiency in production, consumption, and product mix, respectively.

We showed that when certain assumptions are satisfied, an economy in general competitive equilibrium satisfies these three conditions: it is efficient. This result, the first theorem of welfare economics, is the modern equivalent of Adam Smith's doctrine of the natural identity of interests. Loosely speaking, the institutions that permit individuals to realize all the gains possible from their economic union are the institutions of perfect competition.

We also considered the second theorem of welfare economics, which outlines a two-stage procedure for attaining any Pareto-optimal allocation that is possible in the economy. In the first stage, ownership is redistributed among individuals by a set of lump-sum taxes and transfers; in the second stage, efficiency is achieved by relying on perfectly competitive markets. Unfortunately, the lump-sum taxes and transfers envisaged in the first stage are impractical in most real situations.

We found that many things could upset the efficiency applecart. Market power of any sort — monopoly, oligopoly, monopsony — creates inefficiency in any market. As you saw in Problem 15.11, taxes and subsidies also tend to produce inefficiency. And, as we will see in Chapter 17, externalities in consumption and production also mean that competitive general equilibrium is not efficient.

From the perspective of efficiency, the economic world we inhabit is obviously imperfect. As we saw in Chapters 11 through 13, market power is unavoidable in many markets. In addition, externalities such as air and water pollution, which we ignored in this chapter, are an all-too-familiar part of the economic world we inhabit. Furthermore, governments are not about to eliminate their taxing and spending activities, and most of us would not want them to do so. Thus, some form of inefficiency seems to be inevitable.

This predictable inefficiency presents the economist, particularly the policy-making economist, with a real challenge. How do we measure inefficiency? How can we minimize inefficiency? One recent approach — called applied general equilibrium analysis — uses data to build general equilibrium models of the economy and extends the surplus measures familiar from earlier chapters to quantify inefficiency in a general equilibrium framework.[12] These models are one step toward meeting that challenge.

---

[12] See Shoven and Whalley (1987) for a survey of work in applied general equilibrium.

Exercises

1 If a monopolist produces good 1 while the markets for good 2 and both inputs are perfectly competitive, then general equilibrium is inefficient because MRS exceeds MRT for all consumers. Show that a tax on the production of good 2 or a subsidy on the production of good 1 can eliminate the inefficiency of monopoly.

2 Suppose that there are immobile producers of goods 1 and 2 in each of two regions and that both inputs are completely mobile. Suppose too that input 1 is taxed in one region but not in the other. What sort of distortion in the allocation of resources does this produce? Which of the efficiency conditions is violated?

3 Suppose that each firm has monopsony power with respect to input 1 and that no firm has monopoly power. What sort of distortions do these conditions produce? Which of the efficiency conditions is violated? What sort of taxes or subsidies would offset these distortions?

References

Arrow, K. J., and F. H. Hahn (1971), *General Competitive Analysis*, San Francisco: Holden-Day.

Koopmans, T. C. (1957), *Three Essays on the State of Economic Science*, New York: McGraw-Hill.

Shoven, J. B., and J. Whalley (1987), *Applying General Equilibrium*, Cambridge, England: Cambridge University Press.

Stigler, G. (ed.) (1957), *Selections from The Wealth of Nations*, New York: Appleton-Century-Crofts.

Walras, L. (1874, 1877), *Elements d'Economie Politique Pure*, English translation by William Jaffe (1954), *Elements of Pure Economics*, London: Allen and Unwin.

Appendix: Efficiency

In this appendix, we'll use differential calculus and the tools of constrained maximization to develop the conditions for economic efficiency for a very simple economy. We have two goods, goods 1 and 2, each produced by one firm, and two individuals, One and Two. We denote One's consumption bundle by (x_1^1, x_2^1) and Two's by (x_1^2, x_2^2). Notice that subscripts index goods and superscripts index individuals. The two utility functions are $U^1(x_1^1, x_2^1)$ and $U^2(x_1^2, x_2^2)$. We have two inputs, inputs 1 and 2, and a fixed supply of each, denoted by z_1' and z_2'. The input bundle used to produce good 1 is (z_1^1, z_2^1); the bundle used to produce good 2 is (z_1^2, z_2^2). In these input bundles, superscripts index goods; subscripts index inputs. The two production functions are $F^1(z_1^1, z_2^1)$ and $F^2(z_1^2, z_2^2)$.

First, let's simply write down the three conditions for efficiency:

1 Efficiency in consumption requires that

$$MRS^1(x_1^1, x_2^1) = MRS^2(x_1^2, x_2^2)$$

or that

$$\frac{U_1^1(x_1^1, x_2^1)}{U_2^1(x_1^1, x_2^1)} = \frac{U_1^2(x_1^2, x_2^2)}{U_2^2(x_1^2, x_2^2)}$$

2 Efficiency in production requires that

$$MRTS^1(z_1^1, z_2^1) = MRTS^2(z_1^2, z_2^2)$$

or that

$$\frac{F_1^1(z_1^1, z_2^1)}{F_2^1(z_1^1, z_2^1)} = \frac{F_1^2(z_1^2, z_2^2)}{F_2^2(z_1^2, z_2^2)}$$

3 Efficiency in product mix requires that

$$MRT(x_1, x_2) = MRS^1(x_1^1, x_2^1)$$
$$= MRS^2(x_1^2, x_2^2)$$

or that

$$\frac{F_1^2(z_1^2, z_2^2)}{F_1^1(z_1^1, z_2^1)} = MRS^1(x_1^1, x_2^1)$$
$$= MRS^2(x_1^2, x_2^2)$$

Alternatively, since the economy's marginal rate of transformation can be expressed in terms of the marginal products of input 1 or of input 2, efficiency in product mix requires that

$$\frac{F_2^2(z_1^2, z_2^2)}{F_2^1(z_1^1, z_2^1)} = MRS^1(x_1^1, x_2^1)$$
$$= MRS^2(x_1^2, x_2^2)$$

Our task is to show that these three conditions are indeed implied by Pareto optimality. Let's fix the utility level of individual One at, say, u^1. Pareto optimality then demands that we allocate the fixed supplies of the two inputs to the production of the two goods and allocate the resulting quantities of the two goods to the two individuals, so that we maximize Two's utility subject to the constraint that One's utility is equal to u^1. That is, Pareto optimality, or economic efficiency, defines a somewhat complex constrained-maximization problem. We'll see that the solution to this problem implies the three efficiency conditions we set down earlier.

The constrained-maximization problem is this: choose two consumption bundles—(x_1^1, x_2^1) and (x_1^2, x_2^2)—and two input bundles—(z_1^1, z_2^1) and (z_1^2, z_2^2)—to maximize $U^2(x_1^2, x_2^2)$ subject to the following constraints:

$$u^1 = U^1(x_1^1, x_2^1) \tag{1}$$

$$z_1^1 + z_1^2 = z_1' \tag{2}$$

$$z_2^1 + z_2^2 = z_2' \tag{3}$$

$$x_1^1 + x_1^2 = F^1(z_1^1, z_2^1) \tag{4}$$

$$x_2^1 + x_2^2 = F^2(z_1^2, z_2^2) \tag{5}$$

The first constraint is that the bundle allocated to One yields u^1 utility. The second and third constraints are the economy's resource constraints. The fourth and fifth constraints reflect the fact that the two individuals can consume only what the economy produces.

We can simplify the problem by combining constraints to eliminate some of the endogenous variables. First, in equation (5), use equation (2) to eliminate z_1^2 and equation (3) to eliminate z_2^2:

$$x_2^1 + x_2^2 = F^2(z_1' - z_1^1, z_2' - z_2^1) \quad (6)$$

Then write equations (4) and (6) as

$$x_1^1 = F^1(z_1^1, z_2^1) - x_1^2 \quad (7)$$

$$x_2^1 = F^2(z_1' - z_1^1, z_2' - z_2^1) - x_2^2 \quad (8)$$

Now, in equation (1), use equation (7) to eliminate x_1^1 and equation (8) to eliminate x_2^1:

$$u^1 = U^1[F^1(z_1^1, z_2^1) - x_1^2, \\ F^2(z_1' - z_1^1, z_2' - z_2^1) - x_2^2] \quad (9)$$

We are left with just one constraint, equation (9), and only four endogenous variables: Two's consumption bundle, (x_1^2, x_2^2), and the input bundle to be devoted to X_1, (z_1^1, z_2^1).

We've reduced the original problem to this: choose (x_1^2, x_2^2) and (z_1^1, z_2^1) to maximize $U^2(x_1^2, x_2^2)$ subject to one constraint, equation (9). The Lagrangian is

$$L(x_1^2, x_2^2, z_1^1, z_2^1, \lambda) = U^2(x_1^2, x_2^2) \\ + \lambda\{U^1[F^1(z_1^1, z_2^1) - x_1^2, \\ F^2(z_1' - z_1^1, z_2' - z_2^1) - x_2^2] - u^1\}$$

Setting each of the partial derivatives of the Lagrangian equal to zero yields the following characterization of the solution, in which we have suppressed the endogenous variables.

$$U_1^2 - \lambda U_1^1 = 0 \quad (10)$$

$$U_2^2 - \lambda U_2^1 = 0 \quad (11)$$

$$\lambda(U_1^1 F_1^1 - U_2^1 F_1^2) = 0 \quad (12)$$

$$\lambda(U_1^1 F_2^1 - U_2^1 F_2^2) = 0 \quad (13)$$

$$U^1 - u^1 = 0 \quad (14)$$

Conditions (10) and (11) imply that

$$\frac{U_1^1}{U_2^1} = \frac{U_1^2}{U_2^2} \quad (15)$$

which is the condition for *efficiency in consumption*. Conditions (12) and (13) imply that

$$\frac{F_1^1}{F_2^1} = \frac{F_1^2}{F_2^2} \quad (16)$$

$$\frac{U_1^1}{U_2^1} = \frac{F_2^2}{F_1^1} \quad (17)$$

$$\frac{U_1^1}{U_2^1} = \frac{F_2^2}{F_2^1} \quad (18)$$

Condition (16) is the condition for *efficiency in production*. Condition (17) or (18), in combination with condition (15), yields the condition for *efficiency in product mix*.

*16

THE DISTRIBUTION OF INCOME

Chapter 15 explored how well markets performed their allocational function of directing resources to competing uses. In this chapter, we'll consider how well they perform another, equally important function: the distribution of a society's product among its members. By distribution we mean—very loosely—just what share of the national product each person receives. As we turn now to the distributional function of markets, we will be focusing our attention on input markets in a partial equilibrium setting because, in a very real sense, input markets determine the size of everyone's slice of the economic pie. The size of our incomes — our respective claims to the national product — depends primarily on prevailing input prices, including various wage rates. For example, relative shares of the economic pie in a dental office will vary: a dentist may be earning $80 per hour, a dental technician $18 per hour, and a dental receptionist $12 per hour. Even for those who sell resources other than labor, income still depends on the prevailing input prices. One acquaintance who inherited his grandparents' farm in what is now downtown Houston enjoys a relatively large claim to society's product because his land is now

prime real estate. Another who inherited his grandparents' once elegant estate in the decaying core of Chicago has a comparably smaller claim.

One obvious feature of the price system is that some folks get more of the economic pie and others considerably less. A quick tour of any North American city reveals inhabitants ranging from the "filthy rich" to the "dirt poor." We can trace these conspicuous inequalities in personal claims to the national product directly to differences in input prices and input endowments. But are these inequalities in the distribution of wealth and income just? Let us now turn to the issue of distributive justice.

16.1 Distributive Justice

Economist Kenneth Arrow (1976) has noted that what Aristotle called "distributive justice" was not seen as an issue in earlier, more static societies. These societies viewed the prevailing distribution of material goods as unquestionably right, either because they reflected the long-familiar status quo or because their religious systems sanctioned earthly rewards as the workings of a divine justice. As members of a more dynamic society, however, we cannot unthinkingly assert, "What is, is just." We recognize that the distribution of wealth and income is at least in part the handiwork of human beings.

The social and economic institutions we create significantly affect who is rich and who is poor. Just a few of the many institutions affecting distribution in any modern economy are income taxes, inheritance taxes, gift taxes, welfare, social security, collective bargaining, public housing, zoning, public education, minimum wages, rent controls, and agricultural price supports.

Unfortunately, economists have no yardstick comparable to the Pareto criterion to judge whether the market system performs this distributional function well. Indeed, determining what "justice" means is a philosophical rather than an economic issue; even among philosophers, there is no consensus. Broadly speaking, two opposing approaches to this ethical issue have emerged: the productivity principle and the redistributionist principle.

The Productivity Principle

In a nutshell, the **productivity principle** asserts that each of us ought to receive the monetary equivalent of the product created from our human resources, or labor, and from our nonhuman resources, or property. If we set aside the monetary reward to nonhuman resources, the appeal of the principle becomes straightforward: we should reap what we have sown. The harder we work, the more we'll produce and the larger our market reward ought to be.

Although, as economists, we can't agree or disagree with this view, we can clarify the core concept of the productivity principle: the meaning of productivity itself. If it is to serve as a distributional principle, any definition of productivity must fulfill the **product-exhaustion criterion**. If the owners of all

resources receive what their resources produce, then the individual shares of the total product pie must add up to precisely 1. If the sum were less than 1, there would be leftover product that no one had produced; if the sum were greater than 1, there would be too little product to go around.

Surprisingly, a meaning that satisfies the product-exhaustion criterion in any general and interesting set of circumstances is not easy to find. However, we can find one set of circumstances (the case in which all production functions exhibit constant returns to scale) and one definition of productivity (the value of the marginal product) that satisfy the criterion. In other words, if all production functions exhibit constant returns to scale, then paying the owners of each input the value of the input's marginal product will exactly use up what we'll call **the value of the total product**: the sum of all (output) prices multiplied by the quantities produced.

Furthermore, there is a set of institutions (the institutions of perfect competition) that guarantees that the owners of each input do, in fact, receive the value of the input's marginal product in these circumstances. Why? From Section 14.6, we already know that when every input and output market in an economy is perfectly competitive, the owners of each input are paid the value of the input's marginal product.

Product Exhaustion

Let's see why this pattern of input payments just exhausts the value of the total product. We'll look at a firm in long-run competitive equilibrium that uses just two inputs and is producing, say, y^* units of output. If the firm's input bundle is (z_1^*, z_2^*) and if p and (w_1, w_2) are the competitive equilibrium output and input prices, respectively, we want to show that

$$py^* = w_1 z_1^* + w_2 z_2^*$$

The left side is the value of the firm's output, and the right is the sum of the firm's input payments. If, at the level of the firm, the product is just used up, the two sides must be identical. We can rewrite the product-exhaustion requirement as

$$p = \frac{(w_1 z_1^* + w_2 z_2^*)}{y^*} = \text{LAC}(y^*)$$

The second equality follows from the definition of long-run average cost as total cost divided by output. We know from Section 10.6 that price is equal to minimum long-run average cost for any firm in long-run competitive equilibrium. The product-exhaustion criterion is therefore satisfied in a competitive equilibrium.

But just where did the condition of constant returns to scale enter this argument? In long-run competitive equilibrium, each firm is at the bottom of its U-shaped long-run average cost function, operating at the efficient scale of production. As we discovered in Section 9.6, at this level of output the firm experiences constant returns to scale. Therefore, constant returns to scale made an appearance when we observed that p is equal to LAC(y^*) for a firm in long-run competitive equilibrium.

Let's view this result from a slightly different perspective. We have found a definition of productivity that can serve as a principle of distribution because this definition satisfies the product-exhaustion criterion. This definition then raises an important normative question: Is payment in accordance with the value of the marginal product an ethically appealing principle of distributive justice? As economists, we can't answer this question, but we will suggest two thought experiments that are useful in trying to answer it. In both experiments, we'll suppose that the economy produces just one good and then examine how output of that good responds to a change in the *endowment* of an input—that is, in the total amount of an input available in an economy.

Thought Experiments for the Productivity Principle

Imagine an economy in a competitive equilibrium and consider what happens to the total output of the economy if some person —let's call her Rose—simply vanishes, taking her resource endowment, which includes her labor and any other resources she owns, out of the economy. Total output will decrease (approximately) by the amount of Rose's income, since she must have been receiving as income the marginal contribution to the total product of her labor and her other resources. This result follows from the fact that each unit of each input is paid its marginal product in competitive equilibrium. Notice that this exercise, in which there is a *marginal change in the economy's input endowment*, appears to be consistent with the spirit of the productivity principle: Rose appears to have received just what she produced.

Now let's try a second experiment in which there is a *nonmarginal change in the economy's input endowment*. For simplicity, we'll assume that the economy has only two resources (or inputs) and produces only one product. We'll use a specific production function that, we'll assume, describes the entire economy's technology,

$$y = 240(z_1 z_2)^{1/2}$$

Do note, however, that the general nature of the results do not depend on any particular production function.

The marginal product functions associated with this production function are[1]

$$\text{MP}_1 = 120 \left(\frac{z_2}{z_1}\right)^{1/2}$$

$$\text{MP}_2 = 120 \left(\frac{z_1}{z_2}\right)^{1/2}$$

---

[1] We can use calculus to find these marginal product functions. To get MP_1, partially differentiate $240(z_1 z_2)^{1/2}$ with respect to z_1. To get MP_2, partially differentiate with respect to z_2.

Suppose that initially this economy's resource endowment consists of 64 units of input 1 and 36 units of input 2. The economy's total output is then 11,520 units, and the competitive equilibrium input prices are $w_1 = 90$ and $w_2 = 160$. (Since this economy produces only one product, the unit for input prices is the unit in which output is measured.) Now suppose that the quantity of input 2 increases from 36 to 100, while the quantity of input 1 remains at 64. The total output will then rise from 11,520 to 19,200, for an increase of 7680 units. Notice, too, what will happen to input prices: w_1 will increase from 90 to 150, and w_2 will fall from 160 to 96.

What accounted for — or produced — the 7680-unit increase in output? Because only the quantity of input 2 changed, it seems sensible to attribute the increased output to the 74 additional units of input 2. Notice, however, that these 74 units are paid only 7104 (74 times 96) units — not the 7680 units they apparently produced. Thus, in this thought experiment, where the change in an economy's resource endowment is a nonmarginal change, marginal product does not seem to be a sensible measure of productivity, because when the added inputs are paid their marginal product, they do not capture all of the added output.

Notice, too, how dramatic is the change in input prices once the endowment of input 2 increases. The price paid per unit of input 2 drops sharply, while the price paid per unit of input 1 soars. If we want to argue that marginal productivity actually captures the spirit of the productivity principle — that one should reap what one has sown — we must be prepared to accept that the productivity of each of the original 36 units of input 2 decreased from 160 to 96 and that the productivity of each of the original 64 units of input 1 increased from 90 to 150, solely as a result of the increase in the endowment of input 2.

Input Prices and Scarcity

The changes in input prices that arose in the second thought experiment reflect a fundamental reality of the market system: *markets reward scarcity.* As input 1 became scarcer relative to input 2, the price paid per unit went up. This reward to scarcity serves an allocational function by directing resources to the uses in which their marginal productivities are greatest. Think of tennis great Steffi Graf. At least two of her personal characteristics are noteworthy: (1) she is endowed with abundant athletic talent, and (2) she is very wealthy. Most economists would consider her wealth to be a reward for having a scarce natural talent. They are implying not that she is rewarded without working hard at her game, but rather that no matter how hard the vast majority of us worked, we could not put together a tennis game comparable to hers.

The size of any individual's claim on the national product therefore depends on *how scarce his or her salable talents and resources are relative to the whole society's endowment of resources.* If all of us were as talented at tennis as Graf, none of us — including Steffi Graf — would receive a large market reward for it. This insight parallels our earlier lesson from the ticket model in Chapter 10: the initial distribution of resources is crucial in determining the size of personal rewards in a market economy. The larger our initial share of scarce personal or property endowments, the larger will be our slice of the economic pie.

The Redistributionist Principle

The **redistributionist principle** is at odds with the productivity principle. Redistributionists, who find significant economic inequalities ethically unacceptable, argue that wealth and income in the real world should be redistributed from the rich to the poor. The most extreme version of this position is philosopher John Rawls's *difference principle.* Taking equality as a point of reference, Rawls (1971) argues that the only acceptable inequality is one that improves the lot of the worst-off member of society. If we compare all possible distributions of wealth and pinpoint the worst-off member of a society in each distribution, the difference principle asserts that the preferred distribution is the one in which the wealth of the poorest member is largest.

But how do redistributionists conclude that distributive justice demands less inequality? They begin by observing the difficulties in thinking objectively about distribution. For example, they note that taking from the rich and giving to the poor is not nearly as popular among wealthy people as it is among impoverished people. In the attempt to achieve an ethical standard free of personal bias, redistributionists posit a hypothetical circumstance called the *original position.* Arrow (1976), a contemporary proponent of the redistributionist view, has summarized the philosophical arguments for reducing inequality:

The basic presupposition is that any moral judgment must be impersonal. The individual making the judgment cannot take his own situation into account. To the extent that he does, the judgment is one of his own interests and cannot be accounted a moral judgment. A principle of justice or morality is, by its nature, universalizable: an individual cannot defend an allocation of goods to himself unless others benefit similarly from this policy.

The argument has been given modern form in the notion of the "original position" as developed by the economists William Vickery and John Harsanyi and the philosopher John Rawls. To make concrete the concept of an impersonal judgment, they introduce the fiction of an "original position," in which each individual knows all the possible conditions

he or she can be in the society but does not know which particular condition he himself will have. The term "condition" refers to both inherent personal endowment, the individual's capacities and values, and to the social rewards to be received. In the original position, we may imagine the members of the society considering alternative social arrangements for resource allocation. Because of the symmetry of their positions, all would agree in their preferences; hence, they would arrive at a mutually beneficial contract.

The contract would be in effect an arrangement for mutual insurance and have the same advantages. If a group of individuals have the same uncertain prospects, they will each prefer a situation in which beforehand they agree to share their fortunes; those who gain relatively will give up some of their winnings to those who lose relatively. This argument, to be sure, presupposes that individuals may be presumed averse to the bearing of risks; but this is surely a safe assumption.

Thus, the "original position" argument shows that the impersonality which characterizes moral judgment implies that the content of that judgment is an equalization of outcomes. There is considerable room for differences in the precise interpretation of equality. . . . But I would judge that the similarities are much more important than the differences; all tend to lead to the moral obligation to redistribute income and other goods more equally. (pp. 14–15)

The main tenet of the redistributionist principle, then, is that the "insurance contract" resulting from the original-position experiment leads to a more equal distribution of income as a moral principle. Try the following problem to check your understanding of this approach to distributive justice.

PROBLEM 16.1

Put yourself into the following original position. Suppose that tomorrow you will be one of two people, A or B, in a very simple two-person economy that has a fixed endowment of one good, manna. You must choose today how the manna is to be apportioned out between A and B tomorrow, but all you know is this: it is equally probable that you will be A or B. A number R greater than 0 but less than 1 is A's share of manna, and $1 - R$ is B's share. What value of R would you choose?

If you have read the material on expected utility in Chapter 6, try the following problem, designed to reinforce your understanding of Arrow's remarks about risk, insurance, and distribution.

PROBLEM 16.2

Show that a risk-averse person in the original position described in the previous problem, believing that he or she will be either A or B with equal probability, will choose R equal to $\frac{1}{2}$. Notice that if both A and B are risk-averse, they will both choose R equal to $\frac{1}{2}$. In the original position, then, this society of two would unanimously agree on a 50/50 split.

We should underline the fact that this sort of mental experiment does not inevitably lead to the conclusion that equality is necessary for distributive justice. To see why not, let's consider another two-person economy. In the first period, A is alive; in the second period, B is alive. In each period, the endowment of manna is 2 units. In period 1, A can either eat both units of manna or eat one and plant the other. If A eats both, B will have just 2 units of manna in period 2. If A eats just 1 unit, however, the planted manna will triple, so that B will have a total of 5 units in period 2. If you don't know whether you will be A or B, which scheme would you choose in the original position: A gets 1 unit and B gets 5, or A gets 2 units and B gets 2? If you're not too risk-averse, you'll

choose the first; if you are very risk-averse, you'll choose the second. From this, we see that Rawls's difference principle is based on the assumption that people are completely risk-averse.

As we've said, economists have no special expertise on the ethics of distribution and cannot comment on the validity of the redistributionist stance. Nevertheless, if the redistributionist position is accepted as a normative objective, economists can say a great deal about the implication of particular schemes for achieving redistribution.

In the following sections, we'll analyze a range of possible redistributive institutions. As you'll see, many of these schemes inevitably result in a conflict between the demands of redistribution (or equity) and of efficiency. The challenge, therefore, is to design economic institutions that achieve the desired redistribution while minimizing the adverse consequences in terms of efficiency.

16.2 Minimum-Wage Legislation

One of the ubiquitous features of Western economies is minimum-wage legislation designed to provide a "living wage" to workers whose wage rate would otherwise be below a legally designated minimum. In the United States, for instance, the Fair Labor Standards Act of 1938 imposed a minimum wage of $0.25 per hour in specified industries. Periodic updates of the act since 1938 have increased the minimum wage and expanded the number of industries it governs. The objective of the U.S. law — and of similar schemes elsewhere — is clearly to redistribute income to less well-paid members of society.

Yet a recent *Time* magazine article entitled "The Incredible Shrinking Paycheck" posed this question: "Would raising the minimum wage help or hurt the working poor?'' (August 1, 1988, p. 36) In other words, is the objective of redistribution invariably realized under minimum-wage schemes? Do workers in the designated industries actually fare better once a minimum wage is imposed? And whose income drops to compensate for the rise in minimum-wage earners' incomes? Is inefficiency invariably an unfortunate side effect of minimum-wage laws? As you'll see, the answers depend on whether labor markets are perfectly competitive or monopsonistic. In a perfectly competitive labor market, an effective minimum wage creates unemployment or underemployment; redistributes income to workers from those who buy the goods produced in minimum-wage-designated industries; and invariably creates inefficiency. By contrast, in monopsonistic labor markets, a minimum wage is likely to increase employment, redistribute money from monopsonistic firms to their employees, and offset some of the inefficiency associated with monopsony.

To analyze the implications of a minimum wage in these two market settings — perfectly competitive and monopsonistic — we'll think of the labor-supply function as an aggregation of the various reservation wages of workers from lowest to highest. We can then interpret each worker's reservation wage as the value of his or her labor in the best alternative use: work in some other market, work at home, or leisure. For convenience, we'll assume that the first of these is the best alternative. Although this supply function is actually a series of vertical segments ascending from left to right, we'll approximate it by a smooth curve, such as the supply function in Figure 16.1. We'll also assume that all other labor markets and all output markets are perfectly competitive. Given this assumption, for any labor market in equilibrium, the wage rate will be equal to the value of the marginal product.

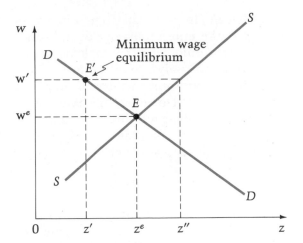

FIGURE 16.1 Minimum-wage legislation in a competitive labor market.

The competitive equilibrium is at point E. Given the minimum wage w', the equilibrium shifts to E'. The wage rises from w^e to w', employment falls from z^e to z', and we have excess supply because z'' individuals want to work at w' but only z' jobs are available.

Competitive Labor Markets

Figure 16.1 presents the basic implications of minimum-wage legislation in a competitive labor market. A minimum wage will alter the prelegislation equilibrium at point E in Figure 16.1 only if it is higher than the competitive equilibrium wage w^e. Accordingly, the minimum wage w' in Figure 16.2 exceeds w^e, and the postlegislation equilibrium shifts to point E', where just z' workers are employed.

We can see from Figure 16.1 that one result of the legislation is inefficiency, because at E' the value of the marginal product of an additional employee — equal to the minimum wage — is higher than the reservation wage at quantity z' on the supply function. In other words, some labor that could have been put to its most productive use in this industry will not be hired.

We can also see that labor is in excess supply at the minimum wage equilibrium: z'' workers would like to be employed at this wage rate, but only z' will be hired. It is tempting to interpret this excess supply as unemployment. However, the unemployment created by the minimum wage will almost certainly be less than $z'' - z'$. We can decompose the excess supply as follows:

$$z'' - z' = (z'' - z^e) + (z^e - z')$$

The first term on the right is the added supply of labor (over and above z^e) that would be forthcoming at wage w' if employment were freely available at this wage. Yet it is unlikely that this component of excess supply in the figure will actually materialize as unemployment. We know that the workers in this group prefer their best alternative option to employment in this market at the competitive equilibrium wage rate, because their reservation wages exceed w^e. Because job openings are few and far between, these workers are not likely to give up their alternative options to look for jobs in this market once the minimum wage is imposed. In all likelihood, they will stay put rather than risk unemployment.

The second term in the decomposition, $z^e - z'$, is the number of workers initially employed at the competitive equilibrium who are laid off once the minimum-wage law is imposed. Even these individuals may or may not show up among the unemployed. If they have no other options, they may continue to search for employment at the higher wage w'. In this case, they will be unemployed. On the other hand, they may seek less attractive employment elsewhere. In this case, they will instead be **underemployed,** in the sense that they accept jobs in which the value of their marginal product is less than w^e. This is just another indication that the minimum-wage equilibrium is inefficient: labor services are not allocated to their most productive uses.

In a competitive market, then, inefficiency is a necessary by-product of an effective minimum-wage law. As labor services are no longer put to their most productive uses, either unemployment or underemployment will signal that inefficiency. From the perspective of efficiency, then, minimum-wage legislation in competitive markets is unsatisfactory.

Nor is the legislation entirely satisfactory from a redistributional perspective. Even though the workers who manage to keep their jobs are better off, laid-off workers are clearly worse off. Moreover, the goods produced by firms employing minimum-wage labor will cost more. In effect, this means that income is redistributed from the buyers of those goods to the minimum-wage workers. Are these buyers the ones who ought to bear the burden of redistribution? Without more information, we can't answer the question.

PROBLEM 16.3

Some people argue that minimum-wage legislation encourages discrimination in hiring. Can you make a supporting argument? Hint: Contrast the employer's costs of discriminating when minimum-wage legislation is and is not in effect.

Monopsonistic Labor Markets

The implications of minimum-wage legislation are very different in monopsonistic markets. Why? Notice that such legislation alters the monopsonist's marginal factor cost function. The monopsonist's prelegislation marginal factor cost function is the line DBC in Figure 16.2. Its postlegislation marginal factor cost function, however, is composed of the two line segments $w'A$ and BC. If it hires an amount of labor less than or equal to z', its marginal factor cost is the minimum wage w'. If it hires beyond that point, its marginal factor cost is segment BC of its original marginal factor cost function because it can hire additional workers only

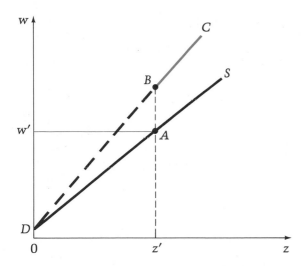

FIGURE 16.2 Minimum wage and a monopsonist's marginal factor cost.

DAS is the supply function and *DBC* is the ordinary marginal factor cost function. Given the minimum wage w', the monopsonist's marginal factor cost function is composed of two segments $w'A$ and BC.

at a wage higher than w'. In Problem 16.4, you can discover the most intriguing implications of a minimum-wage scheme in a monopsonistic labor market.

PROBLEM 16.4

Figure 16.3 illustrates the standard monopsony solution: the monopsonist employs z^* units of labor at a wage rate of w^*. First, show that if the minimum wage is higher than w^* but less than w''' in Figure 16.3, the monopsonist will increase employment. In other words, show that a minimum wage can actually reduce the inefficiency associated with monopsony by inducing the monopsonist to hire more labor. Second, identify the minimum-wage rate in Figure 16.3 that completely eliminates monopsonistic inefficiency. Finally, show that any minimum wage higher than w''' prompts the monopsonist to employ fewer than z^* units of labor. In other words, if the minimum wage is too high, it can increase inefficiency, an increase signaled by reduced employment in the industry.

As you discovered in Problem 16.4, minimum-wage legislation can promote both redistribution and efficiency in a monopsonistic labor market. In fact, if the minimum wage is set astutely, monopsonistic inefficiency can be totally eliminated.

Let's look more closely at the redistributional aspects of the problem in a monopsonistic labor market. Does a minimum wage actually increase workers' incomes? The answer is a carefully qualified yes. As long as the minimum wage is not higher than w''' in Figure 16.3, some workers in the industry will be better off and none worse off. Why? At any minimum wage at or below w^*, the status quo prevails — and legislation is an empty gesture. At rates above w^* but below w''', workers employed before the legislation will be paid more, and new workers will be hired at the new (minimum) wage rate. If the rate is w''', no new workers will be hired, but existing workers will be paid more. In any of these cases, the workers' increase in income is accomplished largely at the expense of the monop-

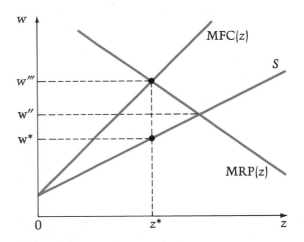

FIGURE 16.3 Minimum wage and monopsony.

In the absence of a minimum wage, the monopsonist hires z^* at wage w^*. Any minimum wage larger than w^* and smaller than w''' causes the monopsonist to hire more than z^*.

sonist. Is the monopsonist the one who ought to bear the burden of this redistribution? Again, the answer is not obvious.

The attractiveness of minimum-wage legislation thus depends on whether labor markets are competitive or monopsonistic. Empirical evidence suggests that labor markets covered by minimum-wage legislation are essentially competitive. This suggests that such legislation is problematical. Workers who remain employed are better off. It is not clear at whose expense this gain is made, however, because we don't know who is footing the bill. Furthermore, by creating unemployment or underemployment, the legislation will hurt some of the people it was intended to help.

Union Wage Rates: Some Analogous Issues

Many people hold strong opinions about unions: they either hate them or love them. Although analyzing the economic consequences of unionization objectively is not easy, we can make a move in that direction by adapting our minimum-wage analysis to apply to union wage rates. In Problem 16.5, you need only reinterpret the symbol w' used above to indicate the minimum wage rate as a union wage rate, because a union wage rate — like a minimum wage — is simply a **wage floor.**

PROBLEM 16.5

What are the redistributional and efficiency implications of a labor union with the power to negotiate a wage rate in a competitive labor market? In a monopsonistic labor market?

PROBLEM 16.6

A hiring hall is common in unionized construction trades and elsewhere. Traditionally, the union member who has been unemployed the longest gets the first available job. The hiring hall thus serves to distribute employment (and unemployment) among union members. If such a union has a fixed membership and (for convenience) a completely wage-inelastic, or vertical, supply function, what is the wage rate that the union would prefer? Hint: Consider the elasticity of demand and also consider the probability of being unemployed.

PROBLEM 16.7

Under seniority rules, if a unionized job is eliminated, the union member most recently hired is laid off. Will a union that has a seniority rule demand a higher wage than one that does not? Assume that in the absence of a seniority rule, each member has the same probability of being laid off if the union-negotiated wage dictates a decrease in employment. Hint: How does the private interest of a member change as his or her seniority changes?

16.3 Wage Floors in a Two-Sector Model

We can explore more deeply the implications of a wage floor, such as a union wage or a minimum wage, by concentrating on a labor market divided into two sectors — say, a union (or minimum-wage-regulated) sector and a nonunion (or non-minimum-wage-regulated) sector. The market might be the construction industry, for instance, in which some workers are unionized and others are not. To keep our model manageable, we'll assume that a total of 100 workers are seeking employment in the two sectors and that, in the absence of a wage floor, workers are perfectly mobile between the two sectors.

First, we'll identify the competitive equilibrium wage and the allocation of the fixed supply of labor to the two sectors as a point of reference. Notice in Figure 16.4 that all four quadrants share an origin at 0 and that the arrows at the ends of the axes indicate the direction in which any variable is increasing. The labor demand functions for sectors 1 and 2 are presented in quadrants I and II. (Notice that in quadrant II, z_2

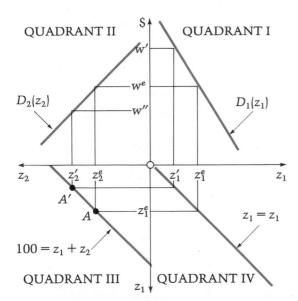

FIGURE 16.4 A wage floor in the two-sector model of the labor market.

A total of 100 individuals seek employment in sectors 1 and 2. Any point on the line $100 = z_1 + z_2$ in quadrant III is an allocation of these individuals to the two sectors. In competitive equilibrium, the wage rate in the two sectors will be identical. Thus, the allocation at A in quadrant III, producing wage w^e in both sectors, is the competitive equilibrium allocation. A minimum wage of w' in sector 1 forces $z_1^e - z_1'$ individuals out of that sector and into sector 2, depressing the wage rate in sector 2 to w''.

increases from right to left along the z_2 axis.) The line in quadrant III labeled $100 = z_1 + z_2$ tells us all the possible allocations of the 100 workers to the two sectors. For example, at point A on this line, z_1^e is allocated to sector 1 and z_2^e to sector 2. The line $z_1 = z_1$ in quadrant IV allows us to project values of z_1 from quadrant III into quadrant I, and vice versa.

To identify the competitive equilibrium, we must find the allocation where the wage rates are identical in both sectors, because if they were unequal, all workers would offer their labor in the higher wage market. The allocation that does the trick is at A in quadrant III. You should check to see

that all the allocations to the right (left) of A imply that the wage in sector 1 will be less than (greater than) the wage in sector 2.

The Underemployment Equilibrium

Now suppose that a wage floor w' is imposed in sector 1. If we ignore the possibility of unemployment for the moment and concentrate on underemployment, we can easily identify the resulting equilibrium: at wage w', only z_1' workers will find a job in sector 1. Projecting this value into quadrant III, we discover that employment in sector 2 will then be z_2' and that the wage rate in sector 2 will fall from w^e to w''. In our two-sector model, then, introducing a wage floor means that some workers are reallocated from sector 1 to sector 2 and that, as a result, the wage rate in sector 2 will drop. Because w'' is less than w', we know that workers are not allocated to their most productive jobs —the wage floor results in an equilibrium with underemployment.

The Unemployment Equilibrium

Let's reintroduce the possibility of unemployment by altering our wage-floor analysis slightly. The crucial factor in determining the effect of wage floors on unemployment is the kind of institution governing the allocation of employment in the high-wage sector. Although we can apply this analysis to any wage floor, including minimum wages, let's talk in terms of a labor market characterized by unionized and nonunionized sectors and assume that the governing institution is what East Coast dock workers used to call "the shape-up." In the shape-up, the union members all turned up at a particular time of day, and a union official picked the members who were to work that day from the assembly. Let's assume, too, that dock workers could choose to look for work in either of two sectors: by joining the union, and therefore participating in the shape-up in sector 1, or by seeking their fortune in the nonunionized sector 2.

We'll now let z_1 be the number of union members looking for work in sector 1. The shape-up, like the hiring hall of Problem 16.6, means that the available employment — or z_1' jobs at wage w' — is shared out among union members. If we assume that the employment is shared equally, then the proportion of time that any union member will be employed is just z_1'/z_1, because z_1' is the number of jobs available in any one period and z_1 is the number of workers chasing those jobs. The expected wage is therefore just w' multiplied by z_1'/z_1, or $(w'z_1')/z_1$.

To find the equilibrium allocation, we'll suppose that workers continue to join the union until the expected wage in unionized sector 1 is just equal to the wage in nonunionized sector 2. The equilibrium is illustrated in Figure 16.5. (For purposes of comparison we have included the underemployment equilibrium from Figure 16.4.) Figure 16.5 is identical to Figure 16.4 in all but one respect — in quadrant I, we have plotted not the demand for labor in sector 1, but instead the expected wage rate in sector 1, $(w'z_1')/z_1$. Notice that the expected wage relationship passes through the point (z_1', w') because when z_1 is z_1', a union member is employed full-time at wage w'. As you can see by trying out alternative allocations, the equilibrium allocation — the one that equates the expected wage rate in sector 1 and the wage rate in sector 2 — is at A''' in quadrant III, and the common expected wage is w'''.

In this equilibrium, z_1''' union members are chasing z_1' jobs in sector 1, and z_2''' nonunion workers are employed full-time in sector 2. In this equilibrium, we have unemployment equal to $(z_1''' - z_1')$, or the distance marked u in quadrant I of Figure 16.5. It is necessarily the case that w'', the sector-2 wage in the underemployment model, is less than w''', the sector-2 wage in the unem-

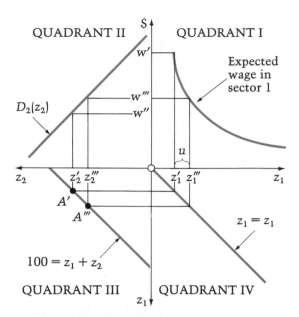

FIGURE 16.5 Wage floors and search unemployment in a two-sector model.

At the minimum wage w', z_1' individuals are hired in sector 1. In quadrant I, we have plotted the expected wage of a job searcher in this sector. In equilibrium, the expected wage is identical in the two sectors. Allocation A''' in quadrant III is the equilibrium allocation because it produces wage w''' in sector 2 and expected wage w''' in sector 1. With z_1''' searchers in sector 1 and only z_1' jobs, the minimum wage creates search unemployment equal to u.

ployment model, which is less than w', the wage in sector 1. As you may want to show, w''' may be smaller or larger than the equilibrium wage in the absence of a wage floor. If it is larger, all workers are better off with the wage floor; if it is smaller, all workers are worse off with the wage floor.

Two sources of inefficiency arise in the unemployment equilibrium. First, u workers are unemployed in each period. Second, the allocation of workers who are employed is inefficient because w' exceeds w'''. In other words, this equilibrium involves both unemployment and underemployment.

PROBLEM 16.8

Michael Todaro (1969) used a two-sector model very much like this one to explain the shanty-towns that lie around the perimeters of most large African cities. These shantytowns are peopled by migrants from the agricultural sector who hope to find high-wage employment in the urban economy. Reinterpret our two-sector model to discover Todaro's explanation.

16.4   Income Maintenance

Despite serious disagreement among members of economically developed societies about how income and wealth should be distributed, people generally agree that no one should live in abject poverty. Given that some minimum standard of living for everyone is an agreed-upon societal objective, what institutional arrangement can best achieve it?

In the last section, we saw some difficulties associated with minimum wages as devices for ensuring a "living wage." In this section, we'll explore three institutions designed to transfer income directly to the poor. The first is an ideal, but impracticable, income-maintenance institution and is compatible with both redistributional and efficiency objectives. The second is a stylized version of the standard welfare system in developed countries and is seriously incompatible with efficiency. The third is a combination of the other two institutions, sometimes called a *negative income tax*, and moderates the gross inefficiency associated with the welfare system.

The Efficient Transfer Mechanism

An economist directly translates "minimum standard of living" into "minimum level of utility." This initial transfer mechanism is concerned, then, not with an income-maintenance program but with a utility-maintenance mechanism. This trans-

fer of income allows someone who is below a socially designated minimum level of utility to attain that target indifference curve. Consider the target indifference curve in Figure 16.6, where x_1 is hours of leisure and x_2 is income (a composite commodity). Suppose, too, that the potential recipient of the income transfer has no access to income other than the opportunity to work at wage rate w. So that we can interpret w as the value of the recipient's marginal product, we'll assume that the economy is perfectly competitive.

In the absence of any income transfer, the potential recipient's opportunities are determined by the budget line $x_2 + wx_1 = wT$, where T is the total time available. Notice that here we can interpret w as the price of leisure, just as we did in Section 5.5. Because this budget line lies below the target

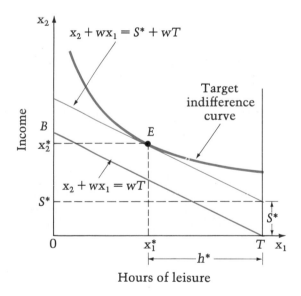

FIGURE 16.6   An efficient income-transfer mechanism.

In the absence of any income transfer, the individual's budget line, $x_2 + wx_1 = wT$, does not permit him or her to reach the target indifference curve. The unconditional income transfer S^* both allows the individual to attain the target indifference curve and is efficient because MRS in the equilibrium at E is equal to the wage rate w.

indifference curve in Figure 16.6, some societal action is needed to boost that person onto the target indifference curve.

Let's look at a scheme that is ideal, in the sense that it achieves the mandated redistribution, and that is consistent with efficiency. From Section 15.5, we know that the single point on the target indifference curve consistent with efficiency is at point E in Figure 16.6, where MRS is equal to w. If this person is given an unconditional transfer of income, or a no-strings-attached gift, just large enough to attain the target indifference curve, then he or she will choose the Pareto-optimal combination of income and leisure. Point E will then be the recipient's utility-maximizing combination. Given the appropriate transfer — equal to S^* in Figure 16.6 — the recipient will work h^* hours, enjoy x_1^* hours of leisure, and have income x_2^*. An unconditional lump-sum transfer of income therefore both accomplishes the mandated redistribution and is efficient.

The lump-sum transfer mechanism is ideal in yet another sense. As you'll see in Problem 16.9, the transfer S^* is the smallest possible transfer that will allow the individual to achieve the target indifference curve.

PROBLEM 16.9

To show that S^* is the minimum transfer, first reproduce Figure 16.6 on the top half of a sheet of paper. Next, construct a diagram on the bottom half in which for every value of x_1, you calculate the amount of income needed in addition to earned income to attain the target indifference curve.

Unfortunately, even though the lump-sum mechanism is efficient, it is not practical. First, we have no systematic way to choose a target indifference curve for each person. Second, even if we had a way, we would still face the overwhelming task of identifying everyone's individual prefer-

ences and everyone's budget line in order to pinpoint subsidy recipients.

Maintenance policies, therefore, are ordinarily formulated in terms of target levels of income rather than utility: they are **income-maintenance programs.** The object of an income-maintenance scheme is to raise the income of anyone below a targeted level up to that level. In all practical income-maintenance schemes, the amount of the income transfer is conditional upon the amount of the recipient's earned income. As you'll see, the conditional nature of such transfers creates a conflict between efficiency and distribution, or equity.

Topping Up and Welfare

The most pervasive conditional transfer mechanism is the familiar welfare system. Although real-world welfare systems are many and diverse, an essential feature of many is a **topping-up mechanism,** whereby the subsidy is just large enough to put the recipient at the mandated income level. The result is that potential recipients can affect the amount of income transferred to them by choosing how much (or how little) income they earn. In fact, they can't avoid making such a choice. And that's the rub.

To see why, suppose that the target level of income is S' and that the potential recipient can work at wage rate w and has no wealth. Let S denote the size of the subsidy actually paid out. If the potential recipient earns as much as or more than S', then he or she will receive no subsidy:

$$\text{If } wh > S' \quad \text{then } S = 0$$

If his or her earned income is below S', however, the amount of the subsidy will be just large enough that the earned income and the subsidy together equal the targeted income level:

$$\text{If } wh < S' \quad \text{then } S = S' - wh$$

We can translate this topping-up mechanism into the kinked budget line *BGE* in Figure 16.7. Segment *BG* corresponds to the case in which earned income exceeds *S'* and no subsidy is paid. Segment *GE* corresponds to the case in which earned income is less than *S'* and a subsidy just sufficient to top income up to *S'* is paid.

Given this topping-up scheme, two solutions to the potential recipient's utility-maximization problem are possible. In one solution, which is not illustrated in Figure 16.7, the individual picks some point on segment *BG* of the kinked budget line *BGE* where earned income exceeds *S*. In this case, he or she gets no income subsidy. In the other solution, the individual picks point *E*

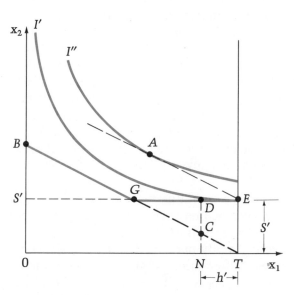

FIGURE 16.7 An inefficient income-transfer mechanism.

Line *BGT* is the no-income-transfer budget line. This transfer mechanism simply tops up the recipient's income to a specified level *S'*. For example, if the recipient works *h'* hours, earning income *NC*, then the income transfer received is *CD* because *NC* + *CD* = *S'*. This mechanism produces the kinked budget line *BGE*, and the recipient chooses point *E*. It is inefficient because the recipient's MRS at *E* is less than the wage rate *w*. The fact that segment *GE* of the budget line is horizontal reflects an implicit tax on earned income at a rate of 100%.

in Figure 16.7. In this case, the recipient does not work, and all of his or her income *S'* comes instead from the public purse.

We see, then, that the topping-up mechanism actually encourages the potential recipient to forgo all income from work (or to conceal any income actually earned). As long as earned income is less than *S'*, the marginal tax rate on earned income is 100%. If the potential recipient in Figure 16.7 considered working *h'* hours instead of zero hours, for instance, his or her earned income would increase from zero to distance *NC*. Yet the income transfer would decrease by precisely the same sum, from *S'* to the distance *CD*, reflecting an implicit tax on earned income at a rate of 100%. The welfare scheme thus fails to provide recipients with any incentive to work. It is obviously inconsistent with Pareto optimality as well because at point *E*, MRS is less than *w*. We know that the potential recipient could attain point *A* in Figure 16.7 by both receiving the transfer *S'* and working. Because he or she would be better off than at point *E* and because no one else would be worse off, we know that the equilibrium at *E* is not efficient. Considerations such as these have led to proposals for a negative income tax, an alternative to the welfare system.

The Negative Income Tax

We'll consider a scheme equivalent to one version of the **negative income tax** (NIT). It combines elements of the efficient lump-sum transfer mechanism and the topping-up mechanism. Though not problem-free, this combined scheme both alleviates the gross inefficiency and perverse lack of work incentives associated with the welfare system and redistributes income to poorer members of society.

The scheme is based on the combination of an unconditional income transfer to everyone, equal to, say, *S"*, and a proportional (but moderate) income tax t on earned income (in the range of a 10% to 25% tax rate rather than the welfare scheme's implicit tax rate of 100%). Under this combined scheme, everyone receives the subsidy S'', pays twh in taxes, keeps $(1-t)wh$ from his or her earned income, and therefore receives a net income of

$$x_2 = S'' + (1-t)wh$$

We can translate this combined scheme into the budget line HES'' illustrated in Figure 16.8.

To compare this mechanism with the welfare topping-up mechanism, we've chosen S'' and t so that the individual achieves indifference curve I' under either transfer scheme. The budget line HES'' is therefore tangent to the indifference curve at point E in Figure 16.8, and the individual is indiffer-

ent between the two schemes. Nevertheless, under the combined mechanism, he or she now supplies h^* hours of labor and earns income equal to wh^*. (The individual's disposable income, including the income subsidy and subtracting taxes payable on earned income, is the larger sum x_2^* in Figure 16.8.) You can see that point E is not an efficient equilibrium because MRS is less than w. Nevertheless, we have offset at least some of the inefficiency associated with the topping-up scheme.

Furthermore, this scheme makes a smaller demand on the public purse. Once we have deducted the taxes paid on earned income from the unconditional subsidy, the net subsidy is just the distance DE in Figure 16.8, an amount much smaller than S', the transfer under the topping-up welfare mechanism.

This combined scheme differs from the proposed NIT only in the actual mechanics of the income transfer. Instead of paying the unconditional subsidy S'' and then collecting the tax on earned income, under the NIT, the government subtracts the income tax due on earned income from S'' and pays only the net subsidy, distance DE in Figure 16.8.

In the case illustrated in Figure 16.8, a negative income tax is preferable to the topping-up, or welfare, scheme because it both avoids totally perverse labor-supply incentives and requires a smaller government subsidy. As you'll discover in Problem 16.10, however, these results are not the invariable outcome of a negative income tax.

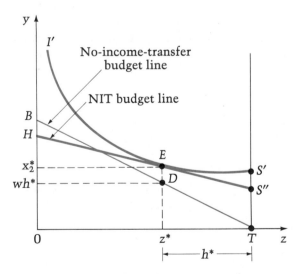

FIGURE 16.8   A negative income tax.

Think of the NIT as offering an unconditional subsidy S'' combined with a proportional tax on earned income, producing the budget line HES''. The individual chooses point E, working h^* hours and receiving the net subsidy DE. The negative income tax avoids the extreme work disincentive inherent in the topping-up mechanism.

PROBLEM 16.10

On a single diagram, draw the budget lines associated with the topping-up and NIT schemes. Let S', the target income under the topping-up mechanism, be greater than S'', the unconditional transfer under the NIT. Show that a person who will receive no subsidy under the topping-up scheme might decide to work less and to receive a subsidy under NIT.

As this problem illustrates, once we leave behind the ideal world of the efficient transfer mechanism, we have no easy answers. In reality, any income-transfer mechanism that has desirable personal and social effects when applied to one person may have just the opposite effects when applied to someone else. Furthermore, conflicts between efficiency and redistributional objectives are inevitable.

These difficulties simply mean that theory can carry us only so far, not that we should throw up our hands in despair. To design a real income-transfer mechanism that successfully minimizes the tension between efficiency and redistribution, good hard evidence is required, and such evidence is being provided. (See Cogan, 1983; Hall, 1975; and Keely, 1977, for example.) Theory thus identifies the potential problems that accompany any income-transfer mechanism; empirical evidence tells us how serious these potential problems are in reality.

Summary

One major task of markets is to allocate resources to competing ends. The question in this context is whether input markets are or are not efficient, and the Pareto criterion provides a precise answer. Another task of markets — and particularly of input markets — is to determine the distribution of wealth and income among the members of a society. The question in this context is whether the resulting distribution is the "right" one. Unfortunately, there is no twin to the economic concept of Pareto optimality that allows us to say whether the market system, or indeed any other set of institutions, performs the function of distribution well. Determining the just distribution of income is essentially an ethical rather than an economic question.

Two opposing philosophical principles have been proposed. The productivity principle is the proposition that each of us ought to receive what we have individually produced. The redistributionist principle is the proposition that a more nearly equitable distribution of wealth and income ought to be a social objective. Advocates of the second position argue first that ethical judgments must be impersonal: the *original position* is a hypothetical situation designed to ensure such impersonality. They also argue that in this original position, each of us would choose a more or less equal distribution of economic rewards. Finally, they assert that what we would choose in this original position is equivalent to what is just in the world we actually inhabit.

We have labeled this the redistributionist principle because it leads to the ethical position that income and wealth ought to be redistributed from the rich to the poor. Judging from the array of redistributional institutions we see in modern economies, it is fair to say that most of us would not regard the distribution arising from pure market institutions as perfectly just. To one degree or another, most of us are redistributionists.

Distribution and efficiency, however, are separate problems. As we saw in considering a range of income-maintenance mechanisms, the institutions that solve one problem regrettably do not solve the other. This presents us with a fundamental social quandary. Once we realize that the efficient income-transfer institutions are not practicable, we must conclude that any institution or set of institutions that effectively redistributes income or wealth will be inconsistent with economic efficiency, at least to some degree. Thus, a conflict between efficiency and distribution is inevitable.

The problem for economists is to design redistributionary institutions that minimize the conflict between equity and efficiency. Yet economic theory alone cannot solve this problem. It can only highlight the problems that we expect to arise in any particular institutional context. To take any further step requires empirical work to determine how serious the potential problems identified by economic theory really are.

Exercises

1   Suppose that in an economy composed of three people, we can measure each person's utility cardinally. Suppose, too, that we can use three possible sets of institutions—A, B, and C—to organize economic activity in this economy. The problem is to choose one of the three sets of institutions. The utility of each person under each set of institutions is given below.

Institution	Utility of 1	Utility of 2	Utility of 3
A	45	45	45
B	75	60	30
C	78	63	21

a   According to Rawls's difference principle, which set of institutions is preferred?

b   Suppose that none of the three people knows which person he or she will be in this economy. What institution would you choose? If each person maximizes expected utility and if each attaches probability $\frac{1}{3}$ to being any one person, which is the preferred set of institutions?

c   Now suppose that each of the three does know which person he or she will be. If the set of institutions is chosen by majority rule, which set will be chosen by self-interested individuals?

2   Hilary hires labor to make fancy fishing lures in a small village. She is a profit maximizer. Her marginal revenue product function is

$$MRP(z) = 130 - z$$

and the supply of labor to her firm is

$$w = 10 + \frac{z}{2}$$

where z is the number of workers she hires and w is the daily wage rate.

a   What wage rate does she pay and how much labor does she hire?

b   Her workers are forming a union and need advice on what wage rate they should seek. Their advisor has told them that they should ask for a wage no lower than $50. Explain why this is good advice.

c   The workers have said that they want to ensure that employment does not fall. Given this objective, what is the maximum wage they should bargain for?

3   This problem provides an illustration of the two-sector model developed in Section 16.3. Labor demand functions in the two sectors are $w_1 = 149 - z_1/2$ and $w_2 = 100 - z_2/2$. There are 200 workers to be allocated to the two sectors.

a   Find the competitive equilibrium allocation and wage rate. Hint: Set z_2 equal to $200 - z_1$ in the second demand function, then set the right-hand sides equal to each other and solve for z_1, the competitive allocation to sector 1.

b   Now suppose that a union wage equal to $100 is established in sector 1 and that available jobs are allocated permanently to a lucky group of 98 workers. Find the underemployment equilibrium.

c   Finally, again suppose that a union wage equal to $100 is established in sector 1, but that jobs in this sector are now allocated by the shape-up (described in Section 16.3). Find the unemployment equilibrium. What is the level of unemployment? What is the wage in sector 2? What is the expected wage of a worker looking for work in sector 1?

d   Illustrate all three equilibria on one carefully drawn graph.

4   Explain (1) why lump-sum, or unconditional, income transfers and taxes are consistent with Pareto optimality; (2) why they are impractical as a means of achieving significant redistribution; and (3) why income transfers and taxes that are conditional on earned in-

come are not consistent with Pareto optimality.

5 Professional associations such as the California Bar Association have considerable leeway in determining both the standards that new entrants must meet and the prices of professional services.

a First, suppose that the professional association can set prices but cannot control entry standards. What are the implications of a price increase when the demand for professional services is price inelastic? In particular, what will happen to the earnings and hours worked of an individual professional in the short run and the long run? What are the implications when demand is price elastic?

b Second, suppose that the association can control entry standards but not prices. What are the implications of increasing the entry standard—say, by requiring entrants to spend an additional term in a training program? In particular, do the established practitioners have private incentives to increase the entry standard?

References

Arrow, K. (1976), *The Viability and Equity of Capitalism*, E. S. Woodward Lectures in Economics, University of British Columbia.

Cogan, J. F. (1983), "Labor Supply and Negative Income Taxation: New Evidence from the New Jersey–Pennsylvania Experiment," *Economic Inquiry*, 21:465–483.

Hall, R. (1975), "Effects of the Experimental Negative Income Tax on Labor Supply," in *Work Incentives and Income Guarantees*, J. Peckman and P. M. Timpane (eds.), Brookings Institute.

Keely, M., et al. (1977), "The Labor Supply Effects and Costs of Alternative Negative Income Tax Programs: Evidence from the Seattle and Denver Income Maintenance Experiments," Stanford Research Institute.

Rawls, J. (1971), *A Theory of Justice*, Belknap Press of Harvard University.

Todaro, M. (1969), "A Model for Labor Migration and Urban Unemployment in Less Developed Countries," *American Economic Review*, 59:138–148.

*17

EXTERNALITIES AND PUBLIC GOODS

Every North American over the age of 40 can remember past cigarette commercial jingles: "I'd walk a mile for a Camel!"; "Call for Philip Morris!"; "Us Tareyton smokers would rather fight than switch!" A few decades ago, smoking was a pervasive, generally acceptable social activity. More recently, a new slogan has superseded those catchy old jingles: "Warning: The Surgeon General Has Determined That Cigarette Smoking Is Dangerous to Your Health." The surgeon general's 1964 report has played a central role in the attitude reversal toward smoking. Today, increasing numbers of people consider cigarette smoking to be not only dangerous to smokers but also obnoxious and dangerous to nonsmokers who share the same air space. In the language of the economist, smokers' behavior imposes an **externality** on their nonsmoking neighbors because it directly affects their well-being. More generally, whenever the behavior of one economic agent affects for better or worse the well-being of another, we say that the agent is imposing an externality, either positive or negative, on the person affected.

The smoker's externality is but one example of a large class of similar problems forming the major focus of this chap-

ter. Virtually all of the following words or phrases—none of which was in common use in 1964—are now both familiar and immediately call to mind important externality problems: acid rain, driftnets, dioxins, PCBs, greenhouse effect, nuclear winter, supertankers, clear-cutting, and ozone layer. So, too, many recent local and international news stories report on issues related to externalities. These are just a brief sample of headlines from a few of those stories: "Must spend billions to fight air pollution, report warns"; "Pulp mill effluents lead to permanent ban on shellfish harvest"; "Hydro demands threaten Grand Canyon"; "A nasty scrap over toxic household waste." Of course, as we noted above, not all externalities are negative. The creation of new public parks, green belts, and recreation areas and the reclamation of marshlands for wildlife habitats are just a few examples of activities associated with positive externalities.

In Section 17.1, we'll use the smoker's example to illustrate why the unrestricted, or blind, pursuit of self-interest does not produce Pareto-optimal results where externalities are concerned; in Section 17.2, we'll develop a taxonomy of externalities; in

Sections 17.3 through 17.6, we'll examine a range of policy responses to problems created by externalities; and in Section 17.7, we'll investigate a set of problems that are different from, but formally similar to, externalities: the provision of public goods.

17.1 The Smoker's Externality: A Representative Case

In Chapter 15, we explored in depth the proposition that competitive markets allocate resources in a Pareto-optimal way. In this chapter, we want to qualify that proposition, showing that markets do so *only in the absence of externalities*. To see how externalities affect Pareto optimality, or efficiency, we'll consider a two-good exchange economy with a negative externality.

Let's begin by imagining an economy in competitive equilibrium that has two types of consumers: smokers and nonsmokers. If we have only two goods in this economy—cigarettes, good 1, and a composite commodity, good 2—then we can represent the smokers' preferences by the standard utility function in which the quantities of cigarettes and of the composite commodity are the arguments. Let x_1' and x_2' be a representative smoker's utility-maximizing bundle, given the price of cigarettes and the smoker's income. (As usual, the price of the composite commodity is 1.)

The nonsmokers' preferences, however, are different. Because nonsmokers presumably will never buy cigarettes, their maximizing consumption bundles will contain only the composite commodity, good 2. If we let x_2^* be a representative nonsmoker's consumption of the composite commodity, x_2^* will be equal to the nonsmoker's income. If these two representative consumers regularly share the same air space, a negative externality may arise as a result of the smoker's consumption decision. It depends on whether the nonsmoker finds second-

hand smoke, or blow-by, objectionable. If so, then the smoker's decision to buy (and smoke) cigarettes is an additional argument in the nonsmoker's utility function because the smoker's decision materially affects the well-being of the nonsmoker.

Now let's take these two people from the larger social context, their maximizing consumption bundles in hand, and form a miniature exchange economy. We'll assume that Shelly is the smoker and Marvin is the nonsmoker. Is the initial endowment in this two-person exchange economy Pareto-optimal? We'll see that it is Pareto-optimal if there is no externality and that it may not be Pareto-optimal if there is an externality.

We can once again use an Edgeworth box diagram, introduced in Chapter 15, to analyze the problem. Let's begin by assuming that Marvin is not bothered by blow-by. When no externality is at stake, we have the situation presented in Figure 17.1. Shelly's origin is the northeasterly corner of the diagram, and her initial endowment of x_1' units of cigarettes and x_2' units of the composite commodity puts her at point E relative to her origin. Her indifference curve through this point is the standard convex curve, labeled s_0. Marvin's origin is the southwesterly corner, and his initial endowment of x_2^* of the composite commodity puts him at point E relative to his origin. Thus, E is the endowment point in this exchange economy.

Notice that Marvin's indifference curves are horizontal lines like the two in Figure 17.1 labeled n_0 and n_1. Why? Marvin doesn't want any of Shelly's cigarettes for his own use, nor does he care how many cigarettes Shelly lights up in their shared air space. In particular, he has no desire to destroy some of her cigarettes to reduce the amount of secondary smoke in the environment. (We'll assume throughout that the cigarettes can be destroyed at no cost.)

Notice, too, that if Marvin's consumption of the composite commodity is fixed at x_2^* and if cigarettes are transferred from

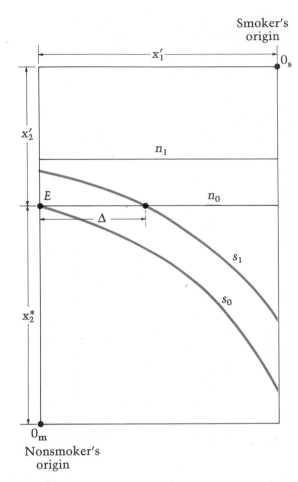

Smoker's origin

O_s

x'_1

x'_2

n_1

E n_0

Δ

s_1

s_0

x^*_2

0_m

Nonsmoker's origin

FIGURE 17.1   **An Edgeworth box for smoking with no externality.**

The smoker's endowment is composed of x'_1 cigarettes and x'_2 of the composite commodity, and the nonsmoker's endowment contains only x^*_2 units of the composite commodity. Hence, the initial endowment is at E. The nonsmoker's indifference curves—n_0 and n_1, for example—are horizontal, reflecting the fact that he is neutral to the smoker's consumption of cigarettes. The initial endowment at E is therefore Pareto-optimal.

Shelly to Marvin, Marvin moves from left to right along the horizontal indifference curve n_0 in Figure 17.1. By contrast, Shelly moves to progressively lower indifference curves. For example, if Δ cigarettes are transferred from Shelly to Marvin, she

moves to the less preferred indifference curve s_1. As we can see from Figure 17.1, in the absence of an externality, the allocation at point E is Pareto-optimal. No other allocation of consumption goods will leave both as well-off.

PROBLEM 17.1

To convince yourself that the market-induced allocation is always Pareto-optimal in this case, identify the contract curve in Figure 17.1.

Now let's assume that Marvin does find blow-by objectionable. Because secondary smoke is now a *negative externality*, the situation is instead the one presented in Figure 17.2. Marvin is now better off as cigarettes are transferred to him because the number of cigarettes in Shelly's hands, and therefore the amount of secondhand smoke in the air, is reduced. (Marvin, of course, simply destroys any cigarettes transferred to him.) Graphically, if Marvin's consumption of the composite commodity is fixed and if Shelly's consumption of cigarettes is reduced—that is, if Marvin moves from left to right along any horizontal line in Figure 17.2—he is better off.

We can deduce from this that Marvin's indifference curves must be negatively sloped. For any small increase in the number of cigarettes allotted to Marvin, there is a compensating decrease in the amount of the composite commodity he consumes that will leave him on the same indifference curve; that is, Marvin is now willing to pay to reduce Shelly's consumption of cigarettes. (For simplicity, we have drawn Marvin's indifference curves in Figure 17.2, n_0 and n_1, not only as negatively sloped but also as convex to the southwesterly origin.)

Is Shelly willing to accept a bribe from Marvin and to hand over some cigarettes in return? The answer is yes. The green area in Figure 17.2 represents all the exchanges of the composite commodity, or money, for cigarettes that both Marvin and Shelly

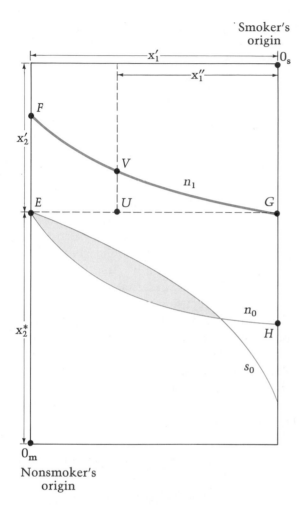

FIGURE 17.2   An Edgeworth box for smoking with an externality.

The initial endowment is at point E, as it is Figure 17.1. In contrast to that figure, here the nonsmoker's indifference curves—n_0 and n_1—are negatively sloped, reflecting the fact that he does find blow-by objectional. (If he were given some of the smoker's cigarettes, he would destroy them, consume less blow-by, and be better off.) In this case, the initial endowment is not Pareto-optimal—any allocation in the green area is Pareto-preferred to it.

would find preferable to the initial allocation at point E. The market solution that generated the initial allocation at point E is therefore not Pareto-optimal, because mutually beneficial swaps are possible.

We can also see why the blind pursuit of self-interest is the ultimate source of that market inefficiency. If Shelly did not smoke any of her cigarettes, Marvin would be at point G on indifference curve n_1 in Figure 17.2 because he could still consume x_2^* of the composite commodity. As Shelly's consumption of cigarettes increases, however, Marvin falls to progressively lower and lower indifference curves until he reaches indifference curve n_0, when Shelly consumes x_1' cigarettes. Shelly's behavior clearly makes Marvin less well-off. We can think of Shelly as imposing an external cost on Marvin.

We can measure this external cost by determining how much Marvin's consumption of the composite commodity must be increased to offset the loss of utility caused by the secondary smoke from any quantity of cigarettes. For x_1' cigarettes, for example, it is the distance EF In Figure 17.2. More generally, for any given quantity of cigarettes smoked, the increase in Marvin's consumption of the composite commodity required to compensate him is equal to the vertical distance from line EG to the indifference curve n_1. If Shelly smokes x_1'' cigarettes, for example, then Marvin requires UV more of the composite commodity to remain as well-off as he would have been in the absence of all smoking.

Although we can identify the cost of the smoker's externality to the nonsmoker, the smoker does not actually bear the costs arising from her behavior. Her failure to bear the costs means, from a social point of view, that she consumes too many cigarettes. We can make the same point by considering the problem from the other side. The nonsmoker is actually willing to pay the smoker to reduce her cigarette consumption. The difficulty is that under the artificial institutional arrangements in this model, he has no way to negotiate with her. Below, we'll see what happens when they can negotiate.

PROBLEM 17.2

What is the maximum amount that Marvin is willing to pay Shelly in Figure 17.2 to reduce cigarette consumption from x_1' to zero?

As the following problem illustrates, the disturbing result illustrated in Figure 17.2 — that in the presence of externalities, market-induced allocations are inefficient — is not inevitable.

PROBLEM 17.3

Construct a diagram analogous to Figure 17.2 in which a negative externality is associated with smoking and yet the market allocation is Pareto-optimal.

In summary, under the ordinary set of market institutions, the smoker has no incentive to take into account the cost she imposes on the nonsmoker, and the nonsmoker has no way to provide her with such an incentive. As a result, the market-induced outcome in the face of the externality may be inefficient.

As we noted earlier, externalities are not always negative. Sometimes one person's consumption of some good increases rather than detracts from the well-being of everyone materially affected by that consumption activity. For example, when one person with a bad cold and hacking cough buys and takes a cough syrup, those who associate with him or her may be the recipients of a positive externality insofar as their exposure to the cold virus (and to the noise, too) is thereby reduced.

PROBLEM 17.4

Suppose that good 1 is of no direct use to Ralph but that when Nancy buys and uses good 1, both Ralph and Nancy are better off. Show that Nancy, left to her own devices, may buy too little of good 1. Can you think of goods other than cough syrup

that fit this framework? How about immunization against communicable diseases such as measles, mumps, and polio?

The smoking and cough-syrup examples are only two of a myriad of real-world externalities, both positive and negative. We can reduce all externalities to the same elements: source(s), carrier(s), and recipient(s). One or more economic agents is the source of the externality; in the smoking example, the source is the smoker. The externality is caused by a carrier; in this case, the carrier of the externality is secondary smoke. One or more economic agents is the recipient of the externality; in our example, the recipient of the external cost is the nonsmoker. The recipient fares better or worse, depending on whether the carrier creates positive or negative externalities or, more simply, external benefits or external costs. Before trying to solve (or even to ameliorate) the many real-world problems arising from externalities, we need to organize them into a few broad categories.

17.2 A Taxonomy of Externalities

We know, at least in theory, that the activity of any economic agent can indirectly affect a host of other economic agents through the operation of the price system. For example, if I decide to buy 100,000 times the number of grapefruit I usually eat, my decision will have an (admittedly small) impact on the price of grapefruit, and that impact will indirectly affect all other grapefruit buyers. Indeed, from a general equilibrium perspective, everything depends on everything else. Any choice a particular economic agent makes potentially has indirect effects on all other economic agents. By contrast, when an externality is at issue, the activity of one economic agent directly affects another economic agent (or agents). Just what do we mean by "direct" in this context?

Consumption – Consumption Externalities

One type of direct impact, called a **consumption – consumption externality**, occurs when consumers are both the source(s) and the recipient(s) of the externality. Massive queuing on a first come, first served basis is an example of a negative consumption – consumption externality: each person in the lineup imposes a negative externality on everyone further down the line. For example, when popular musical groups come to town, their fans often pay a severe time price when they line up to buy tickets — sometimes hours or even days before the tickets go on sale. By contrast, a heavy turnout at that great American institution, the homecoming dance, is a positive consumption – consumption externality because the more people (within reason) who come to see (and to be seen), the merrier.

PROBLEM 17.5

Homecoming dances are usually organized (and often subsidized) by a student organization rather than by "leaving it to the market." Are such dances likely to be provided more efficiently through a student organization or through the market?

Production – Production Externalities

Another type of direct impact, called a **production – production externality**, arises when producers are both the source(s) and the recipient(s) of the externality. A classic case of a negative production – production externality is the pasturing of cows on the commons: any one farmer's productive activity adversely affects that of every other farmer. A major contemporary case is nickel production at INCO in Sudbury, Ontario. INCO's sulfur emissions — the largest single source of acid rain in North America — adversely affect a host of other firms in Canada and the United States. Among the industries thought to be affected are Quebec's maple sugar producers, whose trees produce less sap and die young because of acid rain fallout.

A classic case of a positive production – production externality is the shopping center. The smaller specialty stores benefit from the steady stream of potential customers attracted by the large department stores that are the centerpieces of most such developments.

Consumption – Production Externalities

Another type of direct impact, called a **consumption – production externality**, occurs when one or more consumers are the source(s) and one or more producers the recipient(s) of the externality. One example of a negative consumption – production externality occurred recently in Vancouver, Canada, when certain commercial blueberry producers were forced to take their blueberries off the market because they had been contaminated by lead from the emissions of cars traveling on a nearby highway. An example of a positive consumption – production externality occurs when a private flower garden provides nectar for bees from a neighboring commercial honey producer.

Production – Consumption Externalities

A fourth type of direct impact, called a **production – consumption externality**, arises when one or more producers are the source(s) and one or more consumers the recipient(s) of the externality. Almost inevitably in standard industrial air-pollution problems, producers are sources and consumers are recipients. The 1985 gas leak of methyl isocyanate from a Union Carbide plant in Bhopal, India, which killed more than 2000 people in a 50-square-kilometer area, is just one tragically memorable example of a negative production – consumption externality. A positive production–consumption externality would arise if the bees from a commercial honey producer pollinated the fruit trees of a nearby hobby farmer.

17.3 Responses to Externalities: An Overview

So far, we have learned that externalities can arise between consumers, between firms, or between combinations of the two. When such externalities are positive, resources are **underallocated** to the source of the externality; when they are negative, resources are **overallocated** to the source. What kinds of responses to externalities can help to rectify these allocational distortions? In this section, we'll briefly survey possible responses and then return to look at some of them in greater detail.

Private Negotiations

So far, we have assumed that the source of the externality will turn a blind eye to the effect of its actions on the recipient, and we have seen that this blind self-interest leads directly to inefficiency. Thus, *bargaining* between the concerned parties is an obvious place to seek a remedy.

The parties concerned can actually benefit by recognizing their interdependence and negotiating an alternative, mutually beneficial solution. If the externality is positive, the recipient may be willing to pay the source to increase the amount of the carrier, and the source may be willing to accept. Apple growers in Washington State, for instance, pay an apiary fee to beekeepers for providing bees to pollinate their trees (see Cheung, 1973). If the externality is negative, the recipient may be willing to pay to decrease the amount of the carrier. For instance, a harassed student in the midst of final examinations might be willing to pay the music lover in the neighboring apart-

ment $25 for 10 hours of peaceful study time. If the source and the recipient manage to negotiate a Pareto-optimal private response to the externality, then no real social problem exists.

Internalization

Another remedy is a process called *internalization*, in which a third party, who sees an opportunity to make a private gain from the presence of an externality, intervenes between the source(s) and the recipient(s) and effects an efficient private response. For example, a recent trend among hotel keepers in the United States is to offer their patrons a choice between smoking and nonsmoking rooms. In this way, they can capture the resulting benefit to nonsmokers by charging commensurately higher prices or, more realistically, by avoiding the loss of nonsmoking patrons to competing hotels that offer nonsmoking accommodation. Again, when the problem is internalized by a third party, no real social problem requiring a governmental response arises.

Governmental Responses

As we have seen, then, the fact that externalities are pervasive phenomena does not necessarily imply that governmental intervention must likewise be pervasive. Private parties always have the incentive (and often the means) to resolve the problems created by the blind pursuit of self-interest. Whenever such problems are not privately resolved, however, three sorts of public policy responses are possible. The first approach is to facilitate the negotiation of private solutions by creating property rights. (We'll soon see how property rights help the interested parties to reach a mutually acceptable resolution.) The second approach is to impose public regulations based on cost-benefit analysis. The third is to take no action at all.

Assigning Property Rights

Economists favor using the property-rights approach whenever possible because the problem is thereby resolved by the only parties having the necessary information. For example, suppose that a chemical company is pouring effluent into a river upstream and a household is taking its drinking water out of the same river downstream. In this case, only the chemical company knows the value it places on being able to dump its wastes and only the household knows the value it places on pure drinking water. If property rights to the water are assigned to one party or the other, the two may be able to reach an efficient private solution: under a property-rights approach, each solution is tailor-made by the parties concerned.

Public Regulation

Because the property-rights approach is sometimes unworkable, public regulation based on cost-benefit analysis may be necessary. Many governmental agencies concerned with health, resource management, power, education, and recreation use cost-benefit analysis to regulate externalities. Taxation is one kind of regulation. The heavy taxes imposed on cigarettes and liquor are intended in part to reduce consumption to more socially desirable levels. Bans on certain offensive activities are another regulatory option. For example, playing radios without earphones is now illegal in some New York City and Vancouver parks; smoking is typically prohibited in public buildings, hospitals, and subways; and factories emitting unacceptably high levels of pollutants are sometimes forced to shut down. Regulatory standards are yet another means of controlling externalities. Standards for lead emissions from automobiles and for sulfur emissions from industrial plants are just two of many such governmentally enforced limits.

As we'll see, such regulations are necessarily crude, in the sense that a single solution is imposed on many different problems. Like an off-the-rack pair of jeans, a regulation sometimes fits, but not always. California's automobile emissions standards are applied statewide, for example, even though auto-emissions problems in such areas as Los Angeles, San Francisco, and Tahoe are not the same.

Nonintervention

The third possible governmental response is simply to do nothing. Because regulation itself uses up resources, including the costs of information gathering, administration, and enforcement, the best policy may be no policy. (For instance, though body odor is a negative externality, the problem is simply not significant enough to warrant expensive government regulation.) In the following sections, we'll consider the three major types of responses in more detail and examine the conditions under which each is appropriate.

17.4 Privately Negotiated Solutions

The two-person smoker's externality problem is a useful approximation of many real-world problems well suited to a negotiated solution. Let's imagine that the two consumers are long-term roommates: Sadie is the smoker and Norma the nonsmoker. Because the problem involves only two people and because they interact over a long period of time, the resolution of the problem is best left up to Sadie and Norma themselves. In practice, they'll probably negotiate some solution about when, where, and how much Sadie can smoke in their apartment. But chances are good that they'll spend a great deal of time and energy arguing about their individual rights to their common air space. Sadie may insist that she has every right to smoke in her own home, and Norma may be just as vociferous in claiming her right to breathe unpolluted air.

One solution to the roommates' problem, pioneered by Ronald Coase (1960) and subsequently applied by other economists to a wide range of externality problems, is to endow either of the roommates with the exclusive right to control smoking in their shared environment. This arrangement works by establishing a *default option*: the arrangement that will prevail if no settlement is reached. If Sadie has the exclusive right to the air, she'll presumably smoke as much as she chooses in the apartment if the two can't come to an agreement. Similarly, if Norma has the exclusive right, she'll presumably prohibit all smoking in the apartment if they can't agree on something else.

This default option encourages a negotiated solution by *narrowing the range of possible solutions*. To see how, let's begin by supposing that Sadie has the unbridled right to pollute the apartment's air. The road to a resolution of the externality problem is obvious. Norma will have to either induce Sadie to reduce or eliminate her cigarette consumption or put up with the consequences. As you can see, the possible bargains between the two have shrunk considerably.

The solutions acceptable to both are illustrated in Figure 17.3. Sadie's consumption of cigarettes is on the vertical axis, and her consumption of the composite commodity is on the horizontal axis to the left of 0 in Figure 17.3a. Because by assumption Sadie "owns" the domestic air, she doesn't have to accept any solution less attractive than the default point at E: the solution to her private utility-maximizing problem. On the other hand, Norma's consumption of the composite commodity is on the horizontal axis to the right of 0 in Figure 17.3b, and her income is denoted by N. If Norma fails to negotiate a mutually acceptable alternative, she'll have to accept Sadie's default point E in Figure 17.3a, which leaves her at the corresponding point F in Figure 17.3b.

Relative to the default option, the only solutions acceptable to Norma are those that leave her on or below n_0 (because her utility increases as Sadie's cigarette consumption decreases); the only ones acceptable to Sadie are those that leave her on or above s_0. Solutions that satisfy both conditions leave Sadie in the light green area on or above s_0, and Norma at the corresponding point in the light green area on or below n_0. These are the only possible mutually agreeable bargains because they are the only ones that leave both roommates at least as well-off as they are at the default option.

To understand how the light green area above s_0 and below the dashed curve GBE in Figure 17.3a has been constructed, let's ask: What is the maximum amount Norma would conceivably pay Sadie to reduce her cigarette consumption from x_1' to x_1''? The answer is distance AA', because this is the largest sum that still leaves her on or below n_0. In Figure 17.3a, we have added income AA' to point B' on Sadie's original budget line to find point B. In other words, distance BB' in Figure 17.3a is equal to distance AA' in Figure 17.3b. If this bargain were struck, Norma would be no worse off — and Sadie would be better off.

We can now reverse the argument by asking: What is the smallest sum Norma would have to pay Sadie to reduce consumption from x_1' to x_1''? The answer is the distance $B''B'$ on the left in Figure 17.3a. Finding point A'' on the dashed line $HA''F$ simply means subtracting $B''B'$ from Norma's income and giving that amount to Sadie; that is, distance $B''B'$ is equal to distance $A''A'$. If this bargain were struck, Sadie would be no worse off — and Norma would be better off. In this way, we have demarcated the entire set of possible bargaining solutions. Any such solution will leave Sadie at some point in the light green area in Figure 17.3a and

(a)

(b)

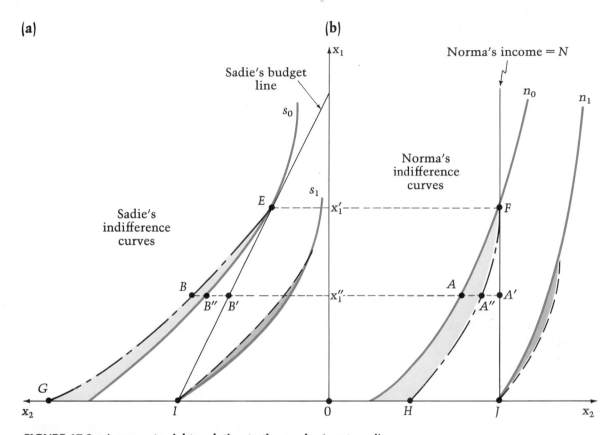

FIGURE 17.3 A property-rights solution to the smoker's externality.

Sadie's cigarette consumption x_1 is measured on the vertical axis, and Sadie's and Norma's consumption of the composite commodity are measured on the leftward and rightward horizontal axes. Norma's indifference curves— n_0 and n_1—are positively sloped, reflecting the negative externality associated with Sadie's habit. The blind pursuit of self-interest puts

Sadie at E in (a) and Norma at F in (b). If Sadie owns their common air space, then Norma must pay Sadie to reduce her cigarette consumption, and possible negotiated solutions lie in the two light green areas. By contrast, if Norma owns their air space, then possible negotiated solutions lie in the two dark green areas.

Norma at the corresponding point in the light green area in Figure 17.3*b*. Which of these bargains Sadie and Norma will actually strike depends on their relative skills as negotiators.

On the other hand, if the property right is Norma's rather than Sadie's, the default option is at J and I in Figure 17.3. In the absence of a negotiated agreement, Norma

need not accept any solution less attractive than a smoke-free environment and an income of N at point J on the right. The corresponding default point for Sadie is point I on the left. Now the shoe is on the other foot: Sadie must bribe Norma for the privilege of smoking in the apartment. The set of possible negotiated solutions that will leave each roommate at least as well-off as she is at the default point is represented by the two dark green areas in Figure 17.3.

Thus, the sets of possible solutions do differ, depending on who "owns" their common air. And ownership has obvious distributional consequences because the resource "owner" is clearly better off. Nevertheless, investing either the source or the recipient with the exclusive property right establishes a natural point of departure for negotiating solutions. In the absence of such a clear default option, the concerned parties might endlessly bicker over respective rights and fail to reach any agreement.

PROBLEM 17.6

Property rights need not be exclusively vested in either the source or the recipient. Suppose that Sadie has the right to smoke only half of her utility-maximizing number of cigarettes. Construct a diagram analogous to Figure 17.3 and identify the range of possible negotiated solutions under this assignment of property rights.

The parable of the two roommates illustrates two important points about externalities. First, when the number of parties directly involved is small and when the externality itself is significant, the concerned parties have every incentive to resolve the problem themselves. From an economic perspective, these privately negotiated settlements are extremely attractive because the concerned parties are the only ones who have the information necessary to create a solution that suits them. A solution hammered out between any two roommates — a smoker and a nonsmoker — is likely to be more satisfactory than one imposed from outside. Second, because many externality problems arise from unspecified or incomplete property rights, one way to facilitate such privately negotiated solutions is to assign property rights, thereby defining the default option and limiting the range of possible solutions.

Is it possible to take advantage of privately negotiated arrangements when the number of sources and recipients is significantly larger? Think of the externality problem associated with residential real estate on a hill rising from the seashore, for example: everyone wants a clear view of the ocean. Owners down the hill can improve their view by building tall houses, but only at the expense of owners up the hill who lose their ocean view. The traditional regulatory solution to this problem — which is, in fact, not "a problem" at all but rather a whole series of discrete externality problems — is to impose a maximum height restriction on everyone. However, because one tall building creates as many different view problems as there are lots behind it and up the hill, only the owners of these building sites know in any precise sense what their particular problem may be. The umbrella, or all-encompassing, regulatory solution of a height restriction is therefore only a rough-and-ready approximation of the tailor-made solutions that individual owners might negotiate for themselves.

PROBLEM 17.7

Suppose that the municipality has imposed a maximum building height restriction of 30 feet on the seaside real estate we have described. Can you devise a better property-rights solution?

The classic externality problem solved by the creation of property rights is the common-property fishery we considered in Chapter 2. As we saw, assigning ownership of the fishing grounds theoretically did away with the externality. A study of oyster production in 1975 provides some empirical support for this view. The evidence indicates that the oyster fishery was more productive in states having a high percentage of privately owned oyster grounds (see Agnello and Donnelley, 1975).

17.5 Internalizing the Externality

We now turn to problem solving through internalization by a third party. Our previous example of department-store and specialized retailers in the same shopping center is an interesting case in point. If we simplify the problem by assuming that the department store is the source of the (positive) externality and the specialized retailers the recipients, then the carrier is the size of the department store. The larger it is, the more traffic it attracts, and the more benefit it confers on the smaller retailers. We can think of the specialized retailers as *free riders* on the retailing opportunities created by the department store, much as the hobos of the 1930s were literally free riders on the nations's railway system.

Imagine a department-store firm bent on blindly pursuing its own self-interest. If it considers establishing a new branch, it will choose to build a store too small to maximize the joint profits of both that new department store and the specialized retail outlets that almost inevitably spring up to take a free ride on its traffic. Why will the store be too small? Because it cannot capture the benefits conferred on the free riders.

We can even imagine a scenario in which the joint profits from the best possible aggregation of retail activity—the best size for the department store and the best types and sizes for the specialized retailers—might be positive, whereas the profit of the department store itself might be negative. In this case, the department store would never establish its branch, even though it would see potential profits from the retail center as a whole.

How can we solve this problem of the free rider? We see the answer across the face of post-1950 North America: the shopping center. We can imagine that the shopping-center developer first calculates the profit-maximizing configuration of stores and then negotiates a series of contracts with the department store and selected specialized retailers. The contracts must guarantee only that each retailer is at least as well-off as it would be in the absence of the shopping center. By putting all the externality-producing activities under one roof, the developer can extract for itself the maximum profit from the retail agglomerate, profit that otherwise would have gone unrealized, given the blind pursuit of self-interest by the large department store. Not surprisingly, the large department stores themselves recognize that potential and often become the prime movers in shopping-center developments. So, too, Cannell Studios recognized a similar potential in the film industry. When it built its new North Shore Studios, it designed a facility in which its own studios occupied only a third of the space. All the remaining space was designated for offices to be rented to other film-related companies, including camera, lighting, and catering firms.

17.6 Regulatory Solutions

When the costs of transacting a private solution to an externality problem are prohibitively high, public regulation is the only effective remedy. Such high costs occur when the number of sources and recipients is relatively large or when direct contact between them is infrequent. For example, smoking in a public elevator, at a bus stop, in the corridor of a hospital, or in any other public place is an ever-changing externality problem; it changes with the number and identity of the smokers and nonsmokers present at any one time. We simply cannot expect the bus riders waiting at Fifth and Main to negotiate a solution to the smoking externality that arises if both smokers and nonsmokers are in the group: the costs of negotiation far outweigh the potential benefits. Neither can we anticipate that a third party will internalize the externality: no private person owns these public places. In this kind of circumstance, governmental regulation is apparently the only feasible option.

Many air and water pollution problems closely resemble the smoker's externality in public places. The number of individuals and firms who contribute to air pollution in Los Angeles, for instance, is as large and as continually changing as the number of individuals and firms who suffer from the resulting smog. Moreover, the air pollution problem changes as the weather changes. For example, the smog is worse when a temperature inversion occurs or when more sunshine drives chemical reactions in the atmosphere.

Because every person and every firm in Los Angeles is both a source and a recipient and because the problem itself is as changeable as the weather, the cost of privately negotiating a solution is prohibitive. And because no one owns the Los Angeles air shed, the problem cannot be internalized by a third party.

When transacting a private solution to an externality is too expensive, regulation becomes an alternative. What first strikes an economist about the regulatory approach is that policymakers need very precise information in order to identify specific regulatory targets. By contrast, the private-property approach requires only that policymakers know the gross features of the problem at hand.

Cost-Benefit Analysis

Economic cost-benefit analysis can be used to generate the information needed to stipulate regulatory targets. We can illustrate this approach by returning once more to the smoking externality. To translate that problem into the language of cost-benefit analysis, we calculate both a representative

smoker's benefits and a representative nonsmoker's costs and then subtract the costs from the benefits to determine the optimal amount of smoking in this two-person case. (Simply for convenience in labeling, we'll assume here that the smoker is male and the nonsmoker female.)

We can identify the smoker's benefit from smoking any given number of cigarettes in Figure 17.4 by using the approach introduced in Section 5.2. The smoker's utility function is $U(x_1, x_2)$, where x_1 is quantity of cigarettes and x_2 is expenditure on all other goods. The smoker's income is B. We'll measure the smoker's benefits

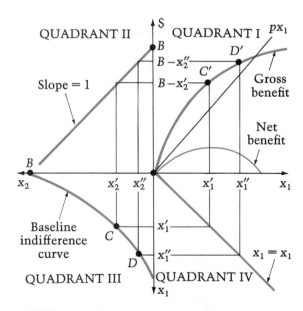

FIGURE 17.4 Gross and net benefit functions.

With no cigarettes, the smoker is at point B in quadrant III on the baseline indifference curve. Using this indifference curve as a point of reference, we have derived the gross benefit function in quadrant I. The gross benefit of x_1' cigarettes is $B - x_2'$ dollars, because if the smoker paid this sum for x_1' cigarettes, he or she would still be on the baseline indifference curve. Projecting $B - x_2'$ and x_1' into quadrant I gives us point C' on the gross benefit function. The line px_1 in quadrant I represents the smoker's expenditure on cigarettes. Subtracting px_1 from the gross benefit gives us the net benefit function.

against a baseline case in which he consumes no cigarettes. Graphically, the smoker's baseline point is at B on the indifference curve BCD in quadrant III of Figure 17.4.

For the moment, we'll ignore the cost of cigarettes and derive the smoker's gross benefit from any quantity of cigarettes. Suppose that the smoker has x_1' cigarettes. Because he can reduce his expenditure on the composite commodity from B to x_2' and still stay on indifference curve BCD, his gross benefit from x_1' cigarettes is $B - x_2'$. In other words, the smoker will voluntarily give up this sum of money for the opportunity to smoke x_1' cigarettes. Using the line whose slope is 1 in quadrant II, we can project the gross benefit $B - x_2'$ into quadrant I. Similarly, using the line $x_1 = x_1$ in quadrant IV, we can project the quantity of cigarettes associated with that gross benefit into quadrant I. The intersection of these two projections at point C' in quadrant I defines one point on the smoker's gross benefit function.

We have derived the entire gross benefit function in just the same way. For instance, the gross benefit of x_1'' cigarettes is $B - x_2''$, defining point D' on the gross benefit function. This function thus tells us, for any number of cigarettes, the maximum amount of money that the smoker is willing to give up to smoke those cigarettes rather than to have none at all.

Now let's find the smoker's net benefit function by subtracting the cost of the cigarettes he buys from the gross benefit function. The line px_1 in quadrant I of Figure 17.4 gives us the cost of consuming any quantity of cigarettes, where p is the competitive equilibrium price of cigarettes. Subtracting px_1 from gross benefit gives us the smoker's net benefit function in quadrant I. This function tells us the smoker's net benefit from consuming cigarettes when he pays the competitive equilibrium price for them. Notice that net benefit from smoking is at a maximum at x_1' cigarettes.

We can also measure the nonsmoker's costs. Given any number of cigarettes, we can simply determine the amount by which we would have to increase the nonsmoker's income, or consumption of the composite commodity, to make her as well off as she would have been in the absence of the secondary smoke. We previously developed a graphic technique for constructing this measure in our discussion of Figure 17.2. We have transposed this measure to Figure 17.5 and labeled it nonsmoker's costs; so, too, we have transposed the net benefit function from Figure 17.4 to Figure 17.5 and labeled it smoker's net benefits.

We can derive the net social benefits function in Figure 17.5 by subtracting the

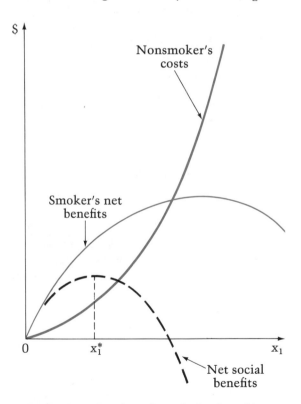

FIGURE 17.5   Cost-benefit analysis of smoking.

The nonsmoker's costs and the smoker's net benefits are plotted in this figure. Subtracting costs from benefits gives us net social benefits. To maximize net social benefit, we should somehow induce smokers to smoke just x_1^* cigarettes.

nonsmoker's costs from the smoker's net benefits. From the perspective of cost-benefit analysis, then, the socially optimal consumption of cigarettes in this illustration is x_1^*. We know that in the absence of control, the smoker will buy and smoke "too many" cigarettes. Thus, if it can be identified, the optimal level of cigarette consumption x_1^* provides a target for policymakers, assuming that the regulatory mechanism is aimed at reducing consumption to that socially optimal level.

Notice that at x_1^*, the rate at which the smoker's net benefits increase is equal to the rate at which the nonsmoker's costs increase; that is, the slopes of the two functions are identical at x_1^*. We can think of the slope of the smoker's net benefit function as the *marginal social benefit* of cigarettes and the slope of the nonsmoker's cost function as the marginal social cost of cigarettes.

At the cost-benefit optimum, the marginal social benefit is equal to the marginal social cost.

We can imagine extending this technique of cost-benefit analysis from our society-of-two to society at large. At least in principle, we can think either of scanning costs and benefits over a large number of individual smokers and nonsmokers, or of directly estimating the costs to nonsmokers as a group and the benefits to smokers as a group. As you'll discover in Section 17.7, however, getting accurate information on personal costs and benefits can be difficult.

In principle, cost-benefit analysis allows policymakers to determine a target level for some activity that produces an externality. In practice, however, serious problems attend applications of cost-benefit analysis. As we saw in the examples concerning bus-stop smoking and Los Angeles smog, what we nominally see as a problem is actually a multitude of problems, because the problem itself changes with each episode. The cost of gathering the information needed for this sort of cost-benefit analysis is simply prohibitive.

The best a cost-benefit analyst can do in such cases is to consider a representative problem that captures the average features of the whole gamut of real problems under study. The regulation resulting from the representative cost-benefit analysis is necessarily an umbrella solution: it covers a whole range of problems and is ideally suited to none. California's statewide auto-emissions legislation, designed to ameliorate air-pollution problems of various descriptions from the Oregon border to the Mexican border, is just one of many examples.

Hitting the Target

Suppose that policymakers, using cost-benefit analysis, have identified a *target* for some externality problem. What kind of regulation will achieve it? We can find no single answer to this question because different problems require different kinds of solutions. Yet economists do have one regulatory rule of thumb: they prefer regulatory mechanisms based on individual choice to mechanisms proscribing individual behavior.

Think of the emissions of sulfur from electricity-generating plants. One regulatory mechanism based on individual choice is to charge an emissions tax of t dollars per unit of sulfur. This regulation leaves the individual electricity-producing firms free to choose any level of emissions they like — as long as they're prepared to pay the price. By contrast, a proscriptive regulatory mechanism is to ban the emission of, say, more than s units of sulfur per kilowatt-hour produced. This ban means that the maximum emissions level applies across the board to every power-generating company.

Assuming that we know the values of s and t that will achieve the target level of sulfur, why is the tax preferable to the ban? If we think of the privilege of emitting sulfur into the atmosphere as an economic resource just like any other, then—in the absence of an externality—the resource is free and requires no regulatory attention. In the presence of an externality, however, only a limited amount of emission will be permitted.

The privilege of emitting sulfur is now a *scarce resource*, and the emissions tax is essentially the price per unit for that privilege. Because all firms face the same price—that is, pay the same emissions tax—the limited amount of sulfur emissions will be allocated to its most productive uses. The tax thus ensures that the limited quantity of emissions will be allocated efficiently, a result we cannot achieve with the blanket proscription.

The U.S. government is currently considering another mechanism that invokes individual choice to allocate emission rights efficiently. Individual polluters would be given marketable emission quotas, or rights. If the firm intended to emit, say, 100,000 tons of sulfur and its quota was only 70,000 tons, it would have to buy emission rights for 30,000 tons of sulfur from other firms. On the other hand, if the firm anticipated emitting less sulfur than allowed by its quota, it could sell its excess emission rights. Like the emissions tax, this marketable emission rights solution ensures that the limited quantity of emissions will be allocated efficiently.

Using this rule of thumb, what kind of regulatory response can you devise to avert a little-publicized tragedy that now threatens much of the United States? The Ogallala Aquifer is a vast underground water reservoir lying beneath much of the Great Plains. Most of the water pumped through the impressive agricultural sprinkling systems that dot this landscape is drawn from the aquifer. As the sprinkling technology has caught on, the demands on the aquifer have grown at such an alarming

rate that it may soon be sucked dry. (The aquifer is so very valuable a resource that proposals have been made to drain the Great Lakes to replenish it.)

The tragedy, of course, is the old problem of the commons in a new guise. Any landowner can tap into the aquifer by drilling a well. The amount of water available to any user of the aquifer next year is virtually independent of how much that person pumps this year, because any individual will use but a tiny fraction of the total. Consequently, no landowner has any incentive to conserve water for future needs. Because access is free to all, the needs of future users of this resource carry no weight in determining its present use.

A simple analogy suggests the absurdity of the problem of the Ogallala Aquifer. Imagine a thousand people on a desert island with just enough water to last them until their rescuers, known to be coming on a specified date, arrive. If each one has a straw in the common drinking supply and if no one can tell how much water anyone else is drinking, the result is almost certainly death for everyone.

PROBLEM 17.8

What sort of regulatory mechanism seems appropriate to control the externality problem associated with the Ogallala Aquifer?

17.7 Public Goods

We now turn from externalities to public goods—goods characterized by a perfect positive externality to the whole community. These public goods are of a different nature from most of the goods (and services) we've considered, which have been characterized by benefits that flow to a particular consumer. When I buy and eat a Granny Smith apple, for instance, I am the only one who gets to enjoy it. Furthermore, the apple itself is no longer available to you or to anyone else. It's simply gone. Such goods are termed **rivalrous**: one person's consumption of a unit of a rivalrous good precludes the possibility of anyone else enjoying it.

Other goods and services — those conferring positive externalities, for example — are to some extent **nonrivalrous**. When I enjoy my flower garden, for instance, my neighbors and occasional passers-by can also take pleasure in it without lessening my own. (Unless, of course, so many come to gawk that they interfere with my pleasure.) So, too, the presence of other sightseers doesn't diminish the pleasure you take in feeling the spray from the awesome force of Niagara Falls (unless the crowds are so large that they interfere with your own enjoyment). Many other goods and services are similarly nonrivalrous, differing only in degree, and a few are even purely nonrivalrous. For instance, my pleasure in the spectacle of Halley's comet zinging through the night sky is in no way diminished by the millions of other eyes turned skyward. So, too, the benefits flowing to you from a national defense program are unaffected by the benefits to me.

Nonrivalrous Goods

Many economists and others take the normative position that, for the sake of efficiency, nonrivalrous goods ought to be provided free of charge. To exclude individuals from the benefit of a nonrivalrous good, they argue, is inefficient, because including them makes them better off and leaves everyone else just as well-off. In other words, the numbers of people who can enjoy the flow of benefits can be increased at virtually no cost.

Indeed, many of the services that governments commonly provide free of charge are, to some degree, nonrivalrous. National defense and navigational safety aids such as channel markers and lighthouses, for example, are, in practice, completely nonrivalrous. Roads and bridges, police and fire protection, and many public health programs — such as compulsory immunization against disease — are, to a considerable extent, nonrivalrous. The argument for publicly provided, nonrivalrous goods implies only that access should be free to all. It does not imply that taxes should not be imposed to provide the goods.

Nonexcludable Goods

Many, but certainly not all, goods and services considered in this section are also **nonexcludable**, meaning that denial of access to the good or service is impossible or at least very costly. In the last century, entrepreneurs built fences along the Niagara Falls gorge and charged tourists to look at the falls through peepholes. In this case, the spectacle of Niagara Falls became an excludable good. But even P. T. Barnum, that masterly entrepreneur, couldn't have denied access to people refusing to pay admission to see Halley's comet. Similarly, New York State can manage to charge tolls for the use of some of its major roads, but the U.S. government would find it impossible to deny the benefits of national defense to selected residents without incurring the considerable expense of deporting them. Thus, nonrivalrous goods may or may not be excludable. By contrast, goods that are rivalrous are necessarily excludable. Once the apple is eaten, it's available to no one else.

Pure Public Goods

Goods that are both completely nonrivalrous and nonexcludable are called **pure public goods.** In many circumstances, if pure public goods are to be produced at all, they will be produced by some public authority rather than by profit-seeking firms, because no firm can profit by providing a nonexcludable good.

One counterexample of a pure public good that is provided privately is "free" commercial TV broadcasting. At least to the viewers themselves, TV watching is both nonrivalrous and nonexcludable. No matter how many millions of people watch a TV program, the individual viewer's pleasure is unaffected, and the programming is available at no cost to anyone with a TV set. Yet, private broadcasting corporations are actually in the business of providing another, both rivalrous and excludable service: a captive audience for advertisers. The programming is merely the bait used to capture the audience. By contrast, ad-free TV programming is produced either by public corporations (such as the BBC in Britain) or by nonprofit organizations (such as PBS in the United States).

PROBLEM 17.9

The invention of cable TV changed forever the face of commercial broadcasting. Viewers can now be excluded from free access to programming if they refuse to pay the installation and monthly charges to private cable TV companies. Is pay TV efficient? Should it be encouraged?

Let's reconsider our short list of nonrivalrous, publicly provided goods. National defense and navigational aids are largely nonexcludable and thus qualify as pure (or nearly pure) public goods. If these are to be available, public agencies must provide them. On the other hand, roads and bridges, as well as police and fire protection, are potentially excludable and therefore are not pure public goods. These potentially excludable, nonrivalrous goods could be provided privately — and at various times and places throughout history, roads, bridges, and police and fire protection have all been financed privately for profit. Yet, the efficiency argument cited earlier suggests that such goods and services ought to be publicly funded instead.

Public Provision of Nonrivalrous Goods

Governments clearly can use some form of cost-benefit analysis to decide how much of a public good to provide. Our analytical tack in this case must be slightly different, however, because we need to imagine that the public good is actually rivalrous rather than nonrivalrous so that we can derive an ordinary demand function that answers the question: How much will an individual demand of the public good at any price p?

The ordinary demand functions for two representative citizens, A and B, are labeled AA' and BB', respectively, in Figure 17.6. If

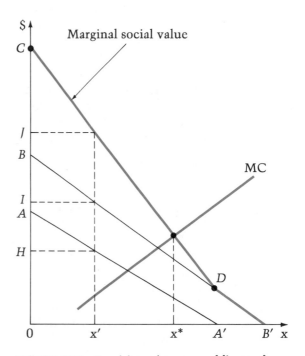

FIGURE 17.6   Provision of a pure public good.

The individual demand functions for this public good are AA' and BB'. Because the good is completely nonrivalrous, to get the marginal social value function, we vertically add the two demand functions. For example, the marginal value of a bit more of the public good when x' is already supplied is $0H$ to person A and $0I$ to person B; the marginal social value is then $0J = 0H + 0I$. The cost-benefit criterion suggests that the public good be supplied up to the point where marginal cost MC is equal to marginal social value, or up to x^* in this illustration.

x' of the public good is supplied, the total value to citizen A is equal to the area under AA' to the left of x'; the total value to citizen B is the area under BB' to the left of x'. (To use these consumer surplus measures, we'll assume that each person's demand for the public good is independent of his or her income.) More important, the marginal values of x' to A and B are the distances $0H$ and $0I$, respectively. Because the good is non-rivalrous, the marginal social value is the *vertical summation* of the two individual marginal values, $0H$ and $0I$, or the distance $0J$. Notice that the vertical summation associated with public goods is different from the horizontal summation associated with rivalrous goods. Because the public good is consumed in its entirety by everyone, vertically summing marginal valuations is the appropriate aggregation procedure.

By vertically summing the individual marginal values for every quantity, we have derived the function labeled "marginal social value" in Figure 17.6. This function is sometimes called the *demand function for public goods*, a potentially confusing label because it does not provide the ordinary information given by a demand function: the quantity demanded of a good for any given price.

From this point on, the cost-benefit analysis is completely straightforward. The optimal amount of the public good is the quantity at which the marginal social value of the good equals the marginal cost of supplying it, or x^* in Figure 17.6.

Cost-Benefit Analysis and Revealed Preference

Although applying cost-benefit analysis to public goods is theoretically straightforward, implementing it can be tricky. The problem is that individual citizens may not reveal their real demand functions for a public good. If the public good is financed by a specially earmarked tax on the citizens who benefit from it and if the more each citizen benefits, the higher his or her tax bill will be, then a self-interested citizen might think twice about reporting personal benefits accurately.

Being only one of a great many who will use the public good, the citizen might assume realistically that the amount supplied will be virtually independent of his or her reported demand function. The cagey response is to underreport the private value of the public good — or even to claim not to value it at all. In this response, we see another example of the free-rider syndrome. The self-interested citizen wants to benefit from the public good without bearing the cost of providing it. If every citizen were similarly tempted to take a free ride, they could all end up with very little of the public good, or perhaps none at all.

On the other hand, if the size of personal tax bills is independent of individually reported benefits, individuals have no incentive to underreport. In fact, they may very well be tempted to overreport. In any event, it seems clear that citizens have no particular incentive to think hard and long about the personal value of any public good and to report that valuation accurately, which makes the whole process of social cost-benefit analysis problematical.

Although these revealed-preference problems are most dramatic in the context of public goods, they also plague the cost-benefit analysis of externalities. Suppose that a nonsmoker is told that the city council is considering a ban on smoking in public places. If asked whether he or she strongly supports the ban, moderately supports the ban, or strongly opposes the ban, the nonsmoker has no reason to weigh the personal costs and benefits thoughtfully or to report accurately. In fact, the nonsmoker may well be tempted to overestimate the value of smoke-free public places. A parallel distortion occurs if the respondent is a smoker. The resulting information from the smokers and nonsmokers whose opinions are solicited is not necessarily useful to policymakers. A hardline economist might even argue that the only useful information this questionnaire provides is a census of smokers and nonsmokers.

Summary

A major theme of economics is that the private pursuit of self-interest produces Pareto optimality, or efficiency. In Chapter 15, we identified the precise set of circumstances in which this theme is a theorem—that is, in which the pursuit of self-interest produces efficiency. We discovered that the absence of market power is essential to this result. Either monopoly or monopsony power upsets the efficiency applecart.

In Chapter 16, we saw that if society at large is not satisfied with the market-determined distribution of wealth, then the institutions used to redistribute wealth inevitably create inefficiency. The general lesson is that taxes or subsidies, like market power, also tend to undermine efficiency.

In this chapter, we began by considering other situations—those involving externalities of any kind—in which the blind pursuit of self-interest again fails to result in efficiency. We then considered a range of possible responses to the problem posed by externalities. In many circumstances, a private resolution is feasible, either through bargaining between the affected parties or through internalization, by putting the problem in the hands of a single decision maker. These private resolutions are appealing to economists because they rely on the only individuals who have the information needed to devise a tailor-made solution: the concerned parties themselves.

However, private solutions are not always feasible. For example, air and water pollution problems are so complicated and involve so many parties that some form of

public regulation seems to be necessary. Given the complexity of such problems, the economist's approach to regulation, which invariably depends on some form of cost-benefit analysis, is necessarily an umbrella approach: one or perhaps a few sets of regulations that can be applied to a great many different externality problems. Although regulation is necessary in these complex cases, the economist's rule of thumb is to rely on private incentives wherever possible. For instance, taxing emissions is preferable to setting emissions standards because it serves to allocate permissible emissions to their most productive uses.

Finally, we turned to the related problem of public goods. A pure public good is both nonrivalrous and nonexcludable. In most circumstances, if such goods are to be provided, they will be publicly provided. Why? Because their nonexcludability means that no profit-seeking firm will ever produce them. Furthermore, even when a nonrivalrous good is excludable, efficiency requires that it be publicly provided at no cost.

In principle, the provision of public goods is straightforward: the rule is to provide the good up to the point where marginal social benefit is equal to marginal social cost. The problem is to estimate marginal social benefit. Here we encounter the revealed-preference problem, a difficulty associated not only with public goods but also with cost-benefit analysis in general. In essence, the problem is to find a mechanism that induces individuals to reveal their true preferences. In the absence of such a mechanism, we are compelled to add public goods to our list of problems that are antithetical to efficiency.

Exercises

1 Interpret the following laws as responses to externalities: Homeowners are required to keep their sidewalks clear of snow and ice. Drivers are required to drive on the right side

of the road. Drivers are allowed to enter an intersection only if the traffic light is green. Dog owners are required to have their pets vaccinated for rabies.

2 Two types of firms emit gunk, a nasty pollutant. There are 10 firms of each type. These firms think of "gunk emissions" as a productive input much like any other, the primary difference being that the price of gunk emissions is currently $0. Their input demand functions for gunk emissions are

$$w_1 = 100 - z_1$$
$$w_2 = 150 - z_2$$

a Given the current price of gunk emissions, how much does each firm emit, and what are total emissions?

b Suppose that we want to reduce gunk emissions to 1000 units in total and that we must use an emission tax T per unit of gunk emitted. What value of T will induce firms to reduce emissions to the target level? Are the 1000 units of the input gunk emissions allocated efficiently among the 20 firms?

c Now suppose that each of the 20 firms is given the right to emit 50 units of gunk and that firms are allowed to buy and sell these rights. What is the aggregate demand for gunk emissions? What is the aggregate supply of emissions? Think of each firm as supplying 50 units. What is the competitive equilibrium price and allocation of gunk emissions? Are the 1000 units allocated efficiently among the 20 firms?

d Finally, suppose that each of the 20 firms is given the right to emit 50 units of gunk and, in contrast to part c, that the firms are forbidden to buy and sell these rights. (In other words, each firm is required to reduce its emissions to 50 units.) Are the 1000 units allocated efficiently among the 20 firms?

3 Mosquito control at the local level is a good example of a pure public good. First, suppose that in an economy-of-two, the two people are identical and each has the following demand function for mosquito control:

$$p = 20 - y$$

where y is quantity of mosquito control. (We are assuming for convenience that their demands for mosquito control are independent of their incomes.) The cost of mosquito control is $10 per unit.

a What is the socially optimal level of mosquito control? Hint: You first need to vertically sum the individual demands.

b Suppose that mosquito control is not publicly provided. If individual 1 provided no mosquito control, how much would individual 2 provide? If individual 1 provided 5 units of mosquito control, how much would individual 2 provide? If individual 1 provided 10 units of mosquito control, how much would individual 2 provide? Building on these results, show that in the Nash equilibrium — where each individual takes the quantity of mosquito control provided by the other as given in choosing how much mosquito control to provide — total quantity provided will be 10 units.

c Now suppose that we have 100 people with this demand function for mosquito control. What is the socially optimal level of mosquito control? Show that in the Nash equilibrium when there are 100 people, the total quantity provided will again be 10 units.

d In the Nash equilibria in parts b and c, there is a free-rider problem. Explain it in detail.

*4 Imagine that a public project costs K and provides benefits to three people: A, B, and C. Let $B_A > B_B > B_C$ be the benefits to the three individuals. Suppose that each must pay one-third of the project's cost. Show that there are circumstances in which two of the three will vote for the project, even though the total benefit from the project is less than its cost. Show that in such circumstances, C will be willing and able to bribe B to vote against the project. Suppose again that only two people will vote for the project but that the project's total benefit exceeds its cost. Is it possible in this case that C will be willing and able to bribe B to vote against the project? Would A be willing to offer B a larger bribe to vote for the project? Do these bribes serve any useful social purpose? Should such bribes be illegal?

References

Agnello, R. J., and L. P. Donnelly (1975), "Property Rights and Efficiency in the Oyster Industry," *Journal of Law and Economics*, **18**:521–533.

Cheung, S. N. S. (1973), "The Fable of the Bees: An Economic Investigation," *Journal of Law and Economics*, **16**:11–13.

Coase, R. (1960), "The Problem of Social Cost," *Journal of Law and Economics*, **3**:1–44.

ANSWERS TO PROBLEMS

PROBLEM 1.1

Profit per unit sold is $P - C$.

PROBLEM 1.2

There are 32 customers between addresses $\frac{1}{2}$ and $\frac{3}{4}$, 96 between $\frac{1}{4}$ and 1, and 16 between 0 and $\frac{1}{8}$.

PROBLEM 1.3

When a is 0, the point of market segmentation is $\frac{3}{8}$, 48 customers shop at All-Valu, and All-Valu's profit is $48. When a is $\frac{1}{4}$, the corresponding values are $\frac{1}{2}$, 64, and $64. When a is $\frac{1}{2}$, the corresponding values are $\frac{5}{8}$, 80, and $80.

PROBLEM 1.4

The relevant diagram is Figure A1.1. The point of market segmentation is again $(a + b)/2$. Because $a > b$, All-Valu will attract the patronage of people who live to the right of $(a + b)/2$. The length of the market segment from $(a + b)/2$ to 1 is $1 - [(a + b)/2]$, and the number of customers All-Valu will attract is then $N[1 - (a + b)/2]$. Profit per unit sold is again $P - C$, and All-Valu's profit is therefore

$(P - C)N[1 - (a + b)/2]$. When a is 1, the point of market segmentation is $\frac{7}{8}$, 16 customers shop at All-Valu, and All Valu's profit is $16. When a is $\frac{7}{8}$, the corresponding values are 13/16, 24, and $24.

PROBLEM 1.5

Figure A1.2 can be interpreted in two ways. First, it gives All-Valu's profit for any location a on Main Street, given that Bestway is located at $\frac{1}{2}$. Second, it gives Bestway's profit for any location b on Main Street, given that All-Valu is located at $\frac{1}{2}$. Hence, given that the other firm is located at $\frac{1}{2}$, either firm maximizes profit by locating at $\frac{1}{2}$. In other words, we have equilibrium when both firms locate at $\frac{1}{2}$.

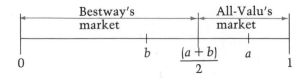

FIGURE A1.1

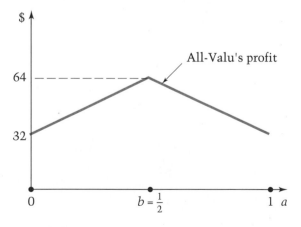

FIGURE A1.2

476

PROBLEM 1.6

Suppose that the firms are located as in Figure A1.3. Now there are two points of market segmentation, x and y, and each firm's market is always exactly half the circumference of the circle, regardless of where the firms are located. Hence, any pair of locations is an equilibrium of locations. We see, then, that market boundaries are critical for minimum differentiation.

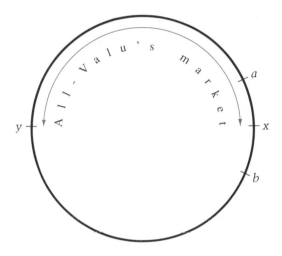

FIGURE A1.3

PROBLEM 1.7

By "eyeballing" this density curve, we can identify the point x such that half the population lives to the left of x and half lives to the right of x. The equilibrium of locations will have the two firms clustered at point x, as in Figure A1.4.

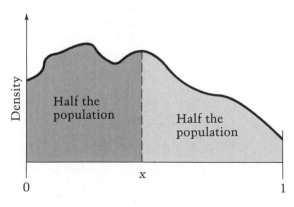

FIGURE A1.4

PROBLEM 1.8

Because All-Valu is worse off in state 2 than in state 2T, state 2 is not Pareto-preferred to state 2T. Because Bestway is worse off in state 2T than in state 2, state 2T is not Pareto-preferred to state 2. In other words, the Pareto criterion does not rank these two states.

PROBLEM 1.9

Suppose that each glutton cares only about his or her own share. Beginning with any value of X, it is impossible to make one glutton better off by increasing his share of the pie without making the other worse off by reducing her share. Hence, given any X, no other state is Pareto-preferred to it. Because no state is Pareto-preferred to any other, any state is Pareto-optimal.

PROBLEM 1.10

Because aggregate profit is identical in all three states, we can rank the states by comparing customers' aggregate transportation costs. These costs are identical in states 2 and 2T. Therefore, the cost-benefit criterion ranks state 2 and state 2T equally. Aggregate transport costs are larger in state 1 than in either state 2 or state 2T. Therefore, the cost-benefit criterion ranks state 2 as better than state 1 and state 2T as better than state 1.

PROBLEM 2.1

The first combination is both in the production possibilities set and on the production possibilities frontier; the second is not in the production possibilities set and it lies above the production possibilities frontier; the third is in the production possibilities set and lies below the production possibilities frontier. The production possibilities frontier is described by the following equation:

$$\text{fish next year} = 300 - \left(\tfrac{5}{3}\right) \text{fish this year}$$

PROBLEM 2.2

At point 0_A, Ted gets 135 fish this year and 75 next year, while Amy gets none in either year. At point B, Ted gets 0 fish this year and 75 next year, while Amy gets 135 this year and 0 next year.

PROBLEM 2.3

The first bundle has 150 fish, the second 160, the third 156, and the fourth 160. Hence, Amy would rank the second and fourth bundles as most desirable, the third bundle as next most desirable, and the first bundle as least desirable.

PROBLEM 2.4

All the points in the dark green triangle in Figure 2.3 are Pareto-preferred to point *B*.

PROBLEM 2.5

This is a dual-purpose institution designed to reduce litter and encourage recycling. It works by creating a private money incentive to return pop bottles to the retailer or a recycling depot.

PROBLEM 2.6

Under the common-property institution, Ted would harvest 75 fish in the second year and his total fish consumption would be 135 fish, while Amy would harvest 75 fish in the second year and her total fish consumption would be 105 fish. Under the private-property institution, Ted would harvest 50 fish in the second year and his total fish consumption would be 110 fish, while Amy would harvest 100 fish in the second year and her total fish consumption would be 130 fish.

PROBLEM 2.7

Whether there are two or four people, we have a common-property institution. When there are two people, if Amy (or Ted) releases one additional fish this year she (or he) will harvest $\frac{3}{2}$ more fish next year; since $\frac{3}{2}$ exceeds one, she (he) will release all her (his) fish. When there are four people, the private return to releasing an additional fish this year is only $\frac{3}{4}$ more fish next year; since $\frac{3}{4}$ is less than 1, no fish are released.

PROBLEM 2.8

Because the demand function for the good shifts up and to the right when the price of a substitute increases, both equilibrium price and quantity increase.

PROBLEM 2.9

Equilibrium price would increase and equilibrium quantity would decrease.

PROBLEM 2.10

For any individual, there are five endogenous variables: fish eaten in each of 2 years, total fish eaten; fish released in the first year, fish harvested in the second year. There are a number of aggregate endogenous variables: total fish eaten in each of two years, total fish eaten over 2 years, total fish released in the first year, total fish harvested in the second year. The exogenous variables include the rate at which fish reproduce, the initial number of fish, the initial distribution of property rights, the property institution, and the number of people.

PROBLEM 3.1

To see that these statements do not violate the transitivity assumption, we can construct the implied preference ordering:

- First: (10, 19)
- Second: (14, 21)
- Third: (15, 8) and (11, 17)
- Fourth: (0, 0)

Since all four preference statements are consistent with this ordering, the transitivity assumption is not violated.

PROBLEM 3.2

Consider just the first two preference statements in the problem, $B_1 \, P \, B_2$ and $B_2 \, P \, B_3$; the transitivity assumption tells us that $B_1 \, P \, B_3$. Now consider this derived preference statement, $B_1 \, P \, B_3$, in conjunction with the third preference statement in the problem, $B_3 \, P \, B_4$; the transitivity assumption tells us that $B_1 \, P \, B_4$, which is what we set out to show. The seven additional statements needed to describe four-term consistency are as follows:

- If $B_1 \, P \, B_2$, $B_2 \, P \, B_3$, and $B_3 \, I \, B_4$, then $B_1 \, P \, B_4$
- If $B_1 \, P \, B_2$, $B_2 \, I \, B_3$, and $B_3 \, P \, B_4$, then $B_1 \, P \, B_4$
- If $B_1 \, I \, B_2$, $B_2 \, P \, B_3$, and $B_3 \, P \, B_4$, then $B_1 \, P \, B_4$
- If $B_1 \, P \, B_2$, $B_2 \, I \, B_3$, and $B_3 \, I \, B_4$, then $B_1 \, P \, B_4$
- If $B_1 \, I \, B_2$, $B_2 \, P \, B_3$, and $B_3 \, I \, B_4$, then $B_1 \, P \, B_4$
- If $B_1 \, I \, B_2$, $B_2 \, I \, B_3$, and $B_3 \, P \, B_4$, then $B_1 \, P \, B_4$
- If $B_1 \, I \, B_2$, $B_2 \, I \, B_3$, and $B_3 \, I \, B_4$, then $B_1 \, I \, B_4$

PROBLEM 3.3

First observe that all bundles fit one of the following categories: (C1) bundles such that quantity of good 1 exceeds 2; (C2) bundles such that quantity of good 1 is less than 2; (C3) bundles such that quantity of good 1 equals 2. All bundles in (C1) are preferred to (2, 3), and (2, 3) is preferred to all bundles in (C2). Now subdivide (C3) as follows: (C3.1) bundles such quantity of good 2 is less than 3; (C3.2) bundles such that quantity of good 2 is greater than 3; (C3.3) bundles such that quantity of good 2 equals 3. Bundle (2, 3) is preferred to any bundle in (C3.1), and any bundle in (C3.2) is preferred to (2, 3). Hence, all bundles B that satisfy B I (2, 3) are in (C3.3). But the only bundle in this category is (2, 3) itself, so we see that (2, 3) is a single-point indifference curve. This argument is easily adapted to show that, for Clem, each conceivable bundle is a single-point indifference curve.

PROBLEM 3.4

The third and sixth preference statements violate the nonsatiation assumption.

PROBLEM 3.5

Pick two bundles B_1 and B_2 such that B_1 P B_2, and call the associated indifference curves I_1 and I_2. Now suppose that I_1 and I_2 intersect. They then have at least one bundle in common—say, B_3. We then infer that B_1 I B_3 and B_3 I B_2, since B_3 is on both indifference curves. Transitivity then implies that B_1 I B_2. But this contradicts the way in which we picked B_1 and B_2—so that B_1 P B_2. What gives rise to this contradiction? The supposition that the two indifference curves intersect. We therefore conclude that they cannot.

PROBLEM 3.6

Consider first the indifference curve $x_1x_2 = 1$. This indifference curve intersects the ray $x_2 = x_1/2$ at the point $x_1 = 2^{1/2}$ and $x_2 = 1/2^{1/2}$. Hence, the rule says to assign utility number $2^{1/2}$ to all bundles on the indifference curve $x_1x_2 = 1$. Similarly, the rule says to assign the number $4^{1/2}$ to all bundles on the indifference curve $x_1x_2 = 2$ and the number $6^{1/2}$ to all bundles on the indifference curve $x_1x_2 = 3$. More generally, the rule says

to assign the number $(2c)^{1/2}$ to bundles on indifference curve $x_1x_2 = c$. The resulting utility function is

$$U(x_1, x_2) = (2x_1x_2)^{1/2}$$

PROBLEM 3.7

Each of the rules assigns a unique number to all bundles on an indifference curve, and each assigns a utility number to all conceivable bundles. Which rules satisfy condition 1 of our definition of a utility function? Choose two bundles,

$$B_1 = (x_1^1, x_2^1) \quad \text{and} \quad B_2 = (x_1^2, x_2^2)$$

on the ray $x_2 = x_1/2$ and suppose that B_1 is farther from the origin than B_2. Hence, x_1^1 exceeds x_1^2 and x_2^1 exceeds x_2^2, and B_1 is therefore preferred to B_2. The crucial question is: Which of the rules invariably assigns a larger number to B_1 than to B_2? Consider rule 1: Is $10x_1^1$ always greater than $10x_1^2$? Yes. For rule 2: Is $(x_1^1)^{1/2}$ always greater than $(x_1^2)^{1/2}$? Yes. For rule 3: Is $(x_1^1 - 5)^2$ always greater than $(x_1^2 - 5)^2$? Not always: let $x_1^1 = 3$ and $x_1^2 = 2$, for example. We conclude that this rules does not define a utility function. For rule 4: Is x_2^1 always greater than x_2^2? Yes.

PROBLEM 3.8

MRS for the first utility function is 1, and MRS for the second utility function is 3.

PROBLEM 3.9

Beginning at bundle (1, 2), draw a horizontal line to the right to get one "arm" of this indifference curve. Along this arm, MRS is 0. The other arm of the indifference curve is the vertical line drawn upward from bundle (1, 2). On this arm, MRS is infinite. The indifference curve has a right-angled kink at bundle (1, 2), and MRS is not defined at this point.

PROBLEM 3.10

The first indifference curve is a line with slope equal to -1 and is weakly convex. The second is a rectangular hyperbola and is convex. The third is a quarter circle and is nonconvex.

PROBLEM 3.11

MRS of good 3 for good 2 is 2. MRS of good 3 for good 1 is 10.

PROBLEM 4.1

The budget line is

$$p_1x_1 + p_2x_2 = M$$

On the x_1 axis, x_2 is zero. Thus, $p_1x_1 = M$ where the budget line intersects this axis. Hence, $x_1 = M/p_1$ at the intersection. Similarly, on the x_2 axis, x_1 is zero. Hence, $p_2x_2 = M$ or $x_2 = M/p_2$ at this point of intersection. The slope of the budget line is $-p_1/p_2$; hence, the individual must give up p_1/p_2 units of good 2 to get an additional unit of good 1. Conversely, he or she must give up p_2/p_1 units of good 1 to get an additional unit of good 2. As p_1 approaches zero, the budget line becomes horizontal; as p_2 approaches zero, it becomes vertical.

PROBLEM 4.2

Consider any bundle $B = (x_1, x_2)$ on the budget line, and suppose that $x_1 < x_2$. The utility associated with the bundle is then $x_1 = \min(x_1, x_2)$. Thus, staying on the budget line, if we increase x_1 by some small amount, utility will increase, and we see that any bundle in which $x_1 < x_2$ cannot be the utility-maximizing bundle. Similarly, any bundle in which $x_2 > x_1$ cannot be the utility-maximizing bundle. Therefore, the quantities of good 1 and good 2 in the utility-maximizing bundle are identical; that is, $x_1^* = x_2^*$. Combining this result with the budget line, we have $p_1x_1^* + p_2x_1^* = M$. Solving for x_1^*, we have $x_1^* = M/(p_1 + p_2)$, which is the demand function for good 1.

PROBLEM 4.3

We need to check each of these for homogeneity of degree zero in p_1, p_2, and M.

1 Is $aM/(ap_1) = M/p_1$? Yes.

2 Is $[(aM)(ap_2)]/(ap_1) = Mp_2/p_1$? No.

3 Is $aM/[(ap_1)^{1/2}(ap_2)^{1/2}] = M/(p_1^{1/2}p_2^{1/2})$? Yes.

4 Is $1 + (ap_2) - 5(ap_1) + (aM)/20 = 1 + p_2 - 5p_1 + (M/20)$? No.

Thus, 2 and 4 are not acceptable demand functions.

PROBLEM 4.4

1 Is $p_1(M/3p_1) + p_2(2M/3p_2) = M$? Yes.

2 Is $p_1(M/5p_1) + p_2(3M/4p_2) = M$? No.

3 Is $p_1[(M/2) + p_2 - p_1] + p_2[(M/2) + p_1 - p_2] = M$? No.

Thus, 1 is the only one of the three systems of equations that satisfies Engel's aggregation. Notice that the demand functions in 1 are also homogeneous of degree zero in M, p_1, and p_2.

PROBLEM 4.5

Good 1 is an essential good in this case, because MRS is infinite where the indifference curve intersects the x_2 axis. Good 1 is inessential if indifference curves intersect the x_2 axis and if MRS is finite at the point of intersection.

PROBLEM 4.6

When good 2 is inessential and good 1 is essential, we must be concerned with the possibility that $x_2^* = 0$. If $\text{MRS}(x_1 = M/p_1, x_2 = 0) > p_1/p_2$, then $x_1^* = M/p_1$ and $x_2^* = 0$. If the inequality is reversed, then $p_1/p_2 = \text{MRS}(x_1^*, x_2^*)$. In either case, $p_1x_1^* + p_2x_2^* = M$.

PROBLEM 4.7

A \$1 increase in either p_1 or p_2 would cause x_1^* to fall from 60 units to 40 units, and a \$2 increase in M would cause x_1^* to increase from 60 units to 61 units.

PROBLEM 4.8

Statement 1 is false, since a negatively sloped IC can indicate either that x_2 is inferior and x_1 normal or that x_1 is inferior and x_2 normal. Statement 2 is true. Statement 3 is true, supposing as we are that there are just two goods and that the nonsatiation assumption is satisfied. Statement 4 is false—in Problem 4.2, for example, both goods are normal.

PROBLEM 4.9

This case is illustrated in Figure A4.1. For simplicity, we have set both p_1 and p_2 equal to \$1. For income greater than \$80, IC in Figure A4.1a is vertical and the Engel curve in Figure A4.1b is horizontal. For income less than $80, the individual spends all income on good 1 and none on good 2.

(a)

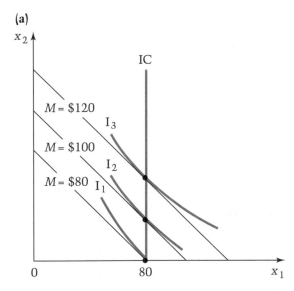

(b)

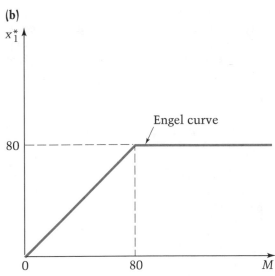

FIGURE A4.1

PROBLEM 4.10

At point D, expenditure on good 1 is $66 and expenditure on good 2 is $44; hence, the income

associated with the compensated budget line is $110. Since prices on the compensated budget line are $p_1 = \$3$ and $p_2 = \$1$, the compensated budget line is $3x_1 + x_2 = 110$. The added income necessary to allow the individual to attain the original indifference curve is $50.

PROBLEM 4.11

See Figure A4.2. The substitution effect leads to an increase in consumption from 14 to 17 units, while the income effect leads to a decrease in consumption from 17 to 12 units. Since consumption decreased when income increased, good 1 is inferior.

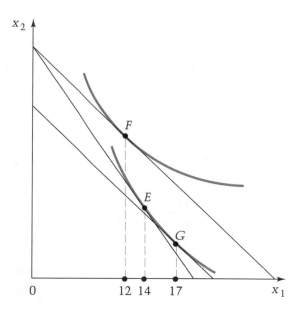

FIGURE A4.2

PROBLEM 4.12

In Figure A4.3, notice that the substitution effect is zero and the compensatory income $45. Since there is no substitution effect, the compensated demand curve is $x_1^{**} = 15$. Given $p_2 = \$1$ and $M = \$30$, the ordinary demand curve is $x_1^* = 30/(1 + p_1)$.

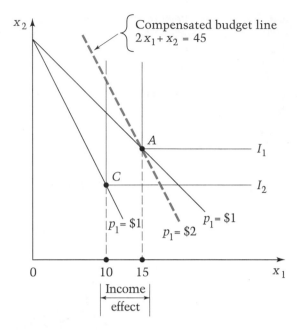

FIGURE A4.3

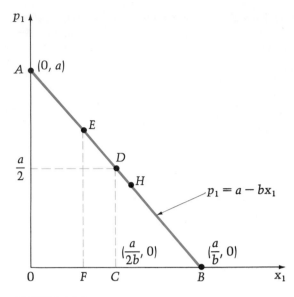

FIGURE A4.4

PROBLEM 4.13

We need the following price-quantity pairs: $p = 9$ and $x_1 = 1$, $p = 8$ and $x_1 = 2$, $p = 3$ and $x_1 = 7$, $p = 2$ and $x_2 = 8$. The two elasticities are then -9 and $-\frac{3}{7}$.

PROBLEM 4.14

In Figure A4.4, we have plotted the linear demand curve $p_1 = a - bx_1$. When $p_1 = a/2$ and $x_1 = a/2b$, the elasticity of demand (at point D in Figure A4.4) is $CB/0C$. But CB and $0C$ are both equal to $a/2b$, and elasticity at point D is therefore 1. Now consider some point to the left of D on the demand function; point E, for example. Elasticity at this point is $FB/0F$. We want to show that $FB/0F > 1$. We know that FB exceeds $a/2b$ and that $0F$ is less than $a/2b$, which establishes the result. An analogous argument establishes that the elasticity at a point such as H to the right of D on the demand function is less than 1. At point A, elasticity is infinite, and at point B it is zero.

PROBLEM 5.1

Figure A5.1 is the graph you need. Because the indifference curve I does not intersect the budget line $p_1x_1 + p_2x_2 = M - tx^*$, the consumer will

choose to remain at point D when the lump-sum tax is substituted for the excise tax.

PROBLEM 5.2

Let x_2 be a composite commodity with price equal to \$1, and m the profit per meal under the first option; that is, let $m = p_1 - 50$. In Figure A5.2, m

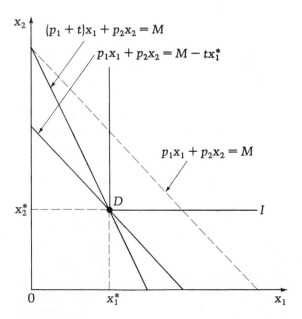

FIGURE A5.1

is, by construction, the profit per meal required to cover the cost per member; that is, $mx_1^* = 1000$. Given this pricing scheme, the representative member chooses point D on indifference curve I. Notice that distance $DC = \$1000 = mx^*$. If the club chooses to sell meals at the $50 per meal cost and to cover overhead costs by a membership fee equal to $1000, the consumer will choose some bundle on segment DE of budget line $50x_1 + x_2 = M - 1000$, a bundle strictly preferred to point D.

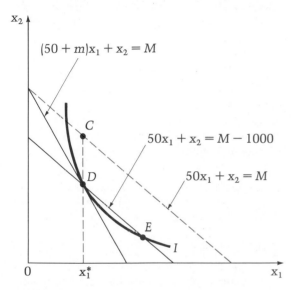

FIGURE A5.2

PROBLEM 5.3

Pick two prices for good 1, $p_1' > p_1''$. On one diagram, use the technique developed in Figure 5.2 to identify the CV associated with each price. You will see immediately that the CV associated with p_1'' exceeds the CV associated with p_1'. This result is consistent with common sense—it says that the value associated with the privilege of buying good 1 at price p_1 decreases as p_1 increases.

PROBLEM 5.4

For this price decrease, the distance labeled CV in Figure 5.3 is the equivalent variation, and the distance labeled EV is the compensating variation.

PROBLEM 5.5

The benefit of a price decrease from $60 to $40 is $500, and the benefit of being able to buy the good

at a price of $50, as opposed to not being able to buy it at all, is $625.

PROBLEM 5.6

Figure A5.3 is useful here. If the price of film is equal to its $1 cost, then the firm's profit is the area of triangle GAF less $5, because the firm just breaks even on its film sales, the area of triangle GAF is the price of the camera, and the cost of producing the camera is $5. At the lower price p_1', the price of the camera increases by the area of the trapezoid $p'GFM$, but the firm incurs a loss on sales of film equal to the area of the rectangle $p'GHM$. The net decrease in its profit, relative to the situation in which film is sold at cost, is the area of the triangle FHM.

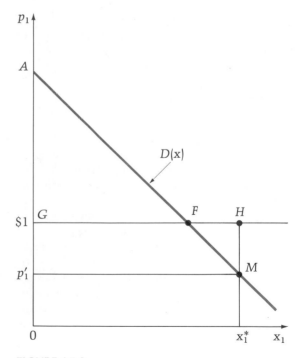

FIGURE A5.3

PROBLEM 5.7

The relevant diagram is Figure A5.4. At wage w', the individual supplies h' hours of labor. At wage w'', larger than w', the individual supplies h'' hours of labor. Notice that h'' is less than h'. Leisure is a normal good in this case.

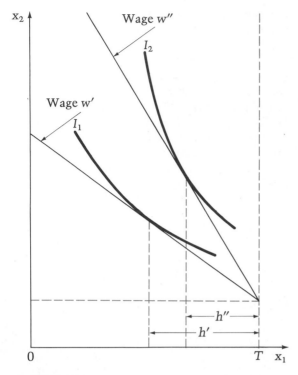

FIGURE A5.4

PROBLEM 5.8

Because B^1 lies above the period-0 budget line, we infer that the expenditure required to purchase B^1 at period-0 prices exceeds actual expenditure or income in period 0. This implies that L exceeds 1. Because B^0 lies above the period-1 budget line, we infer that the expenditure required to purchase B^0 at period-1 prices exceeds actual expenditure or income in period 1. This implies that P is less than 1. To see that it is impossible (without further information) to tell which is the preferred bundle, begin by drawing an indifference curve in Figure 5.13 such that the individual is indifferent between bundles B^0 and B^1.

PROBLEM 5.9

The Paasche and Laspeyres quantity indexes are $\frac{120}{115}$ and $\frac{145}{120}$, respectively. The Paasche and Laspeyres price indexes are $\frac{120}{145}$ and $\frac{115}{120}$, respectively.

PROBLEM 5.10

These present values are $300 when $i = 0$, $272.32 when $i = .05$, $248.68 when $i = .1$, $181.61 when $i = .3$.

PROBLEM 6.1

Only you can answer this question.

PROBLEM 6.2

$950 = (\frac{2}{6})\$1800 + (\frac{1}{6})\$3000 - (\frac{3}{6})\$300.$

PROBLEM 6.3

When he has no initial wealth, Chauncy's expected utility from playing Risk is 4, his reservation price is $0.50, and he'll take A in preference to playing Risk when A is $0.75. When his initial wealth is $1, his expected utility from playing Risk is 7.5.

PROBLEM 6.4

The first object pays $10,000 with probability .25, $6000 with probability .25, and $1000 with probability .5, and its expected value is $4500. The expected values of the other prospects are $5300, $7500, and $6000.

PROBLEM 6.5

For Jack, the number e^* is .75, and for Jane the number e^* is greater than .75.

PROBLEM 6.6

Beginning with prospect $(1/3, 1/3, 1/3)$, the substitution assumption says that we can create another prospect, equally attractive to Jack, by substituting the prospect $(3/4, 0, 1/4)$ for the $6000 prize. In this newly created prospect, the probability of the $10,000 prize is $1/3$ plus $1/3$ times $3/4$, or $7/12$; the probability of the $6000 prize is 0; and the probability of the $1000 prize is $1/3$ plus $1/3$ times $1/4$, or $5/12$. The newly created prospect is then $(7/12, 0, 5/12)$. Similarly, beginning with prospect $(1/2, 1/4, 1/4)$, when we substitute $(3/4, 0, 1/4)$ for the $6000 prize, we get $(11/16, 0, 5/16)$.

PROBLEM 6.7

Jack's utility function is $U(10,000) = 1$, $U(1,000) = 0$, and $U(6,000) = 3/4$ since e^* is $3/4$ for Jack.

PROBLEM 6.8

To find Jack's preference ordering for these prospects, we can compute their expected utilities. For the first prospect, Jack's expected utility is $(1/2$

times 1) plus (1/4 times 3/4) plus (1/4 times 0), or 33/48. The expected utilities for the remaining prospects are, respectively, 28/48, 36/48, 28/48, 30/48, 36/48. Hence, Jack's preference ordering for these prospects is as follows: first, (0, 1, 0) and (3/4, 0, 1/4); second, (1/2, 1/4, 1/4); third, (1/4, 1/2, 1/4); fourth, (1/3, 1/3, 1/3) and (7/12, 0, 5/12).

PROBLEM 6.9

For Melvin, the expected utility of the risky prospect is 2.5, and the expected utility of $25 is 5; hence, he prefers $25. For Jane, the expected utility of the risky prospect is 25, and the expected utility of $25 is also 25; hence, she is indifferent. For Baby Doe, the expected utility of the risky prospect is 2500, and the expected utility of $25 is 625; hence, she prefers the risky prospect.

PROBLEM 6.10

Notice that in the relevant graph, Figure A6.1, EG exceeds EF.

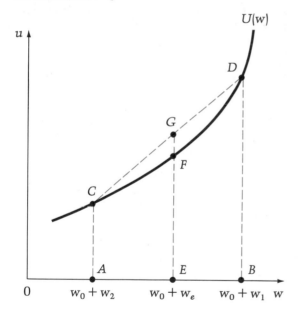

FIGURE A6.1

PROBLEM 6.11

The expected utility of the risk-pooling agreement is $1/100 + (18/100)(1/2)^{1/2}$, and the expected utility with no agreement is $1/10$. As you can easily verify, the expected utility of the risk-pooling agreement is the larger one.

PROBLEM 6.12

In Figure A6.2, I_r is distance HB, whereas $pL = I_s$ is distance AB; AB exceeds HB.

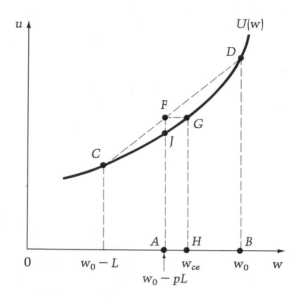

FIGURE A6.2

PROBLEM 6.13

Patricia will not buy this asset alone because $(100)^{1/2}$, her expected utility if she does not buy it, exceeds $(1/20)(10,000)^{1/2}$, her expected utility if she does buy it. If she joins a syndicate with 10 equal partners, her expected utility is $(1/20)(1090)^{1/2} + (19/20)(90)^{1/2}$, which exceeds $(100)^{1/2}$, so she would join the syndicate.

PROBLEM 6.14

If all three groups sold their cars, the market price would be $1920, equal to .6 times $2400 plus .4 times $1200. But this price is not large enough to induce those potential sellers of jewels whose reservations prices are $2000 to part with them. Hence, in equilibrium, all the cars will not be sold. If the last two groups sold their cars, the market price would be $1800, equal to .5 times $2400 plus .5 times $1200. Since $1800 exceeds $1600, in equilibrium, these two groups will sell their cars, but the first group will not. The market failure is that the first group of potential sellers, who would gladly sell their jewels at the $2400 value of a jewel, do not, in fact, sell them.

PROBLEM 6.15

With no signaling, the common wage w would be $s\$50 + (1-s)\$20$. Superior workers will acquire a degree if $10w < 500 - 200$. This inequality reduces to $s < 1/3$. Hence, superior workers will acquire a degree to signal their superior productivity if s is less than $1/3$.

PROBLEM 7.1

The salesperson can offer to pay the customer's premium for the first year. If the customer accepts, he or she gets free insurance for 1 year and the salesperson pockets $500. If the customer then cancels the policy after the first year, the insurance company is an obvious loser. This sort of scam was recently exposed in Ontario.

PROBLEM 7.2

The president is (arguably) the person who makes the decisions that affect the company's profit and therefore the value of its stock. The stock option gives the president an incentive to make decisions that enhance the value of the company's stock. For example, if the president makes a decision that increases the value of the company's stock to $15, the president can make $50,000 by making the appropriate decision, buying 10,000 shares at $10 per share, and then selling the 10,000 shares at $15 per share. If the president fails to make the appropriate decision in the absence of the stock option, then that option is clearly valuable to the company's stockholders — in this case, the stock option means that the value of each share will increase by $5.

PROBLEM 7.3

Regardless of the number of individuals in the partnership, the solution lies on the line $y_R = e_R$ in your diagram. Where? Suppose n is the number of individuals. The solution is at the point on this line where MRS is equal to $1/n$, because each individual gets this fraction of the total income generated by the partnership. As n increases, these solutions move toward the origin; the larger is n, the smaller is each individual's utility at the solution.

PROBLEM 7.4

The appropriate diagram is Figure A7.1. For larger values of B, the partnership is Pareto-preferred,

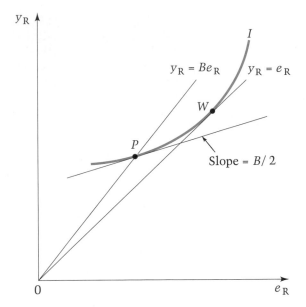

FIGURE A7.1

and for smaller values, the one-person firm is Pareto-preferred.

PROBLEM 7.5

See Figure A7.2.

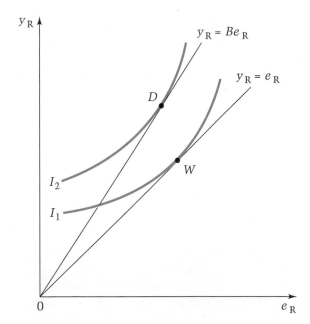

FIGURE A7.2

PROBLEM 7.6

In Figure 7.6, if we interpret e_R as Robert's effort, Robert's income-effort relationship is composed of the two horizontal segments $0e'$ and VG. Supposing that Robert supplies e' units of effort and interpreting e_R as Virginia's effort, Virginia's income-effort relationship is the line labeled $Y_R = Be_R - M/2$ in Figure 7.6.

PROBLEM 7.7

Figure A7.3 is the required diagram.

1 If we increase M by a small amount, the one-person firm is Pareto-preferred.

2 If we increase B by a small amount, the owner-managed firm is Pareto-preferred.

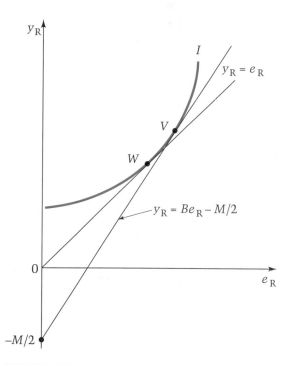

FIGURE A7.3

PROBLEM 7.8

If there is just one worker and if he or she has expended 180 minutes in setup time, then he or she has 300 minutes left. Dividing this time equally between the two stages, he or she can pro-

duce 15 units. If there are two workers and if one specializes in each stage, then the worker in stage 1 can process 42 units, but the worker in stage 2 can process only 36. Thus, we cannot fully utilize the effort of the stage-1 worker. To maximize productivity per worker, we want each worker to specialize, so that he or she incurs only one setup cost, and we want to fully utilize the 8 hours of each worker's time. This means that the number of workers in stage 1—let's call this number N—times 42 must be equal to the number of workers in stage 2—let's call this number M—times 36. That is, we want two integers N and M such that $42N = 36M$, or such that $N/M = 36/42 = 6/7$. Then N equal to 6 and M equal to 7 will do (as will 12 and 14, or 18 and 21, and so on). The 13 workers can produce 252 units.

PROBLEM 7.9

In many cases, it is in the property owner's self-interest. Consider, for example, an owner who is developing a property for resale. The Mechanic's Lien Act assures tradespeople that they will be paid and therefore makes it easier for the property owner to contract with tradespeople. In the absence of such an act, the tradespeople might well demand some other form of assurance that they will be paid, and the assurance is likely to be costly for the property owner.

PROBLEM 8.1

Two units of seviche use all the available red snapper, so the restaurant can make just two units of ceviche. The production function is

$$y = \min(z_1/16, z_2/3, z_3, z_4/8)$$

PROBLEM 8.2

This bundle will produce at most 600 miles, and the speed required is 60 mph. If the car is driven at 40 mph, the truck can be driven only 400 miles, and if it is driven at 80 mph, it can be driven only 450 miles.

PROBLEM 8.3

The equivalent annual rental rate is $121.

PROBLEM 8.4

The total product functions are $120z_1^{1/2}$ when $z_2 = 12$, and $180z_1^{1/2}$ when $z_2 = 27$.

PROBLEM 8.5

The associated marginal product function is

$$MP(z_1) = 1 \quad \text{if } z_1 \leq 10$$
$$MP(z_1) = 0 \quad \text{if } z_1 > 10$$

PROBLEM 8.6

The average product function is

$$AP(z_1) = 120/z_1^{1/2}$$

PROBLEM 8.7

See Figure A8.1.

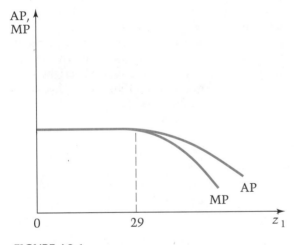

FIGURE A8.1

PROBLEM 8.8

From Problem 8.4, the total product function is

$$TP(z_1) = 180z_1^{1/2}$$

The minimum time necessary to drive y miles is then

$$z_1^* = y^2/32,400$$

and the variable cost function is

$$VC(y) = w_1 y^2 / 32,400$$

PROBLEM 8.9

See $AFC(y)$ in Figure 8.10b.

PROBLEM 8.10

$STC(y)$ is simply $VC(y) + FC$. Since FC does not depend on y, for any y, the slope of $STC(y)$ is equal to the slope of $VC(y)$.

PROBLEM 8.11

Since ACC_2 is always \$5 and ACC_1 is \$5 when N_1 is 3600, if there are more than 3600 commuters, in equilibrium, 3600 will use Route 1 and the rest will use Route 2. If there are fewer than 3600 commuters, all of them will use Route 1.

PROBLEM 8.12

Since MCC_2 is always \$5 and MCC_1 is \$5 when N_1 is 2000, if there are more than 2000 commuters, in the cost-benefit optimum, 2000 should use Route 1 and the rest should use Route 2. If there are fewer than 2000 commuters, all of them should use Route 1.

PROBLEM 9.1

See Figure 9.2.

PROBLEM 9.2

We know that

$$MRTS(z_1, z_2) = MP_1(z_1, z_2)/MP_2(z_1, z_2)$$

This cannot be negative as long as both marginal products are positive. If $MP_2(z_1, z_2)$ were zero, the isoquant would be vertical; if $MP_1(z_1, z_2)$ were zero, the isoquant would be horizontal.

PROBLEM 9.3

The MRTS of wood for coal is 2.5. The MRTS of coal for wood is .4.

PROBLEM 9.4

If $2w_1 < 5w_2$, then $z_1^* = y/5$, $z_2^* = 0$, and $TC(w_1, w_2, y) = w_1 y/5$. If $2w_1 > 5w_2$, then $z_1^* = 0$, $z_2^* = y/2$, and $TC(w_1, w_2, y) = w_2 y/2$. If $2w_1 = 5w_2$, any bundle on the y-unit isoquant is cost minimizing, and $TC(w_1, w_2, y) = w_1 y/5 = w_2 y/2$.

PROBLEM 9.5

The slope is $-w_1/w_2$. The opportunity cost of input 1 in terms of input 2 is w_1/w_2 because, to get an additional unit of input 1, you must give up w_1/w_2 units of input 2. The isocost line intersects the z_1 axis at $z_1 = c/w_1$ and the z_2 axis at $z_2 = c/w_2$.

PROBLEM 9.6

When $w_1 = \$6$ and $w_2 = \$2$, or when $w_1 = \$12$ and $w_2 = \$4$, the conditional input demand functions are $z_1^* = y/60$ and $z_2^* = y/20$. (For each mile, we need 1 minute of the driver's time and $\frac{1}{20}$ of a gallon of gas.) When $w_1 = \$6$ and $w_2 = \$2$, the cost function is $y/5$ (each mile costs \$0.20), and when we double the input prices, it is $2y/5$ (each mile costs \$0.40).

PROBLEM 9.7

Simply reinterpret the argument based on Figure 4.12.

PROBLEM 9.8

First let's show that the cost-minimizing bundle does not change. Given the initial prices w_1 and w_2, at the initial cost-minimizing bundle (z_1^*, z_2^*), we know that $MRTS(z_1^*, z_2^*) = w_1/w_2$. Given the higher prices $2w_1$ and $2w_2$, we must show that MRTS at the initial cost-minimizing bundle (z_1^*, z_2^*) is equal to $2w_1/2w_2$, or that $MRTS(z_1^*, z_2^*) = 2w_1/2w_2$. Canceling the 2s, we have the desired result. Hence the cost-minimizing bundle doesn't change when both input prices double. The second result then follows easily: the cost-minimizing bundle costs twice as much because prices have doubled.

PROBLEM 9.9

Both inputs are normal — as y increases, more of each input is used. When the input prices

are equal, the output-expansion path is the line $z_2 = z_1$.

PROBLEM 9.10

Tipple's expansion path is $z_2 = 10z_1$, since at any point on this ray, MRTS is equal to 10 (or w_1/w_2).

PROBLEM 9.11

No. If the expansion path is one of the two axes, we have an extreme case. If, for example, the expansion path is the z_1 axis, input 1 is normal and input 2 is neither normal nor inferior (since $z_2^* = 0$). Except in these two extreme cases, when the production function is homothetic, both inputs are normal.

PROBLEM 9.12

When $w_1 = w_2 = \$5$, the expansion path is the ray $z_2 = z_1$. The input bundle that minimizes the cost of 1 mile is $z_1 = z_2 = 1/(1200)^{1/2}$, and $Y(s) = s$.

PROBLEM 9.13

The scale elasticity of output is (slope of the tangent line)/(slope of the ray). When $Y(s) = s$, the slope of the tangent line is always equal to the slope of the ray, implying universal constant returns to scale. When $Y(s) = s^{1/2}$, the slope of the tangent line is always less than the slope of the ray, implying universal decreasing returns to scale. When $Y(s) = s^2$, the slope of the tangent line is always greater than the slope of the ray, implying universal increasing returns to scale.

PROBLEM 9.14

The scale elasticity of output is (slope of the tangent line)/(slope of the ray). In Figure 9.9, the slope of the tangent line is greater than, less than, or equal to the slope of the ray as s is less than, greater than, or equal to s'. Hence, we have increasing, decreasing, or constant returns to scale as s is less than, greater than, or equal to s'. $Y(s)/s$ is just the slope of the ray, which is at a maximum when $s = s'$.

PROBLEM 9.15

With $y = s^2$, to produce y units of output, we need $s = y^{1/2}$, which costs $5y^{1/2}$ when $c'' = 5$. With $y =$

$s^{1/2}$, to produce y units of output, we need $s = y^2$, which costs $7y^2$ when $c'' = 7$.

PROBLEM 9.16

See Figure A9.1.

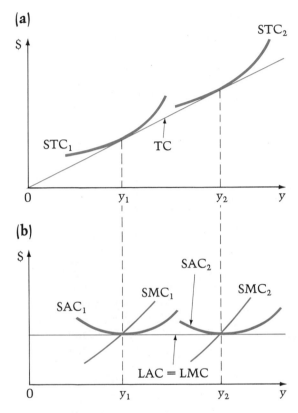

(a)

(b)

FIGURE A9.1

PROBLEM 10.1

The range of equilibrium prices is unchanged. Any price less than or equal to $60 and greater than $50 is a competitive equilibrium price. In this case, only two units are traded in the equilibrium: individuals G and J sell and C and E buy. The final allocation of tickets is the same: individuals A, B, C, D, and E end up with tickets. The individuals who are (unambiguously) better off are those who were initially given tickets this time around but not the first time around. Similarly, those who are (unambiguously) worse off are those who were not initially given a ticket this time but were the first time.

PROBLEM 10.2

There are two competitive equilibria. (1) Consider any price less than or equal to $10. Harry and Sarah will buy or not sell at any such price. Similarly, Jane and Bob will sell or not buy, given that their mate does not end up with a ticket. Therefore, for any such price, we have a competitive equilibrium, with Harry and Sarah holding tickets. This equilibrium is not Pareto-optimal because Jane and Bob together would be willing to offer more than $20 to Harry and Sarah for the pair of tickets, and Harry and Sarah would be willing to accept such an offer. (2) Any price greater than $10 but less than or equal to $20 is a competitive equilibrium price, and the equilibrium allocation at this price leaves the tickets in the hands of Jane and Bob.

PROBLEM 10.3

In this case, any price between $45 and $50 is a market-clearing price; two units are traded; Earl and the suppliers with the three lowest reservation prices lose; the demanders with the two highest reservation prices gain.

PROBLEM 10.4

Because, when price exceeds $12, one individual demands a zero quantity. Distance $0D$ is equal to 21 units.

PROBLEM 10.5

First multiply the right-hand side of the individual demand function by 1000 to get $y = 1000 - p$, and then invert this function to get $p = 1000 - y$.

PROBLEM 10.6

See Figure A10.1. As we have drawn the diagram, the profit-maximizing output is $y^* = 35$. Why does the firm produce anything when its profit is negative? If it produced nothing, its profit would be $-FC$, which is equal to -1 times the area of rectangle $ABCD$. Why? By producing $y^* = 35$, the firm incurs the smaller loss equal to -1 times the area of rectangle $GBCE$. Thus, by producing 35 units, the firm incurs a smaller loss than it would if it produced nothing.

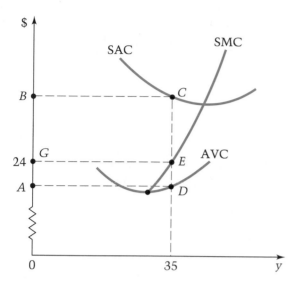

FIGURE A10.1

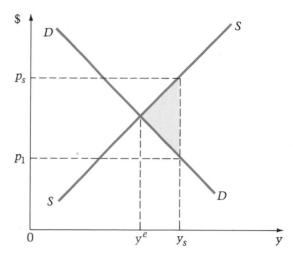

FIGURE A10.2

PROBLEM 10.7

Just multiply quantity supplied by one firm by the number of firms.

PROBLEM 10.8

The $10 excise tax shifts each firm's supply function and the industry supply function vertically upward by $10. If industry demand is perfectly inelastic, equilibrium price increases by $10 and equilibrium quantity does not change. If demand is not perfectly inelastic, equilibrium price increases by less than $10, and quantity decreases.

PROBLEM 10.9

Equilibrium price is $500 and equilibrium quantity is 500 units. Producers' surplus and consumers' surplus are each $125,000.

PROBLEM 10.10

Figure A10.2 is useful. Here, p_s is the support price and y_s the quantity supplied at that price. Suppose that the agency buys all the output y_s and then sells it. The price received will then be p_1. The agency will incur a deficit equal to $(p_s - p_1) \times y_s$. The surplus destroyed is the green area in the diagram. Relative to the competitive equilibrium, it represents the excess of the cost of producing $y_s - y^e$ additional units over the consumers' willingness to pay for those units. Now

suppose that the agency simply buys the quantity that cannot be sold on the market at price p_s and stores it in some warehouse. Its deficit will then be $p_s \times y_s - y_2$ in Figure A10.3 plus storage costs. The surplus destroyed in this bizarre case is the green area in Figure A10.3. Why? This is essentially the policy that the EEC has recently pursued with respect to butter. Millions of pounds of butter were being stored in government warehouses in Europe at the time we wrote this.

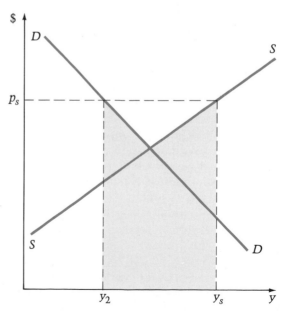

FIGURE A10.3

PROBLEM 11.1

The key to answering this problem is to notice that elasticity is equal to 1 when $y = a/2b$. You may want to review Problem 4.14.

PROBLEM 11.2

Beginning at $y = 11$ in Figure 11.4, the increase in revenue associated with an additional unit of output exceeds the increase in cost, since MR exceeds MC to the right of 11 units of output; hence, profit increases as output increases. Beginning again at $y = 11$ in Figure 11.4, the decrease in revenue associated with 1 less unit of output is less than the decrease in cost, since MC exceeds MR to the left of 11 units of output; hence, profit increases as output decreases. Thus, profit is at a minimum when output is 11 units in Figure 11.4.

PROBLEM 11.3

Let's solve the problem algebraically. The "marginal revenue equals marginal cost" condition is $10 - 2y = 4$, which yields $y^* = 3$. Price is then $p^* = 10 - 3 = 7$, and profit is $3(7 - 4)$, or 9.

PROBLEM 11.4

Beginning at the point where MR = MC, profit falls as the firm produces more output, and profit increases as the firm produces less output. Hence, to maximize profit, the firm produces nothing.

PROBLEM 11.5

The answer to part 1 is to sell 5 books at a price equal to \$35. Profit is \$135. There are obviously unrealized gains from trade equal to \$30 − \$8 plus \$25 − \$8 plus \$20 − \$8 plus \$15 − \$8 plus \$10 − \$8. In part 2, the book vendor sells a book to each individual whose reservation price exceeds \$8. The price charged is the individual's reservation price. The solution is efficient because the only demander who does not buy a book has a reservation price of \$5, which is less than the book vendor's marginal cost.

PROBLEM 11.6

In your diagram, the residual demand function should intersect the entrant's AC function at two levels of output — say y' and y'' — with $y' < y''$. Any level of output for the potential entrant

larger than y' and less than y'' offers the entrant a positive profit; therefore, this is not a case of natural monopoly.

PROBLEM 11.7

Let output y^* be the profit-maximizing output in the absence of the tax. Then $\pi(y^*) > \pi(y)$ for any y not equal to y^*. Given the tax, the firm's profit is just $.9\pi(y)$. Since $\pi(y^*) > \pi(y)$ for any y not equal to y^*, $.9\pi(y^*) > .9\pi(y)$ for any y not equal to y^*. The profit-maximizing output therefore does not change. The monopolist's profit, of course, does change.

PROBLEM 11.8

In each market, it will sell the quantity at which marginal revenue is zero. Hence, it will sell 24 units in the first market and 40 in the second. This result is consistent with the rule we developed.

PROBLEM 11.9

In Figure A11.1, we have drawn both demand and marginal revenue functions and the marginal cost function. The aggregated marginal revenue function is the heavy line composed of MR_1 for y less than y_1^* and $MR_2 = p_2$ for y greater than y_1^*. The profit-maximizing output is y^*, of which y_1^* is sold in the first market at price p_1^*, and $y^* - y_1^*$ is sold in the second market at price p_2.

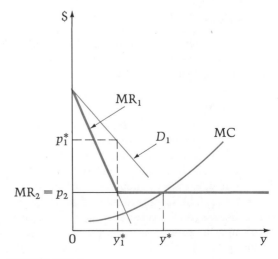

FIGURE A11.1

PROBLEM 11.10

First, Canadian Tire induces buyers with ready cash to part with it rather than to use their credit cards; receiving cash is valuable to Canadian Tire because credit card companies charge the retailer for their services. Thus, there is a form of price discrimination between customers with and without ready cash. Second, among those who receive the cash discount, some proportion do not take it: they lose the Canadian Tire "money" or never return to a Canadian Tire store.

PROBLEM 11.11

1   The profit-maximizing block limit is 21 units, the monopolist's profit is $366 (an increase of $42), and Sam is neither better off nor worse off.

2   The profit-maximizing block limit is 30 units, the monopolist's profit is $420, and Sam is neither better off nor worse off.

PROBLEM 12.1

The payoff matrix is presented below. Payoffs are equal to −1 times the sentence, and hence are negative. F stands for "fink" (provide evidence), and M stands for "mum" (don't provide evidence). In each pair, the first element is Bonnie's payoff and the second Clyde's. Regardless of what Clyde does, fink maximizes Bonnie's payoff. Similarly, regardless of what Bonnie does, fink maximizes Clyde's payoff.

		Clyde's Strategy	
		M	F
Bonnie's	M	−2/−2	−10/−1
Strategy	F	−1/−10	−5/−5

PROBLEM 12.2

The first firm's marginal revenue function is $(100 - y_2 - y_3) - 2y_1$. Setting this equal to marginal cost (40) and solving for y_1^*, we have

$$y_1^* = 30 - \frac{y_2 + y_3}{2}$$

Using the fact that the output of all three firms will be the same in the equilibrium, we set y_1^*, y_2, and y_3 equal to y' in this expression and solve for y', the output of each of the three firms in the Cournot equilibrium: $y' = 15$. Aggregate output is then 45 and price 55. Profit of each firm is 225.

PROBLEM 12.3

Suppose first that there are just three parties to the agreement. The cheater will produce 20 units, aggregate output will be 40 units, and price will be $60. The cheater's profit will be $400, and the inducement to cheat $100 since each firm gets $300 in the collusive agreement. If there were four parties to the agreement, the cheater would produce 18.75 units, aggregate output would be 41.25 units, and price would be $58.75. The cheater's profit would be $351.56, and the inducement to cheat $126.26, since each firm gets $225 in the collusive agreement.

PROBLEM 12.4

Suppose that a collusive solution has been in place for some time and that all sales have included the most-favored-customer clause. Then, by cheating, the firm gets the standard payoff identified above, but it incurs a loss equal to the difference between the collusive price and the discount price times the total quantity sold at the collusive price under the most-favored-customer clause. Therefore, if the most-favored-customer clause has been in effect long enough, no firm will cheat.

PROBLEM 12.5

See Figure A12.1.

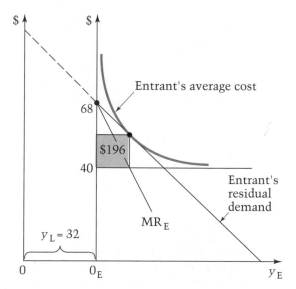

FIGURE A12.1

PROBLEM 12.6

When there is no threat of entry, the statement is true, since marginal revenue is negative in the inelastic portion of the demand curve. However, in the limit-output model, it is entirely possible that the monopolist will produce where demand is inelastic. So, if entry is a possibility, and if we accept the limit output model, the statement is false.

PROBLEM 12.7

In the Bertrand duopoly equilibrium, price is equal to marginal cost. An entrant would therefore anticipate price equal to marginal cost after entry; hence the inducement to entry is $0. Therefore, if K is positive there will be no entry.

PROBLEM 12.8

Given n established firms, an entrant's profit would be $900/(n+1) - K$. The no-entry condition is then $900/(n+1) - K \leq 0$. Industrywide profit, given collusive behavior and sequential entry, is $100 when K is $400 and $100 when K is $100. Using Figure 12.7, we see that industrywide profit, given Cournot behavior and sequential entry, is $500 when K is $400 and $176 when K is $100.

PROBLEM 13.1

Consumers 1 through 6, 19, and 20 prefer A to B and C at a common price. Customers 1, 2, and 19 switch to B, and 3, 4, and 20 switch to C as p_A rises above $p' + e$. Customers 7, 8, and 21 switch from B to A, and 13, 14, and 23 switch from C to A as p_A drops below $p' - e$. At the common price p', customers 7 through 12, 21, and 22 prefer B to A and C. As p_B drops below $p' - e$, customers 1, 2, 15, 16, 19, and 24 switch to B.

PROBLEM 13.2

In Figure A13.1, p^* is the collusive price. If one firm charges p^*, the price that maximizes the other's profit is p'.

PROBLEM 13.3

The collusive solution in Figure A13.2 is for each firm to charge p^* and sell y^*. With the beliefs outlined in the problem, the demand function is the heavy line coincident with dd to the left of y^*

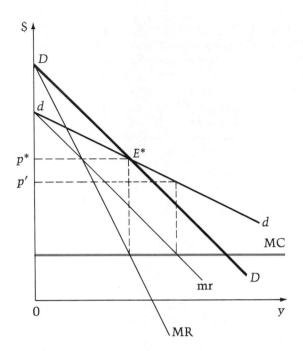

FIGURE A13.1

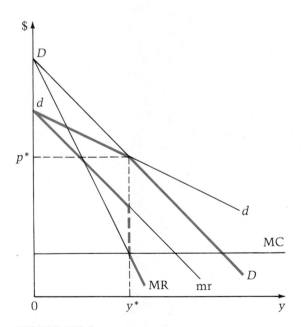

FIGURE A13.2

and coincident with DD to the right of y^*. Similarly, the marginal revenue function is coincident with mr to the left of y^* and with MR to the right of y^*. Notice the discontinuity of the marginal revenue function at y^*, indicated by the heavy dashed line. With these beliefs, firms have no incentive to depart from the collusive solution.

PROBLEM 13.4

Suppose that A is initially available and that B is the second product introduced. When B is introduced, consumers 1 through 6 are no better off. The amounts by which each of consumers 7 through 24 are better off, measured in units of e, are: 1, 1, 2, 3, 2, 3, 0, 0, 1, 2, 0, 1, 0, 0, 1, 2, 0, 1. The total consumers' surplus associated with the second product is thus $20e$. Similarly, the consumers' surplus associated with the fourth product is $6e$. The efficient degree of product diversity is three products because the consumers' surplus associated with the third product is $10e$, which exceeds $K = 8e$, and because the consumers' surplus associated with the fourth product is $6e$, which is less than $K = 8e$.

PROBLEM 13.5

The market boundary between the entrant and the firm to its right is $[p^e + (L/2) - p_E]/2$. Quantity demanded, y_E, is twice this amount. The entrant's demand function is then $p_E = p^e + (L/2) - y_E$. Setting marginal revenue equal to marginal cost c, we have $y_E^* = [p^e + (L/2) - c]/2$, which is equal to $3L/4$ since $p^e - L + c$. The other results follow from substitutions of y_E^* in the entrant's demand and profit functions.

PROBLEM 13.6

An entrant between two firms L units apart would have a market equal to $L/2$, and its profit would be $(L/2) - K$. Notice that $(L/2) - K \le 0$ implies $L \le 2K$, the no-entry condition. An established firm's profit, given L, is $L - K$, which is equal to K when $L = 2K$.

PROBLEM 13.7

From Problem 13.6, we know that the no-entry condition is $L \le 2K$. Because revenue is independent of the number of outlets, the profit-maximizing strategy is to establish as few (evenly spaced) outlets as possible, subject to the no-entry condition: no two outlets can be farther apart than $2K$. If C is the circumference of the circle, then the number of outlets that maximizes your profit is approximately $C/(2K)$.

PROBLEM 14.1

For z just larger then z', $MP(z) > a'$; therefore, beginning at z', profit increases as z increases. Beginning again at z', profit increases as z decreases because $a' > MP(z)$ for z just smaller than z'; therefore, profit is at a (local) minimum at z'. An analogous argument establishes that profit is a maximum at z^*.

PROBLEM 14.2

Profit at z''' is $z''' [AP(z''') - a''']$, which is negative since $AP(z''') < a'''$. By producing nothing, the firm's profit is zero. The firm therefore maximizes profit by hiring no fishers.

PROBLEM 14.3

When $p = \$1$, simply relabel MP as MRP and AP as ARP. When $p = \$2$, shift MP and AP vertically up by a factor of 2 and attach the labels MRP and ARP.

PROBLEM 14.4

Because, by definition, $MRP(z) = MR(y)MP(z)$, we can rewrite the input market profit-maximizing rule, $w = MRP(z^*)$, as $w = MR(y^*)MP(z^*)$. Dividing both sides by $MP(z^*)$, we have $w/MP(z^*) = MR(y^*)$. But $w/MP(z^*)$ is $SMC(y^*)$. Therefore, we can again rewrite the input market rule as $SMC(y^*) = MR(y^*)$, which is the output market profit-maximizing rule.

PROBLEM 14.5

Let y^* denote the positive output at which marginal cost is equal to p. The firm will produce no output if $p < AVC(y^*)$. But from Section 8.5, we know that $AVC(y) = w/AP(z)$. Therefore, we can rewrite the shutdown condition for the output market as $p < w/AP(z^*)$ or as $pAP(z^*) < w$. But, by definition, $pAP(z) = ARP(z)$. Therefore, we can rewrite the shutdown condition as $ARP(z^*) < w$, which is the input market shutdown condition we just defined.

PROBLEM 14.6

By definition, $MRP(z) = MR(y)MP(z)$, and $VMP(z) = pMP(z)$. In a competitive output market, $MR(y^*) = p$; therefore, $VMP(z^*) = MRP(z^*)$ for a firm that is a perfect competitor in its output market. In a monopolistic output market,

$MR(y^*) < p$; therefore, $VMP(z^*) > MRP(z^*)$ in this case. Be sure that you understand these simple but important relationships.

PROBLEM 14.7

The total factor cost of z units is $z(1 + z)$, and the total factor cost of $z + \Delta z$ units is $(z + \Delta z)(1 + z + \Delta z)$. Subtracting the first of these from the second, we have $\Delta z(1 + 2z) + (\Delta z)^2$. To get marginal factor cost, divide by Δz to obtain $1 + 2z + \Delta z$, and let Δz go to zero to get $MFC(z) = 1 + 2z$. More generally, if $S(z) = a + bz$, then $MFC(z) = a + 2bz$.

PROBLEM 14.8

At z^*, MRP is equal to MFC. From Problem 14.7, we know that MFC is $1 + 2z$ in this case. Hence, $10 - z^* = 1 + 2z^*$, or $z^* = 3$, and $w^* = 1 + z^* = 4$.

PROBLEM 14.9

The supply function and the marginal factor cost of each unit are given in Table A14.1. In computing marginal factor cost, we assume that the firm pays the minimum price. When marginal revenue product is 200, the firm buys 5 tons.

TABLE A14.1

Input price	Tons supplied	Marginal factor cost
$w < 105$	0	
$105 \le w < 115$	1	105
$115 \le w < 125$	2	125
$125 \le w < 135$	3	145
$135 \le w < 145$	4	165
$145 \le w < 155$	5	185
$155 \le w < 165$	6	205
$165 \le w < 175$	7	225
$175 \le w < 185$	8	245
$185 \le w < 195$	9	265
$195 \le w$	10	285

PROBLEM 14.10

The demander will obviously pay any supplier $100 per ton for any coal it buys. It will buy the coal supplied by any supplier if $100 plus the transport cost the demander must pay is less than the demander's marginal revenue product, $200. The cost of transporting a ton of coal from the most distant supplier is $95 = 950 \times \$0.10$. The demander therefore will buy all 10 tons. It will pay $1000 in total to the suppliers, and $5 + $15 + $25 + \cdots + $95 to transport the coal.

PROBLEM 14.11

To generate these results, simply observe that when the interest rate increases, the line in quadrant 1 that captures Hotelling's law is steeper, intersecting the locus of market-clearing prices at a point where w_1 is smaller and w_2 larger.

PROBLEM 15.1

At point A, Shelly has 23 units of good 1 and 32 of good 2, while Marvin has 79 units of good 1 and 34 of good 2. At point 0_M, Shelly has 0 units of good 1 and 0 of good 2, while Marvin has 102 units of good 1 and 66 of good 2. At point B, Shelly has 102 units of good 1 and 0 of good 2, while Marvin has 0 units of good 1 and 66 of good 2. At point E, Shelly has 66 units of good 1 and 0 of good 2, while Marvin has 102 units of good 1 and 0 of good 2.

PROBLEM 15.2

Shelly's ordering: first, F; second, D and G; third, A. Marvin's ordering: first, A; second, G; third, D and F.

PROBLEM 15.3

All points in the green area in Figure A15.1 Pareto-dominate point T.

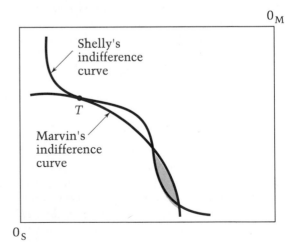

FIGURE A15.1

PROBLEM 15.4

Shelly's net demand for good 1 is 27 units, equal to Marvin's net supply. Marvin's net demand for good 2 is 26 units, equal to Shelly's net supply. If Marvin traded 27 units of good 1 for 26 units of good 2, and Shelly traded 26 units of good 2 for 27 units of good 1, the economy would move from the initial allocation at A to the competitive equilibrium at E^*.

PROBLEM 15.5

Producers of good 1 must use relatively more of input 1 and relatively less of input 2, while producers of good 2 must do the opposite. Yes, it is possible to achieve efficiency in production while maintaining a constant output of good 1.

PROBLEM 15.6

$2, \frac{1}{5}, \frac{1}{3}, 3$.

PROBLEM 15.7

MRT is 1.

PROBLEM 15.8

Less.

PROBLEM 15.9

Supposing that the monopolist produces good 1, the relevant diagram is Figure A15.2. Ms. C's ori-

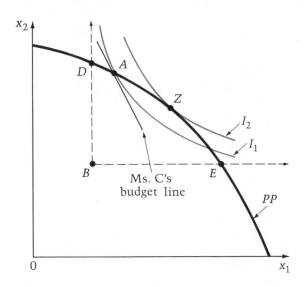

FIGURE A15.2

gin is point B. Initially, she is at a point such as point A in the figure because, as we just discovered, her MRS (at the initial equilibrium) necessarily exceeds MRT when good 1 is produced by a monopolist. When she takes control, she will choose point Z, a point at which she consumes more good 1 and less good 2. At point Z, she is better off, and no one else, including the owner of the firm producing good 1, is worse off, because their consumption bundles have not changed. Therefore, in the general equilibrium, when good 1 is produced by a monopolist, too little of that good is produced.

PROBLEM 15.10

Assume that the price-discriminating monopolist produces good 1; let p_1' and p_1'' be the two prices it charges in the two submarkets and let p_2 be the equilibrium price of good 2. Consumers who face price p_1' will consume a bundle where MRS is equal to p_1'/p_2, and consumers who face price p_1'' will consume a bundle where MRS is equal to p_1''/p_2. The condition for efficiency in consumption—that all consumers' marginal rates of substitution be identical—is therefore violated.

PROBLEM 15.11

Let p_1, p_2, w_1, and w_2 denote equilibrium prices. Each consumer will choose a bundle where MRS $= p_1/(p_2 + t)$, and the economy is efficient in consumption. Each producer will use an input bundle where MRTS $= w_1/w_2$, and the economy is efficient in production. Because the prices firms receive are p_1 and p_2, MRT $= p_1/p_2$. MRT therefore exceeds the common value of MRS, and we do not have efficiency in product mix. Using a diagram like Figure 15.8, you can show that too little of good 2 is produced in general competitive equilibrium when consumption of good 2 is taxed. Similarly, if consumption of good 2 is subsidized, we do not have efficiency in product mix, and too much of good 2 is produced in general competitive equilibrium.

PROBLEM 16.1

This question has no "correct" answer, since each person's response depends on his or her preferences.

PROBLEM 16.2

Suppose that the fixed quantity of manna is 1. In Figure A16.1, the utility associated with $R = \frac{1}{2}$ is AB, which exceeds AC, the expected utility associated with $R = \frac{1}{4}$ (and $1 - R = \frac{3}{4}$). It also exceeds AD, the expected utility associated with $R = 0$ (and $1 - R = 1$). As you can easily verify, the utility associated with $R = \frac{1}{2}$ exceeds the expected utility associated with any other value of R, since the individual is risk-averse.

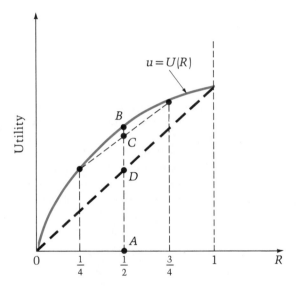

FIGURE A16.1

PROBLEM 16.3

An effective minimum wage implies excess supply; employers therefore can choose among applicants on the basis of sex, race, age, or any other variable at no cost to themselves. In the absence of a minimum wage, there is no excess supply; if the employer does not approve of applicants, it must pay a higher wage to attract more "acceptable" applicants.

PROBLEM 16.4

You can derive these results by constructing the marginal factor cost function implied by different minimum wages (as in Figure 16.3), and then finding the quantity of labor that maximizes the firm's profit.

PROBLEM 16.5

The implications of a union wage w' are identical to the implications of a minimum wage w'.

PROBLEM 16.6

Because the hiring-hall institution distributes unemployment equally and because the supply is completely inelastic, each member wants to maximize his or her earnings. The wage that such a union would seek is the wage at which the elasticity of demand for labor is 1, because the firm's total wage bill is a maximum at this point.

PROBLEM 16.7

In this case, the more junior members of the union bear all the unemployment associated with a higher wage. If the more senior members do not care about the unemployment of junior members, they will favor a much higher wage rate, knowing that they will not be unemployed as a result. The natural coalition is the coalition involving just over half of the most senior members; this coalition will seek the highest wage such that none of them is unemployed.

PROBLEM 16.8

Interpret w' in Figure 16.5 as the high urban wage and $D_2(z_2)$ as the demand for labor in rural areas. Assume a casual labor market, with lots of job turnover, so that each urban worker gets the same share of the available urban employment. Then u is the unemployment rate among urban workers.

PROBLEM 16.9

For any value of x_1, the subsidy required to put the individual on the target indifference curve is the vertical distance from the budget line, $x_2 + wx_1 = wT$, to the indifference curve. This distance is minimized at x_1^*, where the slope of the budget line is equal to the slope of the indifference curve.

PROBLEM 16.10

In Figure A16.2, the individual chooses E_1 on indifference curve I_1 and chooses not to receive the topping-up transfer S'. Given the NIT budget line, the individual chooses point E_2 on indifference curve I_2 and receives the NIT transfer S''.

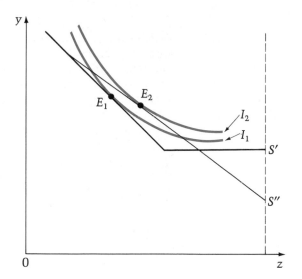

FIGURE A16.2

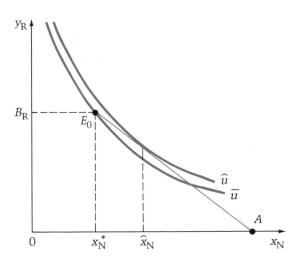

FIGURE A17.1

PROBLEM 17.1

The contract curve is the vertical axis through the nonsmoker's origin in Figure 17.1. Because the nonsmoker never buys cigarettes, any market-induced allocation is on the contract curve.

PROBLEM 17.2

Distance HG in Figure 17.2 is the maximum amount Marvin would pay to reduce Shelly's consumption of cigarettes to 0.

PROBLEM 17.3

In your diagram, the absolute value of the slope of n_0 at the market-induced allocation should be less than the absolute value of the slope of s_0. In this case, s_0 and n_0 have just one point in common, the market-induced allocation, and that allocation is Pareto-optimal.

PROBLEM 17.4

Suppose that Nancy chooses her consumption bundle in the ordinary way, consuming, say, x_N^* of good X. Ralph values only y_R, his consumption of the composite commodity, and x_N, Nancy's consumption of X. Thus, his utility function can be written as $u = U(y_R, x_N)$. If he spends all his income, M_R, on the composite commodity, he will initially be at point E_0 in Figure A17.1. If he considers buying additional X for Nancy, his budget line is E_0A, and he will choose to buy $x_N' - x_N^*$

additional X for Nancy. Ralph is obviously better off, and so is Nancy, because she values her own consumption of X.

PROBLEM 17.5

The market solution is likely to be inefficient for obvious reasons, and a student organization may indeed be able to organize the dance more efficiently.

PROBLEM 17.6

The point to keep in mind in constructing the relevant diagram is that the default option allows Sadie to consume $x_1'/2$ cigarettes.

PROBLEM 17.7

For simplicity, assume that when a downhill owner builds a higher house, the only view that is impaired is the view from the house immediately up the hill. A better institutional arrangement would be to let the default option be a house no higher than 30 feet and allow the neighbors the possibility of negotiating some other solution.

PROBLEM 17.8

One possible mechanism would be to establish a public property right for the whole aquifer and then to charge a fee for every gallon of water pumped from the aquifer. Some form of cost-benefit analysis would be necessary to establish the correct fee.

PROBLEM 17.9

Pay TV is clearly not efficient. It is akin to building a fence around Niagara Falls and charging tourists to look through peepholes in the fence. However, it is not obvious that it is worse than the alternatives. In the next section of the text, we'll encounter the very thorny problems associated with the public provision of a service such as television. Furthermore, current pay TV channels provide many programs that ordinary commercial television stations do not offer. Both the consumers of these services and the firms that provide them are better off.

INDEX